EXAMPLES&EXPLANATIONS

Professional Responsibility

Professional Responsibility

Sixth Edition

W. Bradley Wendel

Professor of Law
Cornell Law School

Wolters Kluwer

Published by Wolters Kluwer in New York.

Wolters Kluwer Legal & Regulatory Solutions U.S. serves customers worldwide with CCH, Aspen Publishers, and Kluwer Law International products. (www.WKLegaledu.com)

To contact Customer Service, e-mail customer.service@wolterskluwer.com, call 1-800-234-1660, fax 1-800-901-9075, or mail correspondence to:

Wolters Kluwer
Attn: Order Department
PO Box 990
Frederick, MD 21705

Printed in the United States of America.

1 2 3 4 5 6 7 8 9 0

ISBN 978-1-5438-0578-9

Library of Congress Cataloging-in-Publication Data

Names: Wendel, W. Bradley, 1969- author.
Title: Professional responsibility / W. Bradley Wendel, Professor of Law,
    Cornell Law School.
Description: A study guide to be used in conjunction with a casebook in the area of Professional
    Responsibility. | New York : Wolters Kluwer, [2020] | Includes
    bibliographical references and index.
Identifiers: LCCN 2019021407 | ISBN 9781543805789
Subjects: LCSH: Legal ethics—United States. | Attorney and client—United States. |
    LCGFT: Study guides.
Classification: LCC KF306.W46 2020 | DDC 174/.30973—dc23
LC record available at https://lccn.loc.gov/2019021407

About Wolters Kluwer Legal & Regulatory U.S.

Wolters Kluwer Legal & Regulatory U.S. delivers expert content and solutions in the areas of law, corporate compliance, health compliance, reimbursement, and legal education. Its practical solutions help customers successfully navigate the demands of a changing environment to drive their daily activities, enhance decision quality and inspire confident outcomes.

Serving customers worldwide, its legal and regulatory portfolio includes products under the Aspen Publishers, CCH Incorporated, Kluwer Law International, ftwilliam.com and MediRegs names. They are regarded as exceptional and trusted resources for general legal and practice-specific knowledge, compliance and risk management, dynamic workflow solutions, and expert commentary.

For Ben and Hannah

Summary of Contents

PART I. THE ATTORNEY-CLIENT RELATIONSHIP   21

PART II. SECRETS AND LIES: PERJURY AND THE PROBLEM OF CLIENT FRAUD   237

Contents

PART III. CONFLICTS OF INTEREST   313

Chapter 13   Overview of Conflicts of Interest   315

Chapter 14   Concurrent Conflicts   329

PART IV. ORGANIZATION AND REGULATION OF THE LEGAL PROFESSION   457

Chapter 18 Attracting Clients: Advertising and Solicitation   459

Chapter 19 Associations of Lawyers   481

Preface

No matter what area of law you choose to specialize in, I guarantee that you will practice the subject of this course. You may never file a motion for summary judgment, appear at a preliminary hearing or sentencing, perfect a security interest, prepare a will, or draft comments on proposed new regulations; but you will, at some time, think about what you are learning in your Professional Responsibility course. You may have to decide whether you can represent a new client in light of your obligations to an existing client. You certainly will have to keep client confidences, and at some point, you may need to assert a privilege covering certain confidential communications to prevent them from being discovered by others. You may bill clients for your services, in which case you need to know the rules governing attorneys' fees, and you may even advertise for business. One way or the other, you will have to know the law of professional responsibility.

One of the major themes of this book is that you cannot understand your duties and responsibilities as a lawyer just by looking at the disciplinary rules, sometimes called "ethics codes" or "rules of ethics." The ABA Model Rules of Professional Conduct, in whatever version they are adopted in your state, are the basis for potential professional discipline by state bar authorities, but this discipline is not the only thing that lawyers must worry about in practice. Your day-to-day actions also will be influenced by the possibility of liability for malpractice to your client, sanctions imposed by a court under its inherent power or rules of procedure, potential loss of entitlement to fees, disqualification from representing a client, and waiver of evidentiary privileges. Not to slight the importance of the disciplinary system, but by the calculations of some scholars, a lawyer is over a *thousand* times more likely to pay out in excess of $10,000 in a malpractice lawsuit, by way of judgment or settlement, than to be disbarred. Which risk do you think is more likely to demand one's attention? Furthermore, many significant areas of professional responsibility law, such as conflicts of interest and the attorney-client privilege, are driven almost entirely by considerations unrelated to professional discipline, such as disqualification and loss of fees in the case of conflicts, or the desire to protect client communications from disclosure in court in the case of the attorney-client privilege. Thus, it is vitally important to consider the whole field of the law governing lawyers—not just the disciplinary rules.

This does not mean that we will not consider the disciplinary rules carefully. In fact, the Model Rules are central to much of the book. In many cases, however, we will move beyond the state bar disciplinary rules and discuss the relationship with other sources of law. For example, the professional duty of confidentiality, stated in Model Rule 1.6, is often confused with the attorney-client privilege, which is a creature of the law of evidence. By looking at the evidentiary privilege with some care, you can see the distinctions and overlap between these two doctrines. Even if your law school course is limited to study of the Model Rules, the contrast with the attorney-client privilege can sharpen your understanding of the precise boundaries of the duty of confidentiality. It is more likely, however, that your Professional Responsibility course will touch on other areas of law, such as the evidence rules governing privileges; the Sixth Amendment doctrines pertaining to ineffective assistance of counsel; the law of agency, partnership, and corporations as it pertains to conflicts of interest; client identification; fiduciary duties; and the tort and regulatory law of fraud.

Thus, the first goal of this book is to integrate these other sources of law with specific professional responsibility rules so that you can get a complete picture of your duties as a lawyer. Unlike some other textbooks, this book does not draw an artificial distinction between analysis of the disciplinary rules and other law that applies to lawyers representing clients. In some places, the result of this integration may be greater complexity and length of treatment, but I believe it is warranted by the importance of understanding the interaction between the bar's own rules and other legal norms that lawyers must take into account. The second goal of the book is to make you aware of the theory and policy reasons underlying the law governing lawyers. Your law school course may be aimed more at ethics (in the philosophical sense of reasoning about right and wrong) than at law. In other words, you may be asked to step back from the law and understand the role of the lawyer in terms of its function in our society, the history of the profession, general rational standards of right and wrong, or the perspective of some other discipline. Although no textbook of reasonable length can do justice to these alternative perspectives on the legal profession, I do hope at least to introduce them and show how they affect the law as it develops.

Acknowledgments

The influence of a number of professional responsibility scholars, several of whom are authors of casebooks and treatises, will be evident in this book. I owe an additional debt of gratitude to the lively and diverse community of lawyers and academics who populate the *legalethics* listserv, whose informative discussions of many issues were extremely helpful to me along the way. A number of those list members generously shared their course materials and exams with me. Special thanks are due to those who maintain free online resources, from which I have frequently learned a great deal: in particular, William Freivogel and Lucian Pera for their electronic newsletter *Ethics and Lawyering Today*, William Freivogel for his online mini-treatise *Freivogel on Conflicts*, and Tom Spahn for his periodic bulletin *Privilege Points*. I also am grateful to my colleagues in other fields who helped clarify specialized points of law as they relate to the professional responsibility issues presented here. Finally, thanks to the many students at Washington and Lee and Cornell who have challenged me to think more carefully about the law of lawyering. At many points in the evolution of this book, I can recall a student pressing a point in class or in an e-mail exchange afterward, and these discussions are often reflected in the text or the examples. As convenient as it would be to blame any remaining errors on my students or the community of professional responsibility specialists, I of course take sole responsibility for them.

Thanks are due to the editorial staff of Wolters Kluwer (formerly Aspen Publishers) over the life of this book, who provided countless suggestions to improve the book in substance and form. It has been a pleasure to work with this excellent team.

Listserv now seems almost as antiquated as rotary-dial phones, and the *legalethics* list has mostly been replaced by the Legal Ethics Forum (LEF) blog as the place for scholars in this field to hang out online. Special thanks to John Steele for his indefatigable energy in keeping the blog running. I am grateful to Andy Perlman (also an essential LEF blogger) for inviting me to serve as a Reporter to one of the ABA Ethics 20/20 working groups, from which I learned a tremendous amount. Bryant Danner at USC has been an enthusiastic adopter of the book and an invaluable source of suggestions for improvement—keep the comments coming, Bry! Among teachers who have adopted the book for use in class, Bill Simon, Brent Landau, and Martha

Acknowledgments

Pacold have also given me helpful comments on the book. Finally, considerable gratitude is owed to Nancy Moore and the rest of the Multistate Professional Responsibility Examination (MPRE) drafting committee for knowing more about the law of lawyering than I ever thought possible and challenging me to keep up.

Citations and Other Stylistic Practices

Other than citations to sources of law, such as disciplinary rules and the Restatement, I will be sparing with cites. In some cases, you may wish to refer to a more detailed reference work for additional guidance, so there are occasional citations to treatises, Restatement commentary, and the like. I have tried to keep footnotes to a minimum, except for citations, but occasionally there is some parenthetical information in a footnote, such as a definition of a word used in the text or an aside on some point that is interesting but peripheral to the discussion in the text. Alterations and omissions to text are indicated by ellipses or brackets, but I have freely italicized text for emphasis without putting "emphasis added" notices everywhere. You can assume that italics are mine unless otherwise indicated.

I will not be a stickler for the *Bluebook* here. Instead, to save space, I will use the following abbreviations.

SOURCES OF LAW

Model Rules	ABA Model Rules of Professional Conduct (as amended by the Ethics 2000 Commission and the Commission on Ethics 20/20)
Rule XX	Model Rule (most current version)
1983 vers.	Version of the Model Rules adopted by the ABA House of Delegates in 1983 and amended through August 2001
Ethics 20/20	ABA Commission on Ethics 20/20, formed in 2009 and active through 2012. Alternatively, the version of the Model Rules proposed by the Ethics 20/20 Commission and adopted by the ABA House of Delegates
Model Code	ABA Model Code of Professional Responsibility (adopted in 1969, as amended through 1981)

EC   Ethical Consideration

DR   Disciplinary Rule

Rest. §XX   Restatement (Third) of the Law Governing Lawyers (2000)

CJC Rule XX ABA Model Code of Judicial Conduct (2010)

cmt.   Comment (to Model Rules, Restatement, or CJC section)

REFERENCE WORKS

H&H   Geoffrey C. Hazard, Jr. & W. William Hodes, *The Law of Lawyering* (3d ed. 2001)

Wolfram   Charles Wolfram, *Modern Legal Ethics* (1986)

R&D   Ronald D. Rotunda & John S. Dzienkowski, *Professional Responsibility: A Student's Guide* (2012–2013 edition)

Unless otherwise specified, the examples and explanations in the book take place in the fictional U.S. State of Perplexity, which has adopted the ABA Model Rules of Professional Conduct (most current version) verbatim as its disciplinary rules.

A brief note about pronouns is also in order. The problem is, of course, that English lacks a third-person singular pronoun that is not gender-specific. Arguably, the masculine pronoun once carried the conventional meaning "he or she," but this usage is increasingly less acceptable. There really is not a good alternative. I tend to use the feminine pronoun generically in academic writing, but I am the first to admit it makes no sense, because "she" has never carried the conventional meaning "he or she." My justification for this practice is based on the observation that people make unconscious use of images in what purports to be purely logical analysis. Try an example. A partner at a law firm gets a call. . . . Stop! You've probably already formed a mental picture of the setting. The partner is a man, probably white, with graying hair, wearing a gray pinstriped suit and conservative tie, in a corner office with spectacular views, sitting behind a mahogany desk on which are piled neat stacks of correspondence and documents. We cannot help using images like this, but it is troublesome that men figure so prominently in our images of people in power. Using the feminine singular pronoun is my feeble effort to introduce alternative images of women as lawyers, judges, and clients. Light a candle or curse the darkness. Some people find this practice distracting, and others will cry "politically correct!" Of course, an equal number of people are distracted or politically provoked by the incessant use of the masculine pronoun. My solution—sure to satisfy no one—is to mix up he and she, pretty much at random, unless it is possible to write around the pronoun in some fashion.

Professional
Responsibility

The Many Ways of Regulating Lawyers

INTRODUCTION

"Every thing is what it is, and not another thing."

—Isaiah Berlin, "Two Concepts of Liberty," quoting Joseph Butler

This may be the course in law school in which there is the most variation in subject matter and emphasis. Torts is torts, evidence is evidence, but students are often unsure of the scope of a course in professional responsibility. This identity crisis is revealed in the variety of course titles used by schools: professional responsibility, the legal profession, lawyers and clients, legal ethics. There seem to be at least two distinct subjects wrapped up together under the label of professional responsibility, one having to do with law, the other having to do with standards of right and wrong that are independent of the law. The American Bar Association (ABA) insists that all accredited law schools require a course in the "history, goals, structure, duties, values, and responsibilities of the legal profession and its members." ABA Standards for Approval of Law Schools, Standard 302(b). This language is pretty broad, and a wide variety of courses can be offered that satisfy the ABA's requirement, as long as the course includes some instruction about the ABA Model Rules of Professional Conduct. Owing to the flexibility of the ABA's standard, and the fact that law professors have many different approaches to the study of the legal profession, you could conceivably study the rules of professional conduct or the law of malpractice and litigation sanctions, or you could take an interdisciplinary approach borrowing from literature, films, moral philosophy, sociology, or theology, in a course called professional responsibility.

Throughout this book, I will talk about both *professional responsibility* and *legal ethics*. The first term is somewhat easier to define. "Professional responsibility" refers to what may be called the law of lawyering or the regulation of lawyers. As a practicing lawyer, you will be subject to legal regulations that are promulgated by many different government bodies, including state bar associations, courts before which you appear, legislatures, and administrative agencies. The highest court in any state has the inherent power to regulate the conduct of lawyers practicing in that state; in practice, the court generally delegates considerable power to a state bar association, which establishes rules of conduct for lawyers and investigates and punishes violations of those rules. In most states, these *disciplinary rules* are patterned after rules drafted by committees of the ABA. You may be subjected to professional discipline (reprimand, suspension, disbarment, and other punishments) for violating these rules. There are plenty of other bad things that can happen to you, though. You may be sued by a client for malpractice, held liable for damages to a third party, disqualified by a court from representing a client, forced to return earned attorneys' fees, held constitutionally ineffective in a criminal defense case, or, in rare cases, even criminally prosecuted.

In each of these cases, the result is driven primarily by *generally applicable law*—that is, rules of procedure, tort principles, or criminal statutes that apply without regard to the state bar disciplinary rules. Sometimes the generally applicable law makes reference to the disciplinary rules, as when failure to comply with the tort-law duty of reasonable care may be proven by the lawyer's failure to comply with a bar association rule. In other cases, the court can either ignore or modify the applicable disciplinary rule. For example, a court may hold a lawyer liable for aiding and abetting her client's fraud on the grounds that the lawyer should have disclosed a particular fact in a transaction, *regardless* of whether the lawyer had a professional obligation to keep the fact secret. Remember that fundamentally, the bar disciplinary rules are really a matter of internal governance of the bar association; they are not binding on courts outside of disciplinary proceedings.

The law is not as much of a mess as you may think after reading the last paragraph. As a practical matter, courts try not to reach results that are wildly at odds with the organized bar's disciplinary rules. They may be influenced by the bar's statements about the obligations of lawyers and may defer to the organized bar as a matter of respect or comity. However, it is a major theme of this book that you must not confine your thinking about the law of professional responsibility to the Model Rules. As we will see again and again, you cannot fully understand your legal obligations as a lawyer without knowing something about tort, contract, agency, procedure, and criminal law. If you are working in a highly specialized area like securities law or financial-institution regulation, you have to know a great deal about the underlying substantive law, too, because it may affect your duties in ways that the disciplinary rules simply do not take into account.

Where does this leave *legal ethics*? There are basically two ways to approach legal ethics. One is to look at the cases and rules that compose the law governing lawyers to see what values, policies, and ideals are embodied in the law. A rule that requires lawyers to keep secrets, where disclosing the information would prevent personal injuries or avert a financial fraud, expresses a strong bias in favor of loyalty to clients and away from some kind of generalized duty on the part of lawyers to do justice or look out for the greater social good. (Of course, one can always respond that justice and social good are more likely to result in the long run if lawyers are primarily concerned with representing their clients' best interests.) You may find competing policies, however, such as the values underlying the rules against presenting perjury at trial. It is fascinating to uncover these policies and see how they affect the outcomes of cases. Getting clear on these underlying values also helps you to predict results where the law is unclear and to become more comfortable with the inevitable "gray areas" in the law in which clear answers are in short supply. In a sense, then, legal ethics is just a name for a system of policy arguments that justify official decisions applying the law of lawyering. To the extent this book addresses legal ethics, it is primarily in this sense.

The second perspective one can take on legal ethics is to stand outside the law altogether and ask whether it is right or wrong to take some action. Suppose the lawyer knows a secret about her client, and knows that several people will be in jeopardy of death or personal injury if the secret is not revealed. Should she keep the secret? Under certain conditions, she would have a legal obligation not to reveal the information, but that obligation is not *necessarily* conclusive of her moral duty. She may have to be a conscientious objector and put aside her fidelity to the law, in favor of a greater moral obligation. How is she to determine the nature of that obligation? That is the subject matter of the academic discipline of *ethics*, usually studied as a branch of philosophy, but which may be encountered in history, literature, political science, theology, sociology, or other fields of inquiry. In the philosophical tradition, ethics is the study of concepts such as goodness, right action, duty, and what ends we ought to choose and pursue as rational beings. It is quite a complex and specialized subject, and you probably will not go into much detail in a law school course. Still, you might encounter concepts borrowed from philosophical ethics, such as values, virtues, duties, consequences, goods, and principles. Alternatively, you might approach the same issues using different terminology, or your instructor might attempt to strip away the jargon altogether and simply get you to think about ethical questions, perhaps by reading novels or watching films. You should pay close attention to the structure of your course, and if your instructor favors interdisciplinary approaches, plan your preparation and study accordingly.

A careful, rigorous exploration of legal ethics in this sense is beyond the scope of this book.

I strongly object to the use of the term "legal ethics" to refer to lawyers' obligations under the state bar disciplinary rules, or the law governing lawyers in general. For one thing, using the term in that way requires invention of an awkward new term, such as "real ethics" to describe what nonlawyers would simply call ethics.[1] Furthermore, some lawyers might be tempted to regard rules of "ethics" as merely aspirational or theoretical, when in fact the rules of professional conduct of the states are *law*, and unpleasant *legal* consequences can attach to their violation. On a related note, because the rules of professional conduct are law, they have intricacies and subtleties of which even morally reflective people may not be aware. Complying with the law of lawyering is not just a matter of "being good," as understood in commonsense moral terms. Most important, referring to lawyers' legal obligations as a matter of ethics suggests that being a good person is primarily a matter of following legal rules. But one can be a complete sleazeball from the standpoint of morality and never violate a single rule in the law governing lawyers. Because there is much more to the moral life than complying with the law, I would not want to contribute to this kind of confusion. In a basically decent society, there will be substantial overlap between legal and moral requirements, but it is important to draw an analytical distinction between the two. As we will see, there are several areas in which the organized bar's disciplinary rules may seem to be at odds with ordinary moral standards.

WHO SHOULD REGULATE LAWYERS?

The Organized Bar: Models and Legally Binding Rules

It is one of the primary characteristics of professions that they are self-regulating. One of the distinctions between a profession, such as law or medicine, and a "mere" business such as plumbing or advertising is that professions carefully control entry and training (through licensing and examination requirements) and continued membership (through disciplinary mechanisms). A plumber who botches a job may be sued by the client, but she is unlikely to be dragged before the Plumber's Disciplinary Board, if there is such a thing, and publicly reprimanded. Lawyers, on the other hand, face internal disciplinary procedures for conduct that violates

---

1. Some people draw a distinction along these lines between ethics and morality. These words are used by some to capture a *different* distinction in moral philosophy, however, so I will not make use of them here. See, for example, Bernard Williams, *Ethics and the Limits of Philosophy* (1985); Avishai Margalit, *The Ethics of Memory* (2002).

professional standards. In this book, I will refer to these internal regulatory standards as the disciplinary rules of a state and talk in terms of whether a lawyer would be subject to discipline for doing such-and-such.[2] Again you should be aware, though, that others may use the term "ethics rules" or "legal ethics" to refer to the same thing, and may ask whether certain conduct is "unethical." Whatever you call them, the idea behind the disciplinary rules is that the legal profession should be self-policing. If the organized bar acts to get rid of the bad apples, the argument goes, the result will be increased public respect for the bar, the enhanced legitimacy of the profession, and less pressure for external regulation of the practice of law.

The disciplinary rules in effect in the vast majority of U.S. jurisdictions are versions of the Model Rules of Professional Conduct, prepared by the ABA. Legally speaking, the ABA is just a trade association, no different from the Piano Tuners Guild or the American Academy of Otolaryngology. It is not empowered to make binding laws any more than these other organizations. The Model Rules are not called "model" for nothing. State courts do, however, have the power to establish legally enforceable disciplinary rules as part of the inherent power of the judiciary. Wolfram §2.2.1. Pursuant to what I refer to as "Track One" inherent authority, the highest court in a jurisdiction can promulgate rules governing the admission, regulation, and discipline of lawyers in that state.[3] When exercising their inherent authority to formulate disciplinary rules, rather than reinvent the wheel, state courts generally have looked to the ABA's models for guidance.

To make your life more complicated, most state courts have not simply adopted the ABA's Model Rules verbatim, but have tinkered around with the ABA versions. As a general rule, the more controversial the ABA rule, the more you can expect the individual states to have fiddled with it. For example, very few states have adopted the model form of Rule 1.6 on confidential client information, which was the flashpoint for a tremendous amount of debate over the initial draft of the Model Rules. These are not cosmetic differences in language, either. In many cases, the fundamental nature of the lawyer's duty varies substantially from the ABA's rule. Although an attorney may be forbidden to disclose something under the Model Rules, the lawyer may be *required* to disclose it under the version of the rules adopted in a given state.

---

2. This corresponds exactly with the definition of "subject to discipline" as used in the Multistate Professional Responsibility Exam (MPRE). On the MPRE, a lawyer is subject to discipline if "the conduct described in the question would subject the lawyer to discipline under the provisions of the ABA Model Rules of Professional Conduct."

3. This is different from the "Track Two" inherent authority of trial courts to regulate the activities of lawyers *appearing before that court*, which is the basis for disqualifying lawyers for conflicts of interest, for example. You should know that Track One and Track Two are my own invented terms, but I think they will help clarify an important distinction between the state's highest court promulgating rules to govern the profession as a whole (Track One) and an individual court punishing a lawyer for engaging in conduct that interferes with that court's ability to administer justice (Track Two).

Throughout the book, I will refer to the *state disciplinary authority*, without regard to the particulars of how it is organized. By that term I mean the official committee, agency, or state bar association that is empowered to draft and promulgate rules of professional conduct, to regulate admission to practice law in a state, and to mete out punishment for lawyers who violate the disciplinary rules.[4]

The situation is even more variable in the federal courts. Federal courts have their own inherent authority to regulate the practice of lawyers who appear in them and are *not* bound to apply the rules of the forum state in which they are located. There are three general approaches that federal district courts follow: (1) adopt the ABA version of the Model Rules; (2) adopt the forum state's version of the Model Rules; or (3) adopt idiosyncratic rules that are not necessarily the same as the ABA or state version of the disciplinary rules. If you practice in federal court, you'll have to pay attention to the approach adopted by a particular court. Often the court will set out in its local rules the rules it intends to follow for the regulation of attorneys practicing in that court.

From time to time, state bar associations and the ABA publish *opinions* explaining how, in their view, a given situation would be treated under the disciplinary rules. In general, those opinions are useful guides to interpreting the disciplinary rules but are not binding on a court in a malpractice, disqualification, or similar proceeding. State opinions may be binding in disciplinary proceedings, depending on the law of that state. We will look at a couple of ABA opinions in some detail, and I frequently will cite ABA opinions where they help interpret a provision of the Model Rules, but state opinions are just too voluminous and diverse to deal with here.

Courts and Legislatures

Despite the rhetoric from the organized bar about how the legal profession should be self-governing, courts get into the act of regulating lawyers all the time.[5] When a judge permits a malpractice action to go to the jury, she is deciding that under a particular set of facts, a lawyer may be liable to pay

---

4. This definition also tracks the MPRE. It provides: "When a question refers to discipline by the 'bar,' 'state bar,' or 'appropriate disciplinary authority,' it refers to the agency in the jurisdiction with the authority to administer the standards for admission to practice and for maintenance of professional competence and integrity."

5. You will occasionally see a reference to the negative inherent power doctrine, which is a kind of analogue to the Dormant Commerce Clause in constitutional law. The idea here is that if state courts have Track One inherent authority to promulgate disciplinary rules, this authority should prevent other branches of government, from any jurisdiction, from regulating the practice of law. A weaker version of this doctrine would hold that courts may be the preferred regulators of lawyers, but that they do share power with the other branches. See Wolfram §2.2.3.

damages to an aggrieved client or third party. That's as good as a disciplinary rule in getting the attention of lawyers. From then on, lawyers in that state will modify their behavior in order not to run afoul of this new rule of tort law. Similarly, when a court sanctions a lawyer for abusing the litigation process — or disqualifies a lawyer from representing a client in a matter — the court is announcing a rule of law that shapes the conduct of lawyers in that jurisdiction. This is regulation of the practice of law, even if it is not set forth in Rule X of the state's disciplinary rules.

Where the regulation of lawyers by a *federal* statute or administrative regulation is involved, don't forget about issues of federal preemption. This has been a running theme throughout the development of the law governing lawyers, and you may see references to the controversy between the Justice Department and state bar authorities over the application to federal prosecutors of the anti-contact rule, Rule 4.2. (See Chapter 3 for more discussion.) A high-profile iteration of this debate arose when the Washington State Bar Association announced that lawyers admitted in Washington would be required to keep information learned in the course of representing clients confidential, even where disclosure would be required by the Securities and Exchange Commission (SEC) regulations promulgated under the Sarbanes-Oxley Act. The SEC's General Counsel responded with a fairly sharply worded letter reminding the Washington bar authorities of a little thing in the U.S. Constitution called the Supremacy Clause. Although the Washington bar refused to back down, the view among most observers who know this area was that the SEC's position is correct as a matter of constitutional law. (The Washington State courts later changed the rule to permit disclosure of confidential information under these circumstances.) The North Carolina bar's ethics committee agreed and issued an opinion stating that an attorney may reveal confidential information where required by the Sarbanes-Oxley regulations, even if the disciplinary rules prohibit disclosure. North Carolina State Bar Ethics Comm., Formal Op. 2005-9.

Although the source of regulatory authority is somewhat different, judicial decisions and disciplinary rules may actually adhere to the same standards. Courts are often willing to borrow from their state's disciplinary rules when deciding whether a lawyer should be punished in some way. A good example is disqualification for conflicts of interest. Trial courts have the authority — what I call Track Two inherent power — to regulate the activities of lawyers who practice before them, and that includes the power to regulate multiple representation. In theory, a court could come up with a set of standards for disqualification that have no relationship whatsoever to the disciplinary rules governing conflicts of interest. But it would be silly to create these rules in a vacuum. The disciplinary rules are well thought out and reflect a lot of study, at both the ABA and the local levels. Their existence also gives lawyers some notice as to what conduct is prohibited. For these reasons, judges often will apply the standards of, say, Model Rule 1.7 on current-client conflicts when deciding whether to disqualify a lawyer. In this way, a body of judicial decisions can grow up around the disciplinary rules, even where lawyers aren't being hauled before a state bar grievance committee for punishment.

I will use the term *generally applicable law* to refer to sources of legal authority, such as cases, statutes, and administrative regulations that apply regardless of whether someone is a lawyer. For example, securities laws prohibit making a false statement of material fact in connection with the purchase or sale of securities. This rule applies to both nonlawyers (for example, securities brokers) and lawyers. Although there are some complications relating to the precise definition of who may be sued for complicity in securities fraud, in general a lawyer may be liable to defrauded investors for making a false statement in connection with the purchase or sale of securities. This is true *regardless* of anything the state bar disciplinary rules might provide. Some of the ugliest situations a lawyer can confront involve conflicts between the duties prescribed by the organized bar and the duties set out by other legal rules. Maybe the rules say that a lawyer must remain silent if the client instructs her not to disclose some fact that would make the client's statement not misleading. If the lawyer had any part in preparing the client's statement, however, the lawyer is looking at some serious financial liability for securities fraud if she doesn't speak up.

Keeping in mind the importance of generally applicable law, we can briefly review the development of the organized bar's disciplinary rules.

A BIT OF ANCIENT HISTORY, AND WHY IT MATTERS

The ABA Canons

The ABA has long been in the business of drafting standards of conduct for lawyers. Its first crack at this task was in 1908 when it issued a series of Canons of Professional Ethics, drawn largely from a series of lectures given in the nineteenth century by an early scholar of legal ethics, George Sharswood. (By the way, please don't write "cannons"—we're not talking about artillery here.) As the name "canons" with all its religious resonance implies, these statements were not black-letter legal rules intended for enforcement by courts or bar associations. Rather, they set out a "general guide" for lawyers. The ABA realized that most lawyers could not comply with all of the Canons all of the time; the Canons were avowedly aspirational or idealistic in nature. Consider, for example, Canon 17: "Clients, not lawyers, are the litigants. Whatever may be the ill-feeling existing between clients, it should not be allowed to influence counsel in their conduct and demeanor toward each other or toward suitors in the case." This standard is plainly not supposed to be the basis for disciplining obnoxious lawyers, but is rather intended to inspire lawyers to try harder not to get too involved emotionally in their clients' cases. In other words, the ABA did not see itself as being in the business of regulating the practice of law. Rather, the drafters of the Canons believed they were simply restating in a formal way the norms and customs of the profession as they were observed by practicing lawyers.

Despite the obviously nonmandatory character of the document, lawyers sometimes got in trouble for violating one of the Canons. Judges have long enjoyed inherent authority to regulate the behavior of lawyers who appear before them. Rather than come up with standards from scratch, courts have frequently looked to the organized bar for guidance on the question of what is appropriate professional conduct for lawyers. Thus, the ABA's Canons started to seep into judicial opinions, in cases where the court was called upon to determine whether one of the lawyers did something wrong. The common law being what it is, some of these earlier opinions got cited over and over, and pretty soon a parallel set of rules had emerged, based on the ABA Canons, but with some wrinkles of their own. In general, these court-made rules were more precisely drawn than the Canons, which made sense in light of their function—not to inspire lawyers to reach new heights of professional excellence, but to set a floor below which professional conduct should not fall.

The Model Code

The ABA took notice of this development and decided to produce a much more detailed set of professional standards, one that would reflect the distinction between ideals and minimum standards. The resulting Model Code of Professional Responsibility (first promulgated in 1970) was divided into canons, ethical considerations, and disciplinary rules, which are grouped by subject matter. The nine canons in the Model Code had the flavor of the old ABA Canons; they were highly general and idealistic in nature. "A lawyer should represent a client zealously within the bounds of the law," said Canon 7, for instance. Ethical considerations, known colloquially as "ECs," were much more specific, but still idealistic in nature. They were not intended to be the basis for professional discipline or civil liability against a lawyer. Rather, they were statements of "best practices" or aspirational guidelines for lawyers seeking to be as responsible as possible. So, for example, under Canon 7 on zealous advocacy within the bounds of the law, EC 7-3 gives some guidance on what a lawyer should do where the law is unclear:

> Where the bounds of law are uncertain, the action of a lawyer may depend on whether he is serving as advocate or adviser. . . . In asserting a position on behalf of his client, an advocate for the most part deals with past conduct and must take the facts as he finds them. By contrast, a lawyer serving as adviser primarily assists his client in determining the course of future conduct and relationships. While serving as advocate, a lawyer should resolve in favor of his client doubts as to the bounds of the law. In serving a client as adviser, a lawyer in appropriate circumstances should give his professional opinion as to what the ultimate decisions of the courts would likely be as to the applicable law.

You get the picture. Obviously, something like EC 7-3 could never be turned into a "black letter" rule and enforced through legal processes.

The only legally enforceable rules in the Model Code are the disciplinary rules, or "DRs," which prohibit specifically described conduct. On the same theme of advocacy within the bounds of the law, here is a rule on disclosing client fraud:

> A lawyer who receives information clearly establishing that [h]is client has, in the course of the representation, perpetrated a fraud upon a person or tribunal shall promptly call upon his client to rectify the same, and if his client refuses or is unable to do so, he shall reveal the fraud to the affected person or tribunal, except when the information is protected as a privileged communication.

DR 7-102(b)(1). Note the *mandatory* language ("shall"), explicit triggers of duty (receiving information "clearly establishing" fraud), and rule-like structure (a general rule with an exception for revealing privileged information), which distinguish DRs from the hortatory canons and ECs. For the most part, when talking about the Model Code, I will refer only to DRs, because you are probably primarily concerned with understanding what a lawyer *must* do. If you are interested in the more aspirational side of the organized bar's approach to professional regulation, you should read through the ECs as well.

The ABA first promulgated the Model Code in 1970 and tinkered around with it until 1981, when the last amended version was issued. States rushed to adopt it and the legal regulation of lawyers, which had been a low-key affair, suddenly took off. Courts began to apply the rules in disqualification proceedings, expert witnesses testified to the standard of care in legal malpractice cases with reference to the rules, and lawyers figured out how to use certain provisions of the rules (such as the prohibition on serving as both an advocate and a witness) as weapons to gain a tactical advantage over their opponents. One result of this explosion in judicial decisions applying the DRs was that weaknesses in the Model Code quickly became apparent and were sharply criticized. The two-tiered structure, with ECs and DRs, was a persistent source of interpretive difficulties. Theoretically, the ECs were not supposed to vary legal duties as stated in the DRs, but some courts (not unreasonably) used the ECs to clarify ambiguities in the language of the black-letter rules. It became quite difficult for lawyers to predict whether they would be subject to professional discipline, because the profusion of sometimes inconsistent ECs made it impossible to settle on a bottom-line rule. In addition, the Model Code failed to cover a number of recurring situations, such as the representation of a new client whose interests were adverse to a former client, and the representation of entity clients. The Model Code also focused principally on litigation and provided little guidance for lawyers involved in counseling, planning, drafting, and transactional matters.

The Model Code is now all but extinct, but you should know about its existence for two reasons: First, some important early cases in the law of lawyering were decided under the Model Code. Because the analysis set out in these cases continues to be influential, you may encounter them in casebooks.[6] Don't be alarmed if you see a bunch of DR and EC references—instead, see if you can translate the Model Code provisions into their Model Rules counterparts and see if the result would be the same. Second, and somewhat more subtly, some states' rules still contain a bit of Model Code language and analysis. For example, in connection with the duty of confidentiality, the Model Code distinguished between "confidences" (communications protected by the attorney-client privilege) and "secrets" (information that lawyers were duty-bound not to disclose). That distinction still exists in the rules of New York, the District of Columbia, Georgia, Virginia, and a few other states, while most states use the Model Rules language of "information relating to representation" to cover both confidences and secrets.

THE MODERN LAW GOVERNING LAWYERS

The Model Rules

As a result of the perceived deficiencies in the Model Code, the ABA quickly moved to revise the rules, appointing a commission chaired by a lawyer named Robert Kutak to study the problem. His name is significant, because you will frequently encounter references to the Kutak Commission. The work of this commission was enormously controversial, in part because of substantive disagreement over the content of particular rules (a noteworthy

---

6. A few examples: *IBM Corp. v. Levin* (conflicts of interest); *In re Fordham* (excessive fees); *Meyerhofer v. Empire Fire & Marine Insurance Co.* (self-defense exception to duty of confidentiality); *SEC v. National Student Marketing Corp.* (assisting client fraud); *In re Himmel* (reporting professional misconduct).

example is the duty of confidentiality, and the scope of exceptions to this rule), but also because the very nature of the commission's project seemed suspect. The Kutak Commission decided to adopt a black-letter set of rules, regulatory in structure, which would establish a minimum standard of conduct for lawyers. The ECs were gone, along with any statements of ideals, aspirations, or "best practices." You can think of the Model Rules as being made up of 100 percent DRs. Legal ethics had become law.

Of course, the commission never intended to preempt the field of morality. There is still plenty of room to argue about whether a lawyer ought to do something, morally speaking. The commission also left some room for individual judgment and discretion, by drafting some rules to state permissions rather than requirements. An example of the former type of rule is Model Rule 1.16(b)(4), which permits but does not require a lawyer to withdraw from representing a client where the lawyer regards the client's objectives as morally repugnant. Nevertheless, you will hear some lawyers and commentators argue that the Model Rules are deficient because they squeezed the morality out of the regulation of lawyers. I tend to think this is a misplaced objection: Morality and legal regulation are different things. Of course, a state can pass a law that tracks the requirements of morality (laws against intentionally killing being the most obvious example), but the existence of a law does not mean that it cannot be criticized in moral terms, or that a person's moral obligations are completely exhausted by following the law. The drafters of the Model Code chose to include a lot of text on the subject of nonlegal moral obligations. That's fine, but remember two things: (1) those moral obligations are still present, even if not written down in the form of ECs; and (2) it's important to keep straight the difference between legal versus moral obligations, or actual duties versus best practices, and including something like ECs can significantly complicate the task of administering the law.

After considerable controversy engendered by the Kutak Commission's proposed draft, the ABA adopted the Model Rules in final form in 1983. By the 1990s, it was apparent that the disciplinary rules were moving in the direction of the Model Rules on a nationwide basis. Less than 20 years after the promulgation of the Model Rules, the ABA appointed a new study group, known as the Ethics 2000 Commission, to consider revisions to the Model Rules. The commission decided to retain the structure, and much of the substance, of the Model Rules. It made significant changes to some rules, however, and generally tightened up the drafting of many provisions. The commission's recommended changes were adopted by the full ABA House of Delegates in 2002, and a couple of amendments regarding confidentiality (Rule 1.6) and entity representation (Rule 1.13) were adopted in 2003. Unfortunately, the ABA cannot seem to resist fiddling around with the Model Rules. In 2009 the ABA created the Commission on Ethics 20/20 (to see with clear vision—get it?) to consider changes to the Model Rules in light of changes in technology and the globalization of the provision of legal services. The Ethics 20/20 Commission did a lot of considering, but not a lot of changing. It proposed two packages of rule amendments, one of which was adopted in August 2012 and the second in February 2013. The amendments make numerous technical changes, many of which simply recognize existing law and state it as black-letter rules. At the risk of offering a broad-brush generalization, no real substantive, important changes to the rules came out of the Ethics 20/20 Commission. That does not mean you should not pay attention to the changes as they are adopted in the states. Many of the amendments clarify the rules in helpful ways.

As of June 2019, all U.S. jurisdictions have adopted disciplinary rules that follow the numbering system of the Model Rules. The content of each state's rules may vary, however, and some states (including New York) retain a great deal of language from the Model Code. In the remainder of the book I will cite the most current version of the Model Rules, *including the Ethics 20/ 20 amendments*. If necessary, I will discuss different versions of the rule, but if you see a citation to "Rule XX," you should assume it is the most current version of the ABA Model Rules. In the real world, however, please make sure to check your state's version of the rule, which may vary in significant respects from the Model Rule version.

The Restatement

You are probably familiar with the Restatements of torts, contracts, property, and other areas of law. Restatements are products of the American Law Institute (ALI), an august body of lawyers, judges, and law professors who study existing legal doctrines and think of ways to improve the law. The law governing lawyers finally got its own Restatement in 2000. Don't be confused by the title, "Restatement (Third) of the Law Governing Lawyers." There was no first or second Restatement. Rather, the ALI is working on the third series of Restatements, and is actually considering subjects like torts for the third time. But the third Restatement of the law of lawyering is its first crack at the subject. So don't go to the library looking for the Second Restatement of the Law Governing Lawyers—it doesn't exist.

Like all ALI Restatements, the Restatement of the Law Governing Lawyers does not *merely* restate existing law. It reflects instead a value judgment about legal rules. Where the law currently in effect is good (for a variety of policy reasons), the Restatement picks up the existing rule. Where the law should be changed in some respect, the Restatement takes a more forward-looking perspective and incorporates a rule its drafters regard as superior (again, on a number of policy grounds) to existing law. An example of this latter category is the rule governing disclosure of confidential information to prevent or rectify the consequences of a client's financial fraud. Rest.

§67. The Restatement drafters preferred a broader scope of authority to disclose than that found in the version of the Model Rules that existed at the time, although the ABA eventually caught up and now Rule 1.6(b)(2),(3) is pretty close to the Restatement position. The point being, however, that because of the mix of actual and desirable legal rules, you have to be careful with any Restatement—don't assume the law of your jurisdiction is the same as the Restatement rule.

Discipline Versus Everything Else

I'll reiterate something mentioned earlier in the chapter, because this is a perennial source of confusion in class: Technically speaking, the state rules of professional conduct, based (everywhere but California) on the ABA Model Rules, exist only for the purpose of establishing when a lawyer will be *subject to discipline* by the authorities in her admitting jurisdiction.[7] The power to admit, regulate, and discipline lawyers is vested in state courts, generally the highest court in the state (although New York has a weird system in which the four Appellate Divisions do the admitting and disciplining). These courts generally maintain variously named grievance or disciplinary committees that investigate allegations of misconduct and recommend discipline to the court.

Having promulgated these nifty disciplinary rules, however, state courts cannot prohibit other uses of them. If they establish standards of professional conduct, what's to stop a trial court from using one of the rules as evidence that a lawyer breached her duty to a client? Remember the idea of negligence *per se* in torts? A safety statute can particularize the duty of reasonable care, so that, for example, a contractor's failure to follow a statute requiring a guardrail on a high floor of a building being constructed can be sufficient evidence of negligence or may even compel a jury to find negligence. The idea isn't really that the jury is enforcing the safety statute, although it does add an additional penalty for its violation. Rather, the idea is that the jury is looking to the statute for guidance to determine what a reasonable person would do in these circumstances. The state rules of professional conduct may similarly be referred to in other contexts, including civil actions for malpractice and breach of fiduciary duty, constitutional claims by criminal defendants citing ineffective assistance of counsel, and efforts by a trial court to regulate the conduct of litigation, including the simultaneous representation of parties with conflicting interests. The rules may not be dispositive—that is, not truly supporting a per se inference of malpractice or some other cause of action—but they are frequently used

---

7. That term is used on the MPRE. When you see a question, "Is the attorney subject to discipline?," think "Did the attorney violate some provision of the ABA Model Rules?"

for guidance by courts. They do not have to be, however; rules of professional conduct are not strictly binding on courts in these contexts.

To keep this straight, simply ask the following question whenever you read a case or deal with an exam question: *Who is trying to do what to the lawyer?* If it is a state grievance or disciplinary committee seeking to have the lawyer suspended, disbarred, or otherwise punished by the licensing authority, then, strictly speaking, the rules of professional conduct are binding on the decisionmaker. See Restatement §5, cmt. b ("Lawyers are subject to professional discipline only for acts that are described as prohibited in an applicable lawyer code, statute, or rule of court"). If, on the other hand, the opposing party in litigation is seeking to have the trial court disqualify an attorney for a conflict of interest, or preclude the admission of evidence obtained in violation of the anticontact rule, or if a former client is suing a lawyer for negligence or disloyalty, then the rules *may*, but need not, be used for guidance.

Example

Who Decides?

Landlord filed an action to evict Tenant for nonpayment of rent on a large parcel of farm land. At the hearing on Landlord's motion for an order of eviction, Landlord was astonished to see her former attorney, Amy, representing Tenant. Amy had drafted the lease agreement and had represented Landlord at the closing of the lease with Tenant six months ago. At the hearing, on behalf of Tenant, Amy now argued that Tenant was entitled to withhold rent because Landlord had not made certain improvements to the property as required by the lease agreement. Landlord was furious, because he remembered discussing that provision of the lease, and Amy had assured him that it did not require making extensive improvements to the land.

Acting through his new attorney, Arnold, Landlord filed a motion with the court to disqualify Amy from representing Tenant. The trial judge denied the motion, stating as follows in a brief written order:

> Landlord claims that Amy is in violation of Rule 1.9(a) of the State of Perplexity Rules of Professional Conduct. That rule provides that a lawyer who has formerly represented a client may not represent another person in a substantially related matter where the interests of the prior and present clients are materially adverse, without the consent of the prior client. It is undisputed that Landlord, the prior client, has not given informed consent to Amy's representation of Tenant. It is also undisputed that the interests of Landlord and Tenant are materially adverse and that the matters—drafting and interpretation of the lease agreement—are substantially related. Nevertheless, the court denies Landlord's motion to disqualify. Comment [20] to the "Scope" section of the Perplexity Rules of Professional Conduct clearly states that "[v]iolation of a

Rule . . . does not necessarily warrant any other nondisciplinary remedy, such as disqualification of a lawyer in pending litigation. The Rules are designed to provide guidance to lawyers and to provide a structure for regulating conduct through disciplinary agencies." This court is not sitting as a disciplinary agency and so therefore declines the invitation to impose sanctions upon Amy. However, the court will refer Amy's conduct to the grievance committee of the Perplexity Supreme Court for further consideration.

What do you think of the trial court's decision? Is the court right, sort of right in a half-baked way, or deeply confused?

Explanation

Who Decides?

The court is somewhere between sort of right and deeply confused. The court is quite correct that it is not required to disqualify Amy because of her clear violation of Rule 1.9(a). (Just to be clear, this example was written to make the rule violation inarguable.) Asking the question above, *who is trying to do what to the lawyer?*, one of the parties in litigation is trying to disqualify the adversary's counsel. This is not a case where a grievance committee is seeking professional discipline. Compare Restatement §5. At the same time, however, the court is not precluded from disqualifying Amy. The court has the inherent authority (Track Two) to regulate the conduct of lawyers appearing before it. Restatement §6(8). It can do so if it determines that Amy has breached a duty of loyalty she owed, and continues to owe, to Landlord. It would be unfair to Landlord to have to litigate this case against her former attorney, Amy, who has behaved disloyally. The court should not have to sit idly by while Landlord's rights are violated in that way. Therefore, it is a reasonable exercise of the court's inherent authority to disqualify Amy.

It's true that Comment [20] from the Scope section of the rules seems to say that they apply only in disciplinary proceedings. But look carefully at the language. It says that violation of a rule does not *necessarily* warrant a nondisciplinary remedy. The court is not compelled to disqualify Amy, since it is not sitting as a disciplinary tribunal. That does not mean that it *may not* disqualify Amy. It only means that there is no *per se* rule requiring disqualification. As we'll see in the discussion of conflicts of interest, disqualification is an equitable remedy. A court may balance equities, including the prejudice to Tenant of being deprived of the attorney of her choice, the nature of Amy's misconduct and the resulting harm to Landlord, and the possibility that Landlord may be using the disqualification motion strategically as a way of driving up Tenant's costs. See Restatement §6, cmt. i. To say the trial court has discretion, however, implies that the trial court might abuse its discretion by refusing to disqualify Amy. That is what happened in the case upon which this example is loosely based, *Carlson v. Langdon*, 751 P.2d 344 (Wyo. 1988).

Note that Amy may also be subject to discipline by the Supreme Court of Perplexity for her violation of Rule 1.9(a). It is fairly rare for lawyers to be disciplined for a single violation of the conflicts rules, but it is possible in theory. If an MPRE question had asked whether Amy was subject to discipline in these circumstances, the answer would be something like "yes, because she represented Tenant in a matter substantially related to her previous representation of Landlord, without Landlord's informed consent."

A WORD ABOUT THE MPRE

Speaking of the MPRE, as of September 2015, 49 states (all but Wisconsin) and the District of Columbia require candidates for admission to practice law to take the Multistate Professional Responsibility Examination. It is administered by the National Conference of Bar Examiners (NCBE), the same folks who bring you the Multistate Bar Examination. The MPRE used to be the subject of ridicule. It tested only the issues in professional responsibility law in which the answer would be the same under the Model Code or the Model Rules, and completely ignored other sources of law, such as procedure, malpractice, and inherent power sanctions (as in the example above). The exam changed, significantly for the better, in 1999. The focus is now on the law governing lawyers generally, including but not limited to the disciplinary rules. To the extent the disciplinary rules determine the answer to a question, they are the rules as set out in the most recent version of the Model Rules:

> The MPRE is based on the law governing the conduct of lawyers, including the disciplinary rules of professional conduct currently articulated in the ABA Model Rules of Professional Conduct, the ABA Code of Judicial Conduct, as well as controlling constitutional decisions and generally accepted principles established in leading federal and state cases and in procedural and evidentiary rules.

The present version of the MPRE consists of 60 multiple-choice questions. The old joke used to be that you should figure out what the second most ethical thing to do would be, and that was the right answer. That's not a smart strategy for taking the MPRE today. Like I said, the exam is much better now, and you will have to be sharp on the law governing lawyers to get the answers right. This book is focused on in-depth analyses of the really challenging areas of professional responsibility, such as conflicts of interest and the intersection of confidentiality rules with duties of candor to the court and to third parties. If you look at the MPRE Subject Matter Outline (linked from the NCBE's Web site), as I strongly recommend you do, you'll see that the exam covers many of these topics in depth. For example, 12–18 percent of exam questions are on conflicts of interest and 6–12 percent are on confidentiality and privilege.

Full disclosure time: I am a member of the MPRE drafting committee, but if you are buying this book for inside dope, you'll be disappointed. This book is written with the objective of helping you understand the subject of professional responsibility, not just passing a test. Having said that, there's no doubt that you're more likely to do better on the MPRE if you have a solid understanding of the subject. I am proud of the work we do as a committee on the MPRE—I really do think it's a serious law-of-lawyering exam and not the bad joke it's sometimes reputed to be. So the best thing to do if you're concerned about the MPRE is take the time to really learn professional responsibility.

For registration and scheduling information, you can visit the National Conference of Bar Examiners Web site at http://www.ncbex.org.

And finally, here's an MPRE-style variation on the preceding example. Although the actual exam does not use proper names, like Amy, this question is in the usual yes, because/no, because format:

Example

Who Decides? (Variation)

Landlord filed an action to evict Tenant for nonpayment of rent on a large parcel of farm land. At the hearing on Landlord's motion for an order of eviction, Landlord was astonished to see her former attorney, Amy, representing Tenant. Amy had drafted the lease agreement and had represented Landlord at the closing of the lease with Tenant six months ago. At the hearing, on behalf of Tenant, Amy now argued that Tenant was entitled to withhold rent because Landlord had not made certain improvements to the property as required by the lease agreement. Landlord was furious, because he remembered discussing that provision of the lease, and Amy had assured him that it did not require making extensive improvements to the land.

Acting through his new attorney, Arnold, Landlord filed a motion with the court to disqualify Amy from representing Tenant. Is Amy subject to disqualification?

A. Yes, because the trial court has the authority to impose professional discipline on lawyers for violation of the rules of professional conduct.

B. Yes, because the trial court has the authority to administer remedies to regulate the course of proceedings before them.

> C. No, because the rules of professional conduct may be relied upon as the basis for a remedy only by a committee of the state's highest court.
> D. No, because the representation of Tenant is not the same matter on which Amy represented Landlord.

Explanation

Who Decides? (Variation)

B is the right answer, which should have been quite clear after the previous example and explanation. The point is merely to illustrate how the same principle can be used as the basis of a multiple-choice question. Note the language in the call of the question, "subject to disqualification." That does not mean the trial court will disqualify Amy — disqualification is an equitable remedy and maybe the trial court will find that the prejudice to Tenant would be too great (although that's doubtful). The "subject to . . ." call, whether discipline, disqualification, civil liability, or some other remedy, simply asks whether there is a legal basis for imposing the remedy.

If you answered A, go back and review the previous discussion on discipline versus other remedies. The trial court cannot impose professional discipline, which is only for the state's highest court acting through duly authorized grievance proceedings. That's why A is wrong, and C is wrong for the mirror image reason — that is, other tribunals may rely upon the rules as a source of guidance when imposing other remedies, such as disqualification. A subtle distinction? Maybe, but get used to reading the options on multiple-choice questions carefully. D is wrong because the matters are substantially related. We haven't gotten to that yet — we'll discuss former-client conflicts in Chapter 16 — but even a cursory reading of Rule 1.9(a) would have revealed the language "the same or a substantially related matter." Get used to reading the rules closely.

And with that, on to the law of professional responsibility!

PART I

The Attorney-
Client Relationship

CHAPTER 2

Formation and Termination

INTRODUCTION

Professional duties generally depend on the existence of a lawyer-client relationship. When a lawyer-client relationship exists, the lawyer owes a range of duties, including acting with reasonable care, keeping the client informed, following the client's lawful instructions where the client is empowered to make decisions, keeping confidences, refraining from representing conflicting interests, and not engaging in self-dealing. Many of these duties, such as the obligation to keep the client's secrets, continue after the termination of the relationship. Others, such as the duty to exercise reasonable care and carry out the client's instructions, end along with the relationship. Finally, the obligation to refrain from representing conflicting interests varies according to whether the relationship is ongoing or terminated. If it is ongoing, the lawyer is prohibited from representing a broader range of conflicting interests—representing clients in unrelated matters may be prohibited if the interests of one "materially limit" the lawyer's ability to represent the other. Thus, it is important that you always figure out whether the lawyer has formed a professional relationship with someone with whom she interacts, and whether that relationship is ongoing or has terminated.

An attorney-client relationship is a consensual one, arising by agreement (express or implied) of the parties. Rest. §14, cmt. b. It is also an *agency* relationship, meaning that one party, the principal, has agreed to grant authority to the other party, the agent, to act on the principal's behalf. An agency relationship is different from a partnership entered into with the expectation of mutual profit. Restatement §16, cmt. b. The agent acts on behalf of the principal, for the principal's benefit, and always giving priority to the principal's interests. Another way to state this is that the lawyer-client agency relationship is fiduciary in nature. In the frequently quoted words of Justice Cardozo, that means the lawyer is "held to something stricter than the morals of the marketplace." Conduct that may be "permissible in a workaday world for those acting at arm's length" may be forbidden in a fiduciary relationship. *Meinhard v. Salmon*, 164 N.E. 545 (N.Y. 1928). As we will discuss in Chapter 3, the contract between the lawyer and client divvies up rights and responsibilities between the parties, subject to two qualifications: (1) *Inherent authority.* Certain rights and obligations may not be varied by contract; they inhere in the very nature of the lawyer-client relationship. For example, a lawyer is never required to follow her client's instruction to perform or assist in unlawful acts or violate a court order. See Rest. §23. (2) *Fiduciary principle.* A lawyer is always required to use competence, diligence, good judgment, and loyalty to carry out the instructions of the client, keeping the client's interests first and not compromising them due to self-interest or the interest of others.

SHALL WE DANCE? FORMATION OF THE RELATIONSHIP

You may think that an attorney-client relationship is a rather formal thing, which must be solemnized with the right form of retainer agreement and a payment of fees. Most professional engagements with clients are formalized to some extent. There is generally an *express* agreement by the lawyer to act on behalf of the client. In other words, a contract establishes an agency relationship. That contract may be simple or elaborate, and may include terms pertaining to the lawyer's fee, the scope of the representation and, as we will see later on, waivers of certain rights the client otherwise would possess. Nevertheless, there are no particular magic words necessary to create an attorney-client relationship. The relationship can be implied from the conduct of the parties. Moreover, no money needs to change hands. An attorney-client relationship may arise out of a seemingly informal consultation, as long as a reasonable person in the client's shoes would interpret the lawyer's conduct as an agreement to provide legal services. And if that relationship does arise, the lawyer will have the full range of professional duties to the "client," including the requirement to keep the client's confidences, the duty to refrain from representing conflicting interests, and the obligation to represent the client diligently and effectively.

There are two different types of implied relationships arising from the conduct of the parties. The first is important as a theoretical matter, but it does not cause too much confusion in the law governing lawyers. For lack of a better name, I will refer to the first type as an "implied-in-fact, full-on professional relationship." (You can abbreviate it as IIFFO if you like, but that's hardly less cumbersome than the name.) In these relationships, the lawyer owes the full range of professional obligations to the client, including competence, communication, diligence, loyalty, and so on. It is really the same thing as a "regular" expressly formed relationship, the only difference being that the agreement of the parties can be inferred from their actions. (Sometimes they arise accidentally, if the lawyer is not careful to avoid creating a reasonable belief on the client's part that she has consented to act on behalf of the client.) The second type of relationship, which I refer to as a quasi-client relationship, is pervasive and troublesome in the law. In a quasi-client relationship, the lawyer owes some professional obligations to the would-be client, but the relationship cannot be characterized as otherwise equivalent to a regular, full-on attorney-client relationship.

Implied-in-Fact, Full-On Professional Relationships

A well-known legal malpractice case illustrates the formation of an implied-in-fact, full-on professional relationship. In *Togstad v. Vesely, Otto, Miller & Keefe*, 291 N.W.2d 686 (Minn. 1980), a potential personal-injury client came to a law office to see whether she (on behalf of herself and her husband) could sue a doctor and hospital for medical malpractice. The lawyer listened patiently, took down the facts, and then said a couple of things, according to the potential client. First, he said he did not think Mrs. Togstad had a legal case. But he also said that he would discuss the case with his partner. The lawyer remembered the conversation slightly differently—he recalled telling Mrs. Togstad that she did not have a case that the firm would be interested in pursuing. In any event, the lawyer called a friend of his who was more knowledgeable about medical malpractice cases, concluded that Mrs. Togstad's case was not worth bringing, and let the matter drop. Mrs. Togstad never consulted another lawyer until after the statute of limitations had passed on her medical malpractice claim.

In the ensuing *legal* malpractice action, the lawyer claimed that there was never an attorney-client relationship between him and Mrs. Togstad. The court, however, observed that Mrs. Togstad relied to her detriment on the lawyer's representation that she did not have a case. The lawyer never told her to seek another opinion, and he certainly never suggested that he was uninterested in the case not because it lacked legal merit, but because his firm did not have much experience with medical malpractice cases. After concluding that an attorney-client relationship had been formed, the court had little trouble concluding that the lawyer's failure to do even minimal research into Mrs. Togstad's claim was malpractice.

According to the Restatement, an attorney-client relationship can be formed by implication from the conduct of the parties as long as two conditions are satisfied: (1) the "client" behaved in such a way that a reasonable person in the lawyer's position would believe that she was being asked to provide legal services; and (2) the "lawyer" behaved in such a way that a reasonable person in the client's position would believe that the lawyer has either agreed to provide legal services or at least not refused to do so. Rest. §14. The Minnesota Supreme Court held in *Togstad* that, although there was some conflict in the evidence, a jury could reasonably conclude that both of these conditions were met. (The Restatement did not exist at the time, but the court's reasoning tracks the rule in Rest. §14 nicely.) First, Mrs. Togstad's actions could only mean that she was asking the lawyer to provide legal services. Second, the lawyer's statement that he did not think Mrs. Togstad had a case but he would discuss it with his partner and get back to her if he changed his mind, could be interpreted by a reasonable person in the would-be client's position as an undertaking by the lawyer to provide legal services. Thus, an agency relationship existed between the parties, and the lawyer had a duty to use reasonable care to protect Mrs. Togstad's interests.

Quasi-Client Relationships

In a full-on professional relationship, express or implied, the lawyer has certain professional obligations. We can call these duties the "Four Cs":

- *Competence*: Providing knowledgeable, skillful, thorough, and effective representation. Rule 1.1.
- *Communication*: Informing the client of all facts the client would need to know to make informed decisions about the matter. Rule 1.4. You might also call this the duty of *candor*, picking up on the language of Rule 2.1, which provides that "a lawyer shall exercise independent professional judgment and render candid advice."
- *Confidentiality*: Keeping absolutely secret all information learned in the course of representing the client, and not using this information in any way that would have an adverse effect on the client. Rule 1.6.
- *Conflicts*: Refraining from representing other clients in the present time or in the future whose interests are opposed in certain ways to the first client, and refraining from self-dealing. Rules 1.7, 1.8. This fourth "C" is often referred to as the duty of *loyalty*.

In a quasi-client relationship, a lawyer owes a subset of these duties to the client, but does not otherwise represent the client. The crucial idea is a bit abstract, but it should become clear from examining the cases; it is the following:

> To the extent a nonclient entrusts some legal interest to a lawyer, in circumstances when it would be reasonable to do so, the lawyer has duties to that person or entity *in respect of that interest*.

The person or entity thus becomes something less than a full-on client, but also not a stranger—hence the term "quasi-client."[1] The lawyer's professional duties correspond to the interest entrusted, but the lawyer does not necessarily represent the quasi-client in general, with respect to the full range of interests. So, for example, if a quasi-client shares confidential information with a lawyer, the lawyer has a duty not to disclose or make adverse use of the information. See Rule 1.6(a), Rule 1.8(b). The lawyer does not necessarily have further duties to the quasi-client, unless the circumstances of the formation of the relationship support them.

Quasi-client relationships pop up all the time in the law governing lawyers, particularly in conflicts of interest cases. For example, in a famous conflicts case, a law firm representing a trade association of which A was a member was disqualified from representing B in a lawsuit against A. *Westinghouse Electric v. Kerr-McGee*, 580 F.2d 1311 (7th Cir. 1978). The firm had never represented A directly, but A had shared confidential information with the trade association client, which in turn had passed it on to the law firm. In frequently quoted language, the court said that "[a] professional relationship is not dependent upon the payment of fees nor . . . upon the execution of a formal contract." But if the formalities of a professional relationship do not determine the scope of a lawyer's duties, what is the standard? The court listed a number of analogous situations, in which the client believed he was consulting the lawyer in a professional capacity, with the intent of obtaining legal assistance. The common denominator in most of these cases, justifying the inference that the client had intended to consult the lawyer in a professional capacity, was *transmission of confidential information* with the expectation that the lawyer would keep it confidential. The members of the trade association had shared information with the law firm because they assumed the trade association, and its law firm, were acting in their interests. Once the firm acquired that information, it had a duty to keep it confidential and to refrain from representing conflicting interests,

---

1. I use the term "quasi-client," but there is no consistently employed description for this type of relationship. Some courts use the term "implied attorney-client relationship" to signify the same thing. See, e.g., *Clark Capital Management Group v. Annuity Investors Life Ins. Co.*, 149 F. Supp. 2d 193 (E.D. Pa. 2001). That is fine as long as you distinguish between quasi-clients and implied-in-fact, full-on clients.

even though it did not have a formal professional relationship with A and the other trade association members.

Most quasi-client relationships arise in this way, so keep your eye on the sharing of confidential information with a lawyer—there's a good chance the lawyer will have professional duties to that person, even in the absence of payment of a fee, an engagement letter, or other indicia of a formal attorney-client relationship. Notice that in the *Westinghouse* case, however, the law firm did not have the full panoply of professional duties to the trade association members. The law firm was obligated only to do or refrain from doing things with respect to the confidential information imparted by the member companies. That means not disclosing it to its other client, Westinghouse, and not using the confidential information adversely to the interests of the member companies. The law firm did not have a responsibility to protect the interests of the member companies in other respects, however, such as by advising them about ways they could act individually to forestall antitrust legislation. For those purposes the trade association was the sole client of the law firm.

Prospective Clients and "Beauty Contests"

Law firms sometimes participate in competitive initial interviews in which lawyers from different firms pitch for a valuable prospective client's business. A "prospective client" is anyone who discusses with a lawyer the possibility of forming a professional relationship. Rule 1.18(a). Whenever there is some kind of large-scale event that promises to generate substantial litigation, there may be a number of parties with potentially adverse interests shopping for lawyers and wanting to interview the top firms in the local area. In the male-dominated parlance of big-firm lawyers, these are called "beauty contests." Beauty contests can be dangerous, because if the lawyer learns confidential information from interviewing Prospective Client A, who chooses not to hire the lawyer, she will be disqualified from representing Prospective Clients B, C, D, and so on, if their interests are adverse to Prospective Client A in the same matter. That is to say, Prospective Client A becomes a quasi-client of the firm, which is obligated in one particular respect, that is, to refrain from accepting the representation of Prospective Clients B, C, or D. See Rule 1.18(c), which is an application of the former-client conflicts rule, discussed in Chapter 16.

Lawyers should be careful not to learn confidential information from prospective clients, in order to avoid being disqualified from representing adverse parties in the future. See some new language added to cmt. [2] to Rule 1.18 by the Ethics 20/20 Commission, advising lawyers to provide "clear and reasonably understandable warnings and cautionary statements" on electronic marketing materials so prospective clients know the lawyer is not undertaking to represent them when they communicate information to the lawyer. In addition, lawyers have a duty of confidentiality with respect to any information learned from a prospective client, quite apart from the rules on conflicts of interest. Rule 1.18(b). If a lawyer learns from the representative of a local corporation that it intends to make a hostile tender offer for another company, the lawyer may not reveal that information, even if the corporation ends up hiring a different lawyer to represent it in the tender offer.

Entity-Constituent Representation

We will encounter the issue of client identity again in connection with conflicts of interest, including in Chapter 5, in connection with the special issues that arise relating to the representation of entities — "organizations as clients," as Rule 1.13 puts it. It is important to flag this issue here, however, because it really is one of the classic quasi-client or implied-in-fact client scenarios. When representing an entity client such as a corporation, partnership, or an unincorporated association (a union, say, or a trade association), the lawyer represents the entity itself, acting through its duly authorized constituents. Rule 1.13(a). What that means is that any flesh-and-blood people the lawyer deals with in the course of the representation are *not* the lawyer's clients. The word "constituents" in Rule 1.13(a) refers to the entity's "officers, directors, employees, and shareholders" or the equivalent in an unincorporated association. Rule 1.13, cmt. [1]. Constituents serve the entity in some capacity, too, and have their own duties to act in the best interests of the entity. In agency law terms, the lawyer and employee are co-agents of the entity. As we will see in Chapter 8, sometimes the communications between lawyers and constituents of an entity client are protected by the entity's attorney-client privilege. But again, it is the entity itself that is the client, not the constituents.

This is all well and good in theory, but in practice the people a lawyer deals with may come to trust and rely upon the lawyer, and may even believe that the lawyer is looking out for their interests *as individuals*, not just insofar as they both serve the interests of the organization. If the lawyer does something to cause a constituent to believe *reasonably* that the lawyer is acting in the individual interests of the constituent, the lawyer may have either an implied-in-fact, full-on attorney-client relationship or a quasi-client relationship with the individual. That means the lawyer may have a conflict of interest, because it may be impossible simultaneously to satisfy obligations the lawyer owes to the entity (such as confidentiality and loyalty) and obligations owed to the individual constituent as a quasi-client. In order to prevent this outcome, the entity-representation rule requires lawyers to explain to constituents that the client itself is the entity, not any individual officers, employees, or other people within the organization. Rule 1.13(f). This is widely known as a "corporate *Miranda*" warning, after the familiar warning to criminal suspects in custody that anything they say "can and will be used against you in a court of law."

Examples

The Usual Preliminaries

1. Capital Group has sued Investors Life for trademark infringement. Investors Life hired a trademark lawyer, David French, to represent it in the litigation. French realized he needed assistance from a litigation specialist, so he called a well-known lawyer in town, Tanya Boomer, to see if she would be willing to associate with him as co-counsel for Investors Life. French and Boomer spoke in general terms about the case, with French describing the trademark infringement case and saying he would expect to use "the usual affirmative defenses." French asked Boomer if she would send some information about the firm, including its experience handling trademark litigation, the background of lawyers who might work on the case, and their billing rates. Boomer said she would be unable to make a decision about representing Investors Life without first running a conflicts check, and French replied that he of course knew that Boomer had to check for conflicts first.

    After running a conflicts check, Boomer learned that her firm represented Capital Group, the plaintiff in the case. She called French and informed him that she would be unable to associate with him as co-counsel. A few weeks later, Investors Life filed a motion to disqualify Boomer's firm from representing Capital Group, arguing that an implied attorney-client relationship was formed by the consultation between French and Boomer.

Lawyers in Cyberspace

2. Hildebrand is a domestic-relations lawyer in the State of Perplexity with significant expertise in international child-custody issues, including the interpretation on the Hague Convention on the Civil Aspects of Child Abduction. He maintains a Web site about international child-custody law, which features articles about the Hague Convention and a list of Frequently Asked Questions (FAQs) and answers. In addition to the articles and FAQs, the Web site has a prominently displayed e-mail link, which reads: "If you have further questions about the international law of child custody, please feel free to contact me for a consultation. I would be happy to discuss your case and perhaps to represent you." Clicking on the link creates an outgoing e-mail message directed to Hildebrand.

Corbin is the father of a small child who is involved in an acrimonious divorce and child-custody proceeding. Without the mother's consent, Corbin took the child to Canada and refused to return to the United States. He became concerned that he might be violating the law, so he did some research on the Internet. By typing "Hague Convention on Child Abduction" into Google, he discovered Hildebrand's Web site. Corbin sent Hildebrand an e-mail message in which he admitted that he had taken the child out of the country without the consent of the mother and requested advice about how to proceed further. A few days passed, during which time Corbin believed he had hired Hildebrand as his lawyer. After a few days, however, Hildebrand sent a message to Corbin that read: "Thank you for your inquiry. Unfortunately, at the present time I am unable to represent you. Best of luck with your legal matter."

A month later, Corbin's wife, who lived in the State of Perplexity, asked Hildebrand to represent her in a proceeding to obtain custody of her child. When Hildebrand agreed and entered a notice of appearance in the custody litigation, Corbin was outraged. He filed a motion to disqualify Hildebrand. What will be the result?

"You're Not Representing Me, Too?"

3. Broadband Corporation is a manufacturer of switching equipment used in computer networks. Like many Silicon Valley companies, it compensates its senior officers in part by granting them generous stock options. These options allow them to acquire shares of stock at the price at which the stock was trading on the date they were issued. Compensating officers with stock options gives them an incentive to increase the stock price of the company, because they will be able to profit from the difference between the price on the date when they exercised their option and the price on the date on which the option was issued. Unfortunately, dishonest officers may also have an incentive to backdate their stock options. This is illegal if it results in corporate shareholders being misled, and can result in significant civil and criminal liability for the corporation.

After being notified of an investigation of backdating by the Securities and Exchange Commission (SEC), Broadband hired a law firm to conduct an internal investigation. The chief executive officer of Broadband instructed the law firm to interview corporate officers, audit the corporation's books, and determine whether illegal activity had occurred. Rheumy is the chief financial officer (CFO) of Broadband. He participated in decisions by senior management to hire the law firm to investigate alleged backdating. As the corporate CFO, he was intimately involved in decisions concerning executive compensation and granting stock options. Rheumy met with two partners from the law firm. During the hour-long meeting, the lawyers explained the nature of the investigation, and told him that there were serious civil and criminal penalties for participating in backdating. Rheumy asked, "Can I trust you?" One of the lawyers replied, "You know we're on the same team." Rheumy then admitted that he had approved granting options to several senior managers and had secretly backdated them to increase their value.

The next day, the two lawyers informed the board of directors of what Rheumy had told them. At the urging of the board of directors of Broadband, the law firm disclosed to the SEC that a senior officer of Broadband had approved the backdating, but it was not company policy and the company had taken disciplinary action against the officer. In fact, Broadband fired Rheumy immediately upon learning of the secret backdating. The SEC then informed the Justice Department about the information it had learned from the law firm, and prosecutors obtained an indictment of Rheumy for criminal securities fraud. Satisfied that the misconduct was solely the responsibility of Rheumy, the rogue officer, the SEC closed its investigation of Broadband.

Outraged, Rheumy filed a lawsuit against the firm, alleging breach of fiduciary duty. The law firm moved to dismiss the lawsuit, arguing that it had an attorney-client relationship only with Broadband, and thus had no fiduciary duties to Rheumy, including obligations of loyalty and keeping confidences. Should the motion to dismiss be granted?

Explanations

The Usual Preliminaries

1. This example is based on a real case, *Clark Capital Management Group v. Annuity Investors Life Ins. Co.*, 149 F. Supp. 2d 193 (E.D. Pa. 2001), and the district court quite properly denied the motion to disqualify the firm for a conflict of interest. It is helpful to consider the *disanalogies* with the *Togstad* case to see why Boomer did not have an implied-in-fact relationship with Investors Life. The most important difference is the varying levels of sophistication of the people dealing with the lawyer in each case. Mrs. Togstad reasonably could have understood the purpose of her conversation with the lawyer as "obtaining legal advice." When the lawyer said, "You do not have a case that we would be interested in pursuing," she focused on the part where the lawyer said she did not have a case. Although the lawyer subjectively intended to emphasize that he did not have the expertise or interest to handle the medical malpractice case, Mrs. Togstad's *reasonable* expectation was that the lawyer had given her legal advice. See Rest. §14(1)(b), which depends on the *reasonable* reliance of the prospective client on the lawyer's apparent undertaking to represent her.

In this case, unlike *Togstad*, French could not reasonably have believed that Boomer was providing legal services during the preliminary consultation. First, he was a lawyer, for Pete's sake. Second, he asked Boomer to send information about firm personnel and their billing rates, suggesting that he was shopping around for co-counsel, not believing he had retained Boomer's firm. Finally, he was not surprised when Boomer said she had to perform a conflicts check. All of these facts show French is sophisticated enough to know that a lawyer cannot commit to representing a prospective client before ensuring that she is not already representing an adverse party. Because French did not have a *justified* expectation that Boomer was providing legal services to Investors Life, the client cannot claim that it has a protectable interest in the information its lawyer shared with Boomer.

Lawyers in Cyberspace

2. This example is based on *Knigge v. Corvese*, 2001 U.S. Dist. LEXIS 10254 (S.D.N.Y. July 23, 2001), the facts of which I have embellished somewhat.[2] For now we will discuss this case mostly under the principles of Restatement §14. You should be aware, however, that there is a provision of the Model Rules dealing with duties owed by lawyers to *prospective* clients. See Rule 1.18. A lawyer may be disqualified from representing a new client, like the wife in this case, even if the lawyer did not end up representing the adverse party.

Don't be fooled by the high-tech setting. This case can be handled as just another example of the rule in Restatement §14 that an attorney-client relationship can be formed without solemn formalities. See Calif. Ethics Op. 2003-161 (communication with prospective client outside office setting can create duty of confidentiality if the lawyer's words or actions would give a reasonable person the belief that the lawyer is being consulted in her professional capacity). Work through the elements of the Restatement rule. Did Corbin manifest an intent that Hildebrand provide legal services, thus satisfying Restatement §14(1)? Yes. Did Hildebrand manifest to Corbin consent to provide legal services, thus satisfying Restatement §14(1)(a)? Subjectively he did not; see his e-mail to Corbin declining to take the case. It's unlikely that Hildebrand's failure to decline representation immediately would be understood by a reasonable person as a failure to manifest lack of consent to represent Corbin. A reasonable person would not expect an immediate response to an unsolicited request for representation. Like Example 1, and like the

---

2. I am grateful to my student Douglas Schnell for bringing this case and related authorities to my attention.

Togstad case, everything here hinges on the reasonableness of Corbin's belief that Hildebrand was his attorney.

Since 2001, when this case was decided, there has been quite a bit of discussion about the impact of the law of lawyering on electronic marketing and client development efforts by attorneys. One of the issues is whether interactive electronic media should be treated as a means by which clients can consult with lawyers. In other words, might a Web site be simply the online equivalent of the office in which Mrs. Togstad met with the lawyer? The ABA Ethics 20/20 Commission recently adopted an amendment to Rule 1.18, cmt. [2], which reads:

> Whether communications, including written, oral, or electronic communica-
> tions, constitute a consultation depends on the circumstances. For example, a
> consultation is likely to have occurred if a lawyer, either in person or through
> the lawyer's advertising in any medium, specifically requests or invites the
> submission of information about a potential representation without clear and
> reasonably understandable warnings and cautionary statements that limit the
> lawyer's obligations, and a person provides information in response.

This comment suggests that Hildebrand really should improve his Web site. He invites would-be clients to e-mail him for a consultation, and does not include a cautionary statement not to share confidential information. Remember that transmission of confidential information is one of the classic ways to form an implied professional relationship.

As mentioned, even if Corbin and Hildebrand did not form an attorney-client relationship, Hildebrand still would have some duties to Corbin as a *prospective* client. See Rule 1.18. Corbin would be a prospective client if he "consults with a lawyer about the possibility of forming a client-lawyer relationship with respect to a matter." Rule 1.18(a). The lawyer must not reveal any information learned from Corbin, such as his admission that he took the child to Canada without permission. Rule 1.18(b). Note, too, that Hildebrand will not be permitted to represent an adverse party, such as Corbin's soon-to-be-ex-wife, in the same matter without the consent of both parties. Rule 1.18(c). This last aspect of the rule foreshadows the analysis of conflicts of interest, later in the book.

"You're Not Representing Me, Too?"

3. This example is based on *U.S. v. Nicholas*, 606 F. Supp. 2d 1109 (C.D. Cal), *rev'd sub nom. U.S. v. Ruehle*, 583 F.3d 600 (9th Cir. 2009), involving a criminal prosecution of executives of Broadcom Corporation for allegedly backdating stock options. The law firm of Irell & Manella represented Broadcom in the internal investigation, and really ticked off the district judge by seeming to lead Ruehle, the CFO of Broadcom, to believe that the firm was also representing him in his individual capacity. (The district

judge actually referred the firm to the California State Bar for potential discipline.) There are a lot of technical issues in the actual case, the most important of which is whether, and under what circumstances, a corporate officer may invoke an individual attorney-client privilege to prevent the disclosure of communications between herself and a lawyer for the organization. See, for example, *In re Grand Jury Subpoena*, 274 F.3d 563 (1st Cir. 2001); *In re Bevill, Bresler & Schulman Asset Mgmt. Corp.*, 805 F.2d 120 (3d Cir. 1986). In the real case, the district judge held that statements made by Ruehle, the CFO, were protected by an individual attorney-client privilege. "Mr. Ruehle reasonably believed that the Irell lawyers were meeting with him as his personal lawyers, not just Broadcom's lawyers." 606 F. Supp. 2d at 1112. The court excoriated the law firm for not giving a "corporate *Miranda* warning" to Ruehle, and said the firm breached its duty of loyalty to him. The court of appeals reversed, avoiding the complicated *Bevill* issues by focusing on the "in confidence" element of the attorney-client privilege. Whether or not Ruehle had a reasonable belief that the law firm was representing him individually, he knew that any statements he made to the firm about stock-option-granting practices would be disclosed to the auditor for Broadcom and ultimately to the government. Because none of the statements were made with an expectation that they remain confidential, there could be no individual or corporate attorney-client privilege in the communications. 583 F.3d at 609-10.

In the simplified version presented here, the question is whether an implied-in-fact full-on relationship or a quasi-client relationship exists between Rheumy and the lawyers for Broadband. I included a little snippet of dialogue, which is deliberately ambiguous, just as in the *Togstad* case. What does it mean when the lawyer says, "You know we're on the same team," in response to Rheumy's question of whether he can trust them? A lot depends on what goes unspoken in that exchange. Rheumy is pretty clearly asking the lawyers whether he *as an individual* can trust them to take care of *his* personal legal interests, including protecting him from criminal liability for participating in the backdating. So why didn't the lawyers just come right out and give the corporate *Miranda* warning? Surely it would have been a simple matter for them to say, "Look, Mr. Rheumy, you have to understand that we are representing Broadband, not you. Our duty of loyalty runs to the corporation. So anything you tell us, we might use against you if it helps our client, Broadband." What do you think would happen then? Rheumy would clam up and the lawyers would learn nothing at the meeting. The lawyers were trying to finesse their disclosure requirement, hoping that they could say just enough to avoid creating some kind of professional relationship with Rheumy, but not so much that they'd scare him into silence. It worked, in the sense that they got the information they needed. Broadband was able to offer up Rheumy as a scapegoat and satisfy the government that it was not involved in the backdating. That's great for the company, but lousy for Rheumy. No wonder he sued for breach of fiduciary duty!

In the real case, it mattered a great deal to the Ninth Circuit that Ruehle was the CFO of Broadcom, and knew perfectly well the purpose of an internal investigation. The court was pretty skeptical that a high-level corporate officer could ever have a *reasonable* belief that an outside law firm, called in to do an internal investigation, would take care of the individual legal needs of an officer. That's particularly true when the officer personally participated in the decision to hire the law firm for the investigation. The real Ruehle was no hayseed, but a sophisticated manager familiar with retaining outside counsel. In this example, however, it would be fair to conclude that the ambiguous dialogue between Rheumy and the lawyers could create a reasonable belief on the part of Rheumy that the law firm was representing him as an individual—that is, that a professional relationship existed between them that was independent of the firm's relationship with the company. Thus, the motion to dismiss the lawsuit should be denied.

For another well-known example of an implied professional relationship between the lawyers for a company and an employee of the company, consider *Perez v. Kirk & Carrigan*, 822 S.W.2d 261 (Tex. Ct. App. 1991). Following a horrific accident (upon which the excellent Russell Banks novel *The Sweet Hereafter* was based, by the way), the lawyer for the company interviewed an employee, Perez, who had been driving a delivery truck that collided with a school bus. The lawyers told Perez that "they were his lawyers too" and that they would keep secret anything he told them. Perez described his role in the accident, and much to his consternation, the lawyers subsequently gave this statement to the local prosecutor, who indicted Perez for manslaughter. Perez successfully sued the lawyers for breaching their duty of confidentiality.

FIFTY WAYS TO LEAVE YOUR CLIENT: TERMINATION OF THE PROFESSIONAL RELATIONSHIP

An attorney-client relationship can end like any other—one of the parties may explicitly call it quits, or the relationship can fail over time, as the bonds that hold the parties together gradually weaken. Unlike nonprofessional relationships, though, there are situations in which the lawyer *must* call it quits. The rule governing *mandatory* withdrawal is stated in Rule 1.16(a). Basically, the lawyer must either refuse to begin representing a client or withdraw from an existing attorney-client relationship if the lawyer is fired by the client, the lawyer is unable, by reason of a physical or mental disability, to represent the client adequately, or the representation would result in a violation of the rules of professional conduct or other law. Examples of the third situation include accepting a new client or continuing an existing relationship that would involve the lawyer in concurrently representing conflicting interests (a violation of the disciplinary rules—see Chapter 15), or where the client's conduct would constitute actionable fraud under tort or securities law (a violation of "other law"). In addition to these three situations in which termination of the relationship is required, there are numerous conditions under which withdrawal is *permissive*—that is, the lawyer or the client may terminate the relationship, but are not required to do so.

In cases where withdrawal is not mandatory, lawyers must be extremely careful to respect the rules on permissible withdrawal. If a lawyer terminates the relationship without good cause—that is, in a situation that is not permitted by the rules—the lawyer may be liable to the client for malpractice or breach of fiduciary duty. Recoverable damages would include the expense of finding substitute counsel on short notice, which may be quite costly.

Client Fires the Lawyer

Clients can fire lawyers for pretty much any reason, good or bad, with only a few exceptions. If the client terminates the professional relationship, the lawyer is obligated to withdraw. Rule 1.16(a)(3). In litigation, the client must seek permission from the court supervising the lawsuit. Rest. §31, cmt. c. In some cases, a court may not permit a client to fire her lawyer too close to trial, because it will seem to be merely a tactical ploy to buy more time. (In the real world, the judge in *Legally Blonde* would not have permitted the defendant to fire the Alan Dershowitz–like lawyer in the middle of trial and retain the law student, never mind that no state permits first-year law students to represent clients in court.) The client is still obligated to pay the lawyer's fee, unless the client has a defense to the contract for fees, based on the lawyer's malpractice or breach of fiduciary duty, or the unreasonableness of the fee.[3]

---

3. There are complex issues of remedies law involved in cases where clients fire lawyers who are compensated on a contingency basis. Many courts permit a fired contingency-fee lawyer to recover the fair value of her services in *quantum meruit*. Rest. §40, cmt. b, Reporter's Note. For a colorful example of this principle in action, see *Mobley Law Firm v. Lisle Law Firm*, 120 S.W.3d 537 (Ark. 2003). After the client asked the lawyer why his case had not progressed, the lawyer responded, "I don't have a speedometer up my ass." The client, unsurprisingly, dumped the lawyer and hired a new lawyer, who settled the client's lawsuit for $50,000. The original lawyer (call him "Speedo") then sued for one-third of the settlement amount—$16,667, representing his full contractual entitlement. The Arkansas Supreme Court, however, found that Speedo was fired for good cause and was entitled only to one-fourth of the $16,667 fee.

There are a few limitations on the client's permission to fire the lawyer at any time, crafted to take into account other interests protected by law. The most significant involves the lawyer as whistleblower. Although a client may fire a *retained* lawyer for any reason, at any time, a client may be limited in its right to fire an *in-house* lawyer—that is, a lawyer employed by the client, not hired as an independent contractor. In-house lawyers are both lawyers and employees, so they might enjoy some of the protections extended to ordinary employees. One of these rights is the protection from retaliatory discharge for bringing safety or regulatory concerns to the attention of management. A few cases have extended protection from retaliatory discharge to in-house lawyers. See, for example, *General Dynamics v. Superior Court*, 876 P.2d 487 (Cal. 1994).

Lawyer Fires the Client

The right of lawyers to discharge clients can be conditional or unconditional. A lawyer can fire a client for any reason as long as it does not create a "material adverse effect on the interests of the client." Rule 1.16(b)(1). In addition, the lawyer may discharge the client even if withdrawal would have a material adverse effect on the client's interests, in one of six situations enumerated in Rule 1.16(b)(2)-(7). The most significant of these grounds is the client persisting in a course of action that the lawyer reasonably believes is criminal or fraudulent, Rule 1.16(b)(2), discovery that the client has used the lawyer's services to perpetrate a crime or fraud, Rule 1.16(b)(3), and a fundamental disagreement with the client's choice of actions, Rule 1.16(b)(4).

Just as in the case of the client firing the lawyer, a lawyer seeking to withdraw during pending litigation must notify the tribunal and seek approval to withdraw. Rule 1.16(c); Rest. §32, cmt. d. This is usually accomplished by filing a motion to substitute counsel. If the court denies the motion, the original lawyer is obligated to continue to represent the client in a manner best calculated to further the legal goals of the client. Rest. §32, cmt. d.

Note that a lawyer *must* withdraw from representation if continuing the representation will result in a violation of the disciplinary rules or other law. Rule 1.16(a)(1). An example of this situation would be where the client has used the lawyer's services to perpetrate a fraud and an ongoing relationship would have the effect of increasing the financial harm to the victims of the fraud. (See the discussion in Chapter 12 of the client fraud problem.) Becoming involved in client fraud is pretty unusual, but a common scenario mandating withdrawal is a conflict of interest. If ongoing representation would result in violation of Rules 1.7, 1.8, or 1.9, the lawyer is required to withdraw from the representation. Lawyers also must withdraw if they are impaired, by a physical or mental disability, from representing their clients competently. Rule 1.16(a)(2).

Breaking Up Is Hard to Do: Relationship Erodes over Time

If both the lawyer and the client agree that the representation is a one-time event (for example, defending a lawsuit, obtaining a trademark, buying a parcel of land), it is easy to figure out when the representation has ended. It ends when the "lawyer has completed the contemplated services." Rest. §31(2)(e). Things get murkier, however, when the scope of the professional relationship is not very clearly defined at the outset, or where the client has used the lawyer's services occasionally over a long period of time. A client may assume that a lawyer is "looking after the client's affairs" in cases where the lawyer thinks the relationship was terminated. See Rule 1.3, cmt. [4]. The risk, however, is that an ongoing relationship creates ongoing duties. As long as the attorney-client relationship persists, the lawyer will be required to communicate relevant information to the client, represent the client diligently, and refrain from representing conflicting interests. (The lawyer's duty of confidentiality continues beyond the termination of the relationship. Rule 1.6, cmt. [18].) To minimize liability risks, lawyers should take affirmative steps to confirm that the professional relationship has ended, such as writing a letter to the client and returning any materials that the client is entitled to possess.

Of course, lawyers hate to end the relationship definitively, preferring to be available to represent the client again in the future. Over time, though, the parties can drift apart, and eventually neither party would reasonably believe that the lawyer is continuing to represent the client. In that case, the relationship can be regarded as having ended. One court has said that the question of whether there is an ongoing attorney-client relationship "turns largely on the client's subjective understanding of whether such a relationship exists, provided that subjective belief is reasonable under all the circumstances." *Oxford Systems v. Cellpro, Inc.*, 45 F. Supp. 2d 1055, 1060 (W.D. Wash. 1999). If you think about it, this is just the flip side of the test in Restatement §14, for whether a professional relationship is formed in the first place. If the client believes there is an ongoing relationship, and a reasonable person in the client's position would believe that the lawyer is still duty-bound to represent the client, then the relationship is continuing.

Clients may *justifiably* believe that the attorney-client relationship is ongoing where a lawyer or law firm continues to send marketing materials like "current developments in the law" newsletters; the firm retains important client documents, such as a corporate minute book; or the client pays any bills the lawyer sends. If the client has used the lawyer's services repeatedly over a course of many years, courts are more likely to conclude that the relationship is ongoing, unless a lengthy period of time has elapsed since the lawyer last performed legal services for the client. On the other hand, a reasonable person might believe the attorney-client relationship has terminated if the client has refused to pay a bill and the lawyer has not followed up to collect the amount due, or if the client has hired other lawyers and the first lawyer is aware of this fact. Courts are more likely to find that the professional relationship has terminated by drift if it was a single, discrete matter instead of a series of matters over time.

We'll talk about this later in the conflicts of interest section, but there's a colorfully named rule, called the "hot potato doctrine," which prohibits lawyers from firing clients just so they can be in a position to take on the more lucrative representation of another client, which would otherwise be prohibited by the conflicts rules. The gist of the hot potato rule is that a lawyer cannot terminate the representation at any point prior to what the parties had considered, *ex ante*, as the natural completion of the matter. See Rest. §132, cmt. c. Any purported termination will be deemed ineffective and the multiple representation must be analyzed as a current-client conflict.

Duties upon Discharge

Whether a lawyer is required to withdraw or does so with permission, for one of the grounds set out in Rule 1.16(b), the lawyer has ongoing duties of loyalty to the now former client. The lawyer must take steps to minimize the harm to the client resulting from withdrawal, including giving notice to the client, allowing time for the client to secure substitute counsel, and returning papers and property that belong to the client. Rule 1.16(d). The lawyer must also refund any unearned amounts advanced by way of a retainer. Not all papers in the client's file belong to the client. Research memos and the like, which reflect the lawyer's work product, may belong to the lawyer. Moreover, state law may permit lawyers to take a "retaining lien" in client property. That means the lawyer can hang on to client property until the client pays fees that are owed to the lawyer.

Following the termination of the attorney-client relationship, the lawyer has an ongoing duty of confidentiality, which lasts forever. Rule 1.6, cmt. [18]; Rule 1.9(c)(2). Lawyers are not only prohibited from disclosing confidential client information pertaining to a former client, but also may not make adverse use to the disadvantage of a former client, unless the information has become publicly known. Rule 1.9(c)(1).

Examples

Dealing with Dodgy Clients

4. Lawyer discovers that Client has used Lawyer's services to prepare and distribute a private placement memorandum for a securities offering which contains materially misleading financial information. Which of the following is a correct statement?
   A. Lawyer may withdraw from the representation of Client, but need not do so.
   B. Lawyer must withdraw from the representation of Client.
   C. Lawyer may withdraw only if withdrawal will not result in prejudice to Client.
   D. Lawyer may not withdraw from representing Client without court permission.

5. During the representation of Client, Lawyer discovers evidence that leads Lawyer to reasonably believe that Client is using Lawyer's services to lay the foundation for a future tax fraud. Must Lawyer withdraw from the representation?
   A. Yes, because the continued representation will result in a violation of other law.
   B. Yes, because Client's course of action involves Lawyer's services in fraudulent conduct.
   C. No, because Lawyer does not know that the representation will result in a violation of other law.
   D. No, because tax fraud is not a violation of the rules of professional conduct.

Explanations

Dealing with Dodgy Clients

4. The answer is (A). See Rule 1.16(b)(3). (B) is *arguably* not the answer because withdrawal is mandatory only if the violation of the rules or other law is in the future. Read Rule 1.16(a)(1) carefully. Although it is beyond the scope of many professional responsibility courses, you should know that, in some circumstances and under some theories of fraud, a client's past fraud may have continuing effect, and a lawyer's failure to withdraw might be tantamount to assisting the fraud. There is a famous case from the 1980s called OPM, in which a law firm's failure to withdraw previous false statements made in opinion letters was deemed to have aided and abetted the client's continuing fraud on several lenders. If you answered (B) for this reason, good for you, but you may not have to incorporate this much understanding of the general law of fraud

into your understanding of professional responsibility. (At least for the purposes of this class; in the real world, failure to think through the intersection between the law of fraud and the duties of lawyers can have disastrous consequences.)

(C) is more clearly not the answer, but make sure you see why: Rule 1.16(b)(1) and (b)(3) are alternatives. The lawyer may withdraw if it can be accomplished without material adverse effect on the client (that is, "prejudice") or the client has used the lawyer's services to perpetrate a crime or fraud. (D) is not the answer because the requirement to seek court permission applies only where the lawyer is representing the client in litigation.

5. I believe the answer is (C). I'm hedging a bit because the rule is frustratingly silent on the mens rea to be applied.[4] Look at Rule 1.16(b)(2). It permits a lawyer to withdraw where the client persists in a course of action that the lawyer *reasonably believes* is criminal or fraudulent. That's helpful; it clarifies that the lawyer need not have actual, subjective knowledge that the client's conduct is criminal or fraudulent — reasonable believe is enough for permissive withdrawal. But this question is asking about mandatory withdrawal. Look at Rule 1.16(a)(1). It says a lawyer must withdraw when the representation will result in violation of the rules or other law (including crimes and frauds), but it does not say whether the lawyer must *know* that this will be the result, must reasonably believe it to be the case, may merely suspect it to be the case, or whether the lawyer's mental state is irrelevant (that is, Rule 1.16(a) is a strict liability rule). It's unlikely that the rule really imposes strict liability, because the rule requires the lawyer to do something. A lawyer has to have some mental state with respect to a factual predicate before she can be required to do something. For this reason, (A) and (B) are probably not the answer. Look at those options and make sure you understand how they differ from (C) in terms of the lawyer's mental state.

---

4. Along with choice of law, mens rea is a significantly under-appreciated aspect of the law governing lawyers. For an excellent article on this topic see Nancy J. Moore, *Mens Rea Standards in Lawyer Disciplinary Codes*, 23 Geo. J. Legal Ethics 1 (2010).

Aspects of an Ongoing Relationship

INTRODUCTION

Lawyers are not just ordinary employees of their clients. They are *professionals*, in the sense that clients expect lawyers to use their specialized knowledge for the benefit of clients in pursuit of objectives that the clients define. The highly technical nature of law practice also creates a relationship of trust, because clients cannot supervise the day-to-day activities of lawyers. Instead, they rely on lawyers to act in their best interests, and they leave the nitty-gritty of the legal work up to the lawyers. The upshot of the professional relationship is that both lawyer and client have spheres of autonomy, where they alone are permitted to make decisions concerning the representation. Only the client may decide whether to settle a lawsuit, for example, but the drafting of the settlement agreement itself is for the lawyer alone.

This chapter deals with the division of decisionmaking authority between lawyers and clients, and the duties that lawyers have in an ongoing relationship to keep their clients in the loop. This chapter also addresses a couple of related issues. The first is the special problem of identifying who has authority to make decisions where the client is an entity, such as a corporation. The second is interference with the attorney-client relationship by the opposing lawyer, either through *ex parte* contacts — that is, talking to the other client outside of the presence of her lawyer — or through secretive information-gathering techniques, such as tape-recording telephone conversations.

DIVISION OF LABOR IN THE ATTORNEY-CLIENT RELATIONSHIP

The whole point of a professional relationship is that the client willingly cedes authority over some part of his affairs to the professional, trusting that the professional will use her expertise and training to further the client's interests. If you go to the doctor, you have the right to set the broad parameters of the relationship — "I want you to look at my sprained ankle" — but you are not entitled to control the precise way in which the doctor diagnoses and treats your condition. If she wants to take an X-ray from three perspectives instead of two because she thinks it would give her a better view of the injury, that is her prerogative. It would be far too cumbersome to require the doctor to explain the reasons for each action and obtain the patient's agreement. At the same time, the patient still has authority to make big decisions, such as whether to operate or to treat a condition medically.

The same kind of division of labor exists for lawyers and clients. The client specifies the legal problem, in broad-brush terms. He might say, "I want you to defend me in this lawsuit," or "I want to set up some kind of entity for my business to minimize my tax liability." Once the client grants this authority, the lawyer pretty much has control over the day-to-day handling of the matter. If a Subchapter S corporation will be more effective than a limited liability corporation, the lawyer should be permitted to structure the client's business in that way, without explaining the ins and outs of the tax code to the client. That is the basic idea behind Rule 1.2(a), which requires the lawyer to abide by the client's decisions concerning the *objectives* of representation, and to consult with the client (but not necessarily obtain the client's permission) regarding the *means* by which the client's objectives are to be pursued. See also Rule 1.2, cmt. [2], which states that the lawyer has authority over "technical, legal, and tactical matters," but that the client has the right to make decisions about such matters as "the expense to be incurred and concern for third parties who might be adversely affected." Technical and tactical matters include questions such as whether to file a complaint in federal or state court, whether to depose a witness or simply rely on an informal interview, and what affirmative defenses a defendant should plead in an answer.

Having said that Rule 1.2(a) contemplates a division of labor, that does not mean that the lawyer can simply force the client to accept the decisions she makes. The rule, and the attorney-client relationship generally, contemplates an ongoing discussion about the way the lawyer carries out the representation of the client. The Restatement, in the introduction to the rules governing the allocation of authority in the attorney-client relationship (§20, *et seq.*), puts it nicely: "A middle view is that the client defines the goals of the representation and the lawyer implements them, but that each consults with the other. Except for certain matters reserved for client or lawyer to decide, *the scope of the lawyer's authority is itself one of the subjects for consultation,* with room for the client's wishes and the parties' contracts to modify the traditionally broad delegation of authority to the lawyer." (Emphasis added.) It really is best to think about the question of authority as a subject for discussion, outside the areas discussed below, of exclusive authority vested in the client.

Some Basic Agency Principles

The disciplinary rules do not create this division of labor out of thin air. In fact, they are largely redundant with the generally applicable law of agency. See generally Deborah A. DeMott, *The Lawyer as Agent,* 67 Fordham L. Rev. 301 (1998). Lawyers are agents for their clients (the principals) and, as such, have express and implied duties to use appropriate skill and diligence to carry out the lawful instructions of their clients. In addition, lawyers belong to a special category of agents called fiduciaries, which means that they occupy a special position of trust with respect to their clients, and have a heightened obligation of loyalty and integrity. You will probably see these words from Judge Cardozo (actually dealing with the duties of trustees) cited to describe the fiduciary duties of lawyers: "A trustee [or lawyer] is held to something stricter than the morals of the marketplace. Not honesty alone, but the punctilio of an honor the most sensitive, is then the standard of behavior." *Meinhard v. Salmon,* 164 N.E. 545 (N.Y. 1928). Courts are utterly intolerant of any kind of self-dealing, divided loyalties, or breaches of trust in the attorney-client relationship. See Rest. §49. Finally, lawyers are more than agents—or a special kind of agent—because their obligations to clients are qualified by duties not to abuse the legal system. These "officer of the court" duties are typified by Rule 1.2(d), which prohibits lawyers from counseling or assisting clients in conduct that the lawyer knows is criminal or fraudulent.

The authority of agents, including lawyers, can take three forms— express, implied, and apparent. *Express* authority is granted by the actual agreement of the parties, often set down in a formal instrument such as an engagement letter. Within certain limits (discussed below), the lawyer and client may agree to modify or limit the scope of the representation. Rule 1.2(c); Rest. §21. *Implied* authority is sort of a default position—it is the authority that must be conferred upon the agent as a result of the creation of a particular kind of principal-agent relationship. Gregory, *supra* §15 ("Implied authority . . . of the agent is a natural consequence of the express authority granted. It is implied from what is actually manifested to the agent by the principal."). There would be no point in having an attorney-client relationship, for example, if the attorney were not empowered to speak on behalf of the client, enter into agreements with others with the consent of the client, and refuse to commit illegal acts. See Rest. §23. The last limitation may seem surprising, but it makes sense given the role of lawyers as representatives of their clients within a system of laws. In that way, lawyers are distinguished from Mafia consiglieri. Within lawful boundaries, however, lawyers have the power to bind their clients by their actions. If a lawyer signs a contract on behalf of her client, it is as though the client signed the contract himself. If a lawyer is negligent in performing some act on behalf of the client, or fails to do something that would have been beneficial to the client, the client is bound by the lawyer's action or inaction, although naturally the client would have a right to sue the lawyer for malpractice. See *Link v. Wabash Railroad Co.*, 370 U.S. 626 (1962).

The least frequently encountered form of authority is *apparent* authority, which is created by an action of the *principal*, not the agent. Suppose the client in a settlement negotiation says to the other party, "Okay, I agree to the terms you propose. My lawyer will draft up an agreement and sign it for me." If the client later regrets agreeing to the settlement but does not communicate her change of mind to the other party, the settlement will still be effective because the lawyer had apparent authority. This is true even though the client ordinarily would be permitted to revoke the lawyer's power to settle the case — usually only clients are empowered to agree to settle a lawsuit. In this case, though, it would be unfair to upset the expectations of the other party, which had reasonably relied on the statement of the client that the lawyer was empowered to draft and sign a settlement agreement. See, for example, *International Telemeter Corp. v. Teleprompter Corp.*, 592 F.2d 49 (2d Cir. 1979). Courts are fairly wary about relying on apparent authority, particularly given the importance to clients of the authority to accept or reject an offered settlement. See, for example, *Makins v. District of Columbia*, 861 A.2d 590 (D.C. 2004) (relying on agency law and Rule 1.2(a), holding that in this case it was unreasonable for opposing party to believe that attorney has settlement authority just because attorney was sent to negotiate); *Covington v. Continental General Tire*, 381 F.3d 216 (3d Cir. 2004) (no apparent authority where clients had not made any communication to opposing counsel to create the impression they had given their attorney the authority to settle).

Allocation of Authority Between Attorney and Client

To paraphrase a lawyer joke, there are some things that even a lawyer may not do. The most significant limitation is that a lawyer shall not counsel a client to engage in criminal or fraudulent conduct, or assist a client in doing something that the lawyer knows is criminal or fraudulent. Rule 1.2(d). The attorney-client relationship is intended to enable individuals and entities to comply with the law, by obtaining expert assistance to accomplish lawful objectives. The professional relationship is not intended to facilitate lawbreaking, by giving the client the tools to do something that is legally forbidden. (By the way, these are the same reasons that underlie the crime-fraud exception to the attorney-client privilege, which we'll consider in Chapter 8.)

As you might imagine, the hard questions concern the boundary between objectives and means. Some decisions are so momentous that they are plainly *solely* within the client's competence. These are enumerated in Rule 1.2(a): in a civil case, whether to settle a case; in a criminal matter, the nature of the plea to be entered, whether to waive a jury trial, and whether the client will take the stand. The Restatement adds to this list the decision to appeal in a civil or criminal case. Rest. §22(1). Only the client may make these decisions, and the lawyer exceeds the scope of her actual authority by making them for the client. The Restatement also gives the client authority to make decisions that are "comparable" to the decision to settle or plead guilty in a criminal case. Rest. §22(1). Examples of comparably significant decisions include entering into a stipulation, consenting to the entry of summary judgment, waiving defenses, and selling real property. Rest. §22(1), cmt. e.

There are some decisions, however, that appear to concern only the means by which the lawyer pursues the client's objectives, but can make all the difference to the outcome of the matter. For example, the lawyer might make a risky tactical decision at trial, such as forgoing the cross-examination of a witness or introducing evidence that could be helpful or harmful to the client, depending on how the jury reacts to it. Must the lawyer obtain the client's permission in these instances? In general, the answer is no. Courts do not wish to erode the professional prerogatives of lawyers, and with good reason. Due to their education and experience, lawyers are expected to know better than their clients what the most effective way would be to realize their objectives. As the Supreme Court has observed, in order to be a successful advocate, a lawyer must sometimes refuse to do something her client desires, such as including a bunch of frivolous grounds for reversal in an appeal. *Jones v. Barnes*, 463 U.S. 745 (1983).[1]

Having said that, the prudent course of action is often to involve the client in the decisionmaking process. Even though the client may not formally have veto power over a decision, it is always possible that the client will later claim that the lawyer's decision was a departure from the required standard of care. There are also some cases holding that it is a violation of the lawyer's

---

1. The dissenting Justices in *Jones* rejected the view that the professional relationship between lawyer and client gave the lawyer broad authority over the means to be employed — in this case, the issues to be raised on appeal. According to the dissenters, the client should have the ability to make these decisions *even* if the lawyer would better able to decide what tactics would be most effective for the client. This is not the view of the Model Rules or the Restatement, but it does show that the profession is divided on how much authority lawyers should have over their clients' cases.

fiduciary duty to fail to follow the explicit instructions of a client. See, for example, *Olfe v. Gordon*, 286 N.W.2d 573 (Wis. 1980). To limit malpractice liability, prudent lawyers can document their clients' consent to risky tactical decisions or deviations from previous understandings in writing.

Even with respect to a "means" decision, which is solely for the lawyer to make, the lawyer still has a duty to "consult with the client as to the means by which" the objectives of the representation are to be pursued. See Rule 1.2(a), citing Rule 1.4. What if the client disagrees with the lawyer's decision? The 1983 version of Rule 1.2(a) basically allowed the lawyer to say "it's my way or the highway." Comment [1] to that rule said that the lawyer is "not required to . . . employ means simply because a client may wish that the lawyer do so," and also said that "the lawyer should assume responsibility for technical and legal tactical issues." Thus, if a decision could properly be characterized as one pertaining to the means by which the representation would be carried out — that is, tactical or technical matters — then the client didn't really have any say. The current version of Rule 1.2(a) eliminates the lawyer's veto power. Comment [2] now provides that clients "*normally* defer to the special knowledge and skill of the lawyer with respect to the means to be used to accomplish their objectives, particularly with respect to technical, legal, and tactical matters." The italicized word is important, however, because it removes any implication that the lawyer has an absolute right to make means decisions. The idea now is that the lawyer and client should consult "and seek a mutually agreeable resolution." If there is an impasse, the lawyer cannot cram her preferred approach down on the client. The parties have to keep talking and, if that is unavailing, the lawyer may have no choice but to withdraw from the representation.

As long as they respect these basic limits, lawyers and clients have the power to agree on the scope of the representation. Rule 1.2(c). Note that this power does not override the allocation of authority given in Rule 1.2(a) and Restatement §§22 and 23. The lawyer and the client cannot agree among themselves that the lawyer will have the final authority on whether the client will plead guilty, or whether to agree to settle a civil action. There is also a basic level of reasonable professional services that an attorney must always provide, no matter what the agreement with the client. Rule 1.2, cmt. [7].[2] Thus, the lawyer and client may agree that the lawyer will undertake preliminary legal research related to a possible lawsuit for $500. Both parties would expect that the lawyer cannot research every possible point of law, and simply would be providing a rough-and-ready analysis. The limitation to "preliminary" research does not excuse sloppiness by the lawyer, however. If the lawyer fails to discover a leading case, directly on point, recently

---

2. See also Rule 1.8(h), which prohibits a lawyer from obtaining a prospective waiver of malpractice liability from the client, unless the client is represented separately for the purposes of the agreement.

decided by the highest court in her jurisdiction, the lawyer still would be liable to the client for malpractice.

The critical requirement for a limitation on the lawyer's authority is that the client must consent after full disclosure — in other words, give *informed consent*. Informed consent is defined in the rules as "agreement by a person to a proposed course of action after the lawyer has communicated adequate information and explanation about the material risks of and reasonably available alternatives to the proposed course of conduct." Rule 1.0(e); see also Rest. §122, cmt. c. Imagine that Sternen believes her boss, Crane, may be sexually harassing her, as well as depriving her of her rights under an employee stock-ownership program (ESOP). You are an experienced employment-discrimination litigator and would like to handle the sexual harassment claim on behalf of Sternen, but you do not know anything about ESOPs. (You think they may be governed by a complex federal statute called the Employee Retirement Income Security Act (ERISA).) You may take Sternen's sexual harassment case and not worry about the ESOP issues as long as you clearly explain to Sternen what you propose to do. The disclosure must be clear, not evasive and legalistic, and in plain language. Do not assume your client knows the difference between a discrimination claim and a claim related to the ESOP. You could include a paragraph like this in the engagement letter:

> You have suggested that Crane has deprived you of your rights under an employee stock-ownership plan (ESOP). This is different from a sex discrimination or sexual harassment claim, and is governed by a completely different set of legal rules. I do not have expertise in the area of ESOPs, and do not agree to represent you or render any legal judgment on the validity of this claim. You should find another lawyer as soon as possible to advise you on matters relating to the ESOP. It is important to talk to someone quickly, because you may lose your legal rights if you wait too long.

As long as Sternen understands this limitation and agrees to it, you are free to represent her in the sexual harassment litigation. Her consent is informed because you, the lawyer, first provided full and candid information about the risks she will incur if she gives consent to the proposed course of conduct.

Informed consent is one of the most important concepts in the law governing lawyers. It recognizes both the lawyer's fiduciary duty to the client and the capacity of competent adult decision-makers to agree to a set of right and duties different from those provided by background law (referred to as "default rules" in the lingo of contract law). The law governing lawyers includes many default rules that can be varied by agreement of the parties. When the lawyer and client agree to change the duties owed by the lawyer to the client, however, the fiduciary nature of the lawyer-client relationship demands that the lawyer first provide a thorough, frank explanation of the risks to the client, in terms the client can understand. In a few cases, the pressures on the fiduciary relationship are so severe that no variation is permitted in the duties owed by the lawyer to the client. These immutable rules are said to be nonwaivable or nonconsentable.

One picky technical issue (a favorite of drafters of multiple-choice questions!) is whether consent, if permitted at all, must be written, "confirmed in writing," or whether it may be oral. Written consent means what it says—the agreement has to be written, and signed by the client. Consent confirmed in writing may start out as oral consent, but must be set down subsequently in writing and transmitted to the person giving the consent. See Rule 1.0(b). If no written or confirmed-in-writing consent is specified, oral consent is sufficient, although of course it's always nice to have written evidence to support one's claim of oral consent. In a few cases, it is necessary only to give notice to a party, not to obtain that party's consent. Here are a few of the rules requiring each of these types of consent:

- No consent permitted (nonwaivable duties): A few categories of concurrent representation conflicts, Rule 1.7(b); preparation of instrument conveying substantial gift to lawyer, Rule 1.8(c); acquisition of media rights in subject of representation, Rule 1.8(d); providing financial assistance to client or acquiring an interest in the subject matter of the litigation, Rule 1.8(e), 1.8(i); sexual relationships with clients, Rule 1.8(j); judge negotiating for employment with party or lawyer involved in matter in which the judge is participating personally and substantially, Rule 1.12(a).
- Written consent: Terms of a contingent fee agreement, Rule 1.5(c), or fee-sharing arrangement between lawyers, Rule 1.5(e). (Likely the language of informed consent is not used because these rules already prescribe the disclosure that must be given to the client.)
- Informed consent, confirmed in writing: Most ordinary concurrent and successive conflicts of interest, Rule 1.7(b)(4), Rule 1.9(a), Rule 1.11(a)(2).
- Written informed consent: Business transactions with clients, Rule 1.8(a).
- Informed consent; may be oral: Limitation on scope of representation, Rule 1.2(c); disclosure or adverse use of confidential information, Rule 1.6(a) and Rule 1.8(b); accepting compensation from third party, Rule 1.8(f); keeping client funds in a state other than the state in which the lawyer's office is located, Rule 1.15(a) (rule says "consent" not "informed consent," but the overall strict fiduciary tenor of the rule implies that informed consent should be required).
- Notice only: Screen employed to protect confidential information of former client in moving-lawyer conflicts situation, Rule 1.10(a)(2)(ii);

screen employed in former government lawyer conflicts situation, Rule 1.11(b)(2); law clerk negotiating for employment with a party or lawyer, Rule 1.12(b) (notice required only to the judge).

A couple of rules also require either an opportunity for the client to consult with independent counsel and written advice concerning the desirability of doing so (for example, Rule 1.8(a)(1) on business transactions; Rule 1.8(h)(2) on settlement of malpractice claims with unrepresented clients or former clients) or actual representation by independent counsel (for example, Rule 1.8(h)(1) on prospective limitations on liability).

Examples

Lawyers and the Chronic

1. Recently voters in the State of Perplexity passed a ballot initiative making the recreational use of marijuana legal in the state. The possession and sale of marijuana remain illegal under federal law, with marijuana classified as a Schedule 1 controlled substance, along with heroin and cocaine. There is no indication that Congress has any intention of removing marijuana from Schedule 1. The Department of Justice under a previous administration had issued a memorandum stating that federal prosecutors will generally exercise their discretion not to prosecute businesses or individuals who are acting lawfully pursuant to state law. There is some concern that a new administration may take a different approach to enforcing the federal statute.

   You have a practice in the State of Perplexity representing small business owners. You assist them with obtaining needed licenses and permits, setting up the entity (such as an LLC or a subchapter S corporation), leasing space, dealing with zoning requirements, and complying with other legal requirements. A man named Calvin Broadus would like to retain you to assist him with all aspects of starting a marijuana dispensary, including forming a corporation, obtaining financing from a bank, securing intellectual property protection for the name of his business, "Half Baked Edibles." Are you permitted to accept this new client?

Can't We All Just Get Along?

2. A group of matrimonial lawyers in the State of Perplexity has discussed the idea of forming a "collaborative family lawyering" practice, representing clients who wish to handle marital dissolution and child custody disputes in an amicable manner. The lawyers have seen many clients' relationships with their ex-spouses and children needlessly harmed by hardball litigation tactics. Thus, they have proposed asking new clients to

sign a retainer agreement with the following terms: The client agrees to try to resolve the dispute through open, good-faith negotiations with all parties present. There will be no formal discovery, but the client agrees to disclose all relevant information voluntarily. The client further agrees that if the collaborative process does not succeed in resolving the dispute, the lawyers will withdraw and not participate in any subsequent litigation.

You are a lawyer with the Perplexity Bar Association and have been asked to provide an opinion on whether this arrangement is permissible under the Model Rules. What is your view? Is this type of practice permissible and, if so, what must the lawyers do to be in compliance with the applicable disciplinary rules?

"I Was Just Doing My Job!"

3. Mega Power Tools hired Jamail to represent it in a product liability lawsuit brought by Prudhomme, a homeowner who injured himself using a Mega 2000 table saw. The representative of Mega who hired Jamail told her that Mega's policy was to defend itself vigorously but fairly, and to contest baseless claims but to settle reasonable ones. In the course of discovery, Jamail learned that the blade guard on the Mega 2000 would occasionally become clogged with sawdust and stick in the open position. Mega had settled several cases in which users were injured by the Mega 2000. Nevertheless, Jamail proceeded to employ "scorched earth" tactics against Prudhomme, filing a barrage of motions, resisting discovery requests, and taking dozens of depositions of Prudhomme's friends and neighbors in a futile attempt to establish that Prudhomme had been snorting cocaine on the day of the accident. When Mega representatives found out about their lawyer's conduct, they were horrified and refused to pay her bill. They also reported her to the state bar authorities in the State of Perplexity. Will Jamail be subject to discipline?

Explanations

Lawyers and the Chronic

1. This is very much a live issue for lawyers in several states — as of summer 2019, Alaska, California, Colorado, Maine, Massachusetts, Michigan, Nevada, Oregon, Vermont, Washington, and the District of Columbia — in which the use of marijuana for recreational purposes is permitted by state law. But a lawyer will notice a problem with the clear language of Rule 1.2(d): "A lawyer shall not . . . assist a client in conduct that the lawyer knows is criminal." Broadus' proposed business would be legal under state law, but that pesky federal criminal statute remains. The Justice Department had previously taken the position that federal prosecutors have better things to do than go after weed entrepreneurs in

states permitting recreational or medical use of marijuana, but that was just a policy — it did not alter an express federal statutory prohibition on the possession and sale of Schedule 1 controlled substances. Declining this representation would be a pity, not least because it deprives Broadus of the assistance of a lawyer in setting up a business that is permitted by state law. However, there is a real risk to your law firm if you assist a client in an unlawful business enterprise.

Note that while Rule 1.2(d) prohibits both counseling and assisting a client in criminal activities, it permits a lawyer to advise on the legal consequences of the client's course of action. This opens the door to relying on the DOJ's nonenforcement policy (if it is still in effect) as a ground for claiming that advice alone does not violate the rule. But the example asks about actively assisting your client, not just providing advice. That's going to be a bit more difficult to square with the language of the rule.

States that have legalized the medical or recreational use of marijuana have taken different approaches to the Rule 1.2(d) problem. An opinion of the Maine Bar prohibits lawyers from providing assistance to medical marijuana businesses that are permitted under state law, because of the federal Controlled Substances Act. See Maine Bar Op. 199 (2010). An ethics opinion in Arizona, by contrast, states that lawyers may assist businesses whose activities are permitted by the state medical marijuana statute, as long as there is no change in the federal nonenforcement policy. See Arizona Op. 11-01 (2011) The Arizona approach is interesting, but seems to me to conflate a legal prohibition with its enforcement. Plenty of laws are at least under-enforced, but a lawyer would still be prohibited by Rule 1.2(d) from assisting a client in violating them. The possession for personal use of weed is a federal crime, even if the feds have said they will not prosecute these violations. In fact, a North Dakota ethics opinion has stated that the personal use of marijuana for medical purposes, in a state (Minnesota) in which this use is permitted by state law, would subject a lawyer to discipline for violating North Dakota Rule 8.4(b) (subjecting a lawyer to discipline for "commit[ting] a criminal act that reflects adversely on the lawyer's . . . fitness as a lawyer in other respects"). See North Dakota Op. 14-02 (2014). Several states (including Alaska, Colorado, Nevada, and Washington) have adopted comments to state versions of Rule 1.2 permitting legal assistance to clients like Broadus, as long as the lawyer advises the client on federal law and there is no change to the Justice Department's policy of nonenforcement.

But it's not clear that adding language to the comments to a disciplinary rule will be enough to make this a riskless proposition for the lawyer. Not only might the enforcement policy change, but there are collateral consequences to the violation of federal law, such as the reluctance of banks to deal with funds derived from marijuana-related businesses, for fear of violating federal money-laundering statutes. Whether to represent the client in this case is a judgment call on which lawyers may reasonably differ.

Can't We All Just Get Along?

2. The concept of collaborative lawyering, in which lawyers and clients mutually agree to use negotiation and cooperation instead of acrimonious litigation, is permissible under the rules. (Most state ethics opinions agree with this position, although Colorado is one conspicuous dissenter.) The important thing to realize is that the lawyer and client may agree that the lawyer will provide something less than the full range of professional services ordinarily available, as long as the limitation is reasonable under the circumstances. Rule 1.2(c). Furthermore, the client must provide informed consent (preferably in writing, although this isn't strictly required by the rule) to the arrangement. Informed consent is a defined term in the Model Rules, which is extremely important. (It will play a substantial role in conflicts of interest analysis.) The client's consent to the collaborative lawyering process will be informed, and thus valid, only if "the lawyer has communicated adequate information and explanation about the material risks of and reasonably available alternatives to the proposed course of conduct." Rule 1.0(e).

In this case, the lawyers should explain to prospective clients that there are risks and benefits to the collaborative dispute resolution process. There may be benefits that can be obtained by playing hardball. A client with greater resources may be able to grind down the opponent and extract concessions. On the other hand, this may be a terrible thing for ongoing relationships with children and ex-spouses. The parties may be in a situation that requires them to deal with each other in a constructive manner for many years. Thus, the very idea of "grinding down the opponent" is out of place in family law disputes. Everyone would be better off if they took a more cooperative approach to resolving the problem. A client may not want to do this and may prefer a bomb-throwing lawyer. That is the client's legal right, as long as he or she does not want the lawyer to do anything in violation of the law. The client would be giving this up by agreeing to the collaborative lawyering process, and that is why the client's informed consent is required. With informed consent, however, this is a reasonable limitation on the lawyer's duties under Rule 1.2(c).

"I Was Just Doing My Job!"

3. This is a question about the distinction between the ends of the representation and the means by which they should be carried out, under Rule 1.2(a) and Rule 1.4(a)(2). One way to attack this question is to note, following *Cool Hand Luke*, that "what we have here is a failure to communicate." Under Rule 1.4(a)(2), the lawyer is required to "reasonably consult with the client about the means by which the client's objectives are to be pursued." But what does it mean to "reasonably consult?" Surely it doesn't mean the lawyer has to talk to the client but is not required to follow the client's reasonable instructions. If the client says, in effect, "no scorched-earth tactics," it would be a mistake to read Rule 1.2(a) as empowering the lawyer to defy those instructions. The whole point of the agency relationship is that the client is the principal, and to the extent reasonably consistent with the nature of the relationship, should be able to call the shots. It's true that the client gave instructions regarding the manner of representation, but the default division of labor doesn't mean the lawyer should be permitted to ignore that instruction, as long as it's reasonable.

Granted, this begs an important question regarding the reasonableness of the client's instructions. Clients cannot be permitted to micromanage the lawyer's efforts, but this isn't micromanaging — it's more like setting the tone or defining the parameters of the representation. In policy terms, the reason clients shouldn't be permitted to micromanage the representation is that lawyers are presumed to have greater expertise regarding tactical decisions. If the lawyer in this case did in fact have superior expertise on the question at issue, I would agree that the decision should be committed to her exclusively. But the decision here did not relate to some arcane technical matter that is outside the client's ability to comprehend. Rather, it was a decision about the general posture to take in litigation, which is something on which clients do have some expertise.

The other way to reach this conclusion under the Model Rules is to characterize the client's statement as relating to the *ends* of the representation, not the *means*. Here, the client seems concerned with not acquiring a reputation as a hardball litigant. Think about how much reputational damage was done to companies like A.H. Robins (from the Dalkon Shield litigation) and the tobacco companies, as a result of their litigation tactics. If a client wishes to avoid this kind of stigma, he should be able to make and enforce a binding agreement with his lawyer not to engage in Rambo tactics. But how does that square with the language of Rule 1.2(a)? The rule sets up a distinction between ends and means, so how do you know which this is? I believe there is not a strict, binary, either/or distinction between ends and means. A decision can be more ends-like or more means-like. As a matter becomes more central to the client's interests, it should be considered as having more of an ends-like quality. You could argue that the client's reputation and goodwill among consumers of its product are sufficiently important that these are decisions relating to the ends of the representation.

When I used this question on a final exam, many students picked up on the client's policy to settle meritorious claims and argued that the client's instruction was a decision regarding settlement, and therefore a clear "ends" decision under Rule 1.2(a). That's not a bad argument, even though ultimately I think it's less persuasive than the one just given, about the client's right to prohibit litigation tactics that might cause reputational harm. The problem is, Rule 1.2(a) requires the lawyer to abide by the client's decision whether to settle, and in this case that decision point hasn't been reached yet. The client does have a policy of behaving reasonably in settlement, but the case hasn't gotten to the point where the client can make an informed settlement decision. The reason, of course, is that the lawyer resorted to tactics that made it less likely that the plaintiff would be able to stay in the litigation long enough to get to the point of settlement negotiations. But the problem is not that the lawyer overrode the client's decision regarding settlement; it is that the lawyer disregarded the client's instruction to behave reasonably toward the adversary.

CLIENTS WITH DIMINISHED CAPACITY

The discussion up until now has assumed that the client is competent to define the scope of the representation and to have a meaningful consultation with the lawyer about the means by which it will be carried out. Suppose, however, that the client is not competent for some reason. The client may be a minor, and thus legally presumed to be unable to make fully considered decisions, or may be elderly and incompetent because of dementia or some other incapacity. Alternatively, the client may have a history of mental illness or be developmentally disabled. In any event, the challenge for the lawyer is how to proceed in light of the client's inability to play the usual role of setting the objectives of the representation.

The Model Rules and the Restatement both deal with the issue of clients with diminished capacity, but they differ in a couple of interesting respects.

They agree that, to the extent possible, the lawyer should try to have a normal lawyer-client relationship. "[A] client with diminished capacity often has the ability to understand, deliberate upon, and reach conclusions about matters affecting the client's own well being." Rule 1.14, cmt. [1]; see also Rest. §24(1). In any event, the lawyer should treat the client with dignity and respect. Rule 1.14, cmt. [2].

It is important to remember that family members and friends may participate in discussions with the lawyer concerning the client's well-being. Nevertheless, unless they are acting as legal guardians for the client, the lawyer should not defer to their wishes. "[T]he lawyer must keep the client's interests foremost and . . . must look to the client, and not family members, to make decisions on the client's behalf." Rule 1.14, cmt. [3]. If a guardian has been appointed, the lawyer generally must defer to the guardian's instructions regarding the client's best interests, unless the lawyer knows the guardian is violating the fiduciary duties she owes the client. Rest. §24(3) & cmt. f; see also Rule 1.14, cmt. [4]. In the absence of a formal guardianship, however, the lawyer should not simply defer to the wishes of family members or friends.

If the client is confused, delusional, unable to communicate with the lawyer, or otherwise impossible to deal with as an ordinary client, the lawyer may seek to have a guardian appointed to make decisions on behalf of the client, or may take some other protective action, such as raising the issue of the client's competence. See Rest. §24, cmt. d. The Model Rules permit this step only where the lawyer *reasonably believes* that the client is at risk of substantial physical, financial, or other harm. Rule 1.14(b). (Note the italicized language — the rule doesn't say the lawyer "suspects" the client may be at risk.) The Restatement permits seeking a guardian only where the client's impairment is severe and no other practical means of protecting the client exists. Rest. §24, cmt. e. If the client is not facing the risk of substantial harm, the lawyer arguably must muddle through and do the best she can to carry on a normal lawyer-client relationship.

What happens in the case in which the client apparently has the capacity to understand the situation and make decisions on her own behalf, but insists on doing something that the lawyer believes, with good reason, to be ill-advised from the point of view of the client's long-term best interests? The Restatement rightly cautions lawyers not to assume that the client has diminished capacity merely because the client "insist[s] on a view of the client's welfare that a lawyer considers unwise or otherwise at variance with the lawyer's own views." Rest. §24, cmt. c. The lawyer's role is to advocate for her client's view about the client's best interests, not to second-guess the client's views. If no guardian has been appointed and the client is truly unable to make an adequately considered judgment about the matter, the Restatement says that the lawyer must "pursue *the lawyer's* reasonable view of the client's objectives or interests as the client would define them if able to make adequately considered decisions on the matter . . ." Rest. §24(2) (emphasis added).

The Restatement's invitation to the lawyer to make her own judgment about the client's best interests raises concerns about paternalism or domination of the client by the lawyer, particularly since the Restatement says this decisionmaking principle applies "even if the client expresses no wishes or gives contrary instructions." *Id.* The comments do caution that a lawyer "should be careful not to construe as proof of disability a client's insistence on a view of the client's welfare that a lawyer considers unwise or otherwise at variance with the lawyer's own views." Rest. §24, cmt. c. But one might still question whether this comment does enough to prevent the lawyer from substituting her own judgment for that of her client. On the other hand, what else is the lawyer to do in a situation in which the lawyer reasonably believes the client unable to make adequately informed decisions? Perhaps the only resolution is to continue the process of dialogue with the client, and intermediaries such as family members and therapists, and to remain open-minded about what is in the client's best interests. *Id.*

DUTY TO COMMUNICATE

A lawyer has a duty to keep a client reasonably informed about the status of a matter, provide information when requested, and give the client sufficient information so that the client can make decisions about the representation where necessary. Rule 1.4. This duty exists in agency law as well. See Restatement (Second) of Agency §381. Rule 1.4 is one of those redundant rules that reminds lawyers of obligations they have anyway, and potentially subjects them to discipline for failing to comply with them. It is true that a lawyer does not need to tell the client everything, such as the fact that a deposition of a third-party witness has been rescheduled for Wednesday instead of Tuesday. Clients are not entitled to micromanage the case, and lawyers are not expected to confirm every little move with the client. When anything of importance happens in the case, however, the lawyer has a duty to communicate it to the client. For example, if the opposing party makes an offer of settlement, Rule 1.4 requires the lawyer to communicate that fact to the client.

Reading Rule 1.4 in conjunction with Rule 1.2 gets you a kind of spectrum of communication obligations, in which the lawyer and client share decisionmaking authority. It goes like this:

3. Aspects of an Ongoing Relationship

Rule 1.4(a)(1)   A lawyer shall inform the client of any decision
or circumstance with respect to which the client's
informed consent is required. Informed consent
means agreement by the client after the lawyer has
communicated adequate information about the
material risks of and reasonably available alternatives
to a proposed course of action. Rule 1.0(e). This is
a two-way communication obligation, in which the
lawyer must defer to the client's instructions. Under
Rule 1.2(a), the client alone has the right to make
major decisions about the matter, such as whether
to settle a civil case or whether to plead guilty in
a criminal prosecution. The lawyer clearly has to
communicate with the client where these decisions
are concerned, and moreover must respect the
client's wishes regarding how to proceed. The same
is true with respect to matters on which the client's
informed consent is required, such as whether to
disclose confidential information, Rule 1.6(a), or
whether to waive a conflict of interest, Rule 1.7(b).

Rule 1.4(a)(2)   A lawyer must reasonably consult with the client
about the means by which the client's objectives are
to be pursued. This is a two-way communication
obligation: It says the lawyer should "consult" with
the client, not merely "inform" the client. Thus,
the lawyer has to listen to what the client says after
being informed of the relevant circumstances. If the
lawyer and the client disagree about the means by
which the lawyer should pursue the client's interests,
the lawyer should consult with the client and try to
come up with a mutually agreeable solution. Rule
1.2, cmt. [2]; Rule 1.4, cmt. [3]. If something is
truly a "means" decision, however, the client does
not have veto power over the lawyer's judgment. If
there is an impasse, the lawyer may decide the best
course of action is to proceed in the way she believes
best calculated to accomplish the client's objectives,
although the lawyer should proceed with caution, as
clients who do not feel like they have been listened
to are prone to file malpractice actions if things don't
turn out well. If the disagreement is serious enough,
the lawyer may withdraw under Rule 1.16(b)(3).

Rule 1.4(a)(3)   A lawyer must keep the client reasonably informed about the status of the matter. This is an ongoing, one-way communication obligation. The lawyer must, on her own initiative, periodically update the client on how things are going, but need not await the client's instructions or advice on how to proceed.

Rule 1.4(a)(4)   A lawyer must comply with reasonable requests for information. This is a one-way communication obligation, triggered by the client's reasonable request. Some clients can pester the heck out of their lawyers, and a lawyer is not required under this rule to respond to every e-mailed question. Client relations considerations, however, should motivate a lawyer to keep the client in the loop. Unreturned phone calls are a major source of client resentment. See Rule 1.4, cmt. [4].

Rule 1.4(a)(5)   A lawyer must consult with the client about any relevant limitation, imposed by the Model Rules or other law, on the lawyer's conduct. This is stated as a two-way communication obligation ("consult" instead of "inform"), but there's really nothing for the client to say in response when the lawyer informs the client that the lawyer is not permitted to do something unlawful.

Rule 1.4(b) essentially just restates the more specific obligations given in Rule 1.4(a): The bottom line is, the lawyer must permit the client to participate meaningfully in the representation. What it means to participate meaningfully depends on how decisionmaking authority is allocated by Rule 1.2 and general agency law principles. In addition, professional traditions, customs, and folklore can tell us something about how the lawyer and client should work together to make decisions, as the following example shows.

Suppose the lawyer believes that the client's decisions are foolish or immoral, but the client has the legal authority to make those decisions. The lawyer still is entitled to try to talk the client out of them. Lawyers are required to be candid with their clients and to exercise independent judgment. Rule 2.1. The rule specifically permits the lawyer to go beyond purely legal considerations in a conversation with the client and refer also to "moral, economic, social, and political factors" that may be relevant to the client's situation. Sometimes a good "Dutch uncle" talk is exactly what the client needs, and "a lawyer should not be deterred from giving candid advice by the prospect that the advice will be unpalatable to the client." Rule 2.1, cmt. [1]. There is a well-known story from the life of Louis Brandeis, a top-flight corporate lawyer who later became a Justice on the U.S. Supreme Court. When Brandeis was in private practice, he had a client who was resisting the demands of his employees for better working conditions. After listening to the client, Brandeis said he thought the workers' demands were fair and that the client ought to comply with them. The client did, and the business continued to be profitable, in part because of harmonious labor-management relations. Brandeis' advice would be permissible under Rule 2.1, even though the client ultimately would have had the authority under Rule 1.2(a) to define his objectives as resisting the workers' demands.[3]

Finally, here is a specific application of the duty to communicate that eluded Jan Schlictmann, the plaintiffs' lawyer in *A Civil Action* (played by John Travolta in the movie): A lawyer representing a party in a civil lawsuit must inform his client of an offer of settlement made by the other side. A lawyer is subject to discipline for failing to do so because Rule 1.4 requires the lawyer to communicate information that the client needs to make informed decisions regarding matters within the scope of her competence, and the client alone has the authority to decide whether to settle under Rule 1.2. In addition, the lawyer may be exposed to a significant malpractice judgment if the lawyer failed to inform the client of a settlement offer and the client lost at trial. The client's cause of action would be for the lawyer's breach of her duty to communicate with the client; this is a tort or agency law claim that overlaps with the disciplinary rule, Rule 1.4.

Examples

Keeping the Client at Arm's Length

4. Enerco is a large energy trading company. Its long-time principal outside law firm is Vincent & Elkton. It is well-known for using creative and aggressive accounting treatment of transactions to bolster its reported earnings, but maintains that the way it accounts for transactions is entirely legal. After a rather alarming letter sent to the CEO by a senior manager in the accounting department, alleging violations of accounting standards and self-dealing by some Enerco officers, the CEO decided to hire a law firm to conduct an investigation of the accounting treatment of certain transactions. He naturally turned to Vincent & Elkton. The firm

---

3. Recall the discussion of termination of representation, from Chapter 2. An attorney has the authority to withdraw from representing the client under Rule 1.16(b)(3), *even* if the withdrawal would have a material adverse effect on the client's interests, if the client "insists on pursuing an objective that the lawyer considers repugnant or imprudent."

was willing to take the matter, but insisted on some limitations on its representation of Enerco. First, it was unwilling to review the details of all the transactions from the ground up and wanted to get all the relevant information from Enerco officers and the independent auditors who had reviewed the transactions. Second, it characterized its representation as a "preliminary investigation," with the purpose of ascertaining whether a more thorough investigation was warranted. May the firm limit its representation in this manner if the client agrees after a full disclosure of the relevant facts?

What Are the Client's Best Interests?

5. Alan Goodman is accused of pushing a young woman to her death in front of a subway train in Gotham City (which is in a Model Rules jurisdiction). Because the act was witnessed by several dozen people, there is no question that Goodman actually pushed the victim; the only issue is whether he is not legally responsible because of his mental illness. He has been diagnosed with schizophrenia and is being treated with antipsychotic medication. From the perspective of trial strategy, his lawyer thinks the medication is working too well. The defense lawyer, Keith Cornfield, wants to take Goodman off his medication so that the jury can see what his mental state was like on the morning of the attack, when he had not been taking his medication. Can he do it, if Goodman agrees? Does it matter that Goodman will "experience the sensation of slowly losing his mind" and may suffer permanent damage, as a psychiatrist at Columbia University testified for the state? (One of Goodman's own treating psychiatrists disagrees with this dire prediction and forecasts no adverse effects for Goodman.) What if Goodman changes his mind after he stops taking his medication?

Explanations

Keeping the Client at Arm's Length

4. This example is based on one of many incidents in the unraveling of Enron in 2001 and 2002. For an excellent analysis of the professional responsibility issues presented by the Enron fiasco, which I have drawn from heavily, see Roger C. Cramton, *Enron and the Corporate Lawyer: A Primer on Legal and Ethical Issues*, 58 Bus. Law. 143 (2002). See also the district court's opinion on the motion to dismiss filed by law firms, accounting firms, and other secondary actors, In re Enron Corp. Securities, Derivative & ERISA Litigation, 235 F. Supp. 2d 549, 593 (S.D. Tex. 2002). We will encounter issues related to Enron at several points in this book.

The issue here is whether the agreement between Enerco and Vincent & Elkton is permissible under Rule 1.2(c), which permits a lawyer to limit the scope of the representation, but only if "the limitation is reasonable under the circumstances." There are a couple of facts that suggest the limitation is not reasonable. For one thing, the accounting manager's letter alleges self-dealing by certain Enerco officers. It would be unreasonable to rely on those officers for reliable facts upon which to base a legal opinion. In order to render even a preliminary judgment about Enerco's exposure to liability, the lawyers should speak to employees not implicated in the misconduct. The outside auditor also may be implicated in the wrongdoing, so the firm should not simply assume that the facts as related by the auditor will be accurate. In addition, the law firm had participated in "papering" some of the transactions that were being questioned, so it is difficult to believe that the firm could be impartial. See *In re Enron*, 235 F. Supp. 2d at 636, 657-658.

Does it make a difference that Vincent & Elkton proposed only to conduct a "preliminary" investigation? Lawyers are allowed to render quick-and-dirty opinions if the client is interested in keeping costs down, or if there is some urgency that requires a speedy response. See, for example, *Lerner v. Laufer*, 819 A.2d 471 (N.J. Super. Ct. App. Div. 2003) (affirming dismissal of a malpractice claim where lawyer had limited scope of his work in writing). For example, "[i]f . . . a client's objective is limited to securing general information about the law the client needs in order to handle a common and typically uncomplicated legal problem, the lawyer and client may agree that the lawyer's services will be limited to a brief telephone consultation." Rule 1.2, cmt. [7]. But calling an investigation "preliminary" does not excuse the lawyer from the responsibility of doing it *properly*. Even if the client's objective is to secure a quickie, seat-of-the-pants opinion about whether wrongdoing had taken place, the lawyers must conduct the investigation in such a way that has a reasonable likelihood of discovering the misconduct. An agreement with the client permitting the lawyers to conduct an unreasonably hasty or slipshod investigation also may violate the prohibition in Rule 1.8(h) on entering into an advance waiver or limitation of a lawyer's malpractice liability to the client, where the client is not separately represented in making the agreement. Talking only to actors who may have been complicit in the wrongdoing is an unreasonable way to conduct the investigation. Lawyers must be extremely careful in these situations, because if they fail to uncover the wrongdoing they were retained to find, they may be sued for malpractice by the client later, if the failure to root out the fraud is the cause of financial harm to the client. For example, a large firm was recently sued by the trustee in bankruptcy for $30 million in compensatory damages and $90 million in punitive damages for negligently ignoring misconduct by the CEO of a client. Matthew Haggman, *Malpractice Suit Against Proskauer Tops* $100M, Miami Daily Business Review (Mar. 26, 2003).

What Are the Client's Best Interests?

5. This problem is based closely upon the case of convicted New York City subway pusher Andrew Goldstein.[4] This is an extremely difficult question, and the disciplinary rules only provide a background; they do not finally resolve the issue one way or the other. The rule on authority, Rule 1.2(a), says that the lawyer has the right to make decisions concerning the means by which the client's objectives will be pursued. It is not entirely clear how Goodman's objectives should be defined, however. One expert on schizophrenia endorsed the lawyer's tactic, arguing from the client's point of view that "I would want the jury to see how psychotic I could be, so the jury does not send me to state prison." But Goodman also may have the objective of maintaining good mental health. This is important because Goodman may change his mind, and decide one day to come off his medication but insist the next day on being remedicated. The lawyer should not take too narrow or legalistic a view of what Goodman's best interests are.

When he is on his medication, Goodman is almost certainly competent to decide to come off his medication for the purposes of trial, but what happens when the unmedicated Goodman demands of his lawyer that he be permitted to go back on medication? The attorney-client relationship during the unmedicated phases will be governed by Rule 1.14, assuming that the lack of medication renders Goodman unable to interact normally with his lawyer. There is some authority that when the client is acting under a disability, and no guardian has been appointed to make decisions for the client, the lawyer must try to make decisions from the perspective of "the lawyer's reasonable view of the client's objectives or interests as the client would define them if able to make adequately considered decisions on the matter, even if the client . . . gives contrary instructions." Rest. §24(2). Does this mean that the lawyer should ignore the subsequent instructions of unmedicated Goodman if medicated Goodman had instructed the lawyer to discontinue the medication for trial? Maybe so, if the lawyer's view is that it would be reasonable for

---

4. Information and quotations in this discussion are taken from Julian E. Barnes, *Second Murder Trial Opens in Subway Shoving Case*, New York Times (Mar. 4, 2000), at B3; David Rohde, *Court Is Told Subway Killer, Off Medication, Hit a Social Worker*, New York Times (Feb. 29, 2000), at B1; David Rohde, *For Retrial, Subway Defendant Goes Off Medication*, New York Times (Feb. 23, 2000), at B1. Goldstein was convicted of second-degree murder, notwithstanding his insanity defense, and sentenced to 25 years to life in prison. David Rohde, *Subway Killer Apologizes at Sentencing*, New York Times (May 5, 2000), at B1.

Goodman to take a narrow view of his "objectives," to include only prevailing on the insanity defense at trial. As a comment to the diminished capacity rule states, in trying to assess the extent of the client's diminished capacity, the lawyer should take into account factors such as "the known long-term commitments and values of the client," Rule 1.14, cmt. [6], which might include Goodman's persistent instructions, when he is lucid, that he should be unmedicated for trial. On the other hand, Richard Uviller, an expert in criminal law and ethics at Columbia, argues that "[a] lawyer's first duty is to preserve his client's health." In that case, the lawyer should respect the instructions of unmedicated Goodman. In either case, the lawyer cannot avoid taking a position on what a reasonable conception of his client's best interests would be.

At a minimum, Cornfield must explain the proposed course of action to Goodman "to the extent reasonably necessary to permit [Goodman] to make informed decisions regarding the representation," Rule 1.4(b), and may refer to "other considerations such as moral, economic, social, and political factors" that might bear on the decision, Rule 2.1. One of the comments to Rule 2.1 notes that a client's situation may implicate matters that are beyond the lawyer's expertise, such as psychiatry. Rule 2.1, cmt. [4]. In those cases, the lawyer should recommend that the client consult with the relevant experts. As the same comment astutely observes, however, the advice of experts may conflict, and in those cases the lawyer may be called upon to give advice on what the client ought to do "in the face of conflicting recommendations of experts." Like the rule on a client with diminished capacity, the rules on communication with clients and candor do not let the lawyer off the hook completely. At some point, a lawyer may have to make a decision about what the client *ought* to do.

Richard Uviller, mentioned above, thinks it is clearly unethical to "make a demonstration" out of Goodman, particularly since the legal issue at trial would be Goodman's state of mind at the time of the pushing, not at trial. Taking Goodman off his medication would make more vivid for the jury the effects of the absence of drug therapy, but Uviller insists that "mental illness is something you don't fool around with," even if it might improve Goodman's chances of prevailing on an insanity defense. In other words, Uviller is saying that respecting the client's best interests creates an overarching obligation on the part of the lawyer not to take any actions that will interfere with the client's mental health.

One might ask if there is an obligation in the rules to protect your client's mental health. I would freely grant that one has a *moral* obligation to protect the health of one's clients, but there does not appear to be a specific *legal* obligation in conflict with the legal obligation to defer to the client's view of what is in his best interests, to the extent possible. But what if the client insists that he's willing to accept the risk of some

65

adverse effect on his mental health in order to avoid prison? It is tempting to argue that the lawyer would be acting paternalistically by refusing to defer to his client in that situation, but remember that it was the lawyer's suggestion in the first place that Goodman stop taking his medication. Thus, it is a bit disingenuous to say that the client's judgment about his best interests was to go off his medication when the interaction with the lawyer is what planted that suggestion in the client's mind in the first place.

INTERFERENCE WITH THE ATTORNEY-CLIENT RELATIONSHIP

Anti-Contact Rule

People hire lawyers so that they do not have to deal directly with their legal problems. They also seek lawyers to protect them from other lawyers, who are not acting in their interests. For these reasons, the disciplinary rules forbid a lawyer from talking to persons who are involved in a matter, if the lawyer knows that those persons are represented by counsel in connection with the matter. Rule 4.2; Rest. §99. (These conversations are sometimes known as *ex parte* contacts, because they take place in the absence of the opposing party's lawyer.) The anti-contact rule relieves represented individuals from the pressure that the opposing lawyer might bring to bear to settle a case, for example, or to provide damaging information. In this way, it protects the integrity of the attorney-client relationship.

Notice some interesting features of the language of Rule 4.2. First, the rule says that a lawyer shall not communicate about the subject matter of a representation with a *person* who is represented by counsel. The word "person" is important in light of the word that had been used in the original version of Rule 4.2, which was "party." "Party" may be taken to have a technical meaning, defined by the law of civil procedure, as the participants in a formal, already commenced lawsuit. The word would rule out disputants who have not yet been made parties to a legal action, such as a potential plaintiff and defendant who are exchanging letters and seeking to settle a case. It also rules out participants in a business transaction whose interests may be adverse, but who are not suing each other (at least not yet). In each of these cases, though, the policies underlying the anti-contact rule still have force. Disputants who have not been made parties to a formal lawsuit may still give up information unwisely to opposing counsel or be induced to settle on unfavorable terms. And participants in a transaction may make concessions unwisely, or share information that they should have kept confidential. The current version of Rule 4.2 substitutes the term "person" for "party." Comment [2] to the rule now makes clear that it applies to "any person who is represented by counsel concerning the matter to which the communication relates." Although it is not explicitly stated in the text of the rule, Rule 4.2 applies to persons who are aligned on the same side of a lawsuit, such as co-defendants. If P is suing D1 and D2, the lawyer for D1 is forbidden to contact both P *and* D2 directly, without the permission of their lawyers.

Second, like many of the disciplinary rules, Rule 4.2 has a mens rea requirement for imposing discipline on the lawyer. In order to be subject to discipline, the lawyer must *know* that the person to whom he talks is represented by counsel in the matter. The word "know" is defined as denoting *actual knowledge* of the fact in question, not just circumstances that should alert a reasonable lawyer to the fact of representation. Rule 1.0(f). Lawyers should be careful, however, because actual knowledge can be inferred from circumstances. *Id.*; Rule 4.2, cmt. [8]. A lawyer cannot willfully blind herself to the obvious. For instance, after a mass disaster such as an airplane crash, it is obvious that the airline will retain counsel to help it deal with the inevitable litigation; for a lawyer to say she didn't "know" the airline was represented by counsel strains credibility. In analyzing a problem under the anti-contact rule, be alert for facts suggesting that the lawyer has actual knowledge of the representation.

Third, the rule is highly protective of the attorney-client relationship, so much so that its protection is *not waivable* by the client. Only the lawyer may consent to direct contact between her client and opposing counsel. The rule provides that the lawyer "shall not communicate . . . unless the lawyer has the consent *of the other lawyer* "to do so (emphasis added). See also Rule 4.2, cmt. [3] ("This Rule applies even though the represented person initiates or consents to the communication."). For example, if the plaintiff wants to talk directly with the defendant's lawyer, the defendant's lawyer had better watch out. Courts have held that this kind of direct communication is prohibited, even if the opposing client initiates the contact. See, for example, *Papanicolaou v. Chase Manhattan Bank*, 720 F. Supp. 1080 (S.D.N.Y. 1989) (disqualifying the lawyer *and the law* firm from continuing to represent the bank, even though the plaintiff himself had initiated the contact with the bank's lawyer). The proper course of action here would be for the defendant's lawyer to say to the plaintiff, "Sorry, but I'm forbidden to talk to you directly without your lawyer's permission. If your lawyer agrees, tell her to call me and give me permission to talk to you. But we cannot continue this conversation now."

Although it is not apparent from the face of Rule 4.2 alone, the rule also applies to *directed* communications using third parties, such as paralegals or investigators—in other words, situations in which the lawyer herself does not communicate with a witness, but instructs another person to make the contact. See Rule 8.4(a) (providing that a lawyer is subject to discipline for violating a rule "through the acts of another"). If the lawyer would be prohibited from talking to a represented person, then the lawyer's agents would be as well. Further support for that view comes from Rule 5.3(c), which provides that the lawyer is responsible for the conduct of a nonlaw-yer employee if that person engages in conduct that would be a violation of the rules, and the lawyer directed the conduct, ratifies it after the fact, or had direct supervisory authority over the employee and an opportunity to prevent the action. Not only would it be too easy to circumvent the anti-contact rule if it applied only to lawyers, but the application to nonlawyer employees also recognizes the reality that it is often nonlawyers, such as paralegals, who do a substantial amount of investigatory work and inter-views of witnesses.

What about *clients* who want to deal directly with the opposing party — would it be an impermissible directed communication for a lawyer to advise her client to initiate settlement discussions directly with the adversary? Comment [4] to Rule 4.2 clarifies that the parties have the right to deal directly with each other, and a lawyer does not violate the rule by "advis-ing a client concerning a communication that the client is legally entitled to make." That position was affirmed in ABA Formal Op. 11-461 (2011), which noted the tension between Comment [4] and the prohibition in Rule 8.4(a) on violating a rule through the acts of another. It concluded that "without violating Rules 4.2 or 8.4(a), a lawyer may give substantial assis-tance to a client regarding a substantive communication with a represented adversary. That advice could include, for example, the subjects or topics to be addressed, issues to be raised and strategies to be used." However, the ethics committee warned against overreaching, such as persuading the opposing party to settle a case, make important admissions, or disclose confidential information.

Remedies for violation of the rule include not only discipline by the state bar authorities, but also disqualification of the offending lawyer from continued representation of the client, and in some cases preclusive sanc-tions, which prevent the offending lawyer from presenting evidence at trial that was obtained through contact with represented nonclients. See, for example, *Kaiser v. AT&T*, 2002 WL 1362054 (D. Ariz. 2002) (disqualifying law firm for engaging in *ex parte* contacts with former manager of adver-sary). The trial court's authority to disqualify a lawyer for violating the anti-contact rule is an example of what I have called Track Two inherent power. See Chapter 1.

Anti-Contact Rule Where an Entity Is the Client

Like the attorney-client privilege (see Chapter 8), the anti-contact rule does not protect individuals only, but also applies to clients who are entities. In other words, the "persons" that are covered by Rule 4.2 include artificial persons such as corporations. The problem is figuring out which employees of a corporation should come under the protective scope of the anti-contact rule. The broadest position is that the opposing lawyer is prohibited from talking with any employee of the corporate client. This certainly would be a clear test, easy to apply in practice. The downside is that it completely would shut down the informal discovery process. The opposing lawyer would be forced to use expensive formal methods like depositions to learn what the corporate employees know. It would be much cheaper and quicker if the lawyer could interview these witnesses informally.

A much narrower position would confine the protection of the rule to the so-called control group—the high-level corporate agents who are responsible for directing the actions of the entity. The control group test makes sense as an analogy with natural persons. The control group "personifies" the corporation because members of that group are empowered to act on behalf of the organization. This test seems too narrow, however, because employees outside the control group can still get the corporation in trouble if they admit to conduct that could be imputed to the corporation for the purposes of liability. Under the tort doctrine of *respondeat superior*, the actions of employees much farther down the corporate hierarchy can subject the employer to liability, as long as they are within the scope of the employee's duties. If the adversary's lawyer is permitted to talk to employees whose liability could be imputed to the corporation, he might be able to trick those employees into making a damaging admission that would subject the corporation to liability. The anti-contact rule is designed to prevent exactly that kind of interference with the attorney-client relationship.

An important case from the New York Court of Appeals (the highest court in that state) included within the protection of the anti-contact rule the following categories of corporate employees: (1) Those whose acts are binding on the corporation—equivalent to the control group. (2) Employees whose acts or omissions can be imputed to the corporation for the purposes of liability. (3) Agents who implement the advice of counsel. *Niesig v. Team I*, 558 N.E.2d 1030 (N.Y. 1990); see also Rule 4.2, cmt. [7]. The Restatement test is very similar to the standard set out in the *Niesig* case and Comment [7] to Rule 4.2. Categories (2) and (3) of the New York rule overlap with the Restatement rule, see Rest. §100(2)(a), (b), but the Restatement has a different third category. Employees are covered by the anti-contact rule if their statements are treated as binding by applicable rules of evidence. Rest. §100(2)(c). There was briefly some uncertainty over the scope of this category, but it has been interpreted as incorporating the common law "judicial admissions" rule, under which certain statements by agents may not be contradicted at trial by the principal. See Rest. §100, cmt. e; *Messing, Rudavsky & Weliky, P.C. v. President and Fellows of Harvard College*, 764 N.E.2d 825 (Mass. 2002). You will encounter this third category of employees only very rarely, but the other two categories are important. For the purposes of working with the Restatement test, concentrate on §§100(2)(a) and (2)(b): When it comes to entities, opposing lawyers should avoid talking with employees who consult with the lawyer on the matter in question, as well as employees who were directly involved with the liability-creating event.

In general, *former* employees are not covered by the no-contact rule. ABA Formal Op. 91-359; Rest. §100, cmt. g. The rule is aimed at protecting the integrity of the attorney-client relationship from interference by outsiders, so once an employee no longer works for the corporation, he or she is not part of the relationship that is safeguarded. Denying access to former employees would impede opposing counsel's access to information, without furthering the policy of facilitating the corporation's relationship with its lawyers. There are a few cases in which courts have prohibited contact with former employees, but only when the former employee had been "extensively exposed" to confidential client information. Rest. §102, cmt. d. These cases often involve aggravating factors, such as a lawyer's specific attempt to obtain confidential documents. See, for example, *Camden v. State*, 910 F. Supp. 1115 (D. Md. 1996) (disqualifying lawyer for violation of anti-contact rule); *Arnold v. Cargill, Inc.*, 2004 WL 2203410 (D. Minn. 2004) (effectively retaining a former manager of defendant corporation as an expert on behalf of the plaintiffs).

Remember that regardless of what test is used in the context of entity representation, the anti-contact rule applies only when a lawyer knows the opposing party is represented by counsel in the matter. Rule 4.2.

Examples

Can We Talk?

6. Pépin was employed as a line cook in B&B's Restaurant, owned by a partnership consisting of Batali and Boulud. He was injured when a grease fire suddenly flared up and alleges that the owners knew of the dangerous condition of the ventilation system in the kitchen but did nothing to correct it. You are representing Pépin in his lawsuit. (Small employers such as B&B's Restaurant are not covered by workers' compensation in the state.) Boulud's daughter plays on the soccer team you coach in your spare time, and you frequently chat with him after soccer practices. Is it permissible to ask him, the next time you see him at soccer practice, "How are things going at the restaurant?"

   A. Yes, because this is an innocuous social pleasantry and is unrelated to the representation of Pépin.

   B. Yes, because the defendant in the lawsuit is B&B's Restaurant, not Batali or Boulud individually.

C. No, because by failing to disclose to Boulud the representation of Pépin, you are essentially making a false statement of fact to a third party.

D. No, because as a general partner of B&B's, Boulud is authorized to settle the lawsuit on behalf of B&B's.

Zones of Silence

7. Leonard works for Spur Corporation, a real-estate development company in the State of Perplexity. On his way to inspect a lot for possible purchase, he was involved in a serious auto accident. The lawyer for the other driver wishes to conduct informal interviews with various employees of Spur. Before she can talk to anyone, she receives a letter from the lawyer representing Spur in the accident litigation, instructing her not to violate the anti-contact rule. Can she talk to . . .

- Leonard;
- Mills, who is a regional director of sales and Leonard's immediate supervisor;
- Parker, a mechanic in the motor pool of Spur, who recently worked on the brakes of the car that Leonard was driving;
- Robinson, the director of human resources for Spur, who conducted a routine background check after interviewing Leonard and discovered that he had ten outstanding speeding tickets;
- Splitter, a friend of Leonard's and another employee at the same level in the corporation; or
- Diaw, the chief operating officer of Spur, who has authority to make significant management decisions on behalf of the corporation?

Explanations

Can We Talk?

6. The answer is D. This is a pretty straightforward anti-contact rule question. If you are the lawyer representing Pépin, you are prohibited from communicating about the subject of the representation with a person you know to be represented by counsel. Rule 4.2. Answer A is a huge stretch. Although it's true that you know Boulud socially and might in other circumstances casually ask him how things are going at the restaurant, here it is a transparent attempt to get him to volunteer information about the accident. Answer B implicates the anti-contact rule for entities, discussed in more detail in Example 7. Rule 4.2 talks about a "person . . . represented by another lawyer," but the comments go on to explain that contacts may also be prohibited by agents of a represented

organization. See Rule 4.2, cmt. [7]. The general partner of a partnership has "authority to obligate the organization with respect to the matter," so the *restaurant's* rights under the anti-contact rule prohibit lawyers suing the restaurant from talking to Boulud. Finally, while Rule 4.1(a) prohibits making a false statement of material fact to a third party, silence alone does not violate the disciplinary rules unless it has the effect of assisting a client's criminal or fraudulent act. Rule 4.1(b).

It wasn't one of the choices here, but if you did not know that B&B's Restaurant was represented by counsel in the matter, the anti-contact rule would not prohibit the chat with Boulud.

Zones of Silence

7. This example is drawn from the illustrations to Restatement §100. The categories of employees who are off-limits to the plaintiff's lawyer are set out in Restatement §100(2). See also Rule 4.2, cmt. [7]. The first category consists of employees who regularly consult with the lawyer concerning the matter, or who have the power to compromise or settle the matter. Rest. §100(2)(a). Only Diaw falls into that category. As a regional sales manager, Mills probably does not have the power to settle a significant personal-injury case (he probably does not have any authority over litigation decisions taken by the company at all). He also probably does not regularly consult with the corporation's lawyer on accident litigation.

The second category contains employees whose acts or omissions may be imputed to the corporation for the purpose of civil or criminal liability in the matter in question. Rest. §100(2)(b). This category includes Leonard himself, whose negligent driving could be imputed to Spur, as well as Parker, who may have been negligent in repairing the car, thus contributing to the accident. Robinson might fall within this category as well, if the plaintiff brings a claim against the corporation for negligent hiring or supervision. If Leonard's job requires him to be out on the road frequently, the corporation probably has a duty to make sure that he is not a reckless driver. As soon as the plaintiff discovers that Leonard had ten speeding tickets, he is sure to refocus his case to develop a negligent hiring claim against Spur, in which case informal interviews with Robinson would be prohibited by the anti-contact rule.

Under the Restatement standard, the plaintiff's lawyer can talk to Splitter, who does not have supervisory authority over the matter and who did nothing to contribute to the accident, and therefore does not risk subjecting the corporation to vicarious liability through an improvident admission. There are some courts that apply the anti-contact rule to *all* current employees, however. See Reporter's Notes to Rest. §100. In one of these jurisdictions, contact with Splitter also would be prohibited.

Note that some jurisdictions still apply a strict version of the "control group" test, and permit contact with all employees who are not alter egos of the corporation. A comment to the relevant New Jersey rule limits the anti-contact rule to the "litigation control group," which consists of employees who are responsible for the determination of the organization's legal position in the matter. N.J. Rule of Prof. Conduct 1.13(a). Under the control group or litigation control group tests, the plaintiff's lawyer would be permitted to informally interview all the employees in this example, except for Diaw.

Anti-Contact Rule in Criminal Cases

Nothing in the text of Rule 4.2 expressly limits its application to civil cases, and the potentially broad applicability of the rule has proven to be an occasional headache for law enforcement. Remember that the rule prohibits a lawyer from directing a third person who has contact with a represented nonclient. This would seem to prevent an Assistant U.S. Attorney from working with the FBI to arrange to have an undercover informant talk to the target of an investigation, if the target were represented by counsel in connection with the subject matter of the investigation. If the fictional mobster Tony Soprano wanted to protect himself against informants wearing wires, couldn't he just hire a permanent "in house" lawyer to represent him in all criminal investigations arising out of his "business" activities? That way, if the government directed an informant to trap Tony into an incriminating admission, the statement may have to be suppressed as a remedy for violating the anti-contact rule, because Tony would be "a person . . . represented by another lawyer in the matter." That might be a reasonable way to apply the anti-contact rule, but it is not the law today. Instead, prosecutors have a great deal of latitude to talk to people who are represented by counsel, as long as they do not violate the Sixth Amendment.

One way to read the anti-contact rule to allow government lawyers and their agents to talk to persons suspected of criminal activity is to flesh out the "authorized by law" exception. Rule 4.2 provides that a lawyer may engage in otherwise forbidden *ex parte* contacts if the lawyer is authorized by law to do so. There are constitutional limitations on what contacts are not authorized, which apply when the proceedings against a criminal suspect have become sufficiently formal. The Sixth Amendment's right to counsel attaches upon the commencement of formal judicial proceedings—that is, indictment or arraignment. Because the government does not violate the Sixth Amendment rights of an unindicted target of an investigation by questioning him outside the presence of counsel, the natural reading of the "authorized by law" exception would be that these preindictment interviews are not covered by the anti-contact rule. By reading the "authorized by law" exception together with the Sixth Amendment, courts generally have permitted attorneys for law enforcement agencies to direct the use of informants to gather evidence from unindicted suspects. See also D.C. Bar Legal Ethics Comm., Op. 323 (a lawyer should not be subject to discipline for engaging in deception where the deceptive practices are authorized by law).

Nevertheless, some courts occasionally have expressed impatience with government agents interviewing unindicted criminal suspects in the absence of counsel. In one well-known case, *United States v. Hammad*, 858 F.2d 834 (2d Cir. 1988), the Second Circuit concluded that the government violated the rule by inducing Bad Guy #1 to wear a recording device and try to trap Bad Guy #2 into an incriminating admission. Significantly, however, the government had engaged in other questionable conduct, by creating a dummy subpoena for Bad Guy #1 to wave in front of Bad Guy #2 to scare him into believing that the government had subpoenaed Bad Guy #1 to testify before the grand jury about his dealings with Bad Guy #2. The court specifically stated that in the absence of the type of aggravating misconduct that occurred in that investigation, the contact between the informant (Bad Guy #1) and the suspect (Bad Guy #2) would fall within the "authorized by law" exception. Cases holding that the government lawyer did violate the anti-contact rule generally involve some kind of egregious prosecutorial misconduct, over and above the interview with the suspect. In the absence of some aggravating factor like the sham subpoena in *Hammad*, pre-indictment contact with a criminal suspect (that is, conduct that would not be a Sixth Amendment violation) is not a violation of Rule 4.2.[5]

The *Hammad* case and others like it led to a highly publicized effort by the Justice Department to exempt federal prosecutors from state disciplinary rules. In 1989, then Attorney General Dick Thornburgh issued a memorandum asserting that the Supremacy Clause of the U.S. Constitution prohibited states from enforcing their disciplinary rules against federal government lawyers. (This was probably an overreaction given the narrow scope of the *Hammad* ruling, but at the time it was unclear whether *Hammad* in fact would apply only to cases involving egregious misconduct or would be expanded to prohibit more routine pre-indictment contacts.) The Thornburgh memo

---

5. In fact, some cases have distinguished *Hammad* so severely on its facts that it is fair to say that *Hammad* probably has little precedential value. For example, in *United States v. Grass*, 239 F. Supp. 2d 535 (M.D. Pa. 2003), the district court refused to suppress a tape recording made under the direction of a federal prosecutor where the target of the investigation had been shown a fake letter suggesting that another corporate officer was also a target of the investigation. The court distinguished *Hammad* by pointing out that the letter did not contain a forged signature of the clerk of court, as the dummy subpoena in *Hammad* did. That is an extremely narrow ground for distinguishing the cases, suggesting that various kinds of deception by government investigators will be permitted, notwithstanding *Hammad*.

led to a huge brouhaha, in which the American Bar Association attacked the Justice Department's attempt to exempt itself from the rules applicable to other lawyers and Attorney General Thornburgh responded by accusing the ABA of "lending aid and comfort" to the criminal defense bar in its attempt "to use rules of professional conduct to stymie criminal investigations and prosecutions." Quoted in Stephen Gillers, *Regulation of Lawyers* 116 (5th ed. 1998). The Attorney General under the Clinton Administration, Janet Reno, attempted to turn the rhetorical heat down a notch or two by issuing detailed rules in the Code of Federal Regulations for federal prosecutors. These rules subsequently were invalidated by the Eighth Circuit. *O'Keefe v. McDonnell Douglas Corp.*, 132 F.3d 1252 (8th Cir. 1998). The denouement to this drama was provided by a federal statute, commonly known as the McDade Amendment, which provides that an attorney for the federal government is subject to the rules of professional conduct governing lawyers in the state in which the lawyer's activities occur. 28 U.S.C. §530B.

After the McDade Amendment was enacted in 1998, you might think the situation has reverted back to *Hammad*, where government lawyers are prohibited from talking to represented nonclients who are the targets of an investigation. For the most part, though, courts considering the issue after the McDade Amendment have made liberal use of the "authorized by law" exception to Rule 4.2 when the contact occurs prior to indictment. See, for example, *United States v. Grass*, 239 F. Supp. 2d 535 (M.D. Pa. 2003). In other words, as long as the contact does not violate the Fifth Amendment (prohibiting custodial interrogations outside the presence of counsel where the suspect has requested a lawyer be present) or the Sixth Amendment (prohibiting postindictment contact with represented defendants), it is authorized by law. Outside the scope of the Fifth and Sixth Amendments, the target of a criminal investigation in federal court can expect little in the way of protection from the anti-contact rule and the supervisory power of federal courts over the conduct of federal prosecutors.[6] The situation may be different in state courts, however, so you should pay attention to the law in your jurisdiction on the boundaries of the "authorized by law" exception to the local version of Rule 4.2.

---

6. The supervisory power permits federal courts to exclude evidence even in cases where the government did not violate a specific constitutional right of the defendant. Courts apply it inconsistently and, as some have argued, too enthusiastically. Sara Sun Beale, *Reconsidering Supervisory Power in Criminal Cases: Constitutional and Statutory Limits on the Authority of Federal Courts*, 84 Colum. L. Rev. 1433 (1984). If a court did not apply the "authorized by law" exception to Rule 4.2, the source of its authority to suppress the evidence resulting from the contact would be its inherent supervisory power.

Attorneys' Fees and Transactions with Clients

4

REASONABLENESS OF FEES

The basic rule here is simple — an attorney must charge a reasonable fee. But what is reasonable can vary considerably under the circumstances. Attorney fees can be challenged under both contract law principles and the disciplinary rules. In contract law, defenses such as unconscionability are available for a client to assert in an action by the lawyer to recover payment. See, for example, *Brobeck, Phleger & Harrison v. Telex Corp.*, 602 F.2d 866 (9th Cir. 1978) (approving a contingent fee of $1 million, concluding it was not unconscionable). In addition, there are various implied terms of reasonableness in a typical attorney-client engagement contract; numerous cases arise out of fee disputes, in which a court essentially requires a lawyer to show that her services were worth the amount charged. See, for example, *Jenkins v. District Court*, 676 P.2d 1201 (Colo. 1984) (citing cases); *Newman v. Silver*, 553 F. Supp. 485 (S.D.N.Y. 1985) (breach of fiduciary duty action against lawyer for charging excessive fees). Thus, the law of contracts supports a rule that a lawyer may not recover a fee unless it is reasonable. "[I]n fee disputes between a lawyer and client, a fee will not be approved to the extent that it violates [the requirement that it be reasonable under the circumstances] even though the parties had agreed to the fee." Rest. §34, cmt. a.

When it comes to professional discipline, though, bar authorities are not so quick to impose it. "For a variety of reasons, discipline may be withheld for charging a fee that would nevertheless be set aside as unreasonable in a fee-dispute proceeding." Rest. §34, cmt. a. One might say that the law of contracts is harder on lawyers than the law of attorney discipline. This makes a certain amount of sense. Bar disciplinary authorities struggle to make do with limited funding and tend to have other fish to fry—lawyers who steal from their clients, neglect cases entirely, and are completely incompetent. Because the law of contracts probably does a pretty good job of policing excessive fees, disciplinary authorities may reasonably defer to private litigation between clients and lawyers to take care of the problem. A somewhat more cynical reason for deferring to contract law is that the possibility of professional discipline for excessive fees is controlled by other lawyers, who may not be interested in limiting the economic opportunities of their professional colleagues. See Wolfram §9.3 ("Lawyers will always be inadequate enforcers of fee limitations because their economic hearts aren't in it."). Occasionally, though, an attorney's fee is so egregious that the bar has to step in, just to underscore its independent commitment to a rule that attorneys must charge reasonable fees.

In economic terms, all fee arrangements create *agency costs* for the client, related to the client's inability to monitor the attorney's performance to make sure it is in the client's best interests, and not self-serving for the attorney in some way.[1] Hourly fees pretty obviously create an incentive for the attorney to "run the meter" by performing tasks that do not substantially improve the client's outcome in the matter, but yield more income for the lawyer. The agency problem arises from the nature of professional services. Suppose a lawyer says it is necessary to take five additional depositions in a civil case. How is the client supposed to know whether the further discovery will make a good outcome more likely or whether it is merely a way for the lawyer to pad the bill? Some clients have responded to this agency problem by either having in-house lawyers to monitor the performance of outside counsel or submitting lawyers' bills to an auditor for evaluation. But it is generally only institutional clients such as large corporations that can employ these sorts of mechanisms to ensure the reasonableness of their lawyers' fees. Individuals and small businesses remain vulnerable to overcharging.

Both the Model Code and the Model Rules forbid charging excessive fees. Actually, the Model Code prohibited charging "clearly excessive" fees, while the Model Rules require that the lawyer's fee not be "unreasonable." Compare Rule 1.5(a) with DR 2-106(A), (B). The difference between the Model Code and the Model Rules simply may be one of emphasis, or the Model Code may impose a higher burden on the disciplinary authorities (showing clear excessiveness) as compared with the Model Rules (showing unreasonableness). In any event, those terms *clearly excessive* and *reasonable* are defined with reference to a set of factors that is identical in the Model Code and the Model Rules.

---

1. For an early economic analysis of attorney fees—still one of the best—see Kevin M. Clermont & John D. Currivan, *Improving on the Contingent Fee*, 63 Cornell L. Rev. 529 (1978).

1. *Nature of the Matter.* "[T]he time and labor required, the novelty and difficulty of the questions involved, and the skill requisite to perform the legal service properly." Rule 1.5(a)(1). A lawyer should be permitted to charge a higher hourly rate for services that require a great deal of skill and experience, and should be permitted to spend more time on a complex case. A routine litigation matter such as a collection case or a misdemeanor defense, or a simple business transaction like a residential real estate closing, should be relatively inexpensive compared to something like a complex lawsuit in federal court involving expert testimony and novel legal issues.

2. *Opportunity Costs.* "[T]he likelihood, if apparent to the client, that the acceptance of the particular employment will preclude other employment by the lawyer." Rule 1.5(a)(2). A lawyer may be unwilling to work on behalf of one client if that representation will conflict her out of future work for other clients. She also may not want to get tied up with a matter that will be time consuming in the short run, but that will not last for very long, if she thinks that a potential client with a longer-term matter is waiting in the wings. Thus, in some cases, the lawyer should be permitted to charge the client a premium for foregoing other sources of business.

3. *Local Custom.* "[T]he fee customarily charged in the locality for similar legal services." Rule 1.5(a)(3). Although not dispositive, a fee may raise the eyebrows of a court or disciplinary agency if it is way out of line with what other lawyers charge for similar services. If most lawyers bill somewhere between $3,000 and $10,000 to defend a misdemeanor charge of driving while intoxicated, and no one has ever heard of a fee higher than $15,000 for that kind of work, a court will probably look askance on a bill in excess of $50,000. See *In re Fordham*, 668 N.E.2d 816 (Mass. 1996).

4. *Stakes for the Client.* "[T]he amount involved and the results obtained." Rule 1.5(a)(4). It is reasonable to charge the client a higher fee when something of great importance is on the line. The *Brobeck* case mentioned above was literally a "bet the company" appeal — if the client had been unable to settle the lawsuit on appeal, it would have been forced to file bankruptcy. In light of the downside risk for the client, the $1 million fee doesn't sound so bad.

5. *Emergencies.* "[T]he time limitations imposed by the client or by the circumstances." Rule 1.5(a)(5). Suppose a long-time client of a law firm calls and reports that it has just been served with a motion for a temporary restraining order, which would force it to shut down its business. The firm drops everything, puts all available lawyers on the matter, and spends the next 48 hours in a frenzy, preparing a response to the motion. The firm should be able to charge

a premium over its normal rates to compensate for the hassle, the sleepless nights, and the disruption in its other business.

6. *One-shot Versus Repeat Players.* "[T]he nature and length of the professional relationship with the client." Rule 1.5(a)(6). If a client has used a lawyer many times in the past, the client probably trusts the lawyer, and for good reason—the lawyer is unlikely to overreach and bill excessively on one matter, for fear of losing the client's future business. On the other hand, if the client comes to the lawyer with a one-time-only matter, the lawyer may have an incentive to milk that matter for all it's worth, figuring the client is unlikely to place future business with that lawyer anyway (although a lawyer is supposed to charge reasonable fees even to one-shot clients). If a fee is high enough to raise judicial eyebrows, a court may be reassured if the client is a repeat player, because the lawyer's incentive to overcharge the client will be kept in check by the desire to maintain a long-term relationship with the client. Thus, a lawyer charging an unusually high fee may get the benefit of the doubt if the client is one with whom the lawyer has had a lengthy professional relationship.

7. *You Get What You Pay For.* "[T]he experience, reputation, and ability of the lawyer or lawyers performing the services." Rule 1.5(a)(7). One would obviously expect to pay more for a senior partner with 25 years' experience than for a junior associate, fresh out of law school. It also makes sense to pay for reputation, because adverse parties may be more inclined to settle or enter into a transaction on favorable terms if they respect (or fear) the opposing lawyer.

   It is important not to overstate the latitude that an experienced, skillful, or renowned lawyer has when billing clients. If you are billing by the hour, you have to charge the same hourly rate, regardless of whether you are thinking brilliant thoughts or mindlessly putting yellow sticky notes on boxes of documents. If you have a "Eureka!" moment that completely turns the case around, you still are not permitted to jack up your hourly rate for that one moment to reflect the contribution that your epiphany has made to your client's case. In *Fordham*, the lawyer admittedly did come up with an interesting basis for a motion to suppress the critical evidence against his client. The motion was granted and the client got a great result, but the court nevertheless found the lawyer's $50,000 fee unreasonable. See In re *Fordham*, 668 N.E.2d 816 (Mass. 1996).

8. *Who Bears the Risk?* "[W]hether the fee is fixed or contingent." Rule 1.5(a)(8). A contingent fee agreement places the risk of an adverse result on the attorney. If the contingency does not happen—if, for example, the client does not settle or recover a judgment at trial—the lawyer does not get paid. Lawyers therefore charge a premium

for bearing this risk. They try to calculate the chances that the contingency will occur, estimate the likely recovery, and divide by the number of hours they anticipate putting into the case. The hourly rate calculated by this method should exceed the hourly rate the lawyer would charge if she did not have to bear the risk of not getting paid. This risk premium is a legitimate reason why contingent fee recoveries sometimes sound shockingly high. What goes unreported when you hear about whopping contingent fees is the number of cases in which the lawyer has to bear all of the cost of preparing for trial, only to recover nothing.

These factors can be summed up a bit more concisely in this bottom-line rule: *If the client had a free and informed choice before entering into the agreement, and the fee is within the range customarily charged by lawyers in similar representations, it is almost certainly reasonable.* See Rest. §34, cmt. c. I might put it slightly differently, starting with the Restatement formulation. Here's the Wendel principle for reasonable fees: If a fee does not fall within the range customarily charged in the relevant community, then the burden of persuasion is on the lawyer to establish that the fee is reasonable, and in doing so, the lawyer should make an argument based on the factors in Rule 1.5(a). In addition, courts are more likely to permit innovative fee arrangements where the client is a sophisticated entity, such as a corporation, and the lawyer and client freely negotiated the fee agreement. Where individuals are involved, particularly people who do not have much experience with the legal system (such as typical personal-injury, probate, and criminal clients), courts are more likely to scrutinize fees much more carefully for reasonableness. In the *Fordham* case, for example, the lawyer did explain to the client that he was not experienced in criminal-defense work, but it is doubtful that the client fully appreciated that the gold-plated lawyer he was talking to would actually have to teach himself some pretty basic skills to handle the misdemeanor case. Thus, even though the rule does not have an explicit informed-consent provision, courts will often inquire into the quality of the disclosure the lawyer gave to the client, and the client's sophistication and experience in dealing with lawyers.

Examples

Let's Be Reasonable

1. Kovacek hired the law firm of DeWalt, Potter & Huggins to represent him in an age discrimination suit against his former employer. The firm and client agreed to an hourly billing arrangement, with the lead partner billing $255/hr. and the senior associate charging $185/hr. These are comparable billing rates for mid-sized firms in the city. The former

employer, E.F.D. International, has a reputation for defending discrimination lawsuits vigorously. Moreover, as his lawyers told Kovacek, because he had no direct evidence of discrimination, he would have to prove his case indirectly, using a burden-shifting method of proof. Kovacek signed a written fee agreement setting out these terms.

The case went to trial, and the jury awarded Kovacek $700,000 in damages. Unfortunately for Kovacek, the trial judge granted the defendant's motion for a judgment notwithstanding the verdict. This judgment was affirmed on appeal. The firm billed him a total of $230,000 for its services. Kovacek paid $120,000, but refused to pay more after coming to the conclusion that the firm's fees were excessive because the lawyers were spending too much time on the case. "This is just a garden-variety age discrimination case," he said. "And besides, I got nothing out of the case. Nothing! I'm not paying another $110,000 to get nothing in return."

Is the firm entitled to recover its fee from Kovacek? To ask the question differently, is the firm subject to discipline for charging Kovacek $230,000 for handling the case?

2. Suppose instead that the firm told Kovacek it would handle his age discrimination lawsuit for a flat fee of $50,000. Kovacek paid the fee, and the law firm started working on his case. A week after the firm sent a demand letter to the former employer, the employer offered to settle the case by reinstating Kovacek and paying him $100,000. Kovacek was ecstatic, and directed his lawyer to accept the offer. He then said to his lawyer, "Since this case was resolved so quickly, I don't think you should get 50 thousand bucks for doing one week's work." The lawyer replied, "A deal's a deal — there's always a risk in any flat-fee arrangement. If this case had dragged on for years, we would have lost money. Pay up."

Can the firm keep the entire flat fee of $50,000? Would it be subject to discipline if it did so?

Explanations

Let's Be Reasonable

1. In the actual case of *DeWitt, Porter, Huggett, Schumacher & Morgan v. Kovalic*, 991 F.2d 1243 (7th Cir. 1993), the trial court instructed the jury to determine the firm's entitlement to recover on the fee agreement based on factors very similar to those listed in Rule 1.5(a). I guesstimated what the inflation-adjusted hourly rates would be today, but they were intended to be ordinary fees for lawyers in a medium-sized firm. (See Rule 1.5(a)(3), the fee customarily charged in the locality.) If the number of hours billed by the lawyers is reasonable in light of the difficulty and complexity of the case, the fee will almost certainly be permitted. Kovacek's argument

is that a "garden-variety" age discrimination suit should not take that much time, but the case did go all the way through trial and then up on appeal. Even though the case may seem simple to the client ("They discriminated against me—what's the problem?"), there may be numerous procedural complexities, difficulties obtaining evidence, and delays created by the defendant's vigorous defense that necessitate spending a lot of time preparing the case. A case like this could easily result in hundreds of hours of billed attorney time over the span of a few years. Thus, the first factor (Rule 1.5(a)(1)) favors the firm. The only factor that seems to work in Kovacek's favor is the fourth (Rule 1.5(a)(4)), namely, the results obtained. But while the result is bad from Kovacek's point of view, it's not necessarily the fault of the firm. Trials are unpredictable, and even competent lawyers lose cases sometimes. We do not know enough about the allegations of discrimination to say one way or the other, but maybe Kovacek had a weak case. Thus, on the facts of this example, there is nothing to suggest that the fee is unreasonable.

Be on the lookout for facts that might suggest unreasonableness—again, not present in this case, but maybe on an exam question. For example, what if the senior associate billed a bunch of time for making routine calls to the court clerk's office, organizing files, photocopying documents, and other tasks that could be (and customarily are) delegated to nonlawyer staff such as paralegals and secretaries? Those charges would likely be deemed unreasonable. See, for example, *In re Green*, 11 P.3d 1078 (Colo. 2000) (cited in R&D §1.5-1(b)). Refer to factors such as Rule 1.5(a)(1) (skill requisite to perform the service) and 1.5(a)(3) (fee customarily charged). Or, suppose the law firm charged 25 cents per page for photocopying, while its expenses for paper, toner, renting the machine, etc., were only 10 cents. Is that permissible? The ABA, in Formal Opinion 93-379 said no, and the firm may charge only the direct cost associated with the service plus a reasonable allocation of overhead expenses directly associated with the provision of the service. Finally, look for straightforward billing fraud, such as charging for time the lawyer did not actually work on the matter.

2. You could analyze this example as an application of the reasonableness rule, but it is also an illustration of a special rule that exists in many jurisdictions regarding *retainers*. See Wolfram §9.2.2. The terminology here can be confusing, so try not to get distracted by it. If the client hands over a chunk of money to an attorney before the attorney has begun to do any work, one of three things can be happening:

A. The client is paying the lawyer to be available to perform services if needed, but no specific representation is contemplated. Businesses often keep an attorney "on retainer" to handle expected problems as they arise. Essentially, the client is paying for the lawyer's availability and promise to take a case on a moment's notice. This is sometimes called a *general retainer* and it is perfectly permissible, as long as the amount of the fee is reasonable in relation to what the client is obtaining — that is, the lawyer's promise to be available to perform services if needed. (The client also obtains the benefit of being able to "conflict out" the lawyer from representing a competitor. See Chapter 15 for the general rule that a lawyer may not represent one current client against another.)

B. The client is putting down a deposit or establishing a fund from which the lawyer will draw down fees as they are earned. A lawyer may require an up-front payment, which will be placed in a trust account. Money will then be transferred from the lawyer's trust account to the lawyer's personal account as the fees accrue. (Often the lawyer will send the client a statement on a monthly basis and transfer the funds at the same time.) Significantly, any amount left in the trust account at the conclusion of the representation is refundable to the client. Indeed, the reason the funds must be kept in the trust account in the first place is that *the money belongs to the client* until it is earned by the lawyer. As long as the lawyer complies with the trust account rule (Rule 1.15(c), discussed below) and refunds any unearned money, this system is an acceptable and normal aspect of law practice. This is sometimes called a "special retainer," but again, it's important not to be caught up in the terminology. What matters is that it is a deposit against future fees to be earned. It is client property until earned, and therefore must be kept separate from the lawyer's funds, in a clients' trust account.

C. The client is paying a flat fee for a specific legal task, and the lawyer gets to keep the fee regardless of how much work she puts into the matter. This arrangement is considered *per se* improper in many jurisdictions, because it interferes with the client's right to fire the lawyer at any time. See, for example, *In re Cooperman*, 633 N.E.2d 1069 (N.Y. 1994). The difference between troublesome flat fees and the more innocuous general retainer is that in the case of flat fees, the lawyer is being compensated for more than just being available (which presumably wouldn't be all that expensive), but is receiving the fee in exchange for performing actual legal services. If the lawyer actually performs the agreed-upon services, the client is not harmed, as long as the amount of the fee is reasonable. By making the fee nonrefundable in all circumstances, though, a lawyer may impermissibly interfere with the client's authority to discharge the lawyer under Rule 1.16(a).

The rule in *Cooperman* is a bit of an anomaly, but it shows something important. Nonrefundable flat fees appear to be the mirror image of contingent fees. Contingent fees shift economic risk to the lawyer; nonrefundable flat fees shift the risk to the client. What is wrong with that? The answer is that the client's right to terminate the attorney-client relationship, for good, bad, or indifferent reasons, is considered almost sacrosanct in the law governing lawyers. That means there are some asymmetries of risk in the lawyer-client relationship. The client may lay off the risk of a lengthy, expensive representation on the lawyer (as would occur with a *refundable* flat fee), but the lawyer may not force the client to bear the mirror-image risk.

CONTINGENT FEES

Most people associate contingent fees with personal-injury cases, but lawyers can handle a wide variety of legal matters on a contingent basis. For example, the firm of Cravath, Swaine & Moore received a $25 million fee upon the closing of the AOL-Time Warner merger. One reason for the increasing interest in contingent fee financing is the recognition by many clients of the incentive it creates for lawyers. If the lawyer will recover the same percentage of a judgment or settlement regardless of how many hours the lawyer puts into the case, the incentive is to handle the case efficiently and not waste time on useless discovery, motions that probably will not be granted (but are not legally frivolous), and gold-standard research into every point of law. Contingent fees also force the lawyer to think about the possibility of recovery, and therefore the legal and factual merit of the case. In a sense, they make lawyers "gatekeepers" of the litigation system, by discouraging the filing of frivolous lawsuits, because a frivolous lawsuit is unlikely to result in a judgment or settlement from which the lawyer can recover a fee.

A typical contingent fee agreement provides that the lawyer is entitled to a percentage (often 33 percent) of any amount that the client may recover as a judgment at trial or in a pretrial settlement. Lawyers are permitted to advance the cost of litigation expenses, such as court-reporter fees, the cost of obtaining deposition transcripts, filing fees, and expert witness fees. The lawyer may be reimbursed for these expenses, even if the client recovers nothing in the litigation, but the client may not realize that the lawyer's fee is calculated as a percentage of the *gross* recovery. For example, assume the client accepts a settlement offer of $100,000, and the lawyer has already advanced payment of $5,000 for expenses. The fee agreement provides for a 33 percent fee, based on the gross recovery. The client's share of the settlement would be calculated as follows:

$100,000.00	Gross recovery
(33,000.00)	Attorney's fee — 33% of gross
(5,000.00)	Reimbursement of expenses
$62,000.00	Net recovery for client

Although this may seem unfair to the client, it is not a violation of the rules governing contingent fees, provided that the basis for calculating the fee was clearly disclosed to the client—for example, in writing signed by the client in Model Rules jurisdictions. Rule 1.5(c). (Rules in some states, including New York, require that the attorney's fee be calculated on the net recovery, less expenses.) Notice that the rule specifically requires the lawyer to notify the client if she will be required to reimburse the lawyer for expenses regardless of whether the client is the prevailing party.

There are a couple of special rules governing contingent fees in addition to the general requirement in Rule 1.5(a) that the fees not be unreasonable. First, contingent fees are flatly prohibited in two categories of cases: criminal defense and many domestic relations matters—specifically those cases in which the payment of a fee is contingent upon obtaining a divorce, or upon the amount of alimony, support, or a property settlement in lieu of alimony or support. Rule 1.5(d). The second rule specific to contingent fees is that contingent fee agreements must be in writing. Rule 1.5(c). An agreement in writing is different from the "consent confirmed in writing" standard used in the conflicts rules. In a conflicts case, the client may orally consent (for example, in a phone call with the lawyer) and the lawyer may subsequently memorialize that consent in a written communication to the client. See Rule 1.0(b) for the definition of "consent confirmed in writing." Rule 1.5(c), however, requires disclosure of the terms of a contingent fee arrangement to be "in a writing signed by the client." The contingent fee rule specifies in considerable detail the information that must be disclosed to the client in the fee agreement, including the percentage of the recovery that will go to the lawyer, whether that percentage is calculated on the gross recovery or the amount recovered after expenses are deducted, and whether the client will be responsible for any expenses even if she is not the prevailing party. Note that even without the requirement of a writing, applicable only to contingent fees, lawyers have an obligation to communicate clearly to their clients the basis of their billing arrangements. Rule 1.5(b).

Much of the discussion of contingent fees centers on some policy concerns they raise. Proponents of contingent fees are impressed with the way they supposedly align the interests of the lawyer and the client. The lawyer wants to work as efficiently as possible, since there is no point in running the meter unless you are billing by the hour. The lawyer also wants a good result for the client, because the more the client recovers, the more the lawyer earns. But are the incentives always matched up? Consider what happens when the lawyer is able to settle a case quickly for less money than the client would be able to recover if the lawyer fought all the way through to trial. Although the client may prefer to go to trial, the lawyer does better *on an effective hourly rate basis* with the quickie settlement.

Hours in Case	Settlement or Judgment	Lawyer's Fee	Hourly Rate
100	$90,000	$30,000	$300
1,000	$180,000	$60,000	$60

If the lawyer is handling many similar cases, there is a risk that she will prefer never to go to trial, since each hour of her time will be worth so much less. Even though the absolute amount of the fee is double if the case goes to trial, lawyers who calculate their effective hourly rate would prefer to settle.

Remember that it is ultimately the client's decision whether to settle a case. Rule 1.2(a). A lawyer who really wants the client to settle early can always put some pressure on the client, though. The lawyer may emphasize the risk of going to trial, may stress the pressing need the client has for the money, and may play up what a good deal the settlement represents. This is not to say that decent, conscientious lawyers do not ignore this incentive and genuinely seek to do what is best for their clients. The incentive is there to arm-twist clients into settling early, however, and it is one reason to think carefully about contingent fees. A lawyer must not *improperly* pressure the client to take the lawyer's advice, such as threatening to withdraw if the client does not agree to an early settlement.

Another criticism of contingent fees that I alluded to earlier is that they stir up litigation, encouraging lawyers to bring frivolous claims in the hopes of winning the lawsuit lottery. This claim is a staple of popular rhetoric about tort reform and the "litigation explosion." Apart from giving no credit at all to lawyers for complying with their obligation not to file frivolous lawsuits (see Rule 3.1; Fed.R.Civ.P. 11), this argument ignores the economic incentives created by contingent fees. The last thing a plaintiff's lawyer wants is to be stuck with a "dog" case — one that eats up a lot of time and offers very little prospect of recovery. Remember that once you are representing a client, you may withdraw from the case only where you can do so without causing prejudice to your client's interests, or under a few other circumstances. (See Chapter 2.) If the case is truly frivolous and the defendant refuses to settle, a lawyer may be duty-bound to slog away on her client's case, in the hopes of recovering some paltry amount at trial. In all likelihood, the trial will end in a defense verdict, and the lawyer will have nothing to show for months, maybe years, of hard work. For these reasons, I tend to think that contingent fees actually help reduce frivolous litigation by forcing lawyers to take a good hard look at the facts and the law to see whether there is a realistic possibility of recovery. Others argue, on the other hand, that contingent fees encourage filing frivolous lawsuits with the hope of obtaining nuisance-value settlements from defendants who would rather pay a few thousand bucks than spend the time obtaining dismissal or summary judgment in the case. Ultimately, this is an empirical question, and the available research appears to show that contingent fee financing has little effect on the number of civil lawsuits filed. See, for example, Thomas J. Miceli, *Do Contingent Fees Promote Excessive Litigation?*, 23 J. Legal Stud. 211 (1994).

Examples

Contingent Fees Without Contingencies?

You work for the state bar's "ethics hotline," which lawyers can call for advice about compliance with the disciplinary rules. Attorney Laura Biden has a couple of questions about contingent fees, both involving insurance coverage disputes.

3. The first case involves a client who was injured in a minor automobile accident. He came to Laura to find out how to make a claim on his insurance policy for $5,000 worth of Personal Injury Protection (PIP) coverage. Laura knows that PIP is a form of no-fault insurance — the insurance company pays a specified amount upon receipt of a claim form completed by the client. May she charge her customary one-third contingent fee to handle the PIP claim?

4. The second case involves a client of the firm, Joseph, whose brother, Stanley, and sister-in-law, Theresa, became fatally ill under mysterious circumstances. Joseph and his mother may be entitled to the proceeds of Stanley's life insurance policy, or the proceeds may be payable to Theresa's mother, depending on which of the two spouses died first. That seemingly simple determination is complicated by the medical evidence — Theresa slipped into a deep coma and was on a respirator for many days — as well as by the need to interpret the simultaneous death provisions in Stanley's insurance policy. Because of the family tragedy, Joseph is short of cash and would prefer to pay Laura on a contingent basis. Can Laura charge her usual one-third fee to represent Joseph and his mother?

Don't Take That Lowball Settlement

5. Lawyer represents Client as the plaintiff in a substantial personal-injury matter. The engagement letter provides that Lawyer is entitled to one-third of the gross recovery by way of settlement or verdict, and in addition that Client must pay Lawyer a $25,000 "low settlement premium" if Client insists on accepting a settlement offer that Lawyer reasonably believes is too low, in light of the facts pertaining to liability

4. Attorneys' Fees and Transactions with Clients

and damages. Lawyer disclosed all these terms in writing to Client and obtained Client's written consent. With respect to the fee agreement:

A. It is permissible, because fees are solely a matter of contract law, and the engagement letter is a valid contract.

B. It is permissible, but only if the case takes longer than anticipated, thus harming the lawyer financially.

C. It is not permissible, because it interferes with Client's absolute authority to decide on what terms to settle the case.

D. It is not permissible, because contingent fees are not permissible in this type of case under Rule 1.5(d).

Left Out in the Cold

6. Client and Lawyer have a 33 percent contingency fee agreement. After a heated argument about politics, Client fires Lawyer and retains New Lawyer. Lawyer had worked 100 hours on the case. Represented by NewLawyer, Client goes to trial and obtains a $100,000 judgment. New Lawyer worked 200 hours on the case. How much may Lawyer recover from Client?

A. Contract damages of $33,000, because Client terminated Lawyer without good cause.

B. Contract damages of $33,000, because Lawyer would be entitled to that amount regardless of whether Client had good cause for termination.

C. Restitution damages of 100 hrs. x Lawyer's reasonable hourly rate, because Client terminated representation for a frivolous reason.

D. Restitution damages of 100 hrs. x Lawyer's reasonable hourly rate, provided that grounds for fee forfeiture do not exist.

Explanations

Contingent Fees Without Contingencies?

3. In a case with no uncertainty, it is unreasonable for a lawyer to charge a contingent fee, which is designed to provide an incentive for a lawyer to accept a risk of nonrecovery. There is no risk that Laura's client will not recover on his PIP policy—all he has to do is fill out the form. It is probably the case that no contingent fee would be appropriate here. See, for example, *Attorney Grievance Comm'n v. Kemp*, 496 A.2d 672, 677-679 (Md. Ct. App. 1985); *Kentucky Bar Ass'n v. Newberg*, 839 S.W.2d 280 (Ky. 1992). Certainly, Laura would not be entitled to her usual one-third fee. The standard fee agreement would result in Laura earning $1,650 for, at most, 20 minutes of work. Charging $5,000 an hour to select and fill out a routine insurance form is plainly unreasonable—none of the

factors in Rule 1.5(a) would permit a fee that large in this case. In any case where the payment of funds to a client is routine or automatic, and not dependent in any way on the skill of a lawyer, a contingent fee would be inappropriate.

4. This case is different from the first one, because there are contested issues surrounding the life insurance policy, and it is not at all certain that Joseph and his mother will be entitled to benefits under Stanley's insurance policy. (By the way, the example is drawn from a disciplinary proceeding brought against the lawyer who represented a family member of some of the victims of the Tylenol tampering case in Chicago in the 1980s. In re Doyle, 581 N.E.2d 669 (Ill. 1991). The legal issues are even more complicated than the example suggests because there were partnership and real property issues entangled with the question of entitlement to the life insurance policy proceeds.) There is a real risk of nonrecovery here, and if Laura wishes to accept that risk by opting for a contingent fee arrangement with her clients, she is entitled to compensation for assuming it. In addition, the skill of the lawyer makes a difference to the outcome, unlike the first case where the only thing required to secure the client's payment was the ministerial act of filling out a form.

Don't Take That Lowball Settlement

5. The correct answer is C. This example ties together not only the material on fees from this chapter, but also the discussion in the previous chapter about the allocation of authority between lawyers and clients. The rule that makes all the difference here is that the decision whether or not to settle a case is the client's alone. Rule 1.2(a). Any provision in an engagement letter that interferes with the client's authority is likely to be looked upon with suspicion by courts and disciplinary agencies. If you were not sure of the answer, you probably could arrive at it by process of elimination. The correct answer cannot be A because based on the Fordham case, fees are not solely a matter of contract law — disciplinary authorities can review fees independently and seek discipline against a lawyer, even if the client would not be entitled to prevail under contract law. B is not the right answer because the whole point of contingent fees is to shift the risk of nonrecovery from the lawyer to the client. If the lawyer has to cover the expenses of litigation for a longer-than-anticipated time, that is just tough luck. I hope it is obvious that D is a silly answer — the only categories of cases in which contingent fees are categorically banned are criminal defense and certain domestic relations cases.

By the way, be extremely wary of any attempt by a lawyer to use money to exert leverage over a client's decisionmaking process. One common kind of misbehavior by lawyers is to try to change the fee arrangement in the middle of the representation, after the client has already invested a great deal of time, trust, and money in the lawyer. In some jurisdictions, any alteration in the fee arrangement after the commencement of representation will be regarded as presumptively fraudulent. Wolfram §9.2.1. To give only one example, a lawyer was disbarred for entering into two contingent fee agreements with a client—one to represent her in an insurance dispute and the other to represent her in a product liability claim—and then later demanding $7,000 in cash as a condition of continuing to work on the product liability lawsuit. In re *Teichner*, 470 N.E.2d 972 (Ill. 1984).

In Opinion 11-458, the ABA discussed midstream modifications of fee agreements. It began with the observation that lawyer-client fee agreements have a dual nature: They are ordinary contracts, governed by ordinary contract law, but due to the fiduciary nature of the lawyer-client relationship, modifications to these contracts are considered suspect once the relationship has commenced. Deriving from Rule 1.5(a), the ABA Committee emphasized that any modification to the original fee agreement must be reasonable. Absent some material change in circumstances that could not have been anticipated by the parties at the time the agreement was entered into, it is unlikely that a midstream modification will be deemed reasonable.

Left Out in the Cold

6. The correct answer is D. Restatement §40 summarizes the law concerning fees upon termination of the attorney-client relationship. The most important thing to note is that the lawyer's entitlement to compensation does not coincide with the lawyer's entitlement to continue representing the client. In other words, the client may have a right to terminate the lawyer-client relationship (see Rule 1.16(a)(3)), but that does not mean the client is relieved from having to pay the lawyer for her services. The law of remedies, specifically the entitlement to recover in *quantum meruit* to avoid unjust enrichment, provides that the lawyer may receive the fair value of her services. *Quantum meruit* recovery balances the client's interests in being able to terminate the professional relationship with the lawyer's interests in getting paid. That is why, in general, courts do not allow the lawyer to recover her fee on the contract. In some instances, however, courts will allow the lawyer to recover the contractually specified fee. The most common situation is where the client in a contingent fee representation discharges the lawyer right before the contingency occurs, to avoid paying the fee. See Rest. §40, cmt. c. In this example the discharge occurred far enough in time from the contingency that the lawyer's recovery should be given by *quantum meruit* principles.

TAKING STOCK IN CLIENTS

The dot-com boom of the late 1990s saw an increase in the number of lawyers who considered taking equity stakes in their clients, in lieu of cash payments for fees. It is becoming common again in the representation of small startup companies, particularly in the technology sector. This kind of financing is not limited to tech startups, however. Lawyers sometimes agree to take an interest in the client's property — perhaps a second mortgage on the client's house — to secure payment of fees. See, for example, In re Snyder, 35 S.W.2d 380 (Mo. 2000); Petit-Clair v. Nelson, 782 A.2d 960 (N.J. Super. 2001). Similarly, clients of patent lawyers may agree to give the lawyer an interest in the patent in exchange for prosecuting the patent, as they are permitted to do under federal law. See 37 C.F.R. §10.64(a)(3). The common denominator in all these transactions is that the lawyer acquires a property or security interest that is at least potentially adverse to the client.[2] Any time a lawyer and a client have adverse interests, you can expect it to raise red flags in the law governing lawyers.

These rules are not limited to transactions in lieu of fees. Any business transaction with a client creates a potential conflict of interest. For this reason, these rules are revisited in Chapter 18, which deals in part with conflicts arising from an interest personal to the lawyer.

Back to the high-tech scenario: Imagine that a group of entrepreneurs, backed with venture capital financing, intend to create Startup.com. They hope to use the cash to pay salaries and buy lavish ads during the Super Bowl. Therefore, to conserve money, they offer a law firm a percentage of the shares to be issued in the initial public offering (IPO) in exchange for handling all the legal work associated with the IPO. Can the firm agree to this arrangement without subjecting itself to either professional discipline or the potential loss of the entitlement to the client's stock? Generally, the answer is yes, but only under stringent conditions. These conditions are spelled out in Rule 1.8(a).

First, the lawyer must fully disclose the terms of the transaction in writing to the client, in language that the client can be expected to understand. Rule 1.8(a)(1). There should be no legalese and evasiveness — this disclosure must be in plain English and clearly state any risks the client faces as a result of the

---

2. You may wonder how investing in clients creates an adversity of interest. After all, both the client and the lawyer want to see the stock price go up, right? The answer is that in some cases, the ownership of client stock may make it difficult for the lawyer to exercise independent professional judgment on behalf of the client. (Compare Rule 2.1.) A clash between the client's interest (stock price going up) and the lawyer's interest in her ability to exercise independent professional judgment might arise if the lawyer is asked to render an opinion on the soundness of a transaction, and the opinion would not be a favorable one. ABA Formal Op. 00-418 states that Rule 1.8(a) applies to investments in clients in lieu of attorneys' fees, because of this potential for conflicts down the road.

transaction. If the client is a sophisticated entity with in-house legal personnel to review the terms of the transaction, the disclosure can include some technical language that would require expertise to appreciate, but if the client is an individual, the disclosure had better be very easy to understand. Second, and perhaps most important, the disclosure must meet the so-called "Stranger Rule." See, for example, *Committee on Professional Ethics v. Mershon*, 316 N.W.2d 895 (Iowa 1982). The Stranger Rule is a judicial interpretation of Rule 1.8(a)(1) that fleshes out the nature of the disclosure that the lawyer must provide to the client. Under the Stranger Rule, the lawyer must warn the client of any risks and downsides to the transaction that an impartial lawyer not participating in the transaction would detect. These disclosures must go above and beyond merely refraining from making active misrepresentations. This is not supposed to be an arm's-length transaction, in which the parties are free to drive hard bargains. Rather, because of the fiduciary nature of the attorney-client relationship, the lawyer must, in effect, give the client impartial advice and full disclosure even if the lawyer would be free to enter into the same transaction with a nonclient without giving similarly robust disclosures.

Third, the lawyer must give the client an opportunity to seek the advice of independent counsel, and confirm this advice in writing. Rule 1.8(a)(2). Independent advice should not be necessary if the lawyer has given adequate Stranger Rule disclosures, but the opportunity to seek a second opinion is nevertheless a prerequisite to a valid transaction with the client. After receiving all of this information and advice, the client must consent to the transaction *in writing*. Rule 1.8(a)(3). Finally, note that full disclosure and informed consent is not enough when dealing with clients. The terms of the bargain must be substantively *fair and reasonable* to the client. Rule 1.8(a)(1). Again, because of the highly fiduciary nature of the attorney-client relationship, the reasonableness standard of this rule is a much lower threshold than an analogous rule for arm's-length transactions, such as the contract law doctrine of unconscionability. Furthermore, the requirement that the transaction be substantively fair creates a lot of risk for lawyers because the fairness of the deal will inevitably be measured after the fact, by a disciplinary authority or court deciding on a contract claim. What may have seemed like a good deal *ex ante* may blow up later, with the result that the lawyer's claim for contract damages may be denied for noncompliance with the disciplinary rule. See, for example, *Avianca, Inc. v. Corriea*, 705 F. Supp. 666 (D.D.C. 1989), *aff'd*, 70 F.3d 637 (D.C. Cir. 1995).

SHARING FEES WITH OTHER LAWYERS

Here's a situation that happens all the time. Client is injured, calls a lawyer listed in the Yellow Pages, and sets up an appointment. Lawyer #1 takes the case, does a little initial investigation, and finds out that the case is going to be a lot more complicated than it first appeared — say, a complex, multiparty product liability action in federal court, rather than a more straightforward state court personal-injury case. Lawyer #1 knows another lawyer in town, Lawyer #2, who works at a firm specializing in sophisticated plaintiff-side tort cases. Can Lawyer #1 and Lawyer #2 agree to split the fees, so that Lawyer #1 receives a "finder's fee," "forwarding fee," or "referral fee" for sending the client to Lawyer #2? Mass-tort cases often employ a large and complicated version of this structure, with numerous lawyers screening cases and signing up clients, who are then passed on to other lawyers for representation in pretrial litigation and at trial. Without some way of regulating the sharing of fees among lawyers in different firms, arrangements like this would be unworkable.

Rule 1.5(e) deals with fee divisions among lawyers *not in the same firm*. Watch out for that fact pattern on an exam — if the lawyers are in the same firm, Rule 1.5(e) is not implicated.[3] For lawyers in different firms, the basic rule is that a lawyer cannot be compensated for assuming an entirely passive role. If the fee is divided between Lawyer #1 and Lawyer #2 on the basis of the amount of work they put into the case — for example, initial discovery versus trial preparation — the division is permissible as long as the client agrees in writing to the fee division and the total fee is reasonable. Lawyers also may share fees if they each assume joint responsibility for the representation as a whole — meaning that each lawyer must agree to be fully liable for malpractice, professional discipline, and court sanctions. On the other hand, if a lawyer does not agree to assume responsibility for the representation, and does not do any work on the case, she cannot receive a referral fee or finder's fee.[4] Lawyers with complementary areas of specialization can, however, agree to a kind of you-scratch-my-back-and-I'll-scratch-yours arrangement, in which they refer cases back and forth to each other, as long as the client is informed of the arrangement and it is not exclusive. Rule 7.2(b)(4).

Fee divisions among *lawyers* not in the same firm should be distinguished from dividing one's legal fees with a nonlawyer. The latter is flatly prohibited by Rule 5.4(a), with a few exceptions for things like internal profit-sharing

---

3. This may be too obscure to ever come up on an exam, but the rule is also not implicated unless a single billing covers the work of lawyers not in the same firm. See Rule 1.5, cmt. [7]. Suppose a client hires a tax lawyer in Firm A and an environmental lawyer in Firm B to provide legal services in support of an acquisition of real property. If Firm A and Firm B send separate bills — as they almost certainly would — for their services to the client, Rule 1.5(e) is not applicable at all.

4. Wolfram describes the practice of paying "forwarding fees" as common, despite the prohibition in the disciplinary rules. See above Wolfram §9.2. Strictly speaking there is no such thing as a referral fee in Rule 1.5(e). The referring law firm must do some work on the case or remain on the hook for malpractice liability. A few states permit so-called "bare" referral fees, so pay attention to your state's version of Rule 1.5(e).

plans. The fee-splitting rule is a significant impediment to the formation of multidisciplinary practices comprised of, say, accountants, engineers, real estate brokers, or physicians, as well as lawyers. It also prevents nonlawyers from owning stock or partnership shares in law firms.

HOLDING CLIENT FUNDS: TRUST ACCOUNTS

Lawyers are required to exercise extreme care with client funds and cannot commingle them with personal money. (The same is true with respect to other kinds of property of clients, such as stock certificates, bonds, bricks of gold, rare art works, etc.) The single most reliable way to get disbarred in many states is to fail to maintain a separate trust account for client funds and to keep one's accounting up to date. State disciplinary authorities take these violations very seriously and seek, and generally obtain, severe penalties for lawyers who are not in compliance with trust accounting standards. In many states, the state bar even sends out inspectors to do on-the-spot audits of lawyers' trust accounts. It is a separate violation to fail to cooperate with these folks. If you are caught commingling funds, it is often automatic disbarment, period, end of story. If you go into practice on your own, make sure you do some reading on how to handle client funds—this is *not* an area where you want to fly by the seat of your pants.[5]

The governing rule is Rule 1.15(a), which states that a lawyer shall hold a client's property separately from the lawyer's own property. For tangible property, that means renting a safety deposit box. Regarding client funds, they should be maintained in a separate account (the trust account) and drawn down only as fees are earned. Unless the client agrees otherwise, the bank account must be maintained in the state in which the lawyer's office is located. State rules often require that the accounts bear interest. Where the amounts in trust accounts are too small, or stay in the account for too short a period of time to permit accurate accounting of the interest earned by individual clients, the interest goes into a common fund.[6] This fund, known as IOLTA (Interest on Lawyers' Trust Accounts) is used to support access to legal service for indigent clients.

---

5. Courts have consistently held that sloppy office procedures do not mitigate the seriousness of the offense of commingling personal funds with client funds. See, e.g., *State ex rel. Nebraska Bar Ass'n v. Statmore*, 352 N.W.2d 875 (Neb. 1984).

6. The Supreme Court has held that the interest generated by these pooled trust funds is the private property of individual clients, *Philips v. Washington Legal Foundation*, 524 U.S. 156 (1998), but that no compensation need be paid by the state since the client suffers no pecuniary loss as a result of the taking of the interest for use by IOLTA-funded programs, *Brown v. Washington Legal Foundation*, 538 U.S. 216 (2003).

Two common situations implicate the trust account rule. First, suppose the client deposits a $10,000 retainer to cover the expected cost of a matter. In that situation, the lawyer is required to deposit the money in her trust account and to transfer funds to her personal account only as the fees are earned. Rule 1.15(c). As a practical matter, this means that on a monthly basis the lawyer calculates the time spent on the client's case, multiplied by the hourly rate, and writes a check for that amount on the trust account to the lawyer's personal account. Any unearned portion of the retainer must be returned to the client at the completion of the representation. The second situation is where the lawyer receives settlement proceeds, for example, in a personal-injury case. That check must be deposited in the lawyer's trust account, not the lawyer's personal account. Rule 1.15(d). If the lawyer is compensated on a contingent basis, the settlement funds often will be made payable to the lawyer and the client, in which case the funds still should go to the trust account. After calculating her share of the proceeds, the lawyer can write a check from the trust account to her personal account and pay the remainder to the client. It would be a big mistake for the lawyer to simply deposit the settlement proceeds in her personal account and pay the client's share from those funds.

One application of the rule against commingling funds is that a lawyer cannot write checks on a client trust account to cover personal or business expenses. In his treatise, Professor Rotunda mentions the observation of a state bar official who noted that lawyers often pay their annual bar dues with checks drawn on client trust accounts. See R&D, Preface, at x. That is a clear violation of the rule, but it is obvious that the lawyers simply do not know it. Why else would they present prima facie evidence of an offense for which they can be disbarred to state disciplinary authorities? Before you ever open, deposit money into, or withdraw funds from a client trust account, do some research and make sure you know the rules.

A final note on the anti-commingling rule: If a dispute arises concerning money or other property in the lawyer's possession, the lawyer should keep that property separate and continue to hold it in trust until the dispute is resolved. Rule 1.15(e). To use simplified numbers, suppose a lawyer is representing a personal-injury client on a standard one-third contingent fee. The lawyer receives $30,000 in settlement proceeds. The hospital that provided medical treatment to the client immediately asserts a lien on $10,000 of the proceeds in recognition of the value of the services it provided. Under state law, the hospital's subrogation claim may be denied if the client is not fully compensated by the settlement. The lawyer anticipates that there will be some further litigation to establish the hospital's right to recover the $10,000 and, let's say, there is a 50 percent chance that the client will be able to retain the $10,000 because he was not fully compensated for his injuries. In this case, the lawyer should: (1) Pay $10,000 to the client, representing the undisputed portion of the client's recovery; (2) cut herself a

$10,000 check for her fee and deposit it in her office account; and (3) hold the remaining $10,000 in her trust account until the dispute between the client and the hospital is resolved. As noted in Comment [4] to Rule 1.15, the lawyer should not attempt to arbitrate the dispute between the hospital and the client.

Examples

Dividing the Pie

7. Gervin works for a large national law firm representing a drug manufacturer in product liability lawsuits all around the country. When the company was sued in State X, Gervin hired a local lawyer, Gilmore, to appear at status conferences, take depositions of local witnesses, and review pleadings for compliance with local court rules. Gervin and Gilmore both bill the client at their usual hourly rates. Is this permissible?

8. Suppose instead that Gilmore's only role is to file a motion to have the court admit Gervin *pro hac vice* — that is, to permit Gervin to function in exactly the same way as a lawyer admitted in State X, but only for the purpose of a particular matter. The *pro hac vice* rules of State X do not require the out-of-state lawyer to associate with local counsel. Gervin's firm pays Gilmore $10,000 for this service. Is that fee permissible?

What's Mine Is Mine, What's Yours Is Yours

9. Attorney Taylor represents Esposito in two separate lawsuits arising out of an accident at work — a workers' compensation claim and an action against the manufacturer of the machine that injured Esposito. When Esposito first met with Taylor, he agreed to a standard one-third contingent fee for Taylor in both matters. As the product liability action against the machine manufacturer dragged on, Taylor started to regret taking it. The defendant's lawyers were dogged and persistent, and Taylor was forced to advance the costs of taking dozens of depositions and hiring numerous experts on the design of industrial machinery.

   Just as things were looking really grim for Taylor, the workers' compensation claim settled, and the insurer delivered a check for $40,000 to Taylor. Taylor deposited the check in his firm's business account and wrote himself a check for $13,200, representing his one-third fee for the workers' compensation case. He deposited that check in his personal bank account. When Esposito asked about the remainder of the funds, Taylor informed him that he needed to advance some of the costs on the product liability action. Esposito protested that he was not supposed to pay a fee unless he recovered damages by way of judgment or settlement. "That's true," said Taylor, "but you're only talking about my fee.

You're still liable for court costs, even if you lose. It says so right here in the engagement letter." Taylor had complied with the requirement in Rule 1.5(c) that he "clearly notify the client of any expenses for which the client will be liable whether or not the client is the prevailing party." Esposito reread the provision in the engagement letter, which he had signed, and agreed to advance $10,000 to Taylor to cover the costs of the product liability litigation.

What, if anything, did Taylor do wrong?

Explanations

Dividing the Pie

7. As long as the client agrees in writing to the billing arrangement, this kind of fee-splitting is perfectly acceptable under Rule 1.5(e). Both Gervin and Gilmore are providing value to the client and billing in proportion to the time they spend working on the case.

8. This example is a bit unrealistic, because most state *pro hac vice* rules do require the out-of-state lawyer to associate with local counsel. (See Chapter 20 on the unauthorized practice of law and multijurisdictional practice.) Assuming that Gervin has not violated the unauthorized practice of law rules in State X, there is still a question regarding whether the billing arrangement violates Rule 1.5(e). It does, because Gilmore is not billing the client in proportion to the value of the services he performs. Filing a motion to have another lawyer admitted *pro hac vice* takes at most a half-hour and is a routine administrative matter in most courts. Gilmore also has not agreed to assume joint responsibility for the representation — that is, he is not liable for Gervin's negligence in handling the case. Also, the fact that the fee is paid by Gervin's firm, not the client directly, suggests that the client may not have agreed to the arrangement and confirmed that agreement in writing.

What's Mine Is Mine, What's Yours Is Yours

9. The lawyer made two huge mistakes here, either of which could result in a severe sanction, including disbarment. See In re Teichner, 470 N.E.2d 972 (Ill. 1984), upon which this example is loosely based. First, he deposited the settlement proceeds in his firm's business account. The check belongs to both Esposito and Taylor; therefore, one-third goes for attorneys' fees and the client gets the rest. Because a portion of the check represents "property of clients . . . that is in a lawyer's possession in connection with a representation," it must be held separately from the lawyer's own property — that is, in a trust account. Rule 1.15(a). As soon as Taylor received the check, he was required to notify Esposito promptly

and deliver Esposito's portion of the funds to him, along with a full accounting, if requested. Rule 1.15(d). The path of the check should be:

deposit to trust account [→] payment of proceeds to Esposito [→] deposit of Taylor's portion to business account

By depositing the check first into his business account, Taylor committed a very serious violation of the disciplinary rules.

The second mistake was to try to hold Esposito's portion of the funds hostage in an attempt to renegotiate the fee agreement. There is not necessarily anything wrong with requiring a client to advance the costs of litigation, as distinct from attorneys' fees, but the lawyer and client must agree on this procedure at the outset of the representation. Once the litigation is under way, the lawyer has a fiduciary obligation to act in the client's best interests. See ABA Formal Op. 11-458. The client should not have to worry that his lawyer will be trying to figure out ways to make more money — he should be able to trust that the lawyer will put his interests first. By coming back to the client and trying to renegotiate the basis for reimbursing expenses, Taylor breached that fiduciary duty. As noted above, mid-course alterations in fee arrangements are presumptively fraudulent in many jurisdictions. For what it's worth, by threatening to hold onto Esposito's portion of the workers' compensation settlement ("exercising dominion" over Esposito's property in a way inconsistent with Esposito's rights), Taylor also committed the tort of conversion. See Dan B. Dobbs, *The Law of Torts* §61 (2000).

Representing Entities and Groups

INTRODUCTION

Relationships with individual clients are complicated enough. The complexity increases exponentially when organizations such as corporations, closely held corporations, partnerships, limited partnerships, trade associations, unions, and government agencies are involved. There are numerous specific problems in the law of lawyering that require a clear understanding of the identity of the client. The most obvious is the application of rules governing conflicts of interest. To look ahead, the concurrent conflicts rule prohibits a lawyer from simultaneously representing clients where the representation of one client has a material adverse effect on the lawyer's ability to represent another. See Chapters 15 and 16. The successive representation rule prohibits a lawyer from representing a new client whose interests are materially adverse to those of a previous client in the same or a substantially related matter. See Chapter 16. In order to work through both of those rules, the attorney must know who her "clients" are in the present, and who they were in the past.

In addition, an attorney may not counsel or assist a client in committing a criminal or fraudulent act (Rule 1.2(d)) and may not remain in a professional relationship where the client's actions will result in a violation of law (Rule 1.16(a)). See Chapter 13. For the purposes of both of these rules, it is important to know who the client is, particularly in light of the duty mentioned above, to represent the best interests of an entity, not those of any of its constituents. Finally, the attorney-client privilege (Chapter 8) and the professional duty of confidentiality (Chapter 9) are specific to a given client, so the lawyer may need to know the identity of the person who is empowered to assert or waive the evidentiary privilege on behalf of the client, as well as be clear on who is outside the protection of the privilege or the duty of confidentiality. An individual corporate officer or director may claim to be a client of the lawyer *as an individual*. If the lawyer does have an individual attorney-client relationship with the officer or director, she would be prohibited from disclosing information she learned from the individual client to the corporation, or from using that information against the interests of the individual.

Client-identification issues do not arise in a vacuum, but as part of the analysis of another issue, such as a conflict of interest or a client-wrongdoing problem. For this reason, you may want to skim over this chapter and refer back to it in more detail when you encounter a client-identification issue as part of another problem later in the book.

COMPLEX CLIENTS: UNDERSTANDING THE BENEFICIARY OF THE LAWYER'S DUTIES

There are two theoretical approaches the law of professional responsibility could take regarding the representation of entities and groups of individuals. The first is *group theory*, which imagines the client as simply a collection of individuals who are represented jointly by the lawyer. The lawyer essentially would be required to juggle all the conflicts that could result from divergence among the individuals and determine whether the interests of the individuals are sufficiently harmonious that she can represent them simultaneously. This process is so cumbersome and fraught with danger for the lawyer that group theory is really not a practical solution to representing organizations. Nevertheless, in a few cases, courts will understand a lawyer's obligations as running to the individuals *as individuals*, even though they are also agents of a legal entity. The most common situation in which this occurs is the representation of closely held corporations, where the lawyer has frequent contact with the individual constituents, who may justifiably believe that the lawyer represents them personally. Group theory is also a good way to understand the relationship between the lawyer and *pre-formalization* constituents of an organization. If three people jointly decide to form a corporation, for example, and they all work with the lawyer to create this new legal entity, the lawyer's clients prior to the incorporation were the three individuals.

If you're ever going to encounter group theory as a way of understanding the representation of organizations, it will be in the context of closely held corporations or partnerships. Imagine that a lawyer represents Click and Clack's Garage, organized as a closely held corporation. When the lawyer needs to know something about the Garage, she talks to either Click or Clack, depending on who is around. Moreover, she occasionally handles legal matters that pertain to Click and Clack as individuals, such as Click's speeding ticket and Clack's divorce. You can understand why, as far as Click and Clack are concerned, the lawyer is *their lawyer*, as individuals and as co-owners of the Garage. They probably do not think about the relationship in formal terms. It probably would surprise them a great deal to learn that the lawyer regarded herself as a representative only of the entity called the Garage, and not of Click and Clack themselves.

To see how this could get messy, imagine that one day Click corners the lawyer at the Garage and says he is sick of Clack and would like to open his own garage. Can the lawyer share this information with Clack? The answer depends on who the lawyer's client is. If it is Click as an individual, it is confidential client information protected by Rule 1.6, and the lawyer would be liable to Click if she disclosed the information to Clack. See Chapter 9. If, on the other hand, the client is the Garage, the lawyer would have an obligation to act in the best interests of the Garage, which probably would require informing Clack of Click's intentions.

Whether the lawyer's client will be deemed to be the entity or a group of individuals depends on the reasonable expectation of the constituents. This is another application of the rule in Restatement §14 on the formation of the attorney-client relationship. (See Chapter 2 and the discussion of the *Togstad* case.) If, under the circumstances, it is reasonable for Click to believe that the lawyer represents him as an individual, the lawyer may not share the information with Clack and may not continue to represent the Garage in matters adverse to Click. See, for example, *Rosman v. Shapiro*, 653 F. Supp. 1441 (S.D.N.Y. 1987). On the other hand, if the lawyer had always observed corporate formalities and had never done anything to lead Click to believe she represented him as an individual, the lawyer's client will be the Garage, and she will be required to report the information to Clack and otherwise to act in the best interests of the Garage.

Although group theory works tolerably well with very small, informal associations, the law in most cases has opted for the *entity theory* of organizational representation. This position is clearly stated in the Model Rules. A lawyer for an entity such as a corporation represents the entity, not individual officers or agents. Rule 1.13(a). That rule is easy enough to state, but hard to put into practice, because an entity can act only through natural persons ("constituents"), who may have their own ideas about the best interests of the organization. However, lawyers often represent entities in which the structures of authority are set out by the applicable substantive law. The relationship between the legal fiction called a corporation and its shareholders, officers, directors, employees, and other agents is given by the law of corporations. Thus, in order to comply with her obligations, a lawyer representing one of these entities must be aware not only of the governing professional responsibility rules, but also of the law establishing the structure of the entity.

The following sections discuss the client identity issue in the context of specific types of organizations and legal problems. The most detailed discussion relates to publicly traded corporations and the related problems of corporate wrongdoing and the Sarbanes-Oxley legislation, shareholder derivative litigation, and complex corporate entities involving separate legal entities. The next sections discuss representing closely held corporations and partnerships, and lawyers who represent government agencies.

Examples

Entities and Groups

1. Lawyer is hired by Homeowners' Association (HOA) comprised of 17 owners of houses in the Shady Acres development. The HOA meets monthly as a committee of the whole, and does not elect a chair with power to act for the HOA. The HOA is in a dispute with the city over who will pay for road maintenance. Homeowner A wants to pay the city to assume maintenance obligations. Homeowner B wants to save money by retaining maintenance. What should Lawyer do?

   A. Have a vote of the HOA, since the HOA is Lawyer's client.

   B. Obtain the informed consent of A and B before proceeding further.

   C. Try to reconcile the interests of A and B somehow, as "counsel for the situation."

   D. Withdraw from the representation.

2. Fairway Corp. is a real estate development company owned by the three sons of George Loewe, Sr. — George Jr., William, and Edward. Each son owned one-third of the outstanding shares of Fairway Corp. According to the bylaws of the corporation, each of the three sons was entitled to elect two directors to the board, with a seventh "outside" director chosen unanimously by the six elected directors. As sometimes happens with family businesses, the three sons had a disagreement about the operation of Fairway Corp. The former outside director resigned, and the three sons could not agree on who should fill that slot. George Jr. and William wanted one candidate, and Edward favored another. So George Jr. and William instructed their directors to adopt a resolution amending the bylaws to permit filling the outside director slot through majority vote. Subsequently, they hired the law firm of Collingwood & Schlesinger to file a lawsuit, on behalf of Fairway, seeking an injunction ordering that the outside slot be filled with their chosen director. What should the law firm do in this situation?

Explanations

Entities and Groups

1. This question is based an illustration from the Hazard and Hodes treatise. See H&H §17.4. You could understand this organization as either an entity or an aggregation of individuals. It is not obvious that it is either one or the other. A good general rule is that "[t]he more formal the association, the longer its duration, and the more elaborately defined its purposes, the more likely it is that the group will be regarded as an entity that is distinct from its individual constituents." H&H §17.4. Extremely informal partnerships and joint ventures may therefore be treated as aggregations of individuals, rather than entities. See, for example, *Bobbitt v. Victorian House, Inc.*, 545 F. Supp. 1124, 1126 (N.D. Ill. 1982) (determining the identity of a client where the lawyer represents a closely held corporation with only a few shareholders and directors is "complex" and "must be determined on the individual facts of each case").

   Rule 1.13(a) and Restatement §96 do not speak in terms of only corporations, but of "organizations." Many judicial decisions apply entity theory to closely held corporations, general and limited partnerships, unions, trade associations, and so on. See ABA Formal Op. 91-361 (applying entity theory to general partnerships). These cases, however, generally depend on the entity having some kind of formal structure, so that the lawyer dealing with the organization can identify the persons who are empowered to act on its behalf. The informal, ad hoc aggregation of homeowners is unlikely to have clear lines of authority established, so it is likely that the HOA should be treated as a bunch of individuals, not a separately entity.

   What difference does it make? We haven't considered the subject of conflicts of interest yet, but you should have at least a rough, intuitive sense that a lawyer trying to represent a group of individuals, on a person-by-person basis, may encounter a situation in which the interests of one clash with the interests of another. If the lawyer actually owes professional duties to both and it is impossible to comply with both duties, then there is a conflict of interest. In this Example, A and B are at loggerheads. If both have an attorney-client relationship with Lawyer (see Chapter 2 for the formation of the professional relationship) and have the capacity under Rule 1.2(a) to direct the representation, then Lawyer may be caught between irreconcilable obligations. For this reason, the safest course of action is probably D, withdraw from the representation. Many lawyers in the real world would probably opt for C, and try to reconcile the interests of the two clients. This may work, but it is dangerous, in the event that one client comes to believe that the lawyer is favoring the other client's interests. Hold the consideration if B to Chapter 14 on concurrent conflicts of interest. For now, it is sufficient to observe that A and B (and the other 15 homeowners) may be able to agree to concurrent representation by Lawyer, but Lawyer will have to explain fully the risks and benefits of proceeding in this way.

Maybe the best answer is one not given above: Work with the members of the HOA to set it up as a formal entity, with clearly defined lines of authority within the organization, and then make clear that Lawyer will represent only the organization. There is some support for the view that after formation of a formal entity, the lawyer's client becomes the entity itself and any previous professional relationships with individuals are terminated. See, for example, *Jesse v. Danforth*, 485 N.W.2d 63 (Wis. 1992); Ariz. Bar Op. 2002-6 (approving same strategy, calling it a form of limited-scope representation); *Manion v. Nagin*, 2004 WL 234402 (D. Minn. Feb. 5, 2004) (applying *Jesse v. Danforth*), *aff'd*, 394 F.3d 1062 (8th Cir. 2005) (agreeing with the application of *Jesse v. Danforth* as a general matter but noting that there may have been a quasi-client relationship with the individual constituent after incorporation).

2. This example is based on *Fairfax Properties, Inc. v. Lyons*, 806 A.2d 535 (Conn. App. 2002), although I made up some of the facts. It is an excellent illustration of a problem that sometimes arises when representing corporations: A lawyer may find herself dealing with many different people who have different ideas about what is best for the corporation. When all the corporate agents with whom the lawyer deals are on the same page about what is in the corporation's best interests, the lawyer may follow the direction of these agents and be assured that she will be acting in the best interests of the entity. But what happens if there are factions struggling for control of the organization? You can't answer that question using the Model Rules alone. Rule 1.13(a) says a lawyer retained by an organization represents the organization *acting through its duly authorized constituents*. The language "duly authorized" refers to corporate law outside the scope of the Model Rules. Thus, in order to decide how to proceed, the lawyers at Collingwood & Schlesinger must first determine whether the two sons who retained the firm, George Jr. and William, have legal authority to act on behalf of the corporation. They probably do not. As shareholders (that is, owners), their operation of the corporation is indirect only. They elect directors using established procedures, and the directors make decisions for the corporation. Corporate law has procedures called derivative actions (discussed later in this chapter) that shareholders may use to enforce their rights, but shareholders are not empowered to hire a lawyer to act directly on behalf of the corporation.

It may be obvious to Collingwood & Schlesinger that the two sons here are acting only on their own, and not claiming corporate authority. But what if the directors they control adopt a resolution *on behalf of the corporation* authorizing the retention of a law firm to obtain an injunction to fill the seventh slot? On its face, that order would not necessarily be invalid. But the dissenting son, Edward, may be able to demonstrate that the directors acted outside their legal authority. There may be (and in most corporations there is) a provision of the bylaws governing amendments and changes to voting rights. Any amendment that effectively denies a minority shareholder the right to object to the actions of the majority shareholders is likely to require the minority shareholder's consent. An actual corporate lawyer, as opposed to a student studying professional responsibility, should inquire into the basis for the directors' actions, examine the corporation's bylaws, and be attentive to the interaction between corporate law and the law governing lawyers. This example brings up a point about the scope of this subject.

Students often ask me if they have to know corporate law for the professional responsibility exam, and you may be wondering the same thing as you read through this chapter. The point of this example, and others like it, is not to see how much you know about corporate law. And although I don't know this for sure, I am fairly confident that your own professional responsibility instructor does not expect you to know a great deal about corporate law. What you should know, however, is that corporate law sets out the rights and duties of various parties, including shareholders, directors, officers, and other agents of the corporation. At many points in the analysis, that law matters more than the Model Rules. You may be expected to identify these areas of interaction and flag a corporate law issue that affects the way the Model Rules should be applied. In this case, you may be expected to say something to the effect that Rule 1.13(a) instructs the lawyer to defer to the directions of the duly authorized constituents of an organization, but where there appears to be a struggle for control of the organization, the lawyer should consult governing corporate law to see which constituents are authorized to act on behalf of the organization. This approach does not require you to resolve the corporate-law questions, but it does show that you are aware that the Model Rules alone do not address all the issues.

PUBLICLY TRADED CORPORATIONS

In contrast with the difficulty posed by cases such as Example 2, where there are feuding factions within the entity, in general when lawyers are representing large, publicly held corporations, the lines of authority are fairly clear. As a matter of corporate law, the corporation is owned by its shareholders, who elect directors to represent their interests. All the directors together constitute a board of directors that may have one or more committees, such as an audit committee (dealing with accounting issues), or a compensation committee to decide on how to reward high-level corporate officers. The directors, in turn, delegate much of the day-to-day operation of the corporation to officers such as the chief executive officer, the chief financial officer, and the general counsel. Sometimes the chief executive officer is also the chair of the board of directors. The officers, in turn, supervise numerous lower-level employees, many of whom have supervisory responsibility over others. Collectively speaking, officers and lower-level employees are all agents of the corporation. The lawyer is an agent, too. Certain agents, such as corporate officers and directors and lawyers retained by the corporation, have heightened fiduciary duties to the corporation, which means that they owe enhanced duties of loyalty and care and must refrain from self-dealing or laboring under conflicts of interest.

All of these things are true as a matter of corporation and agency law. What does the law of lawyering add to this mix? Although the relevant rule, Rule 1.13, looks complicated, it can be boiled down to one essential principle: *The lawyer must act on behalf of the organization, not its constituents.* Of course, corporate personhood is a legal fiction, so the lawyer must interact with the organization through human agents. But the key thing to remember is that those agents have fiduciary duties to the organization, just as the lawyer does. The lawyer's job is not to protect the legal interests of the constituents as individuals (unless, of course, she is hired to represent them in their individual capacity). The corporation's lawyer and its constituents are on the same team, but it is always Team Entity, and protecting the interests of the corporation is the goal for both players.

Structure of Rule 1.13

The rule on representing organizations contains several subsections that deal with disparate professional responsibility issues. They are:

Rule 1.13(a)   Lawyer represents the organization itself, acting through duly authorized (that is, under the terms of the applicable substantive law) constituents.

Rule 1.13(b)   "Up the ladder reporting": A lawyer who knows that an employee of an organization is engaged in wrongdoing that would be harmful to the organization must take remedial action in the best interests of the organization including, unless not necessary in the best interests of the organization, "referring the matter to higher authority in the organization." (Compare the triggering language of the Sarbanes-Oxley regulations, discussed below.)

Rule 1.13(c)　　　Permission to reveal confidential client information, *even if not permitted by Rule 1.6*, if and to the extent necessary to protect the best interests of the organization. This rule is triggered if the highest authority within the organization, such as the board of directors, fails to take appropriate remedial action.

Rule 1.13(d)　　　Essentially limiting permissive disclosure to cases in which the lawyer is counseling the organizational client or representing the client in transactional matters. The lawyer does *not* have permission to disclose confidential client information if the lawyer was retained to conduct an internal investigation of alleged wrongdoing or if the lawyer is defending the organization or one of its constituents against an allegation of wrongdoing.

Rule 1.13(e)　　　If the lawyer is fired for complying with Rule 1.13(b) and 1.13(c), or withdraws under circumstances in which action under these rules would be required, the lawyer should take steps to inform the highest authority.

Rule 1.13(f)　　　"Corporate *Miranda* warnings": Because a lawyer represents the organization itself, and not constituents, Rule 1.13(a), a lawyer may find herself in some ugly conflicts of interest situations if she inadvertently leads a constituent to believe reasonably that the lawyer is representing the constituent in an individual capacity. Thus, the rule requires lawyers to clearly identify the organization as the client when dealing with constituents in cases where the organization's interests are adverse to those of the constituents.

Rule 1.13(g)　　　Multiple representation of the organization and its constituents is permissible only if the requirements of Rule 1.7, the concurrent conflicts of interest rule, are satisfied. Most of this subsection is redundant with the conflicts rules, but the last sentence is important: The organization's consent to waive what would otherwise be a conflict of interest must be given by someone with authority to act on behalf of the organization and who is not individually represented by the lawyer.

One way to see how the provisions of Rule 1.13 operate is to consider the problem of corporate wrongdoing when a lawyer represents an entity whose constituents are engaged in some sort of misconduct—either a breach of the duties they owe to the corporation and its shareholders, or a fraud on some third-party investor, such as a bank.

Corporate Wrongdoing

Suppose you are an in-house lawyer, or an outside lawyer working on a matter for a corporation, and you discover wrongdoing—say, that a bunch of expenses have been incorrectly booked as capital investments, or that corporate officers have been writing loans to themselves from the corporation, or that traders have been artificially pumping up profits using "round-trip trades" with no economic substance.[1] At this moment, you must be perfectly clear that you represent the corporation, not any of the folks you deal with on a daily basis. Of course, that is easier said than done, but in cases of serious corporate wrongdoing, the downside risks of not remembering your fiduciary duty to the corporation are enormous. The question is how, in practical terms, a lawyer can vindicate her obligation to the corporation if the constituents she deals with are implicated in the wrongdoing.

The entity representation rule prescribes a series of responses generally known as "up the ladder" reporting or "running up the chain of command." Under Rule 1.13, if an officer or employee of the corporation is engaged in wrongdoing that is likely to result in substantial harm to the corporation (probably in the form of civil or criminal liability), the lawyer "shall proceed as is reasonably necessary in the best interest of the organization." Rule 1.13(b). Unless it would be unnecessary to refer the matter up the chain of command—that is, the lawyer is able to fix the problem by talking directly to the lower-level employees involved—the lawyer must refer the matter to a higher authority in the organization. If an energy derivatives trader has been fudging the value of assets to make it look like the company is making a greater profit, a lawyer who discovered this wrongdoing would first be required to report the manager to the trader's supervisor, or to the manager of the trading department. If that report was insufficient to prevent the violation of law or substantial injury to the organization, then the lawyer is obligated to report to the highest authority who, under applicable substantive law, can act on behalf of the entity. The highest authority in corporate settings is not God, but generally the board of directors. At each stage of reporting, the inquiry is the same—namely, whether the report and the action taken by the corporate constituent is sufficient to prevent the violation of law or substantial injury to the organization.

---

1. These were the facts of various financial accounting scandals in the early 2000s, including WorldCom, Adelphia, and Enron.

Arguably, Rule 1.13(b) is redundant, and could be eliminated from the rules of professional conduct without changing the lawyer's duties at all. Why is that? Because agency law requires the lawyer to communicate material information to the client. See Restatement (Second) of Agency §381. "The client" in this case—remember the whole point of this discussion— is the entity itself. If lower-level employees are doing something that is likely to get the corporation in trouble, the client needs to know about that. The client in this case would be more senior management or the board of directors—whoever is empowered to act on behalf of the corporation and put a stop to the wrongdoing. See also Rule 1.4(a), which requires the lawyer to communicate reasonably with the client.

Now suppose that the board of directors refuses to act on the lawyer's "up the ladder" report. At one time in the not-so-recent past, that would have been the end of the matter. The lawyer would be obligated by the professional duty of confidentiality to keep silent, subject to the "noisy withdrawal" permission discussed in Chapter 12. The most recent version of Rule 1.13, as amended in August 2003, permits, but does not require, the lawyer to disclose confidential client information to the extent necessary to avoid substantial injury to the organization. Rule 1.13(c). This is sometimes known as "reporting out," as distinguished from the "reporting up" mandated by Rule 1.13(b). Remember that reporting out is permissive ("may reveal"), while reporting up is mandatory ("shall refer the matter to a higher authority"). In reporting out, the lawyer must not over-disclose client confidences. The rule permits disclosure only "to the extent the lawyer reasonably believes necessary to prevent substantial injury to the organization." If the lawyer reasonably believes, for example, that the corporation is proceeding with an offering of securities without making the required disclosures in its registration statements, the lawyer may be justified in informing the Securities and Exchange Commission (SEC) to prevent subsequent injury to the corporation in the form of expensive investor lawsuits. See, for example, *Meyerhofer v. Empire Fire and Marine Ins.*, 497 F.2d 1190 (2d Cir. 1974) (involving this kind of disclosure by a securities lawyer, but analyzed under the self-defense exception to the duty of confidentiality).

Notice that reporting out would also be justified in that case under Rule 1.6(b)(2) and (b)(3), which give the lawyer permission to disclose information to the extent the lawyer reasonably believes necessary to prevent, rectify, or mitigate a serious fraud, in connection with which the lawyer's services have been used. The difference is that Rule 1.13(c) does not require the lawyer's services to have been used in connection with the wrongdoing, but it is necessary that the lawyer first report the information up the ladder, to give the entity's highest authority the opportunity to act. See Rule 1.13, cmt. [6].

Comments to the up the ladder rule, Rule 1.13(b), do caution lawyers not to be hasty in running every concern up the chain of command. It notes that a lawyer should consider factors such as the seriousness of the violation, the apparent motivation of the person involved, and the policies of the organization regarding violations of this type. (In Rule 1.4 terms, the obligation to keep the client *reasonably* informed does not require the communication of every imaginable piece of information the lawyer learns in the course of the representation.) Furthermore, a lawyer should not be too quick to assume that corporate employees are crooks, or that there is no innocent explanation for some event. If the violation is sufficiently serious, however, the lawyer must remember that her duty is to protect the interests of the corporation. To buttress that duty, the law may hold her civilly liable for failing to report up the ladder, if doing so would be in the best interests of the corporation.[2] At some point on the way up the ladder, the lawyer probably will encounter someone who is also motivated to protect the interests of the corporation, and the problem can be solved internally. This should be the case in anything but a seriously dysfunctional corporate culture such as Enron's or Tyco's, in which one all-powerful, high-ranking officer has cowed every subordinate into submission. In an ordinarily law-abiding corporation, however, a lawyer should not have to take the next step of resignation and possibly disclosure.

The Sarbanes-Oxley Act

The Sarbanes-Oxley Act was passed by Congress in 2002 in the wake of accounting scandals at Enron, WorldCom, Global Crossing, and other large corporations. Investors collectively lost billions of dollars, and thousands of employees lost their jobs, in part because the lawyers and accountants who were supposed to prevent financial frauds did not do so. Therefore, numerous provisions in the legislation are targeted at improving the reliability of professional gatekeepers in the legal and accounting professions. The Act and the regulations promulgated under its authority are applicable only to lawyers representing issuers of publicly traded securities, so it is narrower in its scope than Rule 1.13, which covers all lawyers "employed or retained by an organization."

Section 307 of the statute required the SEC to establish rules governing the professional conduct of lawyers who represent issuers of publicly traded securities. The language of Section 307 explicitly directed the SEC to

---

2. For example, in In re *American Continental Corp./Lincoln Savings and Loan Securities Litigation* (Jones Day), 794 F. Supp. 1424 (D. Ariz. 1992), the court said that "where a law firm believes the management of a corporate client is committing serious regulatory violations, the firm has an obligation to actively discuss the violative conduct, urge cessation of the activity, and withdraw from representation where the firm's legal services may contribute to the continuation of such conduct."

include an up the ladder reporting requirement. The SEC therefore issued a rule requiring a lawyer representing an issuer of publicly traded securities to report evidence of a material violation of an applicable securities law or a material breach of fiduciary duty by any corporate officer, director, employee, or agent. See 17 C.F.R. §205.3(b). In brief, the lawyer must report this evidence either to the corporation's chief legal officer (often called "general counsel") or to the chief legal officer and the chief executive officer. If the first report does not produce satisfactory results — that is, remedying the material breach of securities law or fiduciary duty — the lawyer must continue the reporting up to the audit committee of the board of directors, another committee composed of disinterested directors, or the full board.[3] The steps can be summarized as: **Report** (to the general counsel), **Wait** (for a response), **Assess** (the response), and **Report Again** (to a higher authority, if necessary).

A more detailed analysis of the regulations follows. If you are expected to be familiar with the Sarbanes-Oxley regulations for your professional responsibility course, do yourself a favor and work through the language of the regulations, including the defined terms in §205.2, with a sharp pencil. Underline relevant language, circle important terms, make asterisks in the margin, and otherwise get in there and get personal with the language of the regulation. Don't just read passively. For the purposes of this analysis, assume you are an in-house lawyer working for World Crossing Corp., a publicly traded corporation. (That means you are "appearing and practicing before the [SEC]" under §205.2(a)(1).) Your boss is Sarah Senior, the Assistant General Counsel for Regulatory Compliance. Ms. Senior reports to Gina General, the General Counsel of World Crossing. In the course of preparing an SEC filing, you discover that Andrew Fastenloose has engaged in several self-dealing transactions with World Crossing that should have been disclosed to World Crossing shareholders. Your company has not established a Qualified Legal Compliance Committee, which is a whole 'nother subject (as we say in Texas). Your responsibilities are as follows:

1. *Is there a reporting obligation at all?* The triggering standard is found in §205.3(b)(1) ("If an attorney . . . becomes aware of evidence of a material violation . . . by any officer, director, employee, or agent of the issuer"). There is an important series of defined terms in this language: "Evidence of a material violation" means "credible evidence, based upon which it would be unreasonable, under the circumstances, for a prudent and competent attorney not to conclude that it is reasonably likely that a material violation has occurred, is

---

3. There are alternative procedures available for corporations that establish a qualified legal compliance committee, but the basic idea is the same — the lawyer must report the evidence to some "higher authority" within the corporate structure.

ongoing, or is about to occur."§205.2(e).This is the notorious double negative, and some commentators believe it waters down the reporting requirement and encourages lawyers to look the other way. See, for example, Susan P. Koniak, *When the Hurlyburly's Done: The Bar's StruggleWith the SEC*, 103 Colum. L. Rev. 1236 (2003).Admittedly, the grammar of the sentence is pretty lousy, but my own view is that "unreasonable . . . not to conclude" would be interpreted by courts to require reporting whenever a reasonable lawyer would believe a violation is occurring. Resolution of this uncertainty will have to await litigation. In the meantime, all agree that sufficiently compelling evidence would trigger the reporting requirement. If you see a Sarbanes-Oxley hypothetical, chances are there will be some facts that suggest possible wrongdoing. In this example, I preempted the analysis by telling you that Fastenloose has engaged in prohibited transactions, but be alert for a fact pattern that requires you first to determine whether the evidence supports a reasonable belief that the corporate agent has engaged in wrongdoing.

Notice that the reporting obligation is not triggered only by evidence of federal securities fraud, but also by evidence of a "material violation," which is another defined term. Material violation means "a material violation of an applicable United States federal or state securities law, a material breach of fiduciary duty arising under United States federal or state law, or a similar material violation of any United States federal or state law."§205.2(i). Breach of fiduciary duty is a further defined term, and includes "any breach of fiduciary or similar duty to the issuer recognized under an applicable Federal or State statute or at common law, including but not limited to misfeasance, nonfeasance, abdication of duty, abuse of trust, and approval of unlawful transactions."§205.2(d). Approving transactions in which Fastenloose makes a lot of money by dealing with his employer (to whom he owes fiduciary duties) is certainly within the scope of §205.2(d) and §205.2(i).

2. *To whom is the report owed?* Once we're clear that there is a reporting obligation, the question becomes: How should it be discharged? So the analysis picks up again with §205.3(b)(1). After the triggering language ("If an attorney . . ."), the operative portion of the regulation states that "the attorney shall report such evidence to the issuer's chief legal officer . . . or to both the chief legal officer and the chief executive officer." So you report to the General Counsel, right? Well, actually things may be significantly easier for you. A separate provision of the regulations establishes a "safe harbor" for subordinate lawyers. (I know it doesn't sound like much fun to be a "subordinate" lawyer, but in this case it gets you off the hook much more readily.) Subordinate lawyers, defined as lawyers who practice under

the supervision and direction of another attorney, §205.5(a), are permitted to discharge their reporting obligation by going to their bosses. See §205.5(c) ("A subordinate attorney complies with [the reporting obligation] if the subordinate attorney reports to his or her supervising attorney . . . evidence of a material violation. . . ."). If you inform Sarah Senior, you've just made the Fastenloose evidence her problem. See §205.4(c) ("A supervisor attorney is responsible for complying with the reporting requirements of §205.3 when a subordinate attorney has reported to the supervisory attorney evidence of a material violation."). You can sit back and watch her handle things from there. However, if you believe that Sarah has failed to comply with her own reporting obligation, you are permitted to run through the reporting procedures independently. See §205.5(d).

3. *What must the ultimately responsible lawyer do?* Sarah Senior is herself a subordinate, and she reports to Gina General. She is entitled simply to dump the matter on her supervisor's desk and walk away, for the same reason that you are. Eventually, however, all this buck-passing has to stop, and some lawyer has an obligation to follow through with the reporting procedure. The regulations refer to this ultimately responsible lawyer as the "reporting lawyer." The reporting lawyer either has no supervisory lawyer or is concerned that the supervisory lawyer may not satisfy the regulations, so she decides to do it on her own, as permitted by §205.5(d). For the reporting lawyer, the regulations mandate what I call a "report, wait, and assess" procedure:

   a. *Report:* The lawyer reports evidence of a material violation to the chief legal officer or CEO of the corporation. The chief legal officer then has a duty to investigate the allegations of wrongdoing. §205.3(b)(2) ("The chief legal officer . . . shall cause such inquiry into the evidence of a material violation as he or she reasonably believes is appropriate. . . .").

   b. *Wait:* The chief legal officer either (1) takes corrective action, §205.3(b)(2) ("shall take all reasonable steps to cause the issuer to adopt an appropriate response"), or (2) concludes that no material violation has occurred and notifies the reporting lawyer of that conclusion and the grounds for reaching it, §205.3(b)(2) ("shall notify the reporting attorney and advise the reporting attorney of the basis for such determination"). Once again, there is a defined term in here—"appropriate response" is defined in §205.2(b), and basically means either concluding that no wrongdoing has occurred or putting a stop to the wrongdoing.

   c. *Assess:* Significantly, the reporting lawyer cannot simply take the chief legal officer's response on faith. The regulations actually require the lawyer who makes a report to go farther in reporting "[u]nless [the reporting attorney] reasonably believes that the chief legal officer . . . has provided an appropriate response. . . ." §205.3(b)(3). In other words, the reporting lawyer must make an independent evaluation of the appropriateness of the chief legal officer's response. How else would the reporting lawyer be able to have a *reasonable* belief in the appropriateness of the response? Reasonable belief connotes an objective standard of reasonableness, which may require more than simply accepting the chief legal officer's say-so that the evidence was investigated and no wrongdoing was uncovered. Whether the reporting lawyer has any further obligation is an intensely fact-specific question, depending on many factors such as the extent of perceived dishonesty within the corporation and evidence that the chief legal officer may be in cahoots with the alleged primary wrongdoer.

d. *Report Again:* If the reporting lawyer believes that the chief legal officer's response was not appropriate, she shall report the evidence of wrongdoing to either the audit committee of the board of directors or some other suitably disinterested and objective subset of the board. §205.3(b)(3). Similarly, if the lawyer believes that it would be futile to report evidence to the chief legal officer or the CEO (that is, if she reasonably believes they are both crooks), then the lawyer may report directly to the board. §205.3(b)(4).

In effect, §205.3(b)(3) is the almost-final fallback position for a lawyer in a publicly traded corporation. The lawyer may be required to go that far. There may be an "out" at various stages in the reporting up process. The lawyer may be able to report to her supervisory lawyer and be done with it. Alternatively, the chief legal officer may report back and provide an objectively reasonable demonstration that her suspicions of wrongdoing were not well founded.

The very last position, after "reporting up" has been tried and failed, is "reporting out." Ironically, given the enormous controversy and subsequent inaction on the SEC's proposed "noisy withdrawal" provision, the regulations as adopted contain fairly broad authority for the lawyer to disclose confidential client information in certain cases. A lawyer is permitted to report "confidential information relating to the representation" (which, as you will see, is almost identical to the definition of protected confidences in Rule 1.6(a)) to the SEC *without the client's consent* to the extent the lawyer reasonably believes necessary to prevent, rectify, or mitigate the consequences of a material violation by the client. §205.3(d)(2). Although the regulations do not say as much explicitly, I would understand the language "to the extent reasonably necessary" to require that the lawyer first exhaust the up the ladder procedure for preventing wrongdoing.

Corporate Families

Business organizations often consist of affiliated or subsidiary corporations, maybe wholly owned by the parent corporation, perhaps owned in part, with other shareholders having a minority or majority stake in the affiliate. For example, the corporate entity known as Altria Group is the parent company of numerous consumer products companies, including Philip Morris (makers of Marlboro cigarettes) and Kraft Foods (selling food under brands such as Oscar Mayer meats, Post cereals, and Maxwell House coffee). Kraft in turn owns Nabisco, whose brands include Oreo and Nutter Butter cookies. You may be surprised to learn that the ABA has taken the position that representing one member of a corporate family ordinarily does not create an attorney-client relationship with all other affiliated entities. ABA Formal Op. 95-390; see also Rule 1.7, cmt. [34]. Thus, a lawyer who has represented Nabisco in a trademark dispute with another cookie company might conceivably represent a hot dog manufacturer in litigation with Oscar Mayer at the same time. In fact, I would go so far as to interpret Comment [34] as creating a *presumption of nonidentity* of affiliated entities. This presumption may be rebutted if the affiliated entities have a substantial degree of operational overlap — that is, if they share office space, have the same lawyers, share confidential information, work together on projects, and the like. But truly separate divisions, like Nabisco and Oscar Mayer in this example, are generally treated as separate clients.

You should be aware that the ABA committee's opinion produced two vigorous dissents; in any event, an ABA opinion is advisory only, and not binding on state courts that consider issues relating to the representation of corporate families. Courts and ethics opinions use one of two different tests to determine when the presumption is rebutted. The strongest (that is, the one least likely to find identity of clients) is the alter ego test. See, for example, *Brooklyn Navy Yard Cogeneration Partners, LP v. Superior Court*, 70 Cal. Rptr. 2d 419 (Ct. App. 1997); *Reuben H. Donnelley Corp. v. Sprint Publishing and Advertising, Inc.*, 1996 WL 99902 (N.D. Ill. 1996). Other authorities use a multi-factor balancing test. See, for example, *GSI Commerce Solutions, Inc. v. BabyCenter, L.L.C.*, 618 F.3d 204 (2d Cir. 2010); *Certain Underwriters at Lloyd's v. Argonaut Insurance*, 264 F. Supp. 2d 914 (N.D. Cal. 2003); *Discotrade v. Wyeth-Ayerst Int'l Inc.*, 200 F. Supp. 2d 355 (S.D.N.Y. 2002); New York City Bar Formal Op. 2007-03 (setting out "nuanced, fact-specific approach"). I tend to believe the trend is toward recognizing the non-identity of affiliated entities for conflicts purposes, but this remains a fact-specific inquiry. For an elaborate conflicts of interest problem that raises corporate-family issues, see the last example in Chapter 14.

Examples

Who Is the Client?

3. Colicchio is the chief financial officer of Gramercy Corp., and has been notified by the U.S. Attorney's office that he is the target of an investigation into alleged criminal mail and wire fraud at Gramercy Corp. Colicchio retains Loiseau, a lawyer at Sizeable & Snooty, a large law firm with well-known expertise in white-collar crime defense, to represent him in the investigation and any subsequent criminal prosecution. After signing the retainer agreement, Colicchio told Loiseau that he had been maintaining a reserve fund, which he used to manipulate earnings reports; Loiseau realized that this conduct would constitute mail fraud if proven at trial. What must Loiseau do?

   A. Report Colicchio's conduct "up the ladder" within the corporate structure, potentially reporting as far as the board of directors.
   B. Disclose the information to affected investors or the SEC.
   C. Either A or B, depending on which action would best accomplish the goal of protecting investors from fraud.
   D. Remain silent with respect to the information.

Up the Ladder?

4. You are a partner in a law firm representing Blue Devil Chemicals, Inc., a pesticide manufacturer. Your contact at Blue Devil is Shauna Battier, the general counsel. As part of a routine environmental audit, you discover that one of your client's plants has had numerous unreported discharges of various toxic chemicals into an adjacent river. You bring this problem to the attention of Battier, but she directs you not to report. "The EPA and the State Department of the Environment will never detect these discharges," she says. "They have much bigger fish to fry than low-level violations at this plant. I've been in this business for 25 years, and I can guarantee you that nothing will ever become of it. Besides, these reporting obligations are ticky-tacky regulations. The penalty for not reporting is minor—maybe $2,000. Even if we do get caught, we'll just pay the bill. So I'm asking you to keep this matter to yourself and not mention it to anyone else here."

   What must you do, and what can you do?

Advanced Confidentiality Geekery

5. Describe a scenario in which reporting out would be permitted under Rule 1.13(c) but not Rule 1.6(b).

Explanations

Who Is the Client?

3. Gotcha! That was intended to be a trick question, but the point is a serious one. Don't automatically assume that all of the corporate-representation duties apply just because you're representing someone within an organization. It matters a great deal whether your client is the entity (which of course you'll deal with through its agents, who are natural persons) or one of the "constituents" of the organization such as Colicchio. Options A and B are the sorts of things you should think about if you represent the entity. Both Rule 1.13 and the Sarbanes-Oxley regulations require "reporting up" (option A) and may permit "reporting out" (option B) of information regarding wrongdoing by a constituent of the organization. Rule 1.4(a) requires reasonable communication with the client. But if you represent the constituent in his or her individual capacity, these duties don't apply. Here, Loiseau was hired by Colicchio in his individual capacity. Thus, the answer is D.

   To foreshadow the discussion in Chapters 9 and 12 on the duty of confidentiality and client wrongdoing, a lawyer is permitted to disclose confidential information (that is, the admission by Colicchio that he had been manipulating earnings) to prevent, rectify, or mitigate financial harm only if the lawyer's services had been used in the commission of the fraud. See Rule 1.6(b)(2), (b)(3). Where the lawyer is hired after the fact to defend the client, none of the exceptions to the duty of confidentiality apply. That is true of organizations, too, as confirmed by Rule 1.13(d).

Up the Ladder?

4. Thanks to Professor Irma Russell for this example, which implicates numerous disciplinary rules as well as policy issues. On the entity-representation issue, remember that your client is Blue Devil, Rule 1.13(a), and your obligation is to act in the best interests of the organization. Battier is an officer of the corporation, and you know she "refuses to act in a matter related to the representation that is . . . a violation of law which reasonably might be imputed to the organization." Rule 1.13(b). But notice some troublesome language in the same subsection—the violation must be one that is "likely to result in substantial injury to the organization." For the purposes of this example, we can assume that Battier is accurate in her statements that enforcement agencies are unlikely to detect and prosecute the violation and, even if they do, the penalties are likely to be small. It seems, therefore, that a crucial predicate for up the ladder reporting under Rule 1.13(b) is missing—the violation of law is not likely to result in substantial injury to the organization.

But that's just Rule 1.13(b). Remember that Rule 1.13 doesn't occupy the whole field. It merely supplements or explains the duties that a lawyer would have anyway, regarding things like reasonable care and the duty to communicate material information to one's client. Here the general counsel has directed you not to report, but the board of directors may want to know about this. Or maybe they don't—maybe they're happy with Battier's aggressive stance toward complying with environmental regulations. As a lawyer, however, your duty under Rule 1.4(a) is to communicate information that would be material to your client's decisionmaking. In this case, your client is the entity, not the general counsel, so Rule 1.4(a) may require you communicate with the board *even* if this situation doesn't fall within the up-the-ladder provisions of Rule 1.13(b).

What else may you do? You still may resign under Rule 1.16(b)(4), if you regard Battier's stance as something with which you disagree fundamentally. Note, too, that you may not actively participate in any conduct by Blue Devil that is criminal or fraudulent. Rule 1.2(d). Thus, if Battier asks you to prepare documents to be submitted to the State Department of the Environment that fail to disclose the discharges (where this disclosure would otherwise be required), you must refuse; otherwise, you will have assisted the client in committing a fraud on the agency.

The duty of confidentiality is discussed in Chapter 9, but for now you should be aware that a lawyer is generally prohibited from disclosing any information relating to representation of the client. That means no leaks to the newspaper or phone calls to the EPA to report the client's discharges. The only circumstance in this case under which a lawyer would be permitted to disclose is if the pollution discharges are ongoing and disclosure is necessary to prevent "reasonably certain death or substantial bodily harm." Rule 1.6(b)(1). Because the facts of the problem state that all of the discharges were in the past, these conditions are not satisfied. The permissive disclosure aspect of the organizational client rule, Rule 1.13(c), is not triggered unless the violation of law is likely to result in substantial injury to the client.

Advanced Confidentiality Geekery

5. I know, we haven't talked yet about exceptions to the duty of confidentiality in Rule 1.6(b), but the most important ones in connection with entity representation are Rule 1.6(b)(2) and (b)(3), pertaining to financial frauds. This is a technical question and tests whether you're reading the rules carefully. Compare the language of Rule 1.13(c) and the exceptions in 1.6(b)(2) and (b)(3). Rule 1.13(c) says a lawyer may reveal information relating to the representation (that is, confidential information protected by Rule 1.6(a)) even if Rule 1.6 would not permit

it. So now flip over to Rule 1.6(b) and see what is required for that rule to permit disclosure. The most important differences are:

- Rule 1.6(b)(2) and (b)(3) require that the lawyer's services were used in furtherance of the fraud.
- Rule 1.13(c) requires that the lawyer have first reported up the information about wrongdoing and given the highest authority (that is, the board of directors) an opportunity to do something about it.
- Rule 1.6(b)(2) and (b)(3) require that the wrongdoing be reasonably certain to result in injury to the financial interests of another, while Rule 1.13(c) requires that the wrongdoing be reasonably certain to result in substantial injury to the organization.

With that in mind, then, what would the scenario look like in which disclosure is permitted under Rule 1.13(c) but not under Rule 1.6(b)? Well, it would have to be one in which the lawyer's services were not used, the lawyer has reported up the information, and the wrongdoing is reasonably likely to result in substantial injury to the organization. An example might be that the lawyer discovers some kind of self-dealing (and therefore a breach of fiduciary duty) by a high-ranking officer. Because the lawyer's services weren't involved, Rule 1.6(b) doesn't apply, and also it may be the case that the fraud may harm only the organization. That's why you need Rule 1.13(c). If the board of directors won't put a stop to the wrongdoing, the lawyer has discretion (notice the rule says "may reveal") to report the information out, for example, to the SEC or the local prosecutor.

DEALING WITH AGENTS OF THE ENTITY

The theory of the disciplinary rules is clearly that a lawyer represents an organization *itself*, not any individual persons who act on behalf of it. Rule 1.13(a). Of course, an organization can act only through agents who are natural persons, and it is these people who interact with the lawyer on a day-to-day basis. The entity's lawyer might subconsciously come to regard the person she deals with frequently as the "real" client, but this would be a big mistake. The lawyer's duty is always to proceed *in the best interests of the organization*. Rule 1.13(b). Most of the time, the organization's duly authorized constituents do act in the best interests of the entity, so the lawyer's obligation is simply to follow the lawful instructions of these agents. But a lawyer always must be on guard for conduct by corporate employees that would be a violation of a legal obligation owed to the organization, or conduct that is likely to result in substantial injury to the organization.

Suppose you are a lawyer in the legal department of a large, diversified financial services company specializing in trading in energy markets. You work frequently with Alexander Fester, the vice president and chief financial officer. Fester is interested in buying out a partner's share in a joint venture investment, but maintaining the investment off the balance sheets of the company by using a "special purpose entity." You are familiar with these transactions and inform Fester that the company must consolidate the special purpose entity onto its own balance sheets, unless there is an independent investor in the entity with at least 3 percent of equity capital at stake. "Look," says Fester, "I've decided we're going to do it this way. You doggone lawyers are always screwing up deals." You also notice in the documents that Fester is earning substantial "management fees" for setting up these transactions.

This is not a pleasant situation for a lawyer, but you must remember that your duties run to the company, not Fester. If the transactions are not reported correctly, the result could be financial disaster for the company.[4] No matter what Fester says, you should not carry out his instructions. Because you know that Fester is intending to act in a manner that is a violation of a legal obligation to the organization (he is engaging in self-dealing) and in a manner that is likely to result in substantial injury to the organization (by exposing the corporation to civil liability to shareholders), you are required to proceed as necessary in the best interests of the organization. Rule 1.16(b). As discussed above, your next step will be reporting the misconduct "up the ladder" to the chief legal officer and the chief executive officer and, if necessary, to the board of directors.

Remember the problem of implied-in-fact and quasi-clients. A lawyer can acquire professional obligations, including the duty to keep confidences and the duty to refrain from representing conflicting interests, without a formal retainer agreement. All that is necessary is conduct that creates a reasonable expectation by the individual that the lawyer is acting on her behalf. Rest. §14. In the Fester example, you might acquire professional duties to Fester by offering to give him advice on his personal legal liability arising out of the special purpose entity transaction, or by promising that you will keep any information he tells you secret from others at the company.

For this reason, the disciplinary rules caution a lawyer to make sure that a natural person with whom the lawyer interacts does not mistakenly believe that the lawyer is acting to protect her *personal* legal interests. "In

---

4. The retroactive correction of the accounting treatment of the LJM1 and Chewco transactions in the Enron case (on which this example is loosely based) had the effect of reducing shareholders' equity by over $ 1 billion. The resulting obliteration of investor confidence in Enron quickly led to the company's bankruptcy. See the so-called "Powers Report" of the Special Investigative Committee of the Board of Directors of Enron Corp., at pp. 3, 42. See also In re Enron Corp. Securities, Derivative & ERISA Litigation, 235 F. Supp. 2d 549, 614-616 (S.D. Tex. 2002).

dealing with an organization's directors, officers, employees, members, shareholders, or other constituents, a lawyer shall explain the identity of the client when the lawyer knows or reasonably should know that the organization's interests are adverse to those of the constituents with whom the lawyer is dealing." Rule 1.13(f). This is known as a "corporate *Miranda* warning." Like a real *Miranda* warning to a criminal suspect that anything the suspect says can be used in a court of law, a corporate *Miranda* warning cautions that the lawyer may use any statement by the individual for the *corporation's* purposes, not in the interests of the individual. See Example 3 in Chapter 2 for an example of a quasi-client relationship formed between a lawyer and a constituent of an entity client, which could have been avoided by giving a corporate *Miranda* warning.

Examples

I Am Not Your Lawyer

6. In the aftermath of a collision between a delivery truck and a passenger car, a lawyer shows up at the truck driver's hospital bedside, identifies herself as a lawyer "who has been hired by the company," and announces that she would like to learn what happened on the day of the accident. The driver says he is very sorry and asks whether he can reveal something in confidence. The lawyer responds, "As a corporate employee, your statements fall within the company's attorney-client privilege." (See Chapter 8 for more on the privilege for organization clients.) The driver admits that he had deviated from his route in order to go visit his friend who would sell him a bag of marijuana. He had not returned to his delivery route when the accident occurred. Upon learning this fact, the general counsel for the company realizes that he can argue that the driver was on a "frolic of his own," and therefore the company would not be vicariously liable. The general counsel immediately files a motion to dismiss the action against it and a third-party claim against the driver seeking indemnification for the expenses of defending the lawsuit. What recourse does the driver have?

Assisting a Squeeze-Out

7. You represent a three-person general partnership organized to own and operate a large apartment building. The partnership hired Popovich, one of the partners, to operate the building on a daily basis—a full-time job. The managing partner, Nelson, decided to terminate Popovich's services, as permitted by the employment contract between the partnership and Popovich. At the same time, however, the partnership was required to refinance the mortgage on the building, and the lender required each individual partner to assume personal liability at the closing.

Fearful that Popovich would not cooperate in closing the loan, but would instead withdraw from the partnership, Nelson directs you not to inform Popovich about his impending dismissal until a day after the closing. What should you do?

Explanations

I Am Not Your Lawyer

6. This is a variation on the facts of *Perez v. Kirk & Carrigan*, 822 S.W.2d 261 (Tex. Ct. App. 1991), discussed in Chapter 2. Sometimes lawyers try to finesse an interview with a corporate employee, hoping that the employee will reveal useful information that might deflect responsibility away from the corporation. In this case, the lawyer was trying to be clever, but she may have created a reasonable expectation on the part of the driver that the company's lawyers were looking out for his interests. The statement about the corporation's privilege may be true, but it is beside the point. What the driver really is interested in knowing is whether the lawyer represents him. By failing to make it crystal clear that she does not represent his individual interests, the lawyer probably formed an attorney-client relationship under Restatement §14(1)(b). Thus, the lawyer breached her fiduciary duty of confidentiality that she would owe to any client, and owes to the driver by virtue of having formed a professional relationship with him. The driver also may move to disqualify the lawyer and her firm from representing the corporation, on the ground that it has a conflict of interest. As we will see in Chapter 15, a conflict of interest arises when a lawyer cannot discharge her duties of effective representation to two or more clients at the same time. Here, the lawyer would have an obligation to keep the driver's information confidential, not sharing it with the corporation. Simultaneously, however, she would have a duty to communicate this useful information to the company and to use the information to defend the company's interests. Because she obviously cannot fulfill both duties at once, she would be prohibited from representing either the driver or the company.

The safest course of action in this situation would be to give the driver a "corporate *Miranda* warning," advising him that the lawyer's loyalty belongs to the company and not to him personally. The lawyer should say something like, "You must understand, we represent the corporation, not you as an individual. If you provide us with information that is helpful to the corporation, we may use it on the corporation's behalf, against you." Of course, the driver would clam up, but at least the lawyer would not face the consequences of disqualification or a lawsuit for breach of fiduciary duty.

Assisting a Squeeze-Out

7. In the actual case upon which this example is based, *Rice v. Strunk*, 670 N.E.2d 1280 (Ind. 1996), the lawyer attended the closing with "Popovich," and secured the refinancing of the building, including the personal guarantee of Popovich, whereupon Popovich was fired. Popovich sued "Nelson" and the lawyer for fraud and breach of fiduciary duty. Let's look at the issues from the lawyer's point of view. In other words, are there legal arguments the lawyer could offer to avoid liability to Popovich for Nelson's misconduct?

   One argument is that Nelson should be considered the client of the lawyer, since partners share profits and losses equally. Thus, when Nelson directed the lawyer not to inform Popovich of his termination until after the closing, the lawyer simply was obeying the client's lawful instructions. The court rejected that attempt to make Nelson the client, holding that entity theory applies to ordinary partnerships, at least those in which a managing partner has been designated, thus providing a degree of formalization and predictability to the entity's relationship with agents. Therefore, the lawyer's duties run to the partnership itself, not Nelson personally.

   The second argument is that the lawyer satisfies her duties to the partnership by obeying the instructions of Nelson, the managing partner. After all, Nelson is a "duly authorized constituent" through whom the entity acts. Rule 1.13(a). Just as Nelson cannot be considered the lawyer's client, neither can Popovich, so the lawyer has no duties directly to Popovich that were violated by participating in Nelson's ruse. As long as the termination of Popovich did not violate applicable partnership law, the lawyer did not act improperly. The Indiana Supreme Court accepted that argument, and the Restatement takes the same position. See Rest. §96, cmt. g & illus. 2; see also *Skarbrevik v. Cohen, England & Whitfield*, 282 Cal. Rptr. 627 (Ct. App. 1991). The lawyer represents the partnership itself, not any individual constituent, so the lawyer has no duty to protect Popovich against a breach by Nelson of the fiduciary obligation Nelson owes to Popovich.

   There is an important "unless . . ." proviso that must be added to the last sentence. A lawyer has no duty to protect Constituent A against the fiduciary breach of Constituent B, *unless Constituent B breaches a duty owed to the organization.* If the termination of Popovich violates applicable partnership law, and the organization will be sued by Popovich and will suffer financial loss as a result of Nelson's actions, the lawyer may not participate in Nelson's ruse. Rest. §96, illus. 3. "The lawyer must not knowingly or negligently assist any constituent to breach a legal duty to the organization." Rest. §96, cmt. e. If Nelson were engaging in self-dealing, to the detriment of the partnership, the lawyer may not counsel or assist

Nelson's actions. See, for example, *Murphy & Demory, Ltd. v. Admiral Daniel J. Murphy, U.S.N. (Ret.)*, Fairfax (Va.) Circuit Court (June 6, 1994) (not officially published, but reproduced or summarized in many professional responsibility casebooks). Indeed, the lawyer must take steps to prevent Nelson from engaging in self-dealing that would be harmful to the organization. Rest. §96, illus. 1.

It is important to note that the Restatement position, followed in the *Rice* and *Skarbrevik* cases cited above, is not the law in every jurisdiction. Some courts emphasize the fiduciary duties owed by the partners (or shareholders in closely held corporations) to each other, and prohibit the lawyer from assisting one constituent's breach of that duty to another constituent. See, for example, *Cacciola v. Nallhaus*, 733 N.E.2d 133 (Mass. Ct. App. 2000); *Granewich v. Harding*, 985 P.2d 788 (Or. 1999); *Fassihi v. Sommers, Schwartz, Silver, Schwartz and Tyler*, 309 N.W.2d 645 (Mich. App. 1981).[5] Those cases are consistent with the general law of fiduciary relationships. See *Granewich*, 985 P.2d at 793-794 (citing authorities).

Your professional responsibility instructor probably does not expect you to know the details of any particular jurisdiction's law of agency, partnership, closely held corporations, and fiduciary duties. For the purposes of understanding the law of professional responsibility and answering exam questions, it is sufficient to recognize the intersection between the law governing lawyers and generally applicable law. Thus, you can remember the following two-part rule:

1. *Everywhere* it is the law that a lawyer may not assist a constituent in breaching a duty owed to the entity. Self-dealing, such as the president making a "loan" from the entity to himself, is an example of this kind of fiduciary breach.

2. In *some* jurisdictions, if one constituent owes a fiduciary duty to another, the lawyer may not assist in a breach of that duty. Minority shareholders often have protections, under applicable corporate law, from being mistreated by majority shareholders. In some states, a lawyer may not assist the majority shareholder or shareholders in trying to circumvent those protections.

---

5. You should be extremely careful with these cases because they are very fact-specific. For example, in *Fassihi*, the lawyer inadvertently may have created an implied professional (or quasi-client) relationship with Shareholder X in the corporation; thus, the lawyer breached a duty to his own client, not to the entity, by assisting Shareholder Y in freezing Shareholder X out of the corporation. Because of the possible quasi-client relationship with Shareholder X, it is not entirely accurate to read *Fassihi* as standing for the proposition that a lawyer has a duty not to assist the breach of a fiduciary duty owed by one shareholder to another. *Granewich* and *Cacciola* are "purer" examples of liability for assisting a fiduciary breach by one constituent that is owed to another constituent, not the entity itself.

Incompetence: Remedies for Malpractice and Constitutional Ineffectiveness

INTRODUCTION

One obstacle I've encountered with students taking the subject of professional responsibility seriously is the belief that professional discipline is something that happens to "them"—lawyers with substance abuse or mental health issues, grossly incompetent or overworked lawyers, or perhaps those in certain highly contentious practice areas like criminal defense and matrimonial law. When I was in practice, reading the disciplinary pages of my state's bar journal tended to confirm this belief. There were many stories about lawyers with gambling debts, cocaine habits, and the like, which motivated them to "borrow" from their clients' trust account and subsequently get disbarred.

The ABA publishes an annual survey of state disciplinary systems.[1] According to the most recent version, there were 1,187,777 lawyers nationwide who are actively practicing law in 2013. State disciplinary authorities received 43,535 complaints in that year. That's nominally a 3.7% rate of complaints per lawyer, although of course some lawyers may have been the subject of multiple complaints. Of these complaints, 681 were disbarred (either involuntarily or by agreement) and 1,017 were suspended. Doing a bit of arithmetic, that means 3.9% of filed grievances resulted in the most serious sanctions. That's a 0.14% chance, per lawyer per year, of

---

1. I'm grateful to Brent Landau for pointing out these ABA resources to me and correcting the numbers used in previous editions of this book.

disbarment or suspension—doesn't seem like such a big deal. But consider the fact that, according to another ABA resource (*Profile of Legal Malpractice Claims* 2008-2011), attorneys in private practice have between a 4% and 17% chance of being sued in a year, depending on the state in which they practice and their area of specialization. That's a whole lot more significant. Of those filed claims, about 25% result in payouts of $10,000 or greater. Taking the mean likelihood of getting sued (10.5%), you can calculate that lawyers nationally have about a 2.63% per year likelihood of paying out a significant malpractice judgment or settlement. Last bit of math, I promise: The bottom line is that lawyers are about 19 times more likely to pay out on a malpractice claim than to be hit with the most serious disciplinary sanctions.

THE DUTY OF COMPETENCE

Lawyers are subject to professional discipline for failing to provide competent representation to a client. Rule 1.1. A lawyer's general education and experience may be sufficient to enable her to provide competent representation on some matters, but in other cases the lawyer may not be competent to undertake representation without specialized training. Rule 1.1, cmt. [1], [2]. In the latter instance, the lawyer should either spend some time to get "up to speed" on the new area of law or associate with another lawyer who is already an expert in the area. Rule 1.1, cmt. [4]. In an emergency it may be necessary for a lawyer to sort of wing it, relying on generalized experience and training. The classic example is a phone call in the middle of the night from a friend who just got stopped by the cops and wants to know whether it's advisable to refuse to take a breathalyzer test. A lawyer without specialized criminal defense experience may not know the right answer, but Rule 1.1, cmt. [3], permits the lawyer to give her best advice under the circumstances. If there is time to consult a specialist, however, the lawyer should refer the prospective client to another lawyer who truly know that area of practice.

A lawyer must make reasonable efforts to *maintain* competence. That includes keeping informed on changes to the law. Rule 1.1, cmt. [8]. Most states have a requirement that lawyers participate in Continuing Legal Education (CLE) programs and report a certain number of credit hours per year. In addition to satisfying state CLE requirements, a lawyer should make sure to stay up to date on new cases, statutes, and regulations in her area of specialization. If any of you have tried to help your parents use their iPhone or their computer, you will appreciate this additional aspect of the duty to maintain competence: Comment [8] also requires lawyers to stay current on "the benefits and risks associated with relevant technology."

That means understanding, for example, the risks of disclosing confidential information associated with electronic communications and information storage technologies. See ABA Formal Op. 477R (2017). Is unencrypted e-mail secure enough to use to communicate with your client? Is Google Docs safe enough to store confidential information? If you don't know the answer already, you have a duty to conduct a reasonable investigation to determine whether the use of these communication and data-storage technologies are compatible with the duties you owe to your client, including the duty of confidentiality. See also Rule 1.6, cmts. [18]–[19], which provides additional detail regarding the duty to use competence to safeguard confidential client information.

In addition to the duty of competence, a lawyer has an obligation to "act with reasonable diligence and promptness" while working for a client. Rule 1.3. That means returning phone calls right away, not missing filing deadlines, and not getting so bogged down with other cases that it is impossible to provide effective service to each client. This duty applies no matter who the clients are. Lawyers representing indigent criminal defendants — whether as employees of a public defender office or as private appointed counsel — must manage their caseloads in such a way that ensures their ability to provide competent and diligent representation to all clients. See ABA Formal Op. 441 (2006). If necessary to ensure competent representation, a lawyer must seek to avoid appointment to represent additional clients, and must move to withdraw from as many cases as necessary to make it possible to comply with the duties of competence and diligence. The rules of professional conduct in any given state apply by their terms only to lawyers. But that does not mean a lawyer is not responsible for the conduct of nonlawyer assistants, whether employed by the lawyer's firm (such a paralegals) or independent contractors (such as investigators or electronic discovery consultants). Rule 5.3(b) requires a lawyer with direct supervisory authority over a nonlawyer to make reasonable efforts to ensure that the nonlawyer's conduct is compatible with the lawyer's professional obligations to the client. That means the lawyer needs to know enough about the services provided by the nonlawyer to ask the right questions and provide effective supervision.

Even though professional discipline is possible in these cases, it is extremely rare for a lawyer to face discipline for incompetence or procrastination alone. Nevertheless, you should pay close attention to an exam question posing lawyer-competence issues. If the question pertains to *professional discipline*, analyze the issue under Rule 1.1 and 1.3. If the client, not the state disciplinary authority, is bringing the claim against the lawyer, analyze the question in terms of tort law (negligence) and agency law (fiduciary duty) principles, with due regard to whether the disciplinary rules are incorporated somehow into common law causes of action, for example, as *negligence per se* or at least as evidence of the standard of care.

Example

Not My Problem?

1. Jimmy McGill is a lawyer in solo practice, specializing in personal injury law. He filed a lawsuit against a tire manufacturer, seeking damages for a driver who was seriously injured when her sport-utility vehicle rolled over. The manufacturer produced 10 million pages of electronically stored documents, including voluminous engineering test data, in response to McGill's request for production. Feeling overwhelmed by the documents, McGill hired Hamlin's Helping Hands, a provider of electronic discovery support services which advertises extensively in the state's bar journal. If McGill had performed even the most basic investigation, including talking to other plaintiffs' personal-injury lawyers, he would have learned that Howard Hamlin, the owner of the company, had never attended law school and learned all he knows about electronic discovery by working as a paralegal for three years. McGill would also have learned that two other lawyers in the state had been sanctioned for discovery violations which were traceable to errors made by Hamlin's Helping Hands.

   As you might expect, Hamlin's made some mistakes in reviewing the documents produced by the defendant in McGill's case. As a result of a failure to use the correct terms in searching the database of documents, Hamlin's missed several test reports that would have shown that the tire manufacturer knew of a heightened risk of rollover when its tires were used on a certain model of SUV. McGill's client's claims were dismissed on summary judgment, for insufficient evidence of a defect in the tires. Is McGill subject to discipline?

Explanation

Not My Problem?

1. The first thing to notice here is that the mistake was made by an outside vendor of legal-support services, Hamlin's Helping Hands, but the question asks whether the lawyer, McGill, is subject to discipline. Somehow you need a way to connect the negligence of the vendor to McGill's professional obligations. That bridge is found in Rule 5.3(b), which required McGill, as a lawyer having direct supervisory authority over the e-discovery vendor, to "make reasonable efforts to ensure that [Hamlin's] conduct is compatible with the professional obligations of [McGill]." What are McGill's professional obligations? Go back to Rule 1.1. McGill's obligations are to use the knowledge, skill, thoroughness, and preparation required to represent the client effectively. A relatively complex and specialized matter may demand a higher degree of skill and

more extensive preparation. See Rule 1.1, cmt. [1]. Putting Rule 5.3(b) and Rule 1.1 together, McGill owes his client a thorough investigation of the qualifications of any outside vendor of support services. As an ABA ethics opinion notes, at a minimum that would require asking around to get references from other lawyers who have used Hamlin's Helping Hands. See ABA Formal Op. 451 (2008). It may also require — if this can be done easily — investigating any allegations of discovery abuse or negligence attributable to the e-discovery vendor. McGill may also have to conduct further investigation, such as questioning the personnel at Hamlin's who will be working on the case, to ensure that they know how to conduct a thorough document review in a products liability case.

This example does not involve the *vicarious* liability of McGill for the negligence of Hamlin's Helping Hands. Hamlin's truly is an independent contractor, so its negligence is not imputed to McGill for the purpose of discipline. Rather, McGill is subject to discipline for his own independent negligence in failing to investigate and adequately supervise Hamlin's. If McGill himself is clueless about document discovery in complex products liability cases, he will not be able to ask the right questions and provide the kind of supervision that is required by the combination of Rules 1.1 and 5.3.

THE TORT OF MALPRACTICE

Although lawyers sometimes speak loosely of malpractice actions, there is no one single cause of action called "malpractice." A client can sue a lawyer for professional negligence (a *tort* claim), breach of fiduciary duty (a claim brought under *agency* law), or breach of the lawyer's agreement to provide professional services (a *contract* cause of action). Rest. §16. The Restatement sets out the rules governing these claims in more detail in §§48-55. Most of this chapter discusses tort claims for negligence, but remember the other categories of claims, too. In particular, keep the breach of fiduciary duty cause of action in mind when reading about confidentiality and conflicts of interest. A lawyer has an obligation under agency law to give the client her undivided loyalty, refrain from representing conflicting interests, and avoid the disclosure or misuse of the client's confidential information. A lawyer may be liable to the client for breach of fiduciary duty if she violates one of those rules.

An important rule that many lawyers apparently do not know about is that a lawyer cannot request that her client enter into an agreement prospectively limiting the lawyer's liability to the client, without meeting some very stringent conditions. Rule 1.8(h); Rest. §54(2), (4). The lawyer must comply with applicable law (which may hold that prospective liability waivers are void as against public policy), and the client must be represented by an independent lawyer in making the agreement. Rule 1.8(h)(1). As the Restatement rule makes clear, not only would a lawyer be subject to professional discipline for including this kind of provision in a retainer agreement, but in addition the agreement would be unenforceable. A similar rule applies to settlements of malpractice claims, which require the lawyer-defendant to advise the client in writing of the desirability of obtaining separate counsel, and provide a reasonable opportunity for the client to do so. Rule 1.8(h)(2); Rest. §54(4)(b).

A tort action for malpractice is really just a specialized negligence tort, so if you remember the elements of negligence, you will be well on your way to getting a handle on the cause of action for malpractice. There are four elements, each of which has some wrinkles that are peculiar to the law of lawyer malpractice, but by and large track the elements of negligence.

Duty and Standard of Care

Before a duty is owed, there generally must be an attorney-client relationship. There are two significant qualifications to this rule. First, remember from Chapter 2 that an attorney-client relationship does not require a written retainer agreement or any other formal trappings in order to arise. A lawyer may have a professional relationship with, and owe duties to, a person she has consulted with only briefly and informally. Remember the *Togstad* case — if a reasonable person in the client's position would think that the lawyer has undertaken to provide legal services, the lawyer will owe that person a duty of care. See Rest. §14. This is an objective standard. The woman who sought the lawyer's advice in *Togstad* became an implied-in-fact client of the lawyer, quite contrary to the lawyer's subjective intention not to represent her.

Second, there is a trend toward recognizing tort claims by certain categories of third parties — that is, nonclients — who are injured by the lawyer's negligence. This trend goes against the traditional rule, under which an attorney had a duty toward only those persons with whom she was in privity of contract. Modern cases do not require privity to create a duty of care. A lawyer may have a duty toward persons with whom she is not in privity, as long as there are circumstances under which it is fair to extend a duty of care. These circumstances include undertaking legal work for a client, knowing that the client intends to benefit a third party, and expressly inviting a third party to rely on the lawyer's opinion. See Rest. §51.

A common example of a breach of duty owed to someone not in contractual privity is a lawyer who bungles the drafting of a will or trust instrument and deprives the beneficiaries of what they had expected to receive. In an infamous case, the intended beneficiaries of a trust lost $75,000 to the intestate heirs when the lawyer who prepared the trust failed to comply with the Rule Against Perpetuities. *Lucas v. Hamm,* 364 P.2d 685 (Cal. 1961).[2] The court correctly held that the intended beneficiaries could sue the lawyer, even though the lawyer's client was the settlor of the trust. The beneficiaries were not in contractual privity with the attorney, but the attorney did know that one of the primary objectives of his work on behalf of his client was to provide for the trust beneficiaries. Thus, a reasonable lawyer would have taken their interests into account when drafting the trust documents. This result is recognized by the Restatement, which imposes a duty of care on lawyers, in favor of nonclients, where the lawyer knows that the "client intends as one of the primary objectives of the representation that the lawyer's services benefit the nonclient." Rest. §51(3)(a).

An analogous situation creating liability to nonclients is the preparation of opinion letters to facilitate certain transactions. In one well-known case, a federal court held that a lawyer who prepared an opinion letter for the use of a third-party lender, certifying to his client's compliance with the conditions of the loan, could be liable to the lender when the client defaulted on the loan. *Greycas, Inc. v. Proud,* 826 F.2d 1560 (7th Cir. 1987). This is another reasonable result, because the lawyer knew perfectly well that the lender was going to rely on the letter in deciding whether to make the loan. The Restatement now recognizes that a lawyer who invites a nonclient to rely on the soundness of her opinion may be liable to the nonclient for malpractice. Rest. §51(2)(a). This theory of liability can have serious consequences for lawyers who provide opinion letters to facilitate large transactions. Some of the firms that provided legal representation to Enron spent many years embroiled in litigation brought by investors who alleged that the firms had provided bogus opinion letters, allowing fraudulent transactions to close. See *In re Enron Corp. Securities, Derivatives & ERISA Litigation,* 235 F. Supp. 2d 549 (S.D. Tex. 2002). However, reliance by a third party is not an open-ended liability standard. Courts considering the tort of negligent misrepresentation (not just involving lawyers) worry that someone who makes a representation may be faced with almost infinite liability, as the representation is

---

2. The case is notorious because of its other holding—that getting mixed up on the Rule Against Perpetuities was not negligence. Calling the rule a "trap for the unwary," the court said a lawyer of ordinary skill and capacity could not be expected to understand it. That reasoning is baloney. For one thing, the attorney could have read two recent California cases invalidating exactly the kind of bequest he tried to draft. The aspect of the rule that the lawyer missed was so basic it was stated in C.J.S. and Am. Jur. For another, the Rule Against Perpetuities is no more of a trap for the unwary than any other legal rule of some complexity and subtlety. The occupation of lawyer is simply defined by getting these things right. Fortunately, the California Supreme Court got some sense and has been distinguishing *Lucas* ever since. See, for example, *Smith v. Lewis,* 530 P.2d 589 (Cal. 1975). You should not assume that there is some kind of general "trap for the unwary" exception to the duty of care. If there is a complex legal issue involved in representing a client, the lawyer had better get it right, or she may be liable for malpractice.

repeated by one person to another. See, for example, *Ultramares Corp. v. Touche*, 174 N.E. 441 (N.Y. 1931) (Cardozo, J.) (holding auditor liable for negligence could potentially "expose accountants to a liability in an indeterminate amount for an indeterminate time to an indeterminate class"). In order to keep liability for negligent misrepresentation under control, courts will require a showing that the representation was made to a specific third party, for a specific purpose. As the Restatement puts it, the nonclient cannot be "too remote" from the original representation. Rest. §51(2)(b).

A third kind of liability to nonclients involves knowingly providing substantial assistance to the client in breaching a fiduciary duty she owes to a third party. See, for example, *Chem-Age Indus. v. Glover*, 652 N.W.2d 765 (S.D. 2002); *Granewich v. Harding*, 985 P.2d 788 (Or. 1999). This can occur within a partnership or closely held corporation, where the underlying substantive law (that is, state agency, partnership, or corporation law) imposes duties of loyalty running between the "constituents" of the organization. There also may be fiduciary duties running to creditors or other parties in non-arm's-length negotiations. There aren't many cases out there relying on this theory,[3] but it looks like another exception to the traditional privity rule may be emerging.

The standard of care for lawyers is that of the reasonable *professional*, not just the reasonable person. Rest. §52(1). An ordinary citizen might not think to inform a client that the statute of limitation is about to run on her claim, but a lawyer will be expected to do so. The standard of care is even higher for a lawyer who holds herself out as a *specialist* in something like tax or appellate litigation. Lawyers should be careful not to create the expectations of specialized expertise inadvertently, which can happen through the lawyer's advertising and promotional materials. If a Yellow Pages ad says, "I am the best trial lawyer in the state," the lawyer may be held to a higher standard of care than a lawyer who had not made such extravagant claims. Rest. §52, cmt. d.

Breach of Duty

Remember from torts that in professional negligence cases, the definition of reasonable care is provided by the custom among practitioners. In ordinary negligence cases, courts are somewhat suspicious of custom — as Judge Learned Hand said in *The T.J. Hooper*, it is ultimately for courts to say

---

3. *Reynolds v. Schrock*, 142 P.3d 1062 (Or. 2006), limits the *Granewich* case discussed in the text by creating a privilege for lawyers acting on behalf of a client, within the scope of the attorney-client relationship. *Granewich* was distinguishable, because the lawyer's client in that case was the corporation, and the wrongful squeeze-out was perpetrated by a nonclient, the majority shareholder.

what safety precautions an industry must take. When it comes to professions, though, courts reverse themselves and defer to custom. Why is this? Perhaps it is because professions are thought to be self-policing and less likely to follow customs that are systematically harmful to patients or clients. There is also the fear of over-deterrence, or causing professionals to practice "defensively." If the profession cannot set its own definition of reasonable care, courts may set the threshold too high, thereby causing professionals to take unnecessary precautions and driving up the cost of socially valuable services.

The upshot of the rule that "custom is dispositive of compliance with the standard of care" is that virtually every legal malpractice case is going to require the plaintiff to produce expert testimony on this issue. Rest. §52, cmt. g. Otherwise, the trier of fact would have insufficient information from which to judge the defendant's conformity with custom in the profession. There is an exception for cases of negligence that are so glaringly obvious that the jury can readily understand them. The plaintiff may not be required to come forward with expert testimony where, for example, her lawyer had completely failed to take any action at all on the plaintiff's case. The requirement of expert testimony tends to make legal malpractice cases more expensive and difficult to bring, because the plaintiff has to go through the trouble of locating a suitable expert, preparing disclosures of her testimony, and paying her fee. The defendant will, of course, have his own expert, and both experts undoubtedly will be deposed before trial. This procedural hurdle for plaintiffs is one reason that the legal malpractice system cannot be counted on to punish all incidents of incompetence by lawyers.

Custom is determined on a statewide basis, which makes sense considering that lawyers are regulated by the highest court in any given state, not by a national body. The traditional "locality rule" from professional malpractice might apply, so that lawyers are measured against the standard of other practitioners in their hometown, county, or region within a state. But many courts are moving away from the locality rule in legal malpractice cases. Rest. §52 cmt. b; contra *Kellos v. Sawilowsky*, 325 S.E.2d 757 (Ga. 1985); *Rorrer v. Cooke*, 329 S.E.2d 355 (N.C. 1985). By broadening the geographic boundaries in which custom is measured, courts have made it easier for the plaintiff to develop expert testimony favorable to their claims. If custom was measured on a county-by-county basis, it practically might be impossible for an aggrieved client to find an expert, if the lawyers in the locality all stuck together and refused to testify against each other. Lawyers who did testify as plaintiffs' experts might find themselves with fewer referrals from their local colleagues and might receive fewer professional courtesies, such as cooperativeness in scheduling or willingness to grant extensions of time. Now, if a client is suing a lawyer in Rockbridge County, Virginia, she can find a lawyer from Norfolk or Richmond to testify against the defendant, and the plaintiff's expert does not have to fear repercussions in her own community.

One recurring issue is whether the state's disciplinary rules may be used to show the lawyer's nonconformity with the standard of care. The introductory comments to the Model Rules specifically state that violation of one of the rules does not create a cause of action and does not give rise to a presumption that the lawyer has breached a professional duty. Model Rules "Scope," Comment [20]. Despite this admonition in the Model Rules, some courts hold that a plaintiff may use the disciplinary rules to show *negligence per se*—that is, proof of a violation of one of the rules is conclusive on the element of breach of duty. The majority position, however, is that the violation of a disciplinary rule is *evidence* of negligence only, which the trier of fact may consider as an aid to understanding the lawyer's reasonable care duty. Rest. §52(2). You may wonder what courts are doing looking to the Model Rules for guidance in tort cases. In one sense, the disciplinary rules are purely a matter of the internal regulation of the legal profession. Since the general rule of tort law is that professional custom sets the standard of care, however, it is appropriate to look to how the governing body of the profession defines the obligations of its members. It certainly seems more efficient to consider the disciplinary rules on conflicts of interest than to require the plaintiff to prove, from the ground up, how lawyers all over the state handle the question of multiple representations consistent with their fiduciary obligations to each client.

A lawyer does not breach the standard of care by failing to obtain a good result. Just as in torts, the mere fact that there was an accident does not mean the defendant was negligent. A lawyer is required only to act as a *reasonable* professional under the circumstances. If a lawyer did a reasonable amount of investigation, but nevertheless did not find a witness whose testimony could have helped the client's case, the lawyer did not commit malpractice. If the lawyer did a reasonable amount of pretrial preparation but the client did not prevail at trial, the lawyer did not commit malpractice.

In general, a lawyer is not liable for errors in judgment, again as long as the lawyer made a reasonable effort. Wolfram §5.6.2. For example, a lawyer may be called upon to predict how a court will decide an unsettled issue of law. If the lawyer did reasonable legal research and thought carefully about the question, she will not be liable for malpractice just because her prediction turns out to have been incorrect. See 2 Mallen & Smith, *Legal Malpractice* §19:1. However, a lawyer cannot hide behind the "judgment" rule if she failed to do the appropriate amount of legal research and investigation into the facts that a reasonable lawyer would have done in the same circumstances. A lawyer may even be held liable for failing to anticipate a change in the law that would adversely affect the client, and for failing to advise the client of the likelihood of the change, if there is a strong trend in that direction or if there are other signs that would put a reasonable lawyer on notice that further research is necessary. See *Jerry's Enterprises v. Larkin, Hoffman, Daly & Lindgren*, 711 N.W.2d 811 (Minn. 2006) (lawyer may be liable for malpractice where a reasonable real estate attorney would have researched the continuing viability of a legal doctrine that was subsequently modified by the state supreme court, and would have advised the client of the possibility of the change). Thus, while you may encounter the term "judgmental immunity," it is best not to think of it as a true immunity from liability. Rather, if a lawyer asserts that she made a judgment call in resolving an unsettled issue of law, the client has the burden to show that the legal issue was actually fairly well settled or the lawyer did not conduct a reasonable investigation. See 2 Mallen & Smith, *Legal Malpractice* §19:6.

Finally, it is not malpractice for a lawyer to refuse to be a jerk, even if the client insists on it. In a case where the lawyer was defending a hopeless product liability action, the client instructed him to introduce questionable expert testimony and conduct a cross-examination of the plaintiff's expert that the lawyer thought would be a waste of time. *Transcraft, Inc. v. Galvin, Stalmack, Kirschner & Clark,* 39 F.3d 812 (7th Cir. 1994). Although the jury found that the lawyer had been negligent (on another ground), Judge Posner stated that "[r]efusal to violate professional ethics—or even to approach as near to the line as humanly possible—is not professional misconduct." The Restatement commentary takes the same line: "When a lawyer reasonably believes that an act or objective [of the client] is immoral or violates professional courtesy, even if not unlawful, the lawyer may assume that the client would not want that act or objective to be pursued." Rest. §50, cmt. e.

Causation

The element of causation is the reef upon which many legal malpractice claims founder. In order to prove the tort of professional negligence, the plaintiff must show that but for the lawyer's failure to exercise reasonable care, the outcome of the representation would have been different. If the lawyer was representing the client in a litigated matter, in a subsequent malpractice action the client would have to show that she would have prevailed in the underlying litigation, in addition to proving that the lawyer was negligent in representing her. Rest. §53, cmt. b. This is known as the case-within-a-case requirement, and can be a very high burden for plaintiffs to carry.

Consider the following typical scenario. P sues D, a doctor, in a medical malpractice case. On the advice of her lawyer, L, P settles with D for $25,000. Later, P learns that L had not retained a medical expert to review P's chart and erroneously assumed that P had a weak case. P decides to sue L for malpractice. In addition to proving a breach of duty (L's failure to retain an expert), P must show that but for that breach she would have obtained more than $25,000, either by way of judgment or settlement. The emerging rule in most jurisdictions is that a lawyer may be liable for recommending a settlement that is less than what a properly represented client would have accepted. See, for example, *Fishman v. Brooks*, 487 N.E.2d 1377 (Mass. 1986). How is P going to make that showing? Naturally, by retaining the medical expert that her lawyer was supposed to have retained in the first place to establish D's medical negligence. If the case goes to trial, P has to prove two parallel malpractice cases—D's medical malpractice and L's legal malpractice. Each of these cases probably will involve expert testimony, complex factual evidence, affirmative defenses, and difficulties in proof. It can be extremely difficult and expensive to duplicate realistically the proof in the underlying medical malpractice case. Moreover, you can bet that L will defend the legal malpractice case by arguing that the medical malpractice case was a sure loser and that P was lucky to have settled for anything at all. This posture puts L in the odd position of arguing that he agreed to take a lousy case on behalf of P; in other words, P's lawyer is aligned in interests with the doctor!

The "but for" causation rule applied to criminal defense cases produces an even harsher result. In most jurisdictions, the criminal defendant (the plaintiff in the legal malpractice case) must show that he was actually innocent of the crime. The criminal defendant can do this only by having the conviction set aside on direct appeal or collateral attack. Rest. §53, cmt. d, Reporter's Note.

Damages

Prevailing plaintiffs in legal malpractice cases generally can recover the damages that flow "directly and naturally" from the lawyer's negligence. Wolfram §5.6.3. These damages can include pecuniary damages for business losses, the amount the plaintiff would have received at trial, or the additional legal fees necessitated by the first lawyer's malpractice. If the malpractice occurred in litigation, the client may recover the damages that would have been obtained in the underlying action, but for the lawyer's negligence. Rest. §53, cmt. b. The negligent lawyer also may not recover fees for the representation—to put it another way, the fees paid to the negligent lawyer are a recoverable item of damages in the legal malpractice action. Id., cmt. c. If the first lawyer's negligence requires the client to find a new lawyer to fix the problem, the additional fees may be a recoverable item of damages. Id., cmt. f. Some jurisdictions also permit plaintiffs to recover nonpecuniary damages for emotional distress, but usually only in cases of outrageous, willful, or wanton misconduct. Id., cmt. g.

Recovery by a nonclient (third party) on a negligent misrepresentation theory (see Rest. §51) is governed by generally applicable tort principles. Rest. §53, cmt. e. Under the law of negligent misrepresentation, the plaintiff may recover pecuniary damages including the difference between the market value of what the plaintiff received in the transaction and its purchase price, as well as pecuniary losses otherwise suffered as a consequence of the plaintiff's reliance on the misrepresentation, but not expectation or benefit-of-the-bargain damages. See Restatement (Second) of Torts §552B.

In all but two states — Oregon and Idaho — lawyers are not required to carry malpractice insurance. That means that a client harmed by a lawyer's malpractice may not have an effective remedy if the lawyer does not have sufficient assets to satisfy the claim. Many state statutes providing for some type of limited-liability organization, such as a limited liability partnership (LLP) or a professional limited liability corporation (PLLC), require that the organization carry sufficient malpractice insurance in order to qualify. Other states require lawyers to disclose whether or not they have malpractice insurance. In many of these states (17 at last count), the required disclosure is only to a professional regulatory authority (for example, on a periodic renewal of one's license to practice). A prospective client would therefore have to hunt around in regulatory filings to see if a lawyer was insured. In seven states, however, lawyers must disclose directly to clients whether they have malpractice insurance.

Examples

Who's Left Holding the Bag?

2. A law firm in the United States was retained by a real estate investor to represent it in the purchase of a hotel on the Caribbean island of Aruba. Aruba has a civil law system, based on Dutch law. The U.S. law firm retained a lawyer in Aruba who explained that title insurance is unavailable in Aruba. The custom on the island is that a buyer of real estate obtains a certification from a notary (a nonlawyer official common in civil law systems) that the seller has good title to the land being conveyed. The risk of loss in the transaction is on the buyer. An alternative to obtaining the certification from a notary would be to hire a lawyer in Aruba to conduct an investigation of the seller's title, but this would add significant expense to the transaction.

The partner in charge of the representation explained these facts to the client. There is no dispute that the parties both understood the following facts: The purchase price for the hotel was $35 million. Obtaining a certification from an Aruban notary would cost $25,000. Hiring a law firm in Aruba to conduct an investigation of the title would cost $500,000 (that is, 20 times as much as the notary). The client told the partner not to hire a law firm to conduct an investigation, but rather to rely on the certification from the notary.

After the transaction closed, the buyer learned that the swimming pool, tennis courts, and parking lot for the hotel were on land owned by a neighboring resort. The buyer had to pay the neighbor $5 million to acquire that land. Under Aruban law, the notary who provided the mistaken title certification is immune from liability. The client sued the law firm in the United States, alleging that it was negligent in failing to discover the defect in the title. Is the law firm liable to the client for malpractice?

A. Yes, because a reasonable investigation would have revealed the defect in the seller's title.

B. Yes, because it was unreasonable to rely on the advice of the law firm in Aruba regarding the custom in real estate transactions on the island.

C. No, because the client gave informed consent to a limitation on the law firm's representation that was reasonable under the circumstances.

D. No, because the negligence was committed by the Aruban notary, not the law firm.

For Want of a License, the Business Was Lost

3. Michaels is the president of a company that develops luxury condominiums for retirees. He hired attorney Poynter to help him secure all the necessary permits to build condos on the beach in the State of Perplexity. Poynter was an experienced real estate lawyer, but he had never worked on a beachfront project. Unfortunately, he neglected to secure a permit from the Perplexity Coastal Commission (PCC), which regulates beachfront development in order to protect the coastal environment. As soon as Michaels started construction of the condos, the PCC secured an injunction against further building. Michaels hired a new lawyer, but the PCC ruled that he was permanently barred from seeking a license because he already had started construction on the project. Michaels was forced to abandon the project and sell the property at a loss. Can he recover his expected profits from the condo development in a malpractice action against Poynter?

How Wide Is the Circle of Liability?

4. Harris is the lawyer representing Bachman, a real estate developer. Bachman has a parcel of land he would like to sell. The prospective purchaser, Perales, would like to open a child day care center on the lot, so she requested assurances from the seller that the land was suitable for this kind of development. Bachman told Harris to prepare a legal opinion certifying that the land could be used for a day care center. Harris researched the zoning of the land and the building codes, and concluded

that it would satisfy Perales's needs. He wrote a letter stating that the land satisfied all legal requirements for the type of business contemplated by the buyer. After reading the letter, Perales signed a contract to purchase the land.

A. Unfortunately, Harris did not notice a provision of the administrative code of the Department of Health in the State of Perplexity. That code provision required that the land pass a series of percolation tests designed to show whether the soil would permit operation of a septic system. After the sale closed, the engineer hired by Perales to begin constructing the day care center informed her that the land was not suitable for a septic system. (There was no available alternative to the septic system, such as a municipal sewer line.) Perales sued Bachman to rescind the sale, but Bachman had filed for bankruptcy. Perales then sued Harris, seeking damages for the difference in value between the land with a septic system and without. Can Perales recover from Harris?

B. Suppose that instead of missing the administrative code provision, Harris was aware of it, and also was aware that the soil on Bachman's land had failed several percolation tests. Suppose further that Harris prepared a document called the "Legal Report," to inform Bachman of the land's compliance with various zoning, building code, and other legal requirements. If Harris included a sentence reading, "The land has passed the necessary percolation tests and is suitable for a septic system," and Bachman gave the "Legal Report" to Perales, could Perales recover from Harris if she were unable to construct the day care center?

Explanations

Who's Left Holding the Bag?

2. Based on *Sierra Fria Corp. v. Donald J. Evans, P.C.*, 127 F.3d 175 (1st Cir. 1997). You could argue that the answer is either C or D. The analysis under Rule 1.2(c) would support answer C. The idea is that the client, who is a sophisticated real estate investor, had a choice to make: Pay $25,000 for the opinion of the notary, or conduct a full title investigation for $500,000. The client decided to take its chances, and is now stuck with the result. As long as the client gave informed consent to the U.S. law firm's limitation of its duties (that is, to going with the apparent local custom of relying on a notary), then the law firm did not have a duty to investigate title to the swimming pool and tennis courts. If you went with answer D, you might have argued that the U.S. law firm didn't make a mistake; the Aruban notary did. There is one ambiguity in the facts, however. It is unclear whether there was a separate attorney-client

relationship with the Aruban notary. If the U.S. law firm hired the notary essentially as a subcontractor, it may still be liable to the client. If, on the other hand, there was a separate contract between the investor and the notary, there seems to be no duty on the part of the U.S. firm with respect to the title issue.

No valid multiple-choice question would have two arguably right answers. If you went with either C or D and gave the reasons described here, you got this one right.

For Want of a License, the Business Was Lost

3. This example is loosely based on *Miami Int'l Realty Co. v. Paynter*, 841 F.2d 348 (10th Cir. 1988). Go through the malpractice case element by element. Poynter had a duty to his client, Michaels, to "exercise the competence and diligence normally exercised by lawyers in similar circumstances." Rest. §52(1). Would a reasonable professional have missed the requirement of obtaining a permit from the PCC? No—while there are some uncertainties beyond the control of even a careful lawyer, courts uniformly will expect a lawyer to research any applicable statutes and regulations that might apply to the client's situation. Ignorance of the law that could be remedied by doing some research is *not* reasonable. See Wolfram §5.6.2. It is the job of lawyers to know the law. Michaels may be able to argue here that Poynter should be held to a higher standard as an experienced real estate lawyer. Id.; Rest. §52, cmt. d. Even if he does not make that argument, however, Poynter's failure to discover the permit requirement is a breach of the duty of care.

What about causation and damages? Remember that Michaels has to prove a case-within-a-case. He must establish that his condo development otherwise would have been approved and would have made $X in profits if the condos had been built. Proving this element will require testimony from experts, such as economists and marketing specialists, to establish how much Michaels would have earned from the project. In addition, he may recover the fees paid to Poynter, Rest. §53 cmt. c, and the fees paid to the new lawyer that were made necessary by Poynter's negligence, Id., cmt. f.

For a similar case, see *Equitania Ins. Co. v. Sloan & Garrett PSC*, 191 S.W.3d 552 (Ky. 2006). That case is helpful because it clarifies a rule that is sometimes applied too loosely. Courts often say that a lawyer isn't liable for making errors in judgment or for giving advice that turns out to have been erroneous only in hindsight. That is correct as far as it goes, but it is important to keep in mind that the lawyer's judgment must be objectively reasonable under the circumstances. True, no one expects lawyers to be able to predict the future, but lawyers can be expected to do reasonable research into the law and facts. In *Equitania*, the lawyer failed to file an administrative action with the state insurance commission that would have had the effect of blocking a takeover attempt. When the acquired company sued its lawyer for malpractice, the lawyer sought and obtained the following jury instruction at trial:

> [A] lawyer cannot be held responsible for errors in judgment or for advising a course of action even if that course of action ultimately proves to be unsuccessful.

The Kentucky Supreme Court held that the instruction was too broad. A lawyer is not immune from liability for mistakes in judgment. If a reasonable lawyer in the same circumstances would have advised the client to pursue the administrative remedy, then the defendant can be liable for malpractice for failing to give the advice. The damages would be calculated as the additional expenses incurred by the client in fighting the takeover effort, over and above what it would have had to spend on the administrative proceeding.

Another context in which lawyers sometimes assert immunity from liability for making poor judgments is in the giving of settlement advice. Some courts have adopted a *per se* rule that a lawyer can never be held liable for negligence in connection with advising the client whether to settle. See, for example, *Muhammad v. Strassburger, McKenna, Messer, Shilobod and Gutnick*, 587 A.2d 1346 (Pa. 1991). In favor of the *per se* rule is the division of labor recognized in Rule 1.2(a), which commits the decision to settle to the client's sole discretion. On the other hand, many clients rely very much on the advice of their lawyer in deciding whether to exercise their authority to accept an offered settlement. In some cases, the lawyer's faulty advice might have caused the client to make a bad decision, and it seems unfair to saddle the client with the consequences of the lawyer's negligence just because the client has the final say regarding settlements. For the leading case rejecting the *per se* rule and permitting a client to maintain an action against a lawyer for negligent settlement advice, see *Ziegelheim v. Apollo*, 607 A.2d 1298 (N.J. 1992).

How Wide Is the Circle of Liability?

4. I modified the facts of *Petrillo v. Bachenberg*, 655 A.2d 1354 (N.J. 1995), for this example, although part B is pretty close to the actual case.
   A. Whether Harris owes Perales a duty is the only close question in this example. In part A, it is clear that Harris invited Perales to rely on his opinion. Rest. §51(2)(a). There is no reason to prepare an opinion letter, except to induce the reliance of a third party on the representations it contains. In fact, Perales required Bachman to produce the legal opinion letter as a condition of purchasing the land. The

circumstances surrounding the preparation of the letter show that Perales was invited to rely on it. Thus, Harris is liable to Perales if Perales can establish the rest of the malpractice claim.

The analysis of the remaining three elements of the malpractice claim is fairly straightforward. Harris breached his duty (if he owes one!) to Perales by missing the administrative code requirement. Harris has a duty to "exercise the competence and diligence normally exercised by lawyers in similar circumstances." Rest. §52(1). A reasonable professional handling a commercial real estate closing would be expected to know all applicable legal requirements that might pertain to the buyer's contemplated use of the land. There is a causal connection between the breach of duty and the harm, since Perales would not have bought the land if it were not suitable for a day care center because a septic system could not be installed. Finally, there are damages, as measured by the difference between the purchase price of the land and its fair market value. (Although your instructor may not go into damages in this much detail, remember that expectation losses are not recoverable under a negligent misrepresentation theory. See Rest. §53, cmt. e., citing Restatement (Second) of Torts §552B.)

B. The facts in part B present a much closer case. The difference is that Harris did not invite a specific third party to rely on his opinion. Instead, he prepared his opinion for Bachman, leaving the subsequent use of the opinion up to Bachman. Harris might still be liable, though, because the "Legal Report" does not state that it was prepared only for the use of the client, and no one else should rely on it. See Rest. §51, cmt. e ("A lawyer may avoid liability to nonclients . . . by making clear that an opinion or representation is directed only to a client and should not be relied upon by others."). The actual *Petrillo* decision analyzed the lawyer's liability in terms of *foreseeability.* When Harris gave Bachman the report, it arguably was foreseeable that he would give it to prospective purchasers, such as Perales. The dissent in the *Petrillo* case argued that it was not foreseeable that the report would end up in the hands of a prospective purchaser. Perhaps in this situation, the appropriate response is to give the question of foreseeability to the jury, which is the approach followed by the majority in *Petrillo.* In some jurisdictions, however, there may be a rule that a plaintiff in the position of Perales is too remote from the injury-causing event to be owed a duty of care by the lawyer. For that reason, the Restatement limits liability to cases in which there is not such a limitation in generally applicable tort law. Rest. §51(2)(b).

If you encounter a question like this, focus on foreseeability as a possible limitation on the scope of the lawyer's duty and be prepared to argue that the harm either was or was not foreseeable. In torts, questions of duty and foreseeability often are resolved on policy grounds. (Remember *Palsgraf?*) In policy terms, one reason not to impose a duty on a lawyer in the situation of Harris is that expanding the liability of lawyers will drive up the costs of transactions. If lawyers are worried that any document they prepare for a client might end up in the hands of a third party, who will detrimentally rely on that document, they will take much greater care in drafting them. Greater care equals greater time, which equals greater cost to the client. As a result, courts have tended to construe exceptions to the privity requirement narrowly, and impose duties of care in favor of third parties only where it is possible to draw a clear line between cases of liability and nonliability. See, for example, *Prudential Insurance v. Dewey, Ballantine, Bushby, Palmer & Wood*, 605 N.E.2d 318 (N.Y. 1992).

THE SIXTH AMENDMENT

The Sixth Amendment provides that a criminal defendant is entitled to have "the Assistance of Counsel for his defense." This right has been interpreted as guaranteeing counsel that meets at least a baseline of competence. Thus, incompetence by a lawyer may, in some cases, rise to the level of a constitutional violation. If the lawyer is constitutionally incompetent, the only remedy is a new trial at which the accused is provided with competent counsel. Because of the drastic and expensive nature of this remedy, it is unsurprising that the Supreme Court has sought to limit the scope of constitutional ineffectiveness.

Unfortunately, the Sixth Amendment is just about the only potential avenue for obtaining relief if a lawyer's negligence harmed a criminal defendant. Many, if not most, courts refuse to permit a criminal defendant to bring an action for legal malpractice without first obtaining a reversal of the conviction on direct or collateral appeal. See *In re Rantz*, 109 P.3d 132 (Colo. 2005) (citing cases from numerous states on both sides of this issue). A reason often given for this result is that the defendant will not be able to satisfy the requirement of showing but-for causation. See Rest. §53, cmt. [d]. Some courts similarly conclude that the defendant has suffered no damages until he is officially exonerated by the post-conviction relief process. Up until the time of exoneration, the defendant has been treated in a way he legally deserves, and this conclusion of legal desert can be altered only by a legal finding of innocence. Implicit in the reasoning of the majority of courts seems to be a claim that if the defendant is in fact guilty, he will be convicted in a well-functioning trial process, and indeed *ought* to be convicted. It would be a kind of fortuity or windfall if a factually guilty defendant were acquitted solely through the skill of his lawyer. What this reasoning ignores, however, is the role of trial counsel in developing a record, so that the issue of guilt or innocence can be evaluated in a meaningful way. It is a bit disingenuous to look at a trial record where the defendant's lawyer was incompetent and conclude from the lack of evidence of innocence that the defendant must be guilty. Maybe there would have been evidence of innocence if the lawyer had been competent. Perhaps some of the government's witnesses could have been effectively impeached, or evidence supporting an affirmative defense could have been developed.

The *Strickland* Two-Part Test

Strickland v. Washington, 466 U.S. 668 (1984), is the principal case interpreting the Sixth Amendment's guarantee of effective assistance of counsel, and it is worth looking at in some detail. The underlying case in *Strickland* was a death-penalty prosecution for a series of murders and robberies. The lawyer made many strategic decisions—several of which can be characterized as "mistakes"—about which the client later complained. For example, the lawyer did not do much to develop mitigating evidence to be presented at the sentencing phase of trial. (Guilt was not an issue, since the client had pleaded guilty against the attorney's advice.) The lawyer called the defendant's wife and mother on the phone, but did not make any further effort to meet them in person. He also did not order a psychiatric examination of the defendant, which may have revealed clinical levels of depression that could have been used as mitigating circumstances. On the defendant's state petition for collateral relief, the Florida Supreme Court held that even if the lawyer's performance had been deficient, "there is not even the remotest chance that the outcome would have been any different." The accused then filed a petition for *habeas corpus* in U.S. District Court. That court analyzed the case similarly to the Florida Supreme Court, finding no prejudice to the defendant from any mistakes by the lawyer. The Court of Appeals, however, took a different approach, concluding that ineffectiveness does not depend on a showing of prejudice.

The Supreme Court differed from the Court of Appeals. It devised the following bifurcated analysis of ineffective assistance of counsel (IAC). A criminal defendant does not receive effective assistance of counsel, and is entitled to *habeas corpus* relief, if: (1) the lawyer's performance was outside the wide range of professionally competent assistance; and (2) but for counsel's unprofessional errors, the result of the proceeding would have been different.

Performance prong. Under *Strickland*, an IAC claim requires that the petitioner first show that the lawyer's performance fell below some benchmark of competence. The benchmark is provided by "reasonableness under prevailing professional norms." This means that the practices of other criminal defense lawyers, as well as statements by the organized bar about what lawyers ought to do, help the court determine whether a particular lawyer's performance at trial was deficient. State disciplinary rules can be evidence of prevailing professional norms, but there is not a *per se* inference from the violation of a rule to a conclusion that the lawyer fell short of the constitutionally required performance standard. Like the reasonable care standard in torts, the performance prong of *Strickland* is both objective and normative. It is objective in that it refers to what a reasonable lawyer should do, not what the lawyer in the particular case did (or was capable of doing). Like the clueless farmer in *Vaughan v. Menlove*, (1837) 132 Eng. Rep. 490 (C.P.), a lawyer may be liable for failing to do something beyond his or her ability. That means lawyers must spend the time and effort necessary to become competent to represent clients. The standard is normative in that courts do not merely survey the practices of lawyers to see what effective representation requires. The Sixth Amendment should not simply ratify the existing practices of the bar. Rather, courts are making a judgment about what lawyers *ought* to do when representing criminal defendants. See generally Russell Stetler & W. Bradley Wendel, *The ABA Guidelines and the Norms of Capital Defense Representation*, 42 Hofstra L. Rev. 635 (2013).

The Court emphasized that a wide range of tactical decisions are within the lawyer's discretion, and that courts should not be too eager to second-guess counsel's performance. What may appear to be an error in hindsight actually might have been a reasonable judgment at the time. One can imagine a case, for example, where the lawyer might have taken a calculated risk and declined to put on a particular witness, believing the witness to be vulnerable to impeachment. Lawyers should have latitude to make decisions like that, without having their judgments questioned in hindsight by defendants and the courts. "Representation is an art, and an act or omission that is unprofessional in one case may be sound or even brilliant in another." For this reason, the Court in *Strickland* said there should be a strong presumption that counsel's conduct falls within the range of reasonable professional assistance, as long as there was a "meaningful adversarial testing process" at trial.

Nevertheless, there are certain things that a competent lawyer must do. A lawyer must conduct a reasonable investigation including, in a capital case, seeking evidence that would mitigate the client's sentence. *Wiggins v. Smith*, 539 U.S. 510 (2003); *Williams v. Taylor*, 529 U.S. 362 (2000). If a reasonable lawyer would have filed a motion to suppress evidence, it would be ineffective assistance to fail to do so. *Kimmelman v. Morrison*, 477 U.S. 365 (1986). A lawyer must provide objectively reasonable advice, based on knowledge of the law and facts in the client's case, even where the decision in question is one the client has the sole authority to make (compare Rule 1.2(a)), such as pleading guilty. *Lafler v. Cooper*, 132 S. Ct. 1376 (2012) (erroneous advice regarding guilty plea in light of misunderstanding of applicable law); *Padilla v. Kentucky*, 559 U.S. 356 (2010) (failure to advise client of deportation risk). Lawyers must raise applicable defenses that make the best of the available evidence and construct a reasonable trial strategy. See John M. Burkoff & Nancy M. Burkoff, *Ineffective Assistance of Counsel*§7.2. In general, however, courts are extremely reluctant to second-guess any decision that can be characterized as strategic, at least the decision is based on adequate research. *Id.* §7.23 (reporting numerous cases involving decisions whether to call, and how to question, witnesses).

Prejudice prong. The crucial innovation of *Strickland*—if you can call it that—is the adoption of a prejudice analysis, which can deny relief to a defendant with inadequate counsel, even though the lawyer committed unprofessional errors. To prevail on an IAC claim, the petitioner also must establish that "absent the errors, the fact finder would have had a reasonable doubt." There are a few cases in which prejudice should be presumed, but only where there has been an "actual or constructive denial of the assistance of counsel altogether." Examples of a complete denial of counsel would be a lawyer burdened with an actual conflict of interest or a lawyer who is prevented from being present at a critical stage in the proceedings. *United States v. Cronic*, 466 U.S. 648, 659 (1984). (For the Sixth Amendment analysis of conflicts of interest in criminal defense cases, see Chapter 15.) On the other hand, if the defendant enjoys *some* assistance from his lawyer, he must prove that "but for counsel's unprofessional errors, the result of the proceeding would have been different."

The problem with the two-step test is that it too easily collapses into a one-step test. The majority practically invites the evisceration of the reasonableness prong by inviting courts to decide ineffectiveness cases on prejudice. As a result of the emphasis on proving prejudice, courts practically have stopped talking about the awful job done by some trial counsel, because it is easier to dispose of cases on the ground of lack of prejudice. Furthermore, the prejudice inquiry and the related harmless error rule in criminal procedure essentially strip procedural protections from factually guilty defendants. The result is what I call the "guilty as hell" rule—if the evidence at trial against the defendant is overwhelming, it will be extremely difficult to show on *habeas* that a jury would not have convicted absent the lawyer's errors. Thus, incompetence by lawyers often goes uncorrected in cases where the state's case was powerful.

Recent Elaborations on the Right to Effective Assistance of Counsel

After a long period of taking relatively few IAC cases, the Supreme Court has been fairly active in this area recently. In *Lafler v. Cooper*, 566 U.S. 156 (2012), the Court granted relief to a petitioner who had rejected a plea offer after being given shockingly stupid advice by his lawyer. The state offered a deal for a 51–85 month sentence, but the lawyer recommended rejecting it and going to trial. His reason? The state would never be able to prove intent to commit murder because the victim was shot below the waist. Run through the *Strickland* standard in your mind: Prong one, performance — check. The case came down to the prejudice prong of *Strickland*, because the petitioner did make a voluntary decision to go to trial. (Remember that under Rule 1.2(a), the client has the sole authority to decide whether to accept a plea offer.) The petitioner was convicted at trial and sentenced to a mandatory 185–360 month sentence. The Court held that the prejudice prong could be satisfied in this case by showing a reasonable probability that the outcome of the plea-bargaining process would have been different but for the lawyer's error. The Court reached a similar result in *Missouri v. Frye*, 566 U.S. 134 (2012), a case decided along with *Lafler*. The only difference is that, in *Frye*, the lawyer's error was failing to communicate the state's plea offer to the client, not giving boneheaded advice about the likelihood of conviction at trial. Another case involving deficient advice is *Padilla v. Kentucky*, 559 U.S. 356 (2010), in which the lawyer's error was failing to advise the client of the collateral consequences of a guilty plea — in this case, being deported for a drug offense. The Court majority held that a reasonable lawyer would have informed the client of the risk of deportation, to allow the client to make an informed decision whether to go to trial.

While it technically relates to an issue other than the competence of the attorneys involved (whether good cause existed to excuse procedural default), the Court's decision in *Maples v. Thomas*, 565 U.S. 266 (2012), revealed the low quality representation sometimes provided by court-appointed lawyers in capital cases. Compensation for the lawyers in the defendant's state trial court proceedings was capped at $1,000 for pretrial litigation and $40 per hour for in-court work. The defendant was represented in postconviction proceedings — alleging, among other things, ineffective assistance of counsel at trial for failure to raise obvious defenses and to prepare adequately for the penalty phase of trial — by two associates at a prestigious New York City law firm. The two associates left the firm without notifying the state court of their withdrawal and without arranging for substitute counsel. When a notice arrived at the firm informing the lawyers that the state postconviction court had denied their petition for relief, the firm's mailroom sent it back unopened, because the lawyers had left the firm. After the time for filing an appeal of the denial of the petition had passed, the federal district court held that the petitioner had procedurally defaulted on his *habeas corpus* claims, precluding their filing in federal court. The Supreme Court reasoned that, while attorney negligence, such as miscalculating a filing deadline, does not excuse what would otherwise be procedural default, the complete abandonment of a client by his attorney may be sufficient cause to avoid procedural default (citing *Holland v. Florida*, 560 U.S. 631 (2010)). Under agency law, the petitioner's attorneys abandoned him by leaving the firm without arranging for substitute counsel; thus, what would otherwise be a procedural default was excused by circumstances beyond the defendant's control.

Examples

Conflicting Duties

5. McKenna was appointed to represent Clements, who was arrested after being connected with the murder of a woman and the kidnapping of her two children. McKenna met with his client repeatedly in his jail cell and found him extremely difficult to deal with. Although he quickly confessed to murdering the woman, Clements was prone to bizarre ramblings and fantasies, so McKenna had a hard time figuring out what happened to the kids. He was worried that they might be alive, but that time would be running out to rescue them. After a great deal of prodding from McKenna, Clements drew a rough map showing the location of the children. (When asked whether they were alive or dead, Clements said only that Satan had killed the mother, but that Jesus had saved the children.) McKenna never explained to Clements that if McKenna revealed the location of the children to the police—alive or dead—the prosecutor would be able to use evidence derived from this information in the prosecution of Clements. Nevertheless, McKenna had his secretary place an anonymous phone call to the police officers investigating the case, revealing the location given by Clements. The police found the bodies of the two children.

   Clements now claims ineffective assistance of counsel due to Clements's disclosure of the location of the children. In the State of Perplexity, there is a rule on client confidentiality that exactly duplicates Rule 1.6. It provides that a lawyer may not disclose any information relating to representation of a client, except that a lawyer may reveal information to the extent the lawyer reasonably believes necessary to prevent reasonably certain death or substantial bodily harm. Was McKenna constitutionally ineffective?

The Sleeping Lawyer

6. Burnett was accused of capital murder for his role in a botched convenience store robbery. His court-appointed lawyer was Camden. At several points during the six-day jury trial, members of the jury observed Camden "dozing off" at counsel table. Camden even slept during the introduction of critical identification evidence by one of the state's witnesses. Naturally, he did not challenge the admissibility of the evidence or cross-examine the witness. The state's case against Burnett was strong. An eyewitness placed him at the scene of the robbery, and he admitted

to the police that he had taken part in the robbery but was not the person who shot the victim. (Unfortunately for Burnett, he was not aware of the felony murder rule, under which he would be legally liable for someone's death in the course of committing the robbery.) Camden filed a motion to suppress the confession, but it was denied. At trial, Burnett was convicted and lost his direct appeal. On *habeas*, he claims ineffective assistance of counsel. Should the petition be granted by the district court?

A Matter of Judgment?

7. Brandon was indicted for conspiracy to distribute cocaine and for being a prohibited person in possession of a firearm. The firearm charge was based on Brandon's previous conviction for assaulting his live-in girlfriend. It was brought pursuant to a federal statute that makes it a crime for someone convicted of a crime of domestic violence to possess a firearm. 18 U.S.C. §922(g)(9). The statute defines "crime of domestic violence" to include a violent offense against a "person similarly situated to a spouse" of the offender. 18 U.S.C. §921(a)(33)(A)(ii). Brandon's attorney advised him to plead guilty to both charges. As to the firearms charge, she told him that, although there was no controlling authority in the Thirteenth Circuit, two other federal circuit courts had stated in dicta that a live-in girlfriend was a "person similarly situated to a spouse" for the purposes of the firearms statute. The attorney believed that the plea deal offered by the prosecutor was a reasonable one, and that Brandon faced a much longer potential sentence if convicted at trial on the drug and firearms charges.

Six months after Brandon entered a guilty plea, the Thirteenth Circuit held that the firearms statute does not apply where the predicate domestic violence conviction involved a live-in girlfriend. Brandon subsequently filed a *habeas corpus* petition alleging that his attorney provided ineffective assistance of counsel by advising him to plead guilty to the firearms charge. What will the district court likely decide?

Explanations

Conflicting Duties

5. See *McClure v. Thompson*, 323 F.3d 1233 (9th Cir. 2003). The threshold question is whether a possible violation of Rule 1.6 should be the basis of an ineffectiveness claim. The Supreme Court in *Nix v. Whiteside*, 475 U.S. 157, 165 (1986), said that "breach of an ethical standard does not necessarily make out a denial of the Sixth Amendment guarantee of effective assistance of counsel." Disciplinary rules are "only guides" to what is

reasonable; they are not conclusive of the question of reasonableness. *Strickland v. Washington*, 466 U.S. 668, 688 (1984). An important point to take from this example is that simply pointing to the violation of the disciplinary rule is not enough to obtain a writ of *habeas corpus*. Rather, Clements must show that disclosure was unreasonable, as measured by prevailing professional norms.

Fortunately for Clements, this should not be hard to do. If there is any obligation that lawyers uniformly regard as central to their role, it is keeping client confidences. The professional duty of confidentiality is discussed in more detail in Chapter 9, but for now it is sufficient to observe that McKenna's call to the cops would be permissible only if either: (1) Clements gave informed consent to the disclosure; or (2) an exception to the professional duty applied. Regarding informed consent, there is nothing in the facts to suggest that Clements consented at all and, in any event, McKenna failed to explain adequately the risks to Clements associated with disclosing the location of the children. Thus, even if Clements had consented, it would not have satisfied the informed consent requirement. See Rule 1.0(e) (informed consent requires that the lawyer communicate "adequate information and explanation about the material risks of and reasonably available alternatives to the proposed course of conduct").

That leaves the exception for prevention of death or serious bodily harm. Much turns here on the *reasonableness* of McKenna's belief that the children were still alive. As discussed in Chapter 9, if a crime is entirely in the past, a lawyer has no discretion to disclose information pertaining to it under any circumstances. If Clements said, "I killed the kids and the location of their bodies is on this map," it would violate Rule 1.6 to disclose the location to the cops. Moreover, "prevailing professional norms" would roundly condemn this disclosure — no lawyers would regard it as reasonable. But Clements's bizarre ravings made it difficult for McKenna to figure out whether the kids were alive or dead. McKenna did not help himself by failing to conduct a further investigation instead of just assuming the children were alive. He did not even ask Clements directly whether he had killed the children to follow up the comment about Jesus saving them.

In the actual case, the Court of Appeals characterized this as a "close call," but deferred to the district court's findings of fact, which was that the lawyer performed an investigation to the best of his ability, given the circumstances (the need for prompt action and the difficulty in obtaining reliable information from the client). Because the appellate court must defer to the district court's findings of fact, you should not read too much into this case. If the court had reviewed the facts *de novo*, it likely may have found that the lawyer's conduct was not objectively reasonable under the circumstances.

Regardless of whether you agree or disagree with the conclusion on reasonableness, the important things to take from this example are the role of the disciplinary rules in establishing guidelines for reasonableness under *Strickland* and the fact-specific analysis of reasonableness in a case like this one.

Because the court concluded that the lawyer's conduct was reasonable, it did not reach the question of prejudice. You would need to know more facts to analyze prejudice effectively, such as whether the police had other evidence linking Clements to the murder of the children. If there was already sufficient evidence to convict Clements, it is likely that the court would conclude that McKenna's disclosure did not prejudice his client's case. On the other hand, if the police were able to connect Clements with the murder only through his lawyer's disclosure, prejudice would be established.

The Sleeping Lawyer

6. This example is based somewhat loosely on the infamous sleeping-lawyer case, *Burdine v. Johnson*, 262 F.3d 336 (5th Cir. 2001) (*en banc*). Burnett's claim is, first, that falling asleep at trial was "deficient performance" by Camden, in the sense of falling below a minimum standard followed by other criminal defense lawyers. He is probably going to prevail on that element of his ineffective assistance claim. "Prevailing norms of practice" certainly condemn sleeping during any part of trial, let alone during the introduction of eyewitness testimony. It is true that counsel must have wide latitude to make tactical decisions, but falling asleep during the state's case is not a tactic—it is an error. The difficulty for Burnett is going to be in establishing the second element, namely prejudice. The evidence against him is overwhelming. He confessed to taking part in the robbery, and once his motion to suppress the confession was denied, there was little more the state had to prove to convict him of felony murder. Even though Camden's sleeping was unprofessional error, it was not prejudicial. In the actual *Burdine* case, the Fifth Circuit *en banc* held that prejudice should be presumed where the lawyer slept through a substantial portion of the state's case. That is a reasonable prophylactic rule, because it would be difficult for the defendant to demonstrate precisely how counsel's error affected the outcome of the proceedings. Without a presumption of prejudice in this case, however, Burnett's *habeas corpus* petition should be denied.

A Matter of Judgment?

7. This case is based on *Buster v. U.S.*, 447 F.3d 1130 (8th Cir. 2006), although I made up ambiguity in the law where there wasn't any in the real case. In the actual case it was fairly well settled that the firearms statute applied

where the predicate domestic violence conviction involved a live-in girl-friend. In the hypothetical version in the example, however, there was enough ambiguity that the lawyer could characterize her advice as a reasonable strategic decision. There was a benefit to the defendant, in avoiding the possibility of a longer sentence at trial, and the lawyer could reasonably have concluded that the firearms statute would have applied, based on dicta in other circuits. The important point in this example is that the reasonableness of an attorney's decisions—whether in Sixth Amendment IAC or civil malpractice cases—must be evaluated *ex ante*, that is, at the time the decision was made. The fact that the Thirteenth Circuit subsequently came down with a decision that would have made the firearms statute inapplicable to the defendant is irrelevant to the evaluation of the reasonableness of the advice given by the lawyer. It is certainly true that Supreme Court cases like *Lafler* and *Padilla* require the lawyer to give reasonable advice, but the standard is reasonableness under the circumstances, including the state of the law at the time the lawyer gave her advice.

Confidentiality and Secrecy

INTRODUCTION: WHY LAWYERS SHOULD KEEP SECRETS

Many lawyers consider their duty to keep their clients' secrets as one of the most fundamental, even sacred, professional obligations of a lawyer. There is certainly some plausibility to the idea that keeping confidences is close to the very core of what it means to be a lawyer. Imagine what would happen if lawyers and clients had to disclose to the government or to their adversary in litigation what they discussed in private. Clients quickly would come to understand that they should be less than forthcoming with their lawyers. They would certainly not talk about anything they feared might implicate them in wrongdoing or might be embarrassing if disclosed. This would be a disaster for the professional relationship. Lawyers need full and accurate information from their clients in order to advise them. Without knowing everything the client knows, lawyers will not be able to provide helpful advice. They will also be deprived of opportunities to talk clients out of doing something wrong, which many lawyers believe is the essence of their role as client counselors.

Critics of the attorney-client privilege sometimes argue that clients should not have a right to reveal incriminating information about themselves to their lawyers and then expect the lawyers to keep it secret. Aren't lawyers just assisting wrongdoers in avoiding punishment? The following passage from the English law reformer Jeremy Bentham is a famous statement of this view:

> [I]f such confidence, when reposed, is permitted to be violated, . . . the consequence will be, that no such confidence will be reposed. Not reposed?—Well: and if it be not, wherein will consist the mischief? The man by the supposition is guilty; if not, by the supposition there is nothing to betray: let the law adviser say every thing he has heard, every thing he can have heard from his client, the client cannot have any thing to fear from it. . . . What, then will be the consequence? That a guilty person will not in general be able to derive quite so much assistance from his law adviser, in the way of concerting a false defence, as he may do at present.

It seems as though no one is harmed by disclosure of confidential information, at least not from the standpoint of the client's *legal* entitlements. A wrongdoer does not have a right to be found not guilty.

But think more carefully about the variety of clients that may turn up on the lawyer's doorstep. (For now, the discussion will be confined to potential criminal defendants, the subject of Bentham's argument.) Some of them may be flat-out guilty and may have no defense to assert. Others may have done something wrong but have a valid defense. In a well-known example from Monroe Freedman, the defendant is a woman accused of stabbing her husband to death with a kitchen knife. See Monroe H. Freedman & Abbe Smith, *Understanding Lawyers' Ethics* §6.02 (4th ed. 2010). She denies committing the crime, but the physical evidence is overwhelming. In fact, she did stab her husband, but in self-defense after he got into a drunken rage and brutalized her. In a case like this one, it is essential that the lawyer have full information. It also seems reasonable to think that the client would not be as forthcoming without assurances that the lawyer would keep the information confidential and that an opponent in litigation would not be able to compel the lawyer to testify about what the client said. Unless the defendant could trust her lawyer, she might stick with an implausible story that is flatly contradicted by all the physical evidence, thus making her conviction more likely, instead of defending the case on the true and exculpatory facts that she stabbed her attacker in self-defense.

Bentham's argument also assumes that the purpose of the adversary system is only to determine factual truth. Sometimes, however, the system ranks other values higher in importance than determining the truth of what occurred in some past event. The law of evidence is full of rules that block the introduction of probative evidence in order to further other policies. (A familiar example is the prohibition against using evidence of subsequent remedial measures to prove negligence. Federal Rules of Evidence 407.) There are also constitutional doctrines, such as the exclusionary rule and the privilege against self-incrimination, that may require the exclusion of probative evidence if there has been police misconduct. These rules exist for reasons unrelated to finding out the truth of what happened. They instead serve values such as individual privacy and autonomy, or promote ends such as making safety improvements in products by assuring a manufacturer that remedial measures will not be used against it as evidence of tortious conduct. Even if the attorney-client privilege prevents the introduction of truthful evidence in some cases, it can be justified with reference to similar values — for example, encouraging clients to trust their lawyers, protecting a sphere of privacy against government intrusion, and facilitating legal advice that will bring clients into compliance with the law.

Those considerations of trust, privacy, and permitting lawyers to give legal advice that will enable clients to comply with the law are the arguments you are likely to encounter in the debate over confidentiality in the transactional or counseling contexts. Much of the debate within the legal profession in the early 2000s in the wake of the financial accounting scandals concerned confidentiality. Suppose for the sake of argument (although it was generally more complicated than this) that a lawyer working for a publicly traded corporation learns that a manager intends to engage in a self-dealing transaction without providing appropriate disclosures. The lawyer confronts the manager, who tells the lawyer to take a hike. Now what? The traditional view, still asserted very tenaciously by practicing lawyers, is that if the lawyer has not taken affirmative steps to assist the manager's wrongdoing, the lawyer would be committing an unspeakable act of professional betrayal by disclosing the manager's intent to commit fraud. To be a bit more precise, many corporate lawyers have no problem with "reporting up" the information — that is, informing higher-level management of the problem and asking for their help in resolving it. (See Chapter 5 for more discussion of "up the ladder" reporting.)

Whatever a lawyer thinks about "reporting up," however, it is likely that she would be vehemently opposed to "reporting out," or disclosing the prospective fraud to authorities, such as the Securities and Exchange Commission (SEC). The concern is that if clients fear their lawyer will disclose something — rat them out, blow the whistle, snitch, whatever you like to call it — then clients will hold back important information and impair the lawyer's ability to provide useful advice. Notice how this argument neatly avoids the force of Bentham's objection to the privilege. The problem, as Bentham saw it, is that the attorney-client privilege protects scoundrels. But the modern argument for confidentiality is that *everyone* would be hurt by an erosion of the privilege and the duty of confidentiality, because even well-meaning clients may not be forthcoming with their lawyers without assurances of confidentiality. Remember Freedman's example of the client who was afraid to tell her lawyer that she had stabbed her husband. Legally speaking, she was not a wrongdoer, because she acted in self-defense. But she might reasonably have feared that the lawyer would rat her out to the police, so she initially refused to talk about the knife. Similarly, corporate actors dealing with complex legal regulations may worry that they will get in trouble if they reveal something to the company's lawyer. Suppose in the Enron case that the manager's proposed transaction would actually be legal if it were disclosed in a manner that the manager found acceptable. In that case, a win-win resolution would be: Manager informs lawyer, lawyer considers the situation, advises the manager on a lawful way to set up the transaction, the transaction occurs legally, and everyone is happy. That desirable end could not have been achieved if the manager had been reluctant to talk to the lawyer in the first place.

Nevertheless, criticism persists of the near-absolute duty of confidentiality championed by the organized bar and many practicing lawyers. William Simon offers one of the best known academic critiques of professional secrecy. See William H. Simon, *The Practice of Justice: A Theory of Lawyers' Ethics* 54-62 (1998). First, if the involvement of a lawyer in the client's affairs is supposed to deter wrongdoing, the lawyer may need some leverage to dissuade the client from committing illegal acts. Lawyers often talk as though sensible advice will deter the client from a course of action that may involve wrongdoing, but what if the client insists on doing what it wants? If reporting the misconduct up the corporate ladder is ineffective, the lawyer is left without any options for preventing the harm. The threat of disclosure, however, gives the lawyer a card to play. In the case of representing corporations, the lawyer can tell the manager that if he does not provide proper disclosures, the lawyer will be forced to go to the SEC. A lawyer might reply that the threat of disclosure may do some good in some cases, but this good is outweighed by the harm in other cases created by the unwillingness of clients to be candid with their lawyers. To this Simon replies that in many other settings, the law favors disclosure duties over the confidentiality of communications. Take child abuse, for instance. It may happen that doctors, day care workers, and others may be in a position to dissuade an abuser from continuing to harm a child, but the law nevertheless imposes a duty on many professionals to report well-founded suspicions of child abuse.

Simon's second argument is that the fear of diminished candor by clients is unfounded. For one thing, even the most stringent version of the duty of confidentiality is already shot full of holes, permitting disclosure of information to prevent certain kinds of harm and even where the lawyer believes disclosure would be necessary to protect herself from allegations of wrongdoing. Rule 1.6(b)(1), (b)(5) (discussed more fully in Chapter 9). The attorney-client privilege, which protects clients against *compelled* disclosure of confidential information, has even more exceptions, including the crime-fraud exception, requiring revelation of communications where the client's intent was to engage the lawyer's services for the purpose of committing a crime or fraud. (See Chapter 8 for more on these exceptions.) Given all the gaps in the supposedly seamless web of confidentiality duties, it is hard to see how a client would have a firm expectation that the lawyer will not disclose anything she learns from the client. And, in fact, clients tend to believe that lawyers have greater discretion to disclose information than they actually do. Certain categories of clients, particularly criminal defendants, already mistrust their lawyers, no matter what the rules on confidentiality provide.

As with many controversial issues you cover in law school classes, your instructor is probably not trying to convert you to one viewpoint or another. The important thing is to be aware of these policy arguments and to see how they play out in shaping the obligations of lawyers. These controversies are by no means a thing of the past. After the Enron and other financial accounting scandals, in addition to dealing with the requirements imposed by Sarbanes-Oxley, large corporations became concerned over the practice by prosecutors of routinely demanding waivers of the attorney-client privilege, as a condition of deeming the corporation to have cooperated with the government in the investigation. Thus, it would probably be a good idea to think through your position on confidentiality, as well as understanding the doctrine covered in Chapters 8 and 9.

VOLUNTARY AND INVOLUNTARY DISCLOSURE

A critical distinction to keep in mind here is between the professional duty of confidentiality and the attorney-client privilege. Lawyers often confuse the two, sometimes with disastrous results. The professional duty of confidentiality is essentially the same duty that applies to any agent acting for a principal — the Model Rules simply state it more specifically for lawyers. The lawyer's duty runs to the client, and the lawyer's failure to keep her client's secrets may be the basis for an action for breach of fiduciary duty. In addition to being part of the common law of agency, the duty of confidentiality is restated in the professional disciplinary rules. The basic duty is set out in Rule 1.6(a), followed by exceptions to the duty in Rule 1.6(b). Lawyers can be disciplined for disclosing client confidences, in addition to being sued by the aggrieved client for breach of fiduciary duty. Significantly, however, the professional duty of confidentiality cannot be asserted to block production of information or documents obtained from the client. A court can order an attorney to testify about matters that she would be forbidden to disclose by the professional duty of confidentiality. Confidentiality is a duty that runs to the client, but is not something that can be used to resist official demands for information in litigation or a government investigation.

The attorney-client privilege, on the other hand, is a creature of evidence law. It can be asserted in opposition to an official demand for information, such as a subpoena, a deposition question, or an interrogatory. In other words, it protects against compelled disclosure. Along with this enhanced protection comes a limitation—the privilege is narrower than the scope of the professional duty. *A court may order disclosure of information that would be a violation of a disciplinary rule for a lawyer to disclose voluntarily.* In brief, the privilege covers communications between the client and the lawyer, made in confidence, for the purpose of obtaining legal assistance. (These elements will be discussed in quite a bit more detail in Chapter 8.) If some information in the possession of the lawyer or the client satisfies all these elements, *and* there is no applicable exception, *and* the privilege has not been waived, *then and only then* may the lawyer object to disclosing that information on the grounds of the attorney-client privilege.

Beware of some confusing terminology. The Model Code recognized a distinction between *confidences* (matters protected by the attorney-client privilege) and *secrets* (information subject to the professional duty of confidentiality). DR 4-101(A). It is easy to get tangled up in semantic knots here, because the duty of confidentiality pertains to secrets, and the privilege pertains to confidences. The best course of action is to avoid Model Code terminology in your thinking about these issues, but to be prepared to encounter it when you read cases. The Model Rules drop that distinction and refer instead to "information relating to representation of a client." Rule 1.6(a). A few jurisdictions, including the District of Columbia, Georgia, Michigan, and New York, retain Code language in the definition of protected information. The Restatement describes "confidential client information" protected by the professional duty and the attorney-client privilege. Rest. §§60, 68. One casebook employs the term "ethically protected information" to describe information covered by the professional duty, and you sometimes will encounter the term "ethical duty" to refer to the duty of confidentiality. See Stephen Gillers, *Regulation of Lawyers* 28 (7th ed. 2005). The MPRE uses the term "professional rule of confidentiality." To simplify, I will use the terms "professional duty of confidentiality" or "the professional duty," on the one hand, and "attorney-client privilege" or "privilege," on the other.

One more set of rules may create confusion when it comes to secrecy and confidentiality. The work product doctrine, which protects documents prepared by a lawyer in anticipation of litigation, may be invoked in some situations in which a communication also may be covered by the privilege or protected the professional duty. You may or may not study the work product doctrine in a professional responsibility course, but you may remember it from civil procedure. Feel free to skip the detailed discussion of work product if you do not talk about it in class, but you at least should be familiar enough with it to distinguish work-product situations from cases in which the information is covered by the evidentiary privilege or the duty of confidentiality. And also, please, for goodness' sake, do not write that the privilege covers only communications between lawyer and client made in anticipation of litigation. That is a common mistake, involving the importation of one element of the work product doctrine into the attorney-client privilege analysis.

In addition to being somewhat confusing to apply, privilege and confidentiality doctrines are also enormously controversial. Whenever the ABA goes about tinkering with the disciplinary rules, one result is sure to be a kerfuffle over confidentiality. The Kutak Commission that prepared the Model Rules endured an acrimonious debate over the scope of a lawyer's permission to disclose confidential client information if disclosure would be necessary to prevent a client's future crime or fraud. The ABA House of Delegates ended up adopting Model Rule 1.6, a stringent confidentiality rule with very limited exceptions. The Ethics 2000 Commission reconsidered the exceptions to Model Rule 1.6, only to be overruled again in the House of Delegates by lawyers who wished to retain the strict obligation of silence. Then the Enron debacle caused some members of the House of Delegates to rethink their opposition to the proposed exceptions, which would permit disclosure to prevent a client's financial crime or civil fraud, and the ABA *again* amended Model Rule 1.6, this time to add the new exceptions.

As a result of this whirlwind of controversy and amendments, you must be extremely careful to read the most current version of the rule, particularly if you are looking at some old cases that may have been decided under an older version. Numerous state bar associations have had similar debates, and many have adopted versions of Model Rule 1.6 that differ significantly from the ABA's model version. In fact, there is probably more variation in state confidentiality rules than in any other aspect of the law governing lawyers. Thus, when approaching a confidentiality question on an exam, make sure you are clear on which law you are applying — in particular, see whether you are supposed to apply the ABA rule or your state's version, and pay close attention to the specific exceptions in that rule.

Before considering these doctrines in depth, an overview of the relationship between them may be helpful. Keeping these rules straight is important, and that is not hard if you focus on the elements and the distinctions among the rules.

Examples

Getting the Picture

1. The following Venn diagram graphically represents the relationship among the attorney-client privilege ("ACP" on the diagram), the work product doctrine ("WPD"), and the professional duty of confidentiality ("PDC"). The "zones" on the diagram are labeled — for example, Zone #1 is within the privilege but not the work product doctrine, while

Zone #2 is covered by both. Zone #3 is covered by the work product doctrine but not the privilege. Zone #4 is outside both the work product doctrine and the attorney-client privilege. Zones #1 through #4 are all covered by the duty of confidentiality, but Zone #5 is outside the scope of the professional duty.

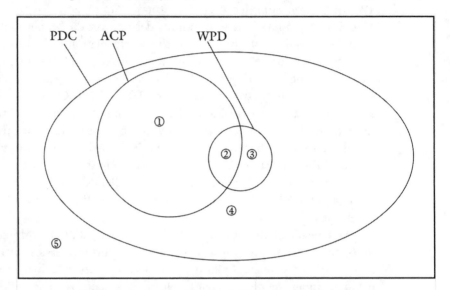

ACP = attorney-client privilege
PDC = professional duty of confidentiality
WPD = work product doctrine

Consider the diagram and decide into which zone the following information falls. Use the thumbnail summary of the relationship among these doctrines in the chart above. Some of the situations present more complex issues that are addressed in successive chapters. For now, make an educated guess about how courts would handle these issues, based on the overview of the confidentiality and privilege doctrines.

A. Interview memoranda summarizing interviews with third-party fact witnesses, who observed an accident involving your client. The interviews occurred after a lawsuit was filed against your client.

B. Your recollection of the stories told by third-party fact witnesses, who observed an accident involving your client. The interviews occurred after a lawsuit was filed against your client.

C. Your recollection of a client's discussion with you of the business opportunities presented by a proposed merger with a competitor.

D. A memo summarizing your thoughts about how to conduct discovery in a case, which witnesses should be deposed, and the affirmative defenses you should assert.

E. A memo summarizing a discussion with your client, held in your office behind closed doors, about whether or not to depose a particular witness.

F. Information about your client's demeanor—for example, whether he appeared nervous when talking to you—sought by a prosecutor to establish that your client intended to flee the jurisdiction at the time he spoke with you.

G. Information pertaining to the guilt or innocence of a potential client who did not choose to retain you as counsel and who confessed his role in an armed robbery the previous day.

H. Your client's intention to file for divorce from his wife. You represent the client only on business matters and will not be handling the divorce proceedings. Assume your client is a public figure, and the impending divorce has been reported accurately in a local newspaper.

I. Your client's statement that it intends to make a tender offer for X Corporation, made in connection with a discussion of whether it is necessary to disclose this information in a filing with the SEC. You would like to buy stock in X Corporation before the tender offer is announced, so that you can cash in when the stock price goes up.

What Is Wrong with This Argument?

2. The following passage appeared in a prominent national magazine for lawyers:

> In the early 1980s the ABA was in the final stages of formulating its Model Rules of Professional Conduct. One of the hottest debates centered on exceptions to the attorney-client privilege. Most states, and the ABA's old code, permitted disclosure of confidences to prevent an economic crime or substantial economic harm to a third party. . . . But after much talk about turning corporate lawyers into client police, the ABA House of Delegates scaled back exceptions to the privilege. The model rules that were adopted in 1983 permitted the disclosure of client confidences only to allow lawyers to defend themselves or to prevent criminal acts likely to result in imminent death or substantial physical harm.
>
> Since then the ABA has held firm on attorney-client privilege, most recently refusing to expand exceptions to the privilege in August 2001.

What fundamental mistake does the author make? Why might it be important to be more precise?

"Let Me Get Back to You on That, Your Honor"

3. A criminal defense lawyer is representing a client on drug charges. She received a call from her client's mother the night before a scheduled court date. The defendant's mother told the defense lawyer that her son

would likely not make it to court the next day, as he just left the house "high as a kite." Drug use would violate a term of the defendant's pretrial release. When the defendant is absent from court the next day, the judge asks defense counsel, "Do you have any information about why your client is absent from court?"

How should the lawyer respond?

A. The lawyer should describe the mother's phone call.
B. The lawyer should ask the judge to excuse her from answering in light of the attorney-client privilege.
C. The lawyer should ask the judge to excuse her from answering in light of her confidentiality obligation.
D. The lawyer should say, "I have no idea where my client is."

Explanations

Getting the Picture

1. A. Zone #3. It is not covered by the privilege because it is not a communication from a client to an attorney, but it is within the protection of the work product doctrine because it is a document prepared in anticipation of litigation. The filing of the lawsuit makes the lawyer's anticipation of litigation reasonable. Watch out for problems where the possibility of litigation is more speculative. There may not be work product protection for documents prepared in the ordinary course of business where litigation is not imminent.

   B. Zone #3 or #4. On one view, represented by the Federal Rules of Civil Procedure, your recollection is not protected by the work product doctrine because it is not embodied in a document or other tangible form, such as a computer file. See Fed. R. Civ. P. 26(b)(3)(A). The Restatement takes a broader view, however, and extends work product protection to "unwritten or oral form" of what would otherwise be attorney work product if it were written down and embodied in a document or tangible thing. See Restatement §87 & cmt. f. The Restatement picks up on the common law of work product, beginning with the Supreme Court's decision in *Hickman v. Taylor*, 329 U.S. 495 (1947). (See further discussion in Chapter 8.) Requiring an attorney to report on an oral statement made to the attorney by a witness tends to reveal the mental processes of the lawyer and would therefore be protected as common law *Hickman* work product, notwithstanding the recollection not being embodied in a document. Thus, in my view the best answer is Zone #3, but this may be a bit inside-baseball for a professional responsibility course. In any event, your recollection of accounts given by third-party witnesses is not covered by the attorney-client privilege because it is not a communication from the client to the lawyer.

C. Zone #4. This conversation, though a communication from a lawyer to a client, is probably not covered by the attorney-client privilege because it is not a communication for the purpose of obtaining legal advice. Rather, the client simply was discussing a business opportunity. Some courts apply the privilege to mixed legal/business advice where the lawyer is an employee of a corporate client and essentially "wears two hats" as a legal and business advisor. Other courts take a strict approach and apply the privilege only to "pure" legal advice.

D. Zone #3. This is a classic example of "opinion" work product, and would not be discoverable even on a showing of substantial need and undue hardship. If the work product doctrine protects anything at all, it is the lawyer's subjective mental impressions, theories of the case, strategies, etc. The problem was written to suggest that no lawyer-client communications are recorded in the memo, so it would not be covered by the privilege, and would not be in Zone #2. If the facts were slightly different, however, and the memo included a summary of a conversation the lawyer had with the client concerning witnesses to depose, etc., then it would be in Zone #2. (In other words, more like problem E, below.)

E. Zone #2. Not only is the memo work product, but the record of the communications with the client, which were made in confidence for the purpose of obtaining legal advice, are covered by the attorney-client privilege.

F. Zone #4. The information falls outside the attorney-client privilege because it is not a "communication" from the client to the lawyer. The client simply *was* acting a certain way; he was not trying to communicate a message. It is still within the scope of the duty of confidentiality, however, because it is information relating to the representation. A difficult variation on this problem concerns the *identity* of a client. Sometimes revelation of the client's identity will be tantamount to revealing a confidential communication—that is, the purpose for which the client sought legal advice. In some cases, this information would be privileged. See, for example, *Baird v. Koerner*, 279 F.2d 623 (9th Cir. 1960), in which the court held that the client's identity was privileged when the client used the lawyer to make a payment of back taxes to the IRS, while shielding the client's identity. *Baird* has been limited practically to its facts, even in the Ninth Circuit, so you should assume that except in a very unusual case, the client's identity is not covered by the privilege.

G. Zone #1. This communication is covered by the privilege, even though a formal attorney-client relationship did not result, as long as the would-be client disclosed confidential information to you with the expectation that you would keep it confidential, and the disclosure was for the purpose of potentially obtaining legal assistance. The information is not in Zone #2 because it was not embodied in any document or other tangible form.

H. Either Zone #4 or Zone #5. The information may be protected by the duty of confidentiality but is not covered by the attorney-client privilege because the communication was not made for the purpose of securing legal advice. (The example asks you to assume that you are not a matrimonial lawyer and represent the client only on business matters; it is likely that the client shared the information with you simply as a social friend.) Whether the duty of confidentiality applies depends on how it is interpreted in your jurisdiction. The version of the duty stated by Model Rule 1.6 applies to all "information related to representation" of the client. One could argue that the information about the divorce is not related to the ongoing representation of the client on business matters. This argument parallels the interpretation of the privilege just given — that the information is not privileged because it was not communicated to the lawyer for the purpose of obtaining legal advice. Courts tend to interpret the agency-law duty of confidentiality more broadly, however, and the comments to the Restatement indicate that it would be covered. "In the course of representation, a lawyer may learn confidential information about the client that is not necessary for the representation but which is of a personal or proprietary nature or other character such that the client evidently would not wish it disclosed. Such information is confidential under this Section." Rest. §59, cmt. b. On this element of the analysis, the information falls into Zone #4.

The other issue here is whether the duty of confidentiality still applies even if the information is publicly available. Some courts hold that the duty applies even where there are other sources of the information. See, for example, In re Anonymous, 654 N.E.2d 1128 (Ind. 1995). The language of Model Rule 1.6 does not provide an exception for information that is generally known, although the rule on adverse use and disclosure of information relating to a former client does permit adverse use and disclosure of information that has become generally known. Rule 1.9(c). It makes sense to interpret Model Rule 1.6 and Model Rule 1.9(c) in a parallel fashion, so that the duty does not extend to generally known information. See R&D §1.61(b). The Restatement avoids these interpretive difficulties by expressly limiting the professional duty by defining "confidential client information" as information relating to the representation, "other than information that is generally known." Rest. §59. I tend to agree that the best interpretation of Model Rule 1.6 is in line with Restatement §59—that is, the duty does not apply to information that is publicly available. This is an argument that the information falls in Zone #5. Again, a careful lawyer would avoid disclosing it even though she may not have an obligation under Model Rule 1.6 to keep it confidential.

I. Depending on subsequent events, either Zone #1 or Zone #4. This sounds like information covered by the attorney-client privilege because it is a communication for the purpose of seeking legal advice. Indeed, if an adversary in litigation subsequently tries to discover what was said between you and the client concerning the tender offer, the communication would be protected by the privilege. If there is no request for information or advice, however, it is covered by the duty of confidentiality only. Note that the duty also covers *use* of confidential client information gained in the course of representation to the disadvantage of the client. Rule 1.8(b).

What Is Wrong with This Argument?

2. See Alison Frankel, *No Confidence*, American Lawyer (Dec. 2002), at 78, 80. The problem with this passage is that the debate on confidentiality in the ABA has *nothing* to do with the attorney-client privilege. The privilege is a creature of evidence law—solely a matter of the common law and rules of evidence of a particular jurisdiction. The ABA has no more power to alter the evidentiary attorney-client privilege than it does the hearsay rule. What the ABA is talking about is the professional duty of confidentiality, which is enforceable by state bar disciplinary authorities. The debate surrounding the drafting of the 1983 and Ethics 2000 versions of the Model Rules centered on the duty of confidentiality. Exceptions to the privilege, like the crime-fraud exception, and various waiver doctrines, are beyond the authority of the ABA or state disciplinary agencies.

There are a couple of reasons why it is important to keep this distinction straight. First of all, there is plenty of information that is not protected by the privilege that is subject to the duty of confidentiality. The article from which this excerpt is taken concerns corporate lawyers who learn that their clients are engaged in illegal activities. These lawyers may learn that information in nonprivileged settings—that is, through independent investigation rather than in communications with their clients; through communications that were not for the purpose of obtaining legal assistance; or in nonconfidential communications, such as conversations in which a stranger to the attorney-client relationship is present. In those cases, the lawyer would need to think through exceptions to the duty, not the privilege. Another reason to keep this distinction straight is that if a court attempts to compel revelation of information, an attorney may object only on the basis of the privilege. A lawyer may not assert professional duty as a ground for refusing to comply with a court order to produce information.

	Attorney-Client Privilege	Professional Duty of Confidentiality	Work Product Doctrine
Source	Law of evidence	Law of agency; state attorney-disciplinary rules	Common law; now codified in Federal Rules of Civil Procedure
Scope	Communications made in confidence from client to lawyer, for the purpose of obtaining legal assistance.	Information "relating to representation of a client," Rule 1.6(a).	Documents and other tangible things prepared by a party or lawyer in anticipation of litigation.
Duration	Forever: Survives termination of attorney-client relationship and death of client. *Swidler & Berlin v. U.S.*, 524 U.S. 399 (1998).	Forever: Survives termination of attorney-client relationship and death of client. Rule 1.6, cmt. [18].	Varies: Narrowest view is protection ends with litigation; broader view is that it extends to *related* litigation; broadest view includes all subsequent litigation.
Who Controls?	Client can assert or waive directly; lawyer can assert or waive as agent of the client, within scope of authority.	Client: There is a duty to keep information secret unless client consents to disclosure.	Varies: Some courts say client and lawyer can assert or waive; some courts permit lawyer to assert over client objection.
Effect	Can be asserted in opposition to an official demand for information, such as a subpoena or deposition question, or to deny admission of evidence at trial. Underlying facts not privileged.	Forbids voluntary disclosure; may not be interposed in response to an official demand for information. Does not bar admission of evidence at trial. Underlying facts are protected. Also, *use* of confidential client information to the disadvantage of the client is prohibited by Rule 1.8(b).	Can be asserted in opposition to a subpoena or discovery request. Underlying facts not protected. Protection of "ordinary" work product may be overridden by showing of substantial need and inability to obtain information elsewhere.

	Attorney-Client Privilege	**Professional Duty of Confidentiality**	**Work Product Doctrine**
Remedy for Breach	Carelessness with privileged communication may lead to waiver; client then would have malpractice action against lawyer.	Lawyer may be subject to professional discipline or lawsuit by client for breach of fiduciary duty.	Failure to assert in opposition to discovery request operates as waiver; client may be able to sue lawyer for malpractice if waiver was negligent.

"Let Me Get Back to You on That, Your Honor"

3. This was one last test of your ability to spot the distinction between the attorney-client privilege and the duty of confidentiality. We'll get deeper into the weeds of these two doctrines in the next chapter, but it is really, really, really important to keep the more general idea in mind: The attorney-client privilege deals with *compelled* disclosure of confidential communications (by official process like a subpoena or questions at trial or in a deposition) and the duty of confidentiality has to do with *voluntary* disclosure of confidential information.

   The trick here is to see that the lawyer has the option of respectfully declining to answer the judge's question. Disclosure of the communication is not really compelled. If the judge said, "Counsel, I am ordering you to tell me whether you know about your client's whereabouts," then the communication would not be protected by the attorney-client privilege. Why not? Because it was with the client's mother, not the client. Thus, (B) can't be the right answer.

   However, (A) is not the right answer because the lawyer still has a duty of confidentiality with respect to the *information* (Rule 1.6(a), and note the distinction between information and *communication*) conveyed by the client's mother. Unless there is an exception permitting disclosure, telling the judge that the client was "high as a kite" would violate the lawyer's duty of confidentiality. We'll talk more about exceptions to the duty of confidentiality in Chapter 9, but for now it is important to note that (1) the exceptions are limited, and (2) the exceptions generally permit, but do not require disclosure. In the variation above, where the judge orders the lawyer to answer the question (most judges wouldn't do that, by the way), then Rule 1.6(b)(6) would permit disclosure notwithstanding the general duty of confidentiality.

   What about (D)? It may be tempting to say this to avoid annoying the judge by declining to answer. The trouble is, it's a false statement. Chapter 10 will take up the issue of false statements made by lawyers

and witnesses, but for now suffice it to observe that Rule 3.3(a)(1) prohibits knowingly making a false statement of fact to a tribunal. "I have
no idea" is false—the lawyer does know, but doesn't want to reveal the
information to the judge.

Thus, the correct answer is (C).

Thanks to Bruce Green for allowing me to use this problem, which
is based on San Diego County Bar Ass'n Op. 2011-1. The opinion concluded: "Attorney's only ethical option is to inform the court respectfully that due to applicable ethical rules she is not at liberty to answer
the question."

CHAPTER 8

Attorney-Client Privilege and Work Product Doctrine

ELEMENTS OF THE ATTORNEY-CLIENT PRIVILEGE

The attorney-client privilege protects information communicated by the client to a lawyer (and, in many jurisdictions, from the lawyer to the client) for the purpose of seeking legal advice. The privilege lasts forever. The Supreme Court has held that as a matter of federal evidence law, if a communication is privileged, the attorney-client privilege survives the death of the client despite a compelling need for the information and even in the context of a criminal investigation. *Swidler & Berlin v. United States*, 524 U.S. 399 (1998). Some states have a different rule and may permit disclosure where the "interests of justice" demand it. Other states recognize a limited "testator's intent" exception where the communication of the decedent would help resolve a dispute among heirs. Pay close attention to your jurisdiction's law.

The classic definition of the privilege sets out eight elements: (1) Where legal advice of any kind is sought (2) from a professional legal advisor in his capacity as such, (3) the communications relating to that purpose, (4) made in confidence (5) by the client, (6) are at his instance permanently protected (7) from disclosure by himself or the legal advisor, (8) except that the protection be waived. 8 Wigmore on Evidence §2292.[1] The elements

---

1. For a recent federal court opinion using the Wigmore factors to analyze the attorney-client privilege, see *United States v. Ruehle*, 583 F.3d 600 (9th Cir. 2009).

from the Restatement are fewer in number, but cover basically the same ground. The attorney-client privilege may be invoked with respect to:

> (1) a communication; (2) made between privileged persons; (3) in confidence; (4) for the purpose of obtaining or providing legal assistance for the client.

Rest. §68.

You should get in the habit of running through each of the elements of the privilege whenever you encounter a lawyer-client communication. Many, many cases turn on whether all of the elements are satisfied. Analyzing element by element will keep you from missing something important. With that in mind, some of the complications that may arise under each of the Restatement elements are below.

Communication

The significance of this element lies in what is not covered by the privilege. Information obtained by the lawyer through observation or investigation is not protected by the attorney-client privilege, because it was not communicated by the client to the lawyer. The identity of a client, the client's appearance, or information such as the kind of car the client was driving is not privileged. The attorney can be compelled to authenticate a photograph of the client or a handwriting sample, for example. See, for example, *In re Grand Jury Proceedings*, 791 F.2d 663, 665 (8th Cir. 1986). Similarly, information learned from nonclient witnesses is not covered by the attorney-client privilege because it did not come in a communication from the client. You may see a question on an exam involving a lawyer doing some investigation as part of the representation of a client and learning facts from persons other than the client. Although any documents containing information learned from those persons may be protected under the work product doctrine (if the documents were prepared in anticipation of litigation), the information they contain is not covered by the attorney-client privilege because it is not a communication from a client to a lawyer.

The traditional attorney-client privilege doctrine covers only communications from the client to the lawyer, not from the lawyer to the client. There is an exception for communications from the lawyer to the client that reveal the content of communications from the client to the lawyer, such as a letter that begins, "You asked me X, and my answer is. . . ." These communications are covered by the privilege, even under the traditional rule. This narrow approach is still followed in some jurisdictions, but the majority rule is that communications are protected in both directions, from the client to the lawyer and from the lawyer to the client.

Privileged Persons

Privileged persons include the lawyer and the client, as well as agents of either the client or the lawyer who facilitate communication between the two, such as interpreters or translators, and agents of the lawyer who facilitate the representation, such as investigators and paralegals. Rest. §71. Privileged persons also can include retained experts, such as accountants or economists, who are retained by the lawyer for the purpose of facilitating the lawyer's provision of legal services to the client. See, for example, In re Grand Jury Subpoena, 2003 U.S. Dist. LEXIS 9022 (S.D.N.Y. June 2, 2003) (communications between target of criminal investigation and public relations firm privileged where public relations firm was hired to create a climate in which it would be more difficult for the U.S. Attorney to indict the target person). On exams, watch out for the presence of persons who are not necessary to the representation or the communication between the lawyer and the client.

It is important that the client consult with the lawyer in her *professional capacity* in order for the communication to be covered by the attorney-client privilege. The question of one's professional capacity can arise where a lawyer also wears another hat, so to speak. For example, the lawyer may be a member of the board of directors of a client corporation. If another director consults the lawyer about a question of business strategy, she is not dealing with the lawyer in her professional capacity; she is dealing with the lawyer as a business advisor, not a legal advisor. Similarly, where a person consults a family friend who is also a lawyer, seeking mixed legal and personal advice, the communication may or may not be privileged, depending on whether the person was dealing with the lawyer in a professional capacity. Resolution of that question will depend on the circumstances of the consultation, including the subjective belief of the person seeking advice, the nature of the advice sought, and the expectations of confidentiality surrounding the communication.

In some cases, communications from *prospective* clients, learned in an initial interview with the attorney, may be protected by the attorney-client privilege. As a general rule, if a prospective client believes she is consulting a lawyer in a professional capacity, and it is reasonable under the circumstances to believe that the lawyer is acting to protect the prospective client's interests—for example, by agreeing to keep the communication confidential—the lawyer will have an obligation not to disclose information learned from the client, Rule 1.18(b), and in addition the communication will be covered by the attorney-client privilege.[2]

---

2. For the privilege, see I Edna Selan Epstein, *The Attorney-Client Privilege and Work-Product Doctrine* 140 (5th ed. 2007) ("What is said in the context of preliminary communications with an eye toward possible representation is generally privileged.").

In Confidence

The communication must be made between the client and the lawyer in private, with no persons present who are not "privileged persons" as discussed above. For example, if a client representative is discussing a product liability issue with a lawyer and a consultant who is working on the design of packaging for the product, the communication will not be privileged because of the presence of the consultant, who is not necessary to assist the lawyer in providing legal services. As mentioned in connection with the "privileged persons" element, be alert for unprivileged third parties, such as a neighbor or friend of the client who attends a meeting with the lawyer to provide comfort and support for the client. (Spouses are covered by a separate marital communication privilege.) If the third party is not a necessary agent to facilitate the lawyer's provision of legal services to the client, his or her presence will destroy the privilege. More dramatically, where the target of a criminal investigation speaks with his lawyer while the cops are searching his house, the communication is not privileged because the client knew of the presence of the third parties. *United States v. Gann*, 732 F.2d 714 (9th Cir. 1984).

The "in confidence" element was not satisfied in a case, involving an internal investigation of misconduct by a corporation and its officers, in which the corporation's management had decided to disclose the results of the investigation to the corporation's auditors and the SEC. *United States v. Ruehle*, 583 F.3d 600 (9th Cir. 2009). The corporation's chief financial officer was unable to assert the privilege with respect to his communications with the corporation's lawyers, because he and other senior management understood that nothing the lawyers learned would be withheld from the government and the auditors.

It is important that the communication *remain* confidential and not be disclosed by either the attorney or the client. An attorney must exercise reasonable care to ensure that confidential information is not disclosed. Carelessness by either the lawyer or the client may operate as a waiver of the privilege. (See the discussion of waiver by inadvertent disclosure, later in this chapter.) If a client deliberately blabs the same information to people other than her lawyer, a court will likely infer that the client did not intend the communication with the lawyer to be confidential.

Purpose

The communication must be made for the purpose of obtaining legal advice—not business advice, public-relations strategies, or friendly counseling. If two friends, one of whom is a lawyer, are talking with each other at a party, the purpose of the communication may be to seek legal advice, but it may be just social chit-chat. Cautious lawyers sometimes preface their comments with little disclaimers, like "Not speaking as your lawyer . . ." to make sure the other party to the conversation knows that the communications are not privileged. A conversation at a party also may fail to qualify for the attorney-client privilege because it was not "made in confidence." Be alert to facts such as the party being very crowded, and the lawyer and the client not making any special effort to talk privately. Another common scenario, discussed above, involves a lawyer, perhaps employed as an in-house counsel, who gives some mixture of legal, strategic, economic, or political advice to a business. The client may consult the lawyer, seeking business advice or legal advice; only communications for the purpose of obtaining legal advice are covered by the attorney-client privilege. Some courts will protect a communication as long as there is a "legal component" to the advice. See, for example, U.S. Postal Service v. Phelps Dodge Refining Corp., 852 F. Supp. 156 (E.D.N.Y. 1994). Others are stricter with the privilege and essentially require that the communication be related to "pure" legal advice. See, for example, Hardy v. New York News, Inc., 114 F.R.D. 633 (S.D.N.Y. 1987).

FACTS NOT PROTECTED

Remember Bentham's argument that the attorney-client privilege is only useful for guilty clients? A similar argument is often made concerning the effect of the privilege on the discovery process and the search for truth. For example, here is a dissenting justice on the Texas Supreme Court objecting to protecting communications between employees and lawyers representing a company after an explosion at a chemical plant: "While a widow plans a funeral, the corporation in whose facility her husband was killed conducts an investigation. . . . As the family buries the victim, the corporation can bury any inconvenient facts it has learned." National Tank Co. v. Brotherton, 851 S.W.2d 193, 207 (Tex. 1993) (Doggett, J., dissenting). Powerful stuff, if accurate. Significantly, however, the privilege does not block disclosure of underlying facts known by the privilege holder. In the ensuing litigation over fault for the chemical plant explosion, if the family's lawyers ask questions of the operations manager to establish sloppiness with regard to safety procedures, the manager must answer truthfully, *even if he has talked to the company's lawyer about those facts.* See Rest. §69, cmt. d. As the Supreme Court said in Upjohn v. United States, 449 U.S. 383 (1981):

> The privilege only protects disclosure of communications; it does not protect disclosure of the underlying facts by those who communicated with the attorney. . . . A fact is one thing and a communication concerning that fact is an

entirely different thing. The client cannot be compelled to answer the question, "What did you say or write to the attorney?" but may not refuse to disclose any relevant fact within his knowledge merely because he incorporated a statement of such fact into his communication to his attorney.

Thus, adversaries in litigation can seek discovery information contained in attorney-client communications through interrogatories or depositions, and the client may not refuse to answer these questions on the basis of the attorney-client privilege.

Examples

It's Element-ary

In the following situations, are the communications covered by the attorney-client privilege?

1. A memo from the chief financial officer of a telecommunications company to in-house counsel, with a copy to an outside accounting firm, discussing plans for acquisition of a competing company and requesting advice about the possible application of antitrust laws.

2. A phone call in the middle of the night from a distraught man to a family friend, who is a lawyer, revealing that he had killed someone and would like to get straight with God and "do whatever else is necessary to make things right." The man agrees with the friend/lawyer that he should sit tight and wait for the police, and that efforts will be made to locate a local rabbi for spiritual counseling.

3. Reports of scientific studies of the addictive effects of tobacco, carried out by an independent research firm at the direction of a cigarette manufacturer, carbon-copied to a law firm engaged in defending the manufacturer against product liability lawsuits.

4. An observation made by the lawyer's investigator, after the client informed the lawyer that he had dumped toxic waste on his land in violation of environmental regulations. Assume the statutes have a civil remedy for violation, but not criminal penalties. Think about the problem in terms of whether a request for information is directed to the client or the lawyer's investigator.

5. A prospective client arrives in an attorney's office one day and asks if she will represent him. The lawyer says, "Sure," whereupon the client reaches into his coat, pulls out a pistol, and plunks it down on the lawyer's desk. "What do I do about that?" he asks. Recovering her composure, the lawyer asks the client what he is doing with the gun. "Well, there's been an armed robbery and a shooting, and maybe somebody will think I have

something to do with it . . . but I don't—I was home watching *American Idol* at the time!" What must the attorney do with the gun?

Explanations

It's Element-ary

1. Here, the element that may not be satisfied is that the communication be made "in confidence" and only among privileged persons. Does the copy to the outside accounting firm destroy the privilege? The presence of agents working under the direct supervision of an attorney, such as associates, paralegals, secretaries, and investigators, does not destroy the privilege. The same rule applies to outside experts retained by the lawyer for the purpose of assisting the lawyer in providing legal advice. If the accounting firm in this example had been hired by the lawyer and directed to provide an analysis of the acquisition to enable the lawyer to evaluate the antitrust implications of the transaction, the copy of the memo to the accounting firm would not destroy the privilege. See, for example, the leading case of *United States v. Kovel*, 296 F.2d 918 (2d Cir. 1961). If the accounting firm had been retained by the client for the purpose of providing general auditing and accounting services, however, sharing the memo with the accounting firm might cause the privilege to be lost because the communication is no longer "in confidence." The analysis turns on whether the accounting firm is assisting the lawyer in providing legal services to the client. One factor that might help answer this question is whether the accountants were hired by the lawyer or the client, but that factor is not dispositive. If you encounter a problem like this one, pay careful attention to all facts that bear on the *purpose* for which the outside expert was retained.

   Another question that sometimes comes up concerning in-house counsel is whether the lawyer is giving strategic or business advice, rather than legal advice. Although an in-house lawyer—that is, one employed by the business itself, rather than an outside law firm—is covered by the privilege just like any other lawyer, there is a danger that the client—here, other agents of the corporation—will communicate on nonlegal matters and therefore destroy the privilege. In this example, the communication pertained to antitrust barriers to the acquisition of another company, which is within the purview of legal advice, so the privilege is not lost on that basis. Be alert, though, to a problem involving mixed business/legal advice, which might show that the lawyer is not being consulted in her professional capacity. If it is possible to characterize the communication as pertaining primarily to business matters, the privilege may be lost.

2. This example turns on whether the friend consulted the lawyer in a personal or professional capacity. It is based on the rather dramatic facts of

People v. Fentress, 425 N.Y.S.2d 485 (Dutchess County Ct. 1980). In *Fentress*, the distraught man was looking for spiritual advice, and did in fact request the presence of a rabbi. But he did not call any old family friend; rather, he called his friend who also happened to be a lawyer. The court stated, "[T]here would be no privilege if Wallace Schwartz [the lawyer] was acting solely as a friend, abjuring professional involvement," but the distressed caller was seeking Schwartz's legal advice along with comfort, support, and moral advice. He testified that he called Schwartz in a professional capacity, and the court noted that the "client's" subjective belief that he is consulting a lawyer *as a lawyer* and not as a friend is sufficient to satisfy this element of the attorney-client privilege. Incidentally, the court went on to hold that the privilege was waived because the caller did not intend to keep the subject matter of the communications confidential; he agreed that the police should come to his house, and it was obvious that when they arrived they would discover the body of his victim. If you see a problem like this, the important thing to recognize is that the analysis turns on whether the client consulted the lawyer in a professional capacity.

Notice that I've been talking as though the midnight caller was a client, even though there was no preexisting attorney-client relationship and the caller never specifically asked the lawyer to represent him. Remember that no formalities, such as an engagement letter or a payment of fees, are required in order to give rise to professional obligations on the part of the lawyer. If a person shares confidential information with a lawyer, in the reasonable belief that the lawyer will be looking out for that person's legal interests, the lawyer has an obligation to keep that information confidential, both as a matter of the professional duty of confidentiality (see Chapter 9) and as an obligation owed to the client to avoid waiver of the attorney-client privilege.

3. Sometimes clients (and lawyers) assume that the attorney-client privilege attaches to any document that is carbon-copied to a lawyer. That is simply not the case. See *U.S. Postal Service v. Phelps Dodge Refining Corp.*, 852 F. Supp. 157, 163 (E.D.N.Y. 1994). What matters is whether the communication is made for the purpose of obtaining legal advice. Moreover, the privilege will not apply to any underlying documents transmitted to an attorney unless the documents would have been privileged in the hands of the client under some independent doctrine such as the Fifth Amendment's privilege against self-incrimination. *Fisher v. United States*, 425 U.S. 391 (1976). In this example, a portion of the communication may be privileged. Suppose the manufacturer wrote a cover memo to the lawyer that said, "The attached documents are reports of some scientific studies concerning the addictive effects of smoking. Do you think they will be helpful to us in upcoming litigation?" The memo itself, but *only*

the memo, would be covered by the attorney-client privilege. The underlying documents — the scientific studies — would not be privileged unless they would be protected from compelled disclosure in the hands of the client. See, for example, *Sneider v. Kimberly-Clark Corp.*, 91 F.R.D. 1, 4 (N.D. Ill. 1980). Resolution of that question is a complex Fifth Amendment inquiry that you probably will not be expected to handle as part of your professional responsibility course. You should, however, be aware of the general rule that simply copying a lawyer on the transmission of documents is insufficient to create an attorney-client privilege, unless the communication is made for the purpose of obtaining legal advice. From a policy standpoint, this makes sense because otherwise a sophisticated client could create a privilege over all of its records simply by routing the documents through a lawyer.

4. First, notice that the investigator is an agent of the lawyer who is necessary to enable the lawyer to carry out her representation of the client. Thus, the use of the investigator does not destroy the privilege. On the question of the relationship between facts and the privilege, the general rule is that facts known by the client are not privileged simply because the client may have communicated those facts to a lawyer. If the client divulges, under the greatest of secrecy, an incriminating fact to the lawyer, the client is not protected by the attorney-client privilege from answering questions truthfully about the fact in question. There is a significant exception to this rule, however, where the lawyer or the client knows facts only by virtue of a privileged communication. In a criminal case, a lawyer may not be compelled to reveal factual information (not the content of a privileged communication) where the client would not be required to testify to those facts because of the Fifth Amendment. That was the situation in the *Fisher* case noted above. Taking that rule one step further, in some instances the attorney-client privilege protects the "fruits" of a confidential communication, so that a lawyer may not be compelled to testify to an observation that resulted from information contained within a confidential communication from the client.

There are a couple of well-known criminal cases in which the client's communication led the lawyers to observe something incriminating, but the lawyers were not required to testify about what they observed. In the famous "hidden bodies" case, a criminal defendant who had been charged with one murder led his lawyers to the site where the body of a second victim was hidden. *People v. Belge*, 372 N.Y.S.2d 798 (Onondaga County Ct. 1975), *aff'd*, 376 N.Y.S.2d 771 (App. Div. 1975). In a subsequent prosecution of the lawyer for violation of a statute requiring that bodies be given a decent burial, the court held that the information about the location of the body was privileged because the lawyer learned about it through a privileged communication from the client. In *People v. Meredith*, 631 P.2d 46 (Cal. 1981), a criminal defense lawyer sent his investigator to a trash can where the defendant had hidden the clothes and wallet of a murder victim. Unwisely, the investigator removed the wallet from the trash can, thereby hindering the ability of law enforcement officers to discover it on their own. Had the investigator not moved the wallet, however, the court would have refused to allow the government to subpoena the investigator to testify about the observation of the wallet, because the location of the wallet was disclosed in a confidential communication by the client.

This case is slightly different. Because it is a civil case, the client has no privilege against self-incrimination. The Environmental Protection Agency (EPA), a state environmental agency, or a private plaintiff simply can take the client's deposition and ask whether he dumped toxic waste on his land. The fact that he confessed this act to his lawyer is irrelevant—he must answer the question truthfully. So the client must answer the question, period. What about the lawyer's investigator? If for some reason the client is not available to answer questions, or the adversary chooses to try to obtain the information directly from the lawyer or the investigator, the issue is whether the lawyer or the lawyer's agent can refuse to testify on the grounds of the attorney-client privilege. Forcing the lawyer or the investigator to reveal facts learned by observation would be tantamount to revealing the content of a privileged communication, because the only reason the lawyer knew about the toxic waste is that the client had revealed its location. Thus, the lawyer and the lawyer's investigator could refuse to answer on the grounds of privilege. See Charles A. Wright, et al., *Federal Practice and Procedure* §5484.

5. This example goes one step beyond the previous example. We are no longer talking about the observation of a gun or toxic waste, but the attorney having physical possession of the gun. The gun is potentially evidence of a crime and could be used to connect the client with the robbery and shooting through ballistics and fingerprint tests or an eyewitness identification. As such, it is extremely valuable to the government. If the gun just disappeared, it would be much harder for the state to prove its case. Because of the importance of physical evidence to the investigation of crimes, criminal statutes prohibit tampering with evidence, and these statutes apply to attorneys with the same force as they would to nonattorneys. If the client's brother took the gun and threw it in the river, he could be prosecuted as an accessory after-the-fact to the shooting and robbery. The same would be true if the lawyer took possession of the gun and locked it in her desk drawer.

There have been cases in which lawyers were severely punished for concealing physical evidence of crimes, and the lawyer in this case must be concerned that she not run afoul of a criminal statute. In one case, the lawyer took marked bills and a sawed-off shotgun from the client and put them in a safety deposit box. *In re Ryder*, 263 F. Supp. 360 (E.D. Va. 1967). The court noted that taking property from a client is not receiving a "communication," so the attorney-client privilege has no application to locking the stuff away in a safety deposit box. By hiding the property, the lawyer in effect made it impossible for the police to find the bills and the shotgun and connect them with the client. The same reasoning applied in the *Meredith* case, cited in the previous example. By taking the wallet out of the trash can, the lawyer not only deprived the government of the opportunity to discover the wallet but obliterated a crucial link in the chain of custody that connected the wallet to the defendant. The court used a nice image to illustrate the problem: "[I]t is as if . . . the wallet in this case bore a tag bearing the words 'located in the trash can by [the victim's] residence,' and the defense, by taking the wallet, destroyed the tag." In this example, the government needs the tag "this gun found in the presence of the defendant" in order to connect the defendant to the shooting, and the lawyer would be destroying the evidentiary value of the location of the gun by accepting it from the client. By taking the gun, the lawyer would impede the government's ability to discover the gun and tie it to the defendant. For this reason, the lawyer may not take possession of the gun.

What if the client had not given the gun to the lawyer? Could the lawyer be compelled to testify that the defendant came into her office with a gun? As a general rule, the identity and appearance of a client are not covered by the attorney-client privilege, because they are not "communications" with the lawyer. See, for example, *In re Grand Jury Subpoena*, 204 F.3d 516 (4th Cir. 2000); *In re Walsh*, 623 F.2d 489, 494 (7th Cir. 1980); but see *State v. Meeks*, 666 N.W.2d 859 (Wis. 2003) (attorney's impressions regarding her client's competency may be protected by attorney-client privilege, because the attorney's impressions regarding competency are necessarily based upon communications between the client and the lawyer). But that result may be different, along the lines suggested by *Meredith*, if the lawyer's testimony about the observation of the gun would be tantamount to revealing a privileged communication. Certainly, the words "I shot someone; now what do I do?" would be covered by the ACP. Logically, a communicative *act* should be treated in the same way as a communication that occurs through words. Imagine this exchange:

Client: I've got a problem.
Lawyer: What's the problem?
Client: You know that shooting that was in the papers last night?
Lawyer: Yes.
Client: Well . . . [pulls out a gun].

The client's act carries exactly the same communicative significance as the statement, "I did it." Any reasonable lawyer would understand it to mean, "I did it." For this reason, the lawyer's observation would be protected to the same extent it would be under *Meredith*. But an observation not related to a communicative act would be treated differently. If, for example, the client came in to see the lawyer and the lawyer noticed he had a distinctive tattoo, the lawyer could be compelled to testify to that observation.

THE ATTORNEY-CLIENT PRIVILEGE FOR ENTITIES

Bentham and Wigmore probably were not thinking about the representation of entities when they wrote about the attorney-client privilege, but for many lawyers, the "client" who can claim the privilege is not an individual but an entity such as a corporation or partnership. Corporations are artificial persons in the eyes of the law, but of course they are composed of many different individual natural persons — for example, shareholders, directors, officers, and lower-level managerial and nonmanagerial employees. Which of these constituents should be deemed to speak for the corporation for the purposes of the attorney-client privilege?

There are important practical considerations at stake here. In order to obtain effective legal assistance, corporations need to have employees who can confidently confide in the entity's lawyer, secure in the knowledge that their communications will not be disclosed to others. On the other hand, if the privilege is too broad, it will shield a wide range of communications from discovery. For example, day-to-day business communications should not be privileged and, arguably, corporate employees who are essentially fact witnesses, as opposed to people who act on behalf of the corporation, should not expect that their statements to the corporation's lawyer will be covered by the privilege. Similarly, if the privilege is too broad, a corporation can create a "zone of silence" by routing routine communication through the legal department.

The most important case on this issue is the decision of the Supreme Court in *Upjohn v. United States*, 449 U.S. 383 (1981). *Upjohn* involved a common scenario — allegations of wrongdoing that prompt the corporation's lawyers to conduct an internal investigation to ferret out possible misconduct by employees. After a routine audit, management at Upjohn believed that employees of some of its foreign subsidiaries had been paying bribes to foreign government officials in violation of a federal criminal statute, the Foreign Corrupt Practices Act. It sent lawyers all over the world to interview employees, and it also sent around some questionnaires regarding possible payments. Apparently, the IRS got wind of these allegations and decided to investigate whether Upjohn had been treating the payments appropriately for tax purposes. It subpoenaed the questionnaires as well as interview memoranda and notes taken by Upjohn's lawyers.

When the IRS filed a petition to enforce its subpoenas, the issue of the scope of the corporate attorney-client privilege was presented to the district court. On appeal from that court's decision, the Sixth Circuit held that the privilege did not cover most of the communications, because its scope is limited to the "control group"—the members of senior management who play a substantial role in corporate decisionmaking. You can see why the control group test would be appealing, because it trades on the analogy between a natural person and a corporation. By making decisions on behalf of the corporation and committing it to a course of action, the control group personifies the corporation. The Supreme Court rejected this test, however, also for understandable reasons. For one thing, the control group may be the official decision makers, but there are plenty of lower-level employees who can commit the corporation to a course of action. For example, if a lawyer decides that a new sexual harassment, drug testing, or antidiscrimination policy should be adopted, the policy will be implemented by supervisory employees below the level of the control group. Furthermore, in order to give good legal advice, an attorney must know information within the possession of the corporate client, and that information is very likely held by employees outside the control group. In the Upjohn case, the managers of foreign subsidiaries were the employees with knowledge of illegal payments. If communications with the company's lawyers were privileged only if they came from the control group, lawyers might not learn of information in the hands of the lower-level managers.

If not the control group, then what? Unfortunately, the Court was not very clear. It held that the notes reflecting the employees' responses to the lawyers' questioning, as well as the written answers to the questionnaires, were within the corporate attorney-client privilege. But when it gave its reasoning, the Court provided such a laundry list of factors that it is difficult to tell which are the rationale for the decision. There are at least a dozen possible elements of the Upjohn test, as the Court sets it out: The communications were (1) made by Upjohn employees (2) to counsel for Upjohn (3) acting as such (4) at the direction of corporate superiors (5) in order to secure legal advice from counsel. (6) The information was not available from upper-echelon management, (7) concerned matters within the scope of the employees' corporate duties, (8) and was given by the employees with an awareness that they were being questioned for the purposes of the corporation obtaining advice. (9) The communications identified the general counsel as the author of the documents, and (10) were accompanied by a statement of policy respecting the payments and the company's willingness to comply with the law. Finally, (11) the communications were considered highly confidential when made and (12) have been kept confidential by the company.

Lower courts applying Upjohn have been forced to grapple with this proliferation of potential elements, and the result is a privilege whose contours are not especially predictable or clear. No one wants to apply a 12-element test, so courts sometimes play up some elements and de-emphasize others in order to create a simpler standard. See Reporter's Note to Rest. §73. To make things even more uncertain, Upjohn was a case applying the Federal Rules of Evidence, so it is binding in federal courts as an interpretation of federal law, but it is not a decision that applies in state courts. State courts have their own rules of evidence. In fact, some states, such as Illinois, even follow the pre-Upjohn control group test. See, for example, *Consolidation Coal Co. v. Bucyrus-Erie Co.*, 432 N.E.2d 250 (Ill. 1982); *State v. Ogle*, 682 P.2d 267 (Or. 1984).

The bottom line is that you have to pay attention to your jurisdiction's law. There are several competing tests floating around. Assuming the other elements of the attorney-client privilege are satisfied, a court would ask one of these further questions:

- *Control Group.* Was the communication made by an employee of the corporation who directs the entity's actions in response to legal advice? Despite the suggestion to the contrary in the Court of Appeals opinion in the Upjohn case, many courts held that the employee does not have to be a member of senior management. See, for example, *Philadelphia v. Westinghouse*, 210 F. Supp. 483 (E.D. Pa. 1962).
- *Subject Matter.* Was the communication intended to enable the attorney to give legal advice to the entity? The Restatement's version of the test privileges communications "concern[ing] a legal matter of interest to the organization," as long as they are disclosed only to agents of the organization who reasonably need to know about the information in order to act on behalf of the organization. Rest. §73.
- *Vicarious Liability.* Was the communication made concerning the conduct of an agent that is within the agent's scope of employment, and liability for which may be attributed to the organization? See *Samaritan Foundation v. Goodfarb*, 862 P.2d 870 (Ariz. 1993).[3]

If in practice you encounter a question about the application of the attorney-client privilege to an entity client, do yourself and your client a big favor

---

3. Whether the acts of an employee can be imputed to the corporation for the purposes of vicarious liability is also an element of the test for the anti-contact rule as applied to entity clients. See Rest. §100(2)(b); *Niesig v. Team I*, 558 N.E.2d 1030 (N.Y. 1990). Chapter 3 discusses the anti-contact rule in more detail. The policies behind the attorney-client privilege and the anti-contact rule overlap somewhat—both are concerned with protecting the attorney-client relationship from outside interference, for example—but there are important differences, too. The most significant is that the anti-contact rule does not shut down discovery of information entirely, but merely requires the adversary to employ formal methods of discovery, such as interrogatories or depositions, rather than informal *ex parte* questioning of witnesses.

and research the question carefully in a good reference work. Start with the excellent two-volume treatise published by the ABA Section on Litigation, Edna Selan Epstein, *The Attorney-Client Privilege and the Work-Product Doctrine* (5th ed. 2007) or for questions related to entity representation, John W. Gergacz, *Attorney-Corporate Client Privilege* (2000). For the purposes of your professional responsibility course, pay attention to whether your instructor wants you to use the Restatement test, the law in your jurisdiction, or whether you will be expected to argue about the application of the *Upjohn* factors based on policy considerations.

Difficult issues can arise when a corporate officer tries to assert an *individual* attorney-client privilege with respect to communications she made with the corporation's lawyer. In general, a lawyer representing an organization represents the organization itself, acting through its duly authorized constituents. Rule 1.13(a). The officer and the lawyer are both agents who owe fiduciary duties to the organization itself. There may be situations in which the same lawyer can represent both the individual and the organization simultaneously, as long as the simultaneous representation does not violate the current-client conflicts of interest rule. Rule 1.13(g). Even where the lawyer represents the individual officer, however, the officer's communications may not be privileged *in her individual capacity*, if they relate to matters within her duties to the corporation. *In re Grand Jury Subpoena*, 274 F.3d 563 (1st Cir. 2001); *In re Bevill, Bresler & Schulman Asset Mgmt. Corp.*, 805 F.2d 120 (3d Cir. 1986). This is a fairly technical analysis, and you probably won't have to be familiar with all the details of cases like *Bevill*, at least not in an introductory professional responsibility course. You should be prepared to spot this issue, however, whenever you see a lawyer representing a corporation and having confidential conversations with an individual constituent.

Another tricky issue pertains to the decision to assert or waive the privilege. Suppose a corporation retains a law firm to conduct an investigation of alleged wrongdoing — let's say, something like dumping toxic waste. In the course of the investigation, lawyers speak to a middle-level employee who admits engaging in the wrongdoing. Now suppose the State Department of Environmental Protection seeks to penalize the corporation for the illegal dumping. The general counsel decides on a strategy of cooperation with the government, and offers to turn over statements showing that the dumping was the result of a single "rogue" employee, not a company-wide policy. Is there anything the employee can do to prevent the company from throwing him under the bus? The short answer is, no. The employee's statements to the company's law firm are within the company's attorney-client privilege. However, the decision to assert or waive the privilege is for the company, not the employee, to make. Why? Because it's the company's privilege! And, from the law firm's point of view, the company is the client — see Rule 1.13(a). After you have resolved the issue of which constituents of the organization are within the organization's privilege, there is a separate question: Who is "a responsible person acting for the organization for th[e] purpose" of asserting or waiving the privilege? See Rest. §73, cmt. j. The answer will generally be someone within the control group — i.e., someone empowered, under applicable law, to act on behalf of the organization. I know this sounds weird, because *Upjohn* rejected the control group test, but that is only for the first question, not the second.

Example

Witnesses or "Parties"?

6. Lewis was working on a switching crew in a railyard when he fell under a railroad car and lost his leg. At the time of the accident, Lewis and three other members of the crew were working for the San Antonio, Austin, and Houston Railroad Company. Immediately after the accident, a "risk management officer," who was a lawyer working for the Railroad, interviewed Lewis and the other three members of the crew. No member of the corporation's management directed the crew members to answer questions; they voluntarily provided the information to the attorney, who recorded their answers in interview memoranda, which were kept in a locked filing cabinet in the lawyer's office. After Lewis filed a lawsuit against the Railroad under the Federal Employees' Liability Act (red flag — this is in federal court, so *Upjohn* applies), his lawyer demanded that the Railroad produce copies of the interview memoranda. The Railroad refused, citing the attorney-client privilege. Should the district court compel production of the documents?

Explanation

Witnesses or "Parties"?

6. The facts here are taken from *Leer v. Chicago, Milwaukee, St. Paul & Pacific Railway Co.*, 308 N.W.2d 305 (Minn. 1981), although I disagree with the court's analysis of the privilege issue. The Railroad is the defendant in the case, so the question is whether the statements by the switching crew members are encompassed by the corporation's attorney-client privilege. Under the control group test, they would not be. No matter how you characterize the decisions the corporation would make in response to legal advice about the accident, there is nothing the crew members could do to implement the advice. They are low-level employees with no supervisory authority over any of the Railroad's activities. Because this is in federal court, post-*Upjohn*, the control group test is no longer good law. Thus, you must apply *Upjohn* to these facts.

First of all, notice how many of the "elements" of the *Upjohn* "test" are not present here: the crew members did not speak at the direction of corporate superiors; the employees may or may not have been aware that the risk management officer was questioning them for the purpose of providing legal advice; and there was no elaborate policy accompanying the statements describing the corporation's willingness to comply with the law. Is this case distinguishable from *Upjohn*? In order to answer that question, you have to consider the policies behind the attorney-client privilege. As the Court in *Upjohn* observes, the attorney-client privilege encourages full and frank communications between lawyers and clients, which permits the lawyer to give legal advice to the client on the basis of full and accurate information. In many instances, lower-level employees have the information that lawyers need to provide advice, so it is important not to draw the boundaries too narrowly around employees whose communications are covered by the corporate attorney-client privilege. On the other hand, it is important not to draw the boundaries too broadly, or the effect will be to convert ordinary fact witnesses to persons whose statements are swept within the corporate attorney-client privilege. (*Samaritan Foundation v. Goodfarb*, 862 P.2d 870 (Ariz. 1993), makes this point clearly. See also Rest. §73, cmt. b.)

In light of the policies behind the attorney-client privilege, it should not matter whether the crew members were directed by corporate superiors to give testimony. It is in the best interests of the Railroad that its lawyer be able to learn quickly any facts that are relevant to its legal liabilities. The crew members, as agents of the corporation, also have the authority to discuss the accident with a lawyer when it is within the scope of their duties on behalf of the corporation. Rest. §73, cmt. h. The employees were acting within the scope of their corporate duties at the time of the accident, so they should be permitted to convey information about the accident to the Railroad's lawyer.[4] The lawyer needs to know what the switching crew members witnessed, so she can prepare a defense to any subsequent lawsuit[5] and possibly improve safety procedures to prevent future accidents.

Interestingly, if a member of the corporate control group happened to be at the site of the accident when it happened, her statements would not necessarily be covered by the Railroad's attorney-client privilege under *Upjohn*. Suppose the chief financial officer, Martha Muckety-Muck,

---

[4.] The court in the actual case said, "the witnessing of an accident was not within the scope of the employees' duties," so their statements were not privileged. 308 N.W.2d at 309 n.8. That is just a bizarre argument. There are no employees of any corporation whose duties can be described as "witnessing accidents," so by the court's logic, no information pertaining to accidents would ever be covered by a corporation's attorney-client privilege.

[5.] Note that "anticipation of litigation" is *not* an element of the attorney-client privilege, but of the work product doctrine.

had decided to eat her lunch on an embankment overlooking the switching yard. She would not be acting within the scope of her corporate duties at the time of the accident and thus should be treated more like an ordinary fact witness. This distinction matters because of the emphasis in Upjohn on creating a free flow of information between employees, who have the relevant information, and the lawyer, and in turn from the lawyer to employees who are in a position to act on the legal advice. Note that Restatement §73 does not include this limitation that the agent's communication must concern action within the scope of her corporate duties, only that it pertain to legal matters of interest to the organization.

EXCEPTIONS TO THE PRIVILEGE AND WAIVER

Strictly speaking, a *waiver* occurs when an otherwise-privileged communication is lost through some act of the lawyer or the client. Putting the privileged communication in issue and intentionally disclosing it are examples of conduct resulting in a waiver. *Exceptions* are sort of like the failure of an element of the attorney-client privilege, in the sense that if the communication falls within an exception, the privilege never existed at all. A further complication results because sometimes the same facts may support a conclusion either that no privilege existed in the first place or that the communication was privileged but the privilege was waived. For example, suppose a lawyer and client are talking in an open conference room at the lawyer's firm, and there are unknown persons walking around. You could argue either that the communication was not made "in confidence," and therefore that the privilege never attached to begin with, or that there was a waiver of the privilege by subsequent disclosure of the communication. It really does not matter to the bottom line—either way, evidence of the communication will be admissible—but you should be clear on whether you are analyzing the existence of the elements of the privilege or the elements of a waiver or exception doctrine.

Crime-Fraud Exception

You may remember the quotation from Jeremy Bentham at the beginning of Chapter 7. Bentham's beef with the attorney-client privilege was that innocent people have no need of it, so its effect is to enable criminals to escape detection and punishment. One undercurrent to this argument is that the privilege may shield unlawful activities from detection by the authorities. If the client had not used the lawyer's services in connection with the wrongdoing, that is pretty much true—the privilege does prevent the government from compelling the lawyer to testify as to what the client said to her. The reason for permitting the attorney-client privilege here is that we want individuals to seek legal advice if they are accused of committing a crime. The picture is very different, though, if the client has used or intends to use the lawyer's services to commit a crime or fraud. We do not want lawyers being used to facilitate crimes and frauds, even though the privilege properly complicates after-the-fact prosecution of crimes in which the lawyer's services were not used. Moreover, lawyers have an independent obligation under the disciplinary rules not to counsel or assist a client in committing a crime or fraud. Rule 1.2(d). For these reasons, there is an exception to the attorney-client privilege for communications made by the client for the purpose of obtaining the lawyer's assistance to commit a criminal or fraudulent act. Rest. §82. If the prosecutor can establish that the client used the attorney's services to commit an unlawful act, the communications between the lawyer and the client will not be protected by the attorney-client privilege.

There are a couple of things to note about the crime-fraud exception. First, the attorney does not have to share the client's purpose in order for it to apply. In other words, the lawyer may be an unwitting and completely innocent participant in the criminal or fraudulent conduct, but the communications nevertheless may be subject to the crime-fraud exception. Second, the crime-fraud exception is not just something for prosecutors to invoke. Parties in civil litigation also may seek to discover communications otherwise protected by the attorney-client privilege if they can show that the adversary's purpose in obtaining legal assistance was to commit a crime or fraud. Finally, the crime-fraud exception may apply even in cases where the client's conduct does not fall within the technical definition of a crime or fraud in the jurisdiction. There are some reported cases applying the crime-fraud exception to acts of deception, misconduct, false suggestion, and suppression of truth. A pattern of stonewalling or discovery abuse, for example, might be sufficient to trigger the crime-fraud exception in some jurisdictions.

These principles are nicely illustrated in a case called (with standard blandness reflecting the secrecy of grand jury proceedings) In re Grand Jury Subpoena, 445 F.3d 266 (3d Cir. 2006). The grand jury in that case issued a subpoena for documents, including e-mails, between "the Organization" and another target of the grand jury investigation. The executive director of "the Organization" met with her lawyer to discuss compliance with the subpoena. On the basis of the conversation with the lawyer, the executive director figured out which e-mails the government was interested in and failed to take any action to stop the deletion of the e-mails. Upon learning of the destruction of the e-mails, the grand jury issued a second subpoena to the lawyer, seeking to learn what he had discussed with the executive director. The trial court ordered the attorney to testify, and the court of appeals affirmed, making several points that are important to remember. Notice that the attorney did nothing wrong. He merely discussed the contents of the subpoena with the executive director so she could comply with it. Because the executive director used information gleaned from the attorney to commit the crime of obstruction of justice, the communication loses the privilege it would otherwise have had. In the words of the Restatement, the client "consults a lawyer for the purpose, later accomplished, of obtaining assistance to engage in a crime or fraud. . . ." Rest. §82(a).

A technical matter concerns the way in which a party seeking discovery may establish that the crime-fraud exception is satisfied. After all, if the purpose of the attorney-client privilege is to protect information from disclosure to the court, how is the court supposed to decide whether the information at issue was communicated for the purpose of furthering the client's crime or fraud? The courts have worked out a rather ingenious solution, involving gradually increasing burdens of proof. *United States v. Zolin*, 491 U.S. 554 (1989). First of all, the showing required to invoke the crime-fraud exception is lower than the burden of proof for the underlying crime or fraud. Courts often state the standard as a "reasonable basis" or "probable cause" to believe that the client's objective in seeking legal advice was to commit a crime or fraud. See, for example, *In re Grand Jury Subpoena*, 417 F.3d 18 (1st Cir. 2005). Second, the trial court has discretion to examine documents *in camera* — that is, in chambers, out of sight of the party seeking disclosure — to determine whether they contain evidence that the client's purpose was to commit a crime or fraud. In order to justify *in camera* review, the party seeking disclosure must make a relatively minimal threshold showing on the basis of unprivileged material, establishing the basis for a good-faith belief that *in camera* review will reveal evidence of the client's purpose. Thus, with a relatively small showing, a party can cause the adversary's attorney-client privilege to unravel using the crime-fraud exception, the stepwise burdens of proof, and possibly *in camera* review by the trial court.

Intentional Revelation and "Selective Waiver"

The privilege is "owned" by the client in the sense that the client has the right to assert or waive it. As the client's agent, though, the lawyer has the power to assert or waive it, too. (Some states limit the lawyer's power to waive the attorney-client privilege in criminal cases.) If the lawyer deliberately discloses information protected by the attorney-client privilege to strangers to the attorney-client relationship, the protection of the privilege is waived because the information is no longer confidential. This seems reasonable, but consider cases in which the lawyer is required to disclose privileged materials to outsiders, either as a condition of a business transaction or as part of a scheme of government regulation. In transactions, lawyers are familiar with the "due diligence" process in which the parties send lawyers to examine one another's records to make sure that there is a basis for the representations that parties have made to each other. In the regulatory context, a client may be required to share certain information with government agencies, such as the EPA, the Securities and Exchange Commission (SEC), or the Occupational Safety and Health Administration (OSHA). The question is whether these "selective" disclosures waive the attorney-client privilege with respect to subsequent litigation against third parties. For a while, it seemed that there was a genuine split of authority, but now there appears to be a strong trend opposing selective waiver. That is, the majority rule is that any disclosure of privileged material to someone not a "privileged person" will waive the privilege with respect to others.

For a good example, consider In re Columbia/HCA Healthcare Corp. Billing Practices Litigation, 293 F.3d 289 (6th Cir. 2002). The alleged wrongdoer was a hospital that had allegedly engaged in Medicare and Medicaid fraud. During the investigation, the target, Columbia/HCA, agreed to produce some documents it had prepared as part of an internal investigation of possible wrongdoing. It entered into a confidentiality agreement with the Justice Department, which provided that the disclosure of the documents "does not constitute a waiver." Subsequently, several private insurance companies sued Columbia/HCA, seeking to recover overpayments, and demanded production of the documents that had been shared with the government. The court disagreed strongly with the concept of selective waiver, noting that the purpose of the attorney-client privilege was to protect the relationship of trust and confidence between attorney and client. Permitting the client to share privileged information with others does not in any way strengthen the attorney-client relationship. The dissenting judge noted that a rule barring selective waiver would greatly increase the cost to corporations of cooperating with the government, thereby increasing the cost of enforcing the law. The private parties who are denied access to the documents are in no worse position than they would have been absent the waiver, and the government has an opportunity to conclude its investigation more quickly and inexpensively.

Although a few other courts permit selective waiver, or at least permit it when the government agrees to a confidentiality order, and despite the dissent's logic, it is safe to say that the decision in Columbia/HCA represents the majority position. However, some jurisdictions (particularly the Eighth Circuit, in Diversified Indus. v. Meredith, 572 F.2d 596 (8th Cir. 1978)) continue to permit a party to disclose information to government investigators and subsequently assert the attorney-client privilege in that information. State courts are all over the place on this issue, so please be careful and do your research if you encounter selective waiver in practice.

Inadvertent Disclosure

There are several different categories of inadvertent waiver of the attorney-client privilege: "elevator talk," "leaving things lying around," "failure to object," and the "oops!" scenario in discovery. Note that each of these situations also may involve a breach of the professional duty of confidentiality, subjecting the lawyer to liability for malpractice. The professional duty of confidentiality requires the lawyer to use reasonable care to protect the client's confidences, and in some of the scenarios described here, the lawyer failed to comply with this standard of care.

"Elevator talk" means gabbing with another lawyer from your office about a case as you ride down the elevator of your building. The elevator stops on a different floor, and an attorney from another firm gets on board, just as you tell your friend about an important confidential communication from a client in a case you are working on. That conversation waives the attorney-client privilege with respect to the communication, because the communication was disclosed, albeit accidentally, to a third party. It also breaches the professional duty of confidentiality, because you have an obligation to keep confidential all information relating to representation of the client. You obviously do not have to be on an elevator for this to happen. One common inadvertent waiver situation is having drinks with your friends after work, chatting about cases. If a group of lawyers (or non-lawyers, for that matter) at an adjoining table hears the conversation, you have waived the privilege with respect to confidential communications and breached the professional duty of confidentiality with respect to anything you discussed pertaining to your client's case.

Leaving things lying around can waive the attorney-client privilege and breach the professional duty of confidentiality if you do not take sufficient precautions to safeguard confidential documents. Suppose you are at a settlement conference with the other party and her lawyer, and you are all sitting around the same conference table. When it comes time to break for lunch, take the confidential documents with you, because if you leave them available for anyone to see, you have not taken sufficient care to keep the communications confidential. The result may be different if the adversary actually has to go rooting around a big pile of documents to find the confidential information. There are some cases holding that it is professional misconduct for a lawyer to go digging through the other side's papers, and that the privilege is not waived in these circumstances. See, for example, *Lipin v. Bender*, 644 N.E.2d 1300 (N.Y. 1994). There are a few cases taking the "leaving things lying around" rule to extremes. One court actually held that throwing away confidential documents without shredding them was a waiver of the attorney-client privilege, because the adversary may comb through the trash and read the documents. *Suburban Sew 'N' Sweep, Inc.*

v. Swiss-Bernina, Inc., 91 F.R.D. 254 (N.D. Ill. 1981). Applying the "expectation of privacy" rule much more sensibly, a court held that sending e-mails does not waive the attorney-client privilege, even though it may be possible for the adversary to obtain the e-mail through some kind of electronic skull-duggery. City of Reno v. Reno Police Protective Ass'n, 59 P.3d 1212 (Nev. 2002), as modified, 2003 Nev. LEXIS 25 (Nev. May 14, 2003).

Failure to object to a discovery request on the basis of the attorney-client privilege can waive the privilege. Rest. §86(2). Without going into too much civil procedure here, remember that if you object to a request for production that calls for privileged documents, you must set forth the basis of your objection with particularity, so that the requesting party can assess the validity of your privilege claim and decide whether to seek an order compelling production of the document. See Federal Rules of Civil Procedure 26(b)(5). This is generally done through a "privilege log," which describes the document without revealing privileged matters. Courts may hold that the failure to prepare an adequate privilege log waives the privilege that otherwise would have applied to the documents. Because the lawyer is the agent of the client, acting within an area of the lawyer's implied authority, the lawyer's carelessness may effectively waive the client's privilege. If the privileged information is sufficiently sensitive, you can expect the client to sue the lawyer for malpractice for negligently failing to object.

In the "oops!" scenario in discovery, the attorney is reviewing boxes of documents, preparing to produce some of them in response to a discovery request. The lawyer inadvertently puts privileged documents in the "to be produced" pile, and off they go to the adversary. (This also can happen when an attorney or secretary hits the wrong speed-dial button on the fax machine, sending privileged documents to the opposing lawyer instead of the client.) The next day, realizing his mistake, the lawyer places a frantic phone call to the adversary, begging her to return the documents. The question is whether the attorney-client privilege on the documents is waived, or whether the lawyer producing the documents can continue asserting it. Courts are divided, with some maintaining that the privilege is per se waived by production, regardless of its accidental nature, and some looking at the context of the production.[6] The courts following the contextual approach generally consider the size of the production — for example, they are less likely to find waiver where four privileged documents were produced along with 120,000 pages of unprivileged material — the care the lawyer took

---

6. The per se approach is sometimes called the "Crown Jewels" approach after the great evidence scholar John Henry Wigmore, who said that a lawyer must treat privileged information like the Crown Jewels. For a modern example, see In re Sealed Case, 877 F.2d 976 (D.C. Cir. 1989). The Crown Jewels approach is particularly harsh because courts treat the revelation of confidential information as prima facie evidence that the lawyer has not treated with the requisite degree of care.

setting up document-review procedures, and whether the lawyer sought return of the privileged documents immediately upon realizing the mistake. See, for example, *Lois Sportswear, U.S.A. v. Levi Strauss & Co.*, 104 F.R.D. 103 (S.D.N.Y. 1985) (no waiver where 30,000 documents reviewed, 16,000 produced, and 22 privileged documents inadvertently produced). The contextual approach of *Lois Sportswear* and similar cases is now recognized in Fed. R. Evid. 502, which provides that a disclosure does not waive the attorney-client privilege if it was inadvertent, the privilege holder took reasonable steps to prevent disclosure, and the privilege holder took prompt action to rectify the error.

Regarding the responsibilities of the *receiving* lawyer, Model Rule 4.4(b) requires a lawyer who receives a document and knows or reasonably should know that it was inadvertently sent to notify the sender. This rule reverses an ABA opinion, Formal Op. 92-368, which had said that the receiving lawyer must return inadvertently produced documents unread to the sender. See ABA Formal Op. 05-437 (sensibly recognizing that new Rule 4.4(b) supersedes previous guidance that lawyers should refrain from examining the materials). Model Rule 4.4 punts the question to the generally applicable law of attorney-client privilege of what further steps the receiving lawyer should take. As discussed above, some courts may hold that the documents remain privileged, and therefore must be returned to the sender. The sending lawyer should be prepared to assert the privilege and will have the burden of demonstrating that all elements of the privilege (including nonwaiver through inadvertent production) are satisfied. Rest. §86(3). Courts following the "Crown Jewels" approach, on the other hand, would permit the receiving attorney to make use of the now-unprivileged documents.

Putting Assistance or Communications in Issue

There are many labels used to describe this kind of waiver. You'll sometimes see it called waiver by reliance on advice of counsel, by injection (of an issue into the litigation), or anticipatory waiver. Restatement §80 calls it waiver by putting assistance or communications in issue, so that's what we'll call it here. Regardless of the label, the basic idea can be captured in a hackneyed metaphor: The attorney-client privilege is supposed to be a shield, not a sword. It would be unfair to the opposing party if a party used part of a privileged document to support a claim or defense, but held the rest of the document back. The opposing party would have no way of knowing whether the undisclosed part of the document contradicted or added essential context to the portion that was disclosed. For this reason, a rule has developed that if a party discloses part of a privileged communication, all communications on the same subject matter lose their privileged status.

See, for example, *Hearn v. Rhay*, 68 F.R.D. 574 (E.D. Wash. 1975); 8 Wigmore, *Evidence* §2328.

Although waiver by putting a communication in issue can happen in many different contexts, the most common scenario for this kind of waiver is where one party uses legal advice as part of a claim or defense. Suppose, for example, that the defendant in a patent infringement action claims "advice of counsel" as a defense to a claim of willful infringement. The defendant would like to introduce as evidence the lawyer's opinion that its invention does not infringe the plaintiff's patent. It would be unfair to the plaintiff, however, if the defendant could introduce bits and pieces of that communication into evidence, while blocking access to the rest of the communication. Maybe farther on down the memo, the lawyer qualified the advice, saying, "But under such-and-such circumstances, the invention might infringe the patent." The plaintiff obviously would love to find out that damaging information. For this reason, if one party introduces part of a communication covered by the attorney-client privilege, the privilege is waived for any related communication—the rest of the hypothetical memo, as well as other communications between the lawyer and the client pertaining to the *same subject matter*. See Rest. §80; Rest. §79, cmt. f.

There are lots of tests out there for determining when one part of a privileged communication pertains to the same subject matter as another part which has been disclosed. See, for example, *United States v. Skeddle*, 989 F. Supp. 905 (N.D. Ohio 1997). But the analysis can be boiled down to a fairly simple question: Is additional disclosure required to prevent the partial disclosure from distorting the truth?

Waivers of Work Product Protection

Work product protection can also be waived, but under different circumstances as compared with waivers of the attorney-client privilege. Privilege and work product are rooted in different policies. The attorney-client privilege is based on the need for a confidential relationship between attorney and client. The confidence necessary to this relationship can be destroyed by sharing communications with strangers to the relationship. The work product doctrine, on the other hand, is justified with reference to the functioning of the adversary system. The basic idea is that opposing counsel should not be able to prepare a case on "borrowed wits" by peeking into her adversary's thoughts and impressions. The conditions under which waiver will occur are given by these policies. *Any* disclosure of attorney-client privileged communications to someone other than the lawyer or client (or the agent of one or the other) is inconsistent with the trust and confidence essential to the attorney-client relationship, and thus causes a waiver of the privilege. On the other hand, only disclosures of work product that are inconsistent with an adversarial system of litigation are contrary to the purposes for which work product protection is granted.

An example of the difference between privilege and work product waivers comes from the criminal prosecution of Martha Stewart for insider trading. *U.S. v. Stewart*, 287 F. Supp. 2d 461 (S.D.N.Y. 2003). Stewart wrote an e-mail to her attorneys giving her account of the facts surrounding the stock trades in question. She then forwarded a copy of the e-mail to her daughter. The original e-mail was covered by the attorney-client privilege and the work product doctrine (mentally run through the elements to be sure you can say why). The government contended, however, that Stewart waived the privilege and work product protection by disclosing the e-mail to her daughter. The district court concluded that Stewart did indeed waive the privilege, but that the e-mail was still covered by work product protection. It noted that work product protection is waived only where disclosure by the client makes it more likely that *the adversary* will obtain the document. Forwarding the e-mail to her daughter did not increase the risk that the government would obtain the e-mail; thus, it did not waive work product protection.

Examples

Communications with a Crooked Client

7. Chan is in the import-export business. Unfortunately, he gets a little greedy and decides to cheat on his taxes. The income taxes on his business are calculated on the basis of revenue, which is simply the sale price of goods minus their cost. Thus, Chan realizes that by altering the invoices for imported goods obtained from Hong Kong, he can record an artificially high cost of goods sold, thereby lowering his reported income. The problem with this scam is that the Customs Service charges import duties based on the cost of goods sold, and the duty payments to Customs are based on the true price, not inflated for the purpose of income tax evasion.

   Chan becomes concerned that the IRS and the Customs Service may communicate and learn that the costs for imported goods reported to Customs are lower than the costs reported to the IRS for the purpose of income tax calculations. He hires a law firm, Stone & O'Hare, and tells his lawyer that he is worried about having inadvertently under-reported the cost of imported goods to the Customs Service. The lawyers prepare amended disclosures and file them with Customs, and Chan pays the additional import duties. (The additional duties are far less than the income tax saved by using inflated costs of the imported goods.) Subsequently, one of Chan's employees becomes disgruntled and tells the IRS about the tax scam. The IRS subpoenas the lawyers from Stone & O'Hare to testify before a grand jury about the conversations they had with Chan concerning the amended Customs disclosures. The firm moves to quash the subpoena on the basis of the attorney-client privilege, and the government responds that the privilege is lost due to the crime-fraud exception. What should the district court do?

Burn, Baby, Burn!

8. A man came to see a lawyer after being fired from his job as the super-intendent of an apartment building. After reviewing the man's employ-ment contract, the lawyer concluded, "It looks like they can terminate your employment for pretty much any reason, so I don't think you have a cause of action." The man responded, "Yeah, well it will be a real shame when their building 'accidentally' burns down." When the lawyer looked shocked, the man said, "Oh, come on—I was only joking."

   Nevertheless, the lawyer was concerned that the man, who had access to private areas of the building, might commit arson. After think-ing about it for a while and consulting with a law school classmate, she decided to call the police. (The lawyer relied on Rule 1.6(b)(1), permit-ting disclosure where reasonably necessary to prevent reasonably certain death or substantial bodily harm.) The police obtained a search warrant for the man's apartment. In it they found several containers of gasoline and a large box of matches. In the ensuing prosecution of the man for attempted arson, the district attorney subpoenaed the lawyer to testify about any conversations she had with the man about his intentions. The lawyer moved to quash the subpoena. Should the court grant the motion or require her to testify at trial against her client?

Letting the Cat out of the Bag

9. A group of plaintiffs in a securities fraud case have sought to take the deposition of William Walters, a partner in the law firm representing Silverman & Baggs, an investment bank that underwrote a large offering of railroad bonds. They also are demanding discovery of a memo pre-pared by Walters in the course of representing his client. Walters and his firm prepared offering documents for the securities and had extensive discussions with the railroad about what disclosures it should make in the documents. Before any civil lawsuits had been filed, the SEC began investigating the railroad and its investment bankers. Walters advised his client, Silverman & Baggs, that it should partially waive the attorney-client privilege and disclose to the SEC some communications from Walters to representatives of the investment bank. The client agreed and disclosed a portion of a memo written by Walters to Silverman & Baggs, as well as some advice given by Walters to his client.

In the private securities fraud action, Silverman & Baggs claims that it did not *knowingly* make any false statements in its offering documents. Walters has claimed the attorney-client privilege with respect to the document and the testimony sought by the private plaintiffs in the securities fraud action. He has, however, offered to share with the plaintiffs the portions of his testimony and the memo that he revealed to the SEC. Should the trial court permit discovery of the remainder of the communications?

Explanations

Communications with a Crooked Client

7. This example is based on an important appellate decision on the crime-fraud exception, *United States v. Chen*, 99 F.3d 1495 (9th Cir. 1996), which affirmed the district court's denial of the attorneys' motion to quash the grand jury subpoenas. The crime-fraud exception applies when a client consults a lawyer for the purpose of obtaining assistance to engage in a crime or fraud. All that is relevant here is the *client's* purpose, not the lawyer's knowledge or intention with respect to the client's crime or fraud. In the actual case, the district court made a finding of fact that the lawyers were entirely innocent of the client's criminal purpose. Nevertheless, it concluded that the lawyer should be required to testify before the grand jury. Although the lawyers had no improper motive, the client's purpose was to use the amended disclosures to cover his tracks, concealing evidence of the tax fraud by harmonizing the amounts reported to Customs with the amounts reported to the IRS.

   Concealing an ongoing or past fraud is conduct by the client that destroys the attorney-client privilege. Note, however, that if Chan had come to Stone & O'Hare after being indicted for tax fraud, seeking assistance in defending himself against those charges, any communications he had with the firm would be privileged. The crime-fraud exception does *not* apply to communications pertaining to wholly past crimes or frauds. Unless the client's criminal or fraudulent actions are contemplated for the future, or ongoing, he may communicate with the lawyer about them in order to obtain legal advice. The reason Chan's conduct destroyed the exception here is that he was trying to conceal — in the present and in the future — evidence of his crime and avoid detection.

Burn, Baby, Burn!

8. This example is based on the well-known case, *Purcell v. District Att'y*, 676 N.E.2d 436 (Mass. 1997). At the outset, note once again the distinction between the duty of confidentiality and the privilege. Is the lawyer

permitted to drop a dime to the police and warn them of the man's threat to burn down the building? Under Rule 1.6(b)(1), yes, if the lawyer reasonably believed it necessary — that is, if she reasonably believed that he might be even a little bit serious about his threat.

The next question is whether the lawyer may be compelled to testify to any communications she had with the man about his intentions. You might be tempted to go straight for the crime-fraud exception. . .but not so fast! Is the communication covered by the privilege at all? It occurred in the course of a conversation about the client's legal problem, but was the joke (or not a joke) about burning down the building made "for the purpose of obtaining . . . legal assistance"? See Rest. §72. I think the answer is clearly no. The whole point of the attorney-client privilege is to allow clients to obtain advice where the lawyer's skill and training in the law would be valuable to the client. Here, the man was not seeking advice about whether it was legal to burn down the building — he knew it wasn't. However, the Massachusetts court in *Purcell* remanded to the trial court to determine whether the comment about starting a fire was made for the purpose of receiving legal advice. 676 N.E.2d at 441. Only after the trial court determined that the privilege applied should it consider the crime-fraud issue. There is no record of what was determined on remand, but I sure hope the trial court found that this communication was not for the purpose of obtaining legal advice.

On the crime-fraud issue, the court also punted to the trial court. I'm a bit dubious that the exception applies, because the man wasn't seeking legal advice on how to commit arson without being detected, or whether it is legal to commit arson. He was just talking in the presence of a lawyer. That's not the same thing as obtaining assistance from the lawyer to engage in the crime. See Rest. §82. Here's an advanced privilege and waiver point: The lawyer's voluntary disclosure of the client's statement, permissible under Rule 1.6(a), does not waive the attorney-client privilege. Why not? Because the lawyer's disclosure would be effective to waive the privilege only if the lawyer had authority to do so, and "[u]nauthorized disclosure by a lawyer not in pursuit of the client's interests does not constitute waiver . . . ." Rest. §79, cmt. c.

Letting the Cat out of the Bag

9. Yes, the *entire* memo and the substance of Walters' advice to Silverman & Baggs is discoverable. See *In re Penn Central Commercial Paper Litigation*, 61 F.R.D. 453 (S.D.N.Y. 1973). Because the investment bank's knowledge is at issue in the securities fraud action, the plaintiffs are entitled to know what the representatives of the bank knew and when they knew it. They may have learned some interesting things in their conversations with Walters and from the memo he prepared, but the plaintiffs will never

know one way or the other if these communications are kept secret. Naturally, the client is entitled to keep these communications absolutely secret, but it is not permitted to reveal only the good parts and continue to keep the bad parts secret. That would be unfair to the adversaries in litigation. Thus, the privilege is waived.

There are two different waiver doctrines that could be used to analyze this case, and you should try to keep them straight. First, Walters could have waived the privilege (with the client's consent) by disclosure of privileged communications to the SEC. Many, if not most, courts hold that an intentional revelation of a communication to a government agency waives the privilege with respect to subsequent litigation not involving the government—including, for example, a private securities fraud lawsuit. Edna Selan Epstein, *The Attorney-Client Privilege and the Work-Product Doctrine* 342-343 (4th ed. 2001). Because Walters has agreed to share this portion with the plaintiffs, you do not need to analyze the issue of waiver by production to the government. The second waiver doctrine is the rule of waiver by putting in issue. If Walters is willing to disclose portions of his communications with Silverman & Baggs, we can infer that those portions are favorable to his client's case. But who knows what is in the remainder of the memo and the rest of the conversation he had with his client? As a basic rule of forensic fairness, the plaintiffs are entitled to see the hidden parts of the memo and ask Walters questions about the rest of the advice he gave to his client.

NO "BORROWED WITS": THE WORK PRODUCT DOCTRINE

You are a smart, diligent, well-prepared lawyer who thinks hard about your client's cases. As you prepare for trial, it occurs to you that you may be able to defend a lawsuit in a novel and interesting way. You write a memo to the file outlining your strategy and explaining how you will marshal legal and factual support for your theory. The next day, you receive a discovery request from your opponent that says, "Please produce all documents outlining your trial strategy." If you had to give up your memo, your opponent would get a free ride on your hard work. That is not how the adversary system is supposed to work. For all its flaws, one good thing about the adversary system is that lawyers can contribute something distinctive to their clients' cases. Also, although lawyers certainly have some duties to the court and to the system of justice as a whole, in the American system they are primarily concerned with their clients' cases. Your client, not the opponent, is supposed to be the one who benefits from your brilliant insight and diligent preparation.

The theory behind the work product doctrine is that lawyers should enjoy some protection for their private thoughts. Lawyers should be able to consider their clients' cases, gather information, make decisions about what is relevant and what is not, and come up with theories of the case and trial strategies without having to disclose all these mental processes to their opponents. Beyond mental processes and strategies, the work product doctrine also starts from the assumption that lawyers should not have to turn over the fruits of their labors to their litigation adversaries, who are just sitting on their duffs and not running around interviewing witnesses and preparing for trial.

The work product doctrine originates with a Supreme Court case called *Hickman v. Taylor*, 329 U.S. 495 (1947), but it has been developed and codified extensively since then. Application of the doctrine is now largely controlled by Federal Rule of Civil Procedure 26(b)(3), part of the discovery rules. As the Federal Rules formulate it, the work product doctrine protects *documents* or other tangible things,[7] but not the information contained within the documents, that were prepared in *anticipation of litigation*. The Federal Rules are not intended to supplant *Hickman*, however, so there remains a common law of work product, separate from the Rules. See II Edna Selan Epstein, *The Attorney-Client Privilege and the Work-Product Doctrine* (5th ed. 2007), at 815 (regarding intangible material, "whether a deponent may be required to disclose work product in her answers is governed not by the rule, but by *Hickman*"). The Restatement reflects both common law and the Rules, so its definition of work product includes "tangible material or its intangible equivalent in unwritten or oral form." See Rest. §87(1). The Restatement definition also requires that work product materials be prepared by a lawyer; that element is not part of the federal rule. (You don't often encounter would-be work product that is not prepared by a lawyer.)

Note a couple of key differences between the work product doctrine and the attorney-client privilege. Work product protection is narrower than the attorney-client privilege, because the privilege applies to all confidential communications between lawyers and clients for the purpose of seeking legal advice, including a witness's recollection about the substance of that communication. A discussion of the legal aspects of a proposed business transaction would be covered by the attorney-client privilege, but a memo summarizing that conversation would *not* be protected by the work product doctrine, because the memo was not prepared in anticipation of litigation. On the other hand, the work product doctrine is broader than

---

7. "Other tangible things," by the way, refers to photographs, drawings, charts, computer data, and other bearers of information that might not be characterized as documents. I use the word "documents" as a shorthand, but you should understand that it also covers things like computer files.

the attorney-client privilege because it extends to information learned in the course of investigation or interviews with nonclient witnesses. The privilege is applicable only to communications between the lawyer and the client.

A key distinction when applying the work product doctrine is between "ordinary" and "opinion" work product. Remember that the Court in *Hickman* was particularly concerned with protecting the theories, opinions, and strategic thinking of counsel, which are the core of the adversary system. These mental impressions, which have come to be known as "opinion" work product, are therefore entitled to the highest degree of protection. The Restatement defines *opinion work product* as that which "consists of the opinions or mental impressions of a lawyer; all other work product is ordinary work product." Rest. §87(2). The Federal Rules are to the same effect: "[I]n ordering discovery of [ordinary work product], the court shall protect against disclosure of the mental impressions, conclusions, opinions, or legal theories of an attorney or other representative of a party concerning the litigation." Fed. R. Civ. P. 26(b)(3). Everything else is *ordinary work product*.

The significance of the distinction is that the other party may obtain discovery of ordinary work product upon a showing of substantial need and inability to obtain the equivalent through other means. Suppose there is an accident with one eyewitness. The defendant's lawyer interviews the witness, who subsequently dies. If the plaintiff's lawyer files a motion to obtain discovery of a memorandum of this interview prepared by the defendant's lawyer, the court will probably grant it under the "substantial need and inability to obtain" exception. Rest. §88. Opinion work product, by contrast, is hardly ever discoverable, except under extraordinary circumstances. Rest. §89. The most common of these "extraordinary circumstances" is when a party puts the advice of counsel in issue in the litigation, such as by asserting the lawyer's opinions and judgment as a defense. In patent infringement cases, for example, the defendant may assert the advice of counsel as a defense to a claim of willful infringement. The defendant's lawyer would not be permitted to assert absolute protection for what otherwise would be opinion work product in this case, because of the unfairness to the plaintiff. If the defendant wants to rely on advice of counsel, the adversary is entitled to know exactly what the lawyer said to the client.

Like the attorney-client privilege, the work product doctrine does not protect *facts* learned by the lawyer in the course of preparing for litigation. The Restatement is perfectly clear about this, see §87(1), where the definition of work product specifically excludes "underlying facts." It would have been nice if there were similarly explicit text in the rules governing the attorney-client privilege, but no matter, the rule is the same regarding underlying facts.

Examples

Find the Privileged Docs

If you practice as a civil litigator, you are likely to have a "document review" project at some point in your career. Your job will be to look through boxes of documents and pull out those that you may avoid producing in discovery on the grounds of the attorney-client privilege or the work product doctrine. If you are a transactional lawyer, you still need to be aware of these rules whenever you counsel clients and would like your advice to remain confidential in any subsequent litigation.

Thus, for the following documents, evaluate whether they may be withheld from discovery, under either the attorney-client privilege or the work product doctrine. Why or why not? If there is additional information you need to make the judgment, please indicate what you need to know and why. You may not know some of the specific rules implicated by these documents, but you should be able to spot the issues and suggest how they should be resolved.

10. A memo written by a lawyer in the General Counsel's office, addressed to the General Counsel, the chief financial officer of the client corporation, and an outside environmental consultant hired by the client, analyzing the environmental consequences of the proposed purchase of a parcel of land. The memo concludes that building on one part of the land may not be feasible because of the Endangered Species Act. The memo is headed "PRIVILEGED AND CONFIDENTIAL — ATTORNEY WORK PRODUCT."

11. An e-mail from the manager of a Danny's restaurant, to the vice president of human resources (who is not a lawyer) at Danny's headquarters, with a copy to the General Counsel's office, seeking advice regarding an employee the manager is considering firing. The employee may be covered by Title VII. The manager sought information about Danny's procedures for terminating employees.

12. A file memo prepared by an outside lawyer who sits on the board of directors of a client corporation, summarizing a conversation between the lawyer and another director, concerning the business opportunities presented by expanding into China, as well as the legal restrictions on giving gifts to foreign government officials.

13. A memo summarizing interviews with witnesses to an accident at a construction site, prepared by a "loss prevention specialist" with the construction company.

14. Handwritten notes taken by a lawyer who attended a strategy session at which the antitrust implications of a pending merger were discussed.

Explanations

Find the Privileged Docs

10. The memo is not covered by the attorney-client privilege unless it is communicated in *confidence*, which it may or may not be. The chief financial officer is certainly within the corporation's privilege under *Upjohn*, but what about the environmental consultant? Because the consultant is just someone the client hired to provide routine environmental advice, she is a stranger to the legal representation, and the communication is not made in confidence. If the lawyer had hired the consultant for the specific purpose of assisting the lawyer in providing legal advice, the communication would remain privileged. You probably are not expected to know this specific rule, but please do make sure you spotted the issue — namely, whether the communication was made in confidence. As for the work product doctrine, the memo was not prepared in anticipation of litigation. It is true that litigation is possible in the future, but courts generally have held that there must be anticipation of imminent, specific litigation, not a generalized threat, in order to satisfy this element of the work product doctrine. See, for example, *Iowa Protection & Advocacy Services, Inc. v. Rasmussen*, 206 F.R.D. 630, 641 (N.D. Iowa 2002) (a government agency's notification that it was beginning an investigation does not give rise to an anticipation of litigation because not all government investigations end in litigation).

    By the way, the "privileged and confidential" language festooning the memo is utterly irrelevant to the analysis. If the document is protected by the attorney-client privilege or work product doctrine, it does not need prominent labels; on the other hand, the document could be stamped "ATTORNEY-CLIENT PRIVILEGE, AND WE REALLY, REALLY MEAN IT!!" and it would not be privileged unless the communication satisfies the elements of the attorney-client privilege and the privilege has not been waived. See, for example, *Lifewise Master Funding v. Telebank*, 206 F.R.D. 298, 301 (D. Utah 2002).

11. The e-mail does not necessarily become a communication seeking legal advice just because it was copied to the General Counsel's office. Whether the e-mail is covered by the attorney-client privilege depends on the sender's purpose — for example, if it was to obtain legal advice, it would be privileged, but if it is to obtain strategic advice from human resources managers, or just to learn about how to go through the company's termination procedures, it would not be privileged. Like the "privileged and confidential" language in the previous example, the mere fact that the e-mail was copied to the general counsel does not automatically make it privileged. *Bell Microproducts Inc. v. Relational Funding*

Corp., 2002 U.S. Dist. LEXIS 18121, at *3-4 (N.D. Ill. Sept. 24, 2002). Furthermore, the e-mail is not protected by the work product doctrine just because it ended up on a lawyer's desk. The Restatement limits work product protection to documents prepared by a lawyer. Rest. §87. If the case ends up in litigation in federal court, which it probably will in this case because the problem involves a federal statute, the Federal Rules of Civil Procedure extend work product protection to parties and their representatives, so the document need not be prepared by a lawyer. Fed. R. Civ. P. 26(b)(3).

No matter who prepares the document, though, it still must be prepared "in anticipation of litigation" to be covered by the work product doctrine. It may seem obvious that if Danny's fires the employee, there will be litigation. Is this enough to satisfy the "anticipation of litigation" element of the work product doctrine? Maybe not. Courts are pretty strict about this element, and generally require a showing that litigation is on the immediate horizon, not just possible at some time in the future. A lawsuit need not have been filed, but there must be a *substantial* probability of *imminent* litigation. See, for example, *Home Ins. Co. v. Ballenger Corp.*, 74 F.R.D. 93 (N.D. Ga. 1977). If an attorney, or a person acting at the direction of an attorney, prepares the document, a court may be more likely to conclude that it was prepared in anticipation of litigation. See, for example, *Thomas Organ Co. v. Jadranska Slobodna Plovidba*, 54 F.R.D. 367 (N.D. Ill. 1972). This one is a close call, but the complete noninvolvement of lawyers (except for receiving the carbon copy) suggests that the manager had a vague sense of trepidation about litigation but was not taking steps to prepare to defend a specific matter.

12. This is the problem of lawyers wearing two hats. The lawyer's conversation with the director may be characterized as business or legal advice. Some courts take a flexible, forgiving approach so that mixed legal and business advice is still privileged. Other courts are harsher and do not protect communications if there is a nonlegal subject mixed in with the legal advice. Again, you may not necessarily know the specific rule in any jurisdiction, but you should have noticed the problem that the lawyer may not be acting in a professional capacity in this case. One of the elements of the attorney-client privilege is that the lawyer must be acting *as a lawyer*, not as a business person, friend, spiritual advisor, etc. The memo summarizing the conversation would not be covered by the work product doctrine because there is no anticipation of litigation. The prospect of some future dispute is not what courts mean when they say litigation must be anticipated. Without a very specific and imminent threat, usually involving specific parties, documents will not be protected by the work product doctrine.

13. The memo may be covered by the work product doctrine if it was pre-
    pared by a lawyer or at the direction of a lawyer. The problem does not
    say whether the "loss prevention specialist" was directed by a lawyer to
    interview the witnesses and prepare the summaries. If so, the interview
    memoranda constitute ordinary work product and may not be discov-
    ered absent the adversary's showing of substantial need and inability to
    obtain the equivalent through other means.

14. This example is tricky if you confuse the attorney-client privilege
    and the work product doctrine. The notes themselves are work prod-
    uct, but only if they are prepared in anticipation of litigation. In this
    case, that element of the work product doctrine is not satisfied. There
    is no imminent threat of a lawsuit from a particular party, just vague
    concerns about "antitrust problems." The notes are not covered by the
    attorney-client privilege unless they are a record of a communication
    from the client to the lawyer. If they are just a record of conversations
    between two nonlawyers, the communications are not protected by
    the attorney-client privilege. Notes like these are privileged only to the
    extent they summarize a conversation between the client and the law-
    yer for the purpose of obtaining legal advice. See, for example, *American
    Nat'l Bank & Trust v. AXA Client Solutions*, 2002 U.S. Dist. Ct. LEXIS 4805 (N.D.
    Ill. 2002) (handwritten notes not privileged because lawyer had not
    communicated them to client).

Professional Duty of Confidentiality

INTRODUCTION

This chapter deals with a lawyer's obligation to hold confidential the information learned in the course of representing a client. The duty of confidentiality arises by virtue of the fiduciary relationship between the lawyer and the client. The law of agency requires any agent — including a lawyer — to keep the principal's secrets. This duty of confidentiality is even more stringent when the agent is a lawyer, because lawyers by necessity learn a great deal of highly sensitive information from their clients. The lawyer-client relationship would not function nearly as well if clients had to worry that the information they shared with lawyers may become public knowledge. Clients would be cagey and close-lipped, refusing to share potentially damaging information with their lawyers. The trouble is, it is precisely that sensitive information that might make all the difference in the client's legal situation. If clients withheld this information from their lawyers, clients would be harmed to the extent that their lawyers would not have a full understanding of their clients' problems and therefore would be unable to provide useful advice.

No one seriously questions the notion that confidentiality is one of the most important duties the lawyer owes to a client. But the extent of that duty continues to engender enormous controversy. To put it more precisely, the disagreement centers on the scope of *exceptions* to the duty of confidentiality.

OUR LIPS ARE SEALED: THE PROFESSIONAL DUTY OF CONFIDENTIALITY

Compelled disclosure by lawyers of confidential client information through subpoenas, depositions, and discovery requests is not the only thing clients fear. They also worry that their lawyers may blab and gossip, reveal confidential information to others, or even use their clients' secrets against them. Suppose, for example, a local developer comes into her lawyer's office to talk about acquiring a parcel of land. She confides in the lawyer that she has done market research and has concluded that the area would support a new casual dining restaurant. She is in discussions with a national chain about becoming a franchisee and opening the restaurant. Now suppose that after having this conversation, the lawyer calls up a competing chain, informs them of the marketing data supplied by the client, and asks about becoming a franchisee of the competitor. He intends to purchase a plot of land across the street from the site under consideration by his client and use it for his own restaurant. This is a betrayal of the client's trust in her lawyer and a breach of the fiduciary duty that the lawyer owes to the client. It is exactly this sort of situation that the professional duty of confidentiality is intended to prevent.[1]

The basic rule of confidentiality, as stated in Model Rule 1.6(a), is very broad. It prohibits a lawyer from revealing *any* information "relating to representation of the client" without the client's informed consent. The definition of protected information is wider in the Model Rules than in the Model Code. The Code, in DR 4-101(A) and (B)(1), prohibited a lawyer from revealing information that the client has requested be held inviolate, or the disclosure of which would be embarrassing or would likely be detrimental to the client. Although by this point in time it's safe to mostly ignore the old Model Code, it's useful to keep it in mind here, because language from the Model Code has stuck around in a few states' versions of the confidentiality rule. See, for example, Michigan Rule of Professional Conduct 1.6, which defines the scope of protected information in Rule 1.6(a) using Code language:

> "Confidence" refers to information protected by the client-lawyer privilege under applicable law, and "secret" refers to other information gained in the professional relationship that the client has requested be held inviolate or the

---

1. You also may see the professional duty of confidentiality called the "ethical duty," but this term is unfortunate, first because it confuses mandatory law and ethics, and second because it does not acknowledge the source of the duty in agency law, not simply the disciplinary rules. For what it's worth, the MPRE uses the term "professional rule of confidentiality" to refer to Rule 1.6.

disclosure of which would be embarrassing or would be likely to be detrimental to the client.

The rule then defines the obligations of lawyers with reference to these defined terms:

> Except when permitted under paragraph (c), a lawyer shall not knowingly:
>
> (1) reveal a confidence or secret of a client;
> (2) use a confidence or secret of a client to the disadvantage of the client; or
> (3) use a confidence or secret of a client for the advantage of the lawyer or of a third person, unless the client consents after full disclosure.

If your professional responsibility course asks you to refer to the law of your jurisdiction, make sure to check the definition of confidential information. Can you think of something that would be covered by the definition of Model Rule 1.6(a) but not the Code language in the Michigan rule set out above?

I will refer to information relating to the representation, and thus protected by the duty of confidentiality, as "confidential client information." With respect to that information, the duty is near absolute, subject to a few exceptions discussed below. For example, a lawyer may not disclose confidential client information even if she reasonably believes it would be helpful to the client to do so, unless the lawyer has implied authorization to disclose. In re O'Neil, 661 N.W.2d 813 (Wis. 2003). In the restaurant example above, the marketing data is information relating to the representation, because the client contacted the lawyer about purchasing a parcel of land for the restaurant. Even though the client did not specifically request the lawyer not to disclose it, and even though it may not be detrimental to the client to reveal the information, it is nevertheless protected as "information relating to the representation." Rule 1.6(a).

In addition to the prohibition on disclosure, all of the disciplinary rules and the law of agency forbid lawyers from using confidential client information against the interests of a current or former client. Rule 1.8(b), 1.9(c); Rest. §60(1)(a) & cmt. j. In our restaurant hypothetical, even if the lawyer did not reveal the marketing data to the competing restaurant chain, he violated the duty of confidentiality by making use of the information in a way that was adverse to his client's interests. It certainly would not benefit the client's business to have a competing franchise open up right across the street. Strangers to the professional relationship may stumble upon this business opportunity, but the lawyer commits a serious breach of his professional obligation by usurping this opportunity for himself.

Note that there is an exception in Rule 1.9(c)(1) permitting the adverse use of the confidential information of former clients if (and only if) that information has become generally known. ABA Formal Op. 17-479 (2017) defines "generally known" as information that is either (a) widely recognized by members of the public in the relevant geographic area; or (b) widely recognized in the former client's industry, profession, or trade.[2] The opinion cites a case giving a helpful example: Although it is true that anyone could go down to the courthouse, look through publicly available records, and learn that X and Y are getting a divorce, that information is not generally known. If X and Y are celebrities, however, and news of their divorce has been splashed across the front page of the tabloids (or today, is all over TMZ), then the information is generally known. "'Generally known' does not require publication on the front page of a tabloid, but it is more than merely sitting in a file in the courthouse." See In re Gordon Props., LLC, 505 B.R. 703, 707 n.6 (Bankr. E.D. Va. 2013). In the restaurant example, the suitability of the parcel for development is not generally known, even though someone could conduct the same kind of market study that the client did.

It is worth emphasizing that the result of the analysis of the restaurant example would be exactly the same even if there was no such thing as state rules of professional conduct. As a fiduciary of his client, the lawyer has an agency law duty to keep the information confidential and not to use information received from the client to her disadvantage. William A. Gregory, The Law of Agency and Partnership §§67-68 (2001). If the client sues the lawyer for usurping her business opportunity, the lawsuit will allege a breach of fiduciary duty under agency law. It might even make reference to the governing disciplinary rules to reinforce the point that the lawyer acted wrongfully. But the lawsuit does not depend on the existence of the disciplinary rules. The lawyer would have these duties anyway.

The duty of confidentiality may extend to *prospective* clients as well. If a person consults a lawyer, believing the lawyer to be acting in a professional capacity in furtherance of that person's interests, the lawyer may have an obligation to keep any information learned from the prospective client confidential. This is true even if the lawyer and the "almost-client" do not formalize their relationship, if they do not continue to work together, or if the "almost-client" does not pay a fee. Rule 1.18(b) states that, even if a prospective client does not retain a lawyer, the lawyer has an obligation not to reveal or use confidential information learned during the initial consultation. Notice an interesting wrinkle. The rule goes on to say that the lawyer may use or disclose information learned, to the extent permitted under Rule 1.9. Recall that Rule 1.9(c) says that a lawyer shall not disclose or

---

2. A controversial case, *Hunter v. Virginia State Bar*, 744 S.E.2d 611, 620 (Va. 2013), held that it would be unconstitutional to prohibit a lawyer from blogging about his representation of clients and disclosing publicly available information. The ABA opinion said that it would not opine on First Amendment issues, but it suggested *Hunter* should be limited to its facts. See ABA Formal Op. 480, p.5, n.20.

make adverse use of information relating to the representation of a former client except where the information has become generally known. Thus, in the case of prospective clients, the rules expressly permit the disclosure or adverse use of generally known information.

The professional duty survives the termination of the attorney-client relationship. To put it another way, lawyers have duties of confidentiality to former clients as well as to current clients. Rule 1.6, cmt. [20]; Rule 1.9(c). The duration of the duty is one reason for the former client conflicts rule, discussed in Chapter 16. The ongoing duty of the lawyer not to disclose a former client's confidences, and not to make adverse use of information learned in the course of the representation, limits the lawyer's ability to represent new clients whose interests are adverse to those of the former client.

It was always clear as a matter of tort and agency law that a lawyer's duty was not only to avoid intentionally disclosing or using confidential information, but also to take reasonable care to protect it. Rule 1.6(c), adopted relatively recently (and thus maybe not in effect in your state), makes this an obligation as a matter of professional discipline as well. Lawyers are now required to make reasonable efforts to protect against the accidental disclosure of confidential client information, and are subject to discipline for failure to do so. For example, a lawyer at a major law firm who accidentally copied a *Wall Street Journal* reporter on an e-mail to other firm lawyers working on a highly confidential matter could be disciplined under Rule 1.6(c) for failing to use reasonable care to prevent the unauthorized disclosure of confidential client information. *See* Debra Cassens Weiss, *Oops! WilmerHale Email to Reporter Reveals Apparent SEC Probe into PepsiCo GC's Departure*, ABA Journal (Sept. 27, 2017). (I suspect the lawyer's first word upon realizing that the Wall Street Journal was cc'ed on the email was not "oops.")

Examples

Loose Lips Sink Ships

1. Appellate specialist Bud Uronner is having a couple of beers with friends from his law firm. The bar is located on the first floor of the building where Bud's firm leases several floors of office space. It is crowded with the usual Friday afternoon customers from the various law, accounting, and financial services firms in the building. Bud tells his friends about a new case he is working on, in which he has thought of a novel procedural tactic. "I'm going to ask the other lawyers whether they will agree to continue the argument until next month. They'll probably agree, just out of courtesy, but they don't know that the judge most likely to rule for them is scheduled for back surgery next month, so he won't be on the panel of judges assigned to hear the appeal." Unfortunately for Bud, an associate at the opposing law firm is seated at the other table. He

overhears the conversation and tells the partner in charge of the appeal not to agree to the continuance, and Bud's client loses the benefit of his little forum-shopping stratagem. Assuming the information about the conversation somehow gets back to Bud's client, is he subject to professional discipline for violating the PDC or a lawsuit for breach of fiduciary duty?

Blogging and Bragging

2. A lawyer represented a famous local chef and restaurant owner, Guy Flowers, in an investigation by the state health department. An inspection had found evidence of the presence of rodents and insects in a restaurant owned by Flowers. The lawyer persuaded the health department not to impose a fine, arguing that the problem was due to an oversight and would not reoccur. Records of the health department investigation, the charging document filed against the restaurant, and the agreed settlement with the department are public records, available for inspection in the health department offices in Capital City.

   The lawyer maintains a blog about law affecting the restaurant industry. She posted a short article with the headline, "Claims of unsanitary conditions in Guy Flowers restaurant are settled," which talked about the high quality of the representation she provided Flowers in the matter. She did not notify Flowers before putting up the blog post. Is the lawyer subject to discipline?

   A. Yes, because she did not notify Flowers before putting up the blog post.
   B. Yes, because she did not obtain Flowers's informed consent to disclose his identity, the representation, and the settlement.
   C. No, because all of the information pertaining to the health department investigation is a matter of public record.
   D. No, because she did not disclose any confidential communications between herself and Flowers that were made for the purpose of providing legal services.

In the Cloud(s)

3. Richmond Avenal is a lawyer who is a keen adopter of technology in his law practice. He was interested in moving his firm's computer files to a data storage site owned and operated by a third party—a so-called cloud computing service. A startup company called LegalCloud had been aggressively marketing its services to lawyers. Without investigating the company's data security measures, Avenal signed up for storage with LegalCloud, and for a fee of $100 per month was able to store all of his client data on file servers operated by LegalCloud. Subsequently a

hacker gained unauthorized access to LegalCloud's servers and released a number of documents that had been stored there. One of the documents was a confidential filing by one of Avenal's clients in a matrimonial proceeding, which described a number of embarrassing incidents. Is Avenal subject to professional discipline?

Explanations

Loose Lips Sink Ships

1. This is a classic example of breaching the duty of confidentiality by careless talk. Lawyers are permitted to talk to others in their firm about cases and share confidential client information. "Lawyers in a firm may, in the course of the firm's practice, disclose to each other information relating to a client of the firm, unless the client has instructed that particular information be confined to specified lawyers." Rule 1.6, cmt. [5]. Indeed, it is this free sharing of information among lawyers within a firm that underlies the imputation of conflicts of interest from one lawyer to others in the same firm. Rule 1.10(a). But lawyers must be extremely careful not to have these freewheeling conversations outside the privacy of their offices. Blabbing about a case while riding on elevators or having drinks in the first-floor bar is an excellent way to disclose your client's confidences. You just never know who is listening. In big office buildings, there may be lawyers from dozens of firms—not just the ones who work in the building, but also lawyers from other firms who are attending depositions, closings, and meetings in your building. Even if you know what all the opposing lawyers look like, you probably do not know all of their friends. Even in a large city, the legal community can be surprisingly small, particularly in any sort of specialized practice area. Thus, a lawyer must take reasonable precautions to ensure against being overheard. Rule 1.6(c). Yakking about the case in a bar is unreasonable, in view of the foreseeable risk of being overheard by someone who might take an interest in the conversation.

Blogging and Bragging

2. Correct answer is (B). This example is meant to reinforce the broad definition of confidential client information. Rule 1.6 applies to all information relating to representation. That includes the identity of the client and the nature of the representation—here, the health department investigation of the rats and cockroaches. ABA Formal Op. 480 (2018) confirms this broad reading of "information relating to representation." The definition of confidential information under Rule 1.6(a) also includes

information that is generally known. The exception for generally known information applies only to the duty not to make adverse use of confidential information, under Rule 1.9(c); it does not qualify the duty not to disclose, under Rule 1.6(a). In any event, the information disclosed would not be generally known under the definition in ABA Formal Op. 17-479 — see the discussion above. For these reasons, option (C) is incorrect.

Option (D) is incorrect because it uses the definition of attorney-client privileged communications in an attempt to narrow the scope of the duty of confidentiality. Remember, "information relating to representation" in Rule 1.6(a) is considerably broader than communications protected by the attorney-client privilege.

Option (A) is a bit tricky. True, the lawyer did not notify Flowers, but even if she had, that would not have made her conduct permissible. She was required to obtain informed consent, which requires an explanation of the risks of, and alternatives to, the lawyer publishing the information. See Rule 1.0(e).

In the Cloud(s)

3. Whenever a new means of communication or information storage is invented, lawyers worry about risks associated with using it. When lawyers first began using e-mail, cordless phones, and cell phones in their practices, there was a flurry of concern that these technologies might be unusually susceptible of being "overheard" through electronic means. (Older analog cellular phones could be monitored using police scanners, as England's Prince Charles found out to his profound consternation after talking dirty with his then girlfriend, now wife, Camilla Parker-Bowles, on an old-school analog cell phone.) With the improvement in these communications technologies, however, there was less of a risk that they would be monitored by others. Accordingly, the ABA Committee on Professional Responsibility issued an opinion stating that sending confidential client information via unencrypted e-mail did not violate the duty, because e-mail communications, even those without fancy privacy protection, do not pose an unreasonable risk of being intercepted. ABA Formal Op. 99-413. In cases involving highly sensitive information, however, a lawyer might be under an obligation to discuss extra security measures with the client.

The ABA Ethics 20/20 Commission made a couple of minor rules changes to address electronic communication and data storage. These changes make abundant sense, and mostly track the law as it existed prior to the 2013 amendments to the Model Rules. What the amendments do is to clarify that a lawyer may be subject to professional discipline for carelessness with client data, as well as potentially being sued for negligence. The first change was to clarify that, as a matter of professional competence, lawyers must be knowledgeable about the risks and benefits of available technology. Rule 1.1, cmt. [6]. As for confidentiality, Rule 1.6(c) now provides that lawyers must exercise reasonable care to safeguard confidential client information. As all of you know from first-year torts, what reasonable care requires varies according to the circumstances. Thus, Rule 1.6, cmt. [19] sets out numerous factors that should be considered in determining whether a lawyer used reasonable care to protect client confidences. These include the sensitivity of the information, the difficulty of implementing security precautions, and the extent to which further security measures make it difficult for the lawyer to represent clients. Fleshing out these factors, an Iowa ethics opinion recommends that lawyers conduct a "due diligence" process on a company with which they contract to provide cloud computing services. This due diligence process should consider factors such as:

- Is the service provider a solid company with a good operating record, and is it recommended by others?
- Does the company's End User License Agreement (EULA) contain limitations on the company's responsibility or damages for breach of the agreement?
- In the event of the company's financial default, will the lawyer lose access to the data?
- Who has access to passwords that are required for access to data?
- Is it possible to encrypt certain data using higher levels of protection if desired?

See Iowa State Bar Assoc. Comm. on Ethics and Practice Guidelines, Opinion 11-01. In this case, Avenal's failure to do any investigation at all of LegalCloud's data protection practices constitutes a failure to take reasonable care to safeguard confidential client information. Thus, he is subject to discipline for violating Rule 1.6(c).

But wait, you might say—isn't the fault that of the outside service provider, LegalCloud, not the lawyer? Maybe, but Avenal has an independent professional duty *himself* to safeguard client confidences. He is not subject to discipline vicariously, due to the cloud-storage vendor's negligence. Rather, the problem is his failure to use reasonable care in vetting the service to make sure it is up to the task. See also ABA Formal Op. 477R (2017), on securing communications of protected client information, and ABA Formal Op. 451 (2008), on outsourcing. (If this example seems familiar, go back and look at Example 1 in Chapter 6 on competence—it's a very similar fact pattern.)

EXCEPTIONS TO THE PROFESSIONAL DUTY

There are some state variations in the scope of the duty of confidentiality—see, for example, the Michigan rule quoted above—but there are a lot of state variations in the exceptions to confidentiality, which permit or require a lawyer to disclose confidential information. If there is any part of the professional responsibility course in which you want to be particularly attentive to local law (assuming, of course, that your instructor does not rely solely on the Model Rules), this would be it. When considering state-by-state variations, please be attentive to the distinction between a permission to disclose (denoted by "may") and a requirement to disclose (indicated by "shall").[3] For example, Illinois Rule of Professional Conduct 1.6(b) states that "[a] lawyer may reveal information relating to the representation of a client to the extent the lawyer reasonably believes necessary . . . to prevent the client from committing a crime in circumstances other than those specified in paragraph (c)." Rule 1.6(c) provides that "[a] lawyer shall reveal information relating to the representation of a client to the extent the lawyer reasonably believes necessary to prevent reasonably certain death or substantial bodily harm." Thus, a lawyer in Chicago would be permitted—but not required—to reveal information to the extent reasonably necessary to prevent a client from committing tax fraud, but would be required to disclose to prevent the client from committing murder or arson.

Exceptions to the duty of confidentiality, as stated in the Model Rules, are considered in the order they are stated in Rule 1.6. The first two exceptions, curiously, are contained in Rule 1.6(a), while the remaining exceptions are in Rule 1.6(b). What difference does this make? I think the answer is that the first two—implied authorization and informed consent—are either/or rules. That is, if the disclosure is authorized, it's authorized, and there is no more to say about the issue. The remainder, however, are all subject to an overarching qualification: Disclosure is permitted, but only to the extent the lawyer reasonably believes necessary to accomplish the purpose of the disclosure. In other words, it is possible to over-disclose, by going beyond the extent of disclosure that would have been adequate. See, for example, In re Bryan, 61 P.3d 641 (Kan. 2003), where a lawyer might have been entitled to disclose some client confidences to respond to allegations of wrongdoing, but went way beyond what was reasonably necessary. Rule 1.6, cmt. [16], also suggests (but does not require) that the lawyer first seek to persuade the client to do the right thing, so that no disclosure would be necessary.

---

3. See Model Rules Scope [14] for the distinction between "shall," "may," and "should."

Authorized in Order to Carry Out
Representation — Rule 1.6(a)

If the professional duty of confidentiality were taken at face value, and a lawyer could never disclose information relating to representation at any time, to anyone, it would be hard to do anything useful on behalf of a client. Lawyers must constantly disclose information to judges, court clerks, and opposing counsel in litigation, or to the lawyers representing other parties in transactions. A simple statement such as "my client is ill and cannot attend the deposition tomorrow" would be a violation of Model Rule 1.6 if the client did not authorize the lawyer to make it. But, of course, it would be unduly cumbersome for the lawyer to seek the client's permission every time she wanted to speak on the client's behalf. Remember, from the client's point of view, the whole point of having a lawyer handle your problems is that you do not have to be involved in every facet of your legal affairs. And remember that the lawyer has authority under Model Rule 1.2(a) to make decisions about the means of representation. While the lawyer must reasonably consult with the client about those means, Rule 1.4(a)(2), that does not mean that every decision requires explicit authorization by the client. In fact, there are broad areas of routine decisions that the lawyer is permitted to make without checking first with the client.

Because the lawyer is authorized by agency law and Model Rule 1.2(a) to make decisions about the representation without consulting the client, we can say that the lawyer has implied authority to act on behalf of the client, as long as the lawyer is pursuing the client's ends as the client defines them. Within this area of authority, therefore, the lawyer also is authorized to make disclosures of confidential client information to the extent they will enable the lawyer to advance the client's ends. That is the permission granted by Model Rule 1.6(a), which is echoed in Restatement §61: "A lawyer may use or disclose confidential client information when the lawyer reasonably believes that doing so will advance the interests of the client in the representation." So, even if the client does not explicitly authorize a disclosure or use of confidential client information, the lawyer does not violate the duty of confidentiality if she is acting in furtherance of her client's interests, within the authority delineated by Model Rule 1.2(a).

A somewhat technical, but important rule connects the duty of confidentiality to the attorney-client privilege: If the lawyer is authorized to disclose a privileged communication between the lawyer and client, then the lawyer's disclosure waives the attorney-client privilege. However, if the disclosure was not authorized, it does not waive the privilege. See Rest. §79, cmt. c. If, for example, a lawyer discloses confidential information to prevent the client from committing a fraud, the lawyer is not subject to discipline because of the exception in Rule 1.6(b)(2) (see below); however, any privilege the client had in the communications disclosed by the lawyer is not waived, because the disclosure was against the client's interests, and therefore not impliedly authorized.

Informed Consent — Rule 1.6(a)

Like many of the rules intended to protect the client's interest, the client may agree to waive the lawyer's duty of confidentiality. Unless the disclosure falls within the lawyer's implied authority, however, the lawyer needs to obtain informed consent to disclose. Rule 1.6(a) ("unless the client gives informed consent"). That means advising the client fully and candidly about the risks and benefits of disclosure. Informed consent is defined by Rule 1.0(e) as agreement *after* the lawyer has given the client "adequate information and explanation about the material risks of and reasonably available alternatives to the proposed course of conduct." Even if it's clear that a reasonable client would consent, the lawyer still needs to explain things to the client and obtain express consent — again, unless this is an area in which the lawyer has implied authority to disclose. Note that the client's informed consent to disclose need not be "confirmed in writing," as would be required for informed consent to a conflict of interest. Compare Rule 1.7(b)(4), Rule 1.9(a). Nevertheless, it is a good idea to confirm the client's consent in writing in the event of a subsequent dispute over whether the disclosure was authorized.

Rule 1.6(b) Exceptions

Model Rule 1.6(b) sets out seven situations in which a lawyer may reveal confidential client information. In other words, disclosure is permissive, not mandatory. In all of the permissive-disclosure situations, the lawyer may disclose information only to the extent the lawyer reasonably believes is necessary to accomplish the objective of the disclosure. Rule 1.6(b). That means, for example, that a lawyer attempting to stop a client's ongoing fraud may contact the victim of the fraud (say, a bank) or law enforcement authorities such as the Securities and Exchange Commission, appealing to the permission in Rule 1.6(b)(2). Informing a reporter for the *Wall Street Journal* is almost certainly not permitted. Even where some disclosure is permitted, over-disclosure of confidential information would violate Rule 1.6 and probably also subject the lawyer to liability for breaching her fiduciary duty to the client.

Furthermore, the lawyer should always explore the possibility that the client would be willing to disclose the information, or otherwise rectify the harm, if only pressed on the matter. Lawyers sometimes assume the worst about their clients, but very few clients are outright crooks, and most are willing to do the right thing if counseled to do so. It is probably fair to say that a lawyer is *required* to consult with the client before disclosing confidential information, even where an exception to Rule 1.6 applies. Comment [16] to Rule 1.6 says that, "[w]here practicable, the lawyer should first seek to persuade the client to take suitable action to obviate the need for disclosure." If you add to that Comment, which is not binding, the duty-to-communicate rule, Rule 1.4, which requires the lawyer "reasonably [to] consult with the client about the means by which the client's objectives are to be accomplished." Rule 1.4(a)(2), there is arguably a duty to remonstrate with the client and seek to either change the client's behavior or obtain informed consent to disclose, before disclosing the information unilaterally.

Disclosure to Prevent Wrongdoing

There is longstanding controversy over the lawyer's authority to disclose client wrongdoing of some sort—criminal conduct, noncriminal conduct threatening bodily harm, financial shenanigans, and so on. Critics of the legal profession argue that the obligation of confidentiality should be modified to permit or require lawyers to disclose confidential information if the disclosure would be necessary to prevent the client's wrongdoing, while defenders of the profession's traditional rule emphasize the values served by confidentiality and warn of an erosion of trust in the lawyer-client relationship that would accompany relaxing the duty. It is extremely important to be clear on what this fight is about. No one, not even the most pro-disclosure zealots, thinks the lawyer ought to be permitted to disclose purely past crimes or frauds in which the lawyer is in no way implicated. The debate instead concerns two tricky situations: (1) future harms caused by the client, generally in cases where the lawyer's services have been used; and (2) past frauds where the lawyer was innocent at the time of the transaction but subsequently learns of the fraudulent nature of the client's activities. As for information relating to purely past conduct, where the consequences of that conduct are entirely in the past, there is practically universal agreement that the lawyer is required to keep those facts secret.

Please be careful not to mix up the crime-fraud exception to the attorney-client privilege (Chapter 8) with any applicable permission to disclose confidential information. The limited exception permitting disclosure of confidential client information in Rule 1.6(b)(2) and (b)(3) applies only to those crimes or frauds that are reasonably certain to result in *substantial* injury to the *financial* interests or property of another, and only where the client used the lawyer's services in connection with the crime or fraud. Compare the scope of the crime-fraud exception to the privilege—a communication occurring where a client consults a lawyer for the purpose of obtaining assistance to engage in (any) crime or fraud. Rest. §82.

Physical Injury to Others (and Crimes) — Rule 1.6(b)(1)

The Model Code permitted a lawyer to reveal the intention of the client to commit *any* crime, no matter how trivial, and the information necessary to prevent the crime. DR 4-101(C)(3). Unlike the crime-fraud exception and the attorney-client privilege, the exception to the professional duty of confidentiality did not require that the client use the lawyer's services to commit the crime. The Model Rules tightened that exception considerably, however, and the 1983 version of the rules permitted disclosure only of information pertaining to future crimes where the client's criminal act was likely to result in death or serious bodily injury. Rule 1.6(b)(1) (1983 vers.). For both the Model Code and the 1983 Model Rules, the permissibility of disclosure turned at least in part on whether the client's act could be characterized as a crime under applicable criminal statutes. That's why I put "(and Crimes)" in the heading above.

The criminal act requirement was removed from the ABA Model Rule in 2002, and that version was subsequently adopted by most states, so now little turns on whether or not the client's act is a crime. The focus is instead on the seriousness of resulting physical harm and the confidence the lawyer has that it may result. If the harm is (1) reasonably certain to occur, and (2) involves death or substantial bodily harm, then the lawyer *may* disclose information (3) to the extent the lawyer reasonably believes necessary to prevent the harm. Rule 1.6(b)(1). In a case in which a criminal defense lawyer may have reasonably believed that an anonymous call to law enforcement could avoid the death of two children, the call would be permissible, even if the client refused to consent to it. See *McClure v. Thompson*, 323 F.3d 1233 (9th Cir. 2003).

Note, however, that this is not the rule governing disclosure of information relating to nonphysical harms, such as financial frauds, regardless of whether they can be characterized as crimes. Under the Model Code, the lawyer would have been permitted to disclose to prevent a future financial harm resulting from a criminal act by the client. But the 1983 version of the Model Rules clearly restricted the permission to disclose to crimes involving physical injury; the permission to disclose to prevent nonphysical harms resulting from client criminal acts did *not* carry over from the Model Code.

Back in the day when the Model Rules prohibited disclosure to save human life, except where the client's act was a crime, professional responsibility instructors liked to show how stringent the duty of confidentiality was by offering dramatic examples where the lawyer would not have permission under the rules to disclose information. An example from many casebooks is *Spaulding v. Zimmerman*, 116 N.W.2d 704 (Minn. 1962), where the defendant's lawyer in a personal-injury lawsuit learns that the plaintiff has a life-threatening injury of which he is unaware. Putting aside the moral issues for a moment (which are what really make *Spaulding* an interesting case), under the 1983 version of the Model Rules the lawyer may not disclose the injury, unless she can somehow persuade the client to give informed consent to the disclosure. The bodily harm exception under the old version of the rules permitted disclosure only to the extent that the lawyer reasonably believed necessary to prevent the client from committing *a criminal* act that the lawyer believed was likely to result in *imminent* death or serious bodily harm. Rule 1.6(b)(1) (1983 vers.). In *Spaulding*, the risk of harm may have been imminent since the plaintiff had an aortic aneurysm that may have burst at any moment, but there was nothing criminal about the defendant's act, which was merely refusing to produce voluntarily information that the plaintiff's lawyer did not request in discovery.

Financial Harms — Rule 1.6(b)(2), (b)(3)

The 2003 amendments by the ABA to Rule 1.6 made the analysis of confidentiality much simpler in the context of financial frauds. Under the current version of the confidentiality rule, a lawyer may disclose confidential client information to prevent, rectify, or mitigate substantial financial injury to a third party caused by the client's crime or fraud, *as long as* the client used the lawyer's services to commit the crime or fraud.[4] Where the fraud was accomplished without the lawyer's services, however, the lawyer has no authority to disclose. The permission to disclose is somewhat confusingly divided between two subsections, (b)(2), which deals with disclosure *before* the lawyer's services were used to commit the crime or fraud, and (b)(3), which applies if the lawyer later learns that her services were unwittingly used to commit the crime or fraud. See Rule 1.6, cmt. [8]. Whether the lawyer is considering disclosing to prevent future fraud or to mitigate the consequences of past fraud, the rules now recognize a permission to disclose, to the extent the lawyer believes disclosure is necessary to avoid substantial harm to the financial interests of a third party.

As discussed elsewhere (in Chapter 5 on representing entities and Chapter 12 on client fraud), the SEC's regulations promulgated under §307

---

4. The term "fraud" is defined in Rule 1.0(d) as "conduct that is fraudulent under the substantive or procedural law of the applicable jurisdiction and has a purpose to deceive." The reference to procedural law suggests that various frauds on the tribunal, such as obstruction of justice, come within this exception. For example, the lawyer would be permitted to disclose confidential information to prevent the lawyer from shredding documents covered by a subpoena.

of the Sarbanes-Oxley Act now require lawyers to follow detailed procedures for reporting evidence of possible wrongdoing up the corporate chain of command. The regulations also permit "reporting out" confidential information to the SEC as necessary to prevent or rectify fraud by the client. 17 C.F.R. §205.3(d). These regulations apply only to lawyers representing publicly traded corporations, however, so in many cases a lawyer will be thrown back into the Model Rules for guidance.

OTHER PERMISSIVE DISCLOSURE SCENARIOS

Securing Legal Advice — Rule 1.6(b)(4)

This section permits a lawyer to disclose confidential information to the extent necessary to secure legal advice (for the lawyer, that is) concerning compliance with the disciplinary rules. Sometimes lawyers are "clients," too, when it comes to figuring out what their obligations are under the increasingly complex disciplinary rules. Arguably, a consultation of this nature is "impliedly authorized" under Model Rule 1.6(a), because obtaining sound legal advice will assist the lawyer in representing the client. See Model Rule 1.6, cmt. [9]. But it is no longer necessary to appeal to the implied authority exception of Model Rule 1.6(a), because there is now an express textual exception for the lawyer obtaining expert assistance on compliance with the disciplinary rules. One problem with the textual exception is that it refers only to "these Rules" — that is, only the state disciplinary rules. As this book emphasizes, however, the law governing lawyers goes beyond the disciplinary rules, and sometimes it is essential to understand how generally applicable law affects a lawyer's duties under the disciplinary rules. For this reason, a sensible interpretation of Model Rule 1.6(b)(2) would permit disclosure to the extent the consultation pertained to the lawyer's compliance with the law governing lawyers generally. Note, however, that this exception does not permit disclosure to another lawyer to obtain expert assistance on some specialized area of law that pertains to the client. It may be that this disclosure is impliedly authorized under Rule 1.6(a), but the disclosure does not come within the exception of Rule 1.6(b)(4).

Self-Defense — Rule 1.6(b)(5)

A lawyer is permitted to disclose information to the extent she reasonably believes necessary in order to defend herself against a charge of wrongdoing connected with her representation of a client. Rule 1.6(b)(5). The most common self-defense situation is a malpractice suit by the client. The lawyer would be unfairly hamstrung in defending this lawsuit if she could not reveal as much of the client's confidences as would be necessary to exonerate herself. The exception also extends to actions against the lawyer brought by third parties based on work the lawyer performed for the client. If a transactional lawyer is sued in a shareholder-derivative action or by the other party in a deal for having aided and abetted the client's fraud, the lawyer would be permitted to disclose confidential client information in self-defense.

A well-known self-defense case is *Meyerhofer v. Empire Fire and Marine Ins.*, 497 F.2d 1190 (2d Cir. 1974). In that case, Goldberg, one of the lawyers for the issuer of securities, had some reservations about the adequacy of the issuer's disclosures in its registration statement and prospectus. He tried to talk the partners in his law firm into disclosing certain payments, but they refused. Rather than take up the matter with the client, which he should have done, Goldberg resigned from the firm and wrote a memo to the SEC detailing his concerns.[5] When investors in the securities issued by the firm's clients took big losses, they considered suing everyone in sight — the issuer, the issuer's law firm, the underwriter, and Goldberg personally. Significantly, they did not actually file a complaint against Goldberg, but advised him that he might be made a defendant. In order to exonerate himself, Goldberg showed the plaintiffs a copy of the memo, indicating that he had tried to have the proper disclosures included in the offering documents. The plaintiffs then dropped plans to sue Goldberg. Once the lawsuit was filed, the law firm representing one of the defendants then moved to disqualify the plaintiffs' law firm, arguing that it had improperly received confidential client information from Goldberg. The court held that Goldberg had acted properly, so the confidential information received by the plaintiffs' lawyers was not "tainted" and should not be the basis for disqualifying the lawyers.

The reason the information was not tainted is the self-defense exception. The court analyzed the issue using the Model Code provision in DR 4-101(C), but exactly the same language is carried over into the Model Rules, in Rule 1.6 (b)(5). A lawyer is permitted to reveal information "to establish a defense to a . . . civil claim against the lawyer based upon

---

5. There are two other professional responsibility issues raised by this case. First, under the entity-representation rule, Rule 1.13(a), Goldberg's client was the corporation itself, not any of its individual officers or directors. See Chapter 5. Second, although it was wise for Goldberg to talk first to the partners in his firm about his concerns, it is important to recognize that he has an independent obligation to comply with the disciplinary rules. Rule 5.2(a). If one of the partners had told him not to worry about the disclosure, Goldberg would have to make a decision for himself about whether that advice was sound. It is true that a subordinate lawyer may act in accordance with the instructions of a supervising lawyer, but only if the supervising lawyer's resolution of an arguable question of professional duty is reasonable. Rule 5.2(b).

conduct in which the client was involved." That is exactly what Goldberg did. Note that the client does not have to be the one accusing the lawyer of wrongdoing in order for the self-defense exception to apply. Notice also that a formal proceeding need not be commenced to permit the lawyer to disclose under the self-defense exception. As a comment to this rule states, the rule "does not require the lawyer to await the commencement of an action or proceeding that charges such complicity." Rule 1.6, cmt. [10].[6] Still, a lawyer should be careful because if the disclosure is made too early, it might be the trigger for the lawsuit, rather than a reaction to it. In this case, Goldberg disclosed the memo only after the plaintiffs advised him that he would be made a defendant. But if Goldberg had disclosed prematurely, he might have given the plaintiffs the information they needed to decide whether to file a lawsuit. In that case, the disclosure would have been impermissible, and Goldberg would have found himself in a whole mess of trouble. His former client could sue him for breach of fiduciary duty for violating Model Rule 1.6, and he could be subject to professional discipline.

The self-defense exception makes some people angry because it appears to undercut the "sacred" duty of confidentiality that lawyers invoke whenever they resist an obligation to disclose confidential information to avoid harms to others. To put it cynically, lawyers think they should be required to keep secrets where disclosure could avoid a grievous harm to others, like the death of the young man in *Spaulding* (see the discussion above) or a massive financial fraud, but they should be permitted to disclose relevant information when their own butts are in the sling. One response to this objection is that without the self-defense exception, the lawyer would be burdened unfairly. H&H §9.22. The client is always free to disclose confidential information, but if the client could prevent the lawyer from disclosing in self-defense, an unscrupulous client could wrongfully accuse a lawyer of misconduct and prevent the lawyer from defending herself. A somewhat less satisfying but perhaps more candid response is simply to admit that the lawyers who draft the disciplinary rules occasionally act in a self-interested manner. R&D §1.16-12. In any event, the self-defense exception has changed remarkably little from the Model Code to the most current version of the Model Rules, so it is a safe bet that it is not going to disappear any time soon.

---

6. As always, please be attentive to variations in your jurisdiction's version of the Model Rules. The self-defense exception in the District of Columbia states precisely the opposite rule to that given in the text here. D.C. Rule of Professional Conduct 1.6(e)(3) permits lawyers to disclose confidential client information "to the extent reasonably necessary to establish a defense to a criminal charge, disciplinary charge, or civil claim, *formally instituted against the lawyer*, based upon conduct in which the client was involved, or to the extent reasonably necessary to respond to specific allegations by the client concerning the lawyer's representation of the client."

Compliance with Law — Rule 1.6(b)(6)

This section helps to mitigate some of the tension created when the disciplinary rules appear to prohibit disclosure in cases where generally applicable law requires it. The text of the 1983 version of Model Rule 1.6 was absolute in its insistence that a lawyer may never reveal confidential client information outside one of the narrow exceptions. This meant that if a court ordered a lawyer to testify about some fact within her knowledge, having considered and rejected a claim of attorney-client privilege, the lawyer would have been prohibited from doing so. That was a troubling result, as commentators recognized, because the disciplinary rules, of which Model Rule 1.6 is a part, are an integral part of a legal system, not something that stands apart from the rest of the law. See, for example, H&H §9.25.

The current version of Model Rule 1.6 accordingly recognizes the commonsense rule that if a lawyer is required to provide information in order to comply with a court order or other law, she is permitted to do so. Rule 1.6(b)(6). The lawyer is required to assert all available nonfrivolous grounds, such as the attorney-client privilege and work product, for resisting disclosure and must consult with the client about appealing any adverse ruling issued by the court. Rule 1.6, cmt. [15]. Once the court has finally ruled, however, disclosure is permitted by Rule 1.6(b)(6), and the lawyer need not fear discipline for breaching the duty of confidentiality. The last example in Chapter 7 imagined a judge demanding that the defense lawyer answer a question about her client's whereabouts. Although the communication was not covered by the attorney-client privilege (because it was with the client's mother), it was within the duty of confidentiality. If the judge in fact ordered the lawyer to answer, Rule 1.6(b)(6) would permit the lawyer to do so without violating the duty of confidentiality.

Conflicts Checking — Rule 1.6(b)(7)

Back in the day, a newly licensed lawyer might hang out a shingle or join a law firm, and then remain in that employment for the remainder of her career. Nowadays lawyers can expect to change jobs many times within a career. Lateral mobility, as it is called, creates numerous issues of professional responsibility. One of the most important is the extent to which a moving lawyer retains duties of loyalty and confidentiality to clients of a former employer. Chapter 16 explains how the law handles conflicts of interest for moving lawyers. For now, suffice it to say that a moving lawyer, and her prospective new employer, will want to ensure that hiring the moving lawyer will not ensnare the new employer in a nasty conflict-of-interest scenario that will result in disqualification of the new employer from the representation of clients whose interests are adverse to those of the moving lawyer's old employer.

The trouble is, the new employer will want to know certain information to determine whether hiring the moving lawyer will create a conflict of interest with other clients of the firm. But that information is almost certainly protected as confidential client information of the moving lawyer. Even the identity of the client and the nature of the matter on which the moving lawyer's old firm represented it is within the scope of Rule 1.6(a) information relating to representation. The moving lawyer therefore seems stuck between a rock and a hard place. Either she keeps the confidences of her old client, thereby creating a risk for the new employer (and thus making the new employer unwilling to hire her), or she risks disclosing protected confidences of the clients of her former employer, thus subjecting herself, and her former employer to potential liability.

Rule 1.6(b)(7), a relatively recently-added exception, permits disclosure of confidential information to the extent the lawyer reasonably believes necessary to detect and resolve conflicts of interest arising from either the lawyer's change of employment or a merger of law firms. The lawyer must ensure, however, that the revealed information will not waive any applicable attorney-client privilege or otherwise prejudice the client. (This is really just a restatement of the overarching principle that disclosure should be no greater than necessary to accomplish the purpose of the exception.) The permission to disclose applies only once substantive discussions about employment have begun. Rule 1.6, cmt. [13]. A lawyer is not allowed to reveal confidential client information during preliminary discussions with a potential new employer.

Examples

Some Exceptional Challenges

In the following scenarios, is the lawyer permitted to disclose the information in question?

4. A lawyer represented a man who had been fired from his job and was seeking unemployment benefits. After a confidential hearing before an administrative law judge, the application was denied because of evidence that the former employee had assaulted another employee. The lawyer billed the $1,500 for her services, but the client refused to pay. When the lawyer wrote a letter demanding payment, the client responded by writing a scathing review of the lawyer on a crowd-sourced review site called Avvo (similar to Yelp or the reviews on Amazon.com). The client called the lawyer's services "lackluster," said she was frequently late in responding to phone calls and e-mails, and said "a trained poodle could have done a better job at my unemployment hearing." The lawyer wrote

a public response on Avvo in which she stated: "I'm sorry for my client, but I can't invent facts that aren't there. If my client hadn't beaten up a co-worker he would not be in this predicament."

5. In the course of working on a client's case, the lawyer runs across an issue that may be governed by federal maritime law. A law school classmate at another firm is a maritime lawyer. The lawyer wants to call up his friend and ask a quick question about the application of maritime law to the case, to see whether additional research or association of specialist co-counsel is required.

6. Attorney Ellen Singer represents Hall Chemical Company, whose owner, Andy Hall, is a notoriously irascible, hard-driving man with limitless contempt for what he regards as needless government regulation. After discovering that Hall had permitted one of his employees to dump 55-gallon drums of toxic chemicals in the woods behind his plant, Singer has been trying to persuade him either to clean up the mess or to notify the Environmental Protection Agency and the state Department of Environmental Protection. Singer is worried that the chemicals may seep into the groundwater, which is the municipal water source for the town. The types of chemicals dumped are known to cause cancer if ingested. If Hall finally refuses to take any remedial action, may Singer disclose the dumping?

7. Christine Collins is a licensed clinical social worker and lawyer, who practices family law. She uses her background as a social worker to address clients' needs holistically, rather than trying to handle their legal problems in isolation from other issues. One of her clients is the husband in a divorce action, who admits that he has had "some disagreements" with his wife over the way he has treated his children. His wife believes he has abused them, physically or sexually. The client admits hitting his children but says it happened only rarely, and only during a particularly difficult period in his life. He swears it will not happen again. His brother, who has helped him emotionally through his divorce, was present during the discussion with Collins.

   Two facts about local law are relevant here. First, the history of abuse may affect the parties' custody arrangements. Second, licensed social workers (among other enumerated mental health professionals) have a duty to report evidence of child abuse to law enforcement officials. Collins believes that the admission by her client satisfies the reporting threshold for the state statute. May or must she report the evidence?

8. Heppner is an attorney for a large firm, the most important client of which is Show Me the Money, Inc. (SMTM). SMTM's basic business plan was to borrow money from banks, use the money to buy expensive computer hardware, and then lease the hardware to businesses. The

difference between the cost of borrowing (interest payments) and the lease payments from the businesses would be the profits of SMTM. At some point, it occurred to one of the partners in SMTM, Wiseman, that it would be possible to make more money by taking out fake bank loans. The bank would be willing to lend money using the lease payments as collateral. In order to obtain loans, however, SMTM needed to present an opinion letter by a lawyer, certifying that various legal requirements had been met in the lease agreement. Heppner and other lawyers prepared these opinion letters, and also drafted the lease agreements and other closing documents. Based on their standard "due diligence" inquiries, everything in the leases appeared legitimate.

One day, Wiseman came to Heppner and informed him that he had been taking out loans using leases on computers that did not exist. Wiseman and his partner had been forging the signatures on lease agreements and presenting them to the bank as collateral for loans. He had tricked the lawyers into preparing opinion letters and lease agreements by altering the documents he had given to them. Wiseman wanted help because his scheme was starting to unwind. Previously, he had been able to cover the interest payments on previous loans by taking out even more fraudulent loans, but now the bank was starting to get suspicious and would not lend any more money to SMTM. Heppner told Wiseman that he had to come clean and inform the bank that many of its loans were extended on the basis of false representations. Wiseman refused to inform the bank, and stormed out of Heppner's office in a rage. "You're my lawyer, not a *&%$!# cop," he roared. "And another thing—you better keep this conversation to yourself, or I'll sue you!" What should Heppner do?

9. James is an attorney admitted to practice in Ohio and Florida. He is currently employed at a law firm in Cleveland, but is considering an offer to move to Miami to work for a law firm there. One of the clients of the law firm in Cleveland is Cavalier Corporation, a large company that manufactures renewable energy systems. It is considering a hostile takeover effort for Heat, Inc., a company based in Miami that designs geothermal heating systems. Cavalier has discussed the potential takeover with mergers and acquisitions lawyers at the Cleveland law firm under the strictest secrecy, believing that if its interest in taking over Heat becomes generally known, other competitors in the green-energy business will realize the value of Heat and drive up its price. It is generally known that the Cleveland firm represents Cavalier Corp. in a variety of corporate matters.

As a senior associate in the corporate department of the Cleveland firm, James worked on other merger transactions for Cavalier Corp., but did not do any work on the proposed hostile takeover of Heat, Inc. James knows that the Miami firm represents Heat, Inc. His offer of employment with the firm is contingent on a satisfactory resolution of a check for conflicts of interest. James reasonably believes that, under applicable moving-lawyer conflicts standards (see Chapter 16), his hiring would not disqualify the Miami firm from continuing to represent Heat, Inc. What information may James disclose to the Miami firm, concerning the Cleveland firm's representation of Cavalier?

Explanations

Some Exceptional Challenges

4. Based on a reported disciplinary action from Illinois, *In re Tsamis*, No. 6288664 (Jan. 15, 2014), in which the lawyer was publicly reprimanded. First, did the lawyer disclose confidential information? Yes — the fact that the client is alleged to have beaten up a co-worker is "information relating to the representation" under Rule 1.6(a). The fact that the hearing was confidential serves to underscore the applicability of Rule 1.6(a), but it is not necessary. Even if the hearing records were public information the lawyer may not disclose the information without the client's authorization, or unless an exception applies.

    Which leads to the applicability of the self-defense exception. Note the italicized language in Rule 1.6(b)(5). A lawyer may disclose information to the extent reasonably necessary "to establish a *claim or defense* on behalf of the lawyer in a controversy between the lawyer and the client, to establish a *defense* to a . . . *civil claim* against the lawyer . . ., or to respond to allegations in any *proceeding* concerning the lawyer's representation of the client." What do the italicized words suggest to you? To my mind they restrict the applicability of the self-defense exception to formal proceedings of some sort, whether disciplinary grievances, malpractice lawsuits, or claims of ineffective assistance of counsel. See also Rule 1.6, cmt. [10], which says a claim giving rise to the self-defense exception "can arise in a civil, criminal, disciplinary, or other proceeding." A client griping on Avvo is not the kind of formal proceeding contemplated by the rule. The comment goes on to say that the lawyer need not await the commencement of formal charges, but in this case there is no connection to any kind of formal proceeding, so the lawyer is not permitted to use the self-defense exception to reveal the information about the client beating up a co-worker.

    You will sometimes hear it said that a lawyer may disclose confidential information in order to collect a fee. Comment [11] to Rule 1.6 does say that a lawyer may "prove the services rendered in an action" as part of collecting a fee, but this means only that the lawyer may disclose information related to the nature and value of the services provided. Disclosing the underlying facts relating to the representation is not permitted here, even if the lawyer is irritated at the client's non-payment of his fee.

A bunch of state ethics opinions reach the same conclusion. See, for example, Texas Bar Op. 662 (2016); Nassau County Bar Ass'n 2016-01; N.Y. State Bar Ass'n Op. 1032 (2014); San Francisco Bar Ass'n Op. 2014-1; Penn. Bar Ass'n Op. 2014-200; L.A. County Bar Ass'n Op. 525 (2012). The Pennsylvania opinion is particularly helpful, and discusses the Illinois reprimand on which this problem is based. Interestingly, Minnesota is considering a new exception, Rule 1.6(b)(8), which would permit a lawyer to "respond to a client's specific and public accusation, made outside a legal proceeding, of misconduct by the lawyer" in certain circumstances.

5. This is a bit of a trick question, because you may be tempted to cite Model Rule 1.6(b)(4) and move on. The problem is that, strictly speaking, the rule permitting disclosure to secure legal advice covers only "advice about the lawyer's compliance with these Rules"—that is, the state disciplinary rules. See also Comment [9] to Rule 1.6, which also talks about "the importance of a lawyer's compliance with the Rules of Professional Conduct." The lawyer in this case probably is permitted to disclose, but you have to argue for it in a different way.

One way to argue for permission is to assume that the client would give the lawyer permission to make a limited inquiry, couched in hypothetical terms, to her friend the maritime lawyer. Thus, the disclosure is "impliedly authorized in order to carry out the representation" of the client under Model Rule 1.6(a). The ABA Committee on Professional Responsibility has interpreted the "implied authorization" exception to include lawyer-to-lawyer consultations where the consultation will further the client's interests by obtaining the benefits of the other lawyer's expertise. ABA Formal Op. 98-411. Even so, the lawyer doing the consulting should take care to keep disclosures of confidential information to a minimum. The comments to the confidentiality rule permit some disclosure as long as the question is couched in hypothetical terms that do not reveal the identity of the client. Rule 1.6, cmt. [4] ("A lawyer's use of a hypothetical to discuss issues relating to the representation is permissible so long as there is no reasonable likelihood that the listener will be able to ascertain the identity of the client or the situation involved."). Don't forget that the safest course of action here may simply be to obtain the client's informed consent to the consultation. Rule 1.6(a).

6. This used to be a common fact pattern used to test your understanding of the bodily harm exception to the rule. Under the 1983 version of Model Rule 1.6, the answer would be "no," Singer cannot disclose unless: (1) dumping the chemicals is a crime under applicable federal or state environmental statutes; and (2) the resulting death or substantial

bodily injury is imminent. Unless you have more information, you probably do not know whether the dumping is a crime, so you would have to answer the question in the alternative—for example, if the dumping is a crime under governing law, then Singer may disclose as long as the second requirement is satisfied. If it is not a crime, however, there is no need to analyze the second element, and disclosure is not permitted. Whether or not it is a crime, however, the dumping is unlikely to lead to *imminent* death or substantial bodily harm, because any harm it causes is likely to take a while to manifest itself. People affected by exposure to toxic chemicals in groundwater may not develop symptoms for many months or even years, making the connection between the dumping and the injury too remote in time to permit Singer to disclose.

All this changed with the 2002 version of Model Rule 1.6, which eliminated: (1) the "criminal act" requirement; (2) the element that the resulting harm be imminent; and (3) the requirement that it be the client's act that threatens harm. In a jurisdiction that has adopted this version of the rule, Singer may disclose, because disclosure would "prevent reasonably certain death or substantial bodily harm." Rule 1.6(b)(1). A comment added to the amended rule recognizes this result exactly:

> [A] lawyer who knows that a client has accidentally discharged toxic waste into a town's water supply may reveal this information to the authorities if there is a present and substantial risk that a person who drinks the water will contract a life-threatening or debilitating disease and the lawyer's disclosure is necessary to eliminate the threat or reduce the number of victims.

Rule 1.6, cmt. [6].

Even though the rule has changed for the better, there are still some traps. Watch out for cases where the harm is not "reasonably certain" to result. What if there is a 40 percent chance that the toxic waste will cause a serious illness? Ten percent? What if the client could eliminate the risk, but only by taking costly precautions? There is no hard-and-fast line here, but the reasonableness standard is intended to make reference to what other similarly situated lawyers would consider likely, in light of the available evidence. See Rule 1.0(h)-(j). If the harm is certain enough that the client would risk civil liability under the circumstances, the harm is "reasonably certain" for the purposes of the bodily harm exception.

7. This example is based on a hypothetical in Robert Mosteller, *Child Abuse Reporting Laws and Attorney-Client Confidences: The Reality and the Specter of Lawyer as Informant*, 42 Duke L.J. 203, 247 (1992). The idea of a lawyer/social worker providing holistic care to clients came from one of my former students, who had exactly this ambition. The attorney-client privilege, which is an evidentiary privilege protecting against compelled disclosure, would bar the lawyer from reporting. That is the whole point of

privileges—they block access to information that otherwise would be available in judicial proceedings. But the professional duty does not serve the same function. It protects the client's legitimate expectation that the lawyer will keep secrets, but it cannot be interposed to block a legal demand for information. Just as a lawyer cannot assert the duty of confidentiality in response to a grand jury subpoena, she cannot rely on the duty to avoid complying with the statute requiring reporting. The attorney-client privilege does not apply here because of the presence of the brother. I threw in the brother just to make it simpler. There actually is a difficult question in many states concerning the interaction between mandatory child-abuse reporting statutes and the attorney-client privilege. Some statutes specifically exempt privileged communications from disclosure, some expressly abrogate the privilege, but others are silent on this point. See Mosteller, *supra*, pp. 218-224. In order to avoid those complexities, I wanted to make clear that this was not a privileged communication because it was not made "in confidence." See Chapter 8 if you are rusty on the elements of the attorney-client privilege.

The "compliance with law" exception in Model Rule 1.6(b)(6) addresses situations like these, and makes clear that the lawyer is not subject to professional discipline as a result of having complied with a state law that requires reporting. Thus, Collins is not subject to discipline. Might she nevertheless face a breach of fiduciary duty lawsuit from her client? Maybe, but not because she violated Model Rule 1.6. The more likely theory is that she failed to *communicate* the relevant circumstances to her client in violation of Model Rule 1.4(a)(1) and (a)(5). The problem is that Collins wears two hats, so to speak. She is both a lawyer and a social worker. Normally, that is beneficial to her clients, who get more complete advice about how to deal with their lives—legal and social problems included. There are some cases, however, in which a client would not want to confide in a lawyer who is not a "pure" lawyer. At the outset of representation, Collins should have explained to her client that because she was both a lawyer and a social worker, she was subject to the reporting statute and would not be permitted to keep confidential any information she learned pertaining to child abuse. The client could give his informed consent to this limitation on Collins's representation of him. Rule 1.2(c). The limitation would be reasonable, particularly in view of the benefit to the client, but Collins would have to provide full disclosure before proceeding. Her failure to do so was a breach of her duty to communicate with her client and could subject her to liability.

If you like, you can make up really tough hypotheticals: Imagine that you're in a jurisdiction with the old version of Rule 1.6, permitting disclosure only where the information pertains to a criminal act committed by the client that the lawyer reasonably believes will result in imminent death or substantial bodily harm. Now imagine that you hear from your client that his brother is abusing the child. (No criminal act by the client.) Or imagine that the abuse is emotional, not physical. (No substantial bodily harm.) Or imagine that the conduct, for whatever reason, falls outside the jurisdiction's criminal prohibition. (No criminal act.) Or imagine that an uncle who is a notorious abuser is coming to visit in a month. (No imminent harm.) Professional responsibility instructors like to do this, to illustrate how harsh the old bodily-harm disclosure rule was. As the old version continues to be phased out in more states, fewer lawyers will need to worry about situations like this, but for a long time this was the "state of play" in discussions of confidentiality.

8. This example is considerably simplified, but based on the well-known *OPM Leasing* case. The best source for the OPM story is Philip B. Heymann & Lance Liebman, eds., *The Social Responsibilities of Lawyers: Case Studies* (1988). OPM really does stand for "Other People's Money," which maybe should have been a red flag to the lawyers that their client was not entirely honest. In any event, the lawyer here has found himself mixed up in his client's wrongdoing, without any intent by the lawyer to assist the wrongdoing. Heppner was duped, as much as the banks were. So this is not a case where the lawyer is trying to dissuade the client from committing fraud and using the threat of disclosing confidences to bring the client into line. In terms of the rules, this does not fall within Rule 1.6(b)(2)'s permission to disclose confidential information to *prevent* the client from committing a fraud. It does fit perfectly, however, into the retrospective disclosure provision of Rule 1.6(b)(3). That rule permits disclosure, to the extent the lawyer reasonably believes necessary, "to prevent, mitigate or rectify substantial injury to the financial interests or property of another that is reasonably certain to result or has resulted from the client's commission of a crime or fraud, in furtherance of which the client has used the lawyer's services."

Running through the elements, Wiseman's act is clearly a fraud and has resulted in substantial injury to the financial interests of the bank, which loaned money it otherwise would not have loaned to SMTM. But what about "prevent, mitigate or rectify"? Does Heppner reasonably believe that disclosure of his knowledge that the loan documents were fraudulent will help the bank in some way? If not, the disclosure is not permissible. In this case, there are probably many steps the bank may take to protect its interests, upon being informed that the loans were fraudulent. It may be able to foreclose on the loans or somehow assert a security interest in assets of SMTM, and it may not know it should do that without being informed of Wiseman's fraud. Importantly, Wiseman and SMTM used Heppner's services to commit the fraud. This isn't a case where Wiseman acted independently and later sought legal advice. If Heppner and his firm had not been involved in this initial wrongdoing, he would have no permission to disclose. But one of the foundational principles of the law governing lawyers is that a lawyer's services should not be used for unlawful purposes. This principle is recognized in Rule 1.2(d) and underlies many other rules, such as the prohibition in Rule 3.3(a) on presenting false testimony. To give effect to that principle in this context, the Model Rules now permit disclosure to lessen some of the harm that would otherwise result from the lawyer's services having been used to commit fraud.

9. James must be very careful here. Yes, it is true that Rule 1.6(b)(7) allows a lawyer to disclose confidential client information for the purpose of checking for conflicts of interest. The discussions with the Miami firm have proceeded to the point at which there are "substantive discussions regarding the new relationship" between James and the firm. See Rule 1.6, cmt. [13]. However, the exception for conflicts-checking does not permit the disclosure of everything. Comment [13] cautions that information should be disclosed only to the extent necessary to detect and resolve conflicts. James reasonably believes that he will not bring a conflict with him to the Miami firm, because while he worked for Cavalier on other matters, he did not perform any work on the proposed takeover of Heat. The trouble is, of course, it is hard to prove a negative. If confidentiality were not a concern, James could say something like, "There is a matter in which the interests of Cavalier and Heat are materially adverse, but I didn't work on it." Of course, revealing this information would probably tip off the Miami firm that Cavalier is considering making a hostile takeover offer for Heat. That disclosure would prejudice Cavalier, and therefore James may not disclose it. Note carefully the exception in Rule 1.6(b)(7), which is reiterated in Comment [13]: Lawyers may not disclose information that would compromise the attorney-client privilege or otherwise prejudice the client.

Thus, James must stay mum about the hostile takeover idea. He may say that he worked on a variety of corporate matters for Cavalier, and none of them involve clients of the Miami firm. Suppose that, having said that and nothing else, James is hired and subsequently Cavalier finds out that one of "its" former lawyers is now working for the Miami law firm representing Heat, Inc. (I put "its" in scare quotes here to flag the issue, to be addressed in Chapter 16, of when a lawyer "represents" a client — that is, does having worked on other matters for the client make James the former attorney for Cavalier for the purposes of conflicts of interest? The short answer is that James has represented Cavalier, but not in the relevant matter.) But suppose Cavalier is outraged about James's move, and wants to make trouble. It may do something like file a motion for an injunction, seeking the disqualification of the Miami law firm from the representation of Heat, on the theory that Heat is now privy to confidential information of Cavalier, learned from its former lawyer. That motion should be denied, but it would be a headache for Heat and the Miami law firm. The prospect of having to litigate disqualification motions makes law firms more reluctant to hire laterally, which impairs the mobility of lawyers. Rule 1.6(b)(7) mitigates this problem to some extent, and courts tend to be suspicious of attempts to disqualify law firms for conflicts of interest, but this example shows that there will always be risks associated with the lateral hiring of lawyers.

PART II

Secrets and Lies: Perjury and the Problem of Client Fraud

Perjury in Civil and Criminal Litigation: The Lawyer's "Trilemma"

10

INTRODUCTION

Many students initially react strongly to the subject of perjury. "It's a crime," says one group, "so why is there any question at all about the lawyer's duty not to assist client perjury?" Interestingly, another group of students usually has the equal but opposite reaction, saying that "[t]ruth is not for the lawyer to decide — it's for the jury — so how can you put the responsibility on the lawyer to police the client's testimony?" When the subject is the lawyer's responsibility to prevent or mitigate client wrongdoing — for example, setting up complex transactions that rely on questionable accounting treatment to conceal expenses from public disclosure — the rhetoric can become even more overheated. On one side, the organized bar tends to fight tooth and nail against any effort to make lawyers "rat out" or "police" their clients or play any kind of evaluative role with respect to the client's conduct. The opposing side — generally legal academics and a few critics within the profession — responds that the role of the lawyer is created within a society governed by the rule of law to ensure that individuals both conform to the law and are protected from abuse at the hands of the state. In some cases, such as defending the accused in a criminal trial, lawyers are justified in taking an adversarial stance toward the rest of the world, favoring the client's interests above all. There are many other contexts, however, in which "my client versus the rest of the world" is not the appropriate attitude to adopt. Planning, counseling, transactional, and regulatory-compliance work require the lawyer to pay more attention to the interests of justice, such as how a transaction will affect unrepresented third parties.

The law of perjury here embodies a delicate balance, which some commentators argue is the wrong one, among three professional duties of the lawyer: (1) to learn as much as possible about the client's case, in order to provide competent representation; (2) to keep confidential any information divulged by the client, so that the client will feel comfortable sharing everything that the lawyer needs to know; (3) not to participate in a fraud on the tribunal. This three-way conflict of duties, often called a "trilemma," is particularly acute in criminal cases where the defendant has a number of constitutional rights that bear on the lawyer's duties. Even in civil cases, though, it may happen that the lawyer will be unable to fulfill all three professional duties. The client may disclose enough information so that the lawyer knows her statement in court was a lie. Alternatively, the client may worry about the lawyer revealing information to the court and will withhold valuable facts that the lawyer could have used in representing the client. As you work through the rules, think about these three professional duties and ask yourself which one is being sacrificed in order to vindicate the others.

In short, the Model Rules emphasize the third duty in the "trilemma," requiring the lawyer to take remedial action to prevent or rectify fraud on the court, even if it requires disclosure of confidential client information. Please be aware, however, that jurisdictions vary tremendously on their approach to this question. Your state may rank the duties differently, and may actually prohibit any action by the lawyer that has the effect of revealing client confidences, even if it is necessary to prevent or rectify perjury.

MODEL RULE 3.3 ON PERJURY

The treatment of perjury under the Model Rules depends on the timing of the act. Perjury cases can be divided into prospective and retrospective—concerning, respectively, what a lawyer's obligations are in advance of trial or a deposition (for example, how to prepare a witness or what to do if the witness indicates she intends to lie) and what a lawyer must do if confronted by perjury in the past, such as a client who unexpectedly lies on the stand.

Get ready to do some flipping around in the rulebook as you work through Rule 3.3. It contains several defined terms, including knowledge (Rule 1.0(f)) and tribunal (Rule 1.0(m)). It also has a kind of internal defined term—"reasonable remedial measures"—which is explained in Comment [10].

Prospective

Active Participation by the Lawyer

First of all, a lawyer must not knowingly make a false statement of fact or law to a tribunal. Rule 3.3(a)(1); cross-reference Rule 1.0(m) for the definition of tribunal. To make this rule concrete, if the judge asks the lawyer at a sentencing hearing, "Does your client have a criminal record?" the lawyer must answer truthfully and would be subject to discipline if she lies.[1] The prohibition on making false statements of fact also extends to referring during closing argument to facts known to be false. Similarly, a lawyer arguing a motion or appeal must not misrepresent the facts in the record in the briefs or during her oral argument. To do so would subject the lawyer to discipline under Model Rule 3.3(a)(1). The lawyer also may not make a false statement of law, so if the judge asks, "Is there a sentencing guideline that covers this case?" the lawyer may argue that a particular guideline is not applicable, but cannot flatly say "no" if there is a guideline on point. Note that the current version of Rule 3.3(a) prohibiting making false statements of fact or law does not cover only "material" false statements, but extends to all false statements.

When the lie is not the lawyer's but the client's, the lawyer must not assist the client's perjury in any way. This prohibition is found in Model Rule 3.3(a)(3), which states that the lawyer shall not offer evidence that the lawyer knows to be false. (Cross-reference Rule 1.0(f) for the definition of knowledge.) If the lawyer calls a witness to testify, with the knowledge that the witness's testimony will be false, the lawyer violates this rule. Note that this rule applies to *any* evidence, not just "material" evidence. To take an even worse case, if the lawyer "engineers" the perjury by telling the witness to lie, the lawyer violates Model Rule 3.3(a)(3), as well as the prohibition in Model Rule 3.4(b) on counseling or assisting a witness to testify falsely.

Rule 3.3(b) requires the lawyer to take reasonable remedial measures, including disclosure to the tribunal if necessary, if the lawyer knows that the client in an adjudicative proceeding "intends to engage, is engaging or has engaged in criminal or fraudulent conduct related to the proceeding." That rule goes beyond false evidence, which is within Rule 3.3(a), and prohibits conduct such as bribery, destroying evidence, or threatening witnesses. Because perjury is a crime, you could interpret Rule 3.3(b) to include false testimony as well, but as a matter of statutory interpretation, the specific duties in Rule 3.3(a) ought to have control over the more general prohibition in Rule 3.3(b).

---

1. The fact of having a criminal record is not protected by the attorney-client privilege, either because (1) it was not a communication from the client to the lawyer (the lawyer probably learned about it through investigation of the case); or (2) it is an underlying fact, not shielded from discovery. See Chapter 8.

Passive Involvement by the Lawyer

One important aspect of the perjury rule is that it is utterly intolerant of a lawyer taking a "hear-no-evil, see-no-evil" approach to client perjury. In other words, the lawyer may not simply stand by while the client testifies falsely, even though the lawyer had no involvement in creating the false story or counseling the client to lie. Suppose the judge addresses the client directly, and the lawyer does not elicit the lie from the client. Is this a violation of the rule? You might think not, but here is an important interpretation of the rule that bears emphasis: *standing by while the client lies is tantamount to assisting the lie.* ABA Formal Op. 87-353. So, if the judge asks the client at the sentencing, "Do you have a criminal record?" and the client falsely answers "no," the lawyer cannot just sit there and say nothing. To remain silent would be a violation of Model Rule 3.3(a)(3). (At this point, the lawyer has a retrospective, or backward-looking, duty to rectify the client's unexpected perjury.) Thinking through a case in a forward-looking way, however, a lawyer must understand that she cannot remain silent while the client lies. But what must the lawyer do? This is where we get to the idea of reasonable remedial measures, in Rule 3.3, cmt. [10].

First, as the lawyer did in Nix v. Whiteside, 475 U.S. 157 (1986), the lawyer should warn the client of the consequences of testifying falsely.[2] These include the possibility that the client will be subject to prosecution for perjury, probably will have his credibility destroyed by the prosecution at trial, and will be subject to sentence enhancements. In addition, the lawyer will have an obligation to take remedial action, including disclosing the client's perjury to the court. If that warning fails to persuade the client not to lie, the lawyer should advise the client that she will be forced to withdraw from representing him. Rule 1.16(a)(1). If the client seems to heed the warning, the lawyer may go ahead with the representation as usual, on the assumption that the client will not lie. (If the client does lie anyway, the retrospective duties discussed below are triggered.) If the client is unusually stubborn and refuses to be talked out of lying, and the lawyer is unable to secure the court's permission to withdraw, then the lawyer's only option is to work around the perjury somehow by questioning the client only on matters about which the lawyer is confident the client will testify truthfully. Rule 3.3, cmt. [6]. Perhaps the lawyer can avoid calling the client as a witness altogether, but a criminal defendant does have a constitutional right to take the stand. See Rock v. Arkansas, 483 U.S. 44 (1987). So, if the defendant

---

2. In that case, the client (who was charged with murder and claimed self-defense) initially told the lawyer that he did not see any weapons in the possession of the decedent. He later changed his story and said that he saw "something metallic" before he stabbed the decedent. The lawyer said he would withdraw if the client insisted on telling the second version of the story at trial.

insists on testifying, there may be little the lawyer can do to prevent the lie, in which case the lawyer will have an obligation to remedy it.

Actual Knowledge of Falsity

A lawyer must not offer evidence she *knows* to be false. Rule 3.3(a)(3). Whatever you think about the possibility of having knowledge in a philosophical sense, the majority of courts are not going to be very impressed with a lawyer's argument that she can never know anything with certainty. Lawyers cannot turn a blind eye to the obvious. As a comment to Rule 3.3 observes, "[a] lawyer's knowledge that evidence is false . . . can be inferred from the circumstances." Rule 3.3, cmt. [8]. Consider the following real example. There was a bank robbery in which the perpetrator used a sawed-off shotgun. The robber made off with over $7,000, including many "bait bills," whose serial numbers had been recorded. The next day, FBI agents raided the defendant's house and recovered $350, some of which was made up of bait bills. The defendant told his lawyer a completely ridiculous story to explain how he came to possess the bait bills. He claimed that a complete stranger had paid him $500 to put a duffel bag in a safe deposit box at a local bank. The lawyer decided to examine the contents of the box, and with his client's permission he opened it and discovered a large quantity of money and a sawed-off shotgun. Can anyone argue with a straight face that the lawyer did not *know* his client was the bank robber? In re Ryder, 263 F. Supp. 360 (E.D. Va. 1967).

Nonetheless, there is nothing wrong with giving the client the benefit of the doubt. Lawyers should not rush to judgment and should not assume their clients are lying. See, for example, *United States v. Midgett*, 342 F.3d 321 (4th Cir. 2003) (lawyer who moved to withdraw after client insisted on presenting "some other dude did it" defense acted improperly; even though the defense lacked corroboration, it cannot be said that the lawyer knew it was false). Every experienced lawyer can tell a story of a case in which she thought the client was lying, but as it turned out, the client was telling the truth. For this reason, many lawyers are extremely unwilling to admit that they ever "know" a fact to be true or false. Plenty of people argue with a straight face that the lawyer in the *Ryder* case still does not know that his client is the bank robber—maybe the client had a good reason to take the duffel bag from a stranger, or maybe the client was just extremely gullible. Yet at some point, most courts will conclude that a lawyer does have knowledge of the truth or falsity of a fact, and that point is well short of absolute, incontrovertible certainty.

There is a distinct minority of courts, however, that is unwilling to accept that a lawyer knows her client is lying unless there is absolute, incontrovertible proof. For example, in *State v. McDowell*, 681 N.W.2d 500

(Wis. 2004), the client told a story to his lawyer that was inconsistent with the testimony of another witness. When the lawyer expressed some doubts and decided that the other witness should not testify, the client said, "I'll say what I need to say to help myself out and if I have something untruthful to say I'll say that. I need to help myself out." The lawyer discussed his concern that the client may perjure himself with the trial judge, and the judge permitted the lawyer to call the client as a witness but have him testify in the form of a narrative. (See below for more on the narrative solution to the perjury problem.) The client was convicted, and on appeal the Wisconsin Supreme Court held that the lawyer's performance at trial was ineffective because he revealed to the trial court *what he believed to be* the client's intent to commit perjury, and he also put on the client's testimony in narrative form. The court said that a lawyer may take remedial measures, such as refusing to assist his client in testifying, only where the lawyer knows *based on an affirmative statement of intent from the client* that the client intends to perjure himself. The client's statement in this case comes pretty close to an affirmative statement of intent, and the client's story utterly defied credibility, but the court nevertheless held that the lawyer's performance was deficient. Importantly, *McDowell* and cases taking a similar hard line on the knowledge requirement involve the representation of a criminal defendant, which creates unique and tricky constitutional issues. A lawyer representing a client in civil litigation is likely to be subject to a slightly less demanding knowledge standard before the obligation to take reasonable remedial measures kicks in.

Retrospective

If the lawyer or a client or witness called by the lawyer offers material evidence[3] that the lawyer later learns is false, even without the lawyer's encouragement or involvement, the lawyer must take remedial measures. Rule 3.3 (a)(3).[4] This duty continues through the termination of the proceedings, Rule 3.3(c), so if a lawyer in a civil case subsequently learns that her client lied in a deposition, she must take remedial measures, even if the deposition happened months ago, as long as the case is still pending. But the duty vanishes at the completion of the proceedings. The proceedings are concluded, for the purpose of the rule, when the court enters final judgment and the judgment is either affirmed on appeal or the deadline for filing a notice of appeal has passed. Rule 3.3, cmt. [13]; Maryland State Bar Op. 2005-15

---

3. In criminal law, material evidence is that which could have affected the outcome of the proceedings. See, for example, Charles E. Torcia, *Wharton's Criminal Law* §591 (15th ed. 1996).
4. Note that the retrospective duty to correct perjury extends only to material evidence, while the prospective duty not to allow perjury applies to all evidence, material or not. Look carefully at the language of Rule 3.3(a)(1) and (a)(3).

(lawyer has obligation to correct perjury if client admits lying while case is pending on appeal). Pay attention to the timing of the discovery of perjury when working through fact patterns. A tricky exam question would be to ask about the lawyer's obligation if she learns after the appeals process is completed of the falsity of her client's testimony at trial. There would be no duty under Model Rule 3.3 to rectify the perjury in that instance, and indeed the lawyer would be required by Model Rule 1.6 to keep confidential the information about the client's past perjury.

The comments to Model Rule 3.3 caution that the lawyer should not immediately assume that revealing the perjury to the court is the best way to rectify the consequences of the falsehood. Rule 3.3, cmt. [10]. Rather, the lawyer should consider a series of increasingly dramatic sanctions, *up to and including disclosure*, but not necessarily disclosure right off the bat. See also Rest. §120, cmt. g. Some commentators have called this stepwise series of remedial measures the "Four Rs":

- **R**ecess the proceedings immediately. If the client lies in a deposition, take a break. If the lie occurs in a trial, ask to approach the bench and seek a recess in the proceedings from the judge.
- **R**emonstrate with the client — that is, try to persuade the client to correct the perjury himself.
- **R**esign, but only if withdrawal will remedy the perjury. This is important. Do not assume that withdrawal will solve the problem. In a civil case, if the lawyer simply withdraws the week after a deposition is taken, and the client obtains new counsel, the new lawyer may have no idea that the client lied at the deposition. The client can continue to maintain the same lie all the way through trial, if necessary, and no one will ever find out. That would be a case in which withdrawal would not effectively cure the perjury.
- **R**eveal the perjury, if it is the only effective response.

Although a lawyer should not leap immediately to the most drastic option of disclosure, remember that the rule *requires* disclosure if it is the only way to rectify the consequences of perjury. Model Rule 3.3(a)(3) underscores the rule that the lawyer may be required to disclose if there is no other way of effectively remedying the perjury.

Disclosure of Adverse Authority

As a general rule, a lawyer does not have a duty to help her adversary avoid making mistakes. If there is a promising legal theory that opposing counsel should have discovered, a lawyer is free to say nothing and watch her opponent blow the case. There is a big, important exception to this principle, however, in situations where the opponent is presenting a legal argument to a court or other tribunal. If the opponent fails to cite legal authority in the controlling jurisdiction for a position that would be directly adverse to a lawyer's case, the lawyer has a duty to disclose it to the court. Rule 3.3(a)(2). The reason for this rule is that judges rely on the legal research performed by lawyers; they have neither the time nor the resources to research every issue for themselves. If a controlling case is not brought to the court's attention, the resulting decision will be wrong on the law, doing a disservice not only to the litigants in the present case, but to others who rely on the accuracy of the court's decision. Note that the rule is not limited to cases. It provides that a lawyer must disclose adverse authority, including statutes and regulations, not disclosed by opposing counsel.

Imagine that Boyd, who is representing the plaintiff in a product liability lawsuit, somehow has failed to notice a new case from the state Supreme Court redefining "design defect" in a way that would be helpful to his client's case. Now suppose that Pantusso, the defendant's lawyer, has moved for summary judgment on the issue of design defect and has not cited the case, assuming Boyd will cite it in response. If Boyd fails to cite the case in his response brief, Pantusso cannot just sit on his hands and keep quiet about the new case. He must disclose the case to the court in his reply brief. Of course, Pantusso may argue that the case is distinguishable and should not be followed by the court — indeed this would be the smart thing to do, rather than just burying the case in a footnote — but he cannot simply avoid mentioning it.

It is tempting to respond that this rule cannot mean very much in practice, because any case can be distinguished by a sufficiently clever lawyer. There is an old joke about a prosecutor who cites a case involving the theft of a brown horse to prove that the defendant is guilty of the crime of horse-theft. "But that case does not apply, your Honor," the defense lawyer replies. "My client was charged with stealing a *white* horse!" A case does not have to be a white-horse case, with no possible basis for distinction, to trigger the application of this rule. Rather, as an ABA ethics opinion from 1949 put it, if the authority would be considered important by the judge or the judge might feel misled if the case later came to light, the lawyer must disclose it. Along these lines, the best statement of the test for the duty to disclose comes from the Hazard & Hodes treatise, which states: "[T]he more unhappy a lawyer is that he found an adverse precedent, the clearer it is that he must reveal it." H&H §29.11. This is what I sometimes call the "Oh, &*!$%" rule — if your reaction to reading a case or statute is an unprintable expletive, you have an obligation to disclose it under Rule 3.3(a)(2) if your adversary fails to cite it.

In this case, compliance with the rules overlaps with good practice, because any smart lawyer, when faced with adverse authority, would cite the case in her brief and then attempt to argue for a persuasive distinction.

If there is a clear distinction, for goodness' sake do not use that as an excuse for not citing the case—discuss the case candidly in your submission to the court and explain why it is distinguishable. If you cannot do that, because there really is not a good distinction, then you clearly have a legal obligation to reveal the authority to the court.

Examples

Liar, Liar?

1. Lawyer is preparing Client for deposition in a sex discrimination lawsuit. One of the issues in the case is whether Client ever said, "I really don't like to work with women; I feel like I can be myself around men." One witness says she heard Client say this in a telephone conversation with someone named Chuck, who was apparently Client's college roommate. Client vehemently denies ever making this statement to Chuck or anyone else. Client tells Lawyer that if he is asked about this statement in his deposition, he will deny having said it. If the question comes up, Lawyer should:

   A. Instruct Client not to answer the question, because the information is protected by the attorney-client privilege.
   B. Do nothing, because Lawyer does not know Client's denial is a lie.
   C. Immediately recess the deposition and instruct Client that he must not deny having made the statement.
   D. Wait until the conclusion of the deposition and instruct Client that he should correct the record to make clear that he is not denying having made the statement.

What a Tangled Web We Weave

2. Haywood is a government lawyer working for the State Department of the Environment on a cleanup action against Schauer Equipment, a business that allegedly contaminated land with toxic chemicals. As part of the action, the Department of the Environment hired Carew, an environmental consultant, to advise on the best method of cleaning the soil. Carew recommended a new, more expensive, but better process that he had helped develop. The defendant would prefer to use a cheaper process, since it will be liable for cleanup costs.

   Carew's resume said that he had received a bachelor's degree in environmental science from Rutgers University and had completed some coursework toward a master's degree in organic chemistry from Drexel University. When Haywood asked him for copies of his diplomas and transcripts, Carew said Rutgers did not process his diploma because of a "paperwork mixup" and that his mother had lost his Drexel transcript.

247

A. Carew's deposition is scheduled for next week. What should Haywood do?

B. Suppose the deposition goes forward and Carew testifies that his resume is accurate. A couple of weeks later, Haywood gets a phone call from the landowner's lawyer, who said that she had spoken to someone at the registrar's office at Rutgers who said that Carew never completed the requirements for his bachelor's degree. Haywood confronts Carew, who admits to falsifying his resume. Now what should Haywood do?

Lies, Damned Lies, and Perjury

3. Is there a violation of Model Rule 3.3 in the following circumstances?

A. Nicole Horvath is a solo practitioner with a busy schedule. She has a civil case with a pretrial conference in Superior Court on the same day a trial is scheduled in a minor criminal matter in District Court. The day before the hearing, she sends a letter to the clerk of Superior Court, copied to opposing counsel, indicating that she is too ill to participate in the pretrial conference. Her opponent finds out from a friend that Horvath actually was trying a case in District Court and refers her to the bar for discipline.

B. Cassie Sanders represents an insurance company and its agent in a coverage dispute with the insured. The policy requires notice of a claim to be given within 60 days of the incident. The insured claims he mailed the notice to the insurance company's agent on the 59th day, which would constitute timely notice under law and the policy, but has no proof of mailing. The insurance company has refused to pay the claim on the ground that notice was not given in a timely manner. The insured takes the deposition of the agent, who states that the notice was never received. A few days later, Sanders runs into the agent at the airport. As they are chatting about the status of several pending cases, the agent tells Sanders that he lied at his deposition and that the notice letter was received on the 60th day, but he shredded it. May Sanders rely on the agent's deposition testimony as the basis for a motion for summary judgment? Must Sanders disclose the false testimony to opposing counsel or the court?

C. Donna Jones is a lawyer representing a state agency in a dispute over a government contract. The opponent filed a motion for summary judgment, and according to the court's pretrial schedule, the state agency's response to the motion for summary judgment was to be filed by May 5, 2000. Because Jones could not comply with that deadline, she filed a motion seeking a 30-day extension of time. It was denied, and the court ordered her to file a response "forthwith." Twelve days later, Jones filed the response. The opponent moved to strike it as untimely, and in response to the motion to strike, Jones quoted the following language from a decision of that state's Supreme Court:

> "Forthwith" means immediately, without delay, or as soon as the object may be accomplished by reasonable exertion. [Citing X v.Y.]

She did not, however, quote the following sentence from the same decision:

> The Supreme Court has said of the word [forthwith] that "in matters of practice and pleading it is usually construed, and sometimes defined by rule of court, as within twenty-four hours."

D. Danielle Ewing is a criminal defense lawyer. Her client was charged with burglary and, on Ewing's advice, accepted a plea deal offered by the prosecutor that would result in a sentence of probation, not jail time. Ewing knows that the prosecutor would not have offered the deal if he knew that the defendant had a criminal record. In fact, as Ewing knows from conducting a database search, the defendant had two prior convictions: one for larceny and one for marijuana possession. At the sentencing hearing, the judge agrees to the proposed sentence of probation, stating, "I am willing to sentence the defendant to probation in light of the fact that he has no prior convictions. Is that right, Mr. Prosecutor?" The prosecutor replies, "That is correct, Your Honor." Ewing says nothing.

Don't Ask, Don't Tell?

4. Duncan files a motion to suppress evidence resulting from an illegal search, citing a state constitutional provision guaranteeing the right of privacy. A week after the motion is filed, the supreme court for the State of Perplexity decides that under the state constitution, a person does not have a reasonable expectation of privacy if an illegal activity is occurring. (There are no challenges based on federal law that can be raised to the search.) For some reason, the prosecutor does not notice this decision, as Duncan can see from the response brief filed after the supreme court decision was announced. At the hearing on the suppression motion, Duncan must:
   A. Disclose the new case if it is directly adverse to the position taken in the suppression motion.
   B. Not disclose the new case, unless the judge asks Duncan a direct question about the continuing vitality of the cases in her motion, in which case she must answer truthfully.
   C. Not disclose the new case, unless Duncan knows that the judge is unaware of the authority.
   D. Disclose the new case, because Duncan has an obligation to disclose information to the extent necessary to avoid committing a fraud on a third party—in this case, the prosecutor.

Explanations

Liar, Liar?

1. The correct answer is B. Remember, the prospective and retrospective duties to take remedial action are triggered only when a lawyer knows that the evidence she will offer, or has offered, is false. Rule 3.3(a)(3). The perjury rules are so clear and categorical that it is tempting to think that a lawyer's client is always lying when he says something inconsistent with other evidence. But, of course, a lawyer has no idea whether the witness or the client is telling the truth, and no principle of professional conduct requires a lawyer to disbelieve her client in a case like this. "A lawyer should not conclude that testimony is or will be false unless there is a firm factual basis for doing so." Rest. §120, cmt. c.

What a Tangled Web We Weave

2. A. The lawyer in the previous example is justified in doing nothing if the client sticks to his story, because there are no facts that put the lawyer on notice that the story may be false. This case is different. Model Rule 3.3(a)(3) provides that a lawyer may not offer evidence that the lawyer *knows* to be false. "Knows" is defined by the Model Rules as "actual knowledge of the fact in question," Rule 1.0(f), but remember that *knowledge can be inferred from circumstances*, and the lawyer cannot ignore an obvious lie. Rule 3.3, cmt. [8]. If the evidence points toward the falsity of the client's story, a lawyer must be very careful. As the case upon which this problem is based says, "a mere suspicion of perjury . . . does not carry with it the obligation to reveal that suspicion to the court under Rule 3.3." *United States v. Shaffer Equip. Co.*, 11 F.3d 450, 459 (4th Cir. 1993). At some point, however, a lawyer's claim to have only a mere suspicion, and not solid evidence of perjury, will begin to ring hollow. This is a close case, because there is no compelling evidence of falsity that no reasonable person could ignore. Carew's explanation for not having supporting documents does sound a bit suspicious, though, like a student claiming that the dog ate his homework.

   Perhaps Haywood should do some "due diligence," including a phone call to Rutgers and Drexel or a demand that Carew find something to substantiate his academic credentials. As the Restatement commentary stresses, however, "[a]ctual knowledge does not include unknown information, even if a reasonable lawyer would have discovered it through inquiry." Rest. §120, cmt. c. At this point, Haywood probably would be safe with a stern warning to Carew that everything on his record must be accurate.

B. This example deals with the retrospective duties contained in Model Rule 3.3(a)(3), which provides that if "a witness called by the lawyer [that is, Carew] has offered material evidence and the lawyer comes to know of its falsity, the lawyer shall take reasonable remedial measures, including, if necessary, disclosure to the tribunal." The only way for Haywood to avoid disclosing the false statements on Carew's resume would be if Carew's academic credentials are not "material" to the litigation. Remember that the retrospective disclosure duties in Model Rule 3.3(a)(3) apply only to material evidence, in contrast to the prohibition in Model Rule 3.3(a)(1) on making false statements of fact or law to a tribunal, which applies to all evidence. Evidence is material if it could have affected the course or outcome of the proceeding. Torcia, *supra* note 3, §591 (citing a gazillion cases). It is not material if offered to prove some collateral matter, such as the time of day a trespass was committed.

Under the generally applicable law of perjury, evidence that is offered to bolster the credibility of a witness is material. Torcia, *supra* note 3, §592. Here, the evidence that Carew had a degree in environmental science and was working toward a graduate degree in organic chemistry helped support his contention that a new, expensive cleanup process was appropriate for this site. Thus, the false statement on his resume was material, and Haywood had a duty to take remedial action. He could call upon Carew to correct the record himself, or he could disclose the perjury to the court, but either way it is the lawyer's responsibility to make sure that the record gets corrected.

Lies, Damned Lies, and Perjury

3. A. This is a clear violation of the rule. Model Rule 3.3(a)(1) states that a lawyer shall not knowingly make a false statement of fact to a tribunal. The lawyer's excuse is false, and knowingly so, since she is well aware of the real reason for missing the pretrial conference. It does not matter that the matter in question—the lawyer's reason for her absence—is not material to the issues in dispute in the litigation. The language in Model Rule 3.3(a)(1) uses the word "material" only with respect to the duty to correct false statements. It also is irrelevant that the statement was made in a pretrial proceeding and not at trial. Do not confuse the forward-looking duty, which does not have a materiality requirement, with the retrospective duty to correct perjury, which applies only to material falsehoods. See, for example, In re Fletcher, 694 N.E.2d 1143 (Ind. 1998); In re Chovanec, 640 N.E.2d 1052 (Ind. 1994).

B. This is not a question about what a lawyer must do with potential or contemplated perjury. Assuming that the lawyer did not know about the shredded letter in advance of the deposition, this is a question about what duties a lawyer has after discovering the client's perjury. Note that if this false statement were made *at trial*, Sanders would have a retrospective obligation to "take reasonable remedial measures, including, if necessary, disclosure to the tribunal." Rule 3.3(a)(3). Sanders should try to convince the agent to correct her testimony on the record but, failing that, she must disclose to the court.

The wrinkle here is that the perjury took place during the discovery process, not at trial. Thus, one might argue that the false statement was not "offered" to a "tribunal," as seemingly required by Model Rule 3.3. (In most cases, a pretrial deposition does not occur before a judge, but is transcribed by a court reporter in the presence of the lawyers for all the parties.) As a result, maybe the applicable rule is Model Rule 4.1, governing false statements to third parties. Because Sanders did not make the false statement herself, Model Rule 4.1(a) does not apply. Under Model Rule 4.1(b), Sanders has an obligation to disclose information to avoid assisting a criminal or fraudulent act by a client, but notice that the rule is "trumped" by the duty of confidentiality stated in Model Rule 1.6. Because information relating to the conversation at the airport would be covered by Model Rule 1.6, Sanders may not disclose the content of the communication *if the applicable rule is Model Rule 4.1*.

Despite this plausible argument for the application of Model Rule 4.1, an ABA ethics opinion states that perjury in pretrial proceedings is governed by Model Rule 3.3. ABA Formal Op. 93-376. It also should be clear that Sanders may not rely on the deposition testimony in support of a motion for summary judgment. (In pretrial motions practice, lawyers generally introduce testimony from discovery depositions by attaching deposition transcripts as exhibits to an affidavit and filing the affidavit along with the motion.) If she files the deposition's transcript and cites to it as evidence that the insured never mailed the notice, Sanders would be making a false statement of fact to a tribunal in violation of Model Rule 3.3(a)(1), and would be offering evidence that she knows to be false in violation of Model Rule 3.3(a)(3). Interestingly, the ABA committee does not stop there. It says that even if the lawyer does not intend to rely on the testimony in a paper filed with the court or in an oral argument, she still has an obligation to correct the record. "[E]ven before these documents are filed there is potential ongoing reliance upon their content which would be outcome-determinative, resulting in an inevitable deception of the other side and a subversion of the truth-finding process which the adversary system is designed to implement." Even though the deposition does not become "evidence" until it is filed with the court or relied upon as the basis for an assertion of fact, its *potential* tainting effect on the litigation process is enough to justify an obligation on Sanders to rectify the perjury either by persuading the agent to correct the record by withdrawing (but only if withdrawal will be sufficient to undo the effect of the false testimony) or by disclosing the perjury to opposing counsel or the court. Rule 3.3, cmt. [10].

C. This example is based on a case in which the lawyer was reprimanded under Federal Rules of Civil Procedure 11, but a similar analysis applies to Jones's conduct under Model Rule 3.3. See *Precision Specialty Metals, Inc. v. United States*, 315 F.3d 1346 (Fed. Cir. 2003). The court considered the lawyer's conduct a deliberate attempt to mislead it into thinking that a 12-day delay could still be considered filing "forthwith." In the example, did Jones "make a false statement of . . . law" to the court by omitting the sentence? There is a great deal of difference in meaning between these two statements:

- "Forthwith" means as soon as possible.
- "Forthwith" means as soon as possible, and courts generally have defined that to mean within 24 hours.

By stating that the X v. Y case stood for the former proposition but not the latter, Jones misrepresented the state of the law to the court in violation of Model Rule 3.3(a)(1). She mischaracterized the meaning of X v. Y just as surely as if she had represented that it stated that "forthwith" means "within two weeks." She arguably violated Model Rule 3.3(a)(2) as well by "fail[ing] to disclose to the tribunal legal authority in the controlling jurisdiction known . . . to be directly adverse to the position of the client." If one understands "authority" as including the omitted sentence, it would be possible to characterize Jones's conduct as constituting a violation of both subsections (a)(1) and (a)(2).

D. This feels kind of sleazy somehow, but a careful reading of the rule shows that Ewing has no obligation to correct the court's misunderstanding about her client's criminal record. See Tex. Ethics Comm. Op. 504 (1994). First, notice that Ewing herself did not make any statement of fact or law to the court, so she did not violate Model Rule 3.3(a)(1). Thus, the case differs from those in which a lawyer makes an affirmative representation to the effect that "my client does not have any prior convictions." See, for example, *Cincinnati Bar Ass'n v. Nienaber*, 687 N.E.2d 678 (Ohio 1997). There is no issue of disclosing adverse legal authority, so there is no violation of Model Rule 3.3(a)(2). Ewing is not "offering evidence," and neither is the client, so she does not violate Model Rule 3.3(a)(3). If the defendant had stated that he had no criminal record, Ewing's silence would be tantamount to assisting the perjury. For that reason, the rule requires a lawyer to take remedial action upon learning of the false statement by the client (or a witness called by the lawyer). But if the lawyer does not "sponsor" the false statement, there is no obligation to correct the court's misunderstanding of the facts.

Don't Ask, Don't Tell?

4. The correct answer is A. This is an application of Model Rule 3.3(a)(2). B is directly contradicted by the rule — the lawyer may not keep silent and hope the judge does not ask an inconvenient question about the new case. There is no requirement in the rule that the judge be unaware of the authority, so C is ruled out. Finally, the rule is not justified in terms of preventing frauds on third parties (which would be a matter for Model Rule 4.1, which is trumped by the duty of confidentiality), but by the duty of candor to the tribunal. Thus, D is not the correct answer.

CRIMINAL CASES: PROFESSIONAL DUTIES IN TENSION

The policy debate surrounding client perjury is sharpest in the context of criminal cases in which the client's procedural rights conflict with the truth-seeking function of the adversarial system. The "trilemma" analysis is most prominently associated with the late Professor Monroe Freedman, who has relentlessly pushed the profession and the academy to think more carefully about the problem of client perjury. See Monroe H. Freedman, *Professional Responsibility of the Criminal Defense Lawyer: The Three Hardest Questions*, 64 Mich. L. Rev. 1469 (1966); Monroe H. Freedman, *Lawyers' Ethics in an Adversary System* (1975); Monroe H. Freedman & Abbe Smith, *Understanding Lawyers' Ethics* (4th ed. 2010). You may end up disagreeing with Professor Freedman — many do — but there is no escaping the power of his analysis. In fact, one of his articles was so provocative that in a rather embarrassing overreaction, then Federal Appellate Judge Warren Burger actually called for Freedman's disbarment.

The point of the trilemma analysis is not that the lawyer should ignore her ethical responsibilities. Rather, it is that the lawyer's ethical responsibilities inevitably require her to sacrifice one of three foundational values, which we can call the "Three Cs" — competence, candor, and confidentiality. The question for attorneys, as a profession, is which values take priority and which are subordinated. Briefly stated, the Model Rules resolve the trilemma in favor of candor to the tribunal in cases of perjury at trial. A lawyer must disclose confidential information to the tribunal, if necessary, to avoid assisting a criminal or fraudulent act by the client. Rule 3.3(a)(3). This means, in some cases, "blowing the whistle" on the client, which appears to contravene the defense lawyer's obligation to provide an effective defense. The lawyer has an obligation to use reasonable skill and diligence in investigating the client's case, including learning the client's version of events. In order to persuade a mistrustful and frightened client to trust her, the lawyer would like to assure the client that she will not disclose any information to the authorities. But in the course of investigating the case and preparing for trial, the lawyer may find out that the client intends to lie. What now? Although the Model Rules clearly answer that the lawyer's overriding obligation is to prevent the client's perjury from tainting the record at trial, the contrary policies are sufficiently weighty that many jurisdictions have not taken this approach.

To make the application of the rule and the underlying policies clear, imagine a prospective perjury situation where the client, a criminal defendant, intends to testify falsely at trial. At this point, you probably are objecting, "Wait—how does the lawyer *know* that the client's testimony will be a lie?" In some cases, there is genuine ambiguity in the evidence, and the lawyer should not assume that the client is being dishonest. There are other cases, however, in which the lawyer knows perfectly well that the client is lying. Lawyers investigate cases, question their clients, talk to witnesses, review the physical evidence, check out alibis, look for inconsistencies, and draw reasonable inferences from the facts as they are known. In some cases, the client admits guilt to his lawyer, but even where the client does not confess, it would be a stretch for a lawyer to say that she would not be persuaded to a "beyond a reasonable doubt" standard of the client's guilt.[5]

The discussion of how the lawyer "knows" actually helps make the point about the first of the Three Cs—*competence*. The Model Rules require the lawyer to take remedial action to prevent prospective perjury or to rectify perjury that has already occurred only where the lawyer *knows* that the testimony was false. Rule 3.3(a). One way out of the trilemma, therefore, would be not to learn facts sufficient to establish knowledge of the falsity of the client's testimony. Without knowing all the facts, however, the lawyer is not going to be in a very good position to represent her client effectively. Some lawyers try to have it both ways by asking their clients to come up with an explanation for the state's charges without telling the lawyer whether or not any of the facts related are true.[6] This technique commonly may be practiced, particularly by lawyers representing sophisticated clients

---

5. A court may nevertheless conclude that a lawyer has no duty to remedy the perjury in these circumstances, but in that case the rationale would have to be the value to criminal defendants of having loyal advocates. In a case like *State v. McDowell*, 681 N.W.2d 500 (Wis. 2004), there is no way a reasonable lawyer could not conclude that the client was lying through his teeth. In that case, the Wisconsin Supreme Court said the lawyer did not "know" the client was going to testify falsely, but that reasoning is specious. The court should have frankly admitted that the lawyer, and any halfway alert human being, knew that the client's story was bogus, but that other policies and values required the lawyer not to take steps to correct the record.

6. Texas trial lawyer Racehorse Haynes supposedly asks clients, "Now why would these police officers be saying all these bad things about you?" A variation is the *Anatomy of a Murder* "lecture," from the novel and film of the same name, in which the lawyer pretends to give neutral advice about the law ("You know, there are three ways to defend against a murder charge . . .") but is in fact suggesting a story to the client. This theme comes up in Chapter 11 in the discussion of witness coaching.

who appreciate that they are supposed to withhold damaging facts, but it merely circumvents the ethical issue. See Kenneth Mann, *Defending White-Collar Crime: A Portrait of Attorneys at Work* (1985). The lawyer is pretending not to know that the client is about to perjure himself, but in fact the lawyer either: (1) has understood the facts of the case and knows perfectly well that the client's story is a lie; or (2) has succeeded in becoming ignorant of the true facts, and for that reason will not be able to represent the client effectively at trial.

One response to the problem of selective ignorance is to enforce a strict duty of *confidentiality*—the second of the Three Cs. If the client were assured that nothing he said to the lawyer would be disclosed to the court or the prosecution, or used against him in any way, he would be more likely to reveal all the relevant facts. Lawyers would love to be able to give this little speech to their clients: "Look, nothing you tell me ever leaves this room, period. It is a sacred professional obligation for me to keep your secrets, and on top of that, the government cannot put me up on the stand and force me to tell what I learned from you. So you should feel free to tell me everything that happened." The trouble is, that speech is not accurate. Under the Model Rules, a lawyer has an obligation to reveal confidential client information if it is the only way to prevent the client from testifying falsely at trial.

The Model Rules stress the obligation of *candor* above all, and insist that the lawyer must never knowingly become an instrument of perjury. That means not only may the lawyer not make misrepresentations of fact or law, Rule 3.3(a)(1), but she may not permit her client's perjury (or a false statement made by a nonclient witness called by the lawyer) to go uncorrected, Rule 3.3(a)(3). The rules impose a duty on the lawyer to *rectify* client perjury, and this duty continues through to the conclusion of the proceedings. Rule 3.3(c). Taking this duty seriously means that the lawyer's obligation of confidentiality is not absolute. If the client reveals facts that show that the story the client is about to tell, or has already told, is a lie, the lawyer's obligation of candor to the tribunal supersedes her duty of confidentiality to the client, and she must take steps to prevent or correct the perjury, up to and including disclosure to the court.

The rules do make a small concession to the duty of confidentiality by requiring the lawyer to first explore remedial measures short of disclosure to the court. Comment 10 to Rule 3.3 sets out a stepwise series of remedies, beginning with first remonstrating with the client—that is, warning the client strongly and in no uncertain terms that he or she had better do the right thing. The lawyer should advise the client that if the client doesn't disclose the false testimony and correct the record, the lawyer will have to do it herself. Note, however, that this first step is the *only* concession to confidentiality. If the lawyer's cajoling does not persuade the client to withdraw or correct the false statement, the lawyer *must* take stronger measures to correct the perjury. The comment goes on to say that if withdrawal is not permitted by the judge, or if it will not rectify the perjury, the lawyer must do whatever is necessary to correct the record, including revealing confidential client information. In criminal cases, the lawyer does not have the option of refusing to permit the client to testify; as a matter of constitutional law, the client may demand to take the stand, and it would be reversible error for the trial court to permit the lawyer to interfere with this right. *Rock v. Arkansas*, 483 U.S. 44 (1987); *United States v. Midgett*, 342 F.3d 321 (4th Cir. 2003).

ALTERNATIVE RESPONSES TO PERJURY IN CRIMINAL CASES

Remember that the Supreme Court did not create a rule of constitutional law that would have required the lawyer to disclose perjury to the tribunal. *Nix v. Whiteside*, 475 U.S. 157 (1986). The Model Rules do recognize this duty but, again, they are only models. States are free to march to different drummers, and, in fact, not every jurisdiction prioritizes candor to the tribunal over the duty of confidentiality to the client. See Rest. §120, cmt. i. Some states permit, or even require, a defense lawyer to continue representing her client to the best of her ability, even if the lawyer knows the client intends to testify falsely. Different judges may even have different preferred ways of handling this situation. In many courts, a defense lawyer can punt the problem to the trial judge, by using some kind of local code, such as "Your honor, I have an ethical problem." Every judge on the bench will know that means the client is going to testify falsely, and then it will be the judge's responsibility to instruct counsel on how to proceed. See, for example, *People v. Andrades*, 828 N.E.2d 599 (N.Y. 2005) (after lawyer said he had "an ethical conflict," trial court figured out that the client intended to perjure himself, but denied the lawyer's request to withdraw, instead ordering the lawyer to present the testimony in narrative form).

"Tell the Court What Happened": The Narrative Solution

The ABA had proposed, but later rejected, a standard for the conduct of criminal defense lawyers that would have permitted the lawyer to call the client as a witness and permit the client to testify in his own words, not in question-and-answer format. Proposed as ABA Standards Relating to the Administration of Criminal Justice, Defense Function Standard 4-7.7 (1991), discussed in H&H §29.17. The idea is to avoid the lawyer's complicity in the perjury. The client may lie, but the lawyer's hands are clean because she has not elicited the perjury at trial. This has always struck me as a sanctimonious solution that permits the lawyer to claim innocence while permitting the client's perjury to infect the trial process. The practical effect of the narrative approach depends on the sophistication of the trier of fact. Judges are perfectly aware of what is going on if the lawyer suddenly stops questioning the client in the usual question-and-answer format and permits the client to tell a rambling story in his own words. They are well aware that the story is false—otherwise, the lawyer would have continued the direct examination in the usual manner. Thus, from the standpoint of the judge, the lawyer has violated her duty of confidentiality (which is what Freedman finds objectionable about the Model Rules approach) by shifting to the narrative format. Jurors, on the other hand, may not be so savvy. In a jury trial, switching to the narrative style may not be tantamount to disclosure of the perjury, but precisely because it does not clue the jury in, it has no prophylactic effect—the perjury comes in as the truth, in the eyes of the jury. On the other hand, if the jury is clever enough to figure out what is going on, then the lawyer again has effectively disclosed the perjury to the trier of fact. See Rest. §120, cmt. i (recognizing this limitation to the narrative approach).

A minority of jurisdictions recognize the narrative approach in the disciplinary rules, as in the District of Columbia, Washington D.C. Rules of Professional Conduct, Rule 3.3(b); by way of an ethics opinion, as in Connecticut, Conn. Bar Formal Op. 42 (1992); or in judicial decisions, as in California, *People v. Johnson*, 72 Cal. Rptr. 2d 805 (Ct. App. 1998); Arizona, *State v. Long*, 714 P.2d 465 (Ariz. Ct. App. 1986); Florida, *Sanborn v. State*, 474 So.2d 309 (Fla. Ct. App. 1985); and New York, *People v. Andrades*, 828 N.E.2d 599 (N.Y. 2004). See also Rule 3.3, cmt. [7] (recognizing that "[i]n some jurisdictions . . . courts have required counsel to present the accused as a witness or to give a narrative statement if the accused so desires, even if counsel knows that the testimony or statement will be false"). Most states, however, follow the Model Rules and subordinate the duty of confidentiality to the lawyer's duty of candor to the tribunal. In these jurisdictions, using the narrative approach would not cure the client's perjury. Finally, there are other courts that regard a request to use the narrative approach as tantamount to *impermissible* disclosure of client perjury. See, for example, *State v. McDowell*, 681 N.W.2d 500 (Wis. 2004) (lawyer's performance was deficient because he permitted client to testify in a narrative format). In these jurisdictions, the duty of confidentiality trumps the duty of candor to the tribunal.

Passing the Buck: Withdrawal

Withdrawal is a superficially satisfying response to the prospect that one's client will commit perjury. It is mandated by the rules—Model Rule 1.16(a)(1) states that a lawyer must withdraw if continuing in the representation will result in a violation of the rules of professional conduct (Rule 3.3 on perjury) or other law (criminal statutes governing perjury). There are two problems regarding withdrawal. The first is that the court may refuse to permit a lawyer to withdraw, particularly if the lawyer's request to withdraw occurs close to the start of trial. Courts are extremely suspicious of criminal defense lawyers' gambits to gain additional time, and are likely to perceive a request to withdraw as simply a ploy. A lawyer may not withdraw from representing a client in litigation except by permission of the court, so if the judge refuses permission, the lawyer is stuck in the case. Rule 1.16(c). The second problem is that even if the court permits the lawyer to withdraw, the lawyer's withdrawal just passes the buck to the next lawyer. The next lawyer will have the same issue if she learns of the client's intention to commit perjury, but, more likely, if the client has any intelligence at all, he will figure out that he should withhold information and tailor the story he tells his lawyer, so that the successor lawyer will never learn of the client's intention to testify falsely. In the end, the system is contaminated by the perjury anyway, the second lawyer is an unwitting accomplice, and the first lawyer may have a clear conscience but has not prevented the trial process from being tainted by the perjury.

For this reason, the Model Rules are quite clear that withdrawal alone may not be a sufficient response to prospective perjury. See the passage quoted above from the comment to Rule 3.3. If the court refuses to permit the lawyer to withdraw, or if withdrawal alone will not alert the trier of fact to the perjury, the lawyer must blow the whistle. Again, however, this advice must be qualified by recognition of the defendant's right to testify in his own defense. A lawyer must be certain that the client's story is a lie before moving to withdraw; otherwise, the lawyer's action will effectively interfere with the client's constitutional right to take the stand. *United States v. Midgett*, 342 F.3d 321 (4th Cir. 2003).

Examples

Surprise and Not-So-Surprise Perjury

5. You are defending Paul Gualtieri against charges of insider trading. Before trial, you went over the testimony that Paul would offer on direct examination. One critical fact pertains to *mens rea*—whether Paul knew a tip from one of his cousins was inside information. On the basis of information from his cousin, Paul bought several hundred shares of stock in Clone-Tech, a company producing anti-cancer drugs. Two days after he bought the shares, Clone-Tech announced FDA approval of a new drug and its share price rose dramatically. Paul maintains that his cousin read in the *Wall Street Journal* about the possibility of the new drug being approved, but you strongly suspect that claim to be false. For one thing, you checked issues of the *Wall Street Journal* for several weeks before the announcement, and there was no news coverage suggesting the new

drug might be approved soon. More damningly for Paul's defense, you know his cousin has a friend who works as a messenger for Clone-Tech and frequently has access to confidential information. The cousin has moved to Brazil, but one of the government's witnesses is a client of Paul's brokerage firm who will testify that Paul gave him a "hot tip" that came from someone on the inside of Clone-Tech. That customer also made a huge profit trading Clone-Tech stock.

A. Paul insists on telling the story about his cousin reading the story in the *Wall Street Journal*. You tell him that he likely will be impeached with evidence that there was no such news coverage in the paper, but he responds that he will testify that he "seems to remember" his cousin telling him about the report, but he could be mistaken. Paul will deny telling the customer that he had a hot inside tip. Rather, he will testify that he told the customer that Clone-Tech was a good company that represented a good long-term investment opportunity. What do you do?

B. Suppose instead that Paul never mentioned the *Wall Street Journal* story. Rather, he told you it was simply a coincidence that he had invested in Clone-Tech and recommended it to clients. As for the client who will testify that Paul gave him a hot inside tip, Paul denies having that conversation and says the client must be embellishing the story in order to obtain leniency from the government in exchange for testimony against Paul. Then, at trial, during direct examination, Paul suddenly blurts out the story about his cousin telling him of the approval, based on a story he read in the newspaper. What do you do?

Whom Do You Believe?

6. You have been appointed by the court (at a scandalously low rate) to defend Gary Brown, a down-and-out young man who lived in an apartment in a ramshackle building with his 65-year-old roommate Bart, an unemployed alcoholic. You meet Gary at the town jail and learn the following:

> Gary confessed to killing Bart at the end of a long day of trying to earn a living as a street musician and panhandler. According to the police report, Gary told the responding officer that he had returned home with a splitting headache to find Bart sitting asleep in front of the blaring television set, an empty jug of Thunderbird wine by his side, reeking of alcohol. Gary roused Bart, told him to turn down the television, and then went to his room to sleep. At about 3:00 A.M., Gary was awakened by the television again. He told Bart that if he did not turn off the television, he would throw him out of the house and he could spend the night in the street. After an exchange of angry words, he threw Bart out onto the porch, which was made of concrete. Gary heard a loud crack and immediately realized he may have hurt Bart. He poured water on him, tried CPR, and called 911. The ambulance

arrived and the EMTs pronounced Bart dead at the scene. The police arrived at the same time, read Gary his *Miranda* rights, and took a statement in which Gary related the foregoing facts.

At your meeting with Gary, he admits to throwing Bart out onto the porch, but insists that he did so only after Bart threatened to kill him. He says that he and Bart actually had stood face-to-face and shoved one another, and that Bart made a move toward the kitchen, where Gary thought he might try to arm himself with a knife. You know from having read the police report that Bart was slightly built, was 65 years of age, and received government disability benefits on account of a back injury he had sustained 15 years ago in a car accident. In addition, the autopsy revealed that his blood alcohol level was over three times the legal limit at the time of his death. Gary is a solidly built 26-year-old and was sober at the time of the death. You therefore doubt that the killing was self-defense. Gary seems apologetic and has no felony record, although he has several misdemeanor convictions for loitering, panhandling, and jumping subway turnstiles.

What are your obligations under the rules of professional conduct? What may or must you do if Gary insists on testifying in his own defense (as he has a right to do) and telling the self-defense story?

Explanations

Surprise and Not-So-Surprise Perjury

5. A. This is a prospective perjury situation. You are faced with the possibility that Paul will testify falsely at trial. Analyzing the example under the Model Rules, your duty is stated in Model Rule 3.3(a)(3) and Model Rule 3.3(b). You may not offer evidence that you know to be false, and this includes calling a witness who you know will testify falsely. Rule 3.3(a)(3). You also must take "reasonable remedial measures," including disclosure to the court if necessary, if you know that your client intends to engage in criminal or fraudulent conduct relating to the proceedings—here, including perjury at trial. Rule 3.3(b).

   Disclosing to the court can be a very tricky matter. For one thing, you may not speak *ex parte* with the judge—that is, without opposing counsel being present. Rule 3.5(b). Thus, whatever you say to the court will be in the presence of the prosecutor, and you obviously do not want to share confidential client information with the Assistant U.S. Attorney. Lawyers usually employ some kind of code words, such as "I have an ethical problem" or "I am concerned about my client's testimony." See, for example, *United States v. Long*, 857 F.2d 436 (8th Cir. 1988); *People v. Andrades*, 828 N.E.2d 599 (N.Y. 2004). The next step is up to the trial judge, who may: order the lawyer to proceed (thus, tacitly permitting the introduction of what the lawyer believes is perjured testimony); order the lawyer to question the client only on "safe" subjects; permit the client to testify in narrative form; or permit the lawyer to withdraw. (Sometimes the trial court will be found on appeal to have acted incorrectly by permitting the lawyer to withdraw. See, for example, *United States v. Midgett*, 342 F.3d 321 (4th Cir. 2003).) For a good discussion of this problem, see H&H §29.21. You may be somewhat reassured to know that these two leading commentators conclude that "a fully satisfactory way of implementing Rule 3.3 . . . has yet to be devised and may never be."

There are a couple of specific issues here. First of all, do you *know* that Paul intends to testify falsely? Both Model Rule 3.3(a)(3) and Model Rule 3.3(b) have a *mens rea* requirement. You must know the evidence to be false in order for the remedial duties to apply. It is tempting to respond that you never really know anything to be true. Maybe Paul's account is correct, and he is just mixed up about what his cousin told him. The standard does refer to actual knowledge, not evidence from which a reasonable person would conclude the testimony is false. See Rule 1.0(f) for a definition of "knowing," but also notice that the definition says that knowledge can be inferred from circumstances. So, while it is true that a lawyer should resolve doubts about the client's truthfulness in favor of the client, "the lawyer cannot ignore an obvious falsehood." Rule 3.3, cmt. [8]. Is it obvious that Paul is lying? Given the complete lack of news coverage in the *Wall Street Journal* and the connection, through Paul's cousin, with someone who has access to confidential information, it strains credibility to suggest that there is an innocent explanation for Paul's knowledge of the upcoming FDA approval. This is about as close to knowledge of falsity as you are going to get. Prospective perjury duties seem to be triggered in this case, but you probably will find many lawyers, and some courts,[7] who would disagree, saying that you do not *know* that Paul's story is false. If you agree with the lawyers who argue that a lawyer never really knows anything, that is fine, but be aware that many courts can and do infer actual knowledge from circumstantial evidence. In this case, the circumstantial evidence makes it pretty difficult to argue that you do not know that Paul's account is false, even though in some philosophical sense you may not have absolute, rock-solid, incontrovertible proof.

The second problem is that Paul has a number of constitutional rights as the defendant in a criminal case. He has the right to defend

---

7. See, for example, the Wisconsin case, *State v. McDowell*, discussed in several places in this chapter.

himself, to take the stand, and to refuse to testify on the basis of the privilege against self-incrimination. He also has broad powers over defense strategy, and has the sole authority to decide whether to plead guilty or whether to waive a jury trial. By refusing to permit him to testify, you might interfere with the exercise of some of these constitutional rights. For this reason, the rules governing perjury are very cautious about the remedial measures a lawyer may take when representing a criminal defendant. For example, a lawyer has discretion in most cases to refuse to offer testimony she reasonably believes is false, but this discretionary permission to refuse *does not apply* in cases in which the evidence is the testimony of the defendant in a criminal matter. Rule 3.3(a)(3). Nevertheless, the disciplinary rules are uncompromising on the lawyer's duty, as an officer of the court, not to knowingly permit the introduction of perjured testimony at trial. You must take some sort of remedial measures to ensure that Paul does not lie on the stand.

The first remedial step you should try is to seek to persuade Paul not to tell the false story. Rule 3.3, cmts. [6] & [10]. If that does not work, you may try to "question around" the false evidence, and ask only questions on direct examination that will not elicit the *Wall Street Journal* story. You also may withdraw from representation, or threaten to withdraw, unless Paul agrees to change his story. See Nix v.Whiteside, 475 U.S. 157 (1986) (no violation of Sixth Amendment where lawyer warned client that he would seek to withdraw and inform judge of false testimony if client persisted in his intention to testify at trial that he saw "something metallic" in the victim's hand). In some jurisdictions, you may be able to avoid discipline by permitting Paul to testify in a "narrative" format—that is, telling his story in a free, unstructured way, without responding to questions on direct examination in the usual way. See Rest. §120, cmt. i (citing authority); Rule 3.3, cmt. [7] (disciplinary rule is subordinate to state law requirements that counsel permit client to testify in narrative form). The narrative approach avoids the moral dilemma for the lawyer, who avoids complicity in the client's perjury by the somewhat artificial expedient of not eliciting the lie from the client. As a practical matter, the narrative solution is a response to the reluctance of courts to allow counsel to withdraw on the eve of trial. In order not to make the situation worse for the lawyer, who has sought to withdraw on the basis of the client's prospective perjury, some jurisdictions permit the lawyer to go ahead, as long as her participation in the perjury is attenuated through the narrative approach. Note, however, that this solution is not approved everywhere, or even in the majority of jurisdictions.

If the narrative solution is not approved in your state, the only acceptable response under Model Rule 3.3 is either to secure a promise from Paul not to lie on the stand or, if he insists on telling the false story, to seek the court's permission to withdraw. You do not have the authority to prevent a criminal defendant from taking the stand. Rest. §120, cmt. i. If the court denies the request to withdraw and you try to question around the false testimony, but Paul still lies on the stand, you are now in the realm of retrospective duties. Example 5(b) deals with your obligations after a client lies.

B. Paul has now offered evidence that you know to be false; thus, you have an obligation under Model Rule 3.3(a)(3) to "take reasonable remedial measures, including, if necessary, disclosure to the tribunal." That rule means what it says. Your obligation is to *remedy the perjury*, period. You should first try to persuade Paul to correct his false testimony. Rest. §120, cmt. h. If that fails, you may make a motion to withdraw, provided that withdrawal will have the effect of curing the perjury by clearly putting the court on notice of the perjury and leaving it up to the judge to take some kind of remedial action, such as declaring a mistrial. As is likely, however, withdrawal alone may not cure the perjury. In that case, you are required to disclose to the tribunal enough information to undo the impact of Paul's false statement. Rule 3.3, cmt. [10]. You have this duty even though you would otherwise be prohibited from disclosing the information by the professional duty of confidentiality. Rule 3.3(c) & cmt. [10]; Rest. §120, cmt. h.

Whom Do You Believe?

6. This problem is adapted from Randy Bellows, "Notes of a Public Defender," in *The Social Responsibilities of Lawyers* 69 (Philip B. Heymann & Lance Liebman, eds. 1988). Remember that the mandatory obligation not to offer false evidence, contained in subsection (a)(3) of the rule, kicks in only where a lawyer "knows" that the client's statement is false. This is actually a *subjective* standard. The Model Rules provide that "knows denotes actual knowledge of the fact in question." See Rule 1.0(f). It is true that knowledge can be inferred from circumstantial evidence, but that does not convert the standard into an objective one. A lawyer has discretion in some cases under Model Rule 3.3(a)(3) not to offer testimony that the lawyer *reasonably believes* is false, but notice that this permission does not apply to the testimony of a defendant in a criminal matter. This rule recognizes Gary's constitutional rights, such as the right to take the stand to testify and the right to defend himself, which would be violated by the lawyer's refusal to permit him to testify. Thus, the rule does not permit a lawyer to take remedial action, *vis-à-vis* Gary's alleged perjury, without knowledge of the falsity of the testimony.

   Nix v. Whiteside addresses only the narrow constitutional issue of whether a lawyer violates the Sixth Amendment by refusing to permit the client to take the stand and offer false testimony. It may be the case that a lawyer would violate the Sixth Amendment by revealing confidences to the court on something less than the client's "clear expression of intent to commit perjury." The constitutional issues are beside the point, however, since the question asked only what your obligations are under the rules of professional conduct if Gary insists on telling his version of the story. The bottom line is, unless you know the story is false, you cannot reveal confidences to the court; the most you can do is try to arm-twist Gary into telling a different story.

Gary's explanation to you of Bart's death is somewhat implausible, but do you "know" that it is false? Let's put the case for letting Gary tell his story in the best possible light: Bart may be meaner and tougher than he looks; also, he was whacked out on Thunderbird and may have become violent suddenly. Also, Gary would have been sleepy and not thinking clearly at 3:00 A.M. On the other hand, if all of this were true, you would expect Gary to have presented this version to the police. It seems like common sense that someone who unburdened himself to the police would want to put himself in the most favorable light possible. Of course, there are responses to this argument: (1) Gary was in a state of shock and confusion after Bart's death and may have told a muddled story to the police; (2) maybe Gary did not tell the self-defense version to the cops because he thought it would be more incriminating than the version he did tell them—only with the benefit of legal advice does he realize that he should have told the truth in the first place; (3) Gary could have been embarrassed to tell the cops he was afraid of a 65-year-old drunk.

It is true that you cannot adopt a strategy of willful blindness, but in the criminal defense context, you practically would have to refuse to learn any contrary facts in order to be accused of being willfully blind. One way to state the standard might be as follows: Unless it is completely irrational to believe your client's story—for example, he says he was abducted by aliens for one night and therefore could not have been at the scene of the crime—or the evidence is so overwhelming that there is absolutely no way your client's story could be true or you have independent knowledge of the falsity of your client's statement, you do not know that your client is about to commit perjury. On these facts, you really do not know that Gary's self-defense story is a lie.

The following are your options at this point. You certainly should warn Gary that perjury is a serious matter and he should not lie in court. If you are feeling nervous about this case, you can seek to withdraw from the representation, but since you are appointed by the court, your request to withdraw very well may be denied, particularly since you cannot reveal the reason for wanting to withdraw unless you know that Gary intends to commit perjury. Withdrawing also passes the buck to the next appointed lawyer. You can try to talk Gary out of telling his story, explaining that he might be subject to a devastating cross-examination if he takes the stand, or that his story simply will fail to persuade the jury. Under *Nix v. Whiteside*, you can push him pretty far—for example, threatening to move to withdraw if you really believe the story is false, but ultimately it is your client's call whether or not to testify. You can, of course, always try to persuade Gary to plead out if the prosecutor has offered a deal. If you are in one of the few states that permits testimony to be presented in narrative form, you can do that, although it does tend to flag for the judge, the prosecutor, and (maybe) the jury that you suspect perjury. Thus, there is little point to using the narrative strategy if you are not required to mitigate what you know to be client perjury; it might even be a violation of your duty of competent representation to employ it. To emphasize, what you *cannot* do is reveal the perjury to the court, even by some indirect form such as citing "ethical problems," if you do not know that Gary is lying.

Attorney Conduct in Litigation: Forensic Tactics, Fair and Foul

INTRODUCTION

We all know that assisting or permitting a client to commit out-and-out perjury is an extremely serious violation of the disciplinary rules and can even constitute a felony. If the client in a deposition testifies that she was in Chicago on March 13, and in fact she was back home in Cedar Rapids, having an affair with her lawyer, both the client and the lawyer are in a lot of trouble. See *Committee on Professional Ethics v. Crary*, 245 N.W.2d 298 (Iowa 1976). Similarly, destroying responsive documents after they have been designated by a subpoena, or flatly refusing to comply with an applicable discovery request, is going to get a lawyer (and the client) in some really hot water—just ask Arthur Andersen.[1] Many cases, however, are not this clear. Much of this chapter deals with deception and with misconduct that lies just beyond the bright-line boundary around outright lying and destruction of evidence. Instead of bald-faced lying, this discussion is about conduct such as deceiving by remaining silent, playing word games to avoid answering a question truthfully, making a statement that is literally true but substantively misleading, taking advantage of an opposing lawyer's mistake or

---

1. The accounting firm Arthur Andersen was prosecuted for obstruction of justice after employees shredded documents relating to the auditing services it provided for Enron. The charges resulted in a huge loss of business for the firm even before the conviction, which interestingly was not based on the shredding but on the alteration of meeting minutes by an in-house lawyer.

inattention, or construing discovery requests narrowly to avoid producing responsive documents.

This is one of the areas of professional responsibility in which you must be the most attuned to generally applicable law. Most of the liability risks faced by lawyers are created by criminal, tort, and procedural law, not the disciplinary rules. The Model Rules do contain some "catch-all" provisions, very broadly drafted, that may encompass the conduct in question. For example, a lawyer may not:

- engage in conduct involving dishonesty, fraud, deceit, or misrepresentation. Rule 8.4(c).
- engage in conduct that is prejudicial to the administration of justice. Rule 8.4(d).

Because these rules are so broad, it is hard to know in advance what conduct is impermissible. There might even be due process problems if the rules were enforced in close cases:

> [T]he breadth of such provisions creates the risk that a charge using only such language would fail to give the fair warning of the nature of the charges to a lawyer respondent . . . and that subjective and idiosyncratic considerations could influence a hearing panel or reviewing court in resolving a charge based only on it.

Rest. §5, cmt. c. For this reason, courts and disciplinary authorities should rely on them infrequently. The Restatement goes so far as to say that if there is a more specific rule on point, a lawyer who complies with that rule should not be subject to discipline under one of the catch-all provisions of the disciplinary rules. Id. As a matter of statutory interpretation, this is a sound position, but be aware that not all courts are so precise. You will sometimes encounter a case of a lawyer who was disciplined under one of the catch-all rules, even though her conduct violated no other, more specific rule.

EX PARTE CONTACTS WITH JUDGES AND JURORS

Lawyers are prohibited from speaking ex parte—that is, outside the presence of the lawyer for the opposing party—with judges and jurors during the pendency of a proceeding. Rule 3.5(b). If you have watched many lawyer shows, you will notice that when one of the lawyers asks permission to approach the bench at trial, the other lawyer comes forward, too. When a judge has a discussion in chambers with one lawyer, the opposing lawyer is there also. The rule is not limited to trials, but is stated in terms of a "proceeding," which includes pretrial and post-trial litigation. The *ex parte* contact rule extends to other kinds of communications with judges and jurors. A common example is sending letters to the court, for instance to confirm a trial schedule or to inform the court of a development in the case. Any correspondence with the court must be copied to opposing counsel, or the lawyer sending the letter has violated Rule 3.5(b). Restatement §113, cmt. c, provides that a written communication is not *ex parte* if it is copied to opposing counsel.

Judges are independently prohibited from initiating *ex parte* contacts with lawyers by Rule 2.9 of the Code of Judicial Conduct. This rule is more detailed than Model Rule 3.5(b) and shows some of the exceptions that have developed to the prohibition on *ex parte* contacts. For example, CJC Rule 2.9(A)(1) permits judges to speak *ex parte* with lawyers as long as the communication does not address substantive matters. A brief call to deal with a minor scheduling issue is therefore permitted by the judge rule. But how does that affect the broader prohibition in the attorney rule? My view is that, if there is an exception in the jurisdiction permitting the contact, then the contact will be "authorized by law" and therefore permissible under Model Rule 3.5(b).

Notice that the prohibition on *ex parte* contacts extends to prospective jurors — that is, members of the venire from which the jury will be drawn — as well as jurors who are seated. The prohibition on *ex parte* communications with judges, jurors, and prospective jurors is limited to the pendency of the proceeding, Rule 3.5(b), but a separate rule prohibits communications with jurors and prospective jurors after discharge, Rule 3.5(c). Many jurisdictions permit post-trial interviews with jurors, and in those states, the contact will be authorized by law and therefore permissible under Rule 3.5(c)(1). Where post-trial contact is not expressly permitted by law, however, the disciplinary rules prohibit it. Wolfram, §11.4.4. And, even if authorized in general, communications are prohibited if a juror has made known a desire not to communicate, or the communications involve misrepresentation, coercion, duress, or harassment. Rule 3.5(c)(2), (3).

TAKING ADVANTAGE OF YOUR OPPONENT'S MISTAKES

The balance of duties in the Model Rules varies according to whether the lawyer is arguably behaving dishonestly toward a court, on the one hand, or toward the adversary or a third party, on the other. You can see this distinction clearly in the relative priority of the duties of candor and confidentiality. When it comes to the client committing a fraud on the *tribunal*, a lawyer has an obligation to disclose any material fact, the disclosure of which would be necessary to prevent the fraud on the court. Rule 3.3(a)(1). This rule expressly trumps the duty of confidentiality. Rule 3.3(c). Similarly, a lawyer has an obligation to disclose adverse legal authority, even if the opposing lawyer did crummy research and failed to discover it. Rule 3.3(a)(2). The priority of these duties is reversed where the object of the deception is a third party — including the opposing party in litigation or a transaction, her lawyer, unrepresented parties, witnesses, investors in a client's business, and everyone else except the court. It appears from Rule 4.1(b) that a lawyer has a similar obligation to disclose a material fact if disclosure would be necessary to avoid assisting a fraudulent act by the client, but notice that this obligation is expressly trumped by the duty of confidentiality stated in Rule 1.6. To put it very bluntly, courts get more protection from fraud than unrepresented third parties, adversaries in negotiations, investors in businesses, and anyone else who deals with a lawyer.

Consider a classic example. You are representing the plaintiff in a lawsuit against a defendant represented by a rather clueless lawyer. The defendant's lawyer does not realize that your claim actually is barred by the statute of limitations. To make the example more realistic, imagine that this is a case in which calculating the relevant limitations period is fairly difficult, and the opposing lawyer has made an understandable technical mistake in applying the law. The defendant's lawyer calls you up and offers to settle for $10,000. You are, of course, entitled to nothing at all, and if the defendant's lawyer had not miscalculated the limitations period, the defendant could prevail on a motion to dismiss. Can you accept the settlement offer?

The ABA says "yes," as long as you do not affirmatively misrepresent the facts or law, which would be a violation of Rule 4.1(a). ABA Formal Op. 94-387. Significantly, you do not have a duty to disclose the running of the limitations period under Rule 4.1(b). Filing and maintaining the lawsuit in the face of the lapsed limitations period is not a "fraudulent act" by the client, because the statute of limitations is an affirmative defense that must be raised by the opponent. The underlying claim — the basis for the lawsuit — is not invalid because of the expiration of the time to file the action, and indeed the court may award judgment to the plaintiff if the defendant does not raise the statute as a defense. For that reason, the ABA stated that filing a time-barred lawsuit is not equivalent to filing a frivolous action (Rule 3.1) or committing a fraud on the tribunal (Rule 3.3(a)).

The committee's conclusion represents a vision of lawyering very different from that contemplated by the rule requiring disclosure of adverse legal authority to the tribunal. In fact, one of the committee members dissented, saying, "I look upon this opinion as Julia Child would regard a fly in her soup." The distaste he feels is a reaction to what he characterizes as a "sly and deceitful" lawyer. Why does the ABA spend so much energy trying to improve the public image of the legal profession, the dissenter asks, when it condones deception and sharp practices by lawyers? This is a reasonable question, and many professional responsibility scholars are troubled by the relative priority of duties of candor and confidentiality in cases involving deception of courts and third parties. The Model Rules are extremely unforgiving of misrepresentations to tribunals, but ironically, courts are in a better position to protect themselves from fraud than are third parties. Courts have the benefit of procedural safeguards against deception — such as cross-examination, rules of evidence, and criminal statutes proscribing perjury and witness tampering — while third parties are pretty much on their own.

There are a few cases that come out the other way. Those cases do not constitute a trend, and the general rule is still that a lawyer is under no duty to correct her adversary's misunderstanding of the facts or law, but you should be aware of them. The best known is *Virzi v. Grand Trunk Warehouse & Cold Storage*, 571 F. Supp. 507 (E.D. Mich. 1983). In that case, the defendant agreed to a relatively high settlement of $35,000 because he believed that the plaintiff would have made an excellent witness at trial. As it turned out, though, the plaintiff had recently died. (The estate of a dead plaintiff is still entitled to recover some of the damages that would have been owed to the decedent during his lifetime.) The defendant never asked whether the plaintiff was still alive, and the plaintiff's lawyer never affirmatively misrepresented anything about his client's health. Nevertheless, the court held that the plaintiff's lawyer should have informed the defendant's lawyer of the death of the plaintiff, and it voided the settlement reached between the parties.

There is a significant distinction between *Virzi* and other cases in which the lawyer exploits her adversary's ignorance — the settlement in *Virzi* was reached in the presence of the trial judge. Thus, the court was able to invoke the more stringent rules on lying to a tribunal, similar to those in Rule 3.3, which create a more robust duty to disclose and are not trumped by the duty of confidentiality. It is not accurate to say that under *Virzi*, a lawyer has a general duty to inform her adversary that he is laboring under a misapprehension of the facts. Rather, the rule in the case is that any statement of fact that is made to one's adversary *and* the tribunal must be evaluated by the stringent rule of Rule 3.3, not the more lenient rule of Rule 4.1.

A different kind of "counsel's mistake" case involves the inadvertent production of privileged documents to the adversary during discovery. If you haven't yet had the pleasure (as a paralegal or summer associate) of participating in a big-case document production, you may not know that hundreds of thousands of pages of documents may be at issue. Teams of lawyers, paralegals, and documents clerks work to assemble the documents for production to the party that has requested them. Documents that are privileged, and therefore not to be produced, must be identified and logged. It sometimes happens that documents get mixed up, and the privileged documents get stuck in one of the boxes to be produced to the adversary. There has been a long-running debate in the profession over what the proper response should be by the lawyer who receives this windfall. For a long time, the ABA took the position that the receiving lawyer was obligated to (1) refrain from examining the materials once she realized they were privileged and had been produced accidentally; (2) notify the lawyer who had inadvertently produced the documents; and (3) follow the instructions of the sending lawyer. ABA Formal Op. 92-368. The ABA committee's reasoning was independent of any consideration of whether the inadvertent production waived the attorney-client privilege. As discussed in Chapter 8, some courts take the position that inadvertent disclosure is an automatic waiver, while other courts take a contextual approach and may not deem production to be a waiver in all cases. Under the ABA committee's approach, however, none of this made any difference; a lawyer was required by this interpretation of the disciplinary rules to refrain from using the (possibly now unprivileged) documents.

This position has changed with the adoption of the new version of Rule 4.4(b). This rule now provides that a lawyer who receives an inadvertently produced document "shall promptly notify the sender," but the receiving lawyer is not obligated to abide by the sending lawyer's instructions. The rule also does not require the receiving lawyer to refrain from looking at the documents. Comment [2] to the rule quite sensibly recognizes that the ultimate decision about what should be done with the document is a function of evidence law: "Whether the lawyer is required to take additional steps, such as returning the original document, is a matter of law beyond the scope of these Rules, as is the question of whether the privileged status of a document has been waived." Recognizing the effect of this rule amendment, the ABA committee has withdrawn its previous opinion requiring cooperation with the sending lawyer. See ABA Formal Op. 05-437.[2]

LYING IN NEGOTIATIONS

In the statute of limitations case, the lawyer could not make an affirmative misrepresentation of a material fact or proposition of law, such as telling opposing counsel "I've researched the statute of limitations and discovered

---

2. This may be beyond the scope of your professional responsibility course, but there has been a tremendous amount of judicial decisionmaking and rule amendments in the area of discovery of electronically stored information. In particular, Fed. R. Evid. 502 and Fed. R. Civ. P. 26(f)(3)(D) recognize the importance of agreements among the parties regarding the preservation of privilege or work product protection in inadvertently produced documents. So-called clawback and quick-peek agreements are often used in discovery in complex cases to reduce the expense and potential for wasteful satellite litigation associated with privilege reviews. Rule 4.4(b) does very little in comparison with the general law of evidence and procedure that applies in this context.

that my claim is not time-barred." See Rule 4.1(a). However, lawyers bluff, puff, and dissemble all the time when negotiating settlements or business transactions. For example, a lawyer might say, "There's no way my client will take anything less than $100,000 to settle this case," even though the client has given the lawyer authority to settle for $75,000. Is this kind of statement covered by the rule as well? The answer is "no," and the justification is one of the least persuasive sleights of hand in the rules. According to the commentary to Rule 4.1, some statements are not taken to be representations of fact. "Under generally accepted conventions in negotiation, certain types of statements ordinarily are not taken as statements of material fact." Rule 4.1, cmt. [2]. So, even though the utterance "My client won't settle for less than $100,000" *sounds* like a statement of fact, it really isn't. Everyone knows that lawyers lie in negotiations. In fairness to the ABA, it is not blessing the practice of lying, but trying to recognize the fact that posturing and bluffing are so common in negotiations that no halfway-sophisticated adversary would take these statements to be factual in nature.

Note, however, that the comment to the rule does not remove all the teeth from Rule 4.1(a). There are still plenty of cases in which a lawyer may be subject to discipline for making a false statement, *even in negotiations*. In all of the following cases, the lawyer was disciplined:

- A lawyer representing a creditor told the debtor that he would lose his driver's license if he did not repay the loan, which was simply not true. In re Eliasen, 913 P.2d 1163 (Idaho 1996).
- A lawyer representing an injured client told health care providers with unpaid bills that his client's verdict was not sufficient to satisfy all outstanding financial obligations, even though the funds were in fact sufficient. Florida Bar v. McLawhorn, 505 So. 2d 1338 (Fla. 1987).
- A lawyer was secretly taping a phone conversation (which was permissible under local law) but specifically stated to the other party that the conversation was not being taped. Mississippi Bar v. Attorney ST, 621 So. 2d 229 (Miss. 1993).
- A lawyer for the plaintiffs told the defendant that he would reveal the identity of one of the defendant's employees who was engaging in misconduct in exchange for a monetary settlement. The lawyer said he had made "confidential arrangements" to learn of the employee's identity. In fact, he had not, and had included that statement in a demand letter "for the purposes of settlement bluster." Ausherman v. Bank of America, 212 F. Supp. 2d 435 (D. Md. 2002).

The lesson of these cases is that you should not place too much reliance on Comment [2] to Rule 4.1, outside of obvious cases of puffery. When the statement pertains to something the parties are haggling over, such as the settlement figure or a sales price, the parties expect a lot of bluffing and posturing. When it comes to facts that are not the subject of the negotiation, however, lawyers must be truthful. It is not possible to say much more here, because resolution of these cases depends a great deal on applicable contract and tort rules, which may vary from one jurisdiction to another. Look for facts that might make a contract voidable at the insistence of the other party or that might constitute misrepresentation as a matter of tort law. You may not be required to know these rules for a professional responsibility exam, but in practice you should certainly be aware of the effect of generally applicable law on what lawyers may permissibly say in negotiations.

As the discussion of *Virzi* in the previous section shows, some courts will regard nondisclosure of a material fact in negotiations as a fraud on the tribunal if the settlement is presented to the court for approval. In the famous *Spaulding v. Zimmerman* case, 116 N.W.2d 704 (Minn. 1962), the defendant's lawyer did not disclose to the plaintiff that his damages were much greater than he realized. The court vacated the settlement after the plaintiff learned the true facts and made a motion to reopen the case. Significantly, because the plaintiff was a minor at the time of the settlement, the court was required to approve the settlement on the basis of its substantive fairness to the plaintiff. What started out as nondisclosure of a material fact to the plaintiff became nondisclosure *to the court* when the defendant presented the settlement for approval. In *Virzi*, the parties entered the settlement at a pretrial conference, in the presence of the judge, so the court was able to characterize the nondisclosure as a fraud on the tribunal. If the fraud is on the tribunal, rather than on a third party, the rules are much more stringent, as discussed above. The fraud on the tribunal rule, Rule 3.3, expressly trumps the duty of confidentiality, Rule 1.6. It also requires the lawyer to take affirmative steps to correct false evidence offered by the lawyer. Rule 3.3(a)(1), (3). The rule on nondisclosure to third parties, Rule 4.1(b), by contrast, is expressly trumped by the duty of confidentiality, Rule 1.6. Watch out for facts that can be characterized as fraud on the tribunal, because the more rigorous duties of Rule 3.3 may apply.

Example

With Friends Like These . . .

1. Johnson was injured when his car was hit by Rodman, a pizza delivery driver. Johnson alleges that he was forced off the road by Rodman's aggressive driving. Rodman responded that Johnson must have simply become distracted and driven off the road. Johnson's attorney asked an associate in her firm, a recent law school graduate (and therefore someone more knowledgeable about social media) to investigate and see if he could learn anything useful about Rodman. The associate discovered Rodman's Facebook page, but his privacy settings only allowed friends

to view his photographs and timeline updates. Since Rodman's publicly viewable information indicated that he liked going to see local bands, the associate created a Facebook account under a false name, indicating that he was a bass player in a local band. He then sent Rodman a friend request, which was accepted. The associate then looked through Rodman's photos and found several of him sitting on a motorcycle, holding a beer, and wearing a t-shirt that said "Born to Be Wild." The associate downloaded the pictures and sent them to the partner representing Johnson.

With trial approaching in two weeks, the partner asked the associate if it would be permissible to introduce the photos downloaded from Rodman's Facebook site. The partner also asked the associate to attend *voir dire* for the jury, surreptitiously review the social media profiles of prospective jurors, and indicate to the partner which prospective jurors seemed, from their online personas, to disapprove of wild young people.

The associate is a classmate of yours from law school, and calls you for advice. What do you say?

Explanation

With Friends Like These . . .

1. You have two potential contacts on social media to analyze here—the friend request to Rodman, the opposing party, and reviewing (but not friending) prospective jurors. Consider the two issues separately, because they implicate different rules.

    With respect to Rodman, I hope you remembered Rule 4.2, the anti-contact rule, from Chapter 3. Look at the specific language. ". . . a lawyer shall not *communicate* about the subject of the representation" with the adverse party. Aha, you think, maybe a friend request is not a communication, and if it is, it may not be about the subject of the representation. Well, a friend request is pretty clearly a communication, so that argument isn't going to work, and since the associate's purpose is to fish around for information that might be harmful to Rodman in the litigation, the communication should be considered related to the representation. Simply viewing the publicly accessible portions of anyone's social media page is not a communication for Rule 4.2 purposes. See, for example, New York State Bar Ass'n Op. 843 (2010); Oregon Bar Op. 2005-164. But the friend request crosses the line. There is a bigger problem, however, and that is the inherent deception in creating the dummy Facebook profile. Rule 4.1(a) prohibits making a false statement of material fact to a third person. Presenting to be a local musician, hoping Rodman will thus be more likely to accept a friend request, would be a violation of this rule. And so have a couple of ethics opinions also concluded. See New York City Bar Formal Op. 2010-2; Philadelphia Bar Ass'n Op. 2009-2.

As for contact with jurors, the on point here is the prohibition on *ex parte* communications with jurors or prospective jurors. See Rule 3.5(b). As with the situation of viewing an opposing party's Facebook page but not making a friend request, the mere accessing and viewing of a prospective juror's social media page is not a prohibited *ex parte* contact. "The mere act of observing that which is open to the public would not constitute a communicative act that violates Rule 3.5(b)." ABA Formal Op. 466 (2014), at 4. However, sending an "access request," such as a friend request on Facebook or a contact request on LinkedIn, would cross the line into a violation of the rule.

Duties of competence and diligence may require investigating available sources of information, including publicly accessible social media profiles. See, for example, N.H. Bar Op. 2012-13/05. Just make sure not to cross the line into deception or prohibited *ex parte* communication.

FRIVOLOUS PLEADINGS, MOTIONS, AND CONTENTIONS

The Model Rules prohibit bringing claims, defending lawsuits, or pressing issues within litigation—for example, seeking relief from the court by way of a motion or trying to get a particular issue before the jury—without a nonfrivolous basis. Rule 3.1. Frivolous discovery requests and objections are prohibited by Rule 3.4(d). In other words, there must be adequate factual and legal support for the position advanced by the lawyer, although the legal basis for the lawyer's contention may be one that is arguable as an extension, modification, or reversal of existing law. The rule is not supposed to inhibit the creativity of lawyers in pressing for changes in the law. The rule specifically exempts criminal defense lawyers in order to conform with the constitutional right a criminal defendant has to "put the state to its proof." The defendant may require the government to prove every element of its case beyond a reasonable doubt, even in the absence of any factual or legal basis for believing that the government will be unable to sustain this burden.

Lawyers tend not to be too focused on Rule 3.1 in practice. The reason is not that state disciplinary authorities are not concerned with frivolous litigation. Disciplinary authorities simply do not have the resources to enforce Rule 3.1 adequately, primarily because of the high information costs associated with understanding the factual and legal record well enough to assess whether a lawyer's position was well grounded. Because they are already well informed about the facts and law at issue in a case, courts are in a better position to enforce norms against frivolous litigation, and they have an array of statutory and rule-based tools for doing so. The most important is Rule 11 of the Federal Rules of Civil Procedure, particularly after its amendment in 1983.

In a nutshell, Rule 11 prohibits filing any paper—such as a complaint, answer, or motion, but not including a discovery request or response, which is handled separately—without a good-faith basis to believe that the factual and legal claims it contains are well grounded. The 1983 amendments to Rule 11 were part of a sweeping package of reforms that were intended to speed litigation, unclog court dockets, and reduce costs. These amendments set the stage for greater judicial control over formerly party-controlled litigation. In general, one can understand Rule 11 as being part of a trend away from conceiving of the litigation system as a purely private, or party-controlled system, with judges serving merely as umpires.

An important aspect of the 1983 amendments was the *objective* standard of reasonableness imposed on lawyers, rejecting the "pure heart, empty head" defense. *Business Guides v. Chromatic Communications*, 498 U.S. 533 (1991). After 1983, the question in evaluating a pleading or motion was whether the lawyer conducted an objectively reasonable investigation into the factual and legal predicates for the paper. The analysis is similar to that in a legal malpractice case—what is reasonable is determined by what a similarly situated lawyer would have done. See Chapter 6. Remember, too, that the standard is an objectively reasonable investigation *under the circumstances*. A lawyer is permitted to file a complaint or answer with less of a factual foundation than the lawyer expects to be able to establish after extensive discovery.

The 1983 amendments were roundly criticized on a number of grounds, including: the potential to chill legitimate advocacy; the disuniformity it created in application among different district and appellate courts; its tendency to spawn extensive satellite litigation, as the lawsuits got bogged down in sanctions proceedings; and the disproportionate impact of the rule on certain types of litigants who needed to push the boundaries of the law more frequently, such as civil rights claimants.

In response to this criticism, Rule 11 was significantly amended again in 1993, with several important changes. The most important is the addition of a "safe harbor" provision, which was designed to reduce the impact of satellite litigation. See Fed. R. Civ. P. 11(c)(1)(A). Under the new version of the rule, the party against whom a Rule 11 motion will be filed must be given an opportunity to withdraw the frivolous contention. The party has 21 days from the service of the notice to file an amended pleading, motion, or whatever, and the moving party may not file the Rule 11 motion until the expiration of the 21-day period. In addition, under the new rule, sanctions are no longer mandatory, but discretionary. See Rule 11(c), which uses the word "may." The new rule also better accommodates discovery procedure. Under Rule 11(b)(3), a pleading is not considered frivolous if the contention is likely to gain evidentiary support after a reasonable period for further investigation. Thus, lawyers are less apt to file Rule 11 motions early on in the proceedings, before there has been an opportunity for the facts to emerge in discovery. At the same time, the rule imposes a continuing duty of good faith on lawyers by covering "later advocating" a position. Rule 11(b). A litigant may believe that a claim will turn out to have evidentiary support after a reasonable opportunity for discovery, but if the hoped-for facts do not emerge, that litigant must drop the claim or face the possibility of sanctions. Finally, the 1993 amendment modifies the rule previously followed in some circuits that Rule 11 applies only to papers as a whole, not to individual contentions within filings. The 1993 version of Rule 11(b)(2) and (b)(3) is deliberately phrased in terms of "claims, defenses, and other legal contentions" and "allegations and other factual contentions," not pleadings or papers as a whole.

Example

When Does an Action Become Frivolous?

2. The law firm of Cooper & Geller represents Discount Menswear, Inc., which, as you might guess, is a discount seller of men's clothing. The president of Discount believes that it is unable to obtain Hickman-Freedom suits for sale because the manufacturer of the suits, Hartz, has exclusive retailer agreements with only a few high-priced men's stores in any given region. A lawyer for Cooper & Geller conducts some preliminary investigation by calling sales managers at men's stores in New York City, Boston, Philadelphia, and Washington, D.C. From these calls, the lawyer concluded that only one store in any metropolitan area sells Hickman-Freedom suits, and that this limitation was due to an exclusive retail agent arrangement imposed by Hartz. Based on that research, Cooper & Geller filed an antitrust lawsuit on behalf of Discount, alleging a nationwide scheme to fix prices and eliminate competition through an exclusive retailer policy and uniform pricing scheme.

Hartz filed an answer to the complaint, denying that it had any exclusive retailer agreement or had imposed a uniform pricing policy. Testimony at the depositions of Hartz managers indicated that the company sold to many different retailers and, in some markets, sold to as many as ten different retailers. As it happened, those markets were mostly in the midwest and western United States, not the four eastern cities contacted by the Cooper & Geller lawyer. After the depositions of Hartz employees had concluded, a lawyer for Hartz sent a letter to Cooper & Geller, which demanded that the firm voluntarily dismiss its lawsuit and threatened to seek Rule 11 sanctions from the district court if it refused to do so.

Did the antitrust complaint violate Rule 11 when it was filed? If not, did the firm subsequently do anything that violated the rule?

Explanation

When Does an Action Become Frivolous?

2. The facts in this example are based on the U.S. Supreme Court case *Cooter & Gell v. Hartmarx Corp.*, 496 U.S. 384 (1989), and the appellate court decision in that case, *Danik, Inc. v. Hartmarx Corp.*, 875 F.2d 890 (D.C. Cir. 1989). Before analyzing the issue of frivolousness, note that the defense firm representing Hartz has not yet successfully gotten the machinery of Rule 11 started. In order to invoke the rule, a lawyer must serve a separate motion on opposing counsel, but not file it with the court. Fed. R. Civ. P. 11(c)(1)(A). Before the 1993 amendments, lawyers commonly wrote letters to each other that threatened Rule 11 sanctions, but under the 1993 version, a lawyer must take the trouble of drafting a formal motion for sanctions and serving it on the adversary. The lawyer accused of misconduct then has 21 days to withdraw or otherwise correct the challenged paper, claim, contention, allegation, or denial. The letter to Cooper & Geller has no legal effect, although the firm nevertheless might be well advised to consider whether it is risking sanctions in the future.

On the issue of frivolousness, it is helpful to consider separately the two questions above — namely, whether the complaint violated Rule 11 as filed, and whether the firm violated Rule 11 by maintaining the action. The duty of a lawyer upon filing a pleading, written motion, or other paper is to make an inquiry that is reasonable under the circumstances into the evidence underlying any allegations and factual contentions made in the pleading. Rule 11(b)(3). Before the discovery process has begun, it is understandable that a party may not have all the evidence it needs to support its factual contentions. Rule 11(b) is written in terms of "an inquiry reasonable under the circumstances" specifically to accommodate the notice pleading system created by the Federal Rules of Civil Procedure. H&H §27.6. In addition, notice that Rule 11(b)(3) permits a lawyer to file a pleading if the allegations and factual contentions it contains are "likely to have evidentiary support after a reasonable opportunity for further investigation or discovery."

The appellate court in the actual case faulted the law firm for a rather superficial initial investigation. It did not believe that calling around to a few men's stores on the East Coast was a sufficient pre-filing investigation, particularly when the complaint alleged a nationwide scheme to fix prices. *Danik*, 875 F.2d at 896. That decision predates the 1993 amendments to the rule, however. As the advisory committee note to the 1993 version makes clear, "sometimes a litigant may have good reason to believe that a fact is true or false but may need discovery, formal or informal, from opposing parties or third persons to gather and confirm the evidentiary basis for the allegation." Even under the 1993 version of the rule, this is a close call. A reasonable investigation *under the circumstances* may require more than just a few phone calls to selected men's stores in four cities. There is probably something the firm could have done that would have approached the more systematic inquiry demanded by the court of appeals in the actual case. It would not take much more, though. Under the notice pleading and discovery system created by the federal rules, a plaintiff can file a complaint without doing anywhere close to the amount of factual investigation that would be required to develop a full evidentiary record—say, one that is sufficient to withstand a motion for summary judgment.

Even if the pre-filing investigation was questionable, once evidence comes to light that undercuts the allegations in the complaint, the firm must proceed very carefully. Rule 11 imposes an ongoing duty to ascertain whether a pleading (or a specific contention within a pleading) is adequately supported. A lawyer is deemed to certify the legal and factual basis for a pleading by "presenting [it] to the court," which includes "signing, filing, submitting, or *later advocating*." Rule 11(b). That means if Cooper & Geller continues to advocate its antitrust complaint, it had better have sufficient evidentiary support for the factual contentions it contains. If the depositions turn up no evidence of a price-fixing scheme, and indeed show that the firm simply was mistaken about the arrangements Hartz has with retailers in different parts of the country, Cooper & Geller must voluntarily dismiss the lawsuit. See H&H §27.6 and Illus. 27-1.

Surveillance, Surreptitious Taping, and Other Sneaky Evidence Gathering

The issue of taping phone conversations gained national attention with the saga of Monica Lewinsky and her "friend" Linda Tripp, but this is something that lawyers have always had to think about. Lawyers also engage in covert surveillance, particularly in personal-injury and domestic-relations cases. (Investigators for the defense in tort cases sometimes lurk near a plaintiff's house, hoping to capture images of a supposedly disabled plaintiff playing basketball or mowing the lawn.) Finally, an evidence-gathering activity for which people tend to have more sympathy is the use of "testers" in employment, housing, and other discrimination cases. See, for example, David

V. Isbell & Lucantonio N. Salvi, *Investigators and Discrimination Testers: An Analysis of the Provisions Prohibiting Misrepresentation Under the Model Rules of Professional Conduct*, 8 Geo. J. Legal Ethics 791 (1995). A public interest law firm might, for example, send a white family and an African-American family to inquire about rental housing; if the landlord offers to rent to one family and not the other, the testers will have developed some evidence of housing discrimination. Even if this purpose is ultimately laudable, the practice does involve some deception, since the testers are misrepresenting their actual intentions to rent housing.

When considering one of these cases, there are two sources of law to consult—generally applicable law and the state disciplinary rules. Many states, as well as the federal government, have criminal statutes prohibiting wiretapping, which includes the taping of telephone calls without the consent of one or both of the parties to the conversation. If a state has a one-party consent rule, lawyers generally may tape phone calls without violating the statute, because the lawyer (or the client) has consented to the recording. Some states have two-party consent rules, however, and in these jurisdictions the taping would violate generally applicable law. As for surveillance, there are state trespass and invasion of privacy laws to consider.

What about the disciplinary rules? There are a few specific rules, such as Rule 4.1(a), which prohibits a lawyer from making a false statement of material fact to a third person, and Rule 4.3, which states that a lawyer should not imply to a third party that he is disinterested in the matter. An example of conduct that violated these rules comes from litigation over a plane crash. *In re Air Crash Disaster*, 909 F. Supp. 1116 (N.D. Ill. 1995). The plaintiffs wanted to know what kind of training the airline's pilots had in dealing with in-flight icing, so they sent questionnaires to the pilots, stating that it was an "independent survey" conducted by the Safety Research Corporation of America.[3] The "research corporation" was actually set up by one of the plaintiffs' experts, for the purpose of gathering information to use in the lawsuit. The court held that the lawyers' failure to disclose that they were working on behalf of the air crash victims, and the implication that the questionnaire was an independent research study, was wrongful. As a remedy, it precluded the plaintiffs from using information obtained from the questionnaires as evidence in the litigation. If you accept that result, what about the discrimination testers? Isn't that the same thing?

---

3. A little review of Chapter 3: Contact with the pilots would not be barred by Rule 4.2, because the protection of the rule belongs to the airline, and the pilots do not fall within any of the three categories of Rest. §100. The acts or omissions of pilots are certainly imputed to the airline for the purpose of vicarious liability, but none of their acts were at issue in this particular crash, which is why Rest. §100(2)(b) does not apply here.

Beyond these explicit prohibitions in the rules, there is a lot of variability in the responses to deception in evidence-gathering, depending on the attitude that the disciplinary authorities take toward the rules. Although legal under generally applicable law, some investigatory practices may strike courts and the bar authorities as "underhanded" or "dishonest" and therefore the occasion for discipline. The basis for discipline is one of the open-ended provisions of Rule 8.4. Subsection (c) states that it is professional misconduct for a lawyer to "engage in conduct involving dishonesty, fraud, deceit, or misrepresentation" and these terms are not limited to conduct that violates a criminal statute.[4] Similarly, subsection (d) prohibits conduct that is "prejudicial to the administration of justice." There are lots of cases out there in which a lawyer is disciplined for engaging in legal conduct that a court concludes involves "deceit" or is prejudicial to the administration of justice. See, for example, *Gunter v. Virginia State Bar*, 385 S.E.2d 597 (Va. 1989), in which the court held that a lawyer who recorded telephone calls had engaged in "conduct involving dishonesty, fraud, or deceit," notwithstanding his acquittal after a criminal trial for violating the Virginia wiretapping statute. There are countless state bar ethics opinions reaching a similar conclusion. See, for example, New York State Bar Ass'n Comm. on Professional Ethics Op. 328 (1974); State Bar of Michigan Standing Committee on Professional and Judicial Ethics Informal Op. CI-200 (interpreting the Code of Professional Responsibility), modified by State Bar of Michigan Standing Committee on Professional and Judicial Ethics Op. RI-309 (May 12, 1998).

Interestingly, the ABA has abandoned its longstanding opposition to the lawful taping of telephone conversations. ABA Formal Op. 01-422. The ABA had previously stated that making a recording of a phone conversation was conduct involving dishonesty or deceit, even if it was made with the consent of one of the parties. ABA Formal Op. 337. It reversed course in 2001, however, admitting that there is no social consensus that the surreptitious taping of conversations is inherently deceitful, absent some kind of relationship of trust. The new opinion also rightly pointed out the different approaches of the Model Code and the Model Rules. The Model Code had an aspirational dimension, and included the broad command to lawyers to "avoid even the appearance of impropriety." Model Code, Canon 9. The Model Rules, by contrast, are supposed to function like a statute, not a statement of "best practices." There is nothing in the Model Rules about avoiding the appearance of impropriety, because the theory of the Model Rules is that the definition of "impropriety" will be spelled out in the black-letter text. I think this is the correct reading of the rules, and for this

---

4. The comments to the Tennessee version of Rule 8.4(c) specifically state that the rule applies to "the secret or surreptitious recording of a conversation or the actions of another." 71 U.S.L.W. 2197, 2200 (2002).

reason I dislike the open-ended prohibitions on "dishonesty" and "deceit." The Restatement takes the same position. "No lawyer conduct that is made permissible or discretionary under an applicable, specific lawyer-code provision constitutes a violation of a more general provision (such as one of the catch-all provisions of Rule 8.4) so long as the lawyer complied with the specific provision." Rest. §5, cmt. c. You should be aware, however, that not all courts and disciplinary authorities take such a hard line, and some may react to sneaky methods of evidence-gathering by holding the lawyer in violation of Rule 8.4(c) or (d).

Example

Gotcha Journalism

3. Osiris is a lawyer in a small town in the State of Perplexity. He represents Hinckley, a local farmer who raises and sells animals for medical research purposes. Hinckley's business has been the target of animal rights activists, who sometimes trespass on his land and vandalize his buildings. Hinckley suspected that a local activist, Sotomayor, was the organizer of some of the raids. He talked to his lawyer, Osiris, to see whether anything could be done. Osiris said he might be able to obtain a protective order keeping Sotomayor off Hinckley's land, but he would need some evidence of Sotomayor's involvement in illegal activity.

   Then Osiris hit upon a plan. He asked his paralegal, Stewart, to pose as a journalist for a national publication and interview Sotomayor. Stewart performed this ruse brilliantly, and Sotomayor admitted that she was one of the leaders of a group of protesters who ransacked facilities engaging in animal research. When Sotomayor was served with an application for the protective order, she was furious about the deception and reported Osiris to the Perplexity Bar Association. Is he subject to discipline?

Explanation

Gotcha Journalism

3. This example is based on *In re Ositis*, 40 P.3d 500 (Or. 2002). *Ositis* is a chapter in an interesting little controversy in Oregon, which began with a case called *In re Gatti*, 8 P.3d 966 (Or. 2000). *Gatti* involved discipline against a private lawyer who posed as a chiropractor to develop evidence that a medical claims-review company was, in essence, defrauding insurance companies. Interestingly, the same lawyer had previously complained to the Oregon State Bar about the practice of *government* lawyers posing as injured workers to develop evidence that chiropractors had been submitting bogus workers' compensation claims. The bar had told

the lawyer, Gatti, that its "preliminary conclusion" was that attorneys with "public authority to root out possible fraud" could use deceptive evidence-gathering techniques without violating the disciplinary rules. So Gatti figured he was in the clear, and was undoubtedly surprised when the trial panel of the Oregon disciplinary board held that *any* lawyer—government or private—who misrepresents his identity while engaged in the practice of law is subject to discipline. The discipline was based on Oregon DR 7-012(A)(5), equivalent to Model Rule 4.1(a), and Oregon DR 1-102(A)(3), equivalent to Model Rule 8.4(c).

This conclusion alarmed a number of professional organizations, including the U.S. Attorney for the District of Oregon, as well as the Oregon Attorney General. These lawyers filed *amicus curiae* briefs in the Oregon Supreme Court urging the court to create an exception for prosecutors who needed to conduct undercover law enforcement operations. Several civil rights groups also filed *amicus* briefs, objecting to the suggestion that only government lawyers should be exempt from the prohibition on deception. Civil rights lawyers have frequently relied upon "testers" to ferret out discrimination, and this practice has long been approved by courts. See, for example, *Richardson v. Howard*, 712 F.2d 319 (7th Cir. 1983). Courts have also approved the use of deception by investigators to develop evidence of infringement of intellectual property rights. See, for example, *Gidatex v. Campaniello Imports, Ltd.*, 82 F. Supp. 2d 119 (S.D.N.Y. 1999); *Apple Corps Ltd. v. International Collectors Society*, 15 F. Supp. 2d 456 (D.N.J. 1998). So Gatti had reason to believe he might be permitted to portray a chiropractor in phone calls to the medical records processing company.

After the case was decided, with no exception for deception by law enforcement lawyers, the Oregon Legislature considered a bill to exempt government lawyers—but not private lawyers—from the rules against deception in evidence gathering. The Oregon Supreme Court, possibly concerned about the legislature interfering with its prerogative to regulate the legal profession, responded by amending the disciplinary rules to exempt "lawful covert activity in the investigation of violations of civil or criminal law or constitutional rights." But this exception would not be not helpful to the lawyer in our example, who is not litigating over any civil or constitutional right.

The point of this example and the discussion of the Oregon controversy is to show that rules of professional conduct, like any legal rules, can be applied either formalistically or purposively. The formalistic application would look at the language of the rules to see whether the rules were literally violated. Rule 4.1(a) states that a lawyer shall not "make a false statement of material fact . . . to a third person." Rule 8.4(a) prohibits violating a disciplinary rule "through the acts of another." The language is pretty clear. Osiris is prohibited by Rule 4.1(a) from posing as a journalist and interviewing the local activist; Rule 8.4(a) extends that prohibition to his direction to the paralegal that he do the same thing. Finally, Rule 8.4(c) prohibits engaging in "conduct involving dishonesty, fraud, deceit or misrepresentation," including the little journalist ruse. This is a formalistic analysis because it relies on the violation of the literal language of these rules.

If this sounds wrong to you, and if you think lawyers should have some latitude to engage in deception in investigation, then you probably tend to approach these rules in terms of their underlying purpose or rationale. A purposive approach would ask what harm the rules seek to prevent and balance that against the good that could be done by permitting a certain amount of deception by lawyers. In some general sense, deception by lawyers is obviously a bad thing. But is the *particular* kind of deception at issue here, where lawyers participate in some kind of undercover "sting" operation, wrongful? In contexts other than attorney discipline, courts permit government lawyers to engage in deception. FBI agents pose as drug users, arms smugglers, and wealthy sheiks interested in bribing members of Congress (remember *American Hustle?*). Lawyers direct these operations and make use of evidence obtained by the undercover agents. This practice is not deemed to violate the constitution or any other rights of the target of the investigation, except in unusual circumstances where government agents overstep the boundaries (as in entrapment cases). Remember that the Sixth Amendment prohibiting any investigative contact with a represented individual is prohibited *after* indictment, but not before.

The legal system appears to tolerate a great deal of deception in the investigation of criminal wrongdoing. Even though employment and housing discrimination aren't crimes, they are still instances of wrongdoing, so we might extend the same reasoning to discrimination testers. What about our hypothetical lawyer Osiris? It is arguable that he was seeking to protect the property rights of his client, Hinckley, by obtaining a restraining order against the animal rights activists? Why should he have fewer rights than government lawyers to engage in deception in the furtherance of protecting rights? But hold on, you might reply; if we let Osiris play this little game, are we opening the door wide to all manner of deception by lawyers? A senior in-house lawyer for computer company Hewlett-Packard resigned, and was actually indicted on several criminal charges, after allegedly supervising an investigation into members of the board of the company, who were thought to be leaking internal board discussions to the press. See Joan C. Rogers, "When Using Investigators, Lawyers Must Set Boundaries of Permissible Conduct," 22 *ABA/BNA Lawyers' Manual on Professional Conduct* 507 (2006). Is it okay to direct an investigation into the board of directors of one's own employer? A prosecutor in Colorado pretended to be a defense attorney to talk a suspect in a gruesome killing into surrendering to law enforcement. In *re Paulter*, 47 P.3d 1175 (Colo. 2002). How do you feel about that kind of deception?

The general or theoretical point to take from this example is that rules may be interpreted formalistically. A formalistic interpretation may seem too narrow, for example, in a case of prohibiting "good" deception, such as the use of testers to discover unlawful discrimination. Or it may seem too broad, for example, if all deception is permitted and it leads to conduct like the lawyers discussed above, who pretended to be conducting a survey on aviation safety when in fact they were trying to discover evidence to use against the airline. To avoid this problem of over- or under-inclusive application of rules, you may prefer a more flexible, contextual, or purposivist approach to interpretation. In that case you might have a disciplinary board ask whether the deception was justified, or whether it served the broader goals of the legal system. Do you trust disciplinary boards to distinguish between "good" and "bad" deception? Do you think lawyers will have sufficient advance notice of what conduct is permissible and when they would be subject to discipline under this more flexible standard? These are questions that should inform your approach to interpreting the disciplinary rules in many contexts, not just the fascinating case of deception by attorneys.

WITNESS COACHING

Witness coaching, or "woodshedding" witnesses (the image is the lawyer hauling the witness out behind the woodshed, in back of the house, for a confidential discussion), happens during the preparation session for a deposition or trial. If the witness is the lawyer's client, or perhaps a close associate, such as an employee of the client, the lawyer may meet with the witness before she gives testimony and discuss the upcoming proceeding. Much of what happens at these sessions is perfectly innocuous. The lawyer will explain, for example, what happens at a deposition—the witness will be sworn in, there will be a court reporter present, the opposing lawyer will ask questions, the lawyer "defending" the deposition may make objections for the record but the witness should still answer, and so on. The lawyer may explain to a nonclient witness something of the factual background of the case and the legal issues in dispute. But these harmless pep talks can start to approach the line separating permissible from impermissible when the lawyer seems to be suggesting testimony the witness should give.

One hard-and-fast guideline is Rule 3.4(b), which states that a lawyer shall not "counsel or assist a witness to testify falsely." This rule really just repeats the prohibition in Model Rule 3.3(a)(3) on offering evidence that the lawyer knows is false. H&H §30.6. If a lawyer knows that a witness does not recall a fact, the lawyer cannot claim merely to be "reminding" the witness of something the witness had forgotten. The fact may be true, but it may be false, and the lawyer runs a real risk of suborning perjury—violating Model Rule 3.4(b) but also being exposed to criminal prosecution—by planting a "memory" in the witness's mind. What happens, though, when the lawyer is not falsifying testimony, but is "true-ifying" it, by helping the witness recall something that the lawyer independently knows to be true? Interestingly, lawyers sometimes claim they know such-and-such to be true, and are confident they are not falsifying evidence, even though in other contexts, such as the prohibition on presenting false testimony, they might claim that lawyers never really know the truth. Setting that little inconsistency aside, a lawyer who engages in "true-ifying" evidence will have committed a serious breach of the disciplinary rules if the testimony turns out to be untrue. In the *Anatomy of a Murder* example, where the lawyer claimed to be merely giving the client a neutral lecture on the law of self-defense, the lawyer had no idea whether the client was temporarily enraged. If the client had not, in fact, been temporarily enraged, the lawyer's "lecture" would be a violation of Rule 3.4(b), even though it was dressed up as a neutral explanation of the law.

Examples

Arm-Twisting the Witness

4. The Resolution Trust Corporation (RTC) filed suit in state court in the State of Perplexity seeking damages from "Boots" Bunco, the former President of Bunco Bank & Trust. Boots Bunco allegedly looted the bank of millions of dollars, and the RTC was seeking to recover funds from Bunco to repay the bank's depositors. One of the lawyers for the RTC, Juan Lascarro, interviewed the former Senior Vice President of Finance at Bunco, Barbara Eckhardt. It was important for the RTC to establish that Boots Bunco personally had authorized a dubious accounting procedure for bad loans, and Lascarro hoped that Eckhardt could provide this evidence. He and Eckhardt talked, and based on that conversation, Lascarro prepared an affidavit for Eckhardt to sign. Eckhardt objected to some of the language, so Lascarro rewrote it, and after another couple rounds of negotiations, Eckhardt signed the affidavit. When the RTC submitted the affidavit in support of its motion for summary judgment, Bunco's lawyer objected that Lascarro had violated Model Rule 3.4(b), prohibiting a lawyer from falsifying evidence. Bunco's lawyer filed a motion to strike the affidavit. What should the trial court do?
   A. Grant the motion as a sanction for violating the anti-contact rule.
   B. Grant the motion, because the court has the inherent power to strike falsified testimony.

C. Deny the motion, if it is satisfied (perhaps after an evidentiary hearing) that Eckhardt's testimony is truthful.

D. Deny the motion, because Model Rule 3.4(b) is a disciplinary rule only, and the court has no power to strike falsified testimony.

"Refreshing" Your Client's Recollection

5. You have just begun work at Sharon & Fudd, a prominent plaintiffs' personal-injury firm, specializing in asbestos litigation. Sharon & Fudd is known for its aggressive—some might say "hardball"—representation of its clients, and also for its track record of securing large jury verdicts and settlements. One of your first assignments is to prepare some of your clients for their upcoming depositions to be taken by lawyers for the asbestos manufacturers. The partner in charge of the case absent-mindedly hands you a packet of documents. "Read this," he says, "it'll help you walk the witnesses through the preparation session. I'm outta here until Monday morning." The depositions are scheduled to begin on Tuesday.

Flipping through the packet, you notice a document captioned "Preparing for Your Depositions," which is apparently to be photocopied and given to the clients. Some excerpts from the memo follow:

> How well you know the name of each product and how you were exposed to it will determine whether that defendant will want to offer you a settlement.
> Remember to say you saw the NAMES on the BAGS. . . .
> It is important to emphasize that you had NO IDEA ASBESTOS WAS DANGEROUS when you were working around it.
> It is important to maintain that you NEVER saw any labels on asbestos products that said WARNING or DANGER. . . .
> You may be asked how you are able to recall so many product names. The best answer is to say that you recall seeing the names on the containers or on the product itself. The more you thought about it, the more you remembered!
> If there is a MISTAKE on your Work History Sheets, explain that the "girl from Sharon & Fudd" must have misunderstood what you told her when she wrote it down.

You are somewhat taken aback by the memo and, being new to the firm, decide to ask someone for guidance. You talk to your assigned "mentor," a senior associate who enjoys a favorable reputation at the firm. She tells you, "Don't worry about the memos. They're protected under the attorney-client privilege and as work product, so there's no way the defendants are going to find out about them. Besides, there's nothing wrong with informing your client about the law. That's all the memo does. Look, our clients aren't the most sophisticated people in the world. They're welders, pipefitters, shipyard workers, you know. They're not too savvy about what goes on in depositions. If we didn't help them prepare, the defendants' lawyers would eat them for breakfast. Relax, you're doing fine."

You obviously are interested in avoiding trouble with the trial court and the state bar disciplinary authorities. Is there anything improper about giving the memo to the witnesses under the law governing lawyers?

Explanations

Arm-Twisting the Witness

4. This example is based on *Resolution Trust Corp. v. Bright*, 6 F.3d 336 (5th Cir. 1993), and reviews some concepts discussed in previous chapters. The correct answer is C. The court does have the inherent power to craft sanctions that would respond to misconduct by lawyers in litigation, so D cannot be the right answer. See Rest. §6(10), which permits the court to deny the admission of evidence wrongfully obtained. In this case, there is no evidence that the affidavit was falsified, so B cannot be correct. Eckhardt objected to some of the language in the affidavit, but she did not dispute the truth of the statements; in fact, she willingly signed the affidavit after the lawyers made some changes to respond to her concerns. There is nothing necessarily improper when lawyers work with a witness to memorialize testimony in a clear written form, as long as the lawyers do not falsify the testimony. Here, having the witness review and sign the affidavit *after* she gave the testimony that was the basis for her sworn statement ensures against falsification of the testimony. Finally, A cannot be the correct answer because Eckhardt is a former employee of Bunco Bank & Trust. See Chapter 3; Rest. §100, cmt. g.

"Refreshing" Your Client's Recollection

5. The memo in this problem was literally cut and pasted from an article in 14 ABA/BNA Lawyers' Manual on Professional Conduct 48-54 (1998). The memo was written by the Dallas-based plaintiffs' firm of Baron & Budd, and its revelation prompted a great deal of discussion about the limits of permissible witness preparation.

This memo goes right up to the edge of permissible witness coaching (under the guise of "advising about the law") and runs the risk of going over the line into suborning perjury, unless the lawyer is sure that all the facts embodied in the memo are true. (The firm became embroiled in litigation over aspects of its conduct in asbestos cases, including allegations that the witness preparation memo is part of a pattern of mail and wire fraud. For this procedural history, see *G-I Holdings, Inc. v. Baron & Budd*,

2004 WL 374450 (S.D.N.Y. 2004).) At the very least, the memo certainly violates the spirit of the discovery rules—a deposition is supposed to be a conversation between the examining lawyer and the witness, not the recitation of a script prepared by the lawyer defending the witness's deposition. But as a matter of black-letter law, it is not entirely clear what prohibits the lawyer from preparing a witness in this manner. The perjury rule, Rule 3.3(a), runs only to evidence that the lawyer knows is false. There is no suggestion that the clients of Sharon & Fudd actually were not exposed to asbestos, and there is nothing in Rule 3.3(a) that directly prohibits "prettying up" the testimony of the witnesses, as long as it is true. The same analysis applies to Model Rule 3.4(b), which prohibits falsifying evidence or counseling a witness to testify falsely.

Thus, if the witness-preparation memo is based on information communicated to the firm by the clients, and the information is factually true, the rules on candor to the tribunal do not support disciplining the lawyer. But if the information in the memo did not come from the clients originally, then the firm is probably counseling perjury. Certain aspects of the memo, such as the reminder that testifying in a certain way would be "better for your case," lend credence to the argument that the firm did not memorialize what the clients had told it, but instead tried to script the clients' testimony in a favorable way. Also, the practice of using questionnaires, intake interviews conducted by paralegals, and memos to clients explaining the nature of their cases suggests that the firm is running a "factory" where there is very little individual client counseling going on. Because the lawyers are unlikely to know the facts that apply to any given client, the memo probably does not represent the testimony that would have been given by the witness without coaching. The lawyers are taking a huge risk by putting words in the witnesses' mouths, because if the words turn out to be false, the lawyers will have violated Rules 3.3(a)(3) and 3.4(b).

FIRST AMENDMENT ISSUES

A fascinating and unfortunately deeply confused area of the law governing lawyers concerns the extent to which courts and disciplinary authorities may limit the speech of participants in the litigation process. Two specific questions frequently arise. First, can the state disciplinary rules prevent a lawyer from making a public statement about a pending trial? Second, can a disciplinary agency impose discipline on a lawyer for criticizing the way a judge handles the case? In both cases, the state's interest in maintaining a fair and efficient judicial system is in tension with either the client's or the lawyer's interest in speaking openly about her involvement in the process. Because judicial proceedings are an important way in which the rights and duties of citizens are settled, they have a "political" aspect, and speech relating to litigation arguably should receive the highest level of First Amendment protection as political speech. See, for example, *Republican Party of Minnesota v. White*, 536 U.S. 765, 792-795 (2002) (Kennedy, J., concurring). Citizens should be informed about what goes on during the litigation process, since the judicial system is such an integral part of the larger system of democratic government. On the other hand, speech connected with judicial proceedings presents special dangers of interfering with the fairness of the process, which itself is a right of constitutional dimensions. Trial by jury presupposes fair-minded jurors who do not approach the factual issues presented with preexisting prejudices and who decide the case based only on the evidence admitted at trial. See Rule 3.6, cmt. [1].

As is the case with restrictions on advertising and solicitation (see Chapter 18), this area of law is shaped substantially by Supreme Court decisions, which are reflected in the disciplinary rules. You really cannot understand the applicable law without considering the constitutional issues, so the following two sections consider both cases and the disciplinary rules.

Trying a Case in the Press

As you might imagine, the theft of $300,000 and a large amount of cocaine from a safety deposit box would be a newsworthy event, particularly when the money and the drugs had been used as part of an undercover police investigation. That is what set the stage for *Gentile v. State Bar of Nevada*, 501 U.S. 1030 (1990), an important decision about the balance between the right to a fair trial and the First Amendment. Soon after the theft, the sheriff named the owner of the safety deposit box company as a suspect, along with two police officers who had access to the box. As the investigation wore on, law enforcement officials increasingly began to focus on the company's owner, even though the evidence exonerating the police officers was ambiguous. Eventually, investigators publicly declared that the two police officers were no longer suspects, and also mentioned that the company's owner, Sanders, had refused to submit to a polygraph examination. Soon thereafter, Sanders was indicted.

Sanders's lawyer was understandably concerned about the effect of the pre-indictment publicity on his client's case. Most potential jurors had been exposed to over a year's worth of news stories reporting on statements made by the police and prosecutors. No one had publicly offered Sanders's account of the events or attempted to rebut the prosecutors' story. Thus, Sanders's lawyer sought to respond to the adverse publicity by holding a press conference at which he sought to blame a police detective for the theft and to explain the focus on Sanders as the result of pressure by police on witnesses to point the finger at Sanders. Sanders was eventually acquitted at trial.

The trouble did not end for his lawyer, Gentile, who was charged with violating a Nevada disciplinary rule governing pretrial publicity. The rule tracked the version of Model Rule 3.6 that was in effect at the time, and prohibited lawyers from making statements having a "substantial likelihood of materially prejudicing" a pending judicial proceeding. The drafters of the rule intended it to incorporate by reference the "clear and present danger" test, which limits the circumstances under which the government may restrict speech to prevent some kind of social harm — here, the harm of interfering with a fair trial. H&H §32.4. The rule did not expressly limit discipline to statements creating a clear and present danger of a harm, however. The rule also contained a list of subjects that are presumed to have a substantial likelihood of creating material prejudice as well as a "safe harbor" list of subjects that presumptively are fair game for public comment. Thus, when Gentile challenged the disciplinary action, he argued not only that the rule was facially unconstitutional because it did not include an explicit clear and present danger requirement, but also that the separate lists of "good" and "bad" statements rendered the rule void for vagueness.

The Court created one of those complex split opinions that you need a scorecard to figure out. There are two principal opinions, by Justice Rehnquist and Justice Kennedy, announcing separate holdings on the facial challenge and the void-for-vagueness argument, respectively. With respect to the facial challenge, the majority opinion written by Justice Rehnquist concluded that a state could limit pretrial statements by lawyers on a showing of less than a clear and present danger of actual prejudice to the rights of a litigant. Although the liberty of the *press* cannot be restricted without a showing of clear and present danger, lawyers, as participants in the trial process, owe a duty to ensure that the proceedings are fair to all the litigants. Thus, the basic standard embodied in the Nevada rule was sufficiently protective of the First Amendment.

That standard today forms the basis for Model Rule 3.6(a): "A lawyer . . . shall not make an extrajudicial statement that the lawyer knows or reasonably should know will be disseminated by means of public communication and will have a *substantial likelihood of materially prejudicing* an adjudicative proceeding in the matter." Please note, however, that a state disciplinary rule or judge-imposed gag order need not be as protective of speech as the Nevada rule. After *Gentile*, the extrajudicial statements of a lawyer may be limited where there is a "reasonable likelihood" of prejudice at trial. See, for example, In re Morrissey, 168 F.3d 134 (4th Cir. 1999); United States v. Cutler, 58 F.3d 825 (2d Cir. 1993). As discussed below, in the section on prosecutorial misconduct, prosecutors are subject to further restrictions on their extrajudicial statements in Rule 3.8(f).

Regarding the second issue, the opinion by Justice Kennedy held that the Nevada rule was void for vagueness, because the categories of presumptively permissible and impermissible statements were not defined with sufficient precision. Indeed, some of the lawyer's statements could have been on both lists! H&H §32.4 n.8. For this reason, the ABA amended Model Rule 3.6 to remove the list of presumptively prejudicial statements, leaving only the "safe harbor" statements that a lawyer may make without fear of discipline. Rule 3.6(b).[5]

The safe harbor subjects include the nature of claims and defenses asserted by the parties, requests for public assistance (such as providing evidence or testimony), warnings of the danger presented by a criminal suspect still on the loose, and any publicly available information. In addition, a lawyer is permitted to respond to public statements made by the adversary—like the extensive comments to the press made by police and prosecutors in *Gentile*—where response is required "to protect a client from the substantial undue prejudicial effect" of those statements. Rule 3.6(c).

Criticism of Judges

The organized bar seems at times to be obsessed with maintaining the public image of lawyers. Complaints about lawyers and lawyer jokes have been around since time immemorial, and seem inevitable given that people generally interact with lawyers only when they have something unpleasant, like a dispute, to deal with. But the profession often has responded to perceived public dislike of lawyers by attempting to manipulate appearances. The stringent restrictions on attorney advertising (which were dramatically upset by the Supreme Court in the Bates decision—see Chapter 18) were justified in large part on the basis of the perceived need to respond to the public's lack of respect for lawyers. In addition to worrying about the image of lawyers, the organized bar is concerned about maintaining public respect for the judicial system, and for this reason has long attempted to prohibit public criticism by lawyers of judges or judicial decisions.

For this reason, the Model Rules prohibit lawyers from impugning the "qualifications or integrity" of a judge or similar adjudicatory official. Rule 8.2(a). The problem with propping up the public's respect for the judicial system by restricting speech critical of judges is that judges are

---

5. The list of presumptively prejudicial statements has been moved to Rule 3.6, cmt. [5], so you still may use these categories for guidance. For example, lawyers should be particularly careful not to state: an opinion about the character or credibility of a party or witness; the results of the performance of a party on a test or examination (such as a polygraph); or an opinion about the guilt or innocence of a criminal defendant. In addition, lawyers should scrupulously avoid disclosing any evidence that is likely to be inadmissible at trial.

political officials, and if there is one thing the First Amendment protects, it is the right to criticize the government. For this reason, the disciplinary rules have been developed to take into account the constitutional protection offered to speech critical of government officials. In particular, Model Rule 8.2(a) incorporates the rule from *New York Times v. Sullivan*, 376 U.S. 254 (1964), that a public official cannot recover for defamation absent a showing that the speaker acted with "actual malice," which is defined as either knowledge of the falsity of the statement or reckless disregard of its truth or falsity. See also Rest. §114, cmt. b. There is a huge body of case law that has grown up around *Sullivan* that imposes additional constitutional requirements in defamation cases against public officials. For example, the First Amendment protects expressions of opinion, as distinct from facts that may be proven true or untrue. *Milkovich v. Lorain Journal Co.*, 497 U.S. 1 (1990). It is an open question in many jurisdictions, even those that have adopted Model Rule 8.2(a), whether the full panoply of constitutional protections, such as the fact/opinion distinction, apply to disciplinary actions against lawyers who criticize judges.

Although a lawyer's comments should enjoy some constitutional protection if they are made in a public forum such as a newspaper (see, for example, *Bridges v. California*, 314 U.S. 252 (1942)), a lawyer does not have the freedom under the First Amendment to disrupt the proceedings by making a series of frivolous objections or launching into a lengthy diatribe about the judge. Rule 3.4(d) prohibits "engag[ing] in conduct intended to disrupt a tribunal," and a series of cases has made it clear that a judge may punish a lawyer for contempt if the lawyer's actions present a clear and present danger of actually interfering with the administration of justice. See, for example, *Offutt v. United States*, 348 U.S. 11 (1954); *Sacher v. United States*, 343 U.S. 1 (1952); *In re Dellinger*, 461 F.3d 389 (7th Cir. 1972) (Chicago Seven trial).

Examples

My Client Is Misunderstood

6. Anthony Alto, a waste management consultant in Old Jersey, was arrested and charged with multiple racketeering violations, including murders allegedly committed in the course of running an organized crime family. After Alto's arrest and indictment, the U.S. Attorney for the District of Old Jersey held a press conference at which he called Alto "a murderer, not a folk hero," listed the charges against him, and predicted that the government would prevail at trial. In response, Alto's lawyer called his own press conference at which he called the prosecutors "publicity-hungry," said the government had "thrown the Constitution out the window," called the government's witnesses "bums," called Alto loyal and honest, and vehemently denied that Alto was a member of the Mafia, which, as

his lawyer pointed out, does not even exist. The disciplinary authorities in Old Jersey have charged Alto's lawyer with violating Model Rule 3.6. Will he be subject to discipline?

Smile When You Call Me That, Mister

7. Witkin is an appellate lawyer representing an insurance company in an appeal from an adverse verdict at trial. The intermediate appellate court of the State of Perplexity affirmed the trial court. Witkin decided to file a petition for discretionary review with the Supreme Court of Perplexity. In the petition, Witkin raised numerous claims of error in the appellate court's reasoning, using fairly strong language for dramatic effect. Here is one passage from the petition: "The Court of Appeals' published Opinion in this case is quite disturbing. It is replete with misstatements of material facts, it misapplies controlling case law, and it does not even bother to discuss relevant cases that are directly on point." Witkin went on to accuse the court of engaging in results-oriented judging, stating: "Indeed, the Opinion is so factually and legally inaccurate that one is left to wonder whether the Court of Appeals was determined to find for [appellee] and then said whatever was necessary to reach that conclusion (regardless of whether the facts or the law supported its decision)."

   The Supreme Court of Perplexity denied the petition for discretionary review, ordered the petition struck as a "scurrilous and intemperate attack on the integrity of the Court of Appeals," and referred the petition to the Perplexity bar association for possible disciplinary action. You are a lawyer for the disciplinary agency—did Witkin violate the applicable rule?

Explanations

My Client Is Misunderstood

6. This example is based on *United States v. Cutler*, 58 F.3d 825 (2d Cir. 1995), which upheld the criminal contempt conviction (not a disciplinary action) of Bruce Cutler, the lawyer representing John Gotti in his racketeering trial. Alto's lawyer has a couple of different arguments available here. The first is that his statements will not have a substantial likelihood of materially prejudicing the trial of Alto. Rule 3.6(a). Remember, a state is not constitutionally required to impose discipline only where a lawyer's statements present a substantial likelihood of materially prejudicing the proceedings; in fact, the local court rule under which Cutler was disciplined restricted extrajudicial speech by lawyers to the extent there is a "reasonable likelihood" of interference with a fair trial. For the purposes of this example, though, use the standard of Model Rule 3.6(a).

Note that the standard is written in terms of *likely* prejudice—the disciplinary authorities in Old Jersey need not show *actual* prejudice to the fairness of the trial proceedings. When assessing the likelihood of prejudice to a judicial proceeding, courts consider factors such as the timing of extrajudicial communications, the frequency of the lawyer's public comments, whether the trial will be before a jury or a judge, whether the information is otherwise available to the public, and the lawyer's intent in making the statements. See Rule 3.6, cmts. [5], [6]; *In re Sullivan*, 586 N.Y.S.2d 322 (App. Div. 1992). A public statement made immediately prior to the beginning of jury selection is much more likely to be prejudicial than one made during the investigative phase of a proceeding. *United States v. Bingham*, 769 F. Supp. 1039 (N.D. Ill. 1991). On the other hand, statements made early in the case can have great impact if the public's interest in the case is high because of the recent arrest and indictment. *Cutler*, 58 F.3d at 837.

This example is a close call, because it is doubtful that a defense lawyer can do much to affect the public attitudes that already have developed in response to a high-profile alleged Mafia boss such as Anthony Alto. (Think about your own beliefs about John Gotti and whether they would be swayed by anything his lawyer might say.) In the actual Gotti case, the lawyer made public comments repeatedly and often in violation of specific instructions by the trial court not to speak about the case. The defiant, repeated, vehement comments of Bruce Cutler are more of a threat to the fairness of the proceedings, as compared with the single press conference in this example. Also, the court in the Gotti trial was applying a much more lenient standard—reasonable likelihood of interference, rather than *substantial* likelihood of *material* prejudice. Thus, the comments made by Alto's lawyer probably do not violate Model Rule 3.6.

Alto's lawyer also can make the "right of response" argument, based on Model Rule 3.6(c). Note, however, that the lawyer's right is limited to what a reasonable lawyer would believe necessary to counter the adverse publicity created by the prosecution. Certainly, Alto's lawyer has some right to rebut the prosecutor's contention that Alto is a murderer, but he must be careful not to go overboard. Calling the witnesses bums and saying the government threw the Constitution out the window is likely to be construed as a statement that goes beyond the right of reply in Model Rule 3.6(c). See H&H §32.7 n.1.

Smile When You Call Me That, Mister

7. The language quoted in the example is taken verbatim from a real case, *In re Wilkins*, 777 N.E.2d 714 (Ind. 2002), detailing the barely contained outrage of the Indiana Supreme Court in response to the suggestion that the Court of Appeals "may have been motivated in their decision making

by something other than the proper administration of justice." The court imposed a 30-day suspension on the lawyer. Never mind that "op-ed" columnists in newspapers, television commentators, legal scholars, and even other judges in dissenting opinions[6] say that sort of thing all the time—the court said it punished the lawyer in order to preserve the public's confidence in the administration of justice. This decision, not the lawyer's comments, is the real outrage. Regrettably, it is not at all atypical of the judicial response to criticism by lawyers of judges.

The difficulty for the lawyer is that the governing rule, Rule 8.2(a), only partially adopts the constitutional principles that would protect a newspaper columnist or law professor from making the very same critical comments. For example, it contains the *New York Times v. Sullivan* actual malice standard, but not the requirement that the government prove the falsity of the statement at issue (see *Philadelphia Newspapers v. Hepps*, 475 U.S. 767 (1986)) or the distinction between constitutionally protected opinion and statements of fact that may subject the speaker to liability (see *Milkovich v. Lorain Journal*, 497 U.S. 1 (1990)). The uncertainty in the law is understandable, because these principles have developed in the context of defamation lawsuits brought by government officials and public figures, often against the news media. Arguably, the need for constitutional protection is greater in these situations than in cases in which attorneys make critical comments in court filings. The lawyer in this example was not exposing wrongdoing or educating the public about the political process. Indeed, it was unlikely that anyone would have read the brief in the actual case, other than the judges on the Indiana Supreme Court, had the case not turned into a big public controversy.

Of course, the lawyer could point to the "private" nature of the speech and argue that the statements in the petition were unlikely, in the extreme, to influence the public's perception of the integrity of the judicial system. It would be one thing if the lawyer had called a press conference to accuse the Court of Appeals of misconduct, but the brief never was intended for public consumption. Ironically, if the lawyer *had* called a press conference, there might be a stronger argument for applying the press-freedom cases, like *Hepps* and *Milkovich*, because of the importance of keeping the public informed about what is going on in the courts. If the judges on the Court of Appeals actually were engaging in corruption (in the sense of failing to follow the law), shouldn't voters know about that misconduct, so they can vote against incumbent judges in an upcoming election?

---

6. A dissenting justice on the Indiana Supreme Court provided some nice examples of critical attacks by U.S. Supreme Court Justice Scalia that make the lawyer's statements in the brief look like tame stuff indeed.

In any event, many courts hold that the First Amendment rules that apply in defamation cases do not carry over to disciplinary actions against lawyers. Other courts grant much more robust constitutional protection to lawyers. See, for example, *Standing Committee v. Yagman*, 55 F.3d 1430 (9th Cir. 1995) (holding that a lawyer could not be disciplined for accusing a judge of being "dishonest" because it was merely rhetorical hyperbole, and that the disciplinary committee did not produce facts to show the *falsity* of the lawyer's claim that the judge was "drunk on the bench"). The U.S. Supreme Court has started to take an interest in these cases. For example, the Court recently treated candidates for judicial office as, roughly speaking, politicians instead of lawyers. *Republican Party of Minnesota v. White*, 536 U.S. 765 (2002). In the absence of some clearer indication from the U.S. Supreme Court about the nature of First Amendment protection to be granted to lawyers who criticize judges, there probably will continue to be tremendous variation in this area of the law. See cases cited in H&H §63.3.

PROSECUTORIAL MISCONDUCT

Public prosecutors have a tremendous amount of power. As a matter of the constitutional separation of powers, they have virtually unreviewable discretion to decide whom to prosecute, and for what offenses. Prosecutors enjoy almost unlimited immunity from civil liability. Prosecutorial discretion, though not truly unfettered, is very lightly regulated. *United States v. Batchelder*, 442 U.S. 114 (1979). Although courts impose some restrictions on discriminatory or vindictive prosecution, these claims tend to be very difficult to prove, particularly after *United States v. Armstrong*, 517 U.S. 546 (1996). In addition, prosecutors can deploy the awesome machinery of the state, supervising investigations by law enforcement officers, seeking wiretaps and searches, and convening grand juries with the power to compel testimony from witnesses. Prosecutors can grant immunity to reluctant witnesses to induce their cooperation, and can decide to dismiss charges or to offer a plea bargain to a defendant in lieu of going to trial.

As Spider-Man would observe, with great power comes great responsibility. There are numerous restrictions on what prosecutors may do. In the most general terms, prosecutors are said to be not ordinary advocates, but ministers of justice and representatives of the sovereign (We the People). *Berger v. U.S.*, 295 U.S. 78 (1935). "A prosecutor has the responsibility of a minister of justice and not simply that of an advocate." Rule 3.8, cmt. [1]. Prosecutors are expected to aim at a just result, not simply seek to convict the accused. The trouble is, prosecutors face political pressures to obtain convictions. State prosecutors are elected officials, and voters tend to be responsive to claims by challengers that the incumbent is "soft on crime." Federal prosecutors are appointed, but are understood to be political appointees who serve at the pleasure of the President. Prosecutors have multiple roles, including both minister of justice and zealous advocate. Thus, platitudes about "strik[ing] hard blows" but not being "at liberty to strike foul ones," *Berger*, 295 U.S. at 88, need to be supplemented with specific, enforceable legal duties that specify how to balance the different aspects of the prosecutorial role.

One source of these duties is the Constitution. As a matter of Fifth and Fourteenth Amendments due process, a prosecutor must disclose material exculpatory evidence to the defendant. *Brady v. Maryland*, 373 U.S. 83 (1963). "Material" evidence means that which would have had a reasonable probability of altering the outcome if it had been disclosed. This duty arises even in the absence of a request from the defendant, *U.S. v. Agurs*, 427 U.S. 97 (1976), but it does not apply at the grand jury stage, *U.S. v. Williams*, 504 U.S. 36 (1992). The Model Rules supplement the obligation stated by *Brady* and its progeny, requiring disclosure of *all* "evidence or information known to the prosecutor that tends to negate the guilt of the accused or mitigates the offense." Rule 3.8(d). Notice that this rule applies to information, not just (admissible) evidence, and requires disclosure not only of exculpatory information—that is, that which establishes innocence—but also that which tends to negate guilt. The *Brady* supplement also applies at sentencing. Similarly, Model Rules 3.8(b) and (c) go beyond the requirements of *Miranda v. Arizona*, 384 U.S. 436 (1966), in requiring not only that prosecutors advise suspects in custody of their right to counsel, but that they give suspects a reasonable opportunity to obtain counsel, Rule 3.8(b), and in the meantime that they do not attempt to obtain waivers of important pretrial rights, such as the right to a preliminary hearing, Rule 3.8(c).

The Model Rules impose additional limitations going beyond the Constitution. Prosecutors may not prosecute a charge that they know is not supported by probable cause. Rule 3.8(a). (Remember that "know" in the Model Rules is defined as actual knowledge—see Rule 1.0(f).) Rule 3.8(e) regulates the issuance of subpoenas to lawyers. Like all lawyers, prosecutors are subject to the limitations of Rule 3.6 on extrajudicial statements to the media that "will have a substantial likelihood of materially prejudicing an adjudicative proceeding in the matter." Rule 3.6(a). In addition, prosecutors may not make public statements that "have a substantial likelihood of heightening public condemnation of the accused." Rule 3.8(f). They also must exercise reasonable care to ensure that law enforcement personnel do not make statements that a prosecutor would be forbidden to make, either by Rule 3.6 or by Rule 3.8(f). Finally, amendments in 2008 establish obligations to address potential wrongful convictions. Upon learning of "new, credible, and material evidence creating a reasonable likelihood" that a convicted defendant is innocent of the crime charged, a prosecutor must disclose that evidence to the defendant and take further steps to investigate whether the defendant was in fact wrongfully convicted. Rule 3.8(g). This duty applies no matter where the conviction occurred. If the conviction occurred in the prosecutor's own jurisdiction, and the evidence is clear and convincing, she must do something further—"seek to remedy the conviction." Rule 3.8(h). Wisconsin became the first state to adopt the wrongful-conviction rules, Rule 3.8(g) and (h). At the time the fifth edition of this book went to press, no other state had followed Wisconsin's lead.

Despite the fairly detailed restrictions in Rule 3.8, discipline for prosecutors is quite uncommon. See Fred Zacharias, *Structuring the Ethics of Prosecutorial Trial Practice: Can Prosecutors Do Justice?* 44 Vand. L. Rev. 45 (1991); Bruce A. Green, *Prosecutorial Ethics as Usual*, 2003 U. Ill. L. Rev. 1573. For this reason, the disbarment of the Durham, North Carolina, district attorney was particularly noteworthy. In the prosecution of three members of the Duke lacrosse team for rape, the D.A., Mike Nifong, committed numerous violations of the disciplinary rules, including failing to turn over exculpatory evidence and making misleading statements to the press. See Robert Mosteller, *The Duke Lacrosse Case, Innocence, and False Identifications: A Fundamental Failure to "Do Justice,"* 76 Fordham L. Rev. 1337 (2007).

12

The Client Fraud Problem

INTRODUCTION

Individuals can commit serious financial frauds, but entity representation is the most common situation in which the problem of a lawyer's complicity in a client's wrongdoing arises. The accounting scandals that came to light with the bursting of the dot-com bubble in the early 2000s focused the attention of the public, legislators, and regulators on the role lawyers played in facilitating or covering up fraudulent transactions. Interestingly, there are still many unanswered questions about the role of lawyers in the financial system meltdown of late 2007, but if history is any guide, lawyers will be found to have had a role in many questionable dealings. Because the issue of lawyer liability for participating in client fraud so frequently arises in the context of corporate representation, it is essential that you understand the material on client identification in Chapter 5. If you encounter the client fraud problem on a professional responsibility exam, it likely is to be intertwined with issues such as conflicts of interest and the attorney-client privilege, which also depend on being clear on the identity of your client.

LAWYER LIABILITY FOR PARTICIPATING IN CLIENT WRONGDOING

Lawyers sometimes forget that they can be held liable in the same way as any nonlawyer for some torts, breaches of fiduciary duty, and securities law violations. See, for example, *Rubin v. Schottenstein, Zox & Dunn*, 143 F.3d 263 (6th Cir. 1998). If you take nothing else from this chapter, remember this: *There is no "acting in a professional capacity" defense to an action for fraud or other civil wrongdoing.* To make the situation even more fraught with peril, a claim for damages may be based on the same kind of conduct that is usually perfectly legitimate, such as drafting documents, negotiating a deal, counseling a client, or sending letters to investors. Having a crooked client is a dangerous situation for a lawyer, because otherwise innocuous activities can become wrongful if done with the intent to assist the client's wrongdoing. The most common claims against lawyers who are involved in their clients' misconduct include: common law fraud, securities fraud, aiding and abetting breach of fiduciary duty, and legal malpractice.

Common Law Fraud

Fraud or misrepresentation is the cause of action resulting from an intentional misrepresentation of material fact that is intended to induce, and does induce, reliance by the plaintiff, which causes financial injury to the plaintiff. See generally Dan B. Dobbs, *The Law of Torts* §470 (2000); Restatement (Second) of Torts §526. It is a somewhat disfavored action, in the sense that it often must be pleaded with particularity and is subject to a higher standard of proof, but there still are plenty of cases in which lawyers are liable for fraud. Moreover, a lawyer may be liable for aiding and abetting fraud, provided that the lawyer acts with the purpose of facilitating the client's fraud. Lawyers may be primarily liable, or liable as aiders and abettors, in cases where the client obtained funds through misrepresentation of material facts, such as by lying about the financial condition of a business or inflating the value of assets used to secure a loan. Fraud cases also may arise out of sales transactions where the client seller (speaking through the lawyer, of course) misleads the purchaser about the condition of the property.

Securities Fraud

Once upon a time, lawyers could be liable as "secondary actors" for securities fraud under federal law. If a client made a false statement in connection with a securities transaction, and the lawyer was involved in the transaction, the lawyer could be liable for assisting the fraud in violation of Securities and Exchange Commission (SEC) Rule 10b-5. A Supreme Court case known as *Central Bank* changed the landscape of secondary liability for securities fraud. *Central Bank of Denver, N.A. v. First Interstate Bank of Denver, N.A.*, 511 U.S. 164 (1994). After *Central Bank*, lawyers no longer can be held liable for their clients' fraudulent statements in connection with securities transactions, but (and this is a big exception) lawyers still can be held liable as primary actors if they fairly can be deemed to be the authors of the fraudulent statements. If a lawyer prepares an opinion letter certifying to the accuracy of a client's financial statements and the client's compliance with various regulatory requirements, the lawyer is a primary actor for the purposes of liability for securities fraud. See, for example, Kline v. First Western Gov't Sec., 24 F.3d 480 (3d Cir. 1994). In addition, the Supreme Court subsequently emphasized the reliance element in 10b-5 actions. Stoneridge Investment Partners LLC v. Scientific-Atlanta, Inc., 552 U.S. 148 (2008). The upshot of Stoneridge is that liability for law firms follows not simply from having made a fraudulent statement but from having been expressly identified to purchasers of securities as the maker of the statement. "To rise to the level of a primary violation, the secondary actor [for example, a law firm] must not only make a material misrepresentation or omission, but the misrepresentation must be attributed to the specific actor at the time of public dissemination." In re Refco, Inc. Securities Litigation, 609 F. Supp. 2d 267 (S.D.N.Y. 2009), aff'd sub nom. PIMCO v. Mayer Brown LLP, 603 F.3d 144 (2d Cir. 2010).

After Central Bank and Stoneridge, it's probably fair to say that lawyers are less exposed to liability for securities fraud than they've ever been. The Refco case cited above bears out that interpretation. In that case, a major law firm helped a client engage in fraudulent "round-trip" loans for the purpose of disguising its financial problems. Lawyers at the firm negotiated the terms of the transactions, drafted documents for the deals, and transmitted copies of the documents to the participants. The documents contained false statements that misrepresented the financial condition of the client corporation. In other words, the lawyers were quite actively involved in the fraud. Nevertheless, because they were not identified as the authors of the false statements, investors who sued the law firm could not satisfy the reliance element of the 10b-5 cause of action. The SEC had argued for a "creator" standard—that is, liability should follow making a false statement. The federal courts instead went with an "attribution" standard, sometimes called the "bright line test," under which secondary actors are liable only for statements that are explicitly attributed to them. See 603 F.3d at 154-155.

Aiding and Abetting Breach of Fiduciary Duty

If a client is a partner in a partnership or an officer or director of a corporation, she has fiduciary duties to the partnership or corporation, as well as fiduciary duties to certain other constituents, such as minority shareholders or other partners. These duties are a function of the substantive law of agency, partnership, or corporations. Be careful here, because in some jurisdictions if the client has a fiduciary duty to X, the lawyer may be liable to X for aiding and abetting the client's breach of duty if the lawyer provides "substantial assistance and encouragement" to the breach. See, for example, *Chem-Age Industries v. Glover*, 652 N.W.2d 756 (S.D. 2002); *Granewich v. Harding*, 985 P.2d 788 (Or. 1999). An example of active participation by the lawyer in the underlying breach of duty would be assisting a majority shareholder in squeezing out a minority shareholder by amending the corporation's bylaws to remove provisions designed to protect the minority shareholder's interests. In other jurisdictions, however, the lawyer for an entity has no duty to avoid assisting the breach by one constituent of a fiduciary duty owed solely to another constituent, as opposed to the entity itself. Rest. §96, cmt. g.

Legal Malpractice

If a lawyer represents a corporation and assists one of its constituents in converting corporate property, usurping corporate opportunities, or some other kind of self-dealing, the lawyer has breached a duty she owes to the corporation to act in its best interests at all times. In a sense, this is similar to the claim for aiding and abetting a breach of fiduciary duty, if the person or entity injured is the lawyer's client. But what if the injured party is a nonclient, such as a shareholder or the other party in a business transaction? The traditional rule is that only persons in contractual privity with the attorney could sue for malpractice, but some courts are willing to relax the privity requirement in some circumstances. If a lawyer prepares an opinion letter for the use of a third party, knowing that the third party will rely on the lawyer's opinion in deciding whether to extend credit to the lawyer's client, the lawyer may be liable for malpractice to the third party, despite a lack of contractual privity. See, for example, *McCamish, Martin, Brown & Loeffler v. F.E. Appling Interests*, 991 S.W.2d 787 (Tex. 1999); *Greycas, Inc. v. Proud*, 826 F.2d 1560 (7th Cir. 1987). The Restatement adopted the emerging rule that lawyers can be held liable for malpractice to nonclients where the injured party relied on the lawyer's opinion or where one of the objectives of the representation was to benefit the injured party. Rest. §51(2), (3). See *In re Enron Corp. Securities, Derivative & ERISA Litigation*, 235 F. Supp. 2d 549, 609 n.46 (S.D. Tex. 2002) (citing cases following the Restatement rule).

The other malpractice scenario related to client fraud is a claim by a successor in interest—that is, new management, a trustee in bankruptcy, or a receiver—alleging that the lawyer permitted a constituent of the organization to commit fraud that led to damage to the organization. (See Rule 1.13(a) for the rule that the lawyer retained by an organization represents the entity itself, not any individual constituents.) This is what happened in the case of *FDIC v. O'Melveny & Myers*, 969 F.2d 744 (9th Cir. 1992) (complicated procedural history not relevant here). In that case, the law firm representing a bank knew or should have known that crooked managers of the bank were engaging in all sorts of book-cooking through inflating the value of assets, engaging in sham sales, and similar shenanigans.[1] The firm failed to conduct a thorough due diligence inquiry to see whether the client was engaging in fraud on investors. Eventually, the bank became insolvent and the FDIC stepped in as a receiver. The FDIC then asserted the claims of investors (which it had acquired in an assignment as part of the process of settling the investors' claims) against the law firm. The law firm attempted to defend this lawsuit by differentiating between a duty to the client, which it conceded it owed, and a duty to investors, which it claimed did not exist. While it may be true that a lawyer would have no duty to investors in the abstract, the court made a very important point here: "Part and parcel of effectively protecting a client, and thus discharging the attorney's duty of care, is to protect the client from the liability which may flow from promulgating a false or misleading offering to investors." That means that the lawyers had an ordinary, negligence-based duty to investigate evidence of wrongdoing by the crooked managers and put a stop to any conduct that might have the effect of exposing the bank to liability for fraud.

DISCIPLINE FOR MAKING FALSE STATEMENTS

Notice that the disciplinary rules have not been mentioned. Lawyers are subject to discipline for making false statements to others or failing to disclose a material fact where disclosure would be necessary to avoid assisting a client's criminal or fraudulent act. Rule 4.1. Remember, though, that the first prohibition is qualified somewhat by the redefinition of "material" in the comments to the rule. Comment [2] says that even if a statement seems like a statement of fact, it may not be considered to be one, depending on the context. In negotiations, for example, lawyers are expected to engage in bluffing or posturing by making statements such as, "My client will not go below $1.5 million to sell the building." This statement would not subject the lawyer to discipline, even if she knows that the client would be happy to sell for $1 million, because the "generally accepted conventions in negotiation" alert the opposing party and lawyer that the statement is not to be taken at face value. Rule 4.1, cmt. [2]. This comment does not create a blanket license to lie, however. Outside of obvious cases of posturing and puffery, courts are willing to discipline lawyers or find them liable for fraud if the lawyer made a false statement. A lawyer for the seller of real property who says, "this parcel is suitable for a septic system," when he

---

1. The bank kept firing accounting firms, which should have been an additional red flag to the law firm, which should have asked the client for a waiver of confidentiality so it could talk to the accounting firms about the circumstances of their dismissal.

knows that the majority of soil tests performed had failed, may be liable to the buyer for fraud, and may be disciplined under Model Rule 4.1(a). See *Petrillo v. Bachenberg*, 655 A.2d 1354 (N.J. 1995) (not specifically addressing discipline).

The rule in subsection (a) is easy to state—do not affirmatively lie. Subsection (b) of Model Rule 4.1 poses a more difficult problem, however, because of the intersection of the attorney's duty of confidentiality and the duty to disclose material facts that may be created by other sources of law, such as those discussed above. The disciplinary rule seems to require disclosure of facts where necessary to avoid assisting a client's criminal or fraudulent act. Rule 4.1(b). But notice something significant about that rule. The duty to disclose is expressly limited by the duty of confidentiality— the rule says the duty applies "unless disclosure is prohibited by rule 1.6." Remember that Model Rule 1.6 covers all "information relating to representation of a client" with only limited exceptions. According to the text of the Model Rules, then, the lawyer appears to have an obligation to keep her mouth shut, even if disclosure otherwise would be necessary to avoid assisting the client's wrongful act.

There is a way out of this uncomfortable dilemma for a lawyer, but only if the relevant jurisdiction has adopted the most recently amended version of Model Rule 1.6. In August 2003, the ABA adopted important amendments to the confidentiality rule that permit (but do not require) the lawyer to disclose confidential client information to the extent the lawyer reasonably believes necessary to prevent, rectify, or mitigate a client's crime or fraud that is likely to result in substantial injury to the financial interests of a third party, as long as the lawyer's services had been used in connection with the client's act. Rule 1.16(b)(2),(3). In order to comply with Model Rule 4.1(b), the lawyer would be required to disclose information to the extent necessary to avoid assisting the client's fraudulent act—disclosure is mandatory under Model Rule 4.1(b) and not prohibited by Model Rule 1.6.

For review, do not forget that the "trumping" effect of Model Rule 1.6 (confidentiality) over Model Rule 4.1(b) (candor in statements to others) is *reversed* in the rules governing statements to a tribunal. Where lies to the court are concerned, Model Rule 3.3(c) explicitly trumps the confidentiality duty as stated in Model Rule 1.6. The theory is that lawyers are "officers of the court," and they bear some responsibility for ensuring that the outcome at trial is not tainted by perjury. When it comes to dealings with third parties, however, the aspect of the lawyer's role that emphasizes loyalty, confidentiality, and diligent representation of the client comes to the fore, and the lawyer is not required to disclose confidential information in most circumstances. The table below summarizes the priority of the duties of confidentiality and candor.

Object of the Fraud	Priority of Confidentiality and Candor	Rule
Court	1. Candor 2. Confidentiality	3.3(c)
Third Party (Model Rules Pre-2003)	1. Confidentiality 2. Candor	4.1(b) + 1.6
Third Party (Post-2003 Version of Model Rules)	1. Candor 2. Confidentiality	4.1(b) + 1.6(b)(2), (3)

Examples

Sales Talk

1. Hurley is representing the seller of a manufacturing business, which is selling all its assets to another corporation. In the course of the negotiations, he makes two statements that are false: (1) "My client will not sell for anything less than $40 million." In fact, the client would be perfectly happy to sell for $30 million. (2) "The machinery in the plant complies with all applicable environmental permits and does not emit volatile organic compounds." In fact, the machinery is out of compliance with the permits and emits volatile organic compounds (VOCs). Is Hurley subject to discipline for making either of those statements?

2. Lawyer represents the owner of a dry cleaning business who wants to sell the business. The owner (Seller) tells Lawyer that one of his former employees used to dump perchlorethylene, or "perc," a solvent used in dry cleaning, into the dirt parking area behind the store. Perc is a hazardous substance that can contaminate the soil and groundwater. Under federal environmental statutes, both Seller and Buyer would be liable for cleanup costs associated with removing perc from the soil. Seller's Lawyer is negotiating with Buyer's Lawyer over the terms of the sale. Buyer's Lawyer asks, "Is there any environmental contamination I should know about?" What may Seller's Lawyer say in response?
   A. "There are no problems." Seller's Lawyer is not permitted to reveal the perc contamination because Seller communicated that information in confidence to his lawyer for the purpose of obtaining legal advice.
   B. "There are no problems." Seller's Lawyer is not permitted to reveal the perc contamination because it is information relating to representation of the client, and the duty of confidentiality trumps the duty to disclose information to third parties.

C. "There are no problems." Under generally accepted conventions of negotiation, Buyer's Lawyer will not accept this statement as a statement of material fact.

D. "There may be some contamination of the soil." If Seller's Lawyer makes an affirmative statement of fact, he must be truthful.

Explanations

Sales Talk

1. The example is based very loosely on *Tekni-Plex, Inc. v. Meyner & Landis*, 674 N.E.2d 663 (N.Y. 1996). In this case, the lawyer made affirmative representations, so we are dealing with Model Rule 4.1(a), not subsection (b) on silence. Both statements are false, so Hurley's only argument is that Buyer's lawyer does not regard them as statements of fact. Hurley cites Comment [2] to Model Rule 4.1: "Under generally accepted conventions in negotiation, certain types of statements ordinarily are not taken as statements of material fact." A clear case of a permitted false statement is 1, the client's demand for no less than $40 million. Lawyers expect this kind of posturing, and no experienced lawyer would expect that Hurley actually means that $40 million is the lowest his client will go. See also Rest. §98, cmt. c: "Certain statements, such as some statements relating to price or value, are considered non-actionable hyperbole or a reflection of the state of mind of the speaker and not misstatements of fact or law." On the other hand, lawyers expect that representations about facts that are not the subject of the negotiation process, but that are important to the way the parties value the deal, are truthful. Statement 2, concerning compliance with the permits and emission of VOCs, is the kind of statement that parties to a negotiation will expect to be truthful.

   Is there a principled distinction between statements 1 and 2? Generally, the line is based on what a reasonable observer would regard as material to the transaction. See Rest. §98, cmt. c., Reporter's Note. In other words, if the statement would not mislead the other party, it may be fair to characterize it as mere puffery and not a statement of material fact. H&H §37.3. You should be very clear on one thing—the negotiation setting does not magically transform all lies into permissible posturing. On this, all of the authorities agree. Wolfram §13.5; H&H §37.3; Rest. §98, cmt. c. For more complex questions, you should check the local law on the tort of misrepresentation, because the professional rules do not supersede generally applicable law. In this case, Hurley's statement 2 about the machinery is material to the transaction, because the buyer would not want to purchase a bunch of machines that were out of compliance with their environmental permits. The buyer would be misled by the statement and might decide to go ahead with the transaction on the strength of Hurley's representation. On the other hand, the buyer is not going to make a decision about whether to go through with the purchase based on statement 1. Hurley can say whatever he wants, but the parties still have to haggle over the price. Statement 1 does not induce the buyer to do something he otherwise would not; it merely prolongs the negotiating process.

2. The correct answer is D. If a lawyer is asked a direct question in negotiations, she must answer truthfully. You may be tempted to answer B, apparently relying on the trumping language in Model Rule 4.1(b). Remember, though, that Model Rule 4.1(b) deals with keeping silent where disclosure would be necessary to make a statement truthful. An affirmative statement of fact—that is, "there are no problems"—falls within Model Rule 4.1(a), which is not trumped by the duty of confidentiality.

CONFIDENTIALITY AND CLIENT FRAUD: RULE 1.6 AND SARBANES-OXLEY

As discussed in Chapter 5 (on representing entities) and Chapter 9 (on confidentiality), under the current version of the Model Rules, a lawyer has permission to disclose confidential client information to the extent the lawyer reasonably believes necessary to prevent, rectify, or mitigate the losses from a client's crime or fraud, where the client's act (1) is likely to result in substantial financial loss to a third party; and (2) the lawyer's services had been used in connection with the client's act. Rule 1.6(b) (2)-(3). The lawyer must first report the misconduct "up the ladder," to the highest authority within the organization. Rule 1.13(b). If the person within the company who is the highest authority permitted to act on its behalf nevertheless fails to take corrective action, the lawyer may reveal confidential information but is not required to do so. Rule 1.13(c).

Under the pre-2003 version of the Model Rules, a lawyer had permission to disclose in a weird roundabout way, using something called a "noisy withdrawal." Professional responsibility textbooks from the 1990s devoted several pages to going through the conceptual gymnastics that were required to create a permission to reveal confidential information when the plain black-letter text of Rule 1.6 prohibited it. The idea was that the lawyer would withdraw from representing the client and indeed may be required to withdraw if ongoing representation would have the effect of aiding and abetting the fraud. As part of the withdrawal, the ABA permitted the lawyer to disaffirm any representations she had made previously in the course of the representation, including opinion letters and the like. Somehow that was supposed to avoid violating Rule 1.6, but of course telling a third party in a transaction that you, the lawyer, no longer stand behind the representations you had made previously on behalf of your client is waving a big red flag indicating that your client is engaging in fraud. If that's not disclosure of confidential information, I don't know what is. At any rate, the current version of the Model Rules retain the old noisy withdrawal procedure in Rule 1.2, cmt. [10] and Rule 4.1 cmt. [3], but it really doesn't do much freestanding work now that there is an express textual permission to disclose confidential information in Rule 1.6(b).[2]

A lawyer representing a publicly traded corporation is subject to regulation by the SEC. As part of the Sarbanes-Oxley Act, 15 U.S.C. §7201, et seq., the SEC issued regulations prescribing procedures lawyers should use upon discovering evidence of possible client wrongdoing. As discussed in more detail in Chapter 5, the regulations require "reporting up" and permit "reporting out." Reporting up means bringing the evidence to the attention of supervisory lawyers, and possibly even the CEO of the corporation or the board of directors, and awaiting a satisfactory response. 17 C.F.R. §205.3(b). Reporting out means disclosing confidential client information to the SEC. 17 C.F.R. §205.3(d)(2). Although the SEC had initially proposed including a noisy withdrawal provision in the regulations, it delayed final consideration after a firestorm of protest from the organized bar. (The adoption by the ABA of amendments to Rule 1.6 and Rule 1.13 took the political pressure off the SEC to act on the noisy withdrawal rule.) Few lawyers seem to have noticed that the regulations as promulgated include an outright permission to disclose confidential information, without going through all the hoopla of the noisy withdrawal procedure.

---

2. The issue is this: Rule 4.1(b) makes a lawyer subject to discipline for failing to disclose a material fact when disclosure is necessary to avoid assisting a fraud by a client. Suppose a lawyer has made a statement of fact, in the form of an opinion letter or otherwise, to a lender in a transaction while representing a client. The lawyer comes to find out the statement is misleading. Comment [3] to Rule 4.1 sets out the remedial actions a lawyer must take: "Ordinarily a lawyer can avoid assisting a client's crime or fraud by withdrawing from the representation. Sometimes it may be necessary for the lawyer to give notice of the fact of withdrawal and to disaffirm an opinion, document, affirmation or the like." Already there's a complication here. In some cases it may be sufficient to withdraw from the representation — that is, withdrawal, without more, avoids assisting the client's fraud. In other cases, however, the lawyer must also disaffirm the statement of fact. When is disaffirmance required? It depends on the applicable substantive law of fraud. You need to know something about fraud law to know when withdrawal alone, without disaffirmance, has the effect of furthering the client's fraudulent act. To underscore this point, the Comment goes on to say: "In extreme cases, substantive law may require a lawyer to disclose information relating to the representation to avoid being deemed to have assisted a client's crime or fraud." Again, the answer turns on general law, not anything peculiar to the law governing lawyers. In all likelihood that knowledge is beyond the scope of a professional responsibility course, but in the real world it may be vital.

Examples

What Did the Client Do, When Did He Do It, and Was the Lawyer Involved?

3. You are a white-collar criminal-defense lawyer. Christopher Imperioli comes into your office one day and explains that his uncle just bailed him out of jail after his arrest for securities fraud. Before you can say a word, he blurts out, "I did it. I took their money. But those people were asking for it. They thought you could just invest in high-tech stocks and make money forever. They deserve to lose their money. I don't want to go to jail for that." Can you disclose Christopher's statement to the FBI?

4. Assume instead that Christopher comes into your office, looking rather nervous. He says, "I saw on TV that the FBI is investigating fraud in the securities brokerage industry. I may have done something that might be regarded as fraudulent. What should I do?" After a lengthy conversation with Christopher, you conclude that he is running a Ponzi scheme: "Investors" give him money, which he claims is invested in high-tech stocks. In fact, there are no stocks. Christopher simply uses the money from new victims of the swindle to pay off previous "investors," and then has to scramble around to find new suckers to keep the money flowing in.

Explanations

What Did the Client Do, When Did He Do It, and Was the Lawyer Involved?

3. Under no circumstances can you disclose this statement. It relates to a wholly past crime and fraud in which your services were not used. On this point, all the authorities agree. Model Rule 1.6(b)(1) limits disclosure to prevent reasonably certain death or serious bodily harm in the future. This case fails on both elements—the act is entirely in the past and it is not likely to result in bodily injury. The Restatement, which is sometimes denounced as radical, still does not permit you to recount Christopher's statement to the authorities. Section 67(2) does permit you to disclose confidential client information when its disclosure is necessary to rectify or mitigate a financial loss, but notice an important condition—"crime or fraud described in Subsection (1)." Turning to paragraph (d) of Subsection (1), notice that the attorney's authority to disclose kicks in only where "the client has employed or is employing [the attorney's] services in the matter in which the crime or fraud is committed." The same qualification exists even in the current version of Model Rule 1.6, which states that the lawyer's permission to disclose exists only

if "the client has used the lawyer's services." Rule 1.6(b) (2)-(3). If you had helped Christopher set up his brokerage business, or drafted some prospectuses that had been distributed to the defrauded investors, you would be permitted to disclose some information, if that were the only way to mitigate the loss to the investors. But absent your involvement in the underlying fraud, there is no permission to disclose. Make sure you understand that even the most radical pro-disclosure rules would not require a criminal defense attorney to disclose an admission by the client of involvement in a past crime in which the lawyer's services were not used.

4. This is a tougher case. You are permitted to defend civil proceedings brought by the investors or a criminal investigation by the FBI. At the same time, however, you cannot do anything that could be construed as assisting Christopher in perpetrating the fraud. Rule 1.2(d). You are required to withdraw from representing him if your legal work would be tantamount to assisting the fraud. Rule 1.16(a). The tricky part is figuring out what you can do without crossing the line into prohibited assistance. The answer will depend on the law governing civil and criminal fraud in your jurisdiction. Although it is dangerous to generalize without doing some specific research, it probably is a safe bet that you may be held liable for aiding and abetting Christopher's fraud if you communicate with new "investors" or reassure past "investors" that everything is on the up-and-up.

Even if you do not communicate with anyone, there is an argument that by continuing to represent Christopher, you are implicitly warranting that the underlying transactions were sound and legal. It is worth quoting this passage from the Restatement commentary, because it seems counterintuitive, and many lawyers are not aware of this interpretation of the law of misrepresentation:

> A lawyer representing a client in a transaction with respect to which the client has made a misrepresentation is not free, after the lawyer learns of the misrepresentation, to continue providing assistance to the client as if the misrepresentation had not been made when the lawyer's continued representation of the client would induce the nonclient reasonably to believe that no such misrepresentation has occurred.

Rest. §98, cmt. c. For this reason, in a jurisdiction that does not have a specific exception to the confidentiality rule permitting disclosure (along the lines of Rest. §67(2) or Rule 1.6(b)(2)-(3)), you may be required to make a noisy withdrawal from representation in order to avoid civil or criminal liability.

Conflicts of Interest

PART III

Overview of Conflicts of Interest

13

INTRODUCTION

Conflicts of interest is a subject that seems to fascinate professional responsibility teachers and befuddle students, in equal proportion. The rules are intricate, technical, and arcane—kind of like the hearsay rule in evidence or the estates in land system in property. If you like that sort of thing, you will love conflicts. But even if you do not value complexity for its own sake, you should pay attention to this subject, because the way courts and bar associations handle conflicts of interest speaks volumes about the ideals of the legal profession they presuppose. For example, if you think one of the purposes of the disciplinary rules is to prevent lawyers from abusing the position of trust they have with clients, you might be inclined to make rules against representing conflicting interests nonwaivable. On the other hand, if you view the lawyer-client relationship as an arm's-length transaction and generally are untroubled by the morals of the marketplace, you may permit clients to waive the protections of the conflicts of interest rules. These debates are ongoing, and you are almost certain to see them played out in the jurisdiction in which you eventually practice law.

One of the tricky things about conflicts cases is the interaction between the interpretation of the legal rules and the policies that justify them. This is true in all areas of the law, of course, but policy reasoning is central to the analysis of the conflicts rules. Thus, this section introduces you to the policies tugging in different directions on courts. The chapters that follow discuss the current-client conflicts rule in general terms

(Chapter 14), the application of the current-client conflicts rule to particular situations (Chapter 15), the former-client conflicts rule (Chapter 16), and special conflicts rules, many relating to personal interests of the lawyer (Chapter 17).

There are essentially four reasons for construing conflicts rules strictly and prohibiting a great many cases of multiple representation. Those reasons are loyalty to one's clients, the related interest of impartiality or independence, the protection of confidential client information, and the systemic interest in the integrity of the adversary process. On the flip side, there are three reasons for construing conflicts rules a bit more loosely, permitting a wider variety of multiple representation. The countervailing policies are the availability to clients of the counsel of their choice, enhancing the economic liberty of lawyers, and preventing the tactical misuse of disqualification motions. These policies can be summarized as follows:

Loyalty

Conflicts of interest rules are deeply rooted in the ideal of lawyers as fiduciaries. Lawyers are expected to put the interests of their clients first always, no matter what other client relationships or personal interests they may have. Clients should not have to worry about being betrayed by their lawyers, and so conflicts rules regulate prophylactically. They prohibit lawyers from getting into certain types of entanglements (with other clients, or in relationships that might create a personal interest) that would tempt them to be less than fully loyal to their clients' interests. The loyalty interest focuses on the lawyer-client *relationship*, not the effect on a specific *representation*. As Rule 1.7, cmt. [6] observes, justifying the prohibition on representing one client whose interests are directly adverse to those of another client, "[t]he client to whom the representation is directly adverse is likely to feel betrayed, and the resulting damage to the client-lawyer relationship is likely to impair the lawyer's ability to represent the client effectively."

Perhaps reflecting the equation of litigation with combat, a lawyer's diminished loyalty is often described using pugilistic metaphors: The lawyer may be tempted to "pull his punches"—that is, not hit as hard as he is capable of—or "take a dive"—that is, fake getting knocked out—when working for Client A, because he is taking into account an interest of Client B. Less colorfully, the comments to the rule on current-client conflict note that there is an interference with the client's expectation of undivided loyalty when a lawyer cannot "consider, recommend, or carry out an appropriate course of action for the client," because the lawyer's ability to do so is materially limited as a result of the lawyer's other responsibilities or interests. Rule 1.7, cmt. [8].

Independence

A lawyer representing a client must be able to exercise independent professional judgment and give the client candid, impartial advice. See Rule 2.1. The interest in impartiality would be threatened if the lawyer's advice was slanted in some way, because of the interests of another client or the lawyer's own interests. In a transactional representation, for example, a lawyer may not be able to advise one client of a way to protect that client's interests without undermining the other client's position. See Rule 1.7, cmt. [8]. The same kind of interference with impartiality may arise where the lawyer's own interests are implicated. A lawyer who serves on the board of directors of a client may have a financial interest in the client taking an action that would be against the client's best interests, such as closing a deal that would result in an increase in the client's share price in the short run, despite misgivings about the wisdom of the deal in the long run.

Another rule aimed at protecting the independent professional judgment of a lawyer is Rule 1.8(f), on the payment of fees by a nonclient. Suppose the adult child of an elderly person comes to a lawyer to seek the lawyer's assistance in preparing a power of attorney, and agrees to pay the attorney for her services.[1] The document would give the child the right to manage the financial affairs of the parent. Even though the child is paying the attorney's fees, the client is the parent. The attorney must consult with the parent to determine what his best interests are, and then act on those interests. As long as the lawyer can exercise this independent judgment, it is okay for the child to pay her fees, but the client—here, the parent—must give informed consent to the arrangement.

Confidentiality

One of the most important duties owed by lawyers to their clients is the obligation not to reveal confidential client information, not to use the information for their own selfish purposes, and not use the confidential information of one client on behalf of another client with adverse interests. Clients should not have to worry that information they disclose to their lawyers will be used against them in the future. In general, if a lawyer acquires confidential client information while working on behalf of a client on Matter X, she may not take on a future case adverse to the client on Matter Y, if the information learned on Matter X may prove helpful to the adversary in Matter Y. For example, if a lawyer represents one spouse in a business transaction and thereby learns a lot of information about her assets, the lawyer may not represent the other

---

1. This example is from Deborah A. Coleman in the Sept. 1997 *ABA Journal*, p. 63.

spouse in a divorce proceeding, because the lawyer will have learned confidential client information during the first representation. The two matters will be deemed "substantially related" for the purposes of Model Rule 1.9 even though they do not seem to have legal issues in common, because of the possibility for use in Matter Y of confidential client information obtained in Matter X in a way that would harm the former client's interests.

Process Integrity

A lawyer representing both the plaintiff and the defendant in litigation would be like a person trying to play both white and black in chess. The player's good intentions would not matter—the game just would not work right. Invariably, she would start to favor white or black, even if only subconsciously, and the structure of the game would break down. That is why lawyers are never permitted to represent clients with adverse interests against one another in the same litigation. In terms of the rules, the conflict presented would be nonconsentable. Even if both clients agreed to the dual representation, there would be a good reason for courts to deny it. That reason is the interest that courts have in the effective presentation of the adversaries' cases by advocates who are thinking about the position of one party only.[2] Courts that emphasize the value of integrity of the adversary process tend to be less willing to permit clients to *waive* or *consent* to conflicts.

You may see some old cases referring to the "appearance of impropriety" as an independent reason to prohibit conflicts of interest. The problem with that standard, as the Restatement quite rightly notes, is that it might be used to prohibit representation that is not improper, but seems improper to an untrained observer. Rest. §121 cmt. c(iv). The occasional outlier case talking about appearance of impropriety tends to use that phrase as a makeweight, in support of a conclusion that was properly reached on other grounds. You should avoid thinking of appearances, apart from actual impropriety, as a reason to prohibit representation.

Client Choice and Availability of Counsel

Overly strict conflicts rules can deprive clients of the lawyer of their choice. For example, suppose the rules treat legal aid organizations and private law firms similarly for the purpose of imputation of conflicts. (Imputation, which

---

2. Rest. §122 cmt. g(iii) states: "When the clients are aligned directly against each other in the same litigation, the institutional interest in vigorous development of each client's position renders the conflict nonconsentable." This is a clear statement of the process-integrity rationale.

is discussed later, means that if one lawyer in an organization is prevented from representing a client because of a conflict of interest, all lawyers in the same organization are similarly conflicted out of the matter.) If there is only one legal aid office in town, low- and middle-income clients may have a hard time securing any legal representation at all if a lawyer in the office previously has represented another client on a similar matter adversely to the new client. Suppose Husband and Wife obtain a divorce, with Husband being represented by Abigail at the legal aid office and Wife representing herself. If Wife later wishes to modify the custody arrangement the parties reached as part of their divorce, she cannot go to Bill at the legal aid office because Abigail's conflict would be imputed to him as well. On the other end of the economic spectrum, rich and powerful clients may be able to deprive their adversaries of effective counsel by "buying up" all the lawyers with a particular specialty, by retaining them for occasional matters, thus creating conflicts of interest.

There is considerable debate over whether sophisticated clients should be given greater latitude to consent to what would otherwise be an impermissible conflict of interest. Experience with hiring lawyers, and often separate representation (in the form of in-house legal departments), gives clients the ability to protect themselves. Thus, if they are willing to accept some risk in exchange for the benefits of retaining a particular lawyer or law firm, they should be permitted to make that cost-benefit tradeoff. There are stray comments here and there in the rules, seeming to bless the idea that the duties owed by lawyers can vary according to the sophistication of the client. For example, in connection with advance waivers of conflicts, the Model Rules say that "if the client is an experienced user of the legal services involved," advance consent is more likely to be upheld. Rule 1.7, cmt. [23]. The rationale here is really about respecting client autonomy — if a well-advised, sophisticated client makes a utility-maximizing decision in connection with the attorney-client relationship, that judgment should be respected. Where inexperienced clients are involved, however, the client is less likely to be able to make a fully informed cost-benefit decision without advice from the lawyer herself. Thus, the lawyer will be expected to be scrupulously impartial in advising the client.

Economic Liberty of Lawyers

Unduly strict conflicts rules could prevent lawyers from ever changing jobs, or would make it very difficult for them to do so. Suppose, to make up an extreme example, that you could never represent a new client in a matter adverse to a case you handled on behalf of a previous client, regardless of whether the matters were related, and that these conflicts are imputed to all lawyers within a firm. No firm would ever hire you, because the new firm would be conflicted out of all matters adverse to your old clients. Conflicts rules are not that strict, of course, but there are plenty of cases in which a firm risks disqualification from a matter because of a new hire or a merger with another law firm. The more stringent the conflicts rules, the harder it is for firms to grow by lateral hires or mergers. In addition, strict conflicts rules would mean that some clients would have a hard time obtaining representation, because law firms would be worried about the conflicts they would create in the future. A firm would therefore refuse to represent the client, or charge a premium fee to compensate the firm for the risk of getting conflicted off a future matter.

Avoiding Game-Playing with Conflicts Rules

It is just a fact about human nature, or at least the nature of lawyers in an adversary system, that whenever a rule exists that can be invoked by an adversary in litigation, lawyers will figure out a way to turn the rule into a weapon to use against their opponents. See the wonderfully titled, and informative, article by John Leubsdorf, *Using Legal Ethics to Screw Your Enemies and Clients*, 11 Geo. J. Legal Ethics 831 (1998). Consider by analogy the experience with Rule 11 of the Federal Rules of Civil Procedure. It sounded like a great idea—giving lawyers authority to police one another's frivolous motions—but Rule 11 created a huge area of satellite litigation. In some cases, the disputes over sanctions motions took up more time and energy than the resolution of the underlying dispute.

Courts take a rather dim view of this kind of strategic use of the conflicts rules, but they sometimes have a hard time figuring out how to prevent game-playing without reaching unprincipled results. Courts that are concerned about misuse of the rules may deny *standing* to nonclients to assert conflicts, despite the value of process integrity noted earlier, or find that the conflict was *impliedly waived*. Alternatively, they may reach for an *estoppel* or *laches* argument if it seems that the party moving for disqualification waited until a late stage in the litigation to raise the conflict. If you get clear on these policies and how they apply to specific cases, you should be better able to understand and predict the legal analysis. For example, if loyalty considerations predominate over confidentiality concerns, a law firm may not be able to employ a "screening" device to continue representing a client after one of its lawyers has been conflicted off the representation. Similarly, if a court is impressed by the need to preserve the integrity of the adversarial process, it may not permit the client to consent to a conflict. In the former-client conflicts area (Chapter 16), the "substantial relationship" test, defining the scope of matters in which a lawyer will be disqualified because of a prior relationship with a client, can be understood either in terms of the confidentiality rationale or as a means of protecting the loyalty interest. You need to be aware of the distinction in order to predict the outcome of cases where the issue is whether two matters are substantially related.

Example

A Rift in the Restaurant Family

The Borman family owns several restaurants in a large city. For many years, their legal work, including trademark prosecution and litigation, was handled by Wagner. After several members of the family had a falling out, they decided to divide the restaurants among two different family groups: Borman East and Borman West. Wagner continued to represent the members of the family in the West group. When one of the restaurants owned by the West family members continued to use a trademark that formerly had been used by the united family, back in the days of peace and harmony, the East family group brought a trademark infringement action against the West group. Wagner, along with co-counsel Spreng (who had never represented anyone in the Borman family), entered a notice of appearance on behalf of the West group.

The attorney for the East families filed a motion to disqualify both Wagner and Spreng. How should the trial judge rule on the motion in light of the policies underlying conflicts of interest rules? Do not worry about the technical rules for now. All you need to know is that, in some cases, a lawyer who formerly represented a client would be prohibited from representing a new client in the same or a substantially related matter on which she represented the old client.

Explanation

A Rift in the Restaurant Family

This example is based on *Brennan's, Inc. v. Brennan's Restaurants, Inc.*, 590 F.2d 168 (5th Cir. 1979). With regard to Wagner, think about the clients' interests and the way they may be harmed by Wagner's change of allegiances. The members of the East group, who used to be part of the united family, may feel betrayed — like Wagner has gone over to the other side. Their feeling of betrayal is reasonable, since Wagner may be, in effect, attacking his own work in the course of representing West. For example, he could argue that West is permitted to use the disputed trademark because the registration of the mark was invalid. To use our terminology, Wagner's representation of the West family members violates East's expectation of *loyalty*. If the conflicts of interest rules are driven by the loyalty rationale, Wagner should be disqualified for turning on his former clients who are now part of the East group.

In addition, Wagner may have learned secret information that the East group would prefer to be kept confidential, not shared with the West group or disclosed to the public. The analysis of the *confidentiality* rationale gets a bit technical at this point. As a matter of evidence law, a client who formerly was jointly represented along with another client cannot assert the attorney-client privilege against the former co-client in subsequent litigation. In other words, since the East and West family members formerly were part of the united Borman family, jointly represented by Wagner, neither group can assert the attorney-client privilege to block discovery of communications between the family members and Wagner. But, Wagner has an independent *professional duty of confidentiality*,[3] separate from the attorney-client privilege, which prohibits him from using information gained in the course of representing East (when the members were part of the united family) to the disadvantage of the former client. This duty underlies Model Rule 1.9(c), one aspect of the former-client conflicts rules, which is discussed in greater detail in Chapter 17. Thus, the confidentiality rationale also supports the disqualification of Wagner. With regard to Spreng, since he never represented the East family members, they cannot claim to feel betrayed by him. But they can complain if Wagner shares confidential information with Spreng, which Spreng can use to their detriment. In the actual case, the trial court did not make a finding as to whether Wagner shared with Spreng any confidential information of the East family members.[4] If he had, then Spreng should be disqualified also. If Wagner did not share this information, then the confidentiality rationale would not provide a basis for disqualifying Spreng. In summary, the following table shows how the motion should be decided, based on the loyalty and confidentiality rationales:

If the conflicts rules are primarily justified by the East group's interest in . . .	then, with respect to Wagner, the trial court should . . .	and, with respect to Spreng, the trial court should . . .
Loyalty	Disqualify him from representing West	Permit him to continue representing West
Confidentiality	Disqualify him from representing West	Disqualify him from representing West, but *only if* Wagner disclosed confidential information to Spreng

In the actual case, the Court of Appeals said that Spreng could continue to represent the West group, unless the East group could show that he had

---

3. See Chapter 7 for the distinction between the duty of confidentiality and the attorney-client privilege.
4. If Spreng and Wagner had practiced together in a firm that represented the united family, Spreng would be presumed to have acquired confidential information from Wagner's client, the united family. See Chapter 16.

acquired confidential information through Wagner. Many commentators read the real case as establishing the independent vitality of the loyalty interest, and showing that a lawyer cannot attack work he previously performed for a client, but the same result—that is, Wagner is out, Spreng is in—can be reached on pure confidentiality grounds as well.

DISCIPLINE AND PUNISH: REMEDIES FOR CONFLICTS

Representing conflicting interests without effective consent is theoretically a basis for professional discipline, although, in practice, state disciplinary authorities are reluctant to get involved in these cases. Conflicts questions are highly fact intensive and often can be resolved only in light of the legal issues in the case; the transaction costs involved tend to deter disciplinary authorities from responding to most conflicts cases. The vast majority of conflicts cases therefore arise either on a motion to disqualify one of the lawyers from representing a client or in an action brought by an aggrieved client for malpractice or breach of fiduciary duty.

Disqualification

Remember that trial courts have the inherent power to regulate those who practice before them. (This is what I have been calling Track Two inherent authority; see Chapter 1.) Trial courts exercise this power to prevent lawyers from proceeding under a conflict, on the grounds that a lawyer with conflicting loyalties undermines the effectiveness of the adversary process. When these decisions are appealed, a body of appellate level precedent develops, regulating the disqualification of lawyers due to conflicts. Because courts have an independent source of authority to disqualify lawyers, they are not obligated to follow the disciplinary rules exactly. For example, there have been cases in which a court refuses to disqualify a lawyer for representing a client in a situation in which the lawyer would be subject to professional discipline. See, for example, *Gerald v. Turnock Plumbing, Heating and Cooling, LLC*, 768 N.E.2d 498 (Ind. Ct. App. 2002). It creates a lot of confusion when courts do not try to harmonize the law of disqualification with the disciplinary rules, and for this reason courts usually are reluctant to deviate from the results dictated by the disciplinary rules, but they can. Another reason for not following the disciplinary rules exactly is that disqualification is an equitable remedy. See Rest. §6, cmt. i. Even if a lawyer violates Rule 1.7 or Rule 1.9, a court might nevertheless deny a motion to disqualify because it is filed in an untimely manner (laches), or because the court believes the party filing the motion is doing so for strategic purposes such as delay or driving up the opponent's costs. A court might also balance the equities on both sides and determine that the harm to the moving party does not outweigh the prejudice to the non-moving party if it is deprived of counsel of its choice.

In addition to ordering disqualification, trial courts in the exercise of their Track Two inherent authority may order the disqualified lawyer to return the fees she had earned in the course of representing the client. Even if the court does not order fee forfeiture directly, the client generally can seek return of fees as a remedy in a civil action for malpractice or breach of fiduciary duty. In an important case on advance waivers of conflicts, discussed in the next chapter, the California Supreme Court held that the fee provisions of an engagement agreement with the client—along with the rest of the contract—were unenforceable due to the law firm's conflict of interest. See *Sheppard, Mullin, Richter & Hampton, LLP v. J-M Manufacturing Co., Inc.*, 6 Cal. 5th 59 (2018).

Malpractice

A lawyer may act negligently by failing to discover a conflict and avoiding the prohibited multiple representation. Alternatively, a lawyer may be deemed to have breached her fiduciary duty by representing conflicting interests. See Rest. §§16(3), 49 (liability for fiduciary breach may result from representing conflicting interests); see also Rest. §49, cmt. c & illus. 1 for the relationship between negligence and breach of fiduciary duty. For example, where a law firm represented the plaintiff in a commercial dispute while simultaneously representing the parent corporation of the defendant in an unrelated matter, the law firm may have harmed the plaintiff's interests by "pulling punches" at trial. See *Weil, Gotshal & Manges v. Fashion Boutique of Short Hills*, 780 N.Y.S.2d 593 (App. Div. 2004).

In terms of recoverable damages, if a lawyer is disqualified from representing a client, the client is harmed not only by having paid for representation that is now useless, but also by the need to go rushing around to find a new firm and get those lawyers up to speed quickly on the case. The client will not be happy about this turn of events, and probably will sue the firm either for negligence (for failing to discover the conflict) or for breach of fiduciary duty. In a litigation case where the firm is disqualified during pretrial proceedings, the damages would be measured by the amount paid to the firm while the firm was violating its fiduciary duty by representing a competing interest, as well as the extraordinary legal expenses proximately caused by the client's need to find substitute counsel in a hurry. These numbers can get big. One bankruptcy court denied $3 million of a firm's $5.2 million fee request because it did not adequately disclose a conflict to the court. *In re Granite Partners*, 219 B.R. 22 (Bankr. S.D.N.Y. 1998).

The most draconian sanction for trying to represent conflicting interests is a criminal conviction for bankruptcy fraud. That is exactly what happened to Milbank Tweed partner John Gellene, who was sent to prison for 15 months and fined $15,000 for failing to disclose a conflict on a bankruptcy filing. *United States v. Gellene*, 182 F.3d 578 (7th Cir. 1999). On top of Gellene's conviction, the firm was ordered to return $1.9 million in earned fees to the client. Gellene's problem was not just the firm's conflict, but his attempt to finesse the disclosure of the firm's representation, to avoid revealing the conflict. This situation is extremely unusual, but it does illustrate the danger of trying to be too clever in avoiding professional obligations.

Example

Looking for Law in All the Wrong Places

Winslow & Jones is a law firm in the state of Perplexity. It has been representing Grayson, Inc., a multinational pharmaceutical company, on matters relating to employee benefit programs, the company's 401(k) plan, and employment issues. When Grayson retained Winslow & Jones, the general counsel of the company signed an engagement letter, which included a broad advance waiver of conflicts of interest. The advance waiver provision stated:

> You [that is, the client] understand and agree that we [that is, the firm] are free to represent other clients, including clients whose interests may conflict with ours in litigation, business transactions, or other legal matters. You agree that our representing you in this matter will not prevent or disqualify us from representing clients adverse to you in other matters and that you consent in advance to our undertaking such adverse representations.

Six months after the engagement letter was signed, Winslow & Jones accepted the representation of a new client, Kaminski Co., which is a competitor in the pharmaceutical industry. On behalf of Kaminski, lawyers in the intellectual property department at Winslow & Jones filed a patent lawsuit in federal court against Grayson, alleging that Grayson had alleged Kaminski's patent. The general counsel of Grayson was furious, and filed a motion in U.S. District Court for the District of Perplexity to disqualify Winslow & Jones from representing Kaminski.

You are the district judge considering the motion. Here is some information you should know about the law:

- The state of Perplexity adopted new rules of professional conduct in 2008 after extensive debate. One hotly contested issue was whether to adopt Comment [22] to ABA Model Rule 1.7, which takes a permissive attitude toward advance waivers of conflict. The rules committee recommended that the state not adopt this comment after hearing testimony from Larissa Volpe, a nationally known legal ethics scholar, who argued that open-ended advance consents were a violation of the profession's core values. The rules, as adopted, do not have a comment permitting broad advance consents.

- The Ethics Committee of the Bar of the State of Perplexity subsequently issued an ethics opinion clarifying the enforceability of advance waivers. It stated that, in limited circumstances, advance waivers would be enforced, but they must identify the adverse party and describe the matter giving rise to the conflict. The Committee cited ABA Formal Opinion 93-372 (1993) as authority for its position.
- In other states, open-ended advance waivers of conflicts have been enforced. See, for example, *Galderma Labs, L.P. v. Actavis Mid Atlantic LLC*, 927 F. Supp. 2d 390 (N.D. Tex. 2013); *Visa U.S.A., Inc. v. First Data Corp.*, 241 F. Supp. 2d 1100 (N.D. Cal. 2003). Several important bar associations, including the New York City Bar, have stated that broad advance waivers are enforceable as long as the client is experienced in hiring lawyers and represented by independent counsel (as is the case here). See, for example, Ass'n of the Bar of the City of New York Formal Op. 2006-1 (2006). In 2005, in Formal Opinion 05-436, the ABA reversed its previous position and now agrees with the emerging national trend to recognize the enforceability of open-ended advance waivers.
- The District of Perplexity is within the U.S. Court of Appeals for the 13th Circuit. There are no cases from the district or from the 13th Circuit that specify the law to be applied in resolving a motion to disqualify a law firm for a conflict of interest.

So, Your Honor, do you grant the motion to disqualify Winslow & Jones? Your options are:

A. Apply the law of the state of Perplexity and grant the motion.
B. Apply the law of the state of Perplexity and deny the motion.
C. Apply national law and grant the motion.
D. Apply national law and deny the motion.

Explanation

Looking for Law in All the Wrong Places

This example is based on *Galderma Labs, L.P. v. Actavis Mid Atlantic LLC*, 927 F. Supp. 2d 390 (N.D. Tex. 2013). Here's the crazy thing: *You could do A, B, C, or D.* If you didn't read this chapter carefully you might go for option A. The firm and the client are both located in the state of Perplexity, and the rules of professional conduct in Perplexity do not permit advance waivers—at least not the open-ended kind used by the firm. But you could also go for option B, because the rules are strictly binding only for the purposes of professional discipline, and you are not on a disciplinary tribunal. You are a trial judge supervising the patent litigation, and your authority flows not from the adoption of rules by the Supreme Court of Perplexity but is inherent in being a court. Because you are exercising your inherent authority, you need not follow the state rules to the letter. You can, but you need not. Remember, too, that disqualification is an equitable remedy and need not automatically follow from a conclusion that a lawyer has violated one of the conflicts rules. You may disqualify, but you need not.

As for C and D, you have a different kind of independence from state law as a result of being a federal district court judge. Lawyers are always subject to discipline in their state of admission — see Rule 8.5(a) — but that's again only a matter of discipline. Many federal courts do in fact apply the national law of lawyering to disqualification motions. See, for example, In re Dresser Indus., 972 F.2d 540 (5th Cir. 1992) (disqualifying a lawyer under national law standards in circumstances in which the lawyer's conduct did not violate the state disciplinary rule). The district court in Galderma said, "[w]ith the ABA canons of ethics [ugh] as a guide, informed by state and local rules, the Court considers the ethical standards relevant to this specific case." 927 F. Supp. 2d at 395. Apart from the bizarre reference to the Canons of Ethics, which haven't been in effect since before the Beatles played on the Ed Sullivan Show,[5] the district court is well within its prerogatives to apply a kind of amalgamated national law of disqualification. In the real case it picked up on the evolving trend toward enforcing open-ended advance waivers and, as a result, denied the motion to disqualify the law firm. You might decide, on the other hand, to give effect to the local policy of your state, which takes a dim view of broad advance consents.

The next chapter starts to get deep into the weeds of conflicts of interest. As you read it, remember that the loosey-goosey approach to law is only for motions to disqualify, which are addressed to the trial court's inherent authority and seek an equitable remedy. For the purposes of professional discipline, the strict letter of the rules applies.

---

5. Justice Scalia has done this, too. See Mickens v. Taylor, 535 U.S. 162, 176 (2002). Would somebody please tell these judges that we have replaced the Canons with the Model Code and then the Model Code with three versions of the Model Rules!

Concurrent Conflicts

INTRODUCTION

This chapter deals with conflicts of interest arising out of the representation of a client, to whom a lawyer owes professional duties such as loyalty, confidentiality, and independence, while the lawyer is encumbered at the same time with another client relationship or interest that potentially interferes with the lawyer's ability to discharge those duties. The problem is therefore known as that of concurrent conflicts of interest. See Rule 1.7(a). More colloquially these can be called "current-client" conflicts, because they arise from the duties owed to a client currently represented by the lawyer or law firm. I will use those terms interchangeably, but note that the Model Rules use the language of concurrent conflicts.

Any concurrent conflicts problem can be handled by breaking it down into four steps: (1) identify client relationships and the matters on which the lawyer or law firm is representing the clients; (2) ascertain whether there is a conflict of interest; (3) determine whether the conflict is consentable; and (4) see whether all affected clients have given informed consent. See Rule 1.7, cmt. [2] for this four-step process.

ANALYSIS OF CONCURRENT CONFLICTS PROBLEMS

Identify Client Relationships

The first step in the conflicts analysis is to determine which of the parties in the dispute is a client of the lawyer or law firm. Remember that the firm may have "quasi-client" obligations to one or more of the parties, even without a formal attorney-client relationship. (See Chapter 2.) If, for example, the firm learned confidential client information of one of the parties when that party was shopping around for representation, the firm may be duty-bound to avoid representing adverse parties, because of its obligation to keep the secrets of the first potential client. A firm also can have quasi-client relationships with constituents of clients, such as members of a trade association, subsidiaries of corporate clients, or even individual corporate officers or employees. Watch out for facts suggesting that a lawyer either has suggested to an individual corporate agent that she will represent him individually, or acquired confidential information pertaining to the individual's situation, not the representation of the entity.

In addition, you may have to work through some of the client-identification problems discussed in Chapter 5. If you see a problem involving, for example, a closely held corporation, or a corporate client and an affiliated entity, be sure to stop and analyze the identity of the clients. Remember that under Model Rule 1.13(a), a lawyer retained by an organization represents the organization itself, acting through duly authorized agents, not any of its human constituents. The lawyer may have a second, concurrent lawyer-client relationship with the constituent, however, which could create a conflict of interest. Another client-identification problem arises in the representation of corporate families with many parent, subsidiary, and affiliated entities. Can a lawyer representing a parent corporation accept the representation of a client with a matter adverse to a subsidiary of the parent? Comment 34 to Model Rule 1.7 states that "the lawyer for an organization is not barred from accepting representation adverse to an affiliate in an unrelated matter, unless the circumstances are such that the affiliate should also be considered a client of the lawyer . . . or the lawyer's obligations to either the organizational client or the new client are likely to limit materially the lawyer's representation of the other client." Circumstances suggesting that the affiliated entity should be considered the lawyer's client include closeness of relationship between the entities (such as sharing management or having interlocking boards of directors) or the sharing of confidential information between the entities.

It is much easier to handle conflicts problems if you draw a picture in the margin of your casebook or in your notes. The drawing does not have to be pretty, but it should capture the relevant relationships among lawyers, law firms, and clients. Your diagram can include features such as lines for attorney-client relationships, lines indicating internal relationships within entities (such as corporate affiliates or officers), arrows showing attorneys moving between firms, notations showing the flow of money in a transaction or contractual obligations among clients, and so on. The explanation following Example 11 has a sample picture illustrating the relationships among the parties.

Identify Conflicts

The second step is to determine whether there are conflicting interests among the clients, or between the interests of one or more clients and the lawyer personally. The very most important piece of advice I can give you about analyzing conflict-of-interest problems is to *think in functional terms.* By "functional" I mean thinking about the core professional obligations a lawyer owes to clients—keeping confidences, giving impartial advice, representing the client's position with vigor, and so on. Then think about how a lawyer's ability or willingness to do these things might be compromised because of the relationship with another client. For example, at a trial involving Bank, might the lawyer be unwilling to conduct a vigorous cross-examination of a witness because that witness is the managing partner of Accounting Firm, an important corporate client of the firm? Does the lawyer possess confidential client information of Bio-Tech, which she might inadvertently leak to her partner, who is representing Pharmaceutical Company and who would dearly love to know that confidential information? Is there some reason that the lawyer cannot take a position that would favor Manufacturer in litigation, because obtaining a favorable result for Manufacturer would by its nature cause harm to Supplier? Or might the lawyer not go all out for a client because she has a personal interest that will be harmed if the client prevails, such as a financial investment in a corporate defendant that the client is suing?

Go ahead and be cynical when thinking functionally. Think about the worst-case scenario. What could a sleazy or careless lawyer do that would harm the interests of one of her clients? The important thing to keep in mind is that the conflicts rules regulate the *risk* of harm to clients. There is no need to show that any client was actually harmed as a result of the concurrent representation. There is a conflict if there is a significant risk that a lawyer cannot consider, recommend, or carry out an appropriate course of action for the client because of the lawyer's other responsibilities or interests. Rule 1.7, cmt. [8]. This risk of harm is evaluated objectively, meaning that it is irrelevant whether the lawyer has pure motives, as long as there is a significant risk that the lawyer might do something to harm the client's interests.

Once you have thought about the lawyer's conduct functionally, in terms of what duties are owed to clients and how the lawyer's capacity to satisfy them may be compromised, it is time to translate this analysis into legal terms, mapping it on to the text of the rules. The concurrent conflicts rule, Rule 1.7, sets out two situations in which a lawyer has a conflict. Considering whether the lawyer can take on a second client whose interests may diverge with the interests of an existing client, the lawyer has a concurrent conflict of interest if:

- "the representation of one client [that is, the prospective new client] will be *directly adverse* to another client," Rule 1.7(a)(1); or
- "there is a significant risk that the representation of one or more clients [again, the new client] will be *materially limited* by the lawyer's responsibilities to another client, a former client or a third person, or by a personal interest of the lawyer," Rule 1.7(a)(2).

Some states use idiosyncratic terminology to describe conflicts. For example, the New York Rules talk about lawyers being involved in representing "differing interests." As that term has been interpreted in cases and ethics opinions, however, it functions very much like the Model Rules categories of direct adversity and material limitation.

Significance of Direct Adversity and Material Limitation Language

In many cases, it is apparent whether a conflict falls under subsection (a)(1) or (a)(2) of the existing rule. Direct adversity would be one client filing a lawsuit against another. For the purposes of the question "Is there a conflict?" *it does not matter whether the actions are unrelated.* See, for example, *IBM v. Levin*, 579 F.2d 271 (2d Cir. 1978); Rule 1.7, cmt. [6]. If Laettner represents Timberwolf Construction Company in litigation against a plumbing subcontractor, he cannot sue Timberwolf in a personal injury case related to a completely different construction site without Timberwolf's consent. Do not forget to look for direct adversity conflicts that occur on the same side of the "v." Co-defendants or co-plaintiffs can have legal positions that are directly adverse. Not all direct adversity conflicts require a filed lawsuit by one party against another—remember, conflicts rules regulate the risk of harm, not actual harm. If the building owner sues Timberwolf and the roofing subcontractor over a leaky roof, there could be direct adversity between the two defendants if both try to blame the other for causing the leaks. The litigation positions of the parties are adverse, and thus there is a conflict under Rule 1.7(a)(1), even without a cross-claim. Direct adversity could also arise in a business transaction where the parties are fighting over how to allocate the risk of some particular contingency. Major commercial transactions almost always present some thorny issue that puts the parties at odds. Some states have a *per se* rule against representing both the buyer and the seller in a commercial transaction, for example, *Baldasarre v. Butler*, 625 A.2d 458 (N.J. 1993), but even in the absence of a strict prohibition on playing both sides in a transaction, it is a reasonable assumption that the parties' interests will be adverse in most complex deals.

Even if there is direct adversity between clients, the conflict still may be consentable under the standards of Rule 1.7(b). See the section on consentable and nonconsentable conflicts in this chapter. Keep these standards straight, because it is possible to get them confused and think, for example, that there is no conflict unless the lawyer is representing both clients in the same litigated matter. That is the test for consentability, not for whether there is a conflict in the first place. Assuming Timberwolf is a sophisticated entity with a long history of dealing with Laettner as counsel, the correct analysis of the example above is that there is a direct adversity conflict under Model Rule 1.7(a)(1), but it is consentable. Students often confuse the "direct adversity" standard of Model Rule 1.7(a)(1) — which answers the "is there a conflict?" question — with one of the categories of nonconsentable conflicts, which is the assertion of a claim by one client against another client in *the same litigation*, see Rule 1.7(b)(3).

Material limitation conflicts are more subtle. They arise out of some other interest that interferes with the lawyer's ability to provide effective, diligent, impartial representation for a client. As Model Rule 2.1 provides, a lawyer is obligated to exercise independent professional judgment. This means that the lawyer's judgment cannot be tainted by the desire to please another client, make money in a deal, find a job for his nephew, or any other interest not shared by the client. The interests in question do not have to be directly opposed, as long as there is some pull on the lawyer's judgment. If there is something about the alignment of the parties and the lawyer's interests that makes you pause and think, "Hmm, I wonder if that's okay," there is probably a material limitation conflict.

As you might expect, there are plenty of gray areas between clear cases of direct adversity or material limitation. In these marginal cases, you can drive yourself nuts trying to figure out whether a particular situation is one of "direct adversity" between two clients under Model Rule 1.7(a)(1), or "material limitation" on the lawyer's ability to represent another client, under Model Rule 1.7(a)(2). If you like, you can think of a continuum of conflicts. With an increase in the severity of the impairment of the lawyer's ability to perform her professional obligations on behalf of both clients, the situation moves from material limitation to direct adversity. Some conflicts cases just kind of feel like direct adversity, others like material limitation. If that sounds too hazy for you, you're in luck. It does not make any difference to the analysis. If there is a conflict, there is a conflict. The lawyer must obtain consent (if the conflict is consentable) in order to proceed. There are not different rules for the handling of direct adversity and material limitation conflicts.

For this reason, the Restatement abandons this distinction entirely, running together the language of materiality and adversity. In the Restatement's definition, there is a conflict of interest "if there is a substantial risk that the lawyer's representation of the client would be materially and adversely affected" by a competing interest. Rest. §121. The Restatement's test does not differ from the Model Rules test—it simply reflects the lack of importance to the rest of the analysis of characterizing a conflict as one of direct adversity or material limitation. Once you have identified a conflict, *the rest of the analysis is the same*, regardless of whether it is one of material limitation or direct adversity.

Actual and Potential Conflicts

Some authorities on the conflicts rules like to divide up the world into "actual" and "potential" conflicts and then map this division onto Model Rule 1.7(a). The idea is that actual conflicts are handled under Model Rule 1.7(a)(1)'s "direct adversity" language, while potential conflicts fall under Model Rule 1.7(a)(2)'s "material limitation" provision. This doesn't work because there are plenty of actual conflicts that do not involve direct adversity. Suppose Carrawell is representing Bank in a big commercial lawsuit against Manufacturer, who is represented by Brand. Now suppose Brand is so impressed by Carrawell's work that he hires her as his personal lawyer in a real estate dispute he is having with a neighbor. Carrawell's representation of Bank is materially limited by her responsibilities to Brand, but there is no direct adversity between Bank and Brand. This is an actual conflict, but one that falls most comfortably within Model Rule 1.7(a)(2). H&H §11.10.

The way out of this confusion is to understand the conflicts rules as *risk rules*, not harm rules. A lawyer has violated Model Rule 1.7 by getting into a position that threatens some important interest of the client, such as the client's interest in a faithful representative without divided loyalties that might compromise her independent judgment. See, for example, *IBM Corp. v. Levin*, 579 F.2d 271 (2d Cir. 1978) ("The fact that a deleterious result cannot be identified subsequently as actually having occurred does not refute the existence of a likelihood of its occurrence.").

The best explanation of this comes from Hazard and Hodes:

> In the modern view, a conflict of interest exists whenever the attorney-client relationship is "at risk," even if no substantive impropriety—such as a breach of confidentiality or less than zealous representation—in fact eventuates. . . . When the risk of substantive harm is small . . . that does not indicate the absence of a conflict of interest, nor does it mean that the conflict is only a "potential" conflict, as is sometimes said. Quite the contrary. *The conflict—the risk—already exists in the here and now*; what is "potential" is the actual harm—the

> actual breakdown of the client-lawyer relationship or actual harm to the quality of the representation.

H&H §10.4 (emphasis added); see also Kevin McMunigal, *Rethinking Attorney Conflict of Interest Doctrine*, 5 Geo. J. Legal Ethics 823 (1992). Repeat after me: The conflict is the risk, not the harm. The conflict is the risk, not the harm. If you see conflicts rules as prophylactic in nature—that is, as preventing a lawyer from getting into a situation in which there might be some harm to the interests of one of the lawyer's clients—you will not be led astray by the actual/potential distinction.

Although the conflicts analysis proceeds in terms of risk, not actual harms to clients, it is not just any risk that will trigger the prohibition on simultaneous representation without informed consent. If the interests of the clients *will be* directly adverse, that is enough. Rule 1.7(a)(1). If the conflict is one that is characterized as a material limitation, however, there must be a significant risk of the impairment of the lawyer's ability to represent the client effectively. Rule 1.7(a)(2).

Apropos of "potential" conflicts, a lawyer has an obligation to keep an eye on developments in a representation, because a conflict may arise where there was not one before. In a case reprinted in many professional responsibility casebooks, a legal services office was representing two classes of plaintiffs: (1) disabled residents seeking better facilities at a state-run facility and (2) female prison inmates seeking equalization of their facilities to be on par with those provided to male inmates. *Fiandaca v. Cunningham*, 827 F.2d 825 (1st Cir. 1987). At the outset, the interests of the clients did not appear to conflict. As the lawyers reasoned, it would be possible to obtain effective relief for both classes without the interests of one class interfering with the interests of the other. But the state made a settlement offer that threw the multiple representation into disarray—it offered to construct a new prison for the female inmates on the grounds of the state facility for the care and treatment of the disabled residents! There was no way the lawyers could evaluate the settlement offer and give advice that was impartial between the client classes. Accepting the offer would be good for the women prisoners, but bad for the disabled residents; declining the offer would be good for the residents, but bad for the inmates. To put it in functional terms, the lawyers would be unable to satisfy their duty of loyalty to the women prisoners because they could not recommend, carry out, or even explain the benefits of the settlement offer, and ensure that the women prisoners gave it careful consideration. The reason they could not satisfy this duty to the women prisoners is their simultaneous representation of the handicapped residents. The same analysis applies to the duty of loyalty owed to the disabled residents. In that case, the lawyers would not be able to oppose the location of a prison on the grounds of the state school, because it was in the interests of the other client class to have the prison built there.

Thus, in this case, a multiple representation that started off presenting no conflicts suddenly turned into one in which the lawyers had a conflict, and maybe even one that was nonconsentable. At the outset, everything looked fine. Representing two classes of plaintiffs like these is bread-and-butter work for legal services offices. There was no reason to think the lawyers in the office would be whipsawed by their competing loyalties to both classes. At the beginning of the representation, there certainly was no actual conflict, and probably not even a potential conflict. As the case wore on, however, an actual conflict arose, maybe even a nonconsentable conflict.

Note that if for some reason the lawyer can foresee at the outset the possibility that the interests of the two classes might diverge at some future time, the lawyer must explain that risk to the affected clients and obtain their consent. The risk must be significant in order to create a conflict under Model Rule 1.7(a)(2), but you can imagine a case in which there would be a significant risk. Maybe there are not that many available state buildings in which a women's prison could be located. Perhaps the state had been talking about evicting the disabled folks and using the facility as a site for a prison. If these facts are known to the legal aid lawyers at the outset, they cannot blithely pretend there are no problems. In our hypothetical case of knowledge of a risk, the lawyers should explain to the clients that the state may do something that puts their interests directly at odds at some later time, and when that occurs, the lawyers may be forced to withdraw from representing one or both classes. That eventuality is exactly the sort of thing that must be explained to the clients in order to obtain their informed consent under Model Rule 1.7(b)(4). See also Rule 1.7, cmt. [18].

Confidentiality-Related Conflicts

Suppose one lawyer in a firm represents Client A, and as a result acquires lots of confidential information about Client A. Another lawyer in the firm represents Client B. Some of the information concerning Client A would be very useful to Client B and detrimental to Client A if disclosed. Does the firm have a conflict?

Many courts and commentators would answer this question in the affirmative, relying on the "risk rules" analysis given above. That is, the conflicts rules regulate the risk that a lawyer will get into a situation in which there is a nontrivial possibility that she will violate a duty owed to a client, such as the duty of loyalty or the obligation to keep confidences. The "risk rules" analysis does seem to slight the first lawyer's duty of confidentiality to Client A. It seems to imply that the lawyer is likely to go blabbing Client A's secrets at the drop of a hat and doesn't give much credit to her commitment, as a professional, to keep secrets. If the lawyer representing Client A actually does comply with the duty of confidentiality (as perhaps we should assume she will), it is harder to see why there is a conflict in this situation. These confidential-information conflicts, in their pure form, arise only from the possession of confidential information; the interests of the clients are not otherwise adverse, and there is no other material limitation on the simultaneous representation of both.

The New York City Bar Association ethics committee has stated that the possession of confidential information of Client A does not, by itself, create a conflict unless the information is so significant to the representation of Client B that the lawyer having the information cannot avoid using it. See New York City Bar Formal Op. 2005-02. "[A] client has no legitimate expectation that a lawyer will use confidential information of another client for the first client's benefit." Thus, the mere fact that the lawyer possesses information from one representation that could be useful in the representation of another does not automatically create a conflict. There must be a further determination that the information is sufficiently material to the second representation. For example, the information may be so important that the lawyer is required to "steer so far clear of disclosing or using the embargoed information" that the lawyer would effectively provide less-than-competent representation to Client B. In that type of situation, there would be a conflict.[2] The opinion also discussed the issue of consentability, which is the next step in the analysis of conflicts.

Ascertain Consentability

The third step, if there are conflicts, is to figure out whether they are consentable. (Some casebooks and commentators use the term "waivable" to mean the same thing.) Most concurrent conflicts are consentable, provided that the client has been given sufficient information upon which to make the decision. This is referred to as the requirement of informed consent. If the lawyer fully explains all the pertinent facts, sets out the client's options, and clearly explains any downside risk to the concurrent representation, the client likely will be able to agree to allow the lawyer to represent multiple clients with conflicting interests. However, there are three categories of non-consentable conflicts established by the Restatement and Model Rule 1.7. If the situation falls into one of these categories, simultaneous representation will be improper, regardless of whether the situation was fully explained to the client and whether the client gave consent.

---

2. As the opinion itself recognized, authority is not unanimous on this point, and there are ethics opinions and cases holding that the mere possession of protected confidences of one client that may be useful to another client creates a conflict. See, for example, *Bank Brussels Lambert v. Fiddler Gonzalez & Rodriguez*, 171 F.3d 779 (2d Cir. 1999) (arguably distinguishable because other grounds existed for concluding that there was a conflict).

Prohibited by Law

A lawyer may not represent two clients, even with consent, if the representation is prohibited by law. Rule 1.7(b)(2); Rest. §122(2)(a). This is a relatively limited category, intended to incorporate by reference generally applicable law governing situations like former government lawyers who are prohibited by criminal statutes from representing certain clients. See Rule 1.7, cmt. [16].

Client Versus Client in the Same Litigation

A nonconsentable conflict is presented by "the assertion of a claim by one client against another client represented by the lawyer in the same litigation or other proceeding before a tribunal." Rule 1.7(b)(3); Rest. §122(2)(b). The traditional rule is that a law firm may not represent a client in any matter in which that client's position would be adverse to that of another existing client. It does not matter that the two matters are not related. *Cinema 5 v. Cinerama*, 528 F.2d 1384 (2d Cir. 1976). In a classic case, Law Firm had represented Twible for many years and was continuing to represent him in a collection action, *Twible v. Debtor. Grievance Comm. v. Rottner*, 203 A.2d 82 (Conn. 1964). A group of lawyers within Law Firm then took the case of O'Brien, who was suing Twible for damages arising out of an assault by Twible on O'Brien. The trial court disqualified Law Firm from both cases (*Twible v. Debtor* and *O'Brien v. Twible*) and ordered it to repay any earned fees. The decision is based on the loyalty rationale (would Twible ever again trust Law Firm after it had accepted the representation of O'Brien?) and the institutional interest in the adversarial presentation of both parties' cases, known as the process-integrity rationale. Although the court did not reach the issue, because Twible did not have an opportunity to give informed consent, the traditional approach would be that this conflict is nonconsentable.

The modern trend, however, is to permit the law firm to represent both clients with consent *provided that* the law firm is not representing them both in the same litigated matter.[3] The firm in the preceding example could have

---

3. See, for example, *Unified Sewerage Agency v. Jelco*, 646 F.2d 1339 (9th Cir. 1981). In that case, the client was a concrete subcontractor, Teeples & Thatcher, which was contemplating suing its general contractor, Jelco. Jelco then approached the law firm and asked whether it would represent it in a dispute with an electrical subcontractor. The law firm advised Jelco of its relationship with Teeples & Thatcher, and said it would represent Jelco only if it consented to the firm's continuing work for Teeples & Thatcher. With advice of its general counsel, Jelco consented. The trial court denied the motion for disqualification filed by the consenting client, which had, in the intervening period, fired the law firm as its representative in the dispute with the electrical subcontractor. The Ninth Circuit affirmed, saying that representation was proper because the client had given informed consent.

represented both Twible and O'Brien, provided it obtained both clients' informed consent. The Restatement rule and Model Rule 1.7(b)(3) therefore reflect a developing trend, not settled law in all jurisdictions.

Remember, however, that it is improper for a lawyer to represent one client in a matter adverse to another client, *even if the second client is being represented on an unrelated matter,* unless both clients give informed consent. There is still a "direct adversity" conflict under Model Rule 1.7(a)(1), even if the lawyer is not representing the clients in the same matter. See the table on page 334 for the difference between the standards for (1) whether there is a conflict and (2) whether the conflict is consentable. It is easy to get these standards mixed up if you are not careful.

Objectively Unreasonable

The final category of nonconsentable conflicts is a catch-all. A lawyer may not represent two clients, even with informed consent, unless "the lawyer reasonably believes that the lawyer will be able to provide competent and diligent representation to each affected client." Rule 1.7(b)(1); Rest. §122(2)(c). The Restatement uses the term "adequate" representation instead of "competent and diligent," but the effect is the same. Unless each client has the same opportunity to achieve a good result with the "conflicted" lawyer as she would with an independent lawyer, the lawyer cannot represent both clients. The key idea here is that there are some situations in which it would be objectively unreasonable for a lawyer to believe that it is possible to be as effective with the dual representation as without it. Rest. §122, cmt. g(iv).

Suppose a lawyer is considering whether to represent both an employee accused of embezzlement and the employer in the action to recover for the losses. After doing some preliminary investigation, the lawyer discovers that the employee had intentionally embezzled funds; yet, in the criminal trial of the employee, he is denying intentional embezzlement. There is no way both clients can come out ahead, because the position taken in one case affects the clients' rights in the other. Either a court decides the money was misplaced accidentally, in which case the employer cannot collect on the bond, or the court characterizes the embezzlement as intentional, in which case the employee goes to jail. This is a zero-sum situation, because the lawyer cannot advance a position favorable to one client without harming the other. It would be objectively unreasonable to believe that either client would not be disadvantaged by the simultaneous representation. Thus, the conflict presented is nonconsentable, and the lawyer cannot represent both parties, even though the lawyer has explained the risks and benefits and secured the clients' rights.

Be sure to analyze the issue of consentability separately from the issue of whether or not there is a conflict. The standards can sound similar, so it is tempting to collapse the analysis into one step. The following table should help you to keep the standards straight.

For example, you may have two clients whose interests are directly adverse (Client A is suing Client B), but the conflict may be consentable if the lawyer is not representing both A and B in the litigated matter.

Is there a conflict?	Is the conflict nonconsentable?
Is the representation of one client directly adverse to the other? Rule 1.7(a)(1).	Will one client assert a claim against another in the same litigation? Rule 1.7(b)(3).
Is the representation of one client materially limited by the lawyer's responsibilities to another client? Rule 1.7(a)(2).	Is it reasonably likely that the lawyer will be unable to provide adequate representation to one or more of the clients? Rule 1.7(a)(1).

See If There Has Been Effective Consent

Finally, if the conflicts are consentable, have all affected clients given informed consent? The key word here is "informed." Informed consent is a concept that has been developed by courts, by analogy with medical malpractice law, to ensure that the affected clients have made a decision to waive conflicts in a knowing, intelligent manner. See Rule 1.0(e) (defining informed consent). The prerequisite to informed consent is full disclosure of all the risks and benefits of a proposed course of action. In a nutshell, the lawyer must provide the kind of information that an impartial lawyer (not laboring under a conflict) would give to the client. If there is a risk to the client, the lawyer must say so. If multiple representation would foreclose a particular strategic move at some later point in the process, the lawyer must explain this to the client clearly, in terms the client can understand. Be on the lookout for fact patterns in which the lawyer provided inadequate disclosure, perhaps because she was trying to finesse it and obtain consent without having to explain some inconvenient facts. A waiver obtained without first providing full information to the client will be deemed unenforceable. This is a very common problem in real conflicts cases, because lawyers don't like to have discussions that will make clients uncomfortable. That may be understandable, but enforceable waivers require full disclosure as a predicate for informed consent.

Remember that *each* affected client must consent after consultation. Rule 1.7(b)(4). If the question is whether a law firm may represent B in light of its existing relationship with A, you may be focusing on the effect of the new client relationship on B, and thinking only about obtaining B's consent. But do not forget that A also must be apprised of the effect of the multiple representation on its interests, and also must provide informed consent. Watch for exam questions in which only one of the clients has consented, if another client's consent is necessary.

The Restatement commentary provides an excellent list of the factors that must be discussed with each client in order to obtain informed consent. Rest. §122 cmt. c(i). Unfortunately, the comments are not reproduced in most professional responsibility rules supplements, so they are quoted here, with some brief explanatory notes:

1. *The interests of the lawyer and the client giving rise to the conflict.* Remember, a material limitation conflict is created if there are attachments, loyalties, financial interests, desires, commitments, or relationships pulling the lawyer in different directions. That is what the Restatement is referring to here — the lawyer may have reasons to act in some way that is not in the client's best interests. Do not just look for other professional relationships with clients. The lawyer's interests here could include: financial investments in clients or third parties who are entangled in a lawsuit or transaction; the lawyer's service on the board of directors of a client or third party; romantic relationships with clients; the lawyer's involvement as an expert witness or consultant in another matter; a client of the firm appearing as an adverse witness in a trial; or the desire to curry favor with a potential client or get back in the good graces of a former client.

2. *Contingent, optional, and tactical considerations and alternative courses of action that would be foreclosed or made less readily available by the conflict.* Imagine an employment discrimination case in which the manager wants to be represented by the employer's law firm. Maybe this is a good idea, maybe not. If the manager had separate counsel, he might be able to argue that he was just following the employer's unwritten policy, or that the employer tolerated the conduct at issue in the case. In other words, he can attempt to shift some of the blame to the employer. He will not be able to do this if he is represented by the employer's lawyer. The manager's course of action of pointing fingers at the employer will be foreclosed by the multiple representation. The employer's lawyer must be very clear about this limitation on the lawyer's ability to handle the case. Despite this foreclosed course of action, it still might be a smart thing to consent to multiple representation if the manager and employer can harmonize

their defenses. If, for example, the events the plaintiff describes did not occur, or they do not amount to actionable discrimination, the manager and the employer can save money and present a united front in their defense.

3. *The effect of the representation or the process of obtaining other clients' informed consent upon confidential information of the client.* In some cases, it may be necessary to reveal secrets of one client in order to fully inform the other client of the nature of the conflict. Suppose Allen is an existing client of a lawyer. The lawyer knows that Allen has been investigated for securities fraud by the Securities and Exchange Commission (SEC), but this information is not publicly known. Now suppose Gates approaches the lawyer about forming a partnership with Allen. Gates and Allen say they want the lawyer to represent them both. In order to obtain Gates's consent to the dual representation, the lawyer must disclose her knowledge about the past investigation of Allen. Otherwise, Gates will not appreciate the risk he is facing when dealing with Allen. But the lawyer has an obligation to keep secret the information relating to Allen's investigation. The lawyer must tell Allen that the process of obtaining Gates's informed consent will require her to divulge the information. If Allen refuses to waive confidentiality, the lawyer cannot obtain informed consent from Gates.

4. *Any material reservations that a disinterested lawyer might harbor about the arrangement if such a lawyer were representing only the client being advised.* One of the fundamental obligations of a lawyer is to exercise independent professional judgment and provide candid legal advice. Rule 2.1. Representing multiple clients may interfere with this independence by making the lawyer less willing to be frank with her client. Imagine a commercial transaction in which the seller is looking for some security in case the buyer defaults. The buyer is a closely held corporation, but the corporation's president offers some personal property as security. An independent lawyer for the seller may look at the arrangement and advise her client, "This isn't a good deal. You could lose your security if the president is personally insolvent." If the same lawyer tries to represent both the buyer and the seller simultaneously, however, she might not be as willing to give this advice. She might instead try to finesse the conflict, saying to the seller, "The security is adequate — you have the right to recover against the president's personal assets if the buyer defaults."

In the second example, the lawyer has not lied to the client, but she still has not been perfectly candid. There is a risk there, and the seller may not appreciate the significance of the security interest in the president's personal property. When representing more than one client, a lawyer must do more than just refrain from actively lying. The lawyer must be completely frank. She must give the very same advice that a disinterested lawyer would—that is, the same advice a lawyer who is not also trying to advance the interests of another client would give. Failure to provide this impartial, candid advice will result in the client's consent being ineffective to cure the conflict.

5. *The consequences and effects of a future withdrawal of consent by any client, including, if relevant, the fact that the lawyer would withdraw from representing all clients.* Suppose Finished Product Manufacturer and Component Parts Supplier are co-defendants in a product liability lawsuit. They would like to be represented by the same firm. Both clients and the lawyer believe their positions can be harmonized because they believe this is a case in which the sole proximate cause of the accident was the plaintiff's misuse of the product. The lawyer still must explain to the clients that their interests may diverge in the future. Maybe it will turn out, after doing some pretrial discovery, that a component part was defective and caused the accident. If that occurred, Finished Product Manufacturer would have the right to file a cross-claim for contribution against Component Parts Supplier.

When the interests of the two parties are no longer harmonious, they are unlikely to want to continue to have the same lawyer representing them. Thus, they may revoke previously given consent to the multiple representation. Withdrawal of consent may be entirely justified, as in this example where the legal position of the parties has become adverse. On the other hand, one of the parties may use withdrawal of consent as a tactical maneuver to harass the other. The following section considers the rules governing the lawyer's obligations when one client has withdrawn consent, continuing with the example of the product liability lawsuit.

Although analyzing this situation requires you to know something about successive, or former-client conflicts (Chapter 16), the law firm would have to withdraw from representing both clients. Rest. §121, cmt. e(i). In a nutshell, if the firm withdrew only from representing Component Parts Supplier, it still would have a former client conflict by virtue of its representation of Finished Product Manufacturer. Model Rule 1.9(a) prohibits a lawyer from representing a client (here, Finished Product Manufacturer) in a matter (the product liability litigation) in which the lawyer had formerly represented another client (Component Parts Supplier) in the same or a substantially related matter (again, the product liability litigation) where the interests of the present and former client are materially adverse. Withdrawing from the representation of Component Parts Supplier makes it a former client, but the lawyer still has duties to the former client, including the duty to refrain from representing adverse interests in related matters. In other cases, though, it may be permissible for the firm to withdraw from representing only one client and continue representing the other.

Requirement of Written Consent

Rule 1.7(b) requires that the client's consent be confirmed in writing. This may be hypertechnical, but note that consent "confirmed in writing" is different from "written consent." See Rule 1.0(b), which includes "a writing that a lawyer promptly transmits to the person confirming an oral informed consent." The requirement of consent confirmed in writing would be satisfied with, for example, an e-mail sent to the client that says, "Pursuant to our conversation earlier today, you have agreed that we can continue to represent XYZ Corporation in regulatory compliance matters . . ." Regardless of what the rule requires, in anything but an emergency situation a lawyer would be crazy not to confirm all clients' consent to the multiple representation in writing. Also, a lawyer would be crazy not to put the *disclosure* to her clients, which is the basis of their informed consent, in writing. A lawyer can accomplish both of these tasks in a well-written "waiver letter" in which the information relevant to informed consent is set forth and the client is asked to indicate her consent by countersigning the letter. The lawyer should keep a copy! For an example of a good written waiver that protected the law firm from being disqualified by a former client, see In re Cerberus Capital Management LP, 164 S.W.3d 379 (Tex. 2005).

"What We Cannot Speak of We Must Pass over in Silence"

Informed consent requires full disclosure. Full disclosure may include information that is covered by the duty of confidentiality owed to another client. If that is the case, the lawyer may obtain the other client's informed consent to disclose the information. If that client refuses to consent, however, the lawyer will be unable to obtain effective consent to the conflict. See Rule 1.7, cmt. [19]. Consider the following example, slightly adapted from the well-known case of IBM v. Levin, 579 F.2d 271 (2d Cir. 1978).

A law firm has two clients — Big Computer Manufacturer and Little Computer Dealer. The firm represents Big in labor and employment matters, and Little in sales contract negotiations with computer manufacturers. Little buys computers from Big but has become increasingly frustrated with what it regards as Big's anti-competitive behavior. Little talks with its lawyers about the possibility of filing an antitrust lawsuit but insists that its lawyers keep this a secret, because it does not want to lose the element of surprise if it does file the lawsuit. Meanwhile, an in-house lawyer at Big asks a lawyer in the labor department at the law firm to handle a union arbitration matter. What would the firm have to discuss with Big in order to obtain Big's informed consent to the concurrent representation of Big and Little? One very important fact would be that other lawyers at the firm are contemplating filing an antitrust action against Big on behalf of Little. Little insists, however, that this information may not be disclosed. That means the firm may not accept the labor matter on behalf of Big. There is simply no way to obtain an effective waiver without informed consent, and full disclosure in this case would include the secret information about the contemplated antitrust action.

Lawyers sometimes try to get cute and finesse the requirement of full disclosure by talking in vague generalities about future adversity. This is a sure way to have the conflict waiver invalidated on a motion to disqualify and probably also to provoke a breach of fiduciary duty action by the aggrieved client as an added bonus.

Advance Waivers

Suppose a lawyer at a firm is approached by Fidelity Insurance Company to work from time to time on relatively discrete, short-term matters involving a type of security in which Fidelity has investments. The problem is that Fidelity is a huge insurance company, and representing it would likely create conflicts for the law firm, if not at the present time, then probably down the road. Can the lawyer ask Fidelity to consent in *advance* to the firm representing other clients with adverse interests? If not, the firm would be forced either to turn away Fidelity or to go through a cumbersome process of obtaining consent every time it started to work on a new matter for the client. Perhaps Fidelity really wants this particular law firm to represent it, and would be deprived of counsel of its choice if the law firm were so skittish about creating conflicts of interest that it would be forced to turn away Fidelity as a client unless Fidelity were willing to waive conflicts in advance. See New York City Bar Formal Op. 2006-1 (discussing changes in the practice of law that have led both clients and lawyers to desire advance waivers in some cases).

In the usual informed-consent scenario, the client's consent is based upon full disclosure of known facts, but where advance waivers are concerned, the client must evaluate risks and contingencies that might occur. In theory, advance waivers are no less effective than contemporaneous waivers, provided that the client gives informed consent in light of the known and reasonably anticipated risks and benefits of providing the waiver. Rule 1.7, cmt. [22] ("The effectiveness of [advance] waivers is generally determined by the extent to which the client reasonably understands the material risks that the waiver entails."). Without some awareness of the type of risk entailed, however, the client's advance consent cannot be said to be "informed." The law of lawyering has adopted an increasingly permissive attitude toward advance waivers. An early ABA opinion takes the traditional, skeptical view of the enforceability of advance waivers: "[I]t would be unlikely that a prospective waiver which did not identify either the opposing party or at least a class of potentially conflicting claims would survive scrutiny," the committee stated. See ABA Formal Op. 93-372. A subsequent ABA opinion, however, is more tolerant of advance waivers, as long as the client is a sophisticated, experienced user of legal services, and the client is fully informed of the circumstances under which a conflict may arise in the future. ABA Formal Op. 05-436. This is more permissive than the requirement that the lawyer forecast the particular party or particular type of legal matter that might create a conflict. Courts that have upheld advance waivers similarly emphasize the factor that the client concerned is a sophisticated consumer of legal services, often advised by its own in-house lawyers. See, for example, *Galderma Labs. L.P. v. Actavis Mid Atlantic LLC*, 927 F. Supp. 2d 390 (N.D. Tex. 2013); *Visa U.S.A., Inc. v. First Data Corp.*, 241 F. Supp. 2d 1100 (N.D. Cal. 2003). See also Rule 1.7, cmt. [22] ("if the client is an experienced user of the legal services involved and is reasonably informed regarding the risk that a conflict may arise, such consent is more likely to be effective, particularly if . . . the client is independently represented by other counsel in giving consent").

Sharp-eyed readers will note that even these increasingly permissive references to advance consent still contemplate the client's awareness of some general category of risk or the circumstances under which a conflict may arise. The final frontier, as it were, for advance waivers is the case of so-called blanket or open-ended waivers, where the client pretty much agrees to waive all future conflicts of any type whatsoever. The New York City Bar is right out there on the leading edge, with Formal Opinion 2006-1, which approves of blanket waivers, but only where the clients are sophisticated in legal matters and where a disinterested lawyer would judge that it would be in the client's best interests to agree to the waiver. The D.C. Bar kind of splits the difference between the New York City Bar and the Model Rules position, stating that an advance waiver will be upheld when "*either* (1) the consent is specific as to types of potentially adverse representations and types of adverse clients . . . *or* (2) the waiving client has available in-house or other current counsel independent of the lawyer soliciting the waiver." D.C. Bar Op. 309 (Sept. 2001).

In 2018 the California Supreme Court decided what will probably become the leading case on advance waivers — *Sheppard, Mullin, Richter & Hampton, LLP v. J-M Manufacturing Co., Inc.*, 6 Cal. 5th 59 (2018). The most important lesson from the *Sheppard Mullin* case is that even if a client has given a fairly broad advance waiver of conflicts, if the law firm knows of another matter that actually creates a conflict of interest, it must disclose this matter to the client. It is not enough to rely on the advance waiver.

Simplifying the facts somewhat, Sheppard Mullin was thinking about taking on J-M Manufacturing as a client. The adverse parties in the matter would be a bunch of public utility districts in the state, including the South Tahoe Public Utility District. Sheppard Mullin already represented South Tahoe in employment matters. South Tahoe had agreed to waive conflicts of interest arising from unrelated matters. The firm included the following language in its engagement agreement with J-M:

> Sheppard, Mullin, Richter & Hampton LLP has many attorneys and multiple offices. We may currently or in the future represent one or more other clients (including current, former, and future clients) in matters involving [J-M]. We undertake this engagement on the condition that we may represent another client in a matter in which we do not represent [J-M], even if the interests of the other client are adverse to [J-M] (including appearance on behalf of another client adverse to [J-M] in litigation or arbitration) and can also, if necessary, examine or cross-examine [J-M] personnel on behalf of that other client in such proceedings or in other proceedings to which [J-M] is not a party provided the other matter is not substantially related to our representation of [J-M] and in the course of representing [J-M] we have not obtained confidential information of [J-M] material to representation of the other client.

The problem was, the firm knew something more than "it may currently or in the future represent" a client with interests adverse to those of J-M. It knew about South Tahoe, but did not tell J-M about its representation of South Tahoe or disclose it in the engagement agreement. The firm was disqualified from representing J-M in what would have been a very lucrative engagement.

There are other important issues in the *Sheppard Mullin* opinion,[4] but for the purposes of this discussion, the thing to remember is that the court held that J-M's consent to the conflict was not *informed* because the lawyers did not tell J-M that it represented South Tahoe. The broad language of the advance waiver was not enough, and it didn't matter that J-M was a sophisticated client represented by its general counsel in negotiating the waiver. This case therefore underscores the principle in Rule 1.7, cmt. [22], that the

---

4. One biggie is whether the conflict of interest renders the entire engagement agreement, including the arbitration and attorneys' fees provisions — unenforceable. The California Supreme Court held that it did. That meant the firm could not recover its contractual fees for approximately 10,000 hours of work it performed on the J-M matter. Ouch! The court did say that the firm may be entitled to recover under a theory of *quantum meruit* for the fair value of its services. A dissenting justice would have denied recovery even in *quantum meruit* — double ouch!

enforceability of advance waivers depends on the extent to which the client truly understood the risks.

Examples

What About Me?

1. The law firm of Modeliste & Purdy is representing a class of small business owners who claim they have been injured by an anti-competitive practice in the trucking industry. Specifically, they allege that trucking companies have been adding undisclosed surcharges to cover rising fuel costs. The class is made up of approximately 500 small business owners. The named plaintiff, the class representative, is Keltner's Knickknacks, Inc. Named partner Modeliste is lead counsel in the class action.

If you're a bit rusty on civ pro, the basic idea is that as long as the representative plaintiff has claims that are typical of the class as a whole, and the named party will fairly and adequately protect the interests of the class, the claims of all class members are brought by the named party on behalf of the class. See Fed. R. Civ. P. 23(a). In this case, the district court found that the fuel surcharges paid by Keltner's Knickknacks to the defendant trucking companies were typical of the fees allegedly tacked on to shipments made by all small business owners; thus, Keltner's Knickknacks was an appropriate representative party.

One of the 500 or so small businesses making up the class in the fuel surcharge litigation is Weinberg's Widgets. The president of Weinberg's Widgets received notice of the fuel surcharge litigation and decided not to opt out of it. As a result, Weinberg's Widgets will be bound by any judgment or settlement in that litigation, but it otherwise has no right to control the conduct of the litigation by Modeliste & Purdy.

Weinberg's Widgets has been involved in a long and acrimonious contract dispute with Gadd's Gizmos. The president of Gadd's Gizmos has decided "enough is enough" and to hire counsel to sue Weinberg's Widgets. The president goes to see Purdy, the other named partner in the Modeliste & Purdy firm. Purdy performs a conflicts check, but somehow does not determine that Weinberg's Widgets is a member of the class represented by the firm in the fuel surcharge litigation. After the complaint in the contract case is filed and served on Weinberg's Widgets, the president of that company hires another law firm which immediately files a motion to disqualify Modeliste & Purdy from representing Gadd's Gizmos. Is it likely that the trial court grant the motion to disqualify the firm?

A. Yes, because the representation of Gadd's Gizmos is directly adverse to another firm client, namely Weinberg's Widgets.

B. Yes, because the representation of Gadd's Gizmos is directly adverse to the class represented by the firm in the fuel surcharge litigation.

C. No, because Weinberg's Widgets is not considered a client of the firm for conflicts purposes.

D. No, because the commercial dispute on which the firm is representing Gadd's Gizmos is not substantially related to the fuel surcharge litigation on which the firm is representing Weinberg's Widgets.

E. No, because it is Purdy, not Modeliste, who is representing a client in a matter directly adverse to Weinberg's Widgets.

What's the Harm?

Analyze the following conflicts problems functionally — that is, in terms of how the lawyer would be prevented from fulfilling her professional obligations to each affected client. Do not worry about the technical analysis using the language of Model Rule 1.7. We will work on the legal analysis starting with Example 5.

2. Husband and Wife come to see a lawyer and explain that they have decided to obtain a divorce and have agreed on how the property will be divided. They think there is no reason to waste the money on two separate lawyers. "Can you draw up the papers?" they ask the lawyer.

3. P is suing A and B for personal injuries. A was the driver of a car who ran into P, and B is a large corporation, A's employer. The police report indicates that A was "on call" with the employer at the time of the accident but was not actually traveling to or from a work-related site. A's liability insurance policy limit is $50,000, and the likely recoverable damages in this case are in excess of $200,000. Can the same law firm represent A and B?

4. A lawyer represents Engine Manufacturer (EM) in a wrongful death lawsuit arising out of a boating accident that allegedly was caused by a defect in either component parts made by EM or negligence in the installation of the parts by Boat Manufacturer (BM). BM is tired of paying a separate lawyer and, with the consent of its lawyer, approaches the lawyer for EM and asks if she will substitute in as counsel for BM as well. Both defendants believe the cause of the accident was reckless operation of the boat by the decedent, but the litigation is in the early stages of discovery.

5. A lawyer represents both a union and a group of workers who have filed a Fair Labor Standards Act (FLSA) claim against a chicken-processing company, claiming it forces them to work after they have clocked out. The union is in the middle of an organization campaign, trying to unionize the workers at the plant. Can the lawyer represent both the union in the organization drive and the workers in the FLSA suit?

Independent Counsel?

6. The law firm of Vincent & Elkton is the principal outside law firm representing Enerco, a large energy-trading firm. For several years, it has assisted the chief financial officer of Enerco in structuring complex entities to take advantage of arcane accounting rules, permitting Enerco to report higher earnings. A senior manager in the accounting department of Enerco has become worried about these transactions. She sent a memo to the chief executive officer of Enerco warning of significant adverse consequences if certain accounting adjustments are not made. The chief executive officer is inclined to hire Vincent & Elkton to investigate the allegations in the manager's letter because lawyers there are familiar with the details of the transactions (having prepared the documents themselves!) and can perform an investigation quickly and inexpensively. Can Vincent & Elkton take the case?

Sauce for the Goose

7. You are a partner at a large Washington, D.C., firm specializing in telecommunications law. Your firm has been approached by Malone and Chambers, two parties who are competing for a single radio broadcasting license to be issued by the FCC. Both potential clients would like your assistance in obtaining the license. Your representation will involve advocacy for the competitors before the FCC, but the administrative proceeding is not judicial in nature. Rather, the FCC will award the license to the applicant whose proposed service best serves "the public interest, convenience, and necessity." 47 U.S.C. §309(a). When there are mutually exclusive applications, the FCC decides who will be the recipient of the license on the basis of criteria such as the degree of the applicant's proposed involvement with the day-to-day management of the radio station, the programming the applicant proposes to provide (whether it is original and different from other radio stations in the market), the applicant's experience in broadcasting, the applicant's involvement in local and civic affairs, and whether the applicant is a woman or person of color.

   Both Malone and Chambers have consented to the dual representation after extensive discussions with your firm, at which the risks of joint representation have been spelled out carefully. Can you take on both Malone and Chambers as clients?

Trust Me, I'm His Lawyer

8. Cohen is a lawyer in a small town in a rural county in the State of Perplexity. He represents a number of local farmers in transactional and

litigation matters. Recently, the operator of a grain elevator sued four farmers, claiming it had issued delivery receipts listing a mistaken quantity of corn. The effect of the error was to unjustly enrich the farmers, so the elevator operator sought return of some of the money it had paid to the farmers. All of the farmers dealt with the elevator through Malkovich, a professional farm manager who also runs his own farm. Malkovich is one of the defendants in the unjust enrichment lawsuit, because his grain was part of the deliveries for which an allegedly mistaken receipt had been issued. Out of a total 22,340 bushels of corn delivered to the elevator, Malkovich claims that approximately 5,000 came from his farm. The rest was delivered by Malkovich, acting as agent for the other three farmers.

In separate conversations with Cohen, two of the other farmers, Broderick and Dafoe, expressed some frustration at Malkovich's management of their farms. They wondered if he had been entirely honest in his dealings with them, and Dafoe said he suspected Malkovich of fudging the delivery receipts to make it appear as though some of the corn from Dafoe had actually come from Malkovich's own farm. (The last farmer, Messier, is happy with Malkovich.) Separately, in a conversation with Cohen, Malkovich blamed the whole mix-up on the elevator operator. He accused the elevator operator of cheating him and the other farmers and insisted that Cohen file a counterclaim for conversion.

Cohen would like to represent all four farmers—Malkovich, Broderick, Dafoe, and Messier—in the dispute with the grain elevator. He believes the joint representation would avoid the duplicative transaction costs that would be imposed on the farmers if they had to obtain separate counsel. Also, there are not many lawyers in the county who have expertise in agricultural contract disputes; Cohen reasonably believes that he is the most competent lawyer in the county at this type of work. Can he represent all four? If so, what steps must he take?

How Informed Is the Consent?

9. After a horrific traffic accident in which a delivery truck owned by Western collided with a truck packed with passengers, the family members of several victims of the accident sought representation in a personal injury lawsuit. Under state law, the contributory negligence of a decedent could be charged to family members seeking to recover from Western. Some of the plaintiffs were heirs of one of the victims who might have been contributorily negligent—others were not. Although the lawyers would have preferred that the plaintiffs not file

cross-claims against each other, it might have been to the advantage of some of the plaintiffs to try to recover from the others, because the heirs of some plaintiffs may have been partially responsible for the accident. Nevertheless, it also might have been reasonable for all the plaintiffs to avoid pointing fingers at each other and proceed solely against Western. The plaintiffs could take the position that none of their family members were responsible for the injuries and that the damages were solely the fault of Western. If the plaintiffs started pointing fingers at each other, things would be a lot easier for Western. It could just sit back and watch the plaintiffs develop evidence of contributory negligence.

The lawyers approached by all the prospective plaintiffs realized there could be a conflict of interest, so they decided to explain the risks and benefits of multiple representation and obtain their clients' consent. They had the clients sign the following waiver of consent letter:

> [A] conflict of interest could arise between the Plaintiffs and members of the different estates of the deceased in the accident object of this case, who are represented by the same attorneys. After amply discussing the matter related with the possibility that a conflict of interest might arise, the effects and consequences related with the same, I have freely and spontaneously consented to continue with our present legal representation in the case.

Is the waiver adequate? If not, how could it be improved?

Bad for Business

10. American Battery Company, Inc. (ABC) manufactures lithium-ion batteries for use in cellular phones and tablet computers. It has sued XYZ Battery Co. (XYZ) for infringing one of its patents. ABC filed a motion to enjoin XYZ from manufacturing or selling any batteries that infringe its patent. The district court granted its motion. The injunction is a gigantic headache for Banana Personal Devices, Inc. (Banana), a large manufacturer of phones and tablet computers, which has an exclusive supply contract with XYZ. Here is the professional responsibility issue: Smith & Knight, the law firm representing ABC in the infringement litigation, is also Banana's long-time outside counsel for corporate financing matters. The General Counsel of Banana is furious over the injunction and its effect on Banana's profits, and has demanded that Smith & Knight withdraw from representing ABC. Setting aside the client relations nightmare this has created for Smith & Knight, must it withdraw? That is, would there be a conflict of interest if it continued to represent ABC and Banana?

Explanations

What About Me?

1. This purpose of this example is to remind you always to analyze the issue of client identification before going through the analysis of conflicts of interest. The specific issue may be a bit obscure—did you read Comment [25] to Rule 1.7?—but the general point is important. Always start by asking whether the party beefing about an alleged conflict of interest is a current or former client of the law firm.

    Options A, B, and C are all getting at the same question: Is Weinberg's Widgets a client of the firm for conflicts purposes? If you didn't know Comment [25], you might reasonably go for A or B. It could be the case that Weinberg's Widgets is straightforwardly a client of the firm for all purposes, in which case A would be the answer. Or, there could be some hybrid civ pro/law of lawyering rule that makes B the answer; that is, it could be the case that representing a class entails disqualification from any representation adverse to a class member. However, Comment [25] clarifies that "unnamed members of the class are ordinarily not considered to be clients of the lawyer for purposes of applying paragraph (a)(1)" of Rule 1.7. (I wrote that Purdy "somehow does not determine" that Weinberg's Widgets is a current firm client. That was deliberately ambiguous between being careless in the conflicts check and correctly determining that there is no client relationship here.) Weinberg's Widgets is out of luck. The firm may represent other clients directly adverse to Weinberg's Widgets, even while representing the class of which it is a member. The answer is C.

    What's the deal with the qualification "ordinarily" in Comment [25]? Notice in the facts it says that Weinberg's Widgets is nothing more than an unnamed class member. If it were separately represented by the firm in other matters, however, it would be a firm client and the firm would be disqualified from representing Gadd's Gizmos. Alternatively, Weinberg's Widgets could be a quasi-client if it shared confidential information with the firm that could be used against it in the representation of Gadd's Gizmos. (The latter possibility is similar to what happened in the *Westinghouse* case, discussed in Chapter 16.) Because none of these facts are present here, however, the example does not fall within the exception to the principle stated in Comment [25] that unnamed class members are not deemed to be clients of the firm for conflicts purposes. The answer is still C.

    Option D raises an interesting possibility. It could be the case that the concurrent conflicts rule does not prohibit a firm's representation of another client in an unrelated matter, even though the representation is adverse to a firm client. The representation of Gadd's Gizmos is clearly unrelated to the subject matter of the representation of the class, including Weinberg's Widgets. Conflicts of interest rules for solicitors (that is, not in-court advocates) in England and Wales permit adverse representation in unrelated matters. American law took a different evolutionary path. A couple of influential early cases, *Cinema 5, Ltd. v. Cinerama, Inc.*, 528 F.2d 1384 (2d Cir. 1976) and *IBM Corp. v. Levin*, 579 F.2d 271 (3d Cir. 1978), are widely understood as prohibiting directly adverse representation in unrelated matters. A scholar has recently argued, however, that this is a misunderstanding of these cases. See Daniel J. Bussel, *No Conflict*, 25 Geo. J. Legal Ethics 207 (2012). That may be right, but for the purpose of discipline, Rule 1.7(a)(1) clearly prohibits directly adverse representation, even in unrelated matters.[5] As I keep harping on, however, disqualification motions appeal to the court's inherent authority, which is not derived from the state rules of professional conduct. It is conceivable that a court might go back into the mists of time and determine that American courts have been misreading *Cinema 5* and *Levin*, and that directly adverse representation in unrelated matters should not subject a lawyer to disqualification. While this is theoretically possible, it is extremely unlikely because (1) the disciplinary rule is clear, and courts try to avoid reaching results in disqualification cases that are inconsistent with the disciplinary rules, and (2) the court has an "out" in the form of Comment [25]—it can simply refuse to disqualify the firm on the ground that Weinberg's Widgets is not a client.

If you went for option E, go back and read Rule 1.10(a). Better yet, write the following sentence ten times: "When lawyers are associated in a firm, none of them shall knowingly represent a client when any one of them alone would be prohibited from doing so by Rule 1.7 or 1.9."

What's the Harm?

2. The risk here is that the lawyer will be unable to explore the alternatives that might be more favorable to Husband or Wife. The spouses may be satisfied with the arrangement they worked out, but what if, subsequently, one of them thinks he or she got a raw deal? That spouse would not have had the benefit of independent, impartial legal advice to assess the situation. The joint representation also may affect the options available to each spouse. Imagine that there is some way of setting up the property division that would be advantageous to one spouse over the other; the lawyer representing both cannot recommend that option, so each spouse, in effect, would get a less effective lawyer than he or she

---

5. The great state of Texas is the only U.S. jurisdiction that does not consider simultaneous adverse representation of a client in an unrelated matter to be a conflict of interest. See Texas Disciplinary Rules of Prof'l Conduct, Rule 1.06(b)(1).

could have with individual representation. Finally, if some sticking point develops during the course of representation, the lawyer would have to withdraw from representing both, which would be expensive. The conflict is probably consentable, as long as the lawyer explains these risks to both Husband and Wife.

3. If the clients were represented separately, B's lawyer would want to deny that A was acting within the scope of his employment; conversely, A's lawyer would want to get B on the hook, to reduce the exposure of A's personal assets to a judgment. Hooking B would almost certainly keep A's share of the settlement within policy limits. There is at least a potential conflict here, depending on the substantive law of your state, regarding B's vicarious liability for A's driving while on call. In addition, there may be a conflict due to the differing settlement postures of the clients and their differing insurance coverage. For example, A's liability insurer might want to just dump policy limits on the table and get out, while it might be in B's interests to contest liability.

4. The thing the lawyer worries about here is some damaging fact coming to light later on in discovery, suggesting that one of the defendants may have a cross-claim against the other. Early in the case, all of the available evidence may, in fact, point toward the plaintiff's recklessness as the sole proximate cause of the accident, but you just never know what might turn up in discovery. From the perspective of the parties at the early stages of litigation, there is a risk that each defendant, if jointly represented, would lose the opportunity to file a cross-claim against the other. Even if each defendant does not want to go so far as to file a cross-claim, each still may wish to defend the case differently at trial. If the two defendants are aware of this risk, they may decide it is worth giving up the opportunity to point fingers at each other, in order to secure the benefits of cooperation. The conflict is probably consentable, but the lawyer has to explain all the risks to both defendants.

5. This problem, based on *Shaffer v. Farm Fresh, Inc.*, 966 F. 2d 142 (4th Cir. 1992), shows the danger of speculating too much about the effects of a joint representation and imagining dangers that do not exist. The district court was worried that the union wanted to use the FLSA case to publicize its organization drive. In other words, it might be in the union's interests for the workers to have a protracted fight with the chicken company, because they might come to hate the employer more and be further motivated to vote to unionize. As a result, the union might put pressure on its lawyer to scotch an early settlement, if in fact one was offered by management. The court of appeals said this kind of reasoning was far too speculative to support the drastic remedy of disqualifying counsel and permitted the lawyer to continue representing both the union and the employees.

Independent Counsel?

6. Obviously, this example is based on one of many incidents in the unraveling of Enron in 2001 and 2002.[6] (Are you getting sick of examples based on Enron?) The conflict presented here is between the interests of Enerco, on the one hand, and Vincent & Elkton and lawyers within the firm, on the other. Remember that a conflict of interest may arise if "there is a significant risk that [the lawyer's ability to provide effective representation to a client] will be materially limited by the lawyer's responsibilities to another client, a former client or third person or by *a personal interest of the lawyer*." Rule 1.7(a)(2) (emphasis added). Conflicts do not just arise between two clients. Here, the interests of Enerco are in having a thorough, impartial, objective investigation of the allegations raised by the accounting manager so that the corporation can take remedial action, if necessary. The firm's interests, by contrast, are in retaining the confidence and trust of Enerco, so that it will continue to use the firm as its principal outside counsel. If the manager's allegations are correct, the firm will have to reveal that it was too aggressive in its use of various accounting stratagems, and that Enerco is potentially exposed to civil and criminal liability as a result. No firm wants to deliver that news, so there is a risk that Vincent & Elkton will "pull its punches," as it were, and not conduct a thorough investigation.

   In addition, if the accounting treatment is so aggressive that it crosses the line into outright fraud, the firm may be liable under federal or state securities law for assisting the client's fraud. (See Chapter 12 for a discussion of the causes of action that may be asserted against a lawyer who may have assisted wrongful conduct by the client.) Facing the prospect of becoming a co-defendant in a lawsuit, the firm may have an incentive to sweep bad facts under the rug, rather than bringing them to the attention of Enerco's management. Thus, there is a conflict here between the interests of Enerco and the personal interests of lawyers within Vincent & Elkton.

Sauce for the Goose

7. This problem is based on Illustration 1 to Restatement §121.[7] Before looking at consent, think about the issue of whether there is a conflict. I hope your answer is a clear "yes." The interests of Malone and Chambers are directly adverse, because each one wants the same

---

6. For an excellent analysis of the professional responsibility issues presented by the Enron fiasco, from which I have drawn heavily, see Roger C. Cramton, *Enron and the Corporate Lawyer: A Primer on Legal and Ethical Issues*, 58 Bus. Law. 143 (2002).

7. I was kind of imprecise with the criteria for awarding licenses, and some of them, such as the preference for women and minority applicants, have been struck down by courts.

thing—the local broadcast license—and there is only one to go around. Moving on, this conflict is nonconsentable, even though Malone and Chambers are not litigation adversaries. This is a good example of zero-sum conflicts. There is no way to get a good result for Malone (the license—hooray!) without harming Chambers (no license—bummer), and vice versa. Every argument the lawyer urges on behalf of Malone hurts Chambers. The fact that Chambers is a woman counts in her favor, but maybe Malone has more experience in broadcasting. Chambers may propose to bring new and different programming to the area, but Malone may propose to be more involved in the day-to-day operation of the radio station. If the lawyer argues the most important criterion should be originality, then Chambers benefits at the expense of Malone. Thus, even though the two potential clients are not asserting claims against one another, the lawyer cannot provide effective representation to both.

Trust Me, I'm His Lawyer

8. The problem is based on *Wendell's Inc.* [no relation] v. *Malmkar*, 405 N.W.2d 562 (Neb. 1987). The actual case (sort of) held that the conflict was not consentable,[8] and I tend to agree. Certainly, there is at least a potential material adversity conflict here, under Model Rule 1.7(a)(2), created by the possibility that Malkovich and Broderick/Dafoe might have inconsistent theories of the case. Malkovich would say the receipts were not mistaken, and that all the corn the receipts show as delivered was in fact delivered. Broderick and Dafoe would say that, too, but also might want to bolster their cases by claiming either that the mix-up was caused by Malkovich's mismanagement or in addition that Malkovich was stealing from them. There easily could be a cross-claim here, filed by Broderick and Dafoe against Malkovich. There also might be some sort of credibility issue if the elevator operator claimed that it mistakenly relied on representations made by Malkovich and the other two farmers wished to respond by essentially aligning with the elevator operator and calling Malkovich's veracity or competence into question. Malkovich, of course, would place all the blame solely on the elevator operator.

Nevertheless, you get the picture. Where two applicants are competing for one license, they have to make an argument for why they should get the license, based on a number of factors.
8. In the actual case, the lawyer did not obtain informed consent from the clients, so the court did not have to reach the issue of consentability. The court, however, included some dicta that created unnecessary confusion in Nebraska law—it said that it "specifically disapproves" of concurrent representation of multiple clients, even with consent. It should have said that cases like this one present nonconsentable conflicts, because there are plenty of other multiple-representation conflicts cases in Nebraska in which the court permitted the representation with consent.

The next step in the analysis is consentability. Even in the absence of a formal cross-claim, the parties' positions are at odds from the outset and there is no way to eliminate the impact this adversity has from Cohen's ability to represent all four effectively. Thus, Cohen cannot "reasonably believe that [he] will be able to provide competent and diligent representation to" each farmer, unaffected by representation of the other clients. See also Rest. §122(2)(c).

One might argue that as long as Cohen explained all these facts to all four farmers, he could obtain their informed consent. The problem with this approach is that it would be extremely difficult for Cohen to obtain informed consent. He basically would have to make Malkovich seem like a really bad guy when talking with Broderick and Dafoe, in order to get them to realize what they would be giving up by agreeing to share a common lawyer with Malkovich. If he soft-pedaled the facts giving rise to the conflict, the consent would be ineffective because it would not be on full disclosure. They would have to agree not to file a cross-claim — client versus client in the same litigation would definitely be nonconsentable, Rest. §122(2)(b) — and in order to make a rational decision about whether it would be a good idea not to cross-claim against Malkovich, they would have to know all the facts about Malkovich's management of their farms. It would be unlikely that Cohen could give this kind of unvarnished opinion without violating his fiduciary obligations to Malkovich. No one in Malkovich's position wants his lawyer running around making him seem like a jerk. (In terms of the policies underlying conflicts cases, you might see this as an interference with Malkovich's interest in Cohen's loyalty.) Furthermore, Broderick and Dafoe might not want word of their suspicions getting back to Malkovich, but Cohen would not be able to obtain informed consent from Malkovich without telling him that his other two clients were unhappy with him, and this unhappiness might result in a cross-claim at some later stage in the litigation. If Cohen obtained a waiver of confidentiality from Broderick and Dafoe, he could make this disclosure, but absent a waiver, he would be violating his duty of confidentiality to Broderick and Dafoe if he shared their concerns with Malkovich.

Perhaps you want to argue that it is possible to harmonize defenses, and have all four farmers argue that the elevator screwed up and Malkovich was blameless. That certainly is what must be true in order for the conflict to be consentable. It would be almost impossible to align the parties' positions, given the mistrust between Malkovich and the other two, concerns about confidentiality, and the likelihood that as the litigation progressed the animosity between the parties only would increase and probably result in a cross-claim.

How Informed Is the Consent?

9. This is a real case, and the district court did something very useful—it spelled out in detail the kind of disclosures that would be necessary in order for the lawyer to secure informed consent. *Figueroa-Olmo v. Westinghouse Elec. Corp.*, 616 F. Supp. 1445 (D.P.R. 1985). The trouble with the lawyers' letter is that there is no way to tell from this waiver what "effects and consequences" the lawyers explained to their clients. One also might wonder what sorts of off-the-record discussions the lawyers had with their clients, trying to persuade them to agree to the joint representation. For this reason, the district court directed the plaintiffs' lawyers to do a better job explaining the risks of concurrent representation to their clients. It ordered the lawyers to give clear explanations and questions to the clients, for example:

> Are you aware that the passengers or driver who died in this accident could be found by the court or by the jury to have been partially or entirely responsible for the damages caused?
> Are you aware that you have the option of suing the heirs of any one of the deceased to recover your damages from the heirs as well as from Westinghouse?
> Are you aware that if any of the deceased or all of them are found to have been entirely responsible for the accident, you will not recover anything?
> Are you aware that by not suing the other plaintiffs' heirs you are abandoning the possibility of obtaining compensation?

Now that is full disclosure! The court-ordered explanations are clear, forceful, expressed in plain language ("you will recover nothing") instead of legalese, and not slanted in favor of multiple representation. If the clients still were willing to consent after reading and understanding those disclosures, the concurrent representation would be permissible. When you consider consent to conflicts, think of this kind of disclosure as a necessary basis for obtaining the informed consent of clients.

Bad for Business

10. This Example is based on a case that got a great deal of attention in the intellectual property community—*Celgard, LLC v. LG Chem, Ltd.*, 594 Fed. Appx. 669 (Fed. Cir. 2014). I'm not sure it's decided correctly; see what you think.

Begin, as always, with Step #1—identify clients. Smith & Knight represents both ABC and Banana. Okay, but the infringement litigation is between ABC and XYZ, and XYZ is not a client of the firm. Move on to Step #2—is there a conflict? As noted in Chapter 13, lawyers are fiduciaries and clients have a reasonable expectation of their loyalty. As Comment

[6] to Rule 1.7 rightly observes, a client would feel betrayed if its lawyer represented another client whose interests are directly adverse, even if the matters are unrelated. Importantly, however, these interests have to be legal, not economic interests to fall within Rule 1.7(a)(1). Granted, beating up on XYZ will have an economic impact on Banana, but adverse effects on a client's business do not generally rise to the level of *legal* conflicts of interest. "[S]imultaneous representation in unrelated matters of clients whose interests are only economically adverse, such as representation of competing economic enterprises in unrelated litigation, does not ordinarily constitute a conflict of interest . . ." Rule 1.6, cmt. [6]. The Federal Circuit in the *Celgard* case said that "[Banana] faces not only the possibility of finding a new battery supplier, but also additional targeting by [ABC] in an attempt to use the injunction as leverage in negotiating a business relationship." Both of those things sound like real bummers for Banana, but again they're not impacts on its legal interests.

While I don't really buy the court's reasoning, it probably made the right call here. Why? Because the law firm and the client had previously agreed that the firm would not represent parties in patent infringement cases against customers of its other clients. Using the party names from the example, Smith & Knight had reassured Banana that it would represent ABC only against other battery manufacturers, not XYZ. The client, Banana, reasonably felt betrayed when Smith & Knight went ahead and represented ABC against XYZ. That's a perfectly good reason to disqualify the firm in this case, but I'm not sure it would be a justification absent the prior agreement between the law firm and its client.

IMPUTATION

Once you have ascertained whether a conflict exists, whether it is consentable, and whether the affected clients have given informed consent, you also must consider whether the conflict is *imputed* to other lawyers in the same organization. The disciplinary rules generally prohibit a lawyer from knowingly representing a client where another lawyer who works in the same firm would be conflicted out of the matter. Rule 1.10(a). So, if Hazard represents Two Pesos, he pretty clearly would be prohibited from representing Taco Cabana on the other side of a hotly contested trade-dress litigation matter with Two Pesos. The imputation rule means that Hazard's partner, Hodes, similarly would be forbidden to represent Taco Cabana. The imputation rule is justified primarily by confidentiality considerations. The concern is that Hazard might accidentally let a secret of Two Pesos slip while she is chatting about her cases with Hodes. We certainly would not want to prevent Hazard and Hodes from talking about their cases, because this kind of informal consultation contributes to the efficiency of law firms (a benefit that is enjoyed by clients), and also just makes work more fun. Loyalty considerations also play a role in justifying the imputation rule, because clients are likely to regard all of the lawyers in a firm as "their lawyer," even if they have no daily contact with most of the lawyers in the firm.

Under the governing rule, Rule 1.10(a), all current-client and former client conflicts are imputed to lawyers working together in the same firm, unless the conflict is based on the personal interest of the lawyer and "does not present a significant risk of materially limiting the representation of the client by the remaining lawyers in the firm." For example, if Sam's wife, Diane, represents the plaintiff, other lawyers in Sam's firm can represent the defendant, as long as they will not be prevented from providing effective representation because of their association with Sam. Note that Sam's relationship with Diane is a personal conflict for him. Under Model Rule 1.7(a)(2), his representation of the defendant would be materially limited by his personal interest—here, his marriage to Diane. Because it is a conflict arising out of Sam's personal interests, however, it is not imputed to the rest of his firm under Model Rule 1.10(a).

A "firm" is defined by Model Rule 1.0(c) as "a lawyer or lawyers in a law partnership, professional corporation, sole proprietorship or other association, or in a legal services organization; or lawyers employed in the legal department of a corporation or other organization." Branch offices of large national law firms count as one "firm" for imputation purposes. *Westinghouse Elec. Corp. v. Kerr-McGee Corp.*, 580 F.2d 1311 (7th Cir. 1978) (involving Washington, D.C., and Chicago offices of Kirkland & Ellis). What about looser associations of lawyers? Sometimes lawyers just starting out will lease a spare room in an existing law office and share the library, photocopier, and secretarial services. The lawyers do not constitute a "firm" unless they hold themselves out to the public as being one firm, or unless they have access to one another's confidential information. Rule 1.0, cmt. [2]. Be careful, though. Listing names together on letterhead or on the office door may be sufficient to justify a court in finding that the lawyers have held themselves out to the public as a firm. *Gosselin v. Webb*, 242 F.3d 412 (1st Cir. 2001).

We will consider the issue of screening in Chapter 16, in connection with the subject of migratory lawyers. The basic idea behind screening is that a law firm may be able to adopt some kind of procedure to separate lawyers working on one matter from lawyers working on another. The result is to cure the imputation of conflicts from one lawyer or group of lawyers to the rest of the firm. These procedures are sometimes called "Chinese walls" or "firewalls," but the Model Rules use the term "screens." Screening has long been one of the most controversial issues related to conflicts of interest.

There is a tremendous amount of variation among jurisdictions in attitudes toward screening. In 2009, the ABA adopted amendments to Rule 1.10(a) permitting screening to cure former-client conflicts associated with a newly hired lawyer. The ABA amendment is unlikely to change the situation in the states, because there has long been a split between states that permit screening to cure imputed conflicts and those that do not. At any rate, the important thing to note, for now, is that even where screening is generally recognized, screens have limited applicability. They are most commonly employed to prevent the imputation of a conflict of a newly hired migratory lawyer to other lawyers in the hiring firm. (This has always been allowed where the incoming lawyer formerly worked in government, Rule 1.11(b); the controversy is over screening for lawyers moving from one private firm to another.) Screening may also be used to cure the imputation of conflicts that arise from interviews with prospective clients. See Rule 1.18(d)(2)(i). Beyond those two applications — incoming migratory lawyers and prospective client interviews — nonconsensual screens are *never* effective to cure the imputation of conflicts.[9] Firms try it all the time, and it never works. If you see a concurrent conflict and an attempt to cure it with a screen, you know it's going to be ineffective.

SUMMING UP

The key to analyzing conflicts cases is to break them down into parts, make sure you apply the right standards, and think in terms of how the lawyer's ability to provide effective representation would be affected by the multiple client relationships. Remember to differentiate between the tests for whether there is a conflict (either direct adversity or material limitation) and whether the conflict is consentable. If the conflict is consentable, make sure the lawyer actually obtains informed consent, after full disclosure and a candid explanation of the risks and benefits of multiple representation. See if you can work through the following example, which brings all these issues together.

Example

Who Owes What to Whom?

11. For a number of years, Davies, Pink & Wormwood (DP&W) represented Federated Insurance in a variety of securities and regulatory transactions. In 1996, DP&W set up a holding company, called Chubby, which

---

9. The word "nonconsensual" is important here because a client may condition its consent to a concurrent representation on the law firm's use of a screening mechanism. The controversy over screening pertains only to the nonconsensual use of screens — to put it bluntly, whether a law firm can force Client A to accept its concurrent representation of Client B, leaving Client A no remedy but to fire the law firm and find new counsel.

purchased all the assets of Federated. The firm ceased to have any dealings with Federated, but continued to represent Chubby. The officers
and general counsel of Chubby care a great deal about what happens
to Federated, because Federated accounts for nearly 90 percent of the
net income of Chubby. Last month, the litigation department at DP&W
was retained by Rockefeller Bank to pursue recovery on $200 million
worth of surety bonds issued by Federated as a guarantor of obligations
of a bankrupt energy-trading company. At the same time, on behalf
of Chubby, securities lawyers in the firm were preparing a filing with
the SEC. The lawyers had to decide how to handle disclosure of the
fact that Federated may have liability to Rockefeller Bank amounting to
$200 million on the surety bonds. Can the firm represent both clients?

Explanation

Who Owes What to Whom?

11. The problem looks fairly complicated, but believe it or not, it is not that
    bad, as long as you do not get confused by all the names and relation-
    ships and carefully work through the step-by-step analysis. *J.P. Morgan
    Chase Bank v. Liberty Mutual Ins. Co.*, 2002 WL 113920 (S.D.N.Y. 2002).
    Draw a picture in the margin representing the lawyer-client relation-
    ships and the transactions at issue. It might look something like the
    picture below. There is no "official" way of symbolizing these cases,
    but you might want to settle on a convention, such as solid lines for
    existing attorney-client relationships and dashed lines for terminated
    relationships; arrows for flows of money or contractual obligations;
    ovals for law firms and rectangles for clients; and so on.

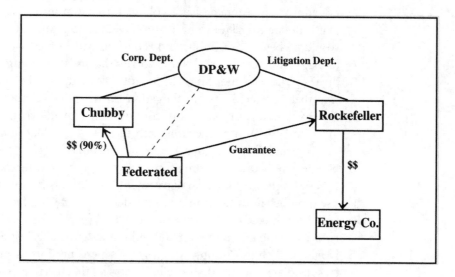

Then go through the steps in the analysis:

Identify client relationships

DP&W represents Chubby and Rockefeller, but not Federated, at least not directly. Thus, you may wonder whether you are representing a client where the representation of that client will be directly adverse to *another client* (Rule 1.7(a)). Maybe not, but nevertheless, this is a material limitation conflict. In some cases, a court might conclude that you are representing two clients who are directly adverse, if Federated and Chubby are alter egos of one another. (The court in the real case ducked that question.) This analysis turns on corporate law, so it probably is beyond the scope of what you will be required to know in a professional responsibility course. You should be aware of it, though, particularly if your teacher expects you to keep a look-out for the influence of other law on professional responsibility problems.

Is there a conflict?

The important thing is to figure out how DP&W's relationship with Chubby affects its ability to represent Rockefeller Bank effectively, and conversely, how its relationship with Rockefeller Bank affects its ability to represent Chubby effectively. Before turning to the legal analysis, make sure you understand factually and conceptually how the interests of the clients create tension for the lawyer. Think about how the lawyer is limited in her ability to provide competent and effective legal services to each client.

- *On behalf of Chubby*: The corporate and securities lawyers have to figure out what to do about disclosing the obligation on the bonds. There might be a way to craft the disclosure so that Chubby does not admit that Federated has an obligation, but instead discloses only that Federated is *alleged* to have an obligation. That kind of disclosure would be better for Chubby and Federated with respect to the litigation against Rockefeller. Chubby worries that its lawyers might "take a dive" on the securities filing, in order to please Rockefeller, by admitting that Federated has an obligation on the bonds. Chubby might also have a concern about the confidentiality of information it has given to DP&W in connection with the SEC filing. Maybe a defense that Federated could ordinarily assert in the bond litigation would not be effective because of some facts known to the securities lawyers at DP&W. Might the litigation department learn of this information and use it on behalf of Rockefeller to the detriment of Chubby?
- *On behalf of Rockefeller*: The litigators at DP&W very much would like to recover on the bonds. But a $200 million judgment against Federated would really hurt Chubby, which gets 90 percent of its income from its subsidiary, Federated. Rockefeller worries that its lawyers are more

concerned with protecting Chubby, so they will unnecessarily complicate the disclosures to the SEC, thus depriving Rockefeller of a way to establish its right to collect on the bonds.

Now that you are clear on the factual nature of the conflict, look at the rules. Arguably, this is not a "direct adversity" conflict under Model Rule 1.7(a)(1), because Federated is not a client of the firm—unless, as suggested above, Federated and Chubby are alter egos. If Federated is sufficiently central to Chubby's business, however, you might characterize this as a direct adversity conflict, even if Federated and Chubby technically are not alter egos for the purposes of corporation law. As the difference between two clients' positions becomes starker, it starts to look more and more like a situation of direct adversity of interests. Whatever you think about direct adversity, there is absolutely no question that this is *at least* a "material limitation" conflict under Model Rule 1.7(a)(2). For the reasons given above, there is substantial likelihood[10] that a lawyer working on each client's case would feel constrained not to take some course of action because it would hurt the other client's legal position.

If you are analyzing the question under the Restatement's test, remember that the Restatement collapses material limitation and direct adversity together, so that the test for the existence of a conflict is whether "the lawyer's representation of the client would be materially and adversely affected by the lawyer's . . . duties to another current client." Rest. §121. The unification of the tests reflects two considerations. First, direct adversity and material limitation are not different concepts, but poles on a continuum. Two clients can have positions that are more or less adverse. The more adverse they become, and the more closely related the interests that give rise to the conflict, the more likely it is that a court will characterize their positions as "directly adverse." Second, in practice it does not matter whether the conflict is the result of direct adversity or material limitation. The rest of the analysis is unchanged. The lawyer still must seek informed consent from the client and must not proceed with multiple representation if either affected client refuses to consent.

---

10. Note that the rule requires that there be "a significant risk" that the representation of one client will be materially limited by the lawyer's responsibilities to the other. See Rule 1.7(a) (2). This language is intended to caution against disqualifying lawyers from representing clients where the potential for conflict is purely speculative or conjectural, and there is no basis in the record for concluding that either of the clients' interests are being affected in some concrete way. As the comment to the rule states, "[t]he mere possibility of subsequent harm does not itself require disclosure and consent." Rule 1.7, cmt. [8]. This problem is way beyond the "mere possibility" stage, and into a very real impairment of the lawyers' ability to represent both clients effectively.

Is it consentable?

The comments to Model Rule 1.7 note that without consent, "a lawyer may not act as advocate in one matter against a person the lawyer represents in some other matter, even when the matters are wholly unrelated." Rule 1.7, cmt. [6]. No kidding — that would be direct adversity between two clients. The interesting question is whether Chubby and Rockefeller could consent to DP&W's representation of both. There are cases going both ways, although the modern trend is to permit clients to consent to being represented by a lawyer who also is representing an adverse party *in an unrelated matter*, provided that the lawyer obtained informed consent after consultation. You should be careful here, because not all courts permit consent in client-versus-client cases. And a lawyer is absolutely, positively prohibited from representing adverse parties in the same litigated matter. Rule 1.7(b)(3); Rest. §122(2)(b). That would be like a person trying to play chess against herself, and because of the courts' interest in the integrity of the adversary process, it is never permissible. In this problem, because Chubby and Rockefeller are highly sophisticated entity clients, they probably would be permitted to consent to the multiple representation, as long as the lawyers provided full *disclosure*.

Did all affected clients give informed consent?

In practice, the requirement of obtaining informed consent is going to be a big impediment to obtaining consent. Do you see why? In order to provide full disclosure, the lawyers may have to reveal confidential client information of one client to the other. Suppose a lawyer from DP&W approaches Chubby to seek consent. Imagine the conversation:

Lawyer: You should know, we are considering taking on a case for Rockefeller Bank, too.

Chubby: What does that have to do with me?

Lawyer: Well, they may be involved in a matter adverse to you.

Chubby: Really? What matter? What's going on?

At this point, the lawyer can either obfuscate or disclose the fact that Rockefeller is contemplating bringing a lawsuit against Federated. But what if Rockefeller's impending lawsuit is a Great Big Secret that Rockefeller does not want Federated to know about? (Maybe there is something Chubby could do to make it harder for Rockefeller to prevail if Chubby gets wind of the impending lawsuit.) If the lawyer tells Chubby, she has breached the firm's duty of confidentiality to Rockefeller, and that is a big problem. But if the lawyer does not inform Chubby of the impending litigation, she has not fully informed Chubby of the risks of accepting DP&W as its lawyers.

It gets uglier. A lawyer from DP&W can always approach Rockefeller and seek a waiver of confidentiality, permitting the firm to share the news of the impending lawsuit with Chubby. If the firm has a waiver, the discussion about multiple representation can proceed. But Rockefeller is highly unlikely to permit revelation if it really values secrecy. Moreover, the firm risks breaching its duty of confidentiality *to Chubby* if it reveals too much in the conversation with Rockefeller.

Without full disclosure, there cannot be informed consent. Obfuscating or waffling about the source of the lawyers' conflicting obligations is a really bad idea, because the "consent" obtained after that conversation will not be effective to cure the conflict. Thus, a conflict may be consentable in principle, but it may be impossible in practice to obtain informed consent, because there would be no way to give full disclosure without violating the duty of confidentiality to one or both clients.

Is the conflict imputed?

Up until now, the discussion has been as though "the lawyer" and "DP&W" are the same thing, even though Rockefeller would be represented by lawyers in the litigation department and Chubby would be represented by corporate and securities lawyers. These departments may be on different floors of the building, or even in different branch offices of the firm. Nevertheless, the different lawyers are treated as one for conflicts purposes. Rule 1.10(a).

Concurrent Conflicts Issues in Specific Contexts

CRIMINAL CASES

Criminal cases differ from civil cases in the importance of the constitutional protections afforded to criminal defendants, particularly the Sixth Amendment right to effective assistance of counsel. Many courts in criminal cases do not even consider state rules of professional conduct, but analyze only decisions interpreting the Sixth Amendment's guarantee. The constitutional issue generally is raised in a *habeas corpus* petition, claiming ineffective assistance of counsel. Thus, there is an overlap between the conflicts analysis here and the issue of ineffective assistance, discussed in Chapter 6. You should look briefly at that discussion if you are unsure of the operation of the *Strickland* test under the Sixth Amendment. See *Strickland v. Washington*, 466 U.S. 668 (1984).

Under *Strickland*, a convicted criminal defendant may obtain a new trial if he can show that counsel's performance fell below an objective standard of reasonableness *and* if this deficient representation created prejudice to the defendant. By "prejudice," the Court means that there is a reasonable probability that the result at trial would have been different. A reasonable probability is one sufficient to undermine our confidence that the trier of fact would have reached the same conclusion. If the evidence against the defendant at trial was overwhelming, courts will often resolve the *Strickland* test on the prejudice element, concluding that the defendant would have been convicted anyway. For this reason, *habeas corpus* petitioners very much would like to establish a rule that prejudice should be *presumed* in certain cases.[1] Then, the convicted person would have to show only that his lawyer made an error, without having the additional burden of establishing that the result at trial would have been different.

Representing conflicting interests is one kind of professional misconduct by criminal defense lawyers that reduces the petitioner's burden under *Strickland*. A series of constitutional cases show the circumstances under which a convicted criminal defendant would be entitled to relief because of a conflict. First, if the defendant's lawyer objects before trial to proceeding with an apparent conflict of interest, the trial court must investigate; failure to conduct an appropriate investigation justifies automatic reversal, without a requirement of showing prejudice. *Holloway v. Arkansas*, 435 U.S. 475 (1978). The theory behind this rule is that a lawyer has an obligation (stated in Rule 1.7) not to represent conflicting interests and to advise the court of a conflict. If the trial court ignores this objection and forces the lawyer to proceed, there is such a high likelihood that the ensuing trial will be unfair to one or more of the defendants that there is just no way the court can rely on the outcome of the trial to ensure fairness. Thus, courts presume prejudice in these instances.

In *Cuyler v. Sullivan*, 446 U.S. 335 (1980), however, the Court refused to extend the automatic-reversal rule to a case in which neither the lawyer nor the defendant objected before trial to the multiple representation. Because the lawyer has an obligation to inform the court of conflicts, if the lawyer does not object, the trial court is entitled to assume that there are no conflicting interests between jointly represented clients, or that all affected clients have accepted whatever risks are created by the conflict. Not all multiple representations present a conflict of interest. It might be a good thing if trial courts had a duty to monitor potential conflicts, as they do in the federal system, see Fed. R. Crim. P. 44(c), but the Supreme Court was unwilling to create a constitutional rule that would require state courts to conduct an investigation into the propriety of multiple representation in every case, absent an objection from counsel.

All is not lost for a client whose lawyer did not object to the multiple representation. The client still can claim ineffective assistance of counsel, by

---

1. "Petitioner," "defendant," and "client" are used interchangeably in this discussion to highlight the fact that many criminal-side conflicts cases arise on *habeas corpus* petitions in federal court.

reason of the conflict, as long as the client can demonstrate that "his counsel actively represented conflicting interests" and that "an actual conflict of interest adversely affected his lawyer's performance." *Burger v. Kemp*, 483 U.S. 776, 783 (1986). Thus, there is a two-part test for ineffective assistance of counsel, where the ineffectiveness is the result of the lawyer representing conflicting interests. In practice, however, the "actual conflict" element tends to collapse into the analysis of "adverse effect." In fact, the Supreme Court has said that "actual conflict of interest" is shorthand for a conflict that affected counsel's performance at trial, as opposed to a mere theoretical division of loyalties. *Mickens v. Taylor*, 535 U.S. 162 (2002). This statement just confirms the practice by courts of running these two prongs of the analysis together. The reason for collapsing these two elements is that the difference between a purely theoretical or potential conflict and an actual conflict depends on whether the multiple representation had some observable effect on the lawyer's performance at trial.

Criminal defense conflicts cases turn, therefore, on the adverse effect element. Note that adverse effect is something less than *Strickland* prejudice, because the petitioner does not have to show a reasonable probability that the result at trial would have been different — that is, that he would have been acquitted but for his lawyer's conflict of interest. Sometimes courts say that prejudice is presumed in conflicts cases. That is a bit misleading, because the petitioner still must show that "counsel is burdened by an *actual* conflict of interest" and that the conflict adversely affected the lawyer's performance. In other words, relying on the multiple representation alone is not enough. The client must point to some concrete act or omission that resulted from the lawyer's inability to represent all of the multiple clients effectively. To put it another way, the client must show that the lawyer was "influenced in his basic strategic decisions" by the need to take account of another person's interests. *Wood v. Georgia*, 450 U.S. 261, 272 (1981).

To get a sense for circumstances in which an actual conflict had an adverse effect on the representation, consider two cases discussed in the *Cuyler* opinion. In one of the cases, the defense lawyer failed to cross-examine a prosecution witness who inculpated one of the defendants, because the lawyer was trying to diminish the co-defendant's guilt. *Glasser v. United States*, 315 U.S. 60 (1942). The Court reversed the conviction because the multiple representation made it impossible for the lawyer to represent the first defendant effectively, by cross-examining the government witness, without impairing the representation of the second defendant. In a later case, by contrast, the defendant was unable to "identify an actual lapse in representation," so *habeas corpus* was inappropriate. *Dukes v. Warden*, 406 U.S. 250 (1972).

The following table summarizes the Sixth Amendment analysis:

Case	If defendant shows...	Then defendant obtains relief...
Holloway v. Arkansas	Timely objection to multiple representation	Automatic reversal; no need to show prejudice or adverse effect
Cuyler v. Sullivan	Actual conflict/"actively representing conflicting interests"	Reversal if the conflict resulted in an adverse effect on the lawyer's performance
Strickland v. Washington	Counsel's acts or omissions were outside the wide range of professionally competent assistance — not limited to representing conflicting interests	Reversal if there is a reasonable probability that, but for counsel's unprofessional errors, the result of the proceedings would have been different

Notice that the petitioner's burden increases as you read down the table. If there is a timely objection on the basis of a conflict and the trial court ignores it, the defendant's burden is nonexistent. In a conflicts case under *Cuyler*, the petitioner must show that the lawyer *actively* or *actually* represented conflicting interests, in the sense of being influenced in her trial strategy by the competent interests. That is more than showing nothing (which is the burden under *Holloway*), but less than the full-on *Strickland* burden of showing a reasonable probability that the result at trial would have been different.

When analyzing criminal defense conflicts cases, look for ways in which the lawyer's duty to D1 prevented him from doing something beneficial for D2. Some of the most common scenarios include:

- D1 and D2 have inconsistent defenses. For example, both defendants may want to claim that they were merely the driver of the getaway car, while the other defendant was the bank robber.
- One defendant has evidence that inculpates the other. For example, D2 may have lent D1 the gun that was used in the shooting, or D2 may have been an intermediary in a drug-distribution chain that ended with D1. The prosecution would therefore like to call D2 as a witness at D1's trial. See, for example, *Wheat v. United States*, 486 U.S. 153 (1988).
- A prosecution witness can put D1 at the scene but not D2. Discrediting the witness's testimony will help D1, but harm D2, because with respect to D2, the testimony is exculpatory. Thus, D2 would like the

jury to believe the witness, but D1 would like to see the witness's credibility undermined.

- In the plea-bargaining stage, one D may want to snitch in exchange for leniency.

Look for something similarly tangible before concluding that multiple representation is a violation of one or more of the defendants' Sixth Amendment rights. There are good reasons that co-defendants may desire joint representation, such as the ability to save on the expense of duplicative investigation and trial preparation. Coordinating defenses also helps resist the divide-and-conquer strategy favored by prosecutors, in which the government pressures one defendant to snitch on a co-defendant in exchange for an offer to plead guilty to a lesser charge. As noted above, if one of the defendants wants to roll over on his fellows, it would be a conflict of interest for the same lawyer to represent both clients. If all of the lawyer's clients are on the same page, however, and wish to maintain that solidarity in the face of prosecution attempts to flip one of the individual defendants, multiple representation might be not only permissible but quite desirable from the defendants' point of view.

The Supreme Court has suggested that the somewhat relaxed standard of *Cuyler*—in which the defendant need only show an adverse effect on the lawyer's performance, not full *Strickland* prejudice in the sense of a reasonable probability that the result at trial would have been different—might not apply to a *former client* conflict. *Mickens v. Taylor*, 535 U.S. 162 (2002). That case involved a lawyer who represented a defendant in a murder case, having previously represented the murder victim in an unrelated criminal matter. Strictly speaking, the Court held only that the defendant had failed to establish that the former client conflict had an adverse effect on his lawyer's performance. The Court noted that the case had been presented on the assumption that *Cuyler* provided the standard for assessing the counsel's performance. Writing for the majority, Justice Scalia questioned whether this assumption is warranted, in light of the reasons underlying the relaxed standard in *Cuyler*. In Justice Scalia's view, *Cuyler* is justified by the high probability of prejudice resulting from concurrent representation of multiple defendants and the difficulty of proving prejudice in those cases. In cases where these concerns are not present, however, the Court (or at least Justice Scalia) appears willing to apply the *Strickland* standard. These cases might include former client conflicts, like the one presented in *Mickens*, as well as personal interest conflicts such as cases in which the lawyer has media rights in the client's case. Keep your eye on this issue, as it is likely to develop through circuit court–level litigation for the time being, and you can expect some variation among the federal circuits.

The preceding discussion has been based on the client's Sixth Amendment right to effective assistance of counsel, but do not forget that a lawyer also may be subject to discipline for violating the local version of Model Rule 1.7 if the clients' interests are sufficiently divergent, and the clients have not consented to the multiple representation. When analyzing a multiple-client representation in a criminal case, be sure to consider both sources of law.

Examples

The Defendant's Burden

1. Lawyer represents Defendant 1 and Defendant 2 in a bank robbery case. At a preliminary hearing, the trial judge asks both defendants whether they are willing to be represented by the same lawyer. They both say "yes." Subsequent to the hearing, Lawyer's investigator talks to a bystander who says she definitely saw Defendant 2 waiting in a getaway car outside the bank. At trial, Lawyer defends the case using an alibi theory—she elicits testimony from both defendants to the effect that they were watching the premiere of the new James Bond movie. Lawyer attempted to impeach the eyewitness by establishing that she did not have a good view of the person in the getaway car. Both defendants are convicted. On federal *habeas*, Defendant 1 claims ineffective assistance of counsel. Should the petition be granted?
   A. No, because neither defendant objected to the dual representation.
   B. No, because Defendant 1 cannot point to any specific action the lawyer would have taken if she had not been concurrently representing Defendant 2.
   C. Yes, because courts presume prejudice in any concurrent representation case where there is a possibility of interference with the attorney's independent judgment.
   D. Yes. Defendant 1 was harmed by the concurrent representation because of Lawyer's desire to protect Defendant 2, which led her to use an alibi defense that is weaker than other defenses that Lawyer could have used.

When Is a Conflict Not a *Cuyler* Conflict?

2. Sanders is appointed to represent Mickey, who is accused of capital murder for killing Hill in the course of a sexual assault. Unknown to Mickey, Sanders had just been appointed to represent Hill in a minor criminal proceeding at the time of the killing. Sanders had met with Hill for about 30 minutes, but had done no other work on the case. Sanders never disclosed to the court that he represented Hill in the other matter. Mickey was convicted and sentenced to death. He now claims on *habeas corpus* that he received ineffective assistance of counsel because

his lawyer was laboring under a conflict of interest, by virtue of having represented Hill.

Having It Both Ways

3. LaRose is a criminal defense lawyer in private practice. He represented Rogers in a murder case, in which the prosecutor was Ms. Able, of the Perplexity District Attorney's office. At the same time, unknown to Rogers, LaRose was under investigation by the Perplexity District Attorney's office for allegedly conspiring with one of his clients to obstruct justice in a drug-distribution case. The lawyer in charge of that investigation was Mr. Baker. Baker notified LaRose that he was a target of the investigation, and the two entered into preliminary negotiations concerning the disposition of the matter.

While the investigation by Baker was ongoing, Rogers's case came up for trial. Rogers strongly believed that there had been police misconduct during the search, that the police had planted evidence linking him with the murder victim, and that the District Attorney's office had conspired with the police to submit a false affidavit in support of the application for a search warrant. He demanded that LaRose file a motion to suppress the evidence on the basis of police and prosecutorial misconduct. "No way," replied LaRose, "that's borderline frivolous. Besides, accusing the DA's office of submitting a false affidavit is sure to really make them mad. We'll do better by seeming reasonable and not slinging around accusations of doctoring the evidence." Over his client's continuing objection, LaRose decided not to file the suppression motion.

After his murder conviction was affirmed on direct appeal, Rogers learned about the investigation of LaRose by the DA's office. He filed a petition for federal *habeas corpus* relief, alleging that LaRose had provided ineffective assistance of counsel. Briefly assess his likelihood of success, considering the case under both *Cuyler* and *Strickland* — that is, assume that *Mickens* creates some uncertainty in the law as to which standard applies.

Explanations

The Defendant's Burden

1. The correct answer is D. Clearly, the answer was not C — the holding of *Cuyler* is that prejudice is not presumed in all concurrent representation cases. Similarly, based on *Cuyler*, A cannot be correct because a timely objection is not required to obtain *habeas* relief for a conflict, provided that there is some kind of actual effect on the representation. B is tricky, but on the facts it is not the correct answer. The lawyer defended the case

on a flimsy alibi theory, rather than putting on the testimony of the witness who inculpated Defendant 2 but did not see Defendant 1. A separate lawyer might have tried to argue that Defendant 2 was involved, but not Defendant 1, rather than having both defendants stand or fall together on the alibi and mistaken identity defense.

When Is a Conflict Not a *Cuyler* Conflict?

2. These are the facts of *Mickens v. Taylor*, 535 U.S. 162 (2002). Remember that criminal-side conflicts cases are governed by constitutional decisions interpreting the Sixth Amendment's guarantee of effective assistance of counsel. In an ordinary Sixth Amendment ineffectiveness case, you would have to run through the *Strickland* two-part test and ask whether there was: (1) an act or omission by the lawyer that falls outside the wide range of reasonable professional judgment (this is a very deferential standard, and courts often will assume that there is a good tactical reason for a lawyer to have done such-and-such); and (2) a reasonable likelihood that the result at trial would have been different. Conflicts reduce this burden somewhat. Mickey can obtain relief if he can show that Sanders actively represented conflicting interests and that this actual conflict adversely affected Sanders's performance at trial. This is a lower threshold than *Strickland* because Mickey does not have to show a reasonable probability that the *result* would have been different; he must show only that Sanders would have done something different (and helpful to Mickey) if Sanders had not been laboring under a conflict.

Factually speaking, what did Sanders do wrong here? First, notice that this is a former client conflicts case. Hill was dead by the time Sanders accepted the appointment to represent Mickey. Remember, though, that Sanders has an obligation to keep information he learned in the course of representing Hill confidential, even after his client is dead. Rest. §60, cmt. e. Perhaps Sanders learned something from Hill that could help Mickey. Mickey's argument is that Sanders would have learned facts that supported Mickey's theory that the sexual relations between Mickey and Hill were consensual. Specifically, Sanders might have learned that Hill was a prostitute. He would be precluded from developing this evidence at trial, however, because he had a continuing obligation to keep it secret. If Sanders had persuaded the jury that the sexual encounter between the defendant and the victim was consensual, maybe the jury would not have found that the murder occurred during the course of another crime, which was a prerequisite to the death sentence imposed on Mickey. The Court was able to duck this question by deferring to the district court, which found after an evidentiary hearing that it would have been impossible to claim that the sexual encounter was consensual, given the forensic evidence presented by the state. Similarly, despite Mickey's contention that his lawyer could have attacked Hill's character at trial (the familiar "blame the victim" strategy), a reasonable lawyer might choose not to do this, for fear it would backfire with the jury. For this reason, the district court concluded that the conflict asserted by Hill was "theoretical" only, not an actual conflict for the purposes of *Cuyler v. Sullivan*.

In the actual case, the Fourth Circuit (*en banc*) concluded that Mickens (the real Mickey) had not shown that a conflict of interest adversely affected the ability of Saunders (a.k.a. Sanders) to represent him effectively at trial. The Supreme Court did not address the question of whether that test (from *Cuyler v. Sullivan*) was the right one to apply in former client conflicts cases or, for that matter, any other kind of conflicts case other than an instance of simultaneous representation of co-defendants. The Court did not have to rule on this question because if Mickens did not meet his burden of showing an adverse effect on his lawyer's performance, then *a fortiori* he could not satisfy the higher burden of showing *Strickland* prejudice. But you can imagine cases that raise the open question flagged by the Court. What about a lawyer who has hornswoggled the client into signing over the rights to make a movie based on the case? That conduct probably violates Rule 1.8(d), and certainly creates a conflict of interest (the lawyer would rather see the case go to trial than accept a plea bargain because plea deals make for pretty boring movies), but it is not a case of concurrent representation of co-defendants like those in *Cuyler* and *Holloway*.

Keep your eye on this open issue, because it may come before the Court in a future term. If you should encounter it on an exam, think about the policies that underlie the rules in these Sixth Amendment cases.

Having It Both Ways

3. This example is based on *Rugiero v. United States*, 330 F. Supp. 2d 990 (E.D. Mich. 2004). As discussed in the explanation to Example 2, the Supreme Court in *Mickens* has strongly hinted that *Cuyler* is appropriate only for simultaneous-representation conflicts. Former-client conflicts (as in the *Mickens* case itself) and personal-interest conflicts like this one may be thrown back into *Strickland*. (If you need a review of *Strickland*, see Chapter 6.) It is considerably easier for the defendant to obtain relief under *Cuyler*, as compared with *Strickland*, so it may make a great deal of difference which framework applies.

Under *Cuyler*, if an actual conflict of interest had an adverse effect on the representation, the lawyer violated the Sixth Amendment. In this case, the conflict arises from the lawyer's desire not to aggravate the prosecutor's office. In Model Rules terms, this would be an instance where the lawyer's interest materially limits his ability to provide effective representation to a client. Rule 1.7(a)(2). But the conflict alone is not enough to make out a Sixth Amendment violation — the petitioner must also show adverse effect defined, as many of you pointed out, as some kind of identifiable, concrete step the lawyer failed to take because of the conflict. A good way to think about the adverse effect standard is in terms of what an impartial, independent lawyer would do if unencumbered by the conflict.

Here, the adverse effect would be the lawyer's refusal to file the suppression motion. This argument is made somewhat more complicated by the fact that the lawyer said the motion was "borderline frivolous." Furthermore, the Supreme Court in *Jones v. Barnes*, 463 U.S. 745 (1983), confirmed the traditional authority lawyers have to make decisions concerning the means by which representation will be carried out. Cf. Rule 1.2(a). However, one might worry that the lawyer's evaluation of the frivolousness of the client's position may be influenced by the lawyer's desire not to make waves with the prosecutor. Criminal defense lawyers file suppression motions all the time, even if it does run the risk of angering the prosecutor (which is, in any event, rather unlikely). Thus, it seems like the lawyer is trying to cover his own behind, not provide the most effective representation to his client. On the other hand, you might have argued for no actual effect on the basis of the lawyer's authority to control the means by which the representation is carried out. See Rule 1.2(a). The Supreme Court in both *Cuyler* and *Strickland* took pains to emphasize that a lawyer's professional judgment should not be evaluated too critically in hindsight, because there might be good tactical reasons for not taking some action that the client would have preferred.

Under *Strickland*, courts are highly deferential to lawyers' strategic decisions. In this case, however, the petitioner may have some hope if he can convince the court that his lawyer's purportedly strategic decision was influenced by his desire not to tick off the prosecutor's office. Courts' assessment of reasonableness is influenced by prevailing professional norms, including the official statements of the organized bar. You might cite Rule 1.7(a)(2) to show that the lawyer committed an unprofessional error. In addition, as noted above, the authority of the defendant to make important strategic decisions is relevant to the analysis of error. If the suppression motion is more like an "ends" decision than a "means" decision, this would add weight to the conclusion that the lawyer committed an unprofessional error.

On the prejudice prong of *Strickland*, it's difficult to evaluate the likelihood that Rogers would have been convicted but for counsel's unprofessional error, because the record a court would use to make this determination was developed by the lousy lawyer. Less theoretically, there aren't enough facts in this problem upon which to base a definitive analysis of prejudice. You don't know what the evidence was that would have been excluded if the suppression motion were granted, and you don't know what other evidence the state introduced. It's reasonable to assume that evidence discovered during a search would be highly probative of guilt, but you don't know for sure. If you see something like this on an exam, be prepared to argue in a hypothetical mode (for example, "If the court is convinced that the result at trial would have been the same regardless of the lawyer's refusal to file the suppression motion—that is, if the evidence that was admitted was cumulative or otherwise not particularly significant—then the court can decide the case on prejudice.").

TRANSACTIONAL MATTERS

The interests of parties in litigation are often made clear through procedural devices—complaints, cross-claims, third-party complaints, and the like. In transactions, there are not the same formal indications of the alignment of the parties, but nevertheless there may be interests that diverge. There may be some aspect of a transaction that will put one or the other of the parties at a disadvantage. For example, in a sales transaction it may be necessary for the buyer to offer some kind of security interest to the seller, and the way the security arrangement is structured may favor either the buyer or the seller. The seller may prefer a lien on the property being sold, while if the buyer is a corporation it may prefer a lien on the corporation's stock. If the buyer goes bankrupt before it finishes paying, the seller would be out of luck if it only had a lien on the buyer's stock.

These are the risks that lawyers in transactional cases haggle about, trying to obtain the best deal for their clients. If one lawyer tries to represent more than one client, though, there is a risk that the lawyer may "sell out" the interests of one client in order to get a better deal for the other. On the other hand, there are good reasons that the parties to a transaction may want only one lawyer to represent all of them. They may have worked out the material terms of the deal and may need the lawyer to serve only as a "scrivener" to memorialize the terms of the arrangement. The deal may be simple and straightforward, such as a residential real estate closing, and the parties may regard having separate lawyers as a waste of money. Even in more complex deals, lawyers sometimes appear to be "deal breakers," who are always thinking in terms of the ways the parties' interests diverge; from the parties' point of view, it may be better to have a single lawyer representing everyone, so that the lawyer will be focused on finding win-win solutions.

The concurrent conflicts rule, Rule 1.7, applies with the same force to transactional work as to litigation. Just as in litigation, the parties' interests may be directly adverse, as in the case of a buyer and seller in negotiations over a transaction. Rule 1.7, cmt. [7]. There also may be cases in which the lawyer's work on behalf of one party to a transaction is materially limited by her representation of another party, another client who is not a party to the transaction, or for some other reason. The tricky question usually is not whether there is a conflict—in general, there will be at least a "material limitation" conflict under Rule 1.7(a)(2) if the lawyer represents more than one party in a deal—but whether the conflict is consentable.

Consentability turns on whether it is possible to harmonize the parties' positions or whether the interests of the parties are "fundamentally antagonistic to each other." Rule 1.7, cmt. [28]. In a simple sales transaction, a single lawyer may be able to represent both the buyer and the seller, with consent, if the parties already have agreed on material terms such as price, time and manner of payment, security arrangements, and so on. As the transaction becomes more complex, however, it may be impossible for the parties to work out the terms for themselves, without the assistance of a lawyer; in that case, the lawyer's involvement would tend to favor one side at the expense of the other, and thereby make the conflict nonconsentable. In some complex deals, a single lawyer may represent multiple parties with consent if it is possible for the lawyer to assist the parties in developing a mutually advantageous arrangement. Generally, this would be possible if the negotiations are not a zero-sum game, so that there would be a solution that is to the advantage of all the parties. It is extremely dangerous, however, to purport to act only as a "scrivener," to memorialize the terms of the transaction independently agreed to by the parties. Most courts will say that, if the lawyer is actually representing either or both parties, the lawyer has duties to use reasonable care to counsel the clients on the terms that would be advantageous to them. As far as I am aware, all arguments that lawyers served as mere scriveners have been rejected in malpractice cases. See, for example, *Simpson v. James*, 903 F.2d 372 (5th Cir. 1990).

Examples

Playing Both Sides

4. Stevens is a real estate lawyer who handles complex commercial real estate transactions. One of his long-time clients is Frances, a developer. Recently, he took a matter on behalf of two sisters, Nieman and Baltasar, who had inherited a sizeable plot of land from their father. The sisters instructed Stevens to find a buyer for the land, which was suitable for subdivision and construction of single-family homes. They told him they would not accept less than $110,000 per lot for the land, and wanted the contract subject only to the contingency of preliminary subdivision

approval. Stevens told Nieman and Baltasar that he represented Frances and asked them to sign a waiver letter. The letter provided, in part:

> You have indicated to us that you represent Frances, the Buyer in the transaction we have discussed. You have pointed out to us potential conflicts of interest if you represent us as Sellers and Frances as Buyer. Notwithstanding such conflicts, we request that you represent us in connection with the sale of the subject property.

After Nieman and Baltasar signed the letter, Stevens prepared a contract conveying the land to Frances for $110,000 per lot. The contract was contingent on Frances obtaining subdivision approval within 18 months.

Near the end of the 18-month contingency period, Frances told Stevens that he had an opportunity to sell the land to Massimo, a major builder of high-end houses, for $200,000 per lot. Frances was worried that he would not be able to obtain subdivision approval in time. He asked Stevens whether he would see if Nieman and Baltasar would agree to extend the contingency period for another six months, in exchange for Frances releasing the $50,000 deposit he had put down. Stevens had this conversation with Nieman and Baltasar, and they agreed to extend the subdivision approval period. Subsequently, Frances obtained the approval, took possession of the land under the contract, and sold it to Massimo, making a profit of $90,000 per lot. When Nieman and Baltasar heard about this transaction, in which Stevens had represented Frances in the sale to Massimo, they were outraged. They sued Stevens for breach of fiduciary duty, claiming he impermissibly represented clients with conflicting interests. Analyze the conflict in this case.

Houston . . . We Have a Problem

5. This example is a review not only of conflicts in transactional matters, but also of other professional obligations. Consider the following sequence of events, and think about the duties owed by the law firm to its clients.

- H and W, a married couple, go to an estate planning partner at the law firm to prepare joint wills. The firm runs a conflicts check, but the paralegal entering the names spells H's last name incorrectly. No conflicts turn up. The partner has H and W sign waiver letters indicating that they consent to the firm representing them jointly for the purpose of preparing the wills.
- The structure of the joint wills is that if either spouse dies before the other, that spouse's property passes to the other, and after the second spouse's death, the property passes to the surviving "issue"—that is, children—of the spouse.

- A different partner in the firm, in the litigation department, takes a new matter for a client, M, who wishes to file a paternity action against the father of her child. As you may have guessed, the father is H. The partner runs a conflicts check, but this time the person entering the names spells H's name correctly, so the firm's representation of H is not discovered.
- On behalf of M, the litigation partner sends a letter to H demanding that he submit to a blood test to establish paternity. H gets a lawyer at a different firm, agrees to the test, and discovers that he has additional "issue" out there in the world.
- M's lawyer requests that H provide financial information. H replies, "You already have it at your firm—you're representing me in my estate planning."

At this point, the firm has three clients—H, W, and M. What duties are owed to each, and what should the firm do?

Explanations

Playing Both Sides

4. This example is based loosely on an important case from the New Jersey Supreme Court, *Baldasarre v. Butler*, 625 A.2d 458 (N.J. 1993). At first, it looks like the lawyer did everything right, but when you go through the analysis in detail, you will see that he deserves to lose this breach of fiduciary duty action. *Baldasarre*, in fact, announced a bright-line rule in New Jersey that "an attorney may not represent both the buyer and the seller in a complex commercial real estate transaction *even if both give their informed consent.*" 625 A.2d at 467 (emphasis added).

   Go through the four-step conflicts analysis discussed in Chapter 14. First, it is easy to identify the clients—they are the sellers and the buyer. Second, is there a conflict? The test for the existence of a conflict is whether under Rule 1.7(a)(1) the interests of Frances and Nieman and Baltasar are directly adverse, or whether Stevens's ability to represent Frances is materially limited by his representation of Nieman and Baltasar, and vice versa, under Rule 1.7(a)(2). What are the interests of both clients? Obviously, they want to get the best possible deal in terms of what they regard as important in the transaction. The sellers wanted as much money as possible and few contingencies in the contract. The buyer wanted to pay as little as possible, but we do not know about other interests—maybe he wanted lots of contingencies so it would be easy to back out of the deal if he could not obtain financing on favorable terms or could not find a buyer for the land. In any event, the nature of the conflict between the buyer and the sellers is that it probably is difficult for one lawyer to come up with a win-win solution. Any contract term that works to the advantage of the sellers is probably not in the interests of the buyer, and any provision that is favorable to the buyer is similarly probably not in the interests of the seller.

At the outset, there may not have been a conflict, but once Massimo comes on the scene, the interests of the two clients certainly are at odds. Remember that an attorney has an ongoing obligation to keep abreast of conflicts. The parties' interests may start out as harmonious, but later may come into conflict because of the actions of others. (Remember the *Fiandaca* case, discussed in Chapter 14, where the state's offer of settlement brought the two classes of plaintiffs into direct conflict.) Massimo offers the opportunity for either the original buyer or seller to make more money, but not both. Either Nieman and Baltasar sell to Massimo for $200,000 per lot, or Frances does, but they both cannot realize the windfall. Stevens could advise both Nieman and Baltasar as well as Frances about Massimo's offer, and suggest that they split the difference, but this advice already represents a second-best outcome for Nieman and Baltasar. If they hold fast on the contingency and allow the contract with Frances to lapse, they can keep control of the property and sell it to Massimo themselves. They only way Frances would have anything to sell to Massimo is if Nieman and Baltasar agree to extend the contingency period, and if they are interested in maximizing their profit, there is no way they would agree to the extension with the knowledge of Massimo's offer. Of course, from the standpoint of Frances, he is worse off if Stevens informs Nieman and Baltasar of Massimo's offer, because he will lose the opportunity buy for $110,000 per lot and immediately turn around and sell for $200,000. He would prefer Stevens keep the information secret from his other clients.

You may see cases where the lawyer claims she was hired only as the "scrivener"—that is, as someone to set down in writing the terms the parties had already agreed upon among themselves. See, for example, *State v. Callahan*, 652 P.2d 708 (Kan. 1982). As the Restatement comments point out, however, "scrivener" is usually the wrong characterization of the lawyer's role, because a lawyer always has a duty to provide independent advice and act in the best interests of each client, in the absence of the client's informed consent to a limited scope of representation. Rest. §130, cmt. b. Maybe, in a very simple transaction, a lawyer could serve as a scrivener. If my neighbors, A and B, agreed between them that A would sell his lawn tractor to B for $1,000 cash, and they for some reason wanted to put this agreement in writing, I suppose I could draft it for them without favoring the interests of one over the other. But as soon as this transaction becomes at all complex, it is unlikely that I could represent both without taking sides, as it were. Suppose B did not pay cash and A wanted some kind of security for the transaction. There are ways of structuring the transaction that are better for A and others that are better for B. Which do I recommend? Maybe the sale price is a lousy deal for A, because for some reason he grossly underestimated the value of his tractor. If I know this, can I advise A not to sell for less than $2,000? Doesn't that harm B?

In short, it is a virtual certainty that any complex transaction will involve at least "material limitation" conflicts under Rule 1.7(a)(2). This is true even where all the parties to the transaction have a common objective, such as forming mutually profitable corporation, partnership, or joint venture. Consider an illustration from the Restatement:

> A, B, and C are interested in forming a partnership in which A is to provide the capital, B the basic patent, and C the management skill. Only C will spend significant amounts of time operating the business. A, B, and C jointly request Lawyer to represent them in creating the partnership. The different contributions to be made to the partnership alone indicate that the prospective partners have conflicts of interest with respect to the structure and governance of the partnership.

Rest. §130, Illus. 4.

A conflict such as the Restatement's example probably is consentable, but the lawyer will have to provide very careful disclosures of the ways in which the clients' interests might diverge. For example, C might come to feel that her skillful management of the enterprise is what has created value for the partners, not B's patent. B may feel frozen out of day-to-day operations and may think that C is not doing enough to maximize the value of his patent. A may want some kind of additional security for her investment, in light of the risky nature of the business, and therefore may demand that the partnership agreement be structured in such a way to give her interests in partnership assets that are superior to those of the other partners. The lawyer will have to explain to A, B, and C that each of them must forego the opportunity to get the best possible deal at the expense of the other partners. If the lawyer can anticipate a contingency under which one of the partners would be better or worse off than the others, she must explain this to the partners as part of the disclosure preceding consent. Again, the partners' consent is required even if all of their interests are aligned at a higher level of generality. They all truly want the partnership to succeed, but how they might fare given the vicissitudes of business depends on how their partnership is structured. As a result, they need to know that they are giving up something of value—the opportunity to have an independent lawyer to protect their interests—in exchange for accepting joint representation.

What about the real estate transaction example considered here? Is the conflict consentable? The New Jersey Supreme Court said "no," but on the basis of a blanket rule that multiple representation is never appropriate in complex commercial real estate transactions. At the outset of representation, the conflict probably was consentable. The clients could have agreed, for example, that there would be no confidentiality among the joint clients. If Stevens learned anything that would be material to the interests of either the buyer or the sellers, he would have to inform all of them. That means in this case telling Nieman and Baltasar of Massimo's offer to purchase for $200,000 per lot. If the lawyer had not obtained waivers of confidentiality in advance from all his clients, though, he might be in a real pickle. He would be precluded by the duty of confidentiality in Rule 1.6 (owed to Frances) from informing Nieman and Baltasar of the offer, but he also would be required by the duty of communication in Rule 1.4 (owed to Nieman and Baltasar) to pass along the information. He simply cannot fulfill one duty without violating the other. Thus, he would have a nonconsentable conflict and would be forced to withdraw from representing both the sellers and the buyer. Remember the standard — a conflict is not consentable if the lawyer does not reasonably believe that he can provide competent and diligent representation to each affected client. Rule 1.7(b)(1). That test is not satisfied here, and the conflict is nonconsentable. If the deal were simpler, and presented fewer opportunities for a skillful lawyer to benefit one client at the expense of the other, the conflict may have been consentable. Other jurisdictions permit simultaneous representation of buyers and sellers in straightforward residential real estate transactions, provided that both parties give informed consent. See, for example, Vermont Bar Ass'n Comm'n on Prof. Resp. Op. 2001-02.

Houston . . . We Have a Problem

5. This is a real case, believe it or not. *A v. B*, 726 A.2d 924 (N.J. 1999). It also is the basis for Rest. §60, Illus. 2 & 3. The case is exactly the sort of thing that gives lawyers the heebie-jeebies, because even a very careful law firm with good conflicts checking procedures got in trouble. (There is one prevention step the firm should have taken, though, which will be discussed.) First, in order to think functionally about the conflicts of interest, think about the duties the firm owes to the two clients, H and M, setting aside for the moment the duty under Rule 1.7 not to represent clients whose interests are directly adverse:

> **To H:** Duty of confidentiality, not to reveal financial information to M, or anyone else, except in response to a legitimate discovery request. Also duty of confidentiality not to reveal existence of extramarital affair to W or anyone else. Rule 1.6.[2]

---

2. Note that the firm has a duty of confidentiality to H with respect to the information learned from M. Do not confuse the duty of confidentiality with the attorney-client privilege, which covers only communications from the client for the purpose of obtaining legal advice. Information learned from third parties is covered by the duty of confidentiality but not the attorney-client privilege. See Chapter 7 for an overview of these rules.

To W: Duty of communication, to keep W informed of developments that she should know about in order to make informed decisions. Rule 1.4. The fact that some of her property might pass to the child resulting from H's extramarital affair is definitely germane to her decision about how to structure her will. The provision leaving property to "all issue" has a different significance if W is aware of H's child by M.

To M: Obligation to be an effective and diligent representative, to investigate the matter thoroughly and obtain information as efficiently as possible. Rule 1.1. This means using informal means of discovery and taking advantage of fortuitously obtained financial information about H.

The point of the analysis of the professional duties is to emphasize that the conflicts rules do not exist in a vacuum. They have the purpose of safeguarding against other professional failures. The reason the firm is prohibited from representing both H and M is that it is impossible to be a complete lawyer for both. Something has to give. One of the duties must end up being subordinated to another, and the client to whom the subordinate duty is owed is not going to be very happy.[3]

So what duty yields to what other duty here? The lawyers in this case said some words you do not necessarily hear every day, "Thank goodness we're in New Jersey!" The reason is that New Jersey has a version of the confidentiality rule that permits (but does not require) a lawyer to disclose confidential client information to the extent the lawyer reasonably believes necessary to "rectify the consequences of a client's . . . fraudulent act in furtherance of which the lawyer's services had been used." New Jersey Rule of Professional Conduct 1.6(c), cited in *A v. B*, 726 A.2d at 927. Citing a number of cases interpreting the crime-fraud exception to the attorney-client privilege, the court held that H's conduct was "fraudulent" for the purposes of the exception to the duty of confidentiality. "[T]he husband's deliberate omission of the existence of his illegitimate child constitutes a fraud on his wife." This is bad for H, but good for the law firm, because now the lawyers can disclose the child to W, who will be in a position to alter her will.

If the firm did not have this permission under the New Jersey version of Model Rule 1.6, it would have been in an insoluble dilemma — either breaching the duty of confidentiality to H, or breaching the duty of communication to W. Outside of New Jersey, the law firm would have been in a real bind. The Restatement recommends a rule that the lawyer would have discretion to disclose the information "if, in the lawyer's reasonable judgment, the immediacy and magnitude of the risk to the

---

3. See Chapter 14 for a discussion of confidentiality-related conflicts and New York City Bar Association Formal Op. 2005-02. Using the reasoning of that opinion, this is a case in which the confidential information of one client is so material to the representation of another client that possession of the information creates a conflict.

affected co-client outweigh the interest of the communicating client in continued secrecy." Rest. §60, cmt. l. The *A v. B* case approves this position and would permit the firm to disclose the illegitimate child, but only if "the other spouse's failure to learn of the information would be materially detrimental to the other spouse or frustrate the spouse's intended testamentary arrangement." *A v. B*, 726 A.2d at 929. As the Reporter's Note to this comment indicates, however, there are no reported cases approving the rule, beyond *A v. B* itself, which was decided under the idiosyncratic New Jersey confidentiality rule.

A careful lawyer could have planned for this contingency. As the court also points out, a lawyer should consider obtaining waivers of confidentiality whenever representing clients jointly. That is, the lawyer should obtain H's and W's informed consent that nothing they tell their lawyer will be confidential from the other co-client, although of course the lawyer will continue to keep the information confidential from the rest of the world. Lawyers should obtain waivers of confidentiality in *any* joint representation, not just estate planning cases, to avoid being whipsawed between professional duties. For example, one favorite fact pattern for professional responsibility exams has the lawyer representing two partners, X and Y, in setting up a partnership. Several months pass, and X comes in to the lawyer's office to confess that he has been embezzling from the partnership. Can the lawyer tell Y? Yes, if the lawyer has planned ahead and obtained waivers of confidentiality from both X and Y. If not, then the lawyer is in the position of a non–New Jersey law firm in the estate planning case.

POSITIONAL ("ISSUE") CONFLICTS

Imagine that you are an associate doing pro bono work for a low-income family that is the debtor in a collection case brought by J.C. Farthing, a large retailer. You want to raise an issue of the constitutionality of a state pretrial attachment statute that allows Farthing to retake possession of the property upon the filing of a complaint. Another client of your firm is another retailer called Steers; it places collection work with a small firm in town and uses your firm for employment and labor cases, as well as commercial lease disputes. You have disclosed this fact to the pro bono client, and after convincing the client that you will be an effective advocate in the case against Farthing despite the firm's representation of Steers, the client agrees in writing to waive conflicts. Steers loves the pretrial attachment statute, and when it reads an article in the local bar newsletter about the associate's challenge to the statute, it calls up the managing partner of the firm and complains. The implicit threat is that it will move to intervene in the Farthing lawsuit and disqualify the firm. Will this conflict result in the firm's disqualification from the pro bono case?

First of all, note that there is no Rule 1.7(a)(1) direct adversity, because the firm is working against J.C. Farthing, not Steers. Is there a Rule 1.7(a)(2) "material limitation" on the lawyer's ability to represent the debtor and on the firm's continuing ability to represent Steers? Analyze the conflict in both directions. Perhaps the associate's desire not to anger partners in the firm, who depend on Steers for a substantial amount of revenue, would materially limit her ability to represent the pro bono client. Going in the other direction, the pro bono case almost certainly does not limit the ability of the firm to work on employment and leasing matters for Steers. To put it bluntly, the firm can ram the pro bono case down Steers's throat, if it wishes. Steers certainly has an expectation that the firm will be loyal to its interests, but this expectation of loyalty cannot be unbounded. Rather, the *justified* expectation of loyalty on the part of Steers does not extend to an ability to restrain the firm from doing anything that would potentially annoy or harm Steers. As long as the precise issue at stake in the pro bono litigation does not arise in cases for which the firm is representing Steers in the same jurisdiction, Steers has nothing to complain about.

Making the problem more difficult, assume the firm represents Steers in collection matters in other jurisdictions, perhaps through a branch office in another state. Does that change the conflicts analysis under Rule 1.7(a)(2)? The modified hypothetical presents what is known as a "positional" conflict. The risk in a positional conflict is that one lawyer in the firm may score a victory for one client that would have the result of establishing an unfavorable precedent, which would be to the detriment of another client of the firm. The ABA's ethics committee has concluded that in some cases, the firm would be required to seek consent of both Steers and the pro bono client:

> [I]f there is a substantial risk that the law firm's representation of one client will create a legal precedent. . .which is likely materially to undercut the legal position *being urged on behalf of the other client*, the lawyer should either refuse to accept the second representation [the pro bono case] or (if otherwise possible) withdraw from the first, unless both clients consent after full disclosure of the ramifications.

ABA Formal Op. 93-377. The italicized language distinguishes the first version of this hypothetical, where the firm did not represent Steers in collection matters. "General antagonism" between clients does not create an impermissible conflict of interest; it must be the result of "conflict in the interests of the clients that are involved in the matters being handled by the lawyer." Rest. §121, cmt. c(iii).

Note, too, that the ABA opinion depends on the two matters being litigated in the same jurisdiction—that is, the language about creating a legal precedent. What if the matters are in different jurisdictions, so that the associate's work for the pro bono client would not create a precedent that harms Steers in the cases for which the law firm is representing it? In that case, the ABA committee says that the lawyer should consider a number of factors. The first is the importance of the issue to the clients' legal position — that is, whether it will create a persuasive precedent that may affect the ultimate outcome of one of the cases. Another way to state this factor is whether the issue is likely to have a significant impact on the law, as in an evolving or developing area of law. In addition, the firm should ask whether either lawyer will be tempted to soft-pedal her advocacy on behalf of one of the clients. Perhaps the firm may try to finesse the conflict by subtly altering the arguments, perhaps to the detriment of one of the clients. If this is a possibility, there is a conflict under Rule 1.7(a)(2), and both clients must consent.

Comment [24] to Rule 1.7 notes that there may be a conflict when the lawyer's representation of one client may create a precedent that seriously would weaken the position taken on behalf of the other client. The likelihood of this risk depends on factors such as the jurisdictions in which the two matters are pending, whether the issues involved in the two cases pertain to substantive matters or are procedural only, and the importance of these legal issues to the clients. See also Rest. §128, cmt. f.

THE "ETERNAL TRIANGLE" FOR INSURANCE DEFENSE LAWYERS

When a lawyer represents someone who is covered by a liability insurance policy, a triangular relationship results. The policy requires the insurance company to defend its policyholder in certain categories of lawsuits (for example, those arising out of an automobile accident), to pay for a lawyer to conduct the defense, and to indemnify the policyholder for any judgment that is entered against her, up to the limits stated in the policy. The lawyer is hired and paid by the insurance company, but charged with the responsibility of defending the policyholder's interests in the lawsuit.[4] In addition, the insurance company may exercise some degree of control over the lawyer's day-to-day work on behalf of the policyholder, often as a cost-control measure. You can see how there would be a potential for the lawyer to feel the pull of competing loyalties — toward the insurance company that is a source of repeat business, which pays the lawyer's bills and supervises the

---

4. The insured/insurer terminology can be confusing, so the parties are referred to as the "policyholder" and the "insurance company" or the "company."

lawyer's work, and toward the client whose interests the lawyer is hired to represent.[5] Hence the image of the triangle.

You may or may not spend much time on issues specific to insurance defense practice. Substantive insurance law matters here, and many professional responsibility teachers do not want to get bogged down on doctrines like equitable subrogation and bad-faith denial of coverage. Even if you do not talk much about insurance defense cases in class, you should make sure you understand the analysis of the professional responsibility issues in this section. It is a good review of matters we have dealt with elsewhere, such as client identification, concurrent conflicts, and the duty of confidentiality.

Client Identification

If the lawyer owes the policyholder a duty to protect its interests, and owes a duty to the insurance company to keep it informed about the progress of the case, keep defense costs under control, and give the insurance company an opportunity to accept or reject settlement offers, it looks like the attorney may have two separate clients. The duties of effective representation and communication are fundamental aspects of the attorney-client relationship, so it seems like this professional relationship exists with respect to both the policyholder and the company. In fact, the traditional view, followed by many courts, is the "dual client doctrine," under which the defense lawyer represents both the policyholder and the insurance company as long as their interests coincide. See, for example, *State Farm Mutual Automobile Ins. Co. v. Federal Ins. Co.*, 86 Cal. Rptr. 2d 20 (1999). Some courts, confusingly, say that the lawyer's primary obligation is to the policyholder, leaving open the possibility that the lawyer may have secondary obligations to the company. Other jurisdictions maintain that the policyholder is the lawyer's sole client for the purpose of professional duties such as communication, confidentiality, and refraining from representing conflicting interests. See, for example, *Atlanta Int'l Ins. Co. v. Bell*, 475 N.W.2d 294 (Mich. 1991). In any jurisdiction, the defense lawyer has the full gamut of professional duties to the policyholder; the only question is whether the lawyer has additional obligations to the company. When you work through these problems, remember that under no circumstances may the lawyer treat the policyholder's interests as secondary to the company's.

---

5. The triangular relationship among insured, insurer, and defense counsel is the subject of countless articles. If you find this issue interesting, or you have technical questions that are beyond the scope of this necessarily brief treatment, check out Douglas R. Richmond, *Lost in the Eternal Triangle of Insurance Defense Ethics*, 9 Geo. J. Legal Ethics 475 (1996) or Robert E. O'Malley, *Ethics Principles for the Insurer, the Insured, and Defense Counsel: The Eternal Triangle Reformed*, 66 Tulane L. Rev. 511 (1991).

The ABA has observed that a lawyer is free to specify the structure of her relationship with the two potential clients, as long as the clients give informed consent. The lawyer and the clients can agree that the lawyer represents (1) the policyholder only; (2) both the policyholder and the company for all purposes; or (3) both the policyholder and the company for all purposes except settlement, in which case counsel represents the policyholder. ABA Formal Op. 96-403. In the absence of an agreement like this, however, courts will fall back on the local default rule — either dual client or single client (policyholder only). If the jurisdiction follows the dual client doctrine, be alert for conflicts and confidentiality issues.

Conflicts

There are several patterns of divergent interests in insurance defense practice. Each of them creates at least a potential conflict of interest under Rule 1.7.

Reservation of Rights

The company's obligation to defend the policyholder in lawsuits arises under its contract of coverage, which may have exclusions for particular kinds of harms. A company may conditionally agree to defend under its policy, believing that it has defenses to coverage. For example, a liability insurance policy may cover negligence but not intentional torts, and the company may suspect that the act in question was intentional. Rather than simply refuse to deny coverage, which creates a risk that the company will be held liable for bad faith, it may defend the action under a reservation of rights. That means it sends a letter to its policyholder notifying her that there may be defenses to coverage, but the company will pay for the defense anyway, leaving the coverage issue to be litigated later.

A reservation of rights letter may put the lawyer in a bind. In the case of an intentional-torts exclusion, the policyholder's interest would be to develop facts that suggest negligence, while the company's interest would be to conduct an investigation and discovery with an aim to finding facts to support an inference of intentional conduct. The lawyer is charged with the responsibility of representing the policyholder's interests, but realistically speaking, the lawyer also is worried about keeping the insurance company happy. It is, after all, paying her bills in this case and may well represent a significant source of business for the lawyer. If the lawyer does "throw" the case for the benefit of the company, however, she runs a serious risk of a malpractice action by the policyholder if the policyholder suffers a judgment at trial in excess of policy limits. For this reason, several states have attempted to deal with this conflict situation by requiring the company to appoint independent counsel, at the company's expense, to represent the policyholder's interests alone. See, for example, *San Diego Fed. Credit Union v. Cumis Ins. Soc'y*, 208 Cal. Rptr. 494 (Ct. App. 1984). Other courts simply have reminded the company that it has a heightened obligation of good faith and must thoroughly investigate the plaintiff's claim; retain competent counsel to defend the policyholder, who regards the policyholder as her sole client; keep the policyholder informed about all material facts affecting the case, including coverage issues; and refrain from treating the company's financial interests as superior to the policyholder's potential exposure. *Tank v. State Farm Fire & Cas. Co.*, 715 P.2d 1133 (Wash. 1986).

In states that do not have formal mechanisms, like in the *Cumis* and *Tank* cases, for dealing with these conflicts, watch out for fact patterns in which the lawyer seems to be favoring the company's interests over those of the policyholder. Remember that a lawyer will be required to treat the policyholder's interests as paramount because of the company's duty of good faith, regardless of whether there are prophylactic measures like independently appointed counsel.

Settlement

Consider a case in which the policyholder defendant has a potential defense to liability, reasonably high policy limits, and substantial exposure to an excess judgment if the plaintiff prevails at trial. Imagine, for example, an auto accident case where the driver has a $100,000 liability policy, the plaintiff's damages may be anywhere from $100,000 to $250,000 at trial, and there is approximately a 25 percent chance of prevailing on a statutory defense. Assume the plaintiff would be willing to settle for policy limits. Now look at the incentives from the point of view of both the company and the policyholder:

	If Settlement	If Going to Trial
Company's perspective	Has to pay $100,000	Worst-case scenario is judgment equal to or in excess of policy limits; downside risk is paying $100,000. Upside is possibly having to pay nothing, if defense verdict.
Policyholder's perspective	Off the hook entirely	May get off the hook, but may have to pay judgment in excess of policy limits if jury comes back with verdict greater than $100,000.

The incentives of the parties are completely adverse. The company would prefer to roll the dice at trial, because even a substantial verdict makes it no worse off than if it had tendered policy limits to settle the case. The policyholder, on the other hand, very much wants to settle — it is not his money — because a verdict in excess of $100,000 will become a personal liability of the policyholder.

Most insurance contracts provide that the company has the right to accept or reject a settlement within policy limits, but it must exercise this discretion in good faith, taking into account the policyholder's interest in not being exposed to a substantial likelihood of an excess judgment at trial. The lawyer always owes a paramount duty to the policyholder. Thus, she must advise the company to accept the settlement if it is in the best interests of the policyholder. This result is reinforced by Rule 5.4(c), which says that a lawyer shall not permit someone who pays the lawyer (that is, the insurance company) to interfere with the lawyer's exercise of independent professional judgment in rendering legal services (that is, representing the policyholder).

Multiple Parties

This kind of conflict scenario is similar to a garden-variety multiple representation; the only difference is that the lawyer is hired by the insurance company to represent multiple insureds on the same policy. Employers and employees, owners and drivers of cars, and general contractors and landowners are often co-insureds on one policy, and a single attorney may be hired to represent both in litigation. The interests of the parties may be harmonious, but they may conflict if one party's interests would be served by defending the case differently — for example, emphasizing the liability of a co-defendant — or even filing cross-claims against co-parties seeking contribution or indemnification. The analysis for one of these problems would proceed under the usual Rule 1.7 criteria.

Duty to Communicate and Confidentiality

In a jurisdiction that follows the dual-client doctrine, the lawyer may have a conflict of duties arising from her obligations: (1) to keep each client informed to the extent necessary to enable the client to make informed decisions about the case, Rule 1.4(b); and (2) to preserve each client's confidences from others, Rule 1.6. Suppose the lawyer discovers some facts that would support a denial of coverage — perhaps evidence that an accident actually was an intentional tort for which coverage would be excluded under a liability policy. The company would love to know these facts, because it could defend the case under a reservation of rights, seeking to deny coverage for the policyholder's liability. The policyholder, on the other hand, would very much like her lawyer to keep this information confidential,

393

because if the company denies coverage, she will have to pay the judgment out of her own pocket. What is a lawyer to do?

The general rule is that the lawyer's primary (or sole, in some jurisdictions) client is the policyholder for the purposes of the duty of confidentiality. Douglas R. Richmond, *Walking a Tightrope: The Tripartite Relationship Between Insurer, Insured, and Insurance Defense Counsel*, 73 Neb. L. Rev. 265, 281 (1994). The lawyer breaches her fiduciary duty to the policyholder by communicating confidential information to the insurer. In one well-known case, a lawyer was retained by an insurance company to represent the policyholder in a personal-injury lawsuit. See *Parsons v. Continental Nat'l Am. Group*, 550 P.2d 94 (Ariz. 1976). The lawyer learned some facts that suggested the plaintiff's injury was the result of an intentional act, and the company then issued a reservation of rights letter. Acting through the lawyer, the company rejected an offer to settle within policy limits. The case went to trial, and the plaintiffs obtained a judgment in excess of the $25,000 limit on the insurance policy. The company disclaimed coverage, but the court held that the company was estopped to deny coverage because the defense lawyer had violated his fiduciary duty to the policyholder. The company was therefore required to pay the excess judgment, on the theory that if the company had not rejected the settlement offer, the policyholder would not have been exposed to the excess liability at trial. You can bet that the company turned around and sued its lawyer for malpractice, for exposing it to the excess liability. See William H. Fortune et al., *Modern Litigation and Professional Responsibility Handbook* §15.11 (1996).

Former-Client Conflicts and Migratory Lawyers

16

INTRODUCTION

This chapter deals with two related situations. In the first, the lawyer does not change firms, but stops representing a client and then picks up a new client whose interests are adverse to the old client. This situation, where all the lawyers stay put, is referred to as a side-switching former-client conflict. In the second scenario, the lawyer changes law firms. This situation is more complicated, because there is a concern not only about the potential personal disqualification of the moving lawyer, but about whether her "taint" is imputed to the new firm, and whether any possible taint can be cured by screening. The second situation is referred to as the problem of "migratory lawyers," a term that always puts me in mind of a herd of caribou crossing the tundra, wearing suits and carrying briefcases. Although they are handled by the same rule on former-client conflicts, migratory lawyer cases introduce additional complications, so those cases are discussed in a separate section.

SIDE-SWITCHING FORMER-CLIENT CONFLICTS

Consider a hypothetical: For many years, your client was Gigantic, a large manufacturer of medical devices. You represented them in a variety of matters, including product liability defense and commercial litigation cases.

Unfortunately for you, Gigantic's general counsel decided last year to consolidate all the company's legal work in five "regional" law firms and fired your firm. Today you get a call from Startup, a much smaller company that also manufactures medical devices. Startup's general counsel tells you that she believes Gigantic has infringed its patent on a machine of some sort. Can you take Startup as a client?

Assuming you are not trying to get back in Gigantic's good graces, which might create a material limitation on your ability to represent Startup — a current-client conflict created by your personal interest, under Model Rule 1.7(a)(2) — you can analyze this situation using the former-client conflicts rule, Model Rule 1.9. Side-switching former-client conflicts are handled by subsection (a) of the rule, which prohibits your firm from representing Startup in the *same* or a *substantially related* matter for which the firm *formerly represented* Gigantic, if the interests of Startup and Gigantic are *materially adverse*, unless Gigantic provides informed consent after consultation. Each of these elements will be analyzed in turn.

Review: Termination of the Attorney-Client Relationship

Chapter 2 discussed how a lawyer or a client can "break up" with the other. Now those rules return with a vengeance. It matters a great deal whether there is an ongoing attorney-client relationship or the relationship is entirely in the past. Why? Because the conflicts rules are stricter on lawyers who intend to represent a new client against the interests of an existing client than they are on a lawyer who wishes to take on a new client against the interests of a former client. A lawyer cannot simultaneously represent two clients whose interests are directly adverse, but a lawyer can take a new matter that is materially adverse to a former client's interests, as long as the two matters are not the same or substantially related.

In the hypothetical involving Gigantic and Startup, it is clear that the client fired your firm. In the real world, however, it is often less clear. No matter how nice it would be to have a clear record, lawyers hate to write letters that say: "Now that we have finished working on this matter, you are no longer our client. We do not represent you in any way, shape, or form." Lawyers want to develop ongoing relationships with clients, who will continue referring business to them. Thus, they encourage clients to think of them as continuing in some kind of professional connection. Maybe the law firm sends out "friends of the firm" newsletters and holiday cards to the former client. Perhaps it continues to hold documents, such as corporate minute books, for the former client. Or, the lawyer and the client may be in a dispute over an unpaid bill, with the implication that the professional relationship will resume on amicable terms once the fee dispute is resolved.

There are a number of cases in which the court had to decide first whether the attorney-client relationship was ongoing—in which case the current-client conflicts rules would apply—or terminated. A good rule to take from these decisions is that an attorney-client relationship is ongoing if: (1) the client subjectively believes that the lawyer is continuing to represent her; and (2) that belief is reasonable in the circumstances. See, for example, *Oxford Systems, Inc. v. Cellpro, Inc.*, 45 F. Supp. 2d 1055 (W.D. Wash. 1999); *Gray v. Gray*, 2002 WL 31093931 (Tenn. Ct. App. 2002). Factors that tend to support a client's reasonable belief in an ongoing relationship include a long history of using the same lawyer or firm; sending promotional materials or "dear friend" letters; retention of client documents; and a relatively short interval between the last legal work performed and the time in which the lawyer seeks to represent a new client with adverse interests. None of these factors alone is dispositive. If a long time has elapsed since the lawyer last performed professional services, the relationship may be considered to have terminated by drift, even though the lawyer kept the client on her mailing list for promotional materials. You should be on the lookout for facts that make the client's subjective belief in an ongoing professional relationship either reasonable or unreasonable.

Analysis of Side-Switching Former-Client Conflicts Problems

Model Rule 1.9(a), governing side-switching former-client conflicts, requires a five-step analysis:

1. Has the lawyer formerly represented a client who might complain about the conflict?
2. What is the nature of the matter for which the lawyer formerly provided representation?
3. Is that matter the same or substantially related to the present matter?
4. Are the interests of the present and former client materially adverse?
5. Did the former client provide informed consent?

Representing a Client

Remember in current-client conflicts cases how important it is to identify existing attorney-client relationships. The same issue recurs in former-client conflicts cases, because there may be some dispute about whether a lawyer formerly represented a client whose interests are now materially adverse to those of a new client. In both contexts, a substantial risk for the lawyer is acquiring professional duties (of keeping confidences and refraining from representing conflicting interest) toward parties the lawyer would prefer not to represent. For example, a lawyer representing a closely held corporation may learn confidential client information from one of the shareholders, personal to the shareholder's legal situation, which the lawyer ought to use on behalf of the entity. If the lawyer does disclose the information to another agent who is authorized to act on behalf of the corporation, the lawyer risks being held liable for breaching her fiduciary duty to the shareholder, *as a separate client*, even though the lawyer is representing the corporation as well. Other kinds of entities present the same difficulty — the lawyer may find herself with multiple client relationships where she had intended only to have one.

An important case illustrating this risk is *Westinghouse Elec. v. Kerr-McGee*, 580 F.2d 1311 (7th Cir. 1978). The large firm of Kirkland & Ellis represented the American Petroleum Institute (API), through its Washington, D.C., office. The API, one of whose members was Kerr-McGee, had hired Kirkland for lobbying projects in Washington. In the course of representing the API, the firm received confidential proprietary information from API members, including Kerr-McGee, which the API had collected to assist in the firm's lobbying efforts. Subsequently, the Chicago office of Kirkland accepted the representation of Westinghouse as the plaintiff in a massive antitrust action against Kerr-McGee and other API members. Kerr-McGee moved to disqualify Kirkland from representing Westinghouse, alleging a former-client conflict. The natural argument in opposition to the motion was, of course, that Kirkland had not "represented a client (Kerr-McGee) in a matter" in which the former client's interests were materially adverse to the interests of the present client, Westinghouse. The district court agreed and refused to disqualify Kirkland, but the Seventh Circuit held that the district court had erred by applying a "narrow, formal agency approach to determining the attorney-client relationship." Rather, the law firm could owe fiduciary duties to Kerr-McGee on the basis of a course of dealing between the parties — creating a "quasi-client" relationship. In particular, the in-house lawyer for Kerr-McGee reasonably believed that Kirkland was working on behalf of not only the API but also its members. The fact that Kerr-McGee and other API members had submitted confidential information to the API, understanding it would be passed along to Kirkland, supported Kerr-McGee's argument that it reasonably believed the firm was looking out for its interests, too. Why else would it permit the firm to receive highly sensitive information?

An application of the rule on former representation of clients is found in Model Rule 1.18, on representing a new client in a matter adverse to one in which a *prospective* client consulted with the lawyer. A lawyer is prohibited from representing new clients with interests adverse to those of a prospective client if the lawyer learned confidential information in the course of the interview with the prospective client. Rule 1.18(c). Suppose, for example, that Wally's Mart is thinking about acquiring a parcel of land and opening a store. A Wally's Mart representative meets with Kramer, a local real estate lawyer, and discusses its intentions. The representative tells Kramer quite clearly that its plans are confidential because it does not want its competitor, Magnet, to realize that the site is available and that, in the judgment of Wally's Mart, the market conditions are right to open a store. Kramer decides not to take the case and is very explicit about not representing Wally's Mart — in other words, this is not a *Togstad*-type scenario in which Wally's Mart is relying on Kramer to perform legal services. (See Chapter 2 for the *Togstad* case.) Nevertheless, if Kramer tried to represent Magnet in an action before the local zoning commission to challenge Wally's Mart's development plans, she would be disqualified. She also would be prohibited from disclosing the information learned from Wally's Mart or using the information to its disadvantage, for instance by calling up Magnet and alerting it to the availability of the parcel and its desirability as a location for a store. Rule 1.6; Rest. §15(1)(a); Rule 1.18(b).

Identify the Matter

A "matter" is not just a lawsuit, but can include a deal, a transaction, or an issue on which the client requires counseling and legal advice. Rest. §132, cmt. d(iii). As this Restatement comment makes clear, a "matter" does not include a legal position taken on behalf of a client, so if the lawyer argues in one case, on behalf of Richards, that a state statute is constitutional, she is not precluded from arguing, on behalf of Watts, that the statute is unconstitutional. Of course, if the matters handled for Richards and Watts are substantially related (as defined next), the lawyer cannot proceed on behalf of Watts without Richards's consent. In addition, there may be cases in which taking adverse positions on behalf of different clients may create a conflict. See the discussion of "positional conflicts" in Chapter 15.

The "Substantial Relationship" Test

Out in the world you may encounter different standards for when two matters are substantially related. Consider three different tests employed by federal courts from the broadest (least permissive of subsequent adverse representation) to the narrowest (most permissive):

- the prior representation is "akin to the present action in a way reasonable persons would understand as important to the issues involved." In re *American Airlines, Inc.*, 972 F.2d 605 (5th Cir. 1992).

- "the lawyer could have obtained confidential information in the first representation that would be relevant in the second." *Analytica, Inc. v. NPD Research*, 708 F.2d 1263 (7th Cir. 1983).
- the relationship between the matters is "patently clear" and the issues "identical" or "essentially the same." *Government of India v. Cook Indus.*, 569 F.2d 737 (2d Cir. 1978).

It's obviously important in practice to know exactly how the substantial relationship test is formulated in your jurisdiction. For the purposes of your professional responsibility course, you should make sure to know what version of the standard you'll have to follow on an exam question. For what it's worth, I tell my students to use the version in Rest. §132. The Restatement test can be understood functionally, as responding to two distinct interests of clients that would be threatened if lawyers were permitted to represent new clients against old ones. Those two interests are the ongoing confidentiality of information and the reasonable expectation of loyalty.

Confidentiality — follow the secrets   A court may analyze the relatedness of two matters in terms of the nature of confidential client information that the lawyer *may have learned* in the course of representing the former client. This is the "follow the secrets" approach, reminiscent of Deep Throat's advice to Woodward and Bernstein to "follow the money." It is the test adopted by the *Analytica* case, above, as well as Restatement §132(2). A comment to Model Rule 1.9 also says the two matters are substantially related if there is a "substantial risk that confidential information as would normally have been obtained in the prior representation would materially advance the client's position in the subsequent matter." Rule 1.9, cmt. [3]. As the comment notes, however, if the new client had access to the information in question, it would not be confidential information of the former client, and the two matters would therefore not be considered substantially related.

The former client does not have to show the confidential information the lawyer *actually* had received. A test that worked by analyzing actual disclosure of information would force the client to disclose these secrets in order to protect them—a highly ironic result indeed. Rather than put clients in this unpleasant dilemma, courts look to the nature of the former representation and the current matter and analyze what sort of information to which a lawyer probably would have had access in the past.[1] If that information

---

1. See Rest. §132, cmt. d(iii): "The substantial-relationship test avoids requiring disclosure of confidential information by focusing upon the general features of the matters involved and inferences as to the likelihood that confidences were imparted by the former client that could be used to adverse effect in the subsequent representation." See also Rule 1.9, cmt. [3] ("A conclusion about the possession of [confidential client] information may be based on the general nature of the services the lawyer provided the former client and information that would in ordinary practice be learned by a lawyer providing such services.").

would be useful in the present representation, the two matters are substantially related. The test is sort of a "virtual" analysis of the rise of transmission of confidential information, using the factual and legal issues in the two matters as a proxy for the risk that secrets of one client could be used by the lawyer to the detriment of the other client in the subsequent representation.

Consider an example. Suppose in our Gigantic/Startup hypothetical that your firm did product liability defense work for Gigantic in a case involving Product X. In order to defend the lawsuit, you had to learn a great deal about Product X, including technical details of how a patented mechanism functions. Now suppose that Startup wants to hire your firm to represent it in a lawsuit alleging that Gigantic's Product X infringes Startup's patent. You can imagine that the information you learned in the course of working on the product liability case could be very useful to Startup in the infringement litigation. This is true even though the legal issues — Is the design defective? Did defendant infringe plaintiff's patent? — are completely different. Remember, for matters to be substantially related, it is not necessary that the underlying *legal* issue be substantially related. Rather, the test is whether resolution of the legal issues in one matter would involve facts that would be relevant in the other matter. Courts follow the secrets not by attempting to discover the actual transmission of confidential client information, but by comparing two matters and making an educated guess as to whether there would be some overlap in the factual information relevant to both.

Loyalty   The trend in the law is toward the "follow the secrets" approach — orienting the analysis of the relationship between matters toward the flow of confidential client information. Despite this overall trend, there is still a lingering effect of the *loyalty* rationale for prohibiting serial representation of clients with opposing interests. The loyalty rationale recognizes that a client would feel wronged, betrayed, or "sold out" if her previous lawyer turned around and represented one of the former client's adversaries. That is true, as far as it goes, but loyalty is a dangerous ground for justifying the former-client conflicts rule, because it may be used to create a broad zone of prohibition on future representation by a lawyer. If after three years passed by without doing any more work for Gigantic, its former law firm represented Humongous in a hostile takeover bid, Gigantic may be upset or feel betrayed, but it has no *justifiable* expectation that its former law firm will not represent any adverse interests. When looking to the loyalty interest to define the scope of the prohibition on representing new clients, it is important to focus on reasonable expectations of loyalty.

There are two particularly egregious situations in which courts will disqualify a lawyer from representing a new client on the basis of loyalty. One is where the lawyer literally switches sides in the middle of a case. This usually happens in migratory lawyer cases, where a lawyer at the law firm representing Plaintiff suddenly takes a job offer at the firm representing Defendant.

The other situation is where the lawyer attacks work she previously had performed for a client. Suppose a lawyer represented Wood in negotiating a contract with Wyman. If the lawyer subsequently seeks to represent Wyman and argue that the contract is invalid and the transaction should be rescinded, the lawyer will be disqualified. In the somewhat crude vernacular of conflicts law, this is known as "fouling one's own nest." Subsequent representation that involves nest-fouling will be prohibited, even if there is no possibility of the lawyer using confidential client information of the former client in the representation of the new client. See, for example, *Eurocom, S.A. v. Mahoney, Cohen & Co.*, 522 F. Supp. 1179 (S.D.N.Y. 1981). The reason sometimes given for preventing nest-fouling is that a lawyer might otherwise have an incentive to create weaknesses in the documents prepared for one client, in the hope of exploiting those weaknesses in the future on behalf of another client. Rest. §132, cmt. b. How often lawyers actually do this is not known; however, it seems a bit implausible to suppose that lawyers actively subvert their current representation of a client because of the risk of a subsequent malpractice action by that client. Because there really are not any good reasons for permitting lawyers to attack their own work, there does not appear to be any harm in an absolute prohibition on nest-fouling by lawyers.

Restatement test   The Restatement defines "substantial relationship" in a way that protects the client's reasonable expectation that the lawyer will keep confidences and not turn against a former client. According to the Restatement, two matters are substantially related if:

1. the current matter involves the work the lawyer performed for the former client; or
2. there is a substantial risk that representation of the present client will involve the use of information acquired in the course of representing the former client, unless that information has become generally known.

Rest. §132. Subsection (1) addresses the client's justifiable expectation of loyalty and subsection (2) deals with the confidentiality interest. The majority of former-client conflicts cases will be handled by subsection (2), which recognizes the "follow the secrets" approach. In addition to taking care of true nest-fouling cases, where the lawyer is attacking his own work, subsection (1) also deals with former joint representation of two clients who have a falling out. The clients may not have had an expectation that information they shared with the lawyer would be kept confidential from the co-client, but in many cases the lawyer would still be prohibited from representing one of the co-clients against the other if their interests diverged at some point during the representation. The lawyer in that case would be disqualified under subsection (1).

Material Adversity

Material adversity refers to the incentives a lawyer has in her representation of a client. See Rest. §132, cmt. e, citing Rest. §121, cmts. c(i) & c(ii). The position of a new client is materially adverse to that of a former client if the lawyer would be limited in performing her professional obligations for either one. See, for example, *Simpson Performance Prods. v. Horn*, 92 P.3d 283 (Wyo. 2004) (material adversity depends on whether subsequent representation threatens "legal, financial, or other identifiable detriment" to former client). If the lawyer for Startup would be unable to use facts learned in the course of representing Gigantic, the lawyer would be faced with the Hobson's choice of either violating her duties of competent representation and communication (Rule 1.1 and Rule 1.4) owed to Startup, or her duty of confidentiality (Rule 1.6) owed to Gigantic. In that case, the interests of the former and present client would be materially adverse.

Consent

Unlike the concurrent conflicts rule, Rule 1.7, the former-client conflicts rule, Rule 1.9, contains no lurking category of nonconsentable (or nonwaivable) conflicts buried in the language of the rule. Under Rule 1.9, all *former-client conflicts are consentable*, provided that the lawyer provides full disclosure to the former client, which is necessary to obtain informed consent. Rest. §122, cmt. g(iv). But that only takes care of the interests of the former client. Consent from the present client may also be required if there is a significant risk that the lawyer's past representation of the former client will materially limit the representation of the present client. Rule 1.7(a)(2). The introduction to the Gigantic/Startup problem alluded to the possibility that the law firm may be trying to get back into the good graces of Gigantic, which had terminated a longstanding professional relationship with the firm. The desire to get back on the company's list of preferred outside counsel might materially limit the firm's representation of Startup by creating an incentive to be less vigorous in litigation than might otherwise be warranted. In that case, even if the representation of Startup is okay under Rule 1.9 (which protects Gigantic's interests), the informed consent of Startup may be required under Rule 1.7(b). In theory some concurrent conflicts under Rule 1.7 are nonconsentable. Although it seems farfetched, one could imagine a situation in which this would be the case: If the matter for Startup is tiny and inconsequential to the firm's bottom line, the litigation against Gigantic would by nature be acrimonious, and the managing partner of the firm really, really wants to curry favor with Gigantic, this may be a case in which no reasonable lawyer would believe it possible to provide competent and diligent representation to Startup. Thus, under Rule 1.7(b)(1), the conflict would not be consentable.

Coming in Second Place in a Beauty Contest

Once upon a time, clients had a long-term relationship with one outside law firm, which handled all of their legal business. In today's market, things are different. Would-be clients frequently shop around for representation and may interview multiple lawyers at different firms before settling on a firm to represent them, often only for the purpose of a single, discrete matter. Perhaps feeling somewhat objectified, lawyers have come to refer to this process as a "beauty contest." The Model Rules include a section intended to deal with the duties owed to these prospective clients. See Rule 1.18. The rule is an application of well-established principles governing the formation of the attorney-client relationship (Rest. §14; see Chapter 2) and the duties that follow from having an attorney-client relationship, including the former-client conflicts rule. See Utah State Bar Op. 05-04 (lawyers owe duties of loyalty and confidentiality to prospective clients, even though state had not yet adopted Rule 1.18); New York City Bar Ass'n, Formal Op. 2006-2 (reaching result similar to Rule 1.18, under New York rules). The prospective client rule shows both how lawyers can get into trouble in connection with beauty contests and how they can protect themselves.

A person who consults a lawyer about the possibility of forming an attorney-client relationship is a prospective client. Rule 1.18(a). At the moment the prospective client consults with a lawyer, the lawyer acquires an obligation to keep confidential any information learned in the course of that consultation. Rule 1.18(b). If the prospective client decides not to retain the lawyer, that lawyer is personally disqualified from representing a new client whose interests are materially adverse to those of the prospective client, in the same or a substantially related matter. See Rule 1.18(c). However, other lawyers in the firm may not be disqualified from representing the new client. Rule 1.18(d)(2) provides for screening the personally disqualified lawyer and notice to the prospective client as a way of avoiding disqualification, as long as the personally disqualified lawyer took reasonable steps to limit exposure to confidential information from the prospective client.

Much the same result could be reached via the ordinary former-client conflicts rule, Rule 1.9(a), as long as you understand that the interview with the prospective client constitutes "represent[ing] a client in a matter" for the purposes of that rule. The only difference between Model Rule 1.18(c) and the ordinary former-client conflicts rule is that the lawyer conducting the interview is disqualified by Model Rule 1.18(c) only where the lawyer obtained information that could be *significantly* harmful to the prospective client. Model Rule 1.9(a) does not contain this qualification, although arguably the lawyer will not be deemed to have represented the prospective client (that is, formed an attorney-client relationship under Rest. §14) unless the information imparted by the prospective client to the lawyer could be significantly harmful if disclosed.

The other way the analysis under the new prospective client rule diverges from the ordinary former-client conflicts analysis is with regard to screening. We will talk more about screening in the Migratory Lawyers section of this chapter, but the idea is that the conflicts of one lawyer that would ordinarily be imputed to other lawyers in the firm under Rule 1.10(a) are contained, and not imputed, if the firm ensures that other lawyers do not learn confidential information from the first client. See Rule 1.0(k) for a definition of screening. The prospective client rule permits the firm to screen the lawyer who conducted the interview from other lawyers in the firm. Rule 1.18(d). If the personally disqualified lawyer is effectively screened, following the procedures in Model Rule 1.18(d), other lawyers in the firm may represent a new client whose interests are materially adverse to those of the prospective client, in the same or a substantially related matter. The screening procedure prevents devious litigants from "tainting" or "conflicting out" entire law firms by participating in a beauty contest and disclosing highly sensitive confidential information that would otherwise require the disqualification of the entire firm from representing adversaries.

Practically speaking, lawyers conducting interviews with prospective clients should protect themselves by obtaining waivers of confidentiality and conflicts of interest from the prospective client. See New York City Bar Ass'n, Formal Op. 2006-2; Virginia State Bar Legal Ethics Op. 1794. These waivers are subject to the usual requirement of informed consent — that is, the lawyer must fully inform the prospective client of the risks and benefits of consenting to disclosure of confidential information and subsequent adverse representation of a different client. It would be a good idea to get these waivers in writing. Note that due to the screening provision of Model Rule 1.18(d), other lawyers in the firm may undertake subsequent adverse representation of other clients, as long as they are effectively screened in a timely manner, even if the interviewing lawyer does not obtain waivers of confidentiality and conflicts. Smart firms have prospective client interview procedures in place to ensure that lawyers participating in beauty contests are automatically screened in the event that the prospective client decides not to hire the firm.

Examples

Leaving with the Client's Playbook

1. Costanza is a lawyer in a medium-sized town who has worked for several years as a defense lawyer in tort cases. One of his most significant clients was Burger Bell, a local chain of fast-food restaurants. Burger Bell was sued occasionally in slip-and-fall cases, where plaintiffs alleged that restaurant employees had left slippery substances on the floor, causing customers to fall and injure themselves. When this happened, the

restaurant would hire Costanza to defend it in the tort litigation. Costanza would discuss various matters with Burger Bell (as he was obligated to under Rule 1.4), such as strategy, how much discovery to do, whether to settle or take the case to trial, what witnesses to call at trial, whether to appeal verdicts, etc. Costanza eventually decided he could make more money representing plaintiffs in tort cases, so he stopped representing Burger Bell.

About a year after Costanza wrapped up his last case for Burger Bell, Benes slipped on a pool of liquid in a Burger Bell and broke her wrist. She hired Costanza to file a lawsuit against Burger Bell. Burger Bell immediately filed a motion to disqualify Costanza from the case, alleging a violation of the former-client conflicts rule. Should the court grant the motion?

Dropping the Client Like a Hot Potato

2. McDonald, Wall & Everett has represented Fission Corp., a pharmaceutical company, in product liability cases for many years. The firm also represents First Bank from time to time, in small and completely unrelated matters. By a strange turn of events, however, the interests of these two clients became adverse. First Bank, through its trust department, is the guardian of the property of Jimmy Harris, a young boy whose serious and disabling injury was allegedly caused by a drug manufactured by Fission. Because the bank has an obligation to conserve the property of Harris, it has entered the litigation against Fission on the side of the plaintiffs. (McDonald, Wall & Everett is not representing First Bank in the litigation, or in any matter relating to administration of Harris's property.) The firm asked the general counsel of First Bank whether she would consent to the firm representing Fission in this matter, but she refused. McDonald, Wall & Everett very much would like to stay in the product liability case on the side of Fission, because it is likely to be a complex, drawn-out (and therefore lucrative) piece of litigation.

   A. Can the firm proceed without First Bank's consent?
   B. What would be the consequence if the firm withdraws from continuing to represent First Bank and decides to represent Fission in the product liability case?

Taint Shopping

3. Tony is considering filing for a divorce from his wife, Carmela. He went to see a matrimonial lawyer at Law Firm #1. At the outset of the conversation, Lawyer A asked for the name of the potential adverse party and said, "Don't tell us anything more until we've had a chance to do a conflicts check." Nevertheless, Tony told Lawyer A that he had numerous

secret bank accounts in the Cayman Islands, and intended to hide assets from Carmela. After the meeting ended, Tony hired Law Firm #2.

After being served with divorce papers, Carmela went to Law Firm #1 and asked Lawyer B to represent her in the divorce proceedings. Can Lawyer B represent Carmela?

Explanations

Leaving with the Client's Playbook

1. This case is similar to *State ex rel. Wal-Mart Stores v. Kortum*, 559 N.W.2d 496 (Neb. 1997), although it is a fairly common fact pattern. This recurring situation even has a name — the problem of "playbook" confidences. (I believe the term originated with Charles Wolfram; see Charles W. Wolfram, *Former-Client Conflicts*, 10 Geo. J. Legal Ethics 677 (1997), although it is now widely used by commentators.) Two steps in the former-client conflicts analysis are easy — Costanza formerly represented Burger Bell, and the interests of Benes and Burger Bell are materially adverse. Rule 1.9(a). That leaves the question of whether the two matters — that is, *Benes v. Burger Bell*, and any other slip-and-fall case Costanza handled for Burger Bell — are substantially related. Burger Bell will argue that substantial relationship should be understood using the "follow the secrets" approach, and that Costanza will be using "information acquired in the course of representing the former client" on behalf of Benes to the detriment of Burger Bell. See Rest. §132(2). It is true, of course, that Costanza learned *something* about Burger Bell in his past life as a defense-side lawyer. He got a feel for how the client defends slip-and-fall cases, how to undermine the plaintiffs' cases, what kind of discovery to seek, and so on. This information definitely will be useful in representing Benes.

   The problem with taking such a broad view of confidential client information is that it seems to require the disqualification of Costanza forever in any tort litigation adverse to Burger Bell. If its attitude toward settling slip-and-fall cases, or its general approach to litigation, is considered confidential client information protected by the former-client conflicts rule, then every subsequent tort case will be "substantially related" to the past work performed by Costanza. But this information is not exactly rocket science, or the secret formula for Coke — any halfway competent plaintiff's personal injury lawyer would know how to litigate a slip-and-fall case and will have a thorough understanding of how defendants approach these cases, too. If Burger Bell is a repeat-player litigant in the community, all local lawyers will have a sense for its particular approach, such as whether it plays hardball in discovery, whether it tends to take cases to trial or prefer to settle, and so on. As a result, it does not make sense to protect this information stringently, at the cost of precluding lawyers like Costanza from taking on cases adverse to a former client in the future.

The Restatement has a good approach to playbook information and a limitation on which possession of this information will be disqualifying:

> A lawyer might also have learned a former client's preferred approach to bargaining in settlement discussions or negotiating business points in a transaction, willingness or unwillingness to be deposed by an adversary, and financial ability to withstand extended litigation or contract negotiations. *Only when such information will be directly in issue or of unusual value in the subsequent matter* will it be independently relevant in assessing a substantial relationship.

Rest. §132, cmt. d(iii).

The variation in the cases often is a result of how client-specific or idiosyncratic the information is. See, for example, *State ex rel. Ogden Newspapers v. Wilkes*, 566 S.E.2d 560 (W. Va. 2002); *Steel v. General Motors Corp.*, 912 F. Supp. 724 (D.N.J. 1995). In *Steel*, a lawyer who used to defend GM in lemon law cases moved to a law firm that represented plaintiffs in lemon law cases against various auto manufacturers. GM argued that the moving lawyer acquired extensive information about the decision-making processes of GM personnel with regard to legal claims, their attitude toward settlements and claim resolution procedures, and the personalities and management styles of specific GM personnel. The court (rightly, in my view) deemed this information sufficiently specific to warrant the disqualification of the new law firm. In other words, the matters were substantially related by virtue of the moving lawyer's access to the former client's playbook. See also *In re Carey*, 89 S.W.3d 477 (Mo. 2002) (disqualification or discipline would be warranted where moving lawyers learned very specific proprietary information about how Chrysler defends class action design-defect litigation, including its hesitancy to implead a particular component parts supplier, its evaluation of the usefulness of certain experts, and its decision tree for analyzing whether or not it should settle cases); *contra In re Drake*, 195 S.W.3d 232 (Tex. Civ. App. 2006) (refusing to disqualify the moving lawyer from representing private clients challenging actions of government agency where the lawyer had learned, from previous government service, information about the "inner workings" of the agency, including its approach to discovery, defense strategy, trial preparation, and attitudes toward settlement).

In the example above, what Costanza learned is fairly generic, but if you encounter a case in which the lawyer has learned truly proprietary, insider, or secret information that would not be common knowledge for any attorney experienced in the area, the case for disqualification — that is, for finding the matters substantially related — grows stronger.

Dropping the Client Like a Hot Potato

2. A. This problem is based on *Harrison v. Fisons Corp.*, 819 F. Supp. 1039 (M.D. Fla. 1993), and should be an easy review of current-client conflicts. Even though the firm is not representing First Bank in the liability litigation or in any matter relating to administration of Harris's property, the bank is still a client of McDonald, Wall & Everett. The interests of Fission are "directly adverse" to those of the bank, so Model Rule 1.7(a)(1) prohibits the firm from representing both clients, without the consent of both clients. Since First Bank has refused to give consent, the multiple representation is prohibited.

B. This is an example of the so-called hot potato rule. If the firm drops First Bank as a client, it can argue that it is not prohibited from representing Fission, because the matter is not "substantially related" to the work the firm performed for the bank. Rule 1.9(a). The rules do not seem to prohibit this maneuver, but courts consistently have refused to allow firms to drop clients solely for the purpose of taking on new matters adverse to the now-former client. One court put the same point colorfully, giving rise to the simile that has entered the professional responsibility lexicon. It said that a lawyer cannot just drop a client "like a hot potato" in order to represent another, more lucrative client. *Picker Int'l. Inc. v. Varian Assoc., Inc.*, 670 F. Supp. 1363, 1365 (N.D. Ohio 1987). Without the hot potato rule, the current-client conflicts rule could be circumvented by permitting the lawyer to fire a client and then take on representation adverse to the former client, as long as the two matters are not substantially related.

Summing up the hot potato rule:

> Withdrawal is effective to render a representation "former" for the purposes of this Section if it occurs at a point that the client and lawyer had contemplated as the end of the representation. . . . If a lawyer is approached by a prospective client seeking representation in a matter adverse to an existing client, the present-client conflict may not be transformed into a former-client conflict by the lawyer's withdrawal from the representation of the existing client. A premature withdrawal violates the lawyer's obligation of loyalty to the existing client and can constitute a breach of the client-lawyer contract of employment.

Rest. §132, cmt. c.

There probably would not be a breach of the client-lawyer contract here because the lawyer has a right to withdraw from representing First Bank at any time, as long as withdrawal does not cause "material adverse effects on the interests" of First Bank. There is nothing in the facts given to suggest that First Bank will be prejudiced by the withdrawal. But it does seem somewhat cavalier for McDonald, Wall & Everett to dump First Bank in favor of doing more lucrative work for Fission. The hot potato rule is motivated by the distaste that courts exhibit when lawyers treat their clients as expendable commodities.

The consequence of firing First Bank and staying in the litigation on the side of Fission probably would be a motion to disqualify, filed by First Bank, which would be granted by the court. This result is harsher than what the rules seem to dictate. Generally, if a conflict arises after a lawyer has begun work on two clients' matters, the lawyer can withdraw from only one of the matters and continue representing the other client, as long as the matters are not substantially related. Rest. §121, cmt. e(ii). Suppose the lawyer is representing Clients A and B, whose interests are initially harmonious, but which come into conflict at some later point in time. Once the lawyer withdraws from Client A's case, Client A becomes a former client, and the propriety of the representation of Client B is judged by Model Rule 1.9(a). If the matters were unrelated, as the work for First Bank and Fission were, the firm should be able to continue representing the remaining client. (The firm must withdraw from representing *both* clients if the matters are related. Rest. §121, cmt. e(i). This situation would be presented if Clients A and B were co-defendants in the same litigation or parties to the same business transaction.) The hot potato rule is therefore stricter than the usual role governing post-representation conflicts, which would allow the firm to stay in on behalf of one of the clients.

There is an exception to the hot potato rule for so-called "thrust upon" conflicts, where the simultaneous representation results not from any action taken by the law firm but from something like a merger among clients. An excellent illustration of this rule in action is *Installation Software Technologies v. Wise Solutions, Inc.*, 2004 WL 524829 (N.D. Ill. 2004). A large law firm represented Installation in intellectual property litigation against Wise, in the United States. At the same time, the firm represented Altiris in Europe and Australia, advising it on corporate, securities, tax, and employment matters. During the litigation, Altiris acquired Wise, which caused the firm to be representing both the plaintiff and the defendant (as a wholly owned subsidiary of a client) in the same litigation. Hello, conflict. The firm first tried to secure consent from Altiris, but it refused to consent, so the firm moved to withdraw from representing Installation. The court denied the motion, noting that Installation would be prejudiced by having to obtain substitute counsel at this late stage in the litigation. The court said the firm should withdraw from representing Altiris to cure the conflict. Altiris cited the hot potato rule, but the court responded that withdrawal from representing Altiris would be permissible in this case because the conflict was thrust upon the firm by Altiris. This decision is almost an equitable one, with the court considering the balance of prejudice (Installation would be harmed more than Altiris by withdrawal, because it would lose counsel in the middle of litigation) and making something like an estoppel argument, because it was Altiris's action that created the problem. See also New York City Bar Ass'n, Formal Op. 2005-5 (in "thrust upon" situations withdrawal from representing both may not be required if one client refuses to consent to simultaneous representation; endorsing a similar balancing approach, with the most important factor being which client will suffer the most prejudice as the result of withdrawal).

Taint Shopping

3. (Fans of *The Sopranos* may recall an episode in which Tony Soprano tries to taint the pool of North Jersey matrimonial lawyers so they cannot represent his wife, Carmela.) Lawyer B at Law Firm #1 is okay here to represent Carmela. There are two alternate, sufficient grounds for this conclusion: (1) Tony was not a "prospective client," entitled to the protection of Rule 1.18, because he communicated the information about his bank accounts with the intention of disqualifying the lawyer from representing Carmela. See Rule 1.18, cmt. [2]. Because Tony is now defined out of the key term "prospective client," what would otherwise be a prohibition in Rule 1.18(c) on representing Carmela does not apply. (2) Lawyer A at Law Firm #1 took "reasonable measures to avoid exposure to more disqualifying information than was reasonably necessary to determine whether to represent" Tony. Rule 1.18(d)(2). If you're going that route, make sure to specify that Law Firm #1 must screen Lawyer A from participating in the representation of Carmela, and must promptly give written notice to Tony. Like I said, these are alternatives, because it is arguable that Tony is not a prospective client. But since the first alternative would require proving Tony's state of mind when he had the initial consultation with Lawyer A, the safe course of action for the firm would be to screen Lawyer A — that is, to treat Tony *as* if he were a prospective client.

There is also alternative (3), Tony providing informed consent to Law Firm #1's representation of Carmela. See Rule 1.18(d)(1). But I think we all know Tony is never going to do that.

MIGRATORY LAWYERS

The side-switching former-client conflicts problem involves a law firm that stays intact, but switches sides in a matter. What happens if, on the other hand, the firm continues representing the old client, but one of its lawyers leaves and starts working at a new firm that has clients adverse to clients of the old firm? Assume the following scenario.

Sutcliffe is a lawyer at Lennon & Harrison, which represents Best Records in a copyright dispute against Martin Records. Harrison is the lead partner on the copyright matter, and Sutcliffe is not involved at all. Of course, Harrison could not just switch sides in the dispute and represent Martin against Best — that would be a clear violation of Model Rule 1.9(a). Moreover, Sutcliffe similarly would be disqualified from representing Martin, because of the imputation rule, Rule 1.10(a). That rule means that any conflicts that are personal to Harrison are imputed to Sutcliffe, and all other lawyers in Lennon & Harrison. Now imagine that Sutcliffe leaves Lennon & Harrison and starts working at McCartney & Starkey, the firm representing Martin Records. Is McCartney & Starkey disqualified from representing Martin? If the imputation of conflicts goes both ways, at Sutcliffe's old firm and his new firm, the answer would be that McCartney & Starkey would be disqualified from the copyright case.

If it helps, draw a picture illustrating the facts:

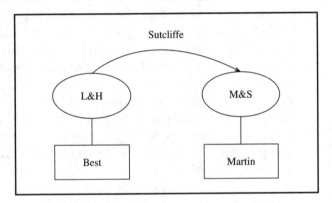

Analysis of Migratory Lawyer Problems

You can analyze this hypothetical, and similar problem, in three steps:

1. While working at the previous firm (Lennon & Harrison), did the moving lawyer (Sutcliffe) represent a client (Best) whose interests are adverse to those of a client (Martin) of the new firm (McCartney & Starkey)?
2. Are the two matters in question the same or substantially related?
3. Is the moving lawyer's "taint" imputed to other lawyers in the new firm (McCartney & Starkey), so that the entire firm is disqualified if the moving lawyer would be personally disqualified?

Definition of "Representation": The *Silver Chrysler* Rule

The former-client conflicts rule is aimed at a lawyer who has formerly represented a client in a matter. Rule 1.9(a); Rest. §132. If it hires Sutcliffe, the first way for McCartney & Starkey to avoid disqualification in the *Best v. Martin* matter is to point out that Sutcliffe did not "represent" Best, for the purposes of the rule. How should we understand "representation"? In line with the general "follow the secrets" approach, most courts define representation in terms of access to confidential client information. If Sutcliffe gained confidential information from Best that could be used by Martin to the detriment of Best, then Sutcliffe will be considered to have represented Best. Sutcliffe, of course, will protest that he did not work on any matters for Best, so he could not have gained any confidential client information. Whether this argument will succeed depends on the status of the *presumption* of access to confidential client information in the jurisdiction.

In all jurisdictions, there is an *irrebuttable* presumption that lawyers within a firm have shared confidential client information among themselves, if the question is whether one lawyer within the firm can take on a new client whose interests are adverse to another firm client. If Sutcliffe stays at Lennon & Harrison, he cannot represent Martin in the dispute with Best, even if Sutcliffe swears that he has never acquired confidential information of Best. In a few jurisdictions, this irrebuttable presumption is extended to lawyers changing firms, so that Sutcliffe will not be able to disclaim having confidential client information of Best, even if he has moved to McCartney & Starkey. The modern rule, recognized in the Restatement and in the majority of jurisdictions, is different. It is a *rebuttable* presumption that Sutcliffe gained confidential client information from Best. If Sutcliffe can make a specific showing that he learned nothing from Best, he may be able to move to McCartney & Starkey without precipitating that firm's disqualification from representing Martin.[2] The answer depends on whether Sutcliffe has a conflict that can be imputed to the new law firm.

The rebuttable presumption that a moving lawyer had acquired confidential information of all the old firm's clients is often called the *Silver Chrysler* rule, after a frequently cited Second Circuit case. *Silver Chrysler Plymouth, Inc. v. Chrysler Motors Corp.*, 518 F.2d 751 (2d Cir. 1975). In that case, an associate at Kelley Drye & Warren, which represented Chrysler Motors Corporation,

---

2. Sutcliffe probably cannot represent Martin personally in the Best versus Martin dispute. For example, California is a jurisdiction that recognizes a rebuttable presumption of sharing confidences in migratory lawyer cases, *Adams v. Aerojet-General Corp.*, 104 Cal. Rptr. 2d 116 (Ct. App. 2001), but even in that state a lawyer would be prohibited from personally working on the opposite side of a matter that her former firm had handled, even though other lawyers at the new firm are not disqualified. *City Nat'l Bank v. Adams*, 117 Cal. Rptr. 2d 125 (Ct. App. 2002).

moved to a firm that represented a Chrysler dealer (Silver) in a dispute over the dealership agreement. The associate had not worked on this particular matter, although he had worked on other Chrysler cases. Even in those cases, though, the associate's involvement was limited to "brief, informal discussions on a procedural matter or research on a specific point of law" — exactly the sorts of things you would expect a junior associate at a firm to do. Because the associate's work for Chrysler was limited to peripheral matters, and because he had not worked on the precise matter in dispute with Silver, the Second Circuit held that the associate had not "represented" Chrysler for the purposes of the former-client conflicts rule, because the associate had not been in a position to acquire confidential information from Chrysler that could be used to Chrysler's detriment in the litigation against Silver. The *Silver Chrysler* rule is recognized in Restatement §132, cmt. h:

> The specific tasks in which a lawyer was engaged might make the access to confidential client information insignificant. The lawyer bears the burden of persuasion as to the issue and as to the absence of opportunity to acquire confidential information. When such a burden has been met, the lawyer is not precluded from proceeding adversely to the former client.

For a subsequent application of *Silver Chrysler*, see *Papyrus Tech. Corp. v. New York Stock Exchange*, 325 F. Supp. 2d 270 (S.D.N.Y. 2004) (presumption of access to confidential information applies where moving lawyer had attended practice group meetings and had received two e-mails from client, even though lawyer never worked on any matter for the firm's former client and had not otherwise received confidential information from the former client).

Under *Silver Chrysler*, the definition of representation is keyed closely to a lawyer's access to confidential client information. Like the use of confidential information to establish whether two matters are substantially related, courts will not insist on examining *actual* confidential information. Rather, they will make educated guesses about what the lawyer probably learned, in light of the nature of the work the lawyer did for the client. Sometimes the party seeking disqualification will submit timesheets to show that the lawyer had extensive involvement in the case. The lawyer trying to avoid disqualification may show, again possibly with timesheets, or perhaps just with an affidavit, that his involvement was merely peripheral. A court will conclude, on the basis of these submissions, whether or not the presumption of acquiring confidential information has been rebutted.

The influence of *Silver Chrysler* on the Model Rules can be seen in the somewhat redundant structure of Model Rule 1.9. Subsection (a) sets out the standard for disqualifying a lawyer who has formerly represented a client. But what does it mean to "represent" a client? *Silver Chrysler* says that representation means having access to confidential client information, so the lawyer would not be disqualified under Model Rule 1.9(a) if he was not in a position to acquire confidential client information. Now look at Model Rule 1.9(b). That section sets out a similar standard for a lawyer who had formerly been associated with a firm that represented a client. It says that the lawyer is personally disqualified if the lawyer had acquired confidential client information from the old client that is material to the matter on which the lawyer seeks to represent a new client. Rule 1.9(b)(2) — voila, *Silver Chrysler*! It is important to recognize that Model Rule 1.9(a) and (b) are not distinct rules. Rather, subsection (b) is really an application of subsection (a), aimed at lawyers changing firms. Subsection (b) clarifies subsection (a) but does not add anything to, or vary, the analysis.[3]

Substantial Relationship

This test is the same as in the side-switching former-client conflicts scenario. The moving lawyer personally would be disqualified from representing a client of the new firm in the same or a substantially related matter as one he had worked on at the old firm. But this standard again calls for some fleshing out — when are two matters substantially related? If you understand substantial relationship using the "follow the secrets" approach, then the test for substantial relationship essentially collapses into the *Silver Chrysler* rule. In other words, if Sutcliffe had not worked on any matters for Best, then two things follow from that fact. First, he did not "represent" Best for the purposes of Model Rule 1.9(a) while working at Lennon & Harrison. That is the *Silver Chrysler* rule. Second, any work he does for Martin, when he starts working at McCartney & Starkey, will not be substantially related to work he did for other clients at Lennon & Harrison.

Using the "follow the secrets" approach is analytically clean, because it enables you to answer two questions at once — whether the lawyer formerly represented a client; and whether the matters at the old firm and the new firm are substantially related. This is the better approach, but note that it might be taken to slight the former client's expectation of loyalty. Best might be annoyed that one of "its lawyers" is now representing Martin, even though the lawyer did not work directly on matters for Best. Thus, a court might interpret the definition of "represented" in Model Rule 1.9(a) as including any case in which the lawyer was formerly associated with a firm that represented the client. As one of the comments to the former-client

---

3. If you are reading old cases, you might notice that the text of Rule 1.9(b) used to reside in Rule 1.10(b). In 1989, the ABA amended those two rules, moving the text of Rule 1.10(b) to Rule 1.9(b), and renumbering the rules accordingly. That restructuring is one reason for the overlap between Rule 1.9(a) and 1.9(b). The reshuffling of the rules also underscores an important point — you need to evaluate migratory lawyer problems using both Rule 1.9, which deals with the *personal* disqualification of the moving lawyer, and Rule 1.10, which addresses the *imputation* of that disqualification to other lawyers in the firm.

conflicts rule observes, "[T]he client previously represented by the former firm must be reasonably assured that the principle of loyalty to the client is not compromised." Rule 1.9, cmt. [4]. The key word in that comment is *reasonably assured*—the principle of loyalty can potentially justify a sweeping prohibition on future representation of adverse interests by former lawyers at a firm that represented a client. In other words, poor Sutcliffe would be turned away from jobs at other firms, because the firms would be worried about being disqualified from representing any clients whose interests were adverse to Best's. At the same comment recognizes, if the loyalty rationale is taken too far, "the result would be radical curtailment of the opportunity of lawyers to move from one practice setting to another and of the opportunity of clients to change counsel." Rule 1.9, cmt. [4]. The best way to put boundaries around the loyalty rationale, so that it does not radically curtail job mobility by lawyers, is to interpret the client's *reasonable* expectation of loyalty so that it is coextensive with the client's expectation of confidentiality.

Jurisdictions that wish to emphasize the loyalty rationale may make the presumption of shared confidences at the old firm (here, Lennon & Harrison) *irrebuttable*. That is, they reject the *Silver Chrysler* rule. If your jurisdiction is one in which loyalty has some independent bite, over and above confidentiality, then the analysis of a migratory lawyer case still would be the same under Model Rule 1.9(a) and 1.9(b). In this case, though, representation under Model Rule 1.9(a) would be understood with reference to the client's expectation of loyalty, and the question under Model Rule 1.9(b)(2) of whether the lawyer had acquired confidential client information would be resolved by applying the irrebuttable presumption of shared confidences.

The "Typhoid Mary" Problem: Imputed Conflicts and Screening

Suppose Sutcliffe had worked on the *Best v. Martin* matter, but intends to have nothing to do with the representation of Martin after he moves to McCartney & Starkey. If his involvement was sufficiently substantial to expose him to confidential client information of Best—that is, under *Silver Chrysler* the presumption of shared confidences is not rebutted—then he is personally disqualified from representing Martin. Is this personal disqualification imputed to the rest of the firm? If it were imputed, Sutcliffe would be a "Typhoid Mary"—he would have a "taint" or "contagion" (courts have an inexplicable fondness for illness metaphors in migratory lawyer cases), which is shared with the other lawyers at McCartney & Starkey. The consequences of hiring a Typhoid Mary would be disastrous. McCartney & Starkey would be disqualified not only from the representation of Martin, but also from any matters in which Sutcliffe would be personally disqualified. The effect of a broad imputation rule would be essentially to freeze lateral hiring of experienced lawyers, particularly in smaller cities or in highly specialized subcommunities of lawyers. As a result, many courts have sought to soften the rule of imputed disqualification of migratory lawyers to avoid unduly restricting lawyers' job mobility.

Softening the harsh rule of imputed disqualification requires *another* rebuttable presumption. Courts will presume that a lawyer in Sutcliffe's position will share confidential information regarding Best with the other lawyers in McCartney & Starkey. Hence, the rule on imputation of conflicts, Rule 1.10(a), which disqualifies any lawyer "associated in a firm" with Sutcliffe—in this case, the new firm of McCartney & Starkey. At one time, the solid majority rule was that the presumption of shared confidences at the new firm is irrebuttable. See, for example, *State ex rel. Freezer Services v. Mullen*, 458 N.W.2d 245 (Neb. 1990). In an increasing number of jurisdictions, however, this presumption (and therefore the imputation of Sutcliffe's "taint") can be rebutted by showing that McCartney & Starkey has put an effective screening mechanism into place, in a timely manner. This is now the position taken by the Model Rules, in Rule 1.10(a).

This is different from the issue of whether Sutcliffe had acquired Best's confidential information in the first place. The *Silver Chrysler* rule pertains to the first presumption, which may be rebuttable if Sutcliffe can show that he did not have access to confidential client information pertaining to Best. Again, the court's decision will not be based on actual confidential material, but on assumptions about what a lawyer in Sutcliffe's position is likely to have learned, given the nature of the work he performed while at Lennon & Harrison. To put it concisely, the first presumption concerns the sharing of information from Best to Lennon & Harrison to Sutcliffe, while the second presumption concerns the sharing of information from Sutcliffe to McCartney & Starkey, which could be disclosed to or used on behalf of Martin.

In order to rebut the second presumption, two things must be true. First, the jurisdiction in question must recognize screening, either by an amendment to the rules or by judicial decision. Second, the elements of an effective screen must be satisfied (see the following section). Screening to cure imputed conflicts is hugely controversial, and it has not been accepted in all jurisdictions. Prior to 2009, the Model Rules did not recognize screening, although many state versions of the rules did. (Some rules supplements for professional responsibility courses include charts showing the state-by-state adoption of screening provisions.) When researching state rules on screening, make sure you differentiate between disciplinary rules and judicial decisions, pursuant to courts' Track Two inherent authority, which may permit screening as a defense to a motion to disqualify a law firm from representing a client. Indiana, for example, has the odd situation of no screening in its disciplinary rules but judicial decisions permitting screening to cure imputation for disqualification purposes. See *Chapman v. Chrysler Corp.*, 54 F. Supp. 2d 864 (S.D. Ind. 1999); *Gerald v. Turnock Plumbing, Heating & Cooling*, 768 N.E.2d 498 (Ind. App. 2002).

The Restatement also recognizes a limited role for screening, but only where the newly hired lawyer does not possess *significant* client information of the former client. Rest. §124(2). The Restatement rule contemplates a kind of intermediate situation, where the lawyer had access to enough confidential client information to have failed to rebut the presumption of shared confidences under *Silver Chrysler*, but where the information is not so significant that the former client would inevitably be harmed by the lawyer changing firms. See Rest §124, cmt. d(i). Consider this "ladder" of increasing access to confidential information by the individual lawyer:

Confidential Information Possessed	Effect
Significant confidences	Lawyer is personally disqualified and screening is not effective to cure imputed disqualification under Rest. §124(2), even in jurisdictions that recognize screening.
Some, but nothing that is likely to be significant in the new matter	Under Rest. §124(2), lawyer is personally disqualified but in a jurisdiction that recognizes screening, lawyer can be screened off; "taint" of incoming lawyer not imputed to firm.
Virtually none; insignificant contact with former client	*Silver Chrysler* — lawyer not personally disqualified; lawyer can represent new client in same or substantially related matter.

By the way, just so we're clear about this, even where it is recognized by rule amendment or judicial decision, screening is effective to cure only certain types of conflicts—principally those created by hiring a lawyer who had formerly worked for a different law firm or a government agency. Screening is almost always permitted to cure conflicts created by the movement of former government lawyers into private practice. Rule 1.11(c). It is now permitted, in the Model Rules and in many states, to cure conflicts created by private lawyers moving from one firm to another. See Rule 1.10(a). In addition, as discussed above, screening may cure imputed conflicts resulting from failed "beauty contests" where the prospective client ends up not retaining the lawyer, and other lawyers in the firm wish to represent another client whose interests are adverse in the same or a substantially related matter. Rule 1.18(d). Otherwise, outside these areas, screening is not effective to cure imputed conflicts. In particular, it may never, never, *never* be used to avoid disqualification of a firm that has a current-client conflict under Model Rule 1.7 and cannot obtain informed consent from all affected clients. Lawyers try screens in current-client conflict situations frequently, but it never works. *Never.* Got that? (At least, I have yet to see a situation in which it is effective. If you are aware of such a case, send me an e-mail with the citation, and I will gratefully acknowledge your research in the next edition of this book.[4])

All this talk about the permissibility of screening pertains only to *nonconsensual* screens. Imagine that Law Firm B hires Moving Lawyer, who formerly worked at Law Firm A and had some peripheral responsibility in the representation of Client A. Law Firm B is representing Client B, who has a lawsuit pending against Client A. The former client complains, worried about sharing of its confidential information. At least two different scenarios may follow:

- Scenario 1: Moving Lawyer calls the general counsel of Client A, explains that she was only peripherally involved in the representation, and is unlikely to possess significant confidential information. She asks the general counsel to consent on behalf of Client A to Law Firm B continuing to represent Client B. The general counsel responds, "Okay, I trust you, but I'm also aware that people can sometimes be careless, so I'll agree to waive any claim we may have of a conflict of interest, *provided that* your new law firm sets up a screen just to ensure against accidental disclosure of confidential information."
- Scenario 2: Moving Lawyer calls the general counsel of Client A, provides the same disclosure, and requests a waiver of the conflict. The general counsel has a conniption, chews out Moving Lawyer for her "betrayal," and adamantly refuses to consent. Moving Lawyer reports back to the managing partner of Law Firm B, who says, "Too bad — we're going to set up a screen, and if Client A moves to disqualify us from representing Client B, we will point to the screen as a reason we shouldn't be disqualified."

Only Scenario 2 is a test case for screening in the sense we're talking about here. Lawyers and clients are always free to condition informed consent on the establishment of a screen, even if nonconsensual screens are not permitted by state rules. Nonconsensual screens, as imagined in Scenario 2,

---

4. Just to be clear, what we're talking about here is *nonconsensual* screening to cure a current-client conflict. A client may condition the grant of a waiver of the conflict on the law firm's compliance with some kind of screening procedure. That's fine, but it's not what we are talking about here. What makes screening controversial is the possibility that a law firm might "cram down" a conflict on a client by accepting the second representation and relying on the screen to solve the problem. That does not work, *ever*, in the context of concurrent conflicts under Rule 1.7.

are controversial because they essentially allow the lawyer to tell the client to get lost when the client expresses concern about loss of control over its confidential information.

Elements of an Effective Screen

Where they are recognized by disciplinary rule or judicial decision, screens have similar elements. Although the precise formulation of the standards for an effective screen varies by jurisdiction, there is broad similarity. Returning to the hypothetical, where a newly hired lawyer (Sutcliffe) formerly worked on a case (*Best v. Martin*) on behalf of a client (Best) who is adverse to a client (Martin) of the hiring firm (McCartney & Starkey) in the same or a substantially related matter in which the interests of the old and new clients are materially adverse, suppose other lawyers at McCartney & Starkey would like to continue representing Martin. In order to do so, they must somehow isolate Sutcliffe from that representation, so that Sutcliffe does not leak confidential information pertaining to Best to the lawyers working on the matter for Martin. In order to be effective to prevent Sutcliffe's taint from "infecting" the entire firm of McCartney & Starkey and requiring its disqualification, the screening process must satisfy several elements. *See* Rule 1.0(k), cmt. [8]; Rest. §124, cmt. d.

1. Strict segregation of paper and electronic files. This may mean locking up case files from *Best v. Martin* in secure cabinets and not giving keys to Sutcliffe; plastering file cabinets with stickers warning Sutcliffe that the files are subject to a screening mechanism; and issuing separate passwords to Sutcliffe and to the lawyers on *Best v. Martin*, so that Sutcliffe cannot look at case documents stored online.

2. Instruction to lawyers in McCartney & Starkey not to communicate with Sutcliffe about *Best v. Martin*. In addition, instructions to Sutcliffe not to reveal confidential client information he learned working for Best to lawyers at the firm working on *Best v. Martin*. This seems to be the most important element. Element 1 seems beside the point — who cares if Sutcliffe learns information about Martin, because he is not working on the case? (Although, the risk would be that Sutcliffe would continue to feel some loyalty to Best and may leak some of Martin's secrets to his former client.) The real danger in a migratory lawyer case is to the former client, in this case Best. If Sutcliffe deliberately or inadvertently discloses Best's confidential information to lawyers working for Martin, Best's interests could be harmed. Thus, it is essential to shut down any lines of communication between Sutcliffe and the lawyers working for Martin, with respect to the *Best v. Martin* litigation.

3. No sharing of fees attributable to the personally disqualified lawyer. The reason for this element is probably to prevent the firm from setting up some kind of *quid pro quo*, where Sutcliffe would get a financial reward for leaking Best's secrets. People often wonder how the prohibition on apportioning fees from the new matter works in practice, because associates and partners are paid out of a common pot of money. Fees received from Martin go into the same pot from which Sutcliffe is paid. The answer is that Sutcliffe can receive whatever salary (as an associate) or share of the profits (as a partner) to which he would otherwise be entitled. The only restriction is that the billings to Martin cannot factor into the bonus or partnership-share calculations of Sutcliffe. Firms have been disqualified for failing to comply with this element of the screening procedure. See, for example, *Norfolk Southern Ry. Co. v. Reading Blue Mountain & Northern RR Co.*, 397 F. Supp. 2d 551 (M.D. Pa. 2005) (citing other grounds for disqualification, including tardy implementation of the screen).

4. Notice to Best of the lateral move of Sutcliffe, so that Best can keep an eye on the progress of *Best v. Martin* to see whether the hiring firm of McCartney & Starkey actually is complying with its screening obligation.[5] If Best starts to worry that its secrets have been compromised, it can file a motion to disqualify McCartney & Starkey. Sometimes, too, the firms involved must submit affidavits, either to Best or to the court, testifying to their compliance with the screening procedure. Screening is still *nonconsensual*, however, in the sense that the firm need only give the former client notice, not obtain its informed consent.

5. As in comedy, with screens *timing is everything*. The screening mechanism must be in place *before* there is any possibility that Sutcliffe could leak Best's confidential client information to the lawyers representing Martin. Usually, this means setting up the screen before Sutcliffe arrives for his first day on the job. There are tons of cases in which a firm has obviously discovered the conflict several weeks, or even months, after hiring a lateral lawyer. It then scrambles around to erect a screen, but courts assume that the damage already has been done. If the screen goes up too late, it will be ineffective to eliminate the imputation of Sutcliffe's conflict. See for example, *Securities Investor Protection Corp. v. Vigman*, 587 F. Supp. 1358 (C.D. Cal. 1984).

6. Some jurisdictions add the requirement that the incoming lawyer (here, Sutcliffe) not process confidential client information that is likely to be *significant* in the matter (here, *Best v. Martin*). This is the position recognized by Restatement §124(2).

---

5. Technically speaking, this is not an element of an effective screen but something else the law firm must do in order to avoid the imputation of the moving lawyer's conflict. Note the structure of Rule 1.10(a)(2), with screening being element (i), written notice to the former client being element (ii), and a certification of compliance provided to the former client as element (iii).

Remember that screening applies only to the lawyer's new firm. If the lawyer does not change firms, there is no way to cure an imputed conflict by screening. Rule 1.10(a). The presumption, embodied in Model Rule 1.10(a), that a lawyer shares confidential client information with others in her firm, is *irrebuttable* in all jurisdictions where the lawyer remains in the same firm. The two-presumption analysis just discussed applies only in migratory lawyer cases. The following table summarizes that analysis:

Migratory Lawyer	Presumption and Effect	Is Presumption Rebuttable?
At old firm	Has acquired confidential information of every client at the firm. If presumption not rebutted (or irrebuttable), then lawyer is personally tainted and cannot represent new clients in the same or substantially related matter materially adverse to former client.	*Yes*, in most jurisdictions, if the lawyer can show either that she was not involved in a particular client's matters, or involvement was so peripheral that lawyer would not have learned confidential client information. *Silver Chrysler.* Lawyer would not be personally tainted and no need to worry about second presumption. *No*, in a few jurisdictions that wish to emphasize the loyalty interest above protection of client confidences.
At new firm	If lawyer is personally tainted, the presumption is that she has shared confidential information with respect to old client with colleagues at new firm.	*Yes*, in a minority of jurisdictions that recognize screening, either by adopting the position of the ABA in Rule 1.10(a), or by judicial decision. *No*, in the majority of jurisdictions that do not accept screening to cure imputed conflicts.

Remember, too, that the analysis in the table only takes care of the question of whether the lawyer acquired a taint by virtue of having represented a client, and the related issue of whether that taint is imputed to the new firm. You still have to address the other issues that arise in former-client conflicts cases, namely (1) whether the two matters are the same or substantially related; (2) whether the position of the clients is materially adverse; and (3) whether the affected client (the former client of the moving lawyer) has given informed consent.

Example

4. After the ABA approved the Ethics 2000 revisions to the Model Rules, the Supreme Court of the State of Perplexity appointed a commission to consider amendments to the Perplexity Rules of Professional Conduct (RPC). The chair of the commission was Barry Rocks, an outspoken critic of screening to cure imputed conflicts of interest. The commission considered a proposed amendment to Perplexity RPC 1.10(a) that would have permitted a law firm to employ a screening mechanism to avoid discipline when a newly hired lawyer would be personally disqualified from representing a new client of the firm, by reason of a former representation. Rocks adamantly opposed this proposal, contending that it would lead to disloyalty to clients and the disclosure of the confidences of former clients. "How can we even call ourselves a profession," Rocks asked rhetorically, "if we allow lawyers to so easily evade their most basic ethical obligations?" The commission voted 11-1 to reject the screening proposal, and when the new Perplexity Rules were adopted, RPC 1.10(a) did not provide for screening to cure imputed conflicts for moving private lawyers (as opposed to government lawyers).

Bonham & Moon, a large law firm, recently hired Watts, a partner from another firm, to head up the litigation practice at Bonham & Moon. At the time the offer to join the firm was made, Watts was at another large firm, which represented Federal Parcel Delivery Service (Federal Parcel) in litigation with Boeing over the conversion of some passenger aircraft to freighters. Watts was one of several partners working on the case for Federal Parcel, but was not the lead attorney on the matter. Boeing was represented in that matter by Bonham & Moon. Before Watts started work at Bonham & Moon, the firm put in place a screening mechanism. Watts agreed not to represent Boeing in the litigation with Federal Parcel. All lawyers in the firm were instructed not to discuss anything with Watts related to his prior representation of Federal Parcel. Watts was required to certify periodically that he had not disclosed confidential information of Federal Parcel. Files relating to the firm's representation of Boeing were kept strictly segregated. After joining Bonham & Moon, Watts accepted the representation of Federal Parcel's arch-rival, United Express, alleging that Federal Parcel's recent acquisition of a chain of copy stores violated antitrust laws. Federal Parcel filed a motion in Perplexity Superior Court to disqualify Bonham & Moon from representing Boeing. The Superior Court denied the motion, reasoning as follows:

> Although we do not approve of the side-switching of attorney Watts, we are mindful of the hardship that Boeing would experience if it were deprived of the counsel of its choice. Federal Parcel has not shown any actual harm as a result of Watts's move to Bonham & Moon. Because Bonham & Moon

has established that it put into place in a timely manner a screening mechanism safeguarding the confidential information of Federal Parcel, we deny Federal Parcel's motion for disqualification.

Did the Superior Court err by denying Federal Parcel's motion to disqualify Bonham & Moon from representing Boeing?

A. No, because courts considering a party's motion to disqualify may consider the state disciplinary rules, but are not required to do so.

B. No, because Federal Parcel did not show any actual harm as a result of Watts's move to Bonham & Moon.

C. Yes, because the Perplexity Rules of Professional Conduct do not permit screening to cure Watts's "taint."

D. Yes, because Watts's move to Bonham & Moon creates an appearance of impropriety.

Explanation

4. The answer is A. After the discussion of the elements of an effective screen, you may have been expecting a question about the specifics of screens, but this is really yet another question about the sources of the law governing lawyers. First of all, notice that your state has refused to amend its version of Rule 1.10(a) to permit screening, following the exhortation of Barry Rocks (professional responsibility teachers will recognize this character). So in theory, the lawyers working on the Boeing matter are subject to discipline because they pick up a conflict of interest from the moving lawyer, Watts. But don't answer C just yet—look carefully at the question. It asks whether the firm should be disqualified from the representation. The court's authority to disqualify the firm arises from its inherent authority, which I referred to in Chapter 1 as Track Two inherent authority, to supervise the conduct of attorneys practicing before it. See Rest. §1, cmt. c. One remedy available to the trial court—wholly apart from discipline by the highest court of the state—is disqualification. See Rest. §6(8). Disqualification is an equitable remedy, however, and trial courts may, in the exercise their discretion, choose not to disqualify a law firm. This may be because they believe the other side is playing games by filing the motion, or because (as is the case here) the court is concerned with the burden that would be imposed on the party that loses the counsel of its choice. See Rest. §6, cmt. i. That's why the answer is A.

   If you answered B, please go back and look at the discussion in Chapter 14 of actual versus potential conflicts, and of harm rules and risk rules. As a general matter, "no harm, no foul" is not a principle of professional responsibility. If you answered D, please show me in the rules where the appearance of impropriety standard is stated. . . . Right, it's not in there. It used to be, but no more.

Lingering Taints of the Departed Lawyer

There is a kind of "reverse imputation" situation, in which the taint of a migratory lawyer persists after that lawyer's departure. In the original hypothetical, Harrison represented Best Records on behalf of Lennon & Harrison. Suppose now that Harrison, not Sutcliffe, leaves the firm, taking his best client (ha ha) with him. After Harrison's departure, the new firm (let's promote Sutcliffe to named partner and call the firm Lennon & Sutcliffe) may represent clients whose interests are adverse to those of Best, even in the same or a substantially related matter, as long as no lawyer remaining in Lennon & Sutcliffe retains confidential client information pertaining to Best. Rule 1.10(b).

Migratory Nonlawyers

The same problem of transmission of confidential client information can occur when a nonlawyer support person, such as a paralegal or secretary, moves from one firm to another. Courts will sometimes analyze these cases exactly as if the newly hired support person had been a lawyer—that is, if that person had worked on substantially related matters while at the old firm, the entire new firm will be disqualified from representing a client whose interests are materially adverse to those of the client of the old firm. See, for example, *Owens v. First Family Financial Servs.*, 379 F. Supp. 2d 840 (S.D. Miss. 2005). However, a comment to the imputation rule, Rule 1.10, says the newly hired support person will not be treated like a lawyer—that is, her conflict will not be imputed to the entire firm; weirdly, however, the comment says the incoming nonlawyer must be screened in a timely manner. See Rule 1.10, cmt. [4]. Alternatively, even in the absence of screening the firm may not be disqualified if the moving nonlawyer employee can show that he or she did not leak any protected confidences of the former firm's clients. See, for example, *Hayes v. Central States Orthopedic Specialists, Inc.*, 51 P.3d 562 (Okla. 2002). Also note that even if Rule 1.10, cmt. [4], doesn't treat moving nonlawyers exactly as lawyers, it's still the case that any lawyer in the firm having direct supervisory authority over the nonlawyer employee must make reasonable efforts to ensure that the support person's conduct is compatible with the rules of professional conduct. Rule 5.3(b). That may mean, for example, ensuring that the new nonlawyer employee does not divulge confidential information from a previous employer.

Examples

Putting the Presumptions to Work

5. O'Connell recently joined the law firm of Leff & Cabranes, after working for many years at Scranton & Artzt. While at Scranton & Artzt, O'Connell represented Gotham Financial Services in litigation involving the sales practices of Gotham's account representatives and managers. Investors have accused Gotham's account representatives of "churning" their accounts, by making needless trades in an effort to increase commissions. As part of O'Connell's representation, she interviewed managers about procedures for hiring, supervising, compensating, and disciplining account representatives, as well as performance expectations and evaluation procedure for both managers and account representatives. In total, she billed almost 1,800 hours in one year to Gotham, and 1,500 the next year.

   Before O'Connell joined Leff & Cabranes, that firm filed an employment discrimination lawsuit against Gotham Financial Services, on behalf of a class of women account representatives, alleging discrimination on the basis of sex, in violation of federal statutes. The action was pending when it hired O'Connell, but she did not have anything to do with it. In fact, she was not even aware of the litigation until the managing partner of Leff & Cabranes informed her that Gotham had filed a motion to disqualify the firm from representing the class of plaintiffs in the discrimination action. Should the district court grant the motion?

An Ounce of Prevention

6. What should O'Connell and Leff & Cabranes have done before O'Connell was hired in order to avoid disqualification from the discrimination action?

Explanations

Putting the Presumptions to Work

5. This example is based on *Mitchell v. Metropolitan Life*, 2002 WL 441194 (S.D.N.Y. 2002), in which the court disqualified the firm of Lieff Cabraser because of its hiring of Fleishman, the former Skadden Arps lawyer. To answer the question in the hypothetical, run through the migratory lawyers analysis of Model Rule 1.9, remembering that you can use subsection (a) or (b). First, did O'Connell formerly represent a client in a matter in which the former client's interests are materially adverse to the new client's? There is a presumption that every lawyer

in Scranton & Artzt shared confidential information of all the firm's clients, including Gotham. That presumption is rebuttable under *Silver Chrysler*, but there is absolutely no way she can establish that the work she performed for Gotham was peripheral or that she was not in a position to acquire confidential client information. You can reach the same result using subsection (b) of Model Rule 1.9, under which O'Connell personally would be disqualified if the firm with which she formerly was associated (here, Scranton & Artzt) had previously represented a client (Gotham) whose interests are materially adverse to those of the new client (the discrimination plaintiffs) and about whom O'Connell had acquired material confidential client information. The bottom line is that her lengthy and extensive exposure to Gotham's sales-practices litigation put her in a position to acquire plenty of confidential client information.

If the matters are substantially related, Leff & Cabranes is disqualified, because the personal conflict of O'Connell will be imputed to the entire firm under Model Rule 1.10(a).[6] Thus, the firm's only hope is to argue that the two matters are not substantially related. Superficially, it seems that they are not. Allegations of account-churning and sex discrimination seem completely distinct. But notice the overlap between the information acquired in one matter and the information that may be useful in the other. Suppose it were the case that Gotham evaluated its account representatives purely "on the numbers" — that is, promotion and compensation decisions were based solely on the amount of sales commissions generated in the relevant period. That would be a dangerous fact in the sales-practices litigation, because it shows that representatives have an incentive to churn accounts. The significance for the conflicts issue, though, is that it also could serve to buttress the sex discrimination claims filed by the plaintiffs. If evaluation and compensation were really a mechanical matter, then it should be easy to correlate account representatives who got promoted with high numbers. If it turns out that some women had high numbers but did not get promoted, this would be *prima facie* evidence of sex discrimination.

Because there is a substantial risk that the *kind of information* O'Connell acquired while representing Gotham could be useful to the plaintiffs in the employment discrimination litigation, the matters are substantially related. Rest. §132(2). The emphasis on "kind of information" is

---

6. This was the court's analysis under the old version of Rule 1.10(a), before the 2009 amendment permitting screening. A court today might decide the case differently, depending on whether the jurisdiction in question had changed its imputation rule to conform to the ABA's new version of Rule 1.10(a).

to underscore that the court will not require a showing of actual transmission of confidential client information. It is enough that Gotham is able to establish a substantial risk that O'Connell would have had access to information that might be useful for the new client's case.

An Ounce of Prevention

6. If the litigation is pending in a jurisdiction that recognizes screening to cure imputed conflicts, the firm should have set up an effective screening mechanism *before O'Connell set foot in the office*. It is vitally important that a screen be in place before there is any possibility of the transmission of confidential client information from the newly hired lawyer to other lawyers working on the new client's matters. Thus, Leff & Cabranes should have discussed O'Connell's potential conflicts with her during the hiring process and should have been prepared either not to make an offer of employment or to research the permissibility and prerequisites for screening in the relevant jurisdiction. These elements vary considerably. Note, for example, that the Restatement would permit screening only where any confidential information communicated to O'Connell is unlikely to be significant in the representation by Leff & Cabranes of the women plaintiffs. Rest. §124(2)(a). Thus, even a jurisdiction that permits screening would require the disqualification of Leff & Cabranes on the facts of this particular case. Pay close attention to local law when analyzing screening.

THE SPECIAL SITUATION OF FORMER GOVERNMENT LAWYERS

The discussion in every casebook of former-client conflicts for former government lawyers observes that government practice generally is less lucrative than working in the private sector. Naturally, lawyers may be motivated to work for the government for ideological reasons, perhaps believing the SEC or the EPA are the "good guys." But other lawyers simply may want to learn useful information, which they subsequently can use on behalf of private clients in similar cases. Many private tax lawyers began their careers at the IRS, for example, and the ranks of criminal defense lawyers are full of former prosecutors. Private-sector lawyers may return to government service, again possibly motivated by idealism, or perhaps to accept an opportunity to serve as an important government official—think, for instance, of Harvey Pitt, a former partner at a Wall Street firm who left private practice to become the chairman of the Securities and Exchange Commission. This cycling of lawyers in and out of government practice is known as the "revolving door," and creates a special kind of former-client conflict situation. Revolving door cases are handled by Model Rule 1.11.[7]

Any conflicts rule addressing former government lawyers will be aimed at preventing corruption of some kind. Two cases in particular are troubling. In the first, a government lawyer throws a case (or "takes a dive") while working for the government agency, in order to curry favor with a prospective private-sector employer. See Rule 1.11, cmt. [4]. The second kind of corruption is the use of insider information, contacts, or intimate familiarity with the internal workings of a government agency to obtain results for a client that a similar lawyer, without the previous experience in government, would be unable to obtain. This second rationale cannot be taken too far, because the whole reason that private-sector firms hire former government lawyers is that they have useful knowledge about how some government agency functions. If they were absolutely prohibited from using that knowledge in any way—for example, if former SEC lawyers were forbidden to work on any securities case for a private client—smart, ambitious lawyers would never choose to work for the government, because they would have to reinvent themselves as completely different kinds of lawyers in private practice. Comment [4] to Rule 1.11 makes that point, too.

The former government lawyer conflicts rule, Rule 1.11, attempts to strike a balance between these competing policies. To see this balance, it is helpful to compare Rule 1.11 with the ordinary former-client conflicts rule, Rule 1.9. The first difference is in the text of the rule: Rule 1.11 essentially incorporates the *Silver Chrysler* rule, but extends it to cases of personal as well as imputed disqualification. Under Model Rule 1.11(a), a former government lawyer is personally disqualified from representing a private client only where the lawyer participated *personally* and *substantially* in the matter when she was working for the government. A lawyer is personally and substantially involved where her involvement goes beyond "mere perfunctory approval or disapproval of the matter in question" and rises to the level of "important, material" work in connection with the matter. Simply being the nominal head of some vast legal department, supervising lawyers working on various matters, does not constitute personal and substantial involvement. See ABA Formal Op. 342. However, where a lawyer worked 382 hours on the defense of an administrative rulemaking proceeding, he cannot deny that he had personal

---

7. You may be wondering why Rule 1.9 does not control these cases, since it applies by its terms to all former-representation conflicts. As a matter of statutory interpretation, the specific controls over the general. If there is a rule, such as Rule 1.11, specific to the situation of former government lawyers, it applies rather than the more general rule, Rule 1.9. In addition, take a look at the text of Rule 1.11(a)(1). It says that a former government lawyer is subject to Rule 1.9(c) (on adverse use of confidential information), but says nothing about Rule 1.9(a) or (b). By negative implication from the inclusion of Rule 1.9(c), you can infer that Rule 1.9(a) and (b) do not apply.

and substantial involvement in the matter. *United States v. Philip Morris, Inc.*, 312 F. Supp. 2d 27 (D.D.C. 2004) (involving former Justice Department attorney who had worked on a Youth Tobacco Rulemaking project while in government practice and subsequently worked for a large law firm representing tobacco company).

Second, the rule defines "matter" rather narrowly in one respect, as compared with Model Rule 1.9(a). A matter includes "any judicial or other proceeding, application, request for a ruling . . . or other particular matter *involving a specific party or parties.*" Rule 1.11(e)(1). That definition rules out something general, like a rulemaking proceeding in which the definition of a statutory term is at issue, or enforcement of a particular set of regulations. As long as the private client was not involved in the proceeding for which the government lawyer had personal and substantial responsibility, it does not matter that the lawyer, now in private practice, will be working on the same kind of case that she had handled previously for the government. A matter is, rather, a "discrete and isolatable transaction or set of transactions between identifiable parties." ABA Formal Op. 342. Thus, an EPA lawyer who had worked on Clean Water Act issues can represent private clients in Clean Water Act cases, as long as the clients were not involved in the particular proceeding for which the lawyer was responsible.

Finally, Model Rule 1.11(a) is broader than Model Rule 1.9 in one respect, because Model Rule 1.11(a) is not limited to cases in which the new client (in the private sector) is taking a position that is materially adverse to the government agency. If the lawyer participated personally and substantially in the matter, she cannot subsequently represent private clients who were mixed up in the matter regardless of the alignment of interests of the parties. For example, a lawyer who worked for the SEC on a civil injunctive action charging securities fraud cannot move to a private firm representing investors against the same defendant in the same securities fraud litigation, even though the SEC and the investors are "on the same side" of the litigation, aligned in interests against the defendant.

The rule prohibiting successive representation of a government agency and a private client is *consentable*, Rule 1.11(a)(2), although some agencies have a policy of never giving consent to adverse representation by their former lawyers who had participated personally and substantially in a matter. See, for example, *Securities Investor Protection Corp. v. Vigman*, 587 F. Supp. 1358 (C.D. Cal. 1984) (SEC has general policy against waiving disqualification). Under the Model Rules, only the government agency must consent, but the Restatement requires consent of both the government agency and the private client. Rest. §133(1). In addition, in contrast with the rule governing former private-sector lawyers, the rule for former government lawyers expressly recognizes *screening* to cure imputed conflicts. Rule 1.11(b). As long as the private firm follows the screening procedure, it must only give *notice* to the government agency, not seek its consent. Rule 1.11(b)(2). Consent, of course, remains an alternative to screening. The procedures for screening former government lawyers are identical with those for lawyers who move from one private-practice setting to another—in fact, the law of screening in private practice is largely derived from cases involving former government lawyers.

The disciplinary rule does not neglect the other side of the revolving door, with lawyers entering government service after working in the private sector. A lawyer now in the government may not participate in a matter in which she had participated personally and substantially while in private practice. Rule 1.11(d)(2)(i). Imputation of these conflicts is handled a bit differently, so make sure to read the rules *and comments* carefully. Where a lawyer enters government service after working in the private sector, her conflicts are not imputed to other government lawyers in the office. See Rule 1.10, cmt. [11]; see also Rule 1.11, cmt. [2] (noting that Rule 1.11 has its own special imputation provisions and the regular imputation analysis under Rule 1.10(a) does not apply).[8]

Finally, the rule provides independent protection to "confidential government information," which is any information obtained by the government, pursuant to its authority, that the government is forbidden to disclose. Rule 1.11(c). Probably the quintessential example is financial information from income tax returns, which is provided by taxpayers to the IRS and which must, by law, be kept confidential. A lawyer who possesses confidential government information, acquired while she was in government service, is forbidden to represent any client in private practice whose interests are adverse to the person to whom the confidential government information pertains, if the case is one in which the confidential information could be used to that person's disadvantage. Rule 1.11(c). In addition to the broad prohibition on the adverse use of (specially defined) confidential government information, a lawyer may not disclose or make adverse use of any information relating to the representation of a former client, which in this case would be a government agency. See Rule 1.11(a)(1) (incorporating Rule 1.9(c) by reference).

---

8. Way deep in the weeds: Notice that Rule 1.11(d)(1) says a current government lawyer, who was formerly in private practice, is subject to Rule 1.9. That means she cannot represent the government in the same or a substantially related matter where the interests of the private party and the government are materially adverse. Given that, why does Rule 1.11(d)(2)(i) go on to prohibit the lawyer from participating in a matter, on behalf of the government, in which the lawyer participated personally and substantially in private practice? Shouldn't Rule 1.9 cover those conflicts? The answer goes back to something noted above, that the former government-lawyer conflicts rule also picks up cases in which the parties' interests are not materially adverse. So a lawyer moving from private practice to government service would be personally disqualified under Rule 1.11(d)(2)(i) but not Rule 1.9.

Summarizing the analysis of former government conflicts under Model Rule 1.11, you should go through the following steps:

1. Identify the matter on which the lawyer worked while in government service and the matter from which a party is now seeking to disqualify the lawyer. See Rule 1.11(e) for a definition of "matter."
2. Was the lawyer personally and substantially involved as a public employee? Rule 1.11(a)(2).
3. If not, is it possible for the lawyer to use information relating to the representation of the government agency to the disadvantage of that agency? Rule 1.11(a)(1), incorporating by reference Rule 1.9(c).
4. Does the lawyer possess "confidential government information" that can be used to the detriment of a third party who provided that information to the government? Rule 1.11(c). There is no consent provision for this rule, because the misuse of confidential government information affects the third parties who provided the information, not the government.
5. Did the appropriate government agency give informed consent? Rule 1.11(a)(2). Note that there is no explicit textual basis in Rule 1.11 for the agency's consent to the adverse use of confidential information, but the duty of confidentiality may generally be waived by the former client. See Rule 1.6(a).
6. If the lawyer is personally disqualified, is the new law firm disqualified by imputation? The new firm can avoid disqualification by timely screening the incoming lawyer from participation in the new matter and giving written notice to the appropriate government agency so that it can ascertain compliance with the screen. Rule 1.11(b).

Example

What the Government Knows Can Hurt You

7. Adams was formerly Assistant Deputy Chief Counsel in the fraud division of the IRS. In that capacity, he supervised lawyers in a number of tax fraud cases, including an enforcement action against Robert Scrunchy, the CEO of Northern Health, who allegedly used an elaborate tax-sheltering scheme to defraud the government out of millions of dollars. Adams left the IRS and took a job at Brown, Cavanaugh & Danforth. Scrunchy's wife, from whom he is separated, seeks to hire Adams to represent her in the divorce proceedings. May Adams represent Scrunchy's wife?

Explanation

What the Government Knows Can Hurt You

7. When you see a former government lawyer problem, it is tempting just to analyze the side-switching aspect of it. Your first instinct may be to observe that Adams would be prohibited from representing someone in the private sector on a matter in which Adams participated personally and substantially while in government service, unless the appropriate agency gives written consent. Rule 1.11(a)(2). Under this rule, Adams would be prohibited from representing Scrunchy in the tax fraud case or representing a private plaintiff suing Scrunchy for misconduct associated with one of the tax-avoidance transactions. (Maybe an investor in Northern Health claims to have been defrauded.) In this respect, the former government lawyer conflicts rule is broader than Model Rule 1.9, because it prevents *any* involvement — not just side-switching — in a matter for which the lawyer had personal and substantial involvement.

   This example is actually an application of a different portion of the former government lawyer conflicts rule. Adams also is prohibited from using "confidential government information" about a person acquired while the lawyer was in government service. Rule 1.11(c). This prohibition extends to any matter in which the confidential government information could be used against the person to whom the information pertains. Here, as a lawyer for the IRS, Adams probably had access to a great deal of confidential financial information filed by Scrunchy. Some of that information may be relevant in the divorce proceedings, as Scrunchy's wife tries to get the best possible division of the marital property. For this reason, Adams cannot represent Scrunchy's wife.

SIDE-SWITCHING JUDGES AND LAW CLERKS

It is not all that common, but judges do step down from the bench and resume the private practice of law. When that happens, they are disqualified from representing a party in connection with a matter in which the judge participated personally and substantially while on the bench. Rule 1.12(a). The "personal and substantial" qualification is intended to exclude from disqualification a judge who was on a multimember court but was not involved in that particular case. See Rule 1.12, cmt. [1]. Suppose a state appellate court has fifteen active judges who sit in panels of three to hear appeals. The case of A versus B was considered by a panel of judges X, Y, and Z. If Judge W retires from the bench and joins the law firm representing A in the A versus B litigation, there is no conflict of interest under Rule 1.12(a).

If, on the other hand, Judge X retires and joints the firm representing A, there is a conflict which is imputed to the entire firm representing A unless a screen, as defined in Rule 1.0(k), is put into place before Judge X joins the firm. See Rule 1.12(c).

Although judicial retirements are relatively uncommon, lawyers do serve with some frequency as mediators and arbitrators—"third-party neutrals" in the jargon of alternative dispute resolution (ADR). Rule 1.12(a) covers former ADR neutrals as well as judges. Note, too, that Rule 1.12(a) applies to all "adjudicative officers," so it includes administrative law judges, members of municipal zoning boards, and the like.

Rule 1.12(b) prohibits judges and ADR neutrals from negotiating for employment while participating personally and substantially in a proceeding. Makes sense, right? Think how a party would feel if its opponent obtained a substantial award in a trial or arbitration proceeding and subsequently learned that the judge or arbitrator had been negotiating to join the law firm representing the opponent while presiding over the proceedings. The potential for corruption in that situation is simply too great, and so the prohibition in Rule 1.12(b) is nonwaivable.

Of more immediate concern to recent law school graduates is the rule on negotiating for employment while serving as a judicial clerk. A law clerk may negotiate for employment with a party or lawyer involved in a matter in which the law clerk is participating personally and substantially, but only after first notifying the judge for whom the law clerk is working. Rule 1.12(b). It is then up to the judge to take any necessary steps, such as reassigning the clerk to other cases.

Personal-Interest Conflicts

17

INTRODUCTION

The preceding chapters have considered conflicts arising from the simultaneous or successive representation of multiple clients. There are also conflicts that arise between the lawyer's own interests and the interests of her client. I will refer to these as either personal-interest conflicts or lawyer-client conflicts. In any case, they are handled by two provisions in the rules. The first is the general concurrent conflicts rule, which states that a lawyer may not proceed without obtaining informed consent, if the lawyer's representation of the client would be materially limited by "a personal interest of the lawyer." Rule 1.7(a)(2). For example, the criminal investigation by a district attorney's office of a lawyer creates a conflict between the personal interest of the lawyer and the interests of a client being prosecuted by a separate lawyer in the same district attorney's office. *Rugiero v. United States*, 330 F. Supp. 2d 900 (E.D. Mich. 2004). The worry here is that the lawyer may be tempted to "pull punches" in representing the client, to avoid angering lawyers in the DA's office who may be deciding whether to proceed with prosecuting the lawyer. The second provision is a rule of its own, Rule 1.8, with several enumerated prohibitions on specific actions that create particularly severe conflicts between the duty of loyal client service and the lawyer's personal interests.

In theory, all conflicts involving personal interests of the lawyer could be analyzed under Rule 1.7(a)(2), but the results of the analysis may differ in subtle ways. For example, the 1983 version of the Model Rules had a specific prohibition on representing a client in a matter directly adverse to a person known to be represented by a specified family member—that is, a parent, child, sibling, or spouse—without the consent of both clients. Rule 1.8(i) (1983 vers.). The 2002 amendments deleted this rule, leaving the prohibition on these conflicts to the general prohibition on personal-interest conflicts in Rule 1.7(a)(2). Where the 1983 rule, a specifically enumerated provision of Rule 1.8, had limited disqualifying relationships to those with parents, children, siblings, and spouses, the present approach relying on the general conflicts rule, Rule 1.7, leaves open the possibility that same-sex relationships, domestic partnerships, close friendships, and similar intimate ties also may be disqualifying.

Why would the Model Rules drafters have opted for the approach of bifurcating the analysis of personal-interest conflicts? There are two principal reasons for the separate treatment of some conflicts in Rule 1.8.

1. *Different waiver standards.* As you know from the last chapter, most conflicts under Rule 1.7(a) are waivable (or consentable—it means the same thing). Some of the specifically enumerated conflicts in Rule 1.8 may be waivable only after the lawyer takes special care in disclosing risks to the client. For example, the rule on business transactions with clients (considered next) has requirements that are more stringent than simply obtaining informed consent: The terms of the deal must be substantively fair and reasonable to the client, the client must have the opportunity to consult with independent counsel, and the consent must be signed by the client (as opposed to being "confirmed in writing"). Rule 1.8(a). The rule on advance waivers of malpractice liability, Rule 1.8(h)(1), requires not only the opportunity to consult independent counsel but actual independent representation of the client in making the agreement, while the provision governing *settlement* of a malpractice claim requires only advice in writing and a reasonable opportunity to consult independent counsel, Rule 1.8(h)(2). The aggregate-settlement rule, Rule 1.8(g), includes specific disclosure requirements, to underscore what informed consent requires in that context.

   Other conflicts are entirely nonwaivable when specifically enumerated in Rule 1.8. Consider the situation of a lawyer drafting a will for a client under which the lawyer will receive a substantial bequest. This should set off alarm bells relating to Rule 1.7(a): Surely the lawyer's representation of the client is materially limited by the lawyer's own interest in receiving the testamentary gift. A lawyer may believe this conflict is consentable under Rule 1.7, but notice the specific prohibition in Rule 1.8(c) on preparing an instrument for a client giving the lawyer a substantial gift. There is no waiver provision in Rule 1.8(c). Personal-interest conflicts are sometimes handled separately under 1.8 to ensure that lawyers do not try to obtain consent to something that poses particularly serious threats to the lawyer's loyalty to her client. Other nonwaivable prohibitions include obtaining media rights in the subject matter of the representation, Rule 1.8(d), and providing financial assistance to a client, Rule 1.8(e).

2. *Different imputation rules.* Ordinarily Rule 1.10 deals with imputation of conflicts of interest to other lawyers in the same firm. It is not written in terms of all conflicts, however, but of prohibitions set forth in Rule 1.7 and 1.9. (Look carefully at Rule 1.10(a)!) Conflicts arising under Rule 1.8 therefore have to be handled by a special imputation rule, which is set out in Rule 1.8(k). That rule states that any conflict arising under Rule 1.8(a) through Rule 1.8(i), inclusive, is imputed to other lawyers in the same firm. That leaves only Rule 1.8(j), the prohibition on sexual relationships with clients. A further implication of the drafting of the Model Rules is that any modification to Rule 1.10, including the permission to use screening to cure imputed conflicts, does not apply to the conflicts regulated by Rule 1.8.

BUSINESS TRANSACTIONS WITH CLIENTS — RULE 1.8(a)

In contracts, you learn that business is governed by the morals of the marketplace, that buyers ought to beware, and that other parties in transactions generally don't owe duties to correct mistakes and look out for inexperienced parties. However, one of the bedrock principles of the law of lawyering is that the lawyer-client relationship is *not* an arm's-length relationship. Rather, it is a *fiduciary* relationship meaning, among other things, that the lawyer must "deal honestly with the client, and not employ advantages arising from the lawyer-client relationship in a manner adverse to the client." Rest. §16(3). Lawyers cannot drive hard bargains in deals with clients. The fiduciary principle extends to all dealings between lawyer and client while the lawyer is representing the client; it is not limited to matters concerning the representation. Thus, if a real estate lawyer is representing a client on the acquisition of Blackacre, the lawyer must act as a fiduciary and deal honestly with the client if the lawyer and client are separately forming a partnership to acquire Whiteacre. One situation that you might not immediately recognize as implicating the transactions-with-clients rule is a fee agreement that is structured to give the lawyer some kind of security interest in the client's assets. In addition to complying with the usual requirement of Rule 1.5(a) that fees be reasonable, the arrangement must also satisfy the transactions-with-clients rule.

The rule is quite broad in scope—it applies to "business transaction[s] with clients" as well as acquisition of "an ownership, possessory, security or other pecuniary interest adverse to a client." However, it should not be interpreted to bar ordinary business transactions with merchants who happen to be clients of the lawyer or law firm. What if a lawyer represents Lowe's—can she shop there? What if a lawyer represents the local bank—can she take out a loan from the bank? It would be ridiculous to go through the requirements of Model Rule 1.8(a) every time the lawyer wanted to do business with a commercial entity who happened to be her client. Fortunately, Comment [1] to the rule says the rule does not apply to "standard commercial transactions between the lawyer and the client for products or services that the client generally markets to others." See also Rest. §126. The reason for this exception is that the lawyer would not have any unfair advantage over the client in these transactions. A can of paint costs the same at Lowe's for the lawyer as it does for a stranger.

Outside the area of standard commercial transactions, in order to avoid discipline, the lawyer must comply with all of the requirements set out in Rule 1.8(a). Discipline for violating this rule can be severe, since the lawyer's conduct may be characterized as a particularly serious breach of fiduciary duties owed to a client. See, for example, In re Lupo, 851 N.E.2d 404 (Mass. 2006) (indefinite suspension of a lawyer who arranged to have himself appointed as a real estate broker for a group of elderly sisters whom he represented as a lawyer). In addition to avoiding discipline, compliance with these requirements is necessary for the agreement between the lawyer and client to be enforceable. Several courts have "imported" the disciplinary rules into contract actions between the lawyer and client, and used a violation of the rules as a basis for rescinding lawyer-client contracts. See, for example, *Passante v. McWilliam*, 62 Cal. Rptr. 2d 298 (Ct. App. 1997); H&H §12.4.

Model Rule 1.8(a) requires:

1. Full disclosure of the terms of the transaction, in terms the client can understand. Rule 1.8(a)(1). Remember that nonlawyers do not necessarily know what an "unperfected" security interest is, or the advantages of taking a first instead of a second mortgage. All of this legal mumbo-jumbo must be explained in plain language to the client.
2. Disclosure *in writing*. Rule 1.8(a)(1). Whenever you see the specific requirement of written disclosure, you can assume this is an area of concern for the drafters of the Model Rules, and they are particularly worried about abuse of the client's interests. Compare, for example, the requirement that the terms of all fee arrangements with new clients be disclosed, *preferably* in writing, Rule 1.5(b), with the requirement that the terms of a contingency fee agreement be disclosed in writing, Rule 1.5(c).

3. Advice to the client from the standpoint of a disinterested lawyer. This so-called "Stranger Rule" is not specifically spelled out in the text of Model Rule 1.8(a), but has been added as a gloss by numerous judicial decisions. See, for example, *Committee on Professional Ethics v. Mershon*, 316 N.W.2d 895 (Iowa 1982). The lawyer cannot negotiate at arm's length with the client, but must advise the client as if the lawyer were evaluating the deal from an outsider's perspective. Here is a good summary of what the lawyer must do:

> [The lawyer] must disclose every circumstance and fact which the client should know to make an intelligent decision concerning the wisdom of entering the agreement. The rule is strict. The lawyer must give the client that information which he would have been obliged to give if he had been counsel rather than an interested party. . . . [F]ull disclosure requires . . . a detailed explanation of the risks and disadvantages to the client which flow from the agreement.

In re *Neville*, 708 P.2d 1297 (Ariz. 1985). I like to summarize the Stranger Rule in this way: A client should never have to protect herself against her own lawyer. It would be perverse to require the client to hire a lawyer to deal with her lawyer. (Not to mention that it would create an infinite regress if the client and the second lawyer tried to negotiate some kind of deal — then the client would need a third lawyer!) The way to ensure that clients never have to protect themselves against their own lawyer is to require lawyers to assume this stance of objectivity and impartiality whenever they advise their clients.

4. The client has a reasonable opportunity to consult independent counsel and is given advice in *writing* by the lawyer about the desirability of having separate representation. Rule 1.8(a)(2). Note the redundant levels of protection in this rule. The Stranger Rule requires the lawyer to give advice from the perspective of an independent lawyer, but in addition to this "virtual" independent advice, the client must have the chance to obtain actual independent advice.

5. The client gives *written* consent to the transaction, in a document indicating the essential terms of the transaction, including whether the client has independent representation. Rule 1.8(a)(3).

6. Finally, in addition to all the rigmarole of disclosure and consent, the terms of the deal must be (objectively!) fair and reasonable to the client. Rule 1.8(a)(1). The lawyer cannot get the better part of the bargain. If there are ways to allocate risks to one party or the other in the transaction, the client cannot be the one who ends up exposed to an unreasonable level of risk while the lawyer is protected. This rule

is sometimes called a "consent plus" rule, meaning that the lawyer will be subject to discipline unless she obtains the client's informed consent *and* the terms of the deal are substantively fair to the client. A case in which the deal was not substantively fair to the client is In re Lupo, 851 N.E.2d 404 (Mass. 2006), in which a lawyer representing an elderly estate-planning client obtained a power of attorney from her and bought her house for $170,000, knowing it was actually worth $240,000.

The requirement of substantive fairness creates a lot of uncertainty and risk for lawyers, because the fairness of the deal inevitably will be evaluated from an *ex post* point of view. In other words, a court or disciplinary authority will judge whether the client got a raw deal *after* the deal has blown up. Some unanticipated contingency may have arisen that made the deal unfavorable to the client, and for this reason, the transaction may be judged to have violated Model Rule 1.8(a). Is this entirely fair to the lawyer? Maybe not, and a better rule might evaluate fairness *ex ante*, from the perspective of the parties at the time the deal was entered into. The fact that clients get the benefit of the doubt when transactions go awry shows, once again, that this is an extremely client-protective rule, and all close calls will be resolved in favor of the client.

ADVERSE USE OF CONFIDENTIAL INFORMATION — RULE 1.8(b)

In Chapter 9, we talked about the professional duty of confidentiality, Rule 1.6. That rule states that a lawyer may not *disclose* information relating to representation of the client without the client's informed consent, unless one of the exceptions applies. There is a separate rule, Rule 1.8(b), prohibiting making use of confidential information adversely to the interests of a current client. There is yet another rule, Rule 1.9(c), which prohibits making use of confidential information adversely to the interests of a former client. Although these provisions are scattered around the Model Rules, they are really just aspects of a single, very simple idea: The lawyer, as a fiduciary, may treat client confidences as sacrosanct and may not do anything with that information that would harm the client, including disclosing it and using it to gain a personal advantage. As noted in Chapter 9, duties relating to confidential information are stated not only in the disciplinary rules but in agency law, so a lawyer may be liable for breach of fiduciary duty, as well as professional discipline, for violating them.

GIFTS TO LAWYERS — RULE 1.8(c)

This is an easy rule to remember, but for some reason lawyers continue to be disciplined for violating it. A lawyer may not *prepare* any kind of instrument, such as a will or trust document, in which the lawyer or a family member — that is, parent, child, sibling, or spouse — will receive any substantial gift from the client. Rule 1.8(c). Period, end of story. The reason for this rule is that the attorney-client relationship is subject to abuse. The confidential and fiduciary nature of the relationship leads clients to trust lawyers and not regard them with the same suspicion they might have for strangers who seek to con them into giving away their property. The rule applies even if the lawyer's motivations are pure. The only exception is where the client is related to the beneficiary, in certain enumerated familial relationships. A lawyer can prepare a will for her spouse or her parents under which she will take property, but as for any other clients, forget about it.

The rule also prohibits *soliciting* a gift, not just preparing an instrument in which the client names the lawyer as a beneficiary. However, a lawyer may *accept* a purely unsolicited gift as long as the lawyer is not involved in preparing any instrument necessary to transfer the title. If your wealthy client wants to give you a valuable painting at the conclusion of a long and mutually beneficial professional relationship, that's fine. See Rule 1.8, cmt. [6] ("If a client offers the lawyer a more substantial gift, paragraph (c) does not prohibit the lawyer from accepting it . . ."). For what it's worth, the Restatement has a different rule; it prohibits *accepting* a gift from a client, not just soliciting it. Rest. §127(2). Notwithstanding the Restatement rule, I'm not aware of a case in which a lawyer was disciplined for merely receiving a gift, not having had any role in soliciting it or preparing documents to effectuate its transfer.

MEDIA RIGHTS — RULE 1.8(d)

Another area with a great deal of potential for abuse is acquiring media rights in clients' cases. For one thing, the client may be desperate and not have much money. A high-profile criminal defense lawyer might be able essentially to extort media rights from the client by agreeing to accept them in lieu of fees. The client really would not be in a position to say "no," even though he would prefer not to give up the media rights. Another problem is that the facts of a case that make for a sensational story, likely to turn into a best-selling book or a blockbuster movie, may not come out unless the case goes to trial. Accordingly, there would be an incentive for the lawyer to try to coax the client into going to trial, instead of accepting a plea bargain in a criminal prosecution.

For these reasons, there is a flat prohibition on a lawyer negotiating for or acquiring any literary or media rights to an account of the client's case, prior to the conclusion of the representation. Rule 1.8(d). This prohibition is nonwaivable. After the case has concluded, the lawyer is in no better or worse position than anyone else to negotiate for the media rights, and cannot "throw" the case to make it more dramatically compelling. After these dangers have been avoided, the lawyer may reach an agreement with the client for media rights.

One detail to note: Rule 1.8(d) prohibits the acquisition of media rights only where they are related to the subject of the representation. A famous athlete may give a lawyer the rights to receive royalties from a forthcoming autobiography in exchange for the lawyer's legal assistance in acquiring a winery without subjecting the lawyer to discipline.

PROBLEMS OF LITIGATION FUNDING AND CLIENT SUPPORT

Financial arrangements between clients and lawyers may be more complicated than simply issuing monthly bills for services rendered, which are paid on a regular basis for clients. As discussed above, lawyers may have a security interest in their clients' assets, to ensure payment of their fees. Those transactions are covered by Rule 1.8(a). In addition, the lawyer may effectively loan the client the value of her services, through contingency fee financing, where the lawyer is paid only at the conclusion of the matter, and only if certain specified conditions occur. Contingency fee financing is often used by plaintiffs' personal-injury lawyers, who receive a percentage of the amount recovered by the client in the form of a judgment or settlement. This structure may create a conflict because the client's incentive may diverge from the lawyer's if the client wishes to accept an early, but relatively parsimonious settlement, and the lawyer would prefer to go to trial, hoping to "ring the bell" by winning a substantial verdict. (See Chapter 4.) Other clients have insurance to pay their legal expenses or may be reimbursed or indemnified by another third party, such as an employer, for legal expenses.

All of these arrangements create the same basic problem—the lawyer's independent professional judgment may be compromised by the lawyer's financial interests. Interference with judgment is a theme in many of the rules dealing with litigation funding. See Rule 1.8(f)(2) (no third-party financing unless there will be no interference with lawyer's professional judgment); Rule 5.4(c) (lawyer shall not permit anyone who pays lawyer to interfere with lawyer's professional judgment); see also Rule 2.1 ("In representing a client, a lawyer shall exercise independent professional judgment and render candid advice."). Nevertheless, the various rules present interesting differences, which is why the Model Rules divide these litigation funding conflicts into several provisions. Make sure you read these provisions in conjunction with the general rule on fees, Rule 1.5, as well as the general prohibition on representing a client without consent where the lawyer's own interests materially limit the lawyer's ability to provide effective representation, Rule 1.7(a)(2).

The law has always been hostile to lawyers taking too much of an entrepreneurial attitude toward litigation. Common law prohibitions on maintenance (lending financial assistance to a party in litigation), champerty (lending money and retaining a security interest in the litigation proceeds), and barratry (stirring up litigation) persist in many states. See, for example, *Rancman v. Interim Settlement Funding Corp.*, 789 N.E.2d 217 (Ohio 2003) (subsequently overruled by legislation). These prohibitions, if read strictly, would prohibit contingency fee financing, but most states now (rather awkwardly) define champerty and maintenance as specifically excluding contingency fees. Some of the conflicts rules discussed below also specifically exclude contingency fees. See, for example, Rule 1.8(e)(1) (prohibiting advancing litigation expenses, but permitting lawyers to advance the costs of their services, via contingency fee financing); Rule 1.8(i)(2) (prohibiting acquiring an interest in a cause of action, but carving out exception for contingency fees). These exclusions are necessary because the economic substance of a contingency fee is a loan: The lawyer provides something valuable to the client (her services) in the present, in exchange for an agreement by the client to pay back the lawyer a specified amount (for example, one-third of the recovery) upon the occurrence of a specified event (judgment or settlement). Yet, direct loans of money to clients are prohibited. The artificial, gerrymander-style exclusion of contingency fees from the operation of these rules has always seemed odd to me, and suggests a certain amount of unresolved tension in this area of the law.

Keeping the Client Afloat — Rule 1.8(e)

Occasionally, a client may lack the resources to await the conclusion of litigation, but would be able to stick it out if a source of funding were available. Imagine a working-class client who is injured in an accident and needs money to replace lost wages and to pay medical bills. In theory, these funds will come from the tortfeasor, but in most cases the client will need to wait for months, or even years, before the defendant offers a reasonable settlement or is ordered to pay a judgment. In the meantime, the client is in dire financial straits. Perhaps having a good feel for the strength of the client's case, a lawyer might offer to lend the client money to tide him over the tough times. Unfortunately for the client, the rules flatly prohibit providing financial assistance to clients, except in the form of contingency fee financing. Rule 1.8(e). In a long, contested case, this means the lawyer may, in effect, lend tens of thousands of dollars' worth of her services to the client, with the hopes of being repaid from the proceeds of a judgment or settlement, but may not lend the client a few thousand dollars to pay bills. The rule permits advancing litigation expenses for all clients, as is customary in contingent fee representations, Rule 1.8(e)(1), and paying court costs and expenses of litigation where the client is indigent. Rule 1.8(e)(2). Because many indigent clients take advantage of contingency fee financing (which is not prohibited by the rule), the permission granted to pay expenses on behalf of indigent clients is primarily relevant in matters in which a contingency fee was not permitted, such as criminal defense representation. Cf. Rule 1.5(d)(2) (prohibiting contingency fees in criminal defense cases).

Although I think this rule is written a bit too broadly, it does have the beneficial effect of prohibiting lawyers from exploiting their knowledge and power to make loans to clients on terms that are unfairly favorable to the lawyer. It also ensures that the lawyer's professional judgment is not clouded by the interest in having loan proceeds paid back. See, for example, *McLaughlin v. Amirsaleh*, 844 N.E.2d 1105 (Mass. App. Ct. 2006) (lawyer who lent client money and obtained mortgage to secure loan acted against client's interest because of his interest in protecting his own security interest). Those concerns are also addressed by Rule 1.8(a), however, so there has to be something else going on to justify a freestanding prohibition on providing financial assistance to clients.

The reason given for having this independent rule, over and above Rule 1.8(a), is that permitting financing for living expenses would "encourage clients to pursue lawsuits that might otherwise not be brought." Rule. 1.8, cmt. [10]. It seems unlikely, however, that advancing financial support would encourage litigation over and above the effect created by contingency fee financing, which is specifically excluded from this prohibition. See Rule 1.8(e)(1). In addition, the rule appears to contemplate that tiding over clients with a loan will encourage lawsuits that should not be brought. If the client's action is meritorious, there seems to be no public policy reason why it ought to be discouraged. The whole point of allowing contingency fee financing is to ensure access to the courts for poor and middle-income people who may have meritorious claims but cannot afford to pay lawyers by the hour. Lawyers accepting cases on a contingency fee basis have an incentive to investigate the merit of a potential client's claim, so that they avoid getting stuck with a "dog" case — that is, one that requires a lot of work (because the lawyer has the duty to provide competent and diligent representation, Rule 1.3), but where the expected payoff is small. See, for example, Herbert M. Kritzer, *Contingency Fee Lawyers as Gatekeepers in the Civil Justice*

System, 81 Judicature 22 (1997). Lawyers lending money on the expectation of being paid back with interest at the conclusion of a lawsuit would have a similar incentive. The rationale given for this rule doesn't hold up, but the rule is enforced anyway.

Investing in Litigation — Rule 1.8(i)

Although this provision is located a few subsections away, it is closely related to the prohibition in Rule 1.8(e) on providing financial assistance to clients in litigation. Not only may the lawyer not advance litigation expenses, but the lawyer is also prohibited from taking any kind of security interest in the cause of action, except for an ordinary lien to secure the lawyer's fee. Rule 1.8(i). Like the former provision, this rule has its origins in the common law doctrines of champerty and maintenance. See Rule 1.8, cmt. [16]. Again, there is an express carve-out for contingency fee financing. See Rule 1.8(i)(2). Because liens on the proceeds of litigation are permitted to secure repayment by clients of attorneys' fees, this rule does not bear on the activities of many lawyers. It really only applies to the case of a lawyer investing in a lawsuit not brought by a client or obtaining a security interest for an amount greater than the (reasonable) accrued fees. However, the rule does prohibit the participation of lawyers in some litigation funding services. The question of the legality of litigation funding activities is interesting, but it is well beyond the scope of most professional responsibility courses, so I will just refer interested readers to some useful articles: Douglas R. Richmond, *Other People's Money: The Ethics of Litigation Funding*, 56 Mercer L. Rev. 649 (2005); James E. Moliterno, *Broad Prohibition, Thin Rationale: The "Acquisition of an Interest and Financial Assistance in Litigation" Rules*, 16 Geo. J. Legal Ethics 223 (2003); Susan Lorde Martin, *Financing Plaintiffs' Litigation: An Increasingly Popular (and Legal) Business*, 33 U. Mich. J.L. Ref. 57 (2000).

Third-Party Fee-Payor Conflicts — Rule 1.8(f)

When a nonclient is paying the attorney, there might be an express or implicit condition attached that the lawyer take account of the interests of the fee payor. For example, suppose a lawyer is retained and paid by a corporation to represent one of its employees who is suspected of wrongdoing. The lawyer must always remember that her client is the employee, and representing the employee effectively might mean making the corporation angry. The Model Rules again underscore the importance of independent professional judgment by forbidding a lawyer to agree to this kind of fee-payment arrangement unless (1) the client consents after consultation — that is, gives informed consent; (2) there is no interference with the lawyer's independent professional judgment; and (3) the lawyer does not violate her duty of confidentiality to the client. Rule 1.8(f).[1] This is another rule, like the rule governing business transactions with clients, that requires "consent plus." The client must not only give informed consent, but two additional requirements must be satisfied: (1) the lawyer must reasonably believe that her independent judgment (see Rule 2.1) will not be affected by any desire she might have to keep the payor happy, and (2) she also must not disclose any confidential client information (see Rule 1.6) to the payor.

For a discussion of other conflicts of interest created by defending an insured client, pursuant to a liability insurance contract, see Chapter 15.

Aggregate Settlements — Rule 1.8(g)

A lawyer representing multiple clients—including, significantly, *classes* of clients—may not participate in making an aggregate settlement of the clients' claims without obtaining informed consent in writing from each affected client. Rule 1.8(g). An aggregate settlement is one in which a lawyer is representing multiple clients and the settlements are somehow linked or interdependent. Example would include (1) the defendant offers $500,000 to settle all cases brought by a single law firm, leaving it to the plaintiffs' lawyers to divvy up the proceeds, or (2) a settlement offer that is contingent on some percentage of the firm's clients accepting the offer.

In order to understand this rule, it is first necessary to understand a little bit about complex litigation and the incentives it creates for lawyers. Suppose there is a case with a large number of parties, such as a mass tort claim against a manufacturer of a product that is believed to have caused injuries. (Asbestos, certain diet drugs, and the painkiller Vioxx are examples of products that have spawned massive litigation of this sort.) Often a single law firm will represent dozens, hundreds, or even thousands of claimants with similar cases, which enables it to handle the claims more efficiently, and also gives it greater leverage in settlement negotiations with defendants. Lawyers naturally tend to think in terms of having an "inventory" of cases, which they can offer to settle all at once with the defendant. Defendants like settling large numbers of cases at one time, because it enables them to better predict their liability exposure in the litigation. Known risks can be insured against and can be understood by investors; unknown risks make investors nervous.

Plaintiffs' lawyers therefore have something valuable to offer defendants, in the form of increased certainty through the ability to settle large

---

1. Just for good measure, there is another provision in the Model Rules reminding lawyers not to permit a person who pays the lawyer's fees to "direct or regulate the lawyer's professional judgment in rendering such legal services." Rule 5.4(c).

numbers of cases at one time. The concern is that they might abuse this power by "selling out" certain categories of claimants in order to reach a deal that may be more favorable to other claimants, and to the lawyers themselves. Consider as an example a product, such as asbestos or pharmaceuticals, where injuries resulting from its use may have already manifested themselves in some users, but where other injuries may be latent for some unknown period of time. Or, a toxic exposure may have injured some victims more severely than others. Depending on how the settlement is structured, some classes may do better than others. For example, a law firm may be willing to accept less compensation for "future" claimants in order to get more money for clients who have present injuries. It may be possible for a firm to set up allocation procedures to ensure that all clients are treated fairly, but even if it does so, it cannot avoid the basic requirement of Rule 1.8(g), that all clients whose claims are settled at one time must give informed consent in writing to the settlement. That would mean that the lawyers would have to explain the significance of the allocation of settlement proceeds and give the clients an opportunity to accept it or reject it. Plaintiffs' lawyers might be tempted to skip this procedural step because it would make it more difficult to negotiate with defendants (who prefer all-or-nothing settlements), and because it would be a big headache to obtain consent from hundreds or thousands of represented plaintiffs, but it is still required by the disciplinary rules.[2]

If you are interested in reading more about these problems, see the very helpful article, Howard M. Erichson, *A Typology of Aggregate Settlements*, 80 Notre Dame L. Rev. 1769 (2005).

Prospective Waivers and Settlements — Rule 1.8(h)

Remember the principle stated above in connection with business transactions with clients: A client should not have to protect herself against her own lawyer. The situation for clients becomes particularly perilous when the lawyer may have failed to perform adequately — that is, he or she may have committed malpractice. (See Chapter 6 for more on legal malpractice.) A lawyer who has already provided inadequate service may not be trustworthy to advise the client further. For this reason, any time there are claims regarding the lawyer's performance of her professional duties, it is crucial that the client be represented by independent counsel. A separate lawyer — that

---

2. Because the harm to be prevented by this rule is sacrificing the interests of one client or set of clients for another, it belongs more naturally as part of Rule 1.7, on current client conflicts. The Restatement version of the aggregate-settlement rule is contained in a comment to the rule on concurrent representation in litigation. Rest. §128, cmt. d(i).

is, actual representation by independent counsel — is required for a client to effectively waive all potential future malpractice claims. Rule 1.8(h)(1). (A common factual setting for actual independent representation is a lawyer obtaining an advance waiver of malpractice liability from the general counsel of a corporate client.) Failure to comply with this rule is also very likely to render the waiver voidable at the client's instance, as a matter of contract law. Simply putting a prospective liability waiver in the engagement letter, as some lawyers have tried to do, is insufficient to waive liability and grounds for professional discipline.

If some dispute does arise over the lawyer's performance, the lawyer may offer to settle the matter. In any such settlement, the lawyer must advise the client in writing of the desirability of having a separate lawyer represent her in the negotiations and must also give the client a reasonable opportunity to obtain independent counsel. Rule 1.8(h)(2). Note that, unlike the situation covered by Rule 1.8(h)(1), the client need not actually be represented by independent counsel. Again, failure to comply with this rule will not only expose the lawyer to professional discipline, but may cause the resulting settlement to be unenforceable.

Sexual Relationships with Clients — Rule 1.8(j)

Sexual relationships with clients are an extremely bad idea. The Model Rules contain a provision, Rule 1.8(j), which prohibit sexual relations between a lawyer and client, unless the personal relationship predated the professional one. (In other words, lawyers can represent their spouses and significant others.) Under the Model Rules, the conflict of interest arising from prohibited sexual relationships with clients is not imputed to other lawyers in the same firm. Rule 1.8(k). What if the client is a corporation? Recall Rule 1.13(a), which specifies that the organization itself, not any individual constituent, is the client. In that case, a lawyer for the entity, whether in-house or outside counsel, may not have a prohibited relationship with any constituent of the organization who supervises, consults with, or directs the lawyer concerning the client's legal matters. Rule 1.8, cmt. [19].

Even if a state did not have a rule specifically addressing the situation, however, there are other adverse consequences of romantic relationships with clients of which a lawyer should be aware. The first is the potential for conflicts of interest. Remember that Model Rule 1.7(a)(2) speaks of conflicts between the interests of a client and "a personal interest of the lawyer." Where a lawyer is involved romantically with a client, the lawyer's interest in continuing the relationship might cause the lawyer to do something not in the client's best interests. And that is putting a relatively benign spin on the matter. There are plenty of not-so-benign cases, in which lawyers essentially extorted sex from clients. Courts consistently hold that the lawyer has an impermissible conflict of interest if his (it is generally a man) interest in obtaining sexual gratification from the client works to the detriment of his representation of the client. See, for example, In re Walker, 24 P.3d 602 (Ariz. 2001) (unconsented sexual touching of client); In re Tsoutsouris, 748 N.E.2d 856 (Ind. 2001) (consensual relationship).

Do not forget that if the bar can discipline the lawyer for having a conflict of interest in this situation, the client probably has a civil remedy for breach of fiduciary duty, and possibly other torts, as well. See, for example, Walter v. Stewart, 67 P.3d 1042 (Utah Ct. App. 2003).

The second problem is that a lawyer who is emotionally involved with a client may not be capable of exercising independent professional judgment, as required by Model Rule 2.1. The lawyer has to be able to give candid advice and a straight assessment of the client's legal situation, even if the news is bad. As the comment to the rule puts it, "[l]egal advice often involves unpleasant facts and alternatives that a client may be disinclined to confront." Rule 2.1, Comment [1]. A lawyer whose emotional ties to the client are so strong that he is unable to provide candid advice would be failing his client, *professionally* speaking.

IMPUTATION OF LAWYER-CLIENT CONFLICTS

Most of the personal-interest conflicts covered by Model Rule 1.8 are imputed to other lawyers in the firm. See Rule 1.8(k) (referring to Rule 1.8(a)-(i)). That means, to review, that if Lawyer A is representing a client, Lawyer B is prohibited from entering into a business transaction with the client, unless she satisfies the procedures of Rule 1.8(a) — that is, full disclosure in writing, substantive fairness, and advice in writing to the client to obtain independent counsel. The only exception to the imputation rule is the conflict created by prohibited sexual relationships between a lawyer and client, which is in Rule 1.8(k). That means Lawyer B can sleep with Lawyer A's client.

ADVOCATE-WITNESS RULE

A conflict of interest may be created if a lawyer is functioning both as a representative of a client and as a witness at trial or in a pretrial deposition. As a consequence, the disciplinary rules prohibit playing both roles. See Rule 3.7. Courts give many reasons for prohibiting the lawyer from acting as both advocate and witness. The prohibition on serving as both witness and advocate is said to prevent prejudice to the client. Prejudice can be the result of the lawyer's inherent ineffectiveness as a witness, owing to the opponent's ability to impeach her for bias. This argument seems to prove too much, however, because *former* lawyers who act as witnesses also may be impeached for bias, and the rule does not cover former lawyers. The other argument from prejudice is that the lawyer's account of events may be inconsistent with the client's, thereby harming the client's case. This seems more likely, but only in some cases; it does not appear to justify a blanket rule against a lawyer appearing as a witness at trial. Two other (inconsistent) reasons for the advocate-witness rule are that a lawyer serving as a witness for her client can cause prejudice to the *opponent*, because the lawyer may have enhanced credibility in the eyes of the jury, and (again, inconsistently) that lawyers are more likely than other witnesses to commit perjury because they have a financial interest in the outcome of the trial. On a related note, some courts argue that the jury might be confused as to how it should evaluate the lawyer's testimony — is it evidence, or is it argument? Taken together, the policy reasons for the advocate-witness rule appear to be an incoherent jumble, but there are cases in which you can see how one or more of them might justify disqualifying the lawyer from serving as counsel.

One final reason for the advocate-witness rule is that lawyers sometimes will attempt to gain a tactical advantage by demanding to take the deposition of opposing counsel, generally on the theory that the other lawyer knows some facts that are at issue in the litigation. Courts tend to be wary of lawyers deposing one another, not only because of the potential for slowing down litigation with disqualification and changing of counsel, but also because depositions of opposing counsel tend to become acrimonious. Because of the possibility for nastiness in cross-examinations of opposing counsel, the Restatement permits lawyers to call opposing counsel at trial only where there is a "compelling need" for the opposing lawyer's testimony. Rest. §108(4). The Restatement rule does not apply directly to pretrial proceedings, but the tendency of judges is similarly to disallow depositions of opposing counsel in the absence of exceptional circumstances.

What would have to happen in order for a lawyer to be both a witness and an advocate? There are several common scenarios:

- The lawyer participates in negotiating a deal and drafting documents. The deal subsequently blows up and litigation ensues. Perhaps an issue in the litigation is whether oral representations were made at the closing of the deal that were fraudulent or that varied the terms of the written documents. Because the lawyer was present at the closing, testimony about her recollection would be useful.
- Similarly, imagine that the lawyer prepares a bankruptcy filing for the client, who is later indicted for bankruptcy fraud. The client takes the Fifth Amendment, and the government would like to call the lawyer

as a witness in the prosecution. (Imagine that the information sought is not protected by the attorney-client privilege, perhaps because the crime-fraud exception applies.)

- The lawyer may be a potential impeachment witness, because she personally conducted witness interviews. Imagine that the lawyer talked to a witness who said he saw the robbery and that the robber was not the defendant. At trial, however, the witness changes his story and says that the defendant was indeed the robber. The lawyer would like to impeach the witness with the prior inconsistent statement. (To prevent this problem, many lawyers assign investigators to conduct witness interviews, or at least have someone else present who could be called at trial as an impeachment witness.)

In cases such as these, the advocate-witness rule requires that the lawyer withdraw from representing the client in some circumstances where the lawyer also will function as a witness in the proceedings. Under Rule 3.7, the standard for disqualifying the lawyer is whether the lawyer is "likely to be a *necessary* witness" in the matter. Rule 3.7(a). The lawyer may remain in the case despite a likelihood of being a necessary witness. If the lawyer can show that disqualification would "work substantial hardship on the client," the lawyer may continue to serve as an advocate. Rule 3.7(a)(3). Notice that the personal disqualification of the advocate-witness rule is *not* imputed to other lawyers in the firm. Rule 3.7(b).

Examples

Business Partner or Lawyer?

1. Petrus hired DeLillo to defend him in a minor traffic matter. The two became friends, played poker together, and from time to time DeLillo provided legal services to Petrus on other matters. Petrus decided to leave the auto body shop where he was employed and start his own business. Together with DeLillo, Petrus toured potential sites for his business, negotiated for the sale of a site, and arranged financing for the acquisition. DeLillo contributed $25,000 of startup capital to the business. He also drafted the documents by which Petrus acquired the land from the previous owners. A different lawyer represented Petrus at the closing, however. After Petrus started the new business, DeLillo received a retainer of $500 per year to be available to handle the shop's legal work.

    The business prospered, but the relationship between DeLillo and Petrus soured. DeLillo eventually decided to "cash out" of the business and demanded that Petrus buy his share. Petrus's response was, "What share? I don't owe you anything, because you violated your duties to me as your client." Can DeLillo recover anything from Petrus?

Insider Trading

2. "Dokey" Dixon is a real estate developer. One day he comes to the office of his lawyer, Louise, to ask for Louise's help in acquiring some land. Dokey tells Louise that he has done extensive market research and concluded that the time would be right to buy some land on the highway north of town and open an outlet mall. He asks Louise to start looking into zoning requirements for the outlet mall. After Dokey leaves, Louise decides she'd like a piece of the action, so she calls up a friend at the bank, obtains a loan, buys an option on a parcel of land on the highway, and finally signs a contract to lease the land to an operator of outlet malls. As a result, Dokey is forced to negotiate with a different operator of outlet malls, who insists on paying less rent due to the competition right across the street. Is Louise subject to discipline?

He Who Pays the Piper

3. Frank Locasio was indicted for criminal violations of the Racketeer Influenced and Corrupt Organizations (RICO) Act, for allegedly taking part in the activities of the Gambino crime family of La Cosa Nostra, commonly known as the Mafia. According to the government, Locasio was the "underboss" of the organization. Much of the government's case was based on the testimony of Sammy "Bull" Gravano, the former consigliere, or advisor, to alleged family boss John Gotti. Locasio wanted to be represented by attorney George Santangelo. The government objected, pointing out that Santangelo had previously served as "house counsel" to Gotti, and that his fees for representing Locasio would be paid by Gotti. Should Santangelo be permitted to represent Locasio?

Who Needs Fees — I'm Writing a Screenplay

4. Rob Anderson represented Bettina Leeks, who was accused of murdering her fifth husband, Joe Bob, and burying his body in a sleeping bag under a planter near the front porch. During a police search of Leeks's property, the police discovered the body of Leeks's fourth husband, Donnie, buried in the same spot. Leeks also had shot her third husband, Bubba, but he survived. Leeks had just obtained a $100,000 life insurance policy on Joe Bob by forging his signature to the application. Not surprisingly, the case attracted a great deal of national attention, and Leeks was profiled on several tabloid television shows. Anderson agreed to represent Leeks on a reduced-fee basis, provided that Leeks would assign any media rights to her story to Anderson. (Anderson had a cousin who worked for a television studio, who told him he could get rich selling the rights to make a made-for-TV movie based on the case.) Leeks readily agreed, and Anderson proved to be a vigorous and capable advocate at trial. Despite

his best efforts, the state's evidence was overwhelming and Leeks was convicted of capital murder. She now seeks *habeas corpus* relief for ineffective assistance of counsel. The state bar authorities also are investigating wrongdoing by Anderson. What will be the result of the bar investigation and the *habeas* petition?

Explanations

Business Partner or Lawyer?

1. This example is taken from *DeLuglio v. Providence Auto Body, Inc.*, 755 A.2d 757 (R.I. 2000). The threshold question is whether Petrus is a "client" of DeLillo, because Model Rule 1.8(a), on business transactions with clients, would not apply if Petrus were only a friend. There may not have been an *express* retainer agreement between DeLillo and Petrus, but the course of dealing between the two suggests that the relationship is professional, not personal. As the court correctly noted, if the "client" subjectively considers the "lawyer" to be providing legal services, and that belief is objectively reasonable, there is an attorney-client relationship between the parties. 755 A.2d at 766. In this example, Petrus's subjective belief that DeLillo was acting as his lawyer was reasonable, in light of DeLillo's willingness to represent Petrus in legal matters from time to time over the course of their relationship.

   Once it is established that DeLillo is acting as Petrus's lawyer, then DeLillo must comply with the terms of Model Rule 1.8(a) in order to have a valid interest in Petrus's business. He failed in several respects. DeLillo did not advise Petrus in writing of the desirability of seeking independent counsel in the transaction and did not obtain Petrus's informed consent to the terms of the transaction. Rule 1.8(a)(2)-(3). The terms of the transaction may have been fair and reasonable to Petrus, but because DeLillo failed to provide the required disclosures, the transaction did not comply with the applicable disciplinary rule. Because of the fiduciary nature of the attorney-client relationship, the lawyer should not be permitted to profit from a transaction in which the lawyer did not comply with the client protective rule on business transactions. For this reason, the court said that the transaction was voidable at the option of the client. 755 A.2d at 770.

Insider Trading

2. I hope this wasn't a hard example to answer. It is a classic case of self-dealing, or misusing confidential client information. Dokey's statement about market research is "information relating to representation of the client" under Rule 1.8(b). (Note that this is the same formulation used

to describe protected confidences in Rule 1.6.) Louise is prohibited from using that information to the disadvantage of her client without the client's informed consent. The client was clearly harmed by the adverse use, because he was unable to lease the land on favorable terms. Not only is Louise subject to discipline for violating Rule 1.8(b), but she is very likely to be sued by Dokey for breaching her fiduciary duty. Rest. §16(3) ("a lawyer must . . . comply with obligations concerning the client's confidences"); §49 ("a lawyer is civilly liable to a client if the lawyer breaches a fiduciary duty to the client set forth in §16(3)").

He Who Pays the Piper

3. This, of course, is a real case, and the names were not altered, since the facts are so familiar. See *United States v. Locasio*, 6 F.3d 924 (2d Cir. 1993). The applicable disciplinary rule is Model Rule 1.8(f), which would prohibit Santangelo from representing Locasio with Gotti paying his fees unless: (1) Locasio gave informed consent to the arrangement; (2) there is no interference with Santangelo's independent professional judgment as a result of the payment of fees by Gotti; and (3) Santangelo protected Locasio's confidential client information. See also Rest. §134. Of these three requirements, the second is the least likely to be satisfied. The concern is that Santangelo's representation of Locasio would be influenced by Santangelo's loyalty to Gotti. Gotti had paid Santangelo's fees before and considered him the lawyer for the family, which was run by Gotti. Moreover, Gotti has a great deal of interest in the way any lawyer handles Locasio's case. As the example of Sammy "the Bull" Gravano shows, family members have a disturbing tendency to turn state's evidence when they are facing life imprisonment. Gotti would like to be able to exert influence over Locasio's lawyer to make sure that he does not offer to plead guilty to some lesser charge in exchange for testimony against Gotti. For this reason, most courts refuse to permit one defendant to pay for counsel for a co-defendant, where there is a realistic possibility that one of the defendants may wish to "flip" on the other and offer testimony favorable to the government. See Rest. §134, cmt. d. Reporter's Note (citing cases). See also Rule 5.4(c), which prohibits a lawyer from allowing a person who pays the lawyer (here, Gotti) to direct or regulate the lawyer's professional judgment in rendering legal services.

Who Needs Fees — I'm Writing a Screenplay

4. This problem is based on *Beets v. Scott*, 65 F.3d 1258 (5th Cir. 1995), the sordid but true story of Betty Lou Beets. The disciplinary action is a slam-dunk, in favor of the bar authorities. Anderson flagrantly violated Model Rule 1.8(d), prohibiting him from acquiring "literary or media rights to

a portrayal or account based in substantial part on information relating to the representation."

The *habeas* question is a closer call. It seems at first that Leeks is out of luck, because Anderson was an effective advocate and the state's case was overwhelming. Under *Strickland v. Washington*, 466 U.S. 668 (1984), the ineffective assistance of counsel claim fails on both prongs—no professional errors by Anderson and, in any event, no prejudice because there is no reasonable probability that the result would have been different with another lawyer. Remember, though, that there are ways to obtain *habeas corpus* relief without showing *Strickland* prejudice or sub-par representation. The most promising is to point to an actual conflict of interest, under *Cuyler v. Sullivan*, 446 U.S. 335 (1980). Notice that Model Rule 1.8(d) is part of a rule titled "Conflicts of Interest . . . Specific Rules." Didn't Anderson actively represent conflicting interests, by taking media rights in Leeks's case while representing her at trial?

The Fifth Circuit said "no." It limited *Cuyler* to cases involving multiple concurrent representation of *clients*, not interests of the lawyer that may diverge from the client's interests. *Cuyler* and the cases it was based upon, including *Glasser v. United States*, 315 U.S. 60 (1942), and *Holloway v. Arkansas*, 435 U.S. 475 (1978), all involved concurrent representation conflicts, not successive representation conflicts (like the one at issue in *Mickens v. Taylor*, 122 S. Ct. 1237 (2002)) or conflicts involving the lawyer's own interests. In other words, prejudice will not be presumed in every case where the lawyer breaches his duty of loyalty to the client (as the lawyer undoubtedly did here). In multiple-representation cases, the client in effect has no lawyer, so it is reasonable to presume prejudice in those cases. In other instances of breaches of loyalty, however, the effect on the representation is not always as severe. In other words, the lawyer may have done a fantastic job representing the client, even though he was laboring under a conflict. That throws the petitioner's *habeas* claim back into *Strickland*, where it is almost certainly a loser.

PART IV

Organization and Regulation of the Legal Profession

CHAPTER 18

Attracting Clients: Advertising and Solicitation

INTRODUCTION

The disciplinary rules deal with advertising and solicitation by lawyers, but this is an area with a significant amount of constitutional overlay. The rules are constantly being fiddled with by state bar associations in order to restrict advertising without running afoul of the First Amendment, while courts often push back on constitutional grounds. Bar association restrictions on advertising still reflect a traditional antipathy toward advertising that has long been a part of professional rhetoric[1] and a more recent backlash against unseemly advertising by lawyers, such as the familiar television ads asking, "Have you been injured?" In general, the organized bar has perceived advertising as one of the principal arenas for a conflict between a vision of the practice of law as a profession and as a money-making enterprise. Bar leaders and judges are constantly going on about the law being a learned profession, not a "mere" business,[2] but many lawyers seem to take their cues from nonlawyer businesspeople. These sorts of arguments about the

---

1. Consider this passage from Canon 27 of the 1908 ABA Canons: "It is unprofessional to solicit professional employment by circulars, advertisements, through touters or by personal communications or interviews not warranted by personal relations. Indirect advertisements for professional employment . . . and all other like self-laudation, offend the traditions and lower the tone of our profession and are reprehensible."

2. Courts really do say this. The New Jersey Supreme Court, for example, wrote that "attorney advertising raises the understandable and realistic concern that the legal profession will degenerate into just another trade." *Petition of Felmeister & Isaacs*, 518 A.2d 188, 193 (N.J. 1986). New Jersey remains one of the most hostile states regarding attorney advertising, as demonstrated in the "Super Lawyers" controversy. See Example 3.

lawyer's role are bound up with the advertising issue in the minds of many lawyers, which is why discussions of advertising often turn surprisingly vehement, and why tasteless ads are frequently a flashpoint for anger at the supposed loss of professionalism by lawyers.

The flipside of a gentlemanly avoidance of self-promotion by lawyers is the issue of access to justice. Paeans to dignity, traditions, and "the tone of our profession" generally originated with elite lawyers serving corporate clients, who had no difficulty attracting business through informal channels—membership in the "right" clubs, living in certain neighborhoods, going to elite churches, and so on. Many of the advertisements and solicitations that most offend bar leaders are targeted at individual clients who are not plugged in to these referral networks. Consider, for example, the clients served by the legal clinic in *Bates*, the injured women sought as clients by the lawyer in *Zauderer*, or the people subject to home foreclosures in *Shapero*. These cases are discussed below. Also, restrictions on advertising and solicitation can be used against public interest lawyers who represent clients in challenges to powerful institutions, such as a class of mothers who had been sterilized in South Carolina as a condition of receiving government benefits. *In re Primus*, 436 U.S. 412 (1978). The organized bar tends to go after personal-injury lawyers hammer and tongs for violating these rules, but oddly enough, no one seems to get all that exercised about large-firm securities lawyers playing golf with the CEO of a big bank.

This may be a bit of an exaggeration, but it is helpful in understanding advertising and solicitation cases to picture a tug-of-war between the organized bar and the Supreme Court. The bar would like to restrict advertising by lawyers as much as possible, but the Court keeps reminding lawyers that most advertising, and some solicitation, is protected by the First Amendment. Other federal courts sometimes stand up to the organized bar, but state courts, for the most part, tend to be more willing to accept the reasons given by the bar for restricting advertising. Maybe that is because many state judges are elected and fear the power of the bar to organize opposition to them in judicial elections. In any event, because of the tension between the bar and the Court, the rules are pretty complicated here. They reflect the bar's constant attempt to enforce rules against advertising and solicitation that are as strict as possible, without running afoul of the Court's free speech cases.

In August 2018 the ABA House of Delegates voted to amend provisions of the Model Rules dealing with advertising and solicitation.

CONSTITUTIONAL DECISIONS

Commercial speech is protected by the First Amendment, albeit to a lesser extent than "core" political speech. *Central Hudson Gas & Elec. Corp. v. Public Service*

Comm'n, 447 U.S. 557 (1980). Lawyers advertising their services or soliciting clients are engaged in commercial speech, if they are seeking to make money on the representation. Lawyers not seeking to attract clients for "pecuniary gain," such as public-interest advocates, may be treated as engaging in political, not commercial speech. Rule 7.3(a); *In re Primus*, 436 U.S. 412 (1978) (law firm working with the ACLU contacted a woman who had been sterilized as a condition of receiving government benefits; solicitation was protected as political speech by the First Amendment). Notwithstanding the First Amendment protections for commercial speech, states may prohibit advertising that is deceptive or misleading. On the other hand, a state cannot ban truthful, nondeceptive advertising by lawyers. Similarly, states cannot prohibit all in-person solicitation of prospective clients, but they can regulate conduct that presents a danger of "fraud, undue influence, intimidation, overreaching, and other forms of vexatious conduct." These principles were established in a line of Supreme Court cases.

Advertising Cases

The case that started the process of constitutionalizing attorney advertising is *Bates v. State Bar of Arizona*, 433 U.S. 350 (1977). The lawyers in *Bates* set up a "legal clinic" that offered routine legal services, such as divorces, name changes, and bankruptcies, at modest prices. The clinic's newspaper advertisement identified the services, listed the prices, and gave the address and phone number of the clinic. That's it. There were no extravagant claims that the lawyers would get millions of dollars of damages, no exhortations to "sue the bastards!" or anything unseemly. Nevertheless, the Arizona bar association was concerned that permitting even this low-key form of advertising would transform the legal profession into a commercial enterprise, encourage litigation, and diminish the public's respect for lawyers.

The Supreme Court struck down Arizona's restriction on *all* advertising by lawyers, but even that decision was by a narrow, 5-4 margin. The Court's holding was modest. It addressed only newspaper publication of truthful advertisements concerning the availability and prices of routine legal services. At the same time, though, some of the Court's statements foreshadowed the much more *laissez-faire* approach to advertising that exists today. It pooh-poohed the argument that advertising tends to "deprofessionalize" lawyers by turning them into businesspeople. "At its core, the argument presumes that attorneys must conceal from themselves and from their clients the real-life fact that lawyers earn their livelihood at the bar." And the Court suggested that the public's lack of respect for lawyers may be caused not by advertising, but by "the profession's failure to reach out and serve the community"—that is, to make legal services more widely available to poor and middle-income clients.

The Court moved beyond *Bates* in two decisions that extended the constitutional protection on advertising to communications dealing with specific legal problems or targeted at specific audiences. In *Zauderer v. Office of Disciplinary Counsel*, 471 U.S. 626 (1985), the Court considered an advertisement by a lawyer directed at women who had been injured by the Dalkon Shield intrauterine device. The ad included a picture of the Dalkon Shield, described complications resulting from its use, and offered to represent women in litigation against the manufacturer. Note that unlike the clinic ad in *Bates*, the lawyer here could not argue that the communication covered only the availability and prices of "routine" legal services. Rather, this ad was targeted at a specific population of clients with a specific legal problem. Still, the ad was truthful and nondeceptive, as the Supreme Court observed, and a state needs to show a substantial government interest for prohibiting the communication of accurate information to the public. The Court noted that stirring up litigation is not necessarily a bad thing — after all, "our society has settled upon civil litigation as a means for redressing grievances, resolving disputes, and vindicating rights when other means fail." As for the state's claim that a restriction on advertising was needed as a prophylactic rule to protect against attorneys using false or misleading advertising to stir up meritless litigation against innocent parties, the Court replied, in effect, that the harms of misleading or false advertising, or frivolous litigation, should be controlled directly, and not indirectly through restrictions on speech.

The Court subsequently extended constitutional protection for advertising to targeted direct-mail communications. *Shapero v. Kentucky Bar Ass'n*, 486 U.S. 466 (1988). The lawyer in *Shapero* sought permission to send mailings to people who were targeted for home foreclosures, warning them that they may have rights under the Federal Fair Debt Collection Practices Act that they might not be aware of. The Court could have treated these communications as "solicitations," but instead it stated that direct-mail contact posed less of a risk of overreaching or unduly influencing the potential client, as compared with face-to-face communications. In direct-mail cases, there is no "trained advocate" in the same room with the potential client, importuning her to sign a retainer agreement. The recipient of the ad can avoid being bothered by simply tossing the mailing in the trash can. Thus, direct-mail communications are treated under the more lenient advertising rules.

A couple of other decisions, while less groundbreaking than *Shapero* or *Bates*, nevertheless illustrate the application of these constitutional principles. A lawyer may announce on his letterhead the fact that he is "a civil trial specialist as certified by the National Board of Trial Advocacy [a private group]," notwithstanding a state bar association rule permitting lawyers to hold themselves out as "certified" only if they are admitted to the patent, trademark, or admiralty bars. *Peel v. Attorney Registration and Disciplinary Comm'n*, 496 U.S. 91 (1990). Similarly, a lawyer may advertise the jurisdictions in which he is admitted to practice law, advertise himself as practicing various areas of law, *In re R.M.J.*, 455 U.S. 191 (1982), advertise that he is certified by a bona fide organization such as the National Board of Trial Advocacy, *Peel v. Attorney Regis. & Discip. Comm'n*, 496 U.S. 91 (1990), or advertise the fact that she is a CPA and certified financial planner (CFP), *Ibañez v. Florida Dep't of Business and Prof'l Regulation*, 512 U.S. 136 (1994). Reading these cases together, you can take away the following principle:

> *States may not ban truthful, non-deceptive advertising by lawyers in print, electronic, or direct-mail advertisements*, although they may impose certain limited restrictions.

The cases also show that a state cannot impose a categorical rule that certain kinds of communications are likely to be inherently deceptive. Rather, the deceptiveness must be evaluated on a case-by-case basis.

Can a state require a lawyer to include disclaimers or specific information that is necessary, in the state's view, in order to make the communication more meaningful to the prospective client? The answer is "yes . . . but." A state may require some additional information in an advertisement, as long as it is related to the purpose of avoiding deception and not unduly burdensome. In the *Zauderer* case—the one involving the ad for Dalkon Shield cases—the Court upheld a state bar requirement that an advertisement for contingency fee cases include the warning that the client will be liable for costs, no matter what the outcome of the litigation. *Zauderer*, 471 U.S. at 652. But the Court refused to permit a state to impose more elaborate requirements in the *Ibañez* case (the one with the lawyer/accountant). *Ibañez*, 512 U.S. at 147. The state rule required anyone who wished to certify herself as a CFP to include the disclaimer that the agency recognizing certified financial planners is a private organization, and that CFPs are not certified by the government. This is an overreaction to a purely hypothetical danger, the Court reasoned. Unless the state can show some specific risk of harm, it cannot require lengthy and burdensome disclosures. "The Supreme Court did not give regulatory authorities a blank check to make every advertisement look like a securities prospectus." R&D §7.0-3(d)(1). But requirements to include more limited, discrete disclaimers that would not dramatically alter the content of an advertisement generally have been permitted. See, for example, *Office of Disciplinary Counsel v. Shane*, 692 N.E.2d 571 (Ohio 1998).

In-Person Solicitation Cases

In person, face-to-face solicitation is given less constitutional protection than advertising, because of the danger that a trained advocate may take advantage of a vulnerable prospective client. Rule 7.3, cmt. [2]; *see also*

Edenfield v. Fane, 507 U.S. 761 (1993). In *Ohralik v. Ohio State Bar*, 436 U.S. 447 (1978), the Supreme Court upheld state restrictions on live and in-person solicitation of prospective clients for pecuniary gain. *Ohralik* involved a most unsympathetic lawyer, who showed up at the hospital bed of an accident victim, wheedled his way into the confidence of the victim's parents, used that access to obtain information about her insurance policy, and then used that information to sign up the victim's passenger as a client. The Court held that the state may discipline a lawyer who solicits clients "in person, for pecuniary gain, under circumstances likely to pose dangers that the State has a right to prevent." As examples of the dangers the state has a right to prevent, the Court cited fraud, undue influence, invasion of privacy, intimidation, and overreaching.

It is worth asking whether a state could discipline a lawyer who does not actually overreach or commit fraud, like the lawyer in *Ohralik*. Picking up on Justice Marshall's concurring opinion, Professor Rotunda argues that the Court might be inclined to permit "benign" commercial solicitation that is noncoercive, nondeceitful, and dignified. Rotunda §46-4. That may not be correct, though, because the Court takes pains to justify the *per se* ban on solicitation as a prophylactic measure, aimed at preventing harm before it occurs. A solicitation that starts out as noncoercive and dignified might change quickly into arm-twisting and deception. Rather than trying to police the specifics of personal interactions between lawyers and prospective clients, a state may decide it is more efficient to prohibit them entirely, particularly because it is difficult to know what goes on in private between a lawyer and prospective client. The better reading of the decision is that face-to-face solicitation is "inherently conducive to overreaching," and a state is justified in prohibiting all solicitation for that reason. Indeed, the Court itself interpreted *Ohralik* as permitting a state to "categorically ban all in-person solicitation." *Shapero v. Kentucky Bar Ass'n*, 486 U.S. 466 (1988).

Even though the Court has given less constitutional protection to solicitation by attorneys, it occasionally has been willing to treat some kinds of direct contact with prospective clients as "political" speech, subject to heightened First Amendment scrutiny. In the case *In re Primus*, 436 U.S. 412 (1978), the Court held that a lawyer working for a nonprofit organization, in coordination with the ACLU, could not be disciplined for meeting with a prospective client and discussing her legal rights. The Court said the lawyer was motivated by the desire to "express personal political beliefs and to advance the civil-liberties objectives of the ACLU," not the prospect of pecuniary gain, and therefore her meetings with the prospective client were protected as political speech and associational activity under the First Amendment.

Putting the lawyer's motive in issue complicates the analysis of in-person solicitation bans. Any lawyer could claim "political" or "ideological" motives for trying to sign up clients. The lawyer in *Ohralik* could argue that by signing up victims of auto accidents as clients, he was making sure that insurance companies play by the rules, and vindicating the compensatory and deterrent purposes of the tort system. That is not necessarily a frivolous argument. There are cases holding that in-person solicitation may be "tinged" with associational values where the underlying litigation is an attempt to vindicate some kind of constitutional rights. See, for example, *Great W. Cities v. Binstein*, 476 F. Supp. 827 (N.D. Ill. 1979), aff'd, 614 F.2d 775 (7th Cir. 1979); *In re Appert*, 315 N.W.2d 204 (Minn. 1981); *In re Teichner*, 387 N.E.2d 265 (Ill. 1979). A comment to the solicitation rule seeks to limit the "non-pecuniary" exception to "public or charitable legal-service organizations," see Rule 7.3, cmt. [5], but of course the ABA does not get to decide what restrictions are constitutional—that is a job for the courts. There is no clear line here. A lawyer working for an organization like the NAACP or the ACLU almost certainly is protected by the First Amendment political speech and associational rights, if she is meeting with prospective clients about some kind of civil rights lawsuit. An ordinary personal-injury attorney meeting with an accident victim probably is not protected. If there is a group of victims, a constitutional right at stake in the lawsuit, and the involvement of a nonprofit legal services organization, the chances increase that a court will grant constitutional protection for the lawyer's in-person solicitation.

Finally, the Court has held that states may place some narrowly drawn limitations on direct-mail "solicitation," even though this kind of communication generally is considered permissible under *Shapero*.[3] In *Florida Bar v. Went For It, Inc.*, 515 U.S. 618 (1995), the Court approved a state rule that imposed a 30-day waiting period for direct-mail contact with accident victims or their relatives. This case was surprising in light of *Shapero*, and the expansive reasoning of the Court has unsettled this area of law. Writing for the majority, Justice O'Connor attempted to justify the 30-day ban on direct-mail contact with accident victims by appealing to their privacy interests, arguing that the state was entitled to protect "the personal privacy and tranquility of citizens from crass commercial intrusion." She also appealed to the state's interest in "maintaining the professionalism of the members of the bar," returning to the pre-*Bates* reasoning that lawyers should not appear to be concerned with making money.

---

3. The 2018 amendments to the Model Rules added a definition of "solicitation." See Rule 1.0(l) A solicitation is defined as a "communication initiated by or on behalf of a lawyer or law firm that is directed to a specific person reasonably believed to need legal services in a particular matter and that offers to provide, or reasonably can be understood as offering to provide, legal services for that matter." A direct mailing is a solicitation under this definition. The interesting question is whether it should be subject to more stringent regulation than mass-media advertisements because it is directed at a specific person. Don't confuse that question with that of the permissibility of stringent regulations on *in-person* solicitation.

Ironically, the state rule at issue in *Went For It* does not prevent insurance adjusters and representatives of the defendant from contacting the victim and trying to arrange to settle the case. What happened to the interest in privacy and mental tranquility? Justice Kennedy has the better argument here, which is that anyone who does not wish to have her privacy intruded upon by a letter from an attorney can just throw the letter in the trash can. As for lawyer professionalism, that argument seemed to have been disposed of by *Bates* and *Zauderer*. Isn't it an important part of professionalism that lawyers advise people of their rights and protect them from being exploited by the defendant's agents? The argument that the Dalkon Shield ad, particularly the illustration of the IUD, would debase the legal profession and ruin its public image was considered and rejected in *Zauderer*.

Examples

Swimming Against the Constitutional Tide

Are the following restrictions on communications with prospective clients by attorneys likely to be held permissible by a court if an attorney challenges them on constitutional grounds?

1. A state disciplinary rule that applies only to television ads and provides that the audio portion of the broadcast be limited to "a single human voice, with no background sound other than instrumental music," and that visual images must be limited to "the advertising lawyer in front of a background consisting of a single solid color or a set of law books in an unadorned bookcase." The rule further requires the advertisement to be "predominantly informational."

2. Here is an example posing an "as applied" constitutional challenge. A law firm has adopted a logo featuring a pit bull wearing a spiked collar, and has obtained the telephone number 1-800-PIT-BULL for its office. The state bar association filed a complaint, alleging that the advertising violated a state rule prohibiting advertising that is "false or misleading." Does the advertisement violate this rule and, if so, would subjecting the lawyers to discipline be consistent with the First Amendment?

3. A state disciplinary rule that requires a lawyer to include the words "Advertising Material" on the outside of the envelope, on any mailing sent to prospective clients.

4. A criminal statute making it a misdemeanor to send letters to defendants facing criminal or traffic-court charges within 30 days of arrest. The state legislature passed the statute to address "feelings of offense caused by attorneys offering their services to people who had been arrested" and to improve the image of the legal profession.

Explanations

Swimming Against the Constitutional Tide

These examples show how much room there is for the bar to tinker with advertising rules while not violating any of the constitutional decisions we have just considered.

1. This hypothetical rule is an amalgam of actual disciplinary rules in effect in New Jersey, Iowa, and Florida. Courts generally have upheld these sorts of restrictions, on the grounds that the restricted aspects of communication—for example, blaring ambulance sirens in the background, a shot of piles of cash falling from the sky, endorsements by former football coach John Madden—present a danger of manipulating consumers into making bad decisions. See, for example, Committee on Prof'l Ethics v. Humphrey, 377 N.W.2d 643 (Iowa 1985). The New Jersey Supreme Court, for example, distinguished between rational and irrational modes of persuasion, and justified its state's rule on the grounds that the rule restricts "emotional, nonrational appeals that have absolutely nothing to do with the attorney's qualifications." Petition of Felmeister & Isaacs, 518 A.2d 188, 194 (N.J. 1986). Television ads, the court reasoned, are particularly apt to be used to manipulate the irrational reactions of consumers, and are more likely to be viewed by a vulnerable population of prospective clients—namely, "the less-affluent, less-educated public." Id. at 195.

   One problem with this reason is that television ads that comply with these regulations will be pretty doggone boring. If all a lawyer can do is appear on screen and intone "Hi, I went to X Law School and have handled lots of accident cases," potential clients are going to learn that they should flip channels or get a refill of their drinks during lawyer ads. The New Jersey court acknowledges this risk, but says the loss of effectiveness is worth the additional protection afforded the public. Television viewers are also savvy enough to know how to change the channel, despite the Iowa court's concern that electronic advertisements intrude themselves onto a captive audience. Humphrey, 377 N.W.2d at 647. Thus, a better analogy would be the Supreme Court's comment in Shapero that the recipient of an unsolicited letter could just throw it away.

   Another problem with these cases is that they overlook a significant line of First Amendment jurisprudence—those cases dealing with communications that depend for their effectiveness on being shocking, absurd, or parodic. Nonrational means of persuasion are entitled to constitutional protection, too. Consider famous messages such as the jacket reading "F—the draft" and the parody of the Campari ad aimed at Jerry Falwell's mother. Cohen v. California, 403 U.S. 15 (1971); Hustler Magazine, Inc. v. Falwell, 485 U.S. 46 (1988). These communications were entitled to protection under the First Amendment, with the Court in these cases explicitly recognizing that the nonrational aspects of the messages were essential to their effectiveness. "F—the draft" is simply a different message from "I oppose the draft." Yet courts often are quick to accept the justification offered by the bar and are not always as critical as they should be. Before *Went For It*, it would be unlikely for the Supreme Court to uphold restrictions such as these, but now that may not be the case. The trend now seems to be that state bars are enacting more onerous restrictions on advertising, state courts are seldom stopping them, and federal courts are occasionally taking the lawyers' constitutional arguments a bit more seriously.

In an important case, the Second Circuit struck down advertising rules adopted in New York that would have, among other things, prohibited attorneys from making communications that "rely on techniques to obtain attention that demonstrate a clear and intentional lack of relevance to the selection of counsel, including the portrayal of lawyers exhibiting characteristics clearly unrelated to legal competence" and that employ a trade name, motto, nickname, or moniker that implies an ability to obtain results in a matter. The rules were invoked in a disciplinary action against a personal-injury law firm in Syracuse that had run television advertisements showing the lawyers towering over tall buildings, running so fast to assist their clients that they appeared as blurs, and providing legal advice to space aliens. The ads also referred to the law firm by the nickname, "The Heavy Hitters." The court, applying the Supreme Court's *Central Hudson* test, conceded that the state has an interest in prohibiting misleading or deceptive advertising, and that this interest is substantial. It concluded, however, that gimmicks like showing the lawyers towering above tall buildings cannot seriously be understood as factual representations, and therefore potentially misleading. Pretending to give legal advice to extraterrestrials may be useful insofar as it is attention-getting, and even if it is irrelevant to the qualifications of the lawyers, it is not misleading to potential clients. Similarly, prohibiting the firm from referring to itself as "The Heavy Hitters" failed the *Central Hudson* test because the nickname was not misleading. See *Alexander v. Cahill*, 598 F.3d 79 (2d Cir. 2010).

2. This example is based on *Florida Bar v. Pape*, 918 So. 2d 240 (Fla. 2005). The reasoning in this opinion is not particularly persuasive, but it illustrates the point made in Explanation 2, above, namely that courts are often so eager to enforce restrictions on attorney advertising that they make some fairly lame constitutional arguments. In this case, the court concluded that the pit bull logo and phone number characterized the quality of the lawyers' services—the lawyers clearly wanted prospective clients to think they were tough, aggressive, and tenacious—and therefore was

inherently misleading. The court interpreted *Zauderer, Bates, R.M.J.*, and *Peel* (discussed above) as prohibiting states from adopting restrictions on advertising that interfere with the right to convey objectively relevant factual information. The rule is not facially invalid, because it purports to regulate only misleading or deceptive communications. But is it invalid as applied to this ad? The lawyers in this case want to convey that they are tough, aggressive, and tenacious, but prefer to do so in a humorous, attention-getting manner. The court said this is a different category of information from that protected in the Supreme Court cases, because it is not objectively verifiable. A lawyer either is or is not representing plaintiffs in Dalkon Shield cases (*Zauderer*) and either is or is not licensed to practice in various states (*R.M.J.*). Here, however, "there is no way to measure whether the attorneys in fact conduct themselves like pit bulls."

Well, okay, but that's a fairly narrow reading of those Supreme Court cases. As suggested in Explanation 1, a broader reading is that states may not prohibit or regulate advertising except to prevent deception and, as the Second Circuit held in *Alexander v. Cahill*, communications relying on gimmicks and non-rational advertising techniques are not deceptive unless a reasonable consumer would regard them as making statements of fact. The Supreme Court cases do permit states to regulate advertising that is inherently deceptive, but the Florida court pretty candidly admits that the problem with the pit bull ad is not that it is deceptive, but that it relies on imagery and associations that are not "factual." That's like the depictions of the lawyers towering over buildings in *Alexander*.

There is some authority to the contrary. For example, New Jersey Committee on Attorney Advertising, Opinion 39 (2006), concluded that advertising oneself as a "Super Lawyer" or "Best Lawyer" is inherently misleading, even if the lawyers are listed in publications called Super Lawyers or Best Lawyers. The New Jersey Supreme Court subsequently vacated that opinion. *See In re Opinion 39 of the Committee on Attorney Advertising*, 961 A.2d 722 (N.J. 2008). The Committee on Attorney Advertising did not give up the fight against hyperbolic claims by lawyers. Despite being reversed by the state Supreme Court, the Committee continues to pro-hibit lawyers from making claims that they are special: "The claim that an attorney is "super," "best," "elite," or in a top percentile of attor-neys, cannot be factually substantiated. Such hyperbolical [sic] words and phrases are utterly and inherently misleading and may not be used in attorneys' communications." N.J. Comm. on Attorney Advertising, Opinion 41 (2010). In contrast with the Second Circuit in *Alexander*, which expressed confidence that prospective clients could separate facts from the ordinary puffery expected in advertising, the New Jersey com-mittee seems to assume that consumers are credulous and easily misled by claims of excellence. *See also* Virginia State Bar Standing Committee on Legal Advertising Opinion A-0114 (even if lawyers are included in a publication called the *Best Lawyers in America*, they may not refer to themselves as the "best" lawyers).

In the Florida case it seems that the dramatization is what the court really objects to, not the potential for deception. As it notes, if it were to permit this ad, "images of sharks, wolves, crocodiles, and piranhas could follow." The problem with images of sharks and wolves is not that potential clients would be deceived, but that they actually might want to retain shark-like lawyers, and the public image of the profession would suffer as lawyers competed to attract clients who were looking for sharks. Under standard commercial speech doctrine, however, that is not a sufficient reason to restrict advertising.

3. A requirement that a direct mailing be labeled "Advertising Material" is fairly common in state rules,[4] and almost certainly is permissible under the standards of *Zauderer* and *Ibañez*. Remember that those cases permit a state to require disclaimers or additional information in attorney communications, as long as they are reasonably related to the purpose of preventing deception and are not unduly burdensome. Here, you can imagine the potential for deception if a mailing from a lawyer is not labeled as advertising. Everyone gets junk mail that is dressed up as some kind of important mailing, in the hopes that the recipient will open it instead of just chucking it in the trash can. Lawyers could do this, too, by making letters look like some kind of official summons. By requiring the envelope to be marked "Advertising Material," the rule prevents this kind of deception. It is not unduly burdensome to require a couple of words on the outside of the envelope. On the other hand, if the rule specified some kind of lengthy disclaimer about how all cases are unique, no one can promise results in any given case and so on, that rule might violate the no undue burden standard. Consider as an example *Mason v. Florida Bar*, 208 F.3d 952 (11th Cir. 2000), which invalidated a rule that required lawyers who advertised listing in a legal rating service, such as the Martindale-Hubbell Directory, to include a full explanation of the rating methodology.

4. This example is based on *Ficker v. Curran*, 119 F.3d 1150 (4th Cir. 1997), which struck down a Maryland statute of this type. A letter to recently arrested criminal defendants ordinarily would be treated as an advertisement by *Shapero* and is presumptively permitted. But the limited nature of the restriction suggests that it may be constitutional under *Went For It*. Do you see any differences between the Maryland statute and the rule in Florida that was upheld in *Went For It*? The court that struck down the

---

4. See Rule 7.3(c). That subsection was deleted by the August 2018 amendments to Rule 7.3. However, it may take some time for this amendment to the Model Rules to be reflected in the rules of a particular state.

statute mentioned several. First, the interests of the recipients of the letters are slightly different. Accident victims and their families may need some time and privacy to come to terms with their grief before dealing with communications from lawyers. Due to the emotional trauma experienced by accident victims, they are perhaps more likely to make bad decisions during the immediate 30-day aftermath of the accident than criminal defendants would be shortly after arrest. Second, criminal defendants must act quickly to preserve their rights, while accident victims have more time. Third, the privacy interests of the two classes of litigants are different. Being arrested is a public event, so criminal defendants already have lost some privacy, while accident victims may choose to remain anonymous.

These may all be distinctions without a real difference. Being arrested would be no picnic, and someone sitting in jail may not be any less emotionally vulnerable than the victim of an accident. (Remember that the Florida rule at issue in *Went For It* is not limited to highly traumatic accidents—fender-benders are covered, too.) Civil litigants have to act quickly to preserve evidence and assert rights, too, particularly if the defendant's lawyers are trying to settle the case rapidly. Finally, the traumatic accidents, like aviation disasters and chemical spills, that really get people upset about lawyer solicitations, are public events that are far more likely to attract widespread attention than someone's arrest on a minor traffic matter. The only distinction that makes any sense is that a criminal defendant has an additional interest of a constitutional dimension—the Sixth Amendment right to counsel—that tips the balance in favor of permitting contact by lawyers. Nevertheless, these are the sorts of arguments you should be prepared to make if faced with a limited ban on some forms of attorney communication with prospective clients.

DISCIPLINARY RULES

Although constitutional law plays an important role in the regulation of advertising and solicitation by lawyers, there are several principles established by the disciplinary rules that are unaffected by the cases discussed above.

As noted, in 2018 the ABA amended the Model Rules dealing with advertising and solicitation. The biggest change was the deletion of Rules 7.4 (on communication of fields of practice and specialization) and 7.5 (on firm names and letterheads). The limitations in those rules are now handled by the general prohibition in Rule 7.1 on false or misleading statements, by a new Rule 7.2(c), and by comments to Rules 7.1 and 7.2. Rule 7.1, Comments [5]-[8], talk about firm names that might be misleading, and

Rule 7.2, Comments [9]-[11], deal with the issues of specialization and certification. My guess is that it will take a while for states to get around to it, so for the foreseeable future you should be prepared to see some variation between the Model Rules and your state's advertising and solicitation rules. The MPRE, however, will use the most recent version of the Model Rules, and that is what I will cite to as well in the discussion that follows.

General Prohibition on False or Misleading Communications

One consistent theme in all of the Supreme Court's commercial speech cases is that a state constitutionally may prohibit false or misleading advertising without violating the First Amendment. See, for example, In re R.M.J., 455 U.S. 191, 203 (1982); see also *Alexander v. Cahill*, 598 F.3d 79 (2d Cir. 2010). Thus, Model Rule 7.1 makes a lawyer subject to discipline for any false or misleading communication about the lawyer's services (including advertising and solicitation). A communication may be deemed false or misleading if it contains a material misrepresentation of fact or law, or omits a fact necessary to make the statement as a whole not misleading.

Remember that, as a gross generalization, the organized bar looks with distaste upon attorney advertising and would prefer to restrict it as much as possible. Because the Supreme Court has permitted the regulation of false or misleading communications by lawyers, you can expect the bar to argue vigorously that any exaggeration, "sales talk," or "puffing" in an advertisement is a false or misleading statement. In one case, a state bar reprimanded a lawyer for using letterhead that said he had "offices" in several locations around the state, when in fact several of the "offices" were just conference rooms that he rented occasionally to hold client meetings. *In re Charges of Unprofessional Conduct Against 95-30*, 550 N.W.2d 616 (Minn. 1996). The state supreme court reversed the discipline against the lawyer, but: (1) it did so in part on the basis that the lawyer had changed his letterhead from "offices located at" to "appointments may be scheduled at," in order to remove any ambiguity; and (2) one justice dissented and would have imposed discipline because of the implication "that this lawyer is the senior or managing partner of a thriving law firm that is so large that it maintains nine offices throughout the metropolitan area."

Even truthful statements can be misleading if they may cause the reader or viewer to form a conclusion about the lawyer that lacks a factual foundation. Rule 7.1, cmt. [2]. One recurring pattern is an advertisement that creates "unjustified expectations" on the part of prospective clients that they will get a particular result. The 1983 version of Model Rule 7.1(b) contained an explicit prohibition on statements that are likely to create an unjustified expectation about results the lawyer can achieve. This rule is now handled as a subset of "false and misleading" communications in the current version of Model Rule 7.1 – see Comment [3]. For example, a lawyer may not create an advertisement featuring a newspaper headline reading "Biker Awarded $250,000 for Accident," because the ad implies that others can expect similar awards in similar cases. Conn. Bar Ass'n Op. 88-3. See also In re Frank, 440 N.E.2d 676 (Ind. 1982) (lawyer's letter recounting his history of successfully plea-bargaining drunk-driving cases "serves to unduly influence the legally unsophisticated persons into believing that the Respondent could and would get a favorable resolution of their case").

Similarly, some states maintain that a lawyer may not use client testimonials (such as, "I didn't think I could recover for my injury, but Attorney X fought for me and got results.") because, again, they create the impression that the lawyer will achieve similar results in future cases. Other jurisdictions permit testimonials, but only as long as there is no way to interpret the communication as promising good results in the future. For example, a client testimonial that "my attorney was always prompt and courteous in handling my case" would not carry any implicit suggestion of future outcomes. See, for example, Phila. Bar Ass'n Op. 91-17 (1992) (permitting "soft endorsement" such as the lawyer always returning telephone calls, appearing concerned, giving the client a "sympathetic ear," and proceeding on a prompt basis).

Another common fact pattern is an advertisement that compares the lawyer's services with those of other lawyers, unless the comparison can be factually substantiated. The 1983 version of Model Rule 7.1(c) had an express prohibition on these advertisements. This rule is now incorporated into the prohibition on "false and misleading" communications in the current version of Model Rule 7.1 – see Comment [3]. Courts and disciplinary authorities are quick to construe a statement about a lawyer's expertise as an illegitimate comparison with other lawyers. The following statements have all been construed to violate this rule: "We Do It Well"; a lawyer is also an "experienced pilot"; and a lawyer provides "big city experience, small town service." *Medina County Bar Ass'n v. Grieselhuber*, 678 N.E.2d 535 (Ohio 1997); *Spencer v. Honorable Justices of Superior Court*, 579 F. Supp. 880 (E.D. Pa. 1984) (rather than refer to himself as an "experienced pilot," lawyer should list hours flown in various types of aircraft, his certification as a flight instructor, and so on); Phila. Bar Ass'n Op. 94-12 (1994) (improper to imply that firm is "somehow better, more friendly and more caring (that is, 'small town') than other city attorneys"). A bland recitation of facts is permissible, so a lawyer may identify herself as a graduate of Local Law School or a member of the Association of Trial Lawyers of America. But a disciplinary authority is likely to react negatively to any explicit suggestion that the lawyer is a better lawyer by virtue of belonging to some organization or having gone to such-and-such a law school.

A couple of other applications of this rule were formerly stated in other rules, but have been brought within the general prohibition in Rule 7.1 on false or misleading statements. (This is a recent change, in August 2018, and your state may not have gotten around to amendment its version of the rules. Be careful!) Former Model Rule 7.4 permitted communications of one's field of practice or specialization as long as the communication is not misleading. That general permission is now in Rule 7.2, cmt. [10]. In addition, a lawyer may not use the magic word "certified" unless the lawyer is approved by an organization that has been approved by an appropriate state authority or the ABA. Former Rule 7.4(d); now Rule 7.2, cmt. [11]. This rule tends to be under-enforced, and if state enforcement authorities did pursue lawyers for claims of certification, they might run into constitutional difficulties. In the *Peel* case, the lawyer described himself as a "Certified Trial Specialist by the National Board of Trial Advocacy." *Peel v. Attorney Registration and Disciplinary Commn.*, 496 U.S. 91 (1990). The Supreme Court said the communication was not misleading because it did not imply official government certification. The National Board of Trial Advocacy was a legitimate organization and had standards for certifying lawyers as trial specialists. It is likely, though not certain, that a court would permit a lawyer to make a truthful, non-deceptive communication of certification by a bona fide professional organization even if it weren't on the state list of approved organizations. Risk-averse lawyers can avoid the whole issue by sticking with the permitted language of "practicing in a particular field of law," under Rule 7.4(a) and not using the word "certified."

Former Rule 7.5(a) prohibited the use of a law firm name that is misleading. One way firm names can be found misleading is by suggesting that the firm is affiliated with the state—for example, the "Virginia Legal Service Office." See current Rule 7.1, cmt. [5]. Watch out for firm names that imply some kind of attributes or experience on the part of the law firm—the name itself may be a violation of the rules, even if the firm does not do anything else wrong. A firm name may include the name of a deceased partner, see Rule 7.1, cmt. [5], but may not include the name of a lawyer holding public office and not actively and regularly practicing with the firm. Rule 7.1, cmt. [11]. When former New York City mayor Rudy Giuliani joined the Houston firm of Bracewell & Patterson in 2005, the firm changed its name to Bracewell & Giuliani. If Rudy had subsequently become Governor of New York, the firm would no longer be able to use the name Bracewell & Giuliani.

Truthful, Non-Deceptive Advertising Is Permitted

Subject to the prohibition on false or misleading communications, lawyers are permitted to advertise in various media—for example, print ads, billboards,

Web sites, television and radio spots, and direct-mail. Rule 7.2(a). Many states require that the lawyer retain a copy of the ad, in case a dispute arises regarding its content, but this rule was deleted by the ABA from Model Rule 7.2 in 2002. Some states even require the lawyer to submit a copy of the ad to the appropriate regulatory authority prior to running it; this requirement probably would be struck down as an unconstitutional prior restraint if the regulator's approval were required before the ad could run, but there are very few decided cases on this point. Wolfram §14.2, at 783. The ABA rule does retain the requirement that the advertisement include the contact information of at least one lawyer or law firm responsible for its content. Rule 7.2(d) & cmt. [12].

Lawyer Referral Services

This is a different topic from mass-media advertising, but it is treated in the same rule, Rule 7.2(b). The issue here is whether a lawyer can pay a fee for referrals. Fees for referrals are prohibited in a wide variety of transactions — they are called "kickbacks" — so it is not surprising that the disciplinary rules restrict the practice for lawyers. Beyond paying to produce advertising, and buying a law practice from another lawyer, a lawyer may not pay for referrals, except in two limited circumstances: (1) a lawyer may pay the customary fee of a nonprofit lawyer referral service established by the appropriate regulatory authority, Rule 7.2(b)(2); and (2) Lawyer A may agree to refer clients to Lawyer B in exchange for Lawyer B agreeing to refer clients to Lawyer A in the future, as long as the client is informed of the nature and existence of the fee arrangement, and it is nonexclusive, Rule 7.2(b)(4). The second arrangement might make sense in a case where the two lawyers had complementary specialties — say, Lawyer A was an expert in patent prosecution and Lawyer B specialized in patent litigation. Note that Lawyer B cannot pay Lawyer A in cash for referrals unless the two lawyers comply with the fee-sharing rule, Rule 1.5(e).[5]

In-Person Solicitation Is More Tightly Restricted

Model Rule 7.3 is the rule on in-person solicitation. Rule 7.3(b) flatly prohibits live, person-to-person contact with prospective clients where the lawyer is motivated by the possibility of pecuniary gain. Any ban on solicitation

---

5. The fee-sharing rule permits lawyers not in the same firm to divide fees among themselves if the division is in proportion to the services performed by each lawyer, or if the lawyers assume joint responsibility for the representation. In addition, the client must agree, in writing, to the arrangement, and the total fee must be reasonable. See Chapter 4 for more on attorneys' fees. This rule should be distinguished from the prohibition on splitting attorneys' fees with nonlawyers, in Rule 5.4(a).

would not be constitutional if it reached in-person solicitation that was not for pecuniary gain, under *Primus*. See *In re Primus*, 436 U.S. 412 (1978). Lawyers may solicit professional employment from other lawyers; family members, friends, or those persons who have a prior professional relationship with the lawyer; or persons who routinely use for business purposes the type of services offered by the lawyer. Rule 7.3(b)(1)(3). The rationale for these exceptions is that the lawyer is less likely to use coercion, fraud, or undue influence on people in these categories.

When you hear the term "ambulance chasing," think solicitation. If a lawyer shows up at the scene of an accident and starts handing out business cards, Model Rule 7.3 is implicated. The same is true if the lawyer's paralegal or a "runner" shows up and starts handing out business cards, because Model Rule 5.3(c) makes a lawyer responsible for the conduct of a nonlawyer that would be a violation of the rules if committed by a lawyer. For example, if Lawyer X directs Paramedic Y to recommend that Victim Z hire Lawyer X as his lawyer, Lawyer X is subject to discipline. The reason is that, if Paramedic Y were a lawyer, she would violate Model Rule 7.3 by soliciting professional employment from Victim Z. Thus, Lawyer X violates Model Rule 5.3(c) by "ordering the conduct involved"—that is, directing Paramedic Y to recommend Lawyer X. This is not as confusing as it sounds. The idea here is that a lawyer cannot circumvent the disciplinary rules by acting as a puppet-master, directing a nonlawyer to do something that the lawyer otherwise would be forbidden to do.

Under the pre-2018 Model Rules, there was some uncertainty over whether targeting an advertisement to a person known to be in need of legal services was sufficient to bring the communication within Rule 7.3's ban on "in-person, live telephone, or real-time electronic contact." (Note that the language of the 2018 amendment now prohibits "live person to person" contact.) Electronic communications made the distinction between mass-media advertising and personal solicitation somewhat blurry. For example, suppose a company purchased a banner ad that appears whenever someone visits a Web site. This would be general, and thus an instance of advertising. But of course everyone knows that Google and numerous other online marketers tailor the content of advertising to the specific user. If someone is running searches for "divorce" or "mesothelioma" or "employment discrimination," he or she may be interested in retaining a lawyer. Does that make an electronic communication a targeted solicitation if it is generated in response to search activity? The Ethics 20/20 Commission considered this question and concluded that search-engine optimization techniques, Facebook ads placed by an algorithm, and similar techniques should be treated in the same way as ordinary mass-media advertising:

> A solicitation is a targeted communication initiated by the lawyer that is directed to a specific person and that offers to provide, or can reasonably be

understood as offering to provide, legal services. In contrast, a lawyer's communication typically does not constitute a solicitation if it is directed to the general public, such as through a billboard, an Internet banner advertisement, a website or a television commercial, or if it is in response to a request for information or is automatically generated in response to Internet searches.

Rule 7.3, cmt. [1]. In any event, it is now clear after the 2018 amendments to the Model Rules that the strict prohibition on in-person solicitation really does apply only to communication that is live. Not necessarily in person — in "meatspace," as the kids say — but in some form that is in real time: "Live person to person contact" means in person, face to face, telephone and real-time person to person communications such as Skype or Facetime, and other visual/auditory communications where the prospective client may feel obligated to speak with the lawyer. Such person to person contact does not include chat rooms, text messages, or other written communications that recipients may easily disregard." Rule 7.3, cmt. [2].

There are a few exceptions to the ban on in-person solicitation, in addition to the situation discussed above of seeking employment where pecuniary gain is not a motive. Even with a profit motive, lawyers may seek business through in-person contact from another lawyer (e.g. the in-house counsel of a prospective corporate client); a person with a prior professional, personal, or familial relationship with the lawyer; and a sophisticated consumer of legal services. See Rule 7.2(b). However, even when the target of the solicitation falls within one of those categories, a lawyer still may not use in-person contact to solicit business if the target has made known her desire not to be solicited, or if the conduct involves coercion, duress, or harassment. See Rule 7.2(c). If your rich uncle owns a business and frequently hires lawyers, he would ordinarily be fair game, due to the familial relationship (Rule 7.2(b)(2)) and his routine use of lawyers for business purposes (Rule 7.2(b)(3)). However, if he tells you to stop pestering him, you can't hit him up at Thanksgiving dinner for legal work (Rule 7.2(c)(1)).

Examples

The Whole Truth?

5. The law firm of Wilmer & Kang ran a television ad that dramatized an auto accident, the hospitalization of one of the victims, and finally, the trial of the victim's case with attorney Kang arguing to the jury. The voice-over begins by saying, "trial is civilized warfare," but assures the viewer that Wilmer & Kang are prepared to "make complicated medical facts clear for the jury" and strive for "victory in the courtroom." Kang is a personal-injury attorney who believes that pretrial settlement of cases

is almost always better for clients than facing the risks of trial. He is an experienced litigator but has never tried a case to a jury. If trial is inevitable in a case, he refers it to a trial lawyer at a different firm in town. Does the firm's television spot violate any disciplinary rules?

Buzz Off!

6. The owner of a local grocery store uses ABC Law Firm to defend minor slip and fall cases that occur in its store. An attorney believes she can provide equivalent quality legal services at a better price. She and the owner each have 7 year-old children who play soccer on a team called the Bumblebees. The attorney walks up to the owner of the store at a soccer game and offers to represent the owner in litigation. The owner was offended that the attorney would try to solicit business at a kids' sporting event, and told her to leave him alone. She did so, and never approached the owner again. The owner filed a grievance with the state disciplinary authority. Is the attorney subject to discipline?

   A. Yes, because the attorney solicited professional employment by live person-to-person contact with the owner, and her motivation was pecuniary gain.

   B. Yes, because the owner is not a lawyer or a family member of the attorney.

   C. No, because the owner told the attorney not to solicit professional employment at the soccer game.

   D. No, because the owner routinely uses another law firm to defend slip-and-fall cases.

Explanations

The Whole Truth?

5. This example is based on In re Zang, 741 P.2d 267 (Ariz. 1987), which upheld discipline against the lawyer for producing an ad falsely implying that he was experienced at trial advocacy, as opposed to litigation. In the example, although Kang is an experienced litigator, his own testimony shows that he avoids trials. (In the real case, the attorney admitted that he is not competent to try a personal-injury case.) By contrast, the advertisement for Wilmer & Kang implies that the lawyers are willing and able to try personal-injury cases to juries. The voice-over states that the lawyers make complicated medical facts clear for the jury and strive for victory in the courtroom. These are not representations about general litigation skill (which the lawyer admittedly has), but specific claims about his ability and experience as a trial lawyer, as well as his belief that cases are won in the courtroom, not through settlement.

The important thing to take from this example is that a court will consider the implied message that a reasonable audience is likely to understand. Even though the advertisement never made an explicit false representation, such as "Attorney Kang has tried 100 cases to juries," the dramatization of his closing argument *suggests* that he is a highly experienced trial lawyer. For this reason, the ad violates the prohibition in Rule 7.1 on false or misleading communications.

Buzz Off!

6. The correct answer is (D). The grocery store owner routinely uses the type of legal services offered by the attorney. See Rule 7.3(b)(3). That's the significance of the fact that he usually employs the ABC Law Firm. (If you're looking at an older version of Rule 7.3(b), the language would be "an experienced user of the type of legal services involved.") I changed the language a little, hoping not to telegraph the answer, but it's saying the same thing as Rule 7.3(b)(3).

Option (A) would be correct but for the list of permitted contacts in Rule 7.3(b).

Option (B) would only trip you up if you forgot about the other category of permitted persons.

Option (C) refers to Rule 7.3(c)(1). Even if the target of an in-person solicitation is within the list of permitted persons in Rule 7.2(b), a lawyer may still be subject to discipline for pestering that person after being asked to stop.

CHAPTER 19

Associations of Lawyers

PRACTICING WITH OTHER LAWYERS

The Model Code appeared to have been written by solo practitioners. There was very little recognition anywhere in it that lawyers frequently practice together, in partnerships or professional corporations. The Model Rules corrected this oversight with a series of provisions governing lawyers in association with other lawyers and nonlawyers. In addition, there are aspects of the general law governing lawyers that apply only in an organizational setting. The Sarbanes-Oxley regulations, for example, provide a safe harbor for junior lawyers who report evidence of wrongdoing to their supervisor. Remember also that as an aspect of practicing together in a "firm," many conflicts of interest that apply to one lawyer in the firm are imputed to all other lawyers in the same firm. Rule 1.8(k), 1.10(a). "Firm" is a defined term in the Model Rules and refers to "a law partnership, professional corporation, sole proprietorship, or other association authorized to practice law; or lawyers employed in a legal services organization or the legal department of a corporation or other organization." Rule 1.0(c).

Responsibilities of Supervising Lawyers

With a few exceptions, most states do not attempt to punish law firms for violations of the disciplinary rules. Individual lawyers within a firm, however, may be subject to discipline for a variety of lapses. Partners in a law firm are required to "make reasonable efforts" to create procedures and structures to ensure compliance by all lawyers in the firm with the disciplinary rules. Rule 5.1(a). Thus, in principle, a partner could be disciplined for failing to implement an adequate conflicts-checking procedure or for failing to train incoming associates on compliance with the duty of confidentiality. In practice, cases in which discipline was imposed have involved extreme conduct, such as creating a "sweatshop" environment for associates in which it is impossible to provide competent legal services to clients because of severe caseload pressures imposed by partners. See, for example, *Attorney Grievance Comm. v. Ficker*, 706 A.2d 1045 (Md. 1998); *Davis v. Alabama State Bar*, 676 So. 2d 306 (Ala. 1996).

Even in the absence of a failure to develop effective firm-wide training and supervision procedures, individual supervisory lawyers still may be subject to discipline for inadequate oversight of another lawyer for whom the supervisor has "direct supervisory authority." Rule 5.1(b). The partner or senior associate in charge of a particular matter therefore is required to ensure that subordinate lawyers on that matter comply with the disciplinary rules. A lawyer also is responsible for the conduct of a lawyer outside the scope of "direct supervisory authority" if the lawyer orders certain conduct or is in a position of managerial authority and has knowledge of the conduct and an opportunity to avoid or mitigate its consequences, but fails to take remedial action. Rule 5.1(c). In agency law terms, the lawyer could be disciplined for *ratifying* the other lawyer's conduct.

The same analysis applies to nonlawyer employees such as paralegals, secretaries, investigators, messengers, and so on. Partners must ensure that there are reasonable firm-wide procedures in place to train and supervise these employees regarding, for example, their obligation to safeguard confidential information. Rule 5.3(a). Partners also must train and supervise those employees over whom they have direct supervisory authority. Rule 5.3(b). And a lawyer may be subject to discipline for ordering or ratifying conduct by a nonlawyer employee that would be a violation of the disciplinary rules if engaged in by a lawyer. For example, if a lawyer is forbidden by Model Rule 4.2 to have contact with a represented nonclient, it would be a violation of Model Rule 5.3(c) for the lawyer to order an investigator to make contact with that person.

The disciplinary rules do not create vicarious liability on the part of partners for the torts or other civil liability of their associates. See Rule 5.1, cmt. [7], which says that *respondeat superior* liability is a question of law beyond the scope of the disciplinary rules. Under generally applicable tort law, however, a law firm is vicariously liable for civil damages legally caused by an employee of the firm acting in the course of firm business. Rest. §58(1). Do not be fooled by the absence of vicarious liability in the disciplinary rules—if a question asks about the civil liability of a firm, think in terms of ordinary agency law principles. If a messenger is involved in an auto accident while driving across town to file papers with the court, the firm will be vicariously liable for injuries caused by the accident.

"Just Following Orders": Responsibilities of Subordinate Lawyers

It would be a big mistake for a junior associate to think that she is not subject to discipline if she simply is acting at the direction of a supervisory lawyer. Every lawyer is individually responsible for following the disciplinary rules, even if working within a hierarchical structure like a law firm. Rule 5.2(a). If a partner orders an associate to commit a violation of the disciplinary rules, the associate must refuse. She may face a Hobson's choice—be punished internally by the partner for failing to carry out instructions or be disciplined by the state bar—but the existence of the order will not get the lawyer off the hook. There is no "Nuremberg defense" to professional disciplinary charges. For example, in *Daniels v. Alander*, 844 A.2d 182 (Conn. 2004), an associate was sitting at the counsel table with a partner when the partner made a misrepresentation to the court. The associate knew the partner's statement was false because he had communicated with the client and knew the real facts. The associate was disciplined under the local version of Rule 3.3 for sitting silently and not correcting the misrepresentation. The Connecticut Supreme Court held that failing to correct the record was a violation of the perjury rule and that there is no sound policy reason to excuse this failure just because the lawyer in question was an associate, acting at the direction of a supervising lawyer.

The disciplinary rules do recognize a limited safe harbor for junior lawyers acting at the direction of supervisors. The subordinate lawyer will not be subject to professional discipline if the action ordered by the supervisor is a "reasonable resolution of an arguable question of professional duty." Rule 5.2(b). If reasonable minds could differ, if the right thing to do in a situation is a matter of professional judgment, and if the supervisory lawyer's decision reflects careful thought, research, and deliberation, only then may the subordinate lawyer follow the instructions of a supervisor. Note an implicit corollary of this rule: *You have a responsibility to do your own research into the law governing lawyers.* Otherwise, you as the subordinate lawyer have no way of knowing whether your supervisor's direction is in fact a reasonable resolution of an arguable question.

A similar safe harbor exists in the Sarbanes-Oxley regulations issued by the Securities and Exchange Commission, which apply to lawyers representing publicly traded corporations. The regulations provide that a subordinate (junior) lawyer has an independent obligation to comply with the regulations and will not be exonerated from responsibility merely because she acted at the direction of a supervising (senior) lawyer. 17 C.F.R. §205.5(b). However, the regulations state that a junior lawyer will have fully complied with her reporting obligation if she reports evidence of wrongdoing to her supervising attorney. §205.5(c). The junior lawyer can still go through the whole "reporting up" procedure on her own if she believes that the supervising lawyer has failed to comply with her obligations under the regulations, but she is not required to do so. §205.5(d).

Outsourcing

The legal services industry is not insulated from large-scale economic forces, including the potential for realizing significant labor cost savings by locating some parts of a production process in low-wage countries or regions of the United States with lower labor costs. Information technology makes it simple and inexpensive to outsource document reviews in civil discovery, due diligence work in corporate transactions, and some aspects of the patent prosecution process. Outsourcing may benefit clients by reducing their costs, in which case sophisticated counsel with in-house legal departments may demand that outside counsel consider it. The ABA had already issued an ethics opinion concluding that there is nothing per se unethical about outsourcing the performance of legal services, as long as the lawyer ensures that they will be performed competently. See ABA Formal Op. 08-451. This obligation follows from Rule 1.1 and Rule 5.1(b).

Outsourcing is not limited to lawyers in the United States; the ABA opinion went on to say that non-American lawyers (from India, for example, which shares the heritage of the English common law with the United States) may also be employed as long as the outsourcing lawyer investigates the legal system of the non-U.S. jurisdiction to ensure that lawyers receive training comparable to that given to American lawyers and that the legal profession in that country adheres to similar core values, particularly the value of confidentiality. The Ethics 20/20 Commission added a comment to Rule 1.1 stating that a lawyer proposing to outsource legal services should obtain the client's informed consent. Rule 1.1, cmt. [6]. (A hyper-technical note about the authority of comments: Because informed consent is mentioned only in the comment, not the text of the rule, a lawyer would not be subject to discipline for failing to obtain informed consent.) The Commission also added comments to Rule 5.3, the rule on supervising nonlawyers, to address the hiring of nonlawyer professionals, such as information technology firms and offsite data storage ("cloud computing") systems, to assist with the provision of legal services. See Rule 5.3, cmts. [3]–[4]. You may recall an example from Chapter 6 about the duties of lawyers using information technology vendors. This is part of the same issue relating to lawyer supervision of nonlawyer assistants.

Intra-Firm Fiduciary Duties

Lawyers who practice within firms are subject not only to the lawyer disciplinary rules, but also to the general law governing the form of organization in which they practice—partnership, professional corporation, limited-liability company (LLC), or whatever. They also are subject to the "constitutional" documents establishing the entity, such as the partnership agreement or articles of incorporation. Together, the general law and the contracts bringing the organization into existence create duties that partners or shareholders owe to one another. For example, depending on how a partnership agreement is drafted, it may be difficult for a law firm to "fire" a partner. The partnership agreement may prescribe procedures for termination and may permit termination only on specified grounds. These duties can run in both directions. Partners may owe fiduciary duties to the partnership and to other partners, which prohibit them from "grabbing and leaving"—that is, departing the firm and taking a bunch of valuable clients with them. Any duties owed to the firm, however, are complicated by the existence of additional fiduciary duties owed directly by the partner to the client. The effect of recognizing the priority of fiduciary obligations to the client may be to weaken the bonds of loyalty that cement partners or shareholders to a law firm; if the duty to the client trumps the duty to the firm, "rainmaker" partners who have the ability to attract clients can threaten to leave with their "book" of business unless they are adequately compensated. See generally Robert W. Hillman, *Hillman on Lawyer Mobility: The Law and Ethics of Partner Withdrawals and Law Firm Breakups* (2d ed. 1998) (looseleaf).

Law firms may try to enhance the duties owed to them by constituents by including provisions in partnership agreements, such as covenants not to compete. A frequently litigated question is whether noncompete agreements violate Rule 5.6, which states that a lawyer may not participate in offering or making an agreement that restricts the right of a lawyer to practice after termination of the relationship with the other contracting party. This rule attempts to prioritize the lawyer's fiduciary duty to clients over any duties the lawyer may owe to a law firm and its constituents. See Rule 5.6, cmt. [1]; Rest. §13, cmt. b. Some courts have held that agreements imposing reasonable financial penalties on departing lawyers are enforceable, because while they may create disincentives to leave, they do not "restrict" practice in violation of the rule. See, for example, *Fearnow v. Ridenour, Swenson, Cleere & Evans PC*, 138 P.3d 723 (Ariz. 2006); *Howard v. Babcock*, 863 P.2d 150 (Cal. 1993). However, even courts that permit enforcement of "reasonable" penalties would not permit an outright prohibition on representing certain classes of clients or practicing within a particular geographic area. The California-Arizona position is decidedly outside the mainstream, so you should generally consider even financial disincentives, and certainly outright noncompete agreements, to be unenforceable against departing law firm partners or shareholders. In addition, restrictive covenants may also be invalid when applied to in-house lawyers. See New Jersey Comm. on Prof'l Ethics Op. 708 (2006).

Associates, as employees (agents) of the law firm (principal), owe the same fiduciary duties that any other agent would owe to her principal. These duties include taking reasonable care to protect the principal's interests, obeying the principal's reasonable instructions, and maintaining the confidentiality of information learned from the principal. See generally William A. Gregory, *The Law of Agency and Partnership* Ch. 7 (3d ed. 2001). Associates may not engage in self-dealing, for example by cutting separate deals with law firm clients to perform services at rates below the rates at which the firm is billing for the associate's services. They may, however, inform clients that they will be changing employers and express their willingness to continue representing these clients at their new employer. *Fred Siegel Co. v. Arter & Hadden*, 707 N.E.2d 853 (Ohio 1999).

Examples

Responsibility up the Chain of Command

1. Flanders is the partner in charge of defending a complex accounting malpractice dispute. Brockman is an associate assigned to work on the same case. Flanders bills approximately 50 hours per month to the client for work on the matter, and Brockman generally bills around 100 hours. The two lawyers consult frequently about Brockman's work, and Flanders reviews all letters and pleadings prepared by Brockman before they are sent out.

   Brockman realizes that it would be helpful to the accounting firm's malpractice case if someone could testify that one of the firm's auditors had specifically warned its client (now the plaintiff in the malpractice case) against using a particular method of accounting. Unfortunately, none of the witnesses who had been deposed would testify that they had communicated this warning to the client. Brockman talks to his friend Wiggums, also an associate in the firm, about this problem. Wiggums, joking around, says that maybe one of the lawyers should impress upon an employee of the accounting firm the importance of this recollection. "Great idea!" exclaims Brockman. "Why don't you do that?" Following this advice, Wiggums subsequently contacts an employee who then changes his testimony. Brockman never informs Flanders of Wiggums's role in talking to the witness.

   If Wiggums persuades the witness to offer false testimony, in violation of Model Rule 3.3(a)(3), will Flanders or Brockman be subject to discipline?

Being a Good Soldier

2. Siegler is a partner in the corporate department of a large law firm; Mendez works frequently with her as a mid-level associate. The firm represents Wolfowitz & Rumsfeld, P.C., a two-person lobbying firm organized as a closely held corporation. One day Wolfowitz comes to see Siegler and Mendez. "I need some help," he says. "I'm getting sick and tired of Rumsfeld. All he does is play golf all the time while I do all the work. I think the clients know it, and I think I could make more money on my own." Wolfowitz asks Siegler to prepare Articles of Incorporation for Wolfowitz Lobbying Group, P.C., and to draft a letter for Wolfowitz's signature to send to clients of Wolfowitz & Rumsfeld announcing the formation of the new firm. After the meeting, Mendez raises a concern. "I think we may represent the firm, Wolfowitz & Rumsfeld, and not Wolfowitz personally," he says. "Even though it is a closely held corporation, the entity is our client, not Wolfowitz individually. Don't we have a conflict of interest by representing Wolfowitz in an action that might be detrimental to the corporation?" Siegler brushes off this advice. "Trust me on this one," she says. "The law of conflicts is a mess when the client is a closely held corporation. I think we have a sufficient relationship with Wolfowitz individually to justify helping him set up a new corporation."

   When Rumsfeld gets wind of these plans, he sues Wolfowitz for breach of fiduciary duty, and Siegler and Mendez for legal malpractice and breach of fiduciary duty. Mendez files a motion to dismiss, arguing that he cannot be liable for his role in the representation, because he was acting at the direction of Siegler. Should the motion be granted?

Explanations

Responsibility up the Chain of Command

1. Analyze the problem lawyer-by-lawyer. Flanders is a partner in a law firm, so he would be responsible for failing to make reasonable efforts to ensure that the firm has adequate procedures in place to ensure that lawyers in the firm comply with the rules. Rule 5.1(a). Nothing in the problem suggests that the Brockman-Wiggums conspiracy is the result of lax training or supervision at a firm-wide level, so Flanders is not subject to discipline under Model Rule 5.1(a). In addition, Flanders has "direct supervisory authority" over Brockman but not Wiggums. If Flanders failed to make reasonable efforts to ensure that Brockman conformed to the disciplinary rules, he would be subject to discipline under Model Rule 5.1(b). Flanders is safe under this rule as well, because he puts sufficient effort into supervising Brockman, by meeting frequently

with the associate and reviewing all his written work before it is sent out. Because Flanders did not order Wiggums to instruct the witness to perjure herself, and was ignorant of Wiggums's involvement in the case, he is not subject to discipline under Model Rule 5.1(c).

Brockman is not subject to Model Rule 5.1(a) at all, because he is not a partner in the firm or a lawyer with comparable managerial authority. Similarly, he does not have "direct supervisory authority" over Wiggums — the two lawyers are on the same level of authority in the firm and, moreover, Wiggums is not working on the accounting-malpractice case. Brockman is subject to discipline under Model Rule 5.1(c)(1), however, for ordering Wiggums to instruct the witness to commit perjury.

Incidentally, although the question does not ask about the discipline of Wiggums, note that he is bound by the disciplinary rules despite having acted at the direction of Brockman. Rule 5.2(a). Brockman is not a "supervisory lawyer," so Wiggums cannot take advantage of the safe harbor in Model Rule 5.2(b); in any event, the safe harbor provision is inapplicable because the direction to engineer perjury is not a "reasonable resolution of an arguable question of professional duty" — it is a flat-out violation, which any reasonably alert lawyer would recognize as such.

Being a Good Soldier

2. This is a really tough situation for the associate, but it is exactly the sort of thing that can happen in practice. See *Murphy & Demory, Ltd. v. Admiral Daniel J. Murphy, U.S.N. (Ret.)*, Fairfax (Va.) Circuit Court (June 6, 1994) (not officially published, but reproduced or summarized in many professional responsibility casebooks). The court in the *Murphy & Demory* case excoriated the partner for not listening to the warnings of several junior associates who had raised the possibility of a conflict of interest in the representation of a corporate shareholder in a transaction adverse to the firm's existing corporate client. (See Chapter 5 for client-identification issues in the representation of closely held corporations, and Chapter 14 for current-client conflicts.) Unfortunately for the associate, the court was "not unsympathetic" to his difficult position, but ultimately held that he was equally responsible for legal malpractice.

First, notice the overlap between the disciplinary rules and the law of malpractice. The disciplinary rules used to simply disclaim any role in setting the standard of care in civil lawsuits against lawyers, but the most current version of the rules adds a sensible qualification that reflects the law in most jurisdictions: "[S]ince the Rules do establish standards of conduct by lawyers, a lawyer's violation of a Rule may be evidence of breach of the applicable standard of conduct." Rule, Scope para. [20]. See also Rest. §52, cmt. f (permitting use of expert testimony or other means to inform the trier of fact of applicable disciplinary rules). Thus, the analysis is the same whether we are analyzing the professional discipline of Mendez or his civil liability to Rumsfeld.

In order for Mendez to take advantage of the safe harbor in Model Rule 5.2(b), he must establish that Siegler's instruction is a reasonable resolution of an arguable question of professional duty. It is not enough for the partner to say, "Trust me." The associate must undertake her own analysis of the law applicable to the lawyer's conduct. As it turns out, the law in this area is indeed a mess, but if Mendez had read the cases carefully, he would have discovered that it is a pretty obvious breach of fiduciary duty that the law firm owes to its client, the corporation, to set up a competing corporation on behalf of one of the shareholders. For the purposes of answering an exam question, you may need additional facts to analyze the underlying substantive issue of the law governing lawyers. Do keep in mind, though, that a lawyer cannot simply follow orders blindly, but must make an independent determination that the supervisor's instructions are reasonable.

PRACTICING WITH NONLAWYERS: THE MDP "PROBLEM"

Not long ago, it seemed as though you could not open a publication aimed at practicing lawyers without seeing a reference to the debate over multidisciplinary practices (MDPs). An MDP is an organization consisting of at least one lawyer and at least one other professional, such as an accountant or financial planner, which is intended to provide integrated professional services to clients. The widespread accounting fraud scandals of 2002 were perceived to have taken some of the wind out of the sails of reformers who sought broader recognition of MDPs, and the Ethics 20/20 Commission rejected any possibility of permitting so-called alternative business structures for lawyers. The Commission co-chairs stated:

> Since its creation in 2009, the Commission has undertaken a careful study of alternative law practice structures. Based on the Commission's extensive outreach, research, consultation, and the response of the profession, there does not appear to be a sufficient basis for recommending a change to ABA policy on nonlawyer ownership of law firms.

See ABA Ethics 20/20 Commission Press Release (April 16, 2012). Despite the issue being pretty much a dead letter at this point, your professional responsibility teacher may find it interesting. The question is why. The answer is likely that considering the MDP issue can be useful as a window into a deeper disagreement over the nature of the legal profession. It is fair to say that most academics tend to be tolerant of the idea of MDPs, while most practicing lawyers range from skeptical to adamantly opposed to any alteration in the traditional lawyer-only structure of professional associations. See Charles W. Wolfram, *Comparative Multi-Disciplinary Practice: Paths Taken and Not Taken*, 52 Case W. Res. L. Rev. 961 (2002). What does that say about the relationship between the legal academy and practicing lawyers? What are the core values of lawyers that MDPs allegedly threaten?

The discussion of MDPs often focuses on the large accounting firms, who wish to sell packages of integrated legal, financial, and strategic consulting services to business clients. This is the Wall Street side of MDPs, but there also is a Main Street side. Imagine a solo practitioner in a small town who does a fair amount of advising small businesses and preparing estate plans for local residents. The lawyer believes that she would be able to provide better service to her clients by associating with a CPA, because the lawyer and the accountant would be more familiar with the client's business, and could work together to solve the client's problems. Also, the association probably would result in a cost savings to clients, because the lawyer and the accountant would not have to, in effect, double-bill for services on which they have overlapping competencies. Similarly, a domestic relations lawyer might wish to form a partnership with a clinical social worker, to provide a package of services to clients going through divorce. This arrangement also would be an MDP.

Whether an MDP is Smith & Jones in Anytown, USA, or a gigantic multinational consulting firm like Ernst & Young, its existence raises certain issues for the lawyer-members under the professional disciplinary rules. The idea behind most of these rules is to protect the independent professional judgment of the lawyer from being influenced by the financial interests of nonlawyer members of the MDP. Interestingly, most of these rules state nonwaivable prohibitions, meaning that an affected client could not provide informed consent to a lawyer engaging in the otherwise prohibited conduct. A business could not, for example, decide that it preferred a lawyer-accountant MDP to provide its auditing and tax-advising services, even after being fully informed of the relevant risks. The specific rules are considered below.

Fee-Splitting

Generally, lawyers are prohibited from dividing earned fees with nonlawyers. Rule 5.4(a). That means that if a lawyer and an accountant cooperate to advise a client on a business transaction, each must bill separately for her services. The rule also means that the accountant cannot share in the lawyer's profits. Suppose a lawyer and an accountant have an arrangement to split net profits 50/50. If the lawyer receives a large windfall in one year—say, from the settlement of a personal-injury case in which the accountant had no role—she may not split those profits with the accountant according to the usual arrangement without violating Model Rule 5.4(a). The rule contains exceptions allowing the acquisition of a law practice from the estate of a deceased lawyer, payments of profit-sharing bonuses to nonlawyer staff, and sharing court-awarded legal fees with a nonprofit organization. None of these exceptions cover a full-on MDP, with lawyers and nonlawyers practicing together in a professional association.

Historically, the rule was aimed mostly at the solicitation of clients by "runners" or "cappers" who would visit hospitals and try to sign up injured patients as clients. See Wolfram §16.5. It is still litigated in cases involving referral arrangements between lawyers and nonlawyers. The rule appears to be invoked most frequently today in the context of referral arrangements. See, for example, *Son v. Margolius, Mallios, Davis, Rider & Tomar*, 709 A.2d 112 (Md. Ct. App. 1998). Today the rule is justified primarily on the grounds of avoiding interference with the independent professional judgment of the lawyer. See Rule 5.4, cmt. [1]. Because standardized financial transactions do not threaten the independent judgment of the lawyer, the fee-splitting rule has been deemed by many state bar ethics opinions not to apply to financial transactions such as accepting credit card payments from clients, even though the merchant agreement between the lawyer and credit card company require the lawyer to pay some percentage of the fee to the bank. See, for example, California State Bar Formal Opinion 2007-172 (citing numerous other state opinions). Secured commercial lending by banks also should not fall within the fee-splitting rule for similar reasons. See, for example, Maine Bar Opinion 152 (1995) (permitting law firm to establish line of credit with bank, secured by firm's receivables).

Partnerships and Corporations with Nonlawyer Members

Reinforcing the rule on fee-splitting is a prohibition on a lawyer forming a partnership with a nonlawyer, if the activities of the partnership include practicing law. Rule 5.4(b). Lawyer Smith and Accountant Jones can share office space and cooperate in representing clients, but they may not form a partnership if the partnership will provide legal services. They also may not practice in the form of a professional corporation if a nonlawyer owns any interest in the corporation, serves as an officer or director, or has the right to direct the professional judgment of the lawyer. Rule 5.4(d); see also Rest. §10(2). A prohibited employment relationship would include working for a management consulting or accounting firm and providing legal services directly to clients of the firm, as opposed to advising the firm itself. A lawyer also may be an employee of a corporation in which nonlawyers have an ownership interest, but only if the lawyer is providing legal services only to that corporation—that is, acting as in-house counsel. Rest. §10, cmt. c. Obviously, law firms have many nonlawyer employees, but paying them a salary does not violate these rules unless the employees have an ownership interest in the firm or the right to control the professional activities of lawyers in the firm.

Many lawyers, particularly in smaller communities, provide ancillary services to clients that are related to the legal work they perform. For example, a lawyer may be a licensed real estate broker, an insurance agent, or a certified financial planner. It is permissible for a lawyer to provide these ancillary services, as long as the lawyer complies with the fee-splitting rule, Rule 5.4(a) (discussed above), by billing separately for the nonlegal services. See Rest. §10, cmt. g.

Professional Judgment

Several disciplinary rules emphasize the concept of professional judgment and prohibit lawyers from getting into any arrangement in which their independence may be compromised. See Rule 5.4(c) (lawyer shall not permit a person who recommends, employs, or pays the lawyer to control the lawyer's professional judgment); Rule 2.1 (lawyer must exercise independent professional judgment); Rule 1.7(a)(2) (conflict of interest if representation may be materially limited by lawyer's own interest or another client's interest); Rule 1.8(f) (lawyer may not accept compensation from a nonclient unless there is no interference with lawyer's independent professional judgment). The essence of all these rules is that a lawyer must be guided by the best interests of the client, and nothing else, in recommending a course of action for the client to follow and in making judgments about how to proceed in representing the client. See also Rule 1.2(a) (client alone has authority to determine objectives of representation). If you encounter any situation in which it appears that the lawyer is being pulled in a different direction, and may be unwilling or unable to put the client's interests first, there may be a prohibited interference with the lawyer's professional independence and judgment.

Attorney-Client Privilege and Confidentiality

Another problem with MDPs is that the lawyer and nonlawyer members may have incompatible confidentiality obligations. Consider the hypothetical association of a matrimonial lawyer and social worker. Suppose they are both in the room when the client admits to having physically abused a child at some point in the past. The client says the abuse has not occurred for several months and promises that it will not happen again. Under these circumstances, where there is no reasonably certain death or substantial bodily harm to prevent, the lawyer is required by Model Rule 1.6 to keep the information confidential. The social worker, on the other hand, may be required by a state statute to report the evidence of abuse. The lawyer and nonlawyer should plan around this situation by obtaining the client's informed consent at the outset of representation to an arrangement respecting confidentiality that does not conflict with either professional's reporting obligations. See Rule 1.6(a) (permitting revelation of confidential information with the client's informed consent). For example, the client may be asked to agree that any evidence of child abuse will be reported to the authorities.

A lawyer and nonlawyer also must be careful not to destroy the attorney-client privilege through the presence of unprivileged persons. See Rest. §68. If a nonlawyer professional facilitates the *legal* representation of the client, her presence would not destroy the privilege. Rest. §70. On the other hand, if the nonlawyer is present to help out with some nonlegal aspect of the client's affairs, the lawyer-client communication may not be privileged. Again, an MDP can avoid interfering with the attorney-client privilege by carefully planning to ensure that only privileged persons are present for sensitive conversations.

Examples

Is the Client in Good Hands?

3. Ginobili is a lawyer in a small city in the State of Perplexity. He also owns an insurance brokerage business, which sells life, automobile, and homeowner's insurance. When a client comes to Ginobili for estate planning advice, his practice is to offer a free "insurance checkup," to make sure the client is adequately insured. If the client does not have life insurance, Ginobili will write a "checkup" letter that urges the client to consider purchasing insurance and mentions Ginobili's insurance brokerage business. Does this practice violate any of the disciplinary rules?

Uber for Lawyers

4. The president of an online lawyer rating company wants to get into the "gig economy," so she proposes the company start a "lawyer sharing service." On the president's proposal, the company would agree to list a number of state-licensed lawyers who are willing to provide a particular service for a flat fee. Lawyers might offer, for example, will preparation for $895 or filing a Chapter 7 bankruptcy petition for $1,450. The

customer pays the company, which in turn pays the lawyer. The lawyer, however, must return 20 percent of the amount as a "marketing fee" to the company. The company does market the lawyers' services. Its website refers to the lawyers as "top-rated," "experienced," and "qualified." It also employs a rating system, from one to five stars, based on customer reviews. You are the general counsel of the company. What do you advise the president—is this new service permissible?

Explanations

Is the Client in Good Hands?

3. First of all, there is nothing wrong with a lawyer operating an "ancillary business" such as an insurance brokerage, as long as the lawyer complies with the disciplinary rules in providing services that are related to the client's legal affairs. Rule 5.7; Rest. §10, cmt. (g). The danger inherent in this sort of arrangement is that the lawyer's independent professional judgment will be compromised. In this case, Ginobili wears two hats—lawyer and insurance broker. Wearing his lawyer hat, Ginobili has an obligation to act in the client's best interests. If the client really does not need life insurance to create an effective estate plan, then Ginobili should not recommend purchasing life insurance. When he is wearing his insurance broker hat, however, Ginobili would like to sell as much life insurance as possible. The practice of doing "insurance checkups" and automatically recommending life insurance is probably an interference with Ginobili's independent professional judgment in violation of Model Rules 2.1 and 1.7(a)(2) (personal interest conflict of interest).

   Note that there is an interference with the lawyer's professional judgment in this case, even though there is only one person in the firm. Think of Ginobili as a one-man MDP. Lawyers who are concerned about MDPs imagine the situation of a nonlawyer business associate—insurance broker, CPA, or whatever—who puts pressure on the lawyer to recommend the associate's products or services, regardless of the client's best interests. But the problem can arise for a solo practitioner as well.

Uber for Lawyers

4. Someday we'll probably see the impact of disruptive technologies on the provision of legal services. As of 2018, however, lawyer regulators have been pretty successful in beating back threats from technologically enabled competitors. Technically the company is not subject to discipline, as it's not a lawyer, but the new business model won't work very well if lawyers are concerned about their exposure to discipline for working

with the company. This example requires you to remember rules discussed in other chapters, as well as considering the fee-splitting rule.

The example kind of telegraphed one of the answers by telling you that the lawyer was required to return 20 percent of her fee to the company. Whether you call it a marketing fee or something else, it is a sharing of the lawyer's fee with a nonlawyer. Thus, it is a violation of Rule 5.4(a). Although the fee-splitting rule was discussed above in connection with multidisciplinary practices, another common application of the rule is to prohibit certain types of marketing arrangements. For example, debt-counseling services sometimes share legal fees with the lawyer to whom they referred a client. That's a violation of Rule 5.4(a) as well as another regulation of the marketing of legal services, Rule 7.2(b). That rule prohibits giving anything of value to a person in exchange for the recommendation of a lawyer, with a few exceptions. Lawyers would violate this rule by promising to pay 20 percent of their fees (the promise is something of value) to the company in exchange for listing them. You might argue that the exception in Rule 7.2(b)(1) applies, allowing the payment of the reasonable costs of otherwise permitted advertisements. That's not a bad argument, but the state ethics opinions that have considered this situation have concluded that 20 percent of the lawyer's fee goes way beyond the cost of advertising (which, after all, is practically zero when it's just a listing on a website).

This example was based on the attempt by the online lawyer rating service Avvo to establish a product called Avvo Legal Services. It was shut down in July 2018 after a string of bar association opinions concluded that lawyers who participate in the service may be subject to discipline. See, e.g., N.Y. State Bar Op. 1132 (2017); Pa. Bar Formal Op. 2016-200; S.C. Op. 16-06; Ohio Op. 2016-3.

The Organized Bar

REGULATING ENTRY INTO THE PROFESSION

Legal Authority to Regulate

As a matter of state constitutional law, the court of last resort in a given state has the inherent power to regulate the activities of lawyers that have effects within the territorial borders of a jurisdiction. This is what I've been calling Track One inherent authority, to distinguish it from the authority of a particular tribunal to regulate the practice of lawyers appearing before it (Track Two). Under Track One inherent authority, the state's highest court can establish rules and procedures for the admission of lawyers to practice; promulgate rules of professional conduct; and administer a system of investigating grievances, holding hearings, and meting out discipline for lawyers who violate the rules. State courts often delegate this power to what are, in effect, administrative agencies of the judicial branch. Remember, though, that the final regulatory authority rests with the state court, even if in practice state courts give a great deal of deference to grievance committees and seldom overturn their recommendations regarding discipline.

You have to be careful when you hear the term "State X Bar Association." Many state bar associations are formally nothing more than trade associations, which lawyers are free to join or ignore if they choose. That is the situation in New York State, where lawyers are admitted by committees of the Appellate Division of the Supreme Court (the intermediate appellate court in the state) and are free to join, or not to join, the New York State Bar Association. In other states, however, there are so-called "mandatory," "integrated," or "unified" bars, meaning that every lawyer who practices in that jurisdiction is required to belong to the bar association. This is the case in Washington State, for example, where admission to practice goes along with membership in the Washington State Bar Association. Regardless of whether there is a voluntary or mandatory bar association, every state has some kind of apparatus for promulgating rules and disciplining lawyers, going under a bewildering variety of names (attorney grievance commission, committee on discipline, committee on professional conduct, etc.).

It is one thing to say that state supreme courts have the inherent authority to regulate the practice of law, and quite another to believe that courts' authority ought to be *exclusive*. This is the position taken by many courts, however, in the face of attempts by legislatures and administrative agencies to regulate the activities of lawyers. Charles Wolfram calls this the "negative inherent powers doctrine," similar to the dormant Commerce Clause in constitutional law. Wolfram §2.2.3. It has its clearest application where a legislature seeks to modify the conditions under which a lawyer may be admitted to practice, disciplined, or disbarred. Courts often hold that these core regulatory functions are reserved to the judiciary. See, for example, *Mississippi Bar v. McGuire*, 647 So.2d 706 (Miss. 1994); *State ex rel. Fiedler v. Wisconsin Senate*, 454 N.W.2d 770 (Wis. 1990); *Bennion, Van Camp, Hagen & Ruhl v. Kassler Escrow, Inc.*, 635 P.2d 730 (Wash. 1981).

There are many cases, though, in which the judicial and legislative branches have *overlapping* jurisdiction over the regulation of lawyers. So, for example, a state statute prohibiting deceptive trade practices might be applied to a law firm that misled clients about their fees, without violating the separation of powers doctrine. *Heslin v. Connecticut Law Clinic of Trantolo & Trantolo*, 461 A.2d 938 (Conn. 1983). Similarly, a state statute regulating the activities of lobbyists does not violate the negative inherent powers doctrine, even though it may incidentally affect lobbyists who are also lawyers. *Florida Ass'n of Professional Lobbyists v. Division of Legislative Information Services*, 431 F. Supp. 2d 1228 (N.D. Fla. 2006). This is true even though some activities of lobbyists—such as providing legal analysis of proposed bills or drafting legislation—would constitute the "practice of law" under state rules.

If you encounter a recently promulgated statute that appears to conflict with some provision of the disciplinary rules, consider whether it may be challenged on separation of powers grounds. As a general rule, if the statute interferes directly with the judiciary's regulation of the profession, it may be vulnerable to challenge under the negative inherent powers doctrine. A statute providing that certain clients may discharge their lawyers "only with just cause" probably would violate the separation of powers between the legislature and the judiciary, because it would conflict with the rule in

Model Rule 1.16(a)(3) that the client can discharge the lawyer at any time, for any reason. See In re Wallace, 574 So. 2d 348 (La. 1991).

Note that various state and federal administrative agencies are permitted to set their own rules for lawyers practicing before them. The most prominent example is the Securities and Exchange Commission (SEC), which extensively regulates the practice of law by lawyers doing securities work. In particular, regulations promulgated under the Sarbanes-Oxley Act of 2002 impose disclosure requirements on lawyers that differ from those in the Model Rules. There is no negative inherent power problem presented by the Sarbanes-Oxley regulations, because the agency does not purport to regulate lawyers generally, but only to the extent that they practice before the SEC. Similarly, the Internal Revenue Service (IRS) regulates the practice of lawyers who represent taxpayers before the Service; Circular 230 governing tax shelter opinions is another example of a regulatory requirement that affects the practice of lawyers, apart from the bar disciplinary rules.

What if the rules issued by a federal administrative agency conflict with the disciplinary rules? This problem was raised in a dramatic fashion during the public comment period on the SEC's proposed regulations under Sarbanes-Oxley. One proposal would have required lawyers to withdraw "noisily"—that is, withdrawing from representing a client and giving notice to the SEC that the lawyer no longer stood behind representations made in a filing with the Commission—in certain cases. The Washington State Bar Association issued an advisory opinion stating that a lawyer who complied with the SEC's rules would be subject to discipline for violating the duty of confidentiality. The General Counsel of the SEC responded by reminding the Washington bar committee of the doctrine of federal preemption, under which inconsistent state regulations may be preempted by federal law, citing several Supreme Court cases including *Sperry v. State of Florida*, 373 U.S. 379 (1963) (federal regulation permitting nonlawyers to represent clients before U.S. Patent Office preempted state unauthorized practice rule which would prohibit the representation).

Most commentators believe the SEC's position on preemption was correct, but the Washington committee stuck to its guns. The issue became moot when Washington adopted a new version of the confidentiality rule that would permit disclosure under circumstances required or permitted by the final SEC regulations. The controversy is worth remembering, however, because it shows that lawyers must be aware of potentially inconsistent obligations imposed by federal and state law.

Requirements for Admission

Most states have similar requirements for admission to practice—for example, graduation from an accredited law school (generally accredited by the

ABA, but sometimes only by a state agency), passing the bar examination, and undergoing a character and fitness review. There are occasional exceptions. Some states allow applicants to "read for the bar," serving a lengthy term as an apprentice in a law office while following a prescribed curriculum. Wisconsin has a "diploma privilege," automatically admitting graduates of in-state law schools who pass the character and fitness review. The ordinary sequence of requirements for admission to the bar—namely, law school + bar exam + character and fitness review—is legally uncontroversial. Some states have adopted additional restrictions, however, and these have been the subject of a great deal of litigation.

Physical Presence Requirements

A number of states require a lawyer to maintain a physical office, not just a post-office box and telephone answering service, or some other form of "virtual" law office, within the borders of the state. That restriction generally has been held to be permissible (see, for example, *Schoenfeld v. State of New York*, 29 N.E.3d 230 (N.Y. 2015); *Tolchin v. Supreme Court of New Jersey*, 111 F.3d 1099 (3d Cir. 1997)[1]), but more substantial restrictions on practice by out-of-state lawyers have been struck down. For example, a state may not require as a condition for admission to the bar that an applicant maintain a home address within a state, as opposed to a business office. *Supreme Court of New Hampshire v. Piper*, 470 U.S. 274 (1985) (in-state residence requirement inconsistent with the Privileges and Immunities Clause of the U.S. Constitution). Extending that rule, the Supreme Court has said that states may not require experienced practitioners who wish to be "waived in" or "admitted on motion"—that is, be admitted without taking the state's bar exam—to maintain residence within the state. *Supreme Court of Virginia v. Friedman*, 487 U.S. 59 (1988).

Character and Fitness Screening

Most states maintain some kind of character and fitness review as part of their bar admissions procedures. These requirements for admission are set out in state statutes. In Virginia, for example, an applicant to sit for the bar exam or to be licensed in that state must be found to be "a person of honest demeanor and good moral character . . . and possesses the requisite fitness to perform the obligations and responsibilities of a practicing attorney at

---

1. In January 2013, the New Jersey Supreme Court repealed that state's *bona fide* office requirement, but a rule of the court continues to require lawyers to be available for in-person consultations with clients if required, and to have an address for the service of process and for files to be inspected by clients and state regulators. See N.J. Rule 1:12-1(a).

law." Va. Code §§54.1-3925.1. Students often ask whether their conviction for such-and-such will prevent them from sitting for the bar exam. Usually, "such-and-such" is a relatively minor infraction that can be characterized as a youthful indiscretion—for example, possessing a small quantity of marijuana, being drunk and disorderly, jumping a subway turnstile, or stealing license plates from police cars as part of a fraternity initiation. Occasionally, though, it is a serious criminal charge. People also worry about the bewildering array of questions on a typical bar application, focused on matters such as pending lawsuits, treatment for mental illnesses or substance abuse, and bankruptcy. What will be disqualifying?

In general, the state disciplinary authorities are looking for evidence of past conduct that is probative of likely future violations of the disciplinary rules. (To put it more controversially but perhaps more accurately, they are looking for evidence that is probative of the applicant's *moral character*, such as a disposition to steal or abuse a position of trust.) The character and fitness screening process is supposed to avoid the necessity of pursuing professional discipline in the future against lawyers who commit violations of the rules of professional conduct. Based on the concerns that bar admissions committees have about future misconduct by lawyers, there are three things that can cause real trouble for an applicant in the character and fitness review process. See H&H §62.7.

1. A *pattern* of lawbreaking that supports an inference of recidivism or a cavalier attitude toward the legal system. A couple of speeding or parking tickets are no big deal. But dozens of traffic tickets may be the basis for denial. See, for example, *Frasher v. Board of Law Examiners*, 408 S.E.2d 675 (W. Va. 1991) (applicant had three DUI convictions and 24 speeding tickets).

2. A smaller number of infractions that reveal *dishonesty* or abuse of a position of trust. See, for example, In re *Mustafa*, 631 A.2d 45 (D.C. App. 1993) (mishandling moot court funds); In re *Simmons*, 584 N.E.2d 1159 (Ohio 1992) (misappropriation of funds from student organization). A conviction for embezzlement, fraud, perjury, or forgery would be a much bigger deal on a bar application than one for manslaughter or driving under the influence. The evidence of dishonesty need not be a criminal conviction—applicants have been denied on character and fitness grounds for academic dishonesty, such as cheating or plagiarism. Violations of a university honor code are a big problem for the same reason. Lawyers have a fiduciary relationship with their clients, which means there are plenty of opportunities to take advantage of the asymmetry of power and knowledge between lawyers and their clients. Bar committees want to make sure that people who have a tendency to take advantage of positions of confidence and trust do not become lawyers.

3. Evidence of *neglect of financial responsibilities*, such as defaulting on student loans or being in arrears on child support obligations. See, for example, *In re C.R.W.*, 481 S.E.2d 511 (Ga. 1997) (applicant defaulted on student loans and had filed two petitions for bankruptcy); *Character and Fitness Comm. v. Jones*, 62 S.W.3d 28 (Ky. 2001) (failure to pay student loans justifies denial of admission). The disciplinary authorities worry that applicants who have played fast and loose with their financial obligations in the past may be more likely in the future to dip into client funds to satisfy their personal debts. Remember that commingling personal accounts and client funds is a very big no-no, Rule 1.15(a), and is likely to lead to disbarment in many states. Bar committees worry that lawyers who have a propensity to get into financial difficulties may steal or "borrow" from clients to pay their debts.

An applicant with one of these problems may still be admitted, but the committee is likely to take a closer look and possibly demand some evidence of rehabilitation. In addition to the three categories above, which make admission questionable, there is one sure-fire way to get denied admissions on character and fitness grounds immediately and without question:

4. *Failure to disclose* information responsive to a question on the application. See, for example, *Radtke v. Board of Bar Examiners*, 601 N.W.2d 642 (Wis. 1999) (applicant accused of perjury in his former job as a history instructor; the perjury probably would not have been disqualifying, but the lack of candor was). Even if it is no big deal, disclose it. A conviction for some ticky-tacky traffic offense? Disclose it. You have to disclose these events even if it means doing a lot of research, dredging up embarrassing memories, publicly admitting that you have a conviction for indecent exposure for that little college streaking incident, and calling up county sheriff's offices in small towns in Texas to find speeding tickets. Of course, you only have to disclose information that is called for by a specific question. If the application does not ask whether you have ever used illegal drugs, you do not need to mention that Grateful Dead concert. But now is *not* the time to draw hairsplitting distinctions and use clever word games to avoid disclosure. If an application asks about drug use (most do not, by the way), it would not be fairly responsive to answer "no" if you "didn't inhale." Remember, the disciplinary authorities are looking for evidence that you are honest, candid, and forthcoming. They may not care that much about the underlying conduct, but they will care a great deal if you seem to be playing games with their admissions process.[2]

---

2. And, if you eventually do gain admission to the bar, you will be deemed to have violated Rule 8.1(a) if the false statement on the application is subsequently discovered. See H&H §62.3 and Illus. 62-1.

The character and fitness review process raises a number of interesting questions when it intersects with other legal entitlements, such as civil rights statutes and the Bill of Rights. For example, state bars once asked routinely about treatment for mental illness, but after the passage of the Americans with Disabilities Act, it is no longer clear that a state can deny admission to an applicant on the basis of a mental disability. See H&H §62.8. It is also true as a matter of constitutional law that a state may deny admission only on the basis of conduct that is *germane* to the practice of law. The fact that an applicant is cohabiting with a member of the opposite sex is not relevant to the applicant's fitness as a lawyer. See, for example, *Cord v. Gibb*, 254 S.E.2d 71 (Va. 1979). Believe it or not, the applicant in that case stipulated that her living arrangement would be considered immoral by community standards — remember, this is the 1970s, in a fairly conservative state. But the Virginia Supreme Court still said the immorality, as conceded, was not germane to the applicant's fitness as a lawyer. Similarly, the First Amendment may prohibit a state from using an applicant's past membership in "subversive" organizations as a basis for denial, although it can still compel an applicant to answer questions about membership. *Law Students Civil Rights Research Council v. Wadmond*, 401 U.S. 154 (1971).

Examples

Who Gets In?

1. You are a member of the Perplexity Committee of Bar Examiners; your job is to review applications for admission and make recommendations concerning the character and fitness of applicants to practice law in the great State of Perplexity. Your committee is considering two applicants:
   * Stewart Gross wrote for a national opinion magazine (before blogs and Twitter, that is, back when serious journalism appeared in print publications) for two years. He wrote numerous articles, some of which received a great deal of attention for their shocking allegations about members of Congress and celebrities. As it turned out, however, many of the salacious "facts" reported in the magazine were outright fabrications. Gross was fired from the magazine after an investigation concluded that 27 of the 42 pieces he had written contained false statements. Gross became depressed and entered therapy. He came to understand his fabrications as a response to the intense pressure he felt, both from his family and the community of political journalists in Washington, D.C., to succeed. After a successful course of therapy he entered law school, where he excelled academically and struck all of his professors as hard-working and honest. Gross disclosed his invention of facts, which he admitted were clear violations of core principles of journalism ethics. But he contended that, with the help

of intensive therapy, his friends and family, and a new relationship, he was a very different person from the one who had fabricated the articles, and therefore posed no risk of engaging in deception as a lawyer.

- Santiago Gomez was brought by his parents from Mexico to the United States when he was 17 months old. He attended high school, college, and law school in the United States. When he was 15 years old, Gomez's father became a lawful permanent resident of the United States and filed a petition for an immigration visa on his son's behalf. Due to an extensive backlog of applications, however, the visa was never issued, and as a result, Gomez continues to live in the United States without proper documentation. He disclosed his undocumented status on his application to the Perplexity bar committee. No federal or state statute renders him ineligible to apply for a license to practice law, but some committee members believe that his presence in the United States without authorization demonstrates contempt for the laws of the country. Employers, including a law firm where Gomez worked as a paralegal, all testify that he is hard-working and honest.

Do you recommend the admission of Gross, Gomez, neither, or both?

Deanie on a Weenie = Application on Ice

2. Pat Conrad is one of those law students who likes to shake things up at his school. He enjoys needling the administration and provoking public controversies. After he was, in his opinion, treated badly by a professor in class discussion, he circulated a memo to his classmates questioning the ethics and integrity of the professor. He wrote a letter to a local newspaper complaining about an increase in student health service fees and accusing the administration of mismanagement. When he received no response from the administration to his complaints about the fee increase, he posted a list of faculty salaries on a student bulletin board. He posted a photograph of "a nude female's backside" in his carrel in the library and threatened to contact the ACLU when a librarian asked that it be removed. When the dean contacted Conrad personally to ask him to remove the photo, Conrad began a public campaign to embarrass the dean. He wrote an editorial in the student newspaper accusing the dean of unethical conduct, threatened to sue the dean for pressuring him to remove the photo, wrote a memo to the university president characterizing the dean as incompetent and requesting that he be fired, and finally, posted fliers advertising the "Deanie on a Weenie" T-shirts he had printed, which depicted a caricature of the dean "sitting astride what appears to be a large hot dog."

When the bar committee on character and fitness for the State of Perplexity sent a routine request for information to Conrad's law school, the dean responded with information about Conrad's conduct. Should his application be denied?

Explanations

Who Gets In?

1. These are two real applicants to the California bar, Stephen Glass and Sergio Garcia, respectively. See In re Glass, 58 Cal.4th 500, 316 P.3d 1199, 167 Cal.Rptr.3d 87 (2014) (denying admission to the fabricating journalist); In re Garcia, 58 Cal.4th 440, 315 P.3d 117, 165 Cal.Rptr.3d 855 (2014) (allowing the undocumented applicant to sit for the bar exam). I modified the facts slightly in the Glass case, because one of the factors that led the California Supreme Court to deny his application was his apparent lack of candor in the application process. I wanted the example to focus solely on the past dishonesty.

   I don't think these cases had to come out the way they did, although they're both fairly well reasoned decisions. The important thing is that you be able to articulate reasons for your recommendation — admit or deny — based on some of the factors courts generally rely on. In the Gross (journalist) case, not only was he dishonest, but he displayed a significant pattern of dishonesty. Twenty-seven out of forty-one articles is a lot. He also occupied a position of trust as a journalist. Many publications do have fact-checkers, but readers rely on the honesty of journalists, and Gross betrayed that trust. As for feeling pressure from his family and friends, hey, that's life! Being a lawyer is not exactly a stress-free job. If he lied because he couldn't handle the pressure of being a journalist, we should worry that he would behave similarly as a lawyer.

   In the case of Gomez, he did something unlawful, and in some sense also engaged in a pattern of unauthorized conduct by remaining in the United States. In the actual Garcia case, the California Supreme Court argued that this conduct did not demonstrate moral turpitude, in contrast with crimes involving "fraud, perjury, theft, embezzlement, and bribery." See 315 P.3d at 116. The mere fact of conduct being unlawful does not demonstrate a lack of fitness to practice law. The court also noted that an immigration violation is not technically a crime. While that is true, it is neither here nor there if the court has to inquire into the underlying conduct to determine whether it involves dishonesty or abuse of power or trust, which fraud, perjury, theft, embezzlement, and bribery all do. So our hypothetical Gomez should probably be admitted.

Deanie on a Weenie = Application on Ice

2. This example is based on a colorful, and probably wrongly decided character and fitness case, In re Converse, 602 N.W.2d 500 (Neb. 1999).[3] We can grant that Conrad's conduct was childish, inappropriate, and annoying. But is that a sufficient reason to deny his application? The court in the actual case thought so. It reasoned that the applicant's *pattern* of personally attacking those with whom he disagrees "[is] not acceptable in one who would be a counselor and advocate in the legal system." In addition, the court noted that he had a tendency to try to resolve disputes in an arena outside the legal process — that is, by writing letters to the president, "op-ed" pieces in the student newspaper, letters to the editor of the local paper, and of course by printing the T-shirts. See *Converse*, 602 N.W.2d at 508-509.

   This argument strikes me as bogus, for a number of reasons. There is nothing necessarily improper about using public relations techniques to resolve disputes. Although some may decry the practice of "trying cases in the press," it is increasingly accepted that part of a lawyer's job in some cases may be to seek to influence the public perception of a client. The court was alarmed that the applicant consistently portrayed himself as the victim and his opponent as the aggressor, but this is not exactly unusual conduct for practicing lawyers. Plaintiffs' personal injury lawyers and criminal defense lawyers, for example, are adept at framing a case as one in which their clients are the victims of another's misconduct. Finally, the court characterized the applicant as hostile, turbulent, intemperate, and threatening, as opposed to someone who was "dedicated to the peaceful and reasoned settlement of disputes." Perhaps it is unfortunate, but there are no disciplinary rules specifically aimed at turbulence, hostility, and intemperateness in practicing lawyers. The character and fitness committee in this case appears to be trying to solve a perceived problem with incivility and aggressiveness among practicing lawyers by screening out applicants who make too many waves. This is dangerous business, though, since making waves is exactly what we want lawyers to do in some cases. Lawyers representing civil rights protesters often cause

---

3. I have taught this case for years and always had a bit of fun at the expense of Paul Converse, the applicant who gave the law school administration a gigantic headache for three years. When one of my students discovered that Converse had been killed while working as a civilian employee in Iraq, a different aspect of Converse's character emerged. See, for example, Sholnn Freeman, "Anxiety Rises over Vulnerable Housing in Iraqi Green Zone," *Washington Post* (Apr. 8, 2008). Converse had worked in Bosnia, Kosovo, and Iraq, and had previously served in local politics. People who knew him described him as spirited and passionate and always interesting to be around. As this explanation indicates, I am generally skeptical of the capacity of bar committees to make reliable judgments about an applicant's moral character. The denouement to the Converse story is additional evidence that moral character can be a subtle thing, not readily susceptible to evaluation in this context.

a lot of hostility and turbulence, but we recognize that they are doing an important job. I am not comparing the applicant in this case to people with legitimate grievances against powerful institutions—he probably is just immature and has an anger-management problem—but I do worry when character and fitness committees read their mandate broadly and try to keep out applicants merely because they are "undesirable."

THE ORGANIZED BAR: REGULATING THE PRACTICE OF LAW

You will frequently hear it asserted that law is a profession, not a "mere" business. Never mind the backhanded criticism of businesspeople—what is that supposed to mean? One characteristic of a profession is that it is self-regulating. Rule 8.3 reinforces professional self-regulation by requiring lawyers to report certain misconduct by other lawyers. Another hallmark of a profession is that it sets high standards for conduct that is in the public interest. Rule 8.4 lists several grounds for imposing discipline on lawyers who engage in conduct that calls into question their fitness to practice law.

Reporting Professional Misconduct

Model Rule 8.3(a) imposes a duty to report to the state disciplinary authority another lawyer's violation of the rules "that raises a substantial question as to that lawyer's honesty, trustworthiness, or fitness as a lawyer." Note that the reporting duty arises only when the lawyer knows of this misconduct. The cynically minded might think that the reporting duty can be ducked by claiming that the information does not rise to the level of knowledge, but just as in the law of perjury, remember that "[a] person's knowledge may be inferred from circumstances." Rule 1.0(f). Thus, a lawyer risks discipline for not reporting professional misconduct where circumstantial evidence would support a finding that the lawyer did in fact know of the misconduct. This seems like a perfect example of self-regulation by the organized bar. If lawyers police one another, there is less need for external regulation of the legal profession.

Ironically, though, the one well-known case that enforced the reporting duty sent shock waves through the bar. *In re Himmel*, 533 N.E.2d 790 (Ill. 1988). In that case, the client hired Lawyer Himmel to recover misappropriated settlement proceeds from Lawyer Casey. Casey agreed to cough up the money, provided that neither the client nor Himmel reported him to the disciplinary authorities. Himmel took the deal and was then suspended for one year by the Illinois Supreme Court. *Himmel* arose under the Model Code. The applicable rule was DR 1-103(A), which required reporting of misconduct, but exempted "privileged information." The Illinois Supreme Court defined "privileged information" as limited to matters covered by the attorney-client privilege, and reasoned that the communication from the client to Himmel was not intended to be kept confidential, since the client told the same story to many others. Thus, Himmel had an obligation to report under DR 1-103 and the reporting obligation was not trumped by the obligation to keep privileged information confidential. The Illinois Supreme Court reasoned that, notwithstanding the client's instruction to refrain from reporting Casey's misconduct, Himmel's obligation as an officer of the court superseded his duty to respect the client's wishes and his duty to obtain the best settlement possible (which probably could be accomplished only by promising secrecy to Casey).

The analysis under the Model Rules would be different. The duty to report in Model Rule 8.3(a) is expressly qualified (in section (c)) by Model Rule 1.6, which is very broad. Model Rule 1.6 forbids disclosure of "information relating to representation of a client" unless the client is about to commit a crime threatening imminent death or serious bodily injury. Thus, the argument is not available in Model Rules jurisdictions that the reporting duty trumps the professional duty of confidentiality. For this reason, *Himmel* is pretty much a dead letter in Model Rules jurisdictions. Interestingly, though, it is still good law in Illinois, even though Illinois is a Model Rules jurisdiction, because the Illinois version of Model Rule 8.3 preserves the distinction between confidences and secrets, carried over from the Model Code.

Extra-Professional Crimes

Rule 8.4(b) subjects a lawyer to discipline for committing a criminal act that reflects adversely on the lawyer's honesty, trustworthiness or, in other respects, fitness to practice law. It is very important to see that this rule is not limited to conduct that occurred in connection with the practice of law. The classic example is a lawyer who serves in a fiduciary capacity for another—let's say, holding a power of attorney over the financial affairs of a wealthy relative or serving as the treasurer of a non-profit organization—who misappropriates funds. That conduct reflects adversely on the lawyer's fitness to practice because lawyers are very often entrusted with the funds of others. (Rule 1.15 on safekeeping of funds and other property reflects the obligation of utmost care with the property of others.) Crimes treated under Rule 8.4(b) often involve dishonesty, but may include other crimes such as drug offenses and driving under the influence of alcohol.

Consider the case of an attorney who placed a GPS tracking device on his ex-girlfriend's car, to follow her and see who she was dating. Assume the conduct is a crime under state law. The question is whether the conduct "indicate[s] lack of those characteristics relevant to law practice." Rule 8.4, cmt. [2]. The Pennsylvania Supreme Court suspended a lawyer from practice for five years under these circumstances. See *Disciplinary Counsel v. Casale*, 2018 BL 315337 (Pa. 8/30/18). What are those characteristics? The court did not say, but presumably they include the resort to extra-legal measures to invade the privacy and potentially threaten another person. The setting of the crime, within a terminated intimate relationship, is also significant since lawyers are frequently subject to discipline under this rule for sexual assaults, stalking, and possessing child pornography.

Notice that the rule says "commit a criminal act," not "be convicted of a crime." A disciplinary authority could punish a lawyer under Rule 8.4(b) without awaiting a criminal conviction, and could even do so under a lower standard of proof—preponderance or clear and convincing evidence, not the criminal standard of proof beyond a reasonable doubt.

Catch-All Misconduct Rules

Rules 8.4(c) and (d) are what I call catch-all misconduct rules, subjecting a lawyer to discipline for "conduct involving dishonesty, fraud, deceit, or misrepresentation" (Rule 8.4(c)) or "conduct that is prejudicial to the administration of justice" (Rule 8.4(d)). We encountered Rule 8.4(c) in Chapter 11, in the example on deceptive tactics used during investigation. For example, a party's attorneys were sanctioned for hiring a private investigator to pose as a customer and talk to the managers of a rival outdoor-equipment dealer to see what brand of snowmobile was selling best. *Midwest Motor Sports v. Arctic Cat Sales, Inc.*, 347 F.3d 693 (8th Cir. 2003). Similarly, there are tons of state and local ethics opinions warning lawyers against social media "catfishing" or "pretexting"—that is, pretending to be a friend of a party in order to connect on Facebook, Snapchat, etc. See, e.g., L.A. County Bar Ass'n Op. 529 (2017); D.C. Bar Op. 371 (2016); N.Y. City Bar Op. 2010-2; Phila. Bar Ass'n Op. 2009-02.

The difficulty with the catch-all rules is their breadth and vagueness. Go back to the example of deceptive investigative tactics in the snowmobile case. The lawyers were sanctioned in that case, but it is generally permissible to use "testers" to develop evidence of discrimination. See, e.g., *Richardson v. Howard*, 712 F.2d 319 (7th Cir. 1983). For example, a lawyer might hire actors to play a black family and a white family, "wire up" one of the actors in each family with a hidden recorder, and have them go in separately to see a landlord to inquire about the availability of apartments. If the landlord is willing to rent to the white family but not the black family, you have evidence of racial discrimination. One could certainly make arguments to distinguish discrimination testers from the private investigator in the snow-mobile case or creating a phony profile on LinkedIn to connect with an opposing party in litigation.[4] The question is whether a lawyer would have sufficient notice, from the language "dishonesty, fraud, deceit, or misrep-resentation" (Rule 8.4(c)) or "prejudicial to the administration of justice" (Rule 8.4(d)), of what conduct is permitted and what is prohibited. Or consider the issue of "ghostwriting" pleadings for pro se litigants—is that conduct involving deceit or misrepresentation? For cases taking contrary positions, see In re Fengling Liu, 664 F.3d 367 (2d Cir. 2011) (refusing to discipline lawyer who engaged in ghostwriting); Duran v. Carris, 238 F.3d 1268 (10th Cir. 2001) (noting that the undisclosed presence of a lawyer gave the pro se litigant an unfair advantage). Nevertheless, the rule has been upheld against constitutional vagueness challenges, with courts saying that a lawyer of common intelligence could figure out what the operative lan-guage means. See, e.g., Florida Bar v. Ross, 732 So. 2d 1037 (Fla. 1998). What do you think?

Despite my slight discomfort with the vagueness of the language of the catch-all rules, they do play an important role in the ecosystem of Professional Responsibility, providing a basis for disciplining lawyers who lie to clients or their professional colleagues, misappropriate funds, engage in frauds on tribunals that are not directly addressed by Rule 3.3 or other rules, intercept electronic communications, and engage in abusive or dis-ruptive behavior.

#UsToo: Discrimination in the Legal Profession

After several years of sometimes contentious debate, the ABA in 2016 adopted a rule prohibiting conduct that the lawyer knows or reasonably should know constitutes harassment or discrimination on the basis of race, sex, religion, national origin, ethnicity, disability, age, sexual orientation, gender identity, marital status, or socioeconomic status. See Model Rule 8.4(g). The rule was adopted in response to, among other evidence, survey data and numerous published decisions showing the pervasiveness of bias and harassment against women and people of color. See Stephen Gillers, *A Rule to Forbid Bias and Harassment in Law Practice: A Guide for State Courts Considering Model 8.4(g)*, 30 Geo. J. Legal Ethics 195, 199-200 (2017). The language "related to the practice of law" was intended to be broader than the "prejudicial to

---

4. For a good analysis of the issue, see David B. Isbell & Lucantonio N. Salvi, *Ethical Responsibility of Lawyers for Deception by Undercover Investigators and Discrimination Testers: An Analysis of the Provisions Prohibiting Misrepresentation Under The Model Rules of Professional Conduct*, 8 Geo. J. Legal Ethics 791 (1995).

the administration of justice" standard from Rule 8.4(d). The latter term has generally been interpreted to mean in connection with pending litigation. The scope of Rule 8.4(g) is intended to reach conduct unrelated to litigation—not only negotiation or transactional practice, but also the management of a law firm and conduct at bar association or continuing legal education programs.

Comments to Rule 8.4 provide some guidance in the interpretation of the key terms "harassment or discrimination." Comment [2] defines discrimination as harmful verbal or physical conduct that manifests bias or prejudice towards others. Harassment includes both sexual harassment (particularly as interpreted by courts applying Title VII of the 1964 Civil Rights Act and similar state anti-discrimination statutes), as well as derogatory or demeaning conduct that is objectively hostile or abusive. Under a hostile-environment theory of discrimination, the plaintiff must show that conduct was either severe or pervasive enough to be hostile to a reasonable person.[5] Lawyers subject to discipline under the rule may challenge it as being unconstitutionally vague, but at least in paradigmatic cases of abuse or harassment, the boundaries around prohibited conduct should be clear. The issue of notice is also handled by the mens rea language in the rule, limiting its application to conduct that the lawyer knows or reasonably should know constitutes harassment or discrimination.

The core application of Rule 8.4(g) is to conduct such as abusive conduct on the basis of a protected classification in the course of dealing with other parties or lawyers. For example, a male lawyer said to opposing counsel, a woman, during a deposition, "I don't have to talk to you, little lady" and "Be quiet, little girl." *Principe v. Assay Partners*, 586 N.Y.S.2d 182 (N.Y. Sup. Ct. 1992). Similarly, a lawyer was sanctioned for incivility—not under a specific bias and harassment rule—for referring in a deposition to a woman lawyer as "babe" and a "bimbo." *Mullaney v. Aude*, 730 A.2d 759 (Md. Ct. Spec. App. 1999). There is no legitimate need for such name-calling, although lawyers do frequently try to rattle their opposing counsel during depositions. Beyond litigation-related misconduct, the rule would clearly apply to

---

5. In the article cited in text, at p. 224, Professor Gillers cites a U.S. Supreme Court case applying the sexual harassment jurisprudence under Title VII. The Court held that, in order to be actionable, conduct must be that which "a reasonable person would find hostile or abusive, and one that the victim in fact did perceive to be so." The Court distinguished actionable harassment from "simple teasing, offhand comments, and isolated incidents." See *Faragher v. City of Boca Raton*, 524 U.S. 775, 787-788 (1998). The trier of fact, such as a disciplinary committee, may have to determine whether words or conduct have crossed the line from "simple teasing" to objectively hostile or abusive behavior. But that's okay—factfinders make similar determinations all the time. Did a party use reasonable care? Was performance of a contract in good faith? Moreover, the existence of difficult borderline cases does not mean there aren't clear, core cases of harassment, such as calling a woman a bitch, using a vulgar anatomical term to refer to her, and telling her to "go home and have babies." See *In re Schiff*, 599 N.Y.S.2d 242, 294 (Sup. Ct. 1993),

prohibit sexual harassment by lawyers of other lawyers or staff within a law firm or other organization.

The rule expressly immunizes lawyers from discipline for decisions regarding the acceptance or rejection of clients or withdrawal from representation. Thus, a matrimonial lawyer may decide to represent only husbands or wives in divorce cases, and an immigration lawyer may represent a client population that is exclusively or disproportionately made up of one ethnic group. Comment [5] permits lawyers to limit their practice to "underserved populations," but the text of Rule 8.4(g) does not depend on whether the population is underserved. Does that mean all discrimination in representation is fair game? Could a law firm have a "white clients only" policy? The answer is almost surely no, but there is admittedly some conflict between the text of the rule and the comment. Matters are a bit clearer for judges. The Code of Judicial Conduct prohibits affiliation with an organization that practices invidious discrimination. See CJC Rule 3.6(A). In historical and social context, there is a difference between the Finger Lakes Women's Bar Association (an organization which exists, and with which judges may associate) and a hypothetical Finger Lakes Men's Bar Association. As the comment to this rule admits, however, in some cases whether discrimination is invidious "is a complex question." CJC Rule 3.6, cmt. [2].

Rule 8.4(g) also does not apply to "legitimate advice or advocacy consistent with" the rules of professional conduct. What work is the word "legitimate" doing here? It could mean simply consistent with the rules of professional conduct, but then it would be redundant, and statutes should be construed to avoid making words superfluous. One exclusion from the anti-bias rule on the grounds of legitimate advocacy is the exercise of peremptory challenges in jury selection. See Rule 8.4, cmt. [5] ("A trial judge's finding that peremptory challenges were exercised on a discriminatory basis does not alone establish a violation" of Rule 8.4(g)). According to the legislative history of a previous, unsuccessful version of the anti-bias rule, the criminal defense bar was concerned that it may be difficult to determine whether striking a juror on the basis of race or some other protected classification was based on a legitimate reason or unconscious bias. See Gillers, *supra*, p. 206.

This leads to the really hard issue related to Rule 8.4(g) — its relationship to the First Amendment rights of lawyers. Conservative scholars, advocacy groups (such as the Federalist Society and the Christian Legal Society), and states' attorneys general, from states such as Tennessee and Texas, have tended to construe the rule as a pure "speech code" that interferes with free and open public discourse. The Texas Attorney General, in an opinion advising against adoption of Rule 8.4(g), picked up on an example given by the late Professor Ron Rotunda: A lawyer is presenting at a Continuing Legal Education program on the use of excessive force by police officers (thus, within the scope of "conduct related to the practice of law"). The lawyer says, "blue lives matter too," commenting on the slogan "black lives matter." Is the lawyer subject to discipline under the rule? It seems unlikely that the stray comment constitutes harassment, but what about discrimination? Comment [3] defines discrimination to include "verbal . . . conduct that manifests bias or prejudice" on the basis of race, among other classifications. The lawyer's statement would be constitutionally protected political speech in virtually any other context. A government employee cannot be fired for making statements about issues regarding race, unless the speech substantially interferes with the government's capacity to conduct its business. See, e.g., *Givhan v. Western Line Consol. School Dist.*, 439 U.S. 410 (1979); *Pickering v. Board of Ed. of Township High School Dist. 205, Will Cty.*, 391 U.S. 563, 568 (1968). Public-employee speech cases take great care not to limit the right of government employees to speak in their capacity as a citizen. Isn't that what lawyers do in many situations? Professor Rotunda's hypothetical lawyer is speaking on his own behalf, on a matter of public concern. Would it be consistent with the First Amendment to permit discipline in that case? Similar issues may arise in connection with the religion clauses of the First Amendment for speech relating to matters like same-sex marriage.

This is a great debate, which may be beyond the scope of your Professional Responsibility class, depending on how much your teacher expects you to know about the First Amendment. If this is within the scope of your class, check out *Garcetti v. Ceballos*, 547 U.S. 410 (2006), for a recent Supreme Court case applying government-employee free speech protections to a prosecutor.

Examples

Sticky Fingers

3. A paralegal met with the managing partner of a law firm. He informed the managing partner that a lawyer he worked with in the firm's estate planning practice had been writing checks on the firm's trust account, payable to himself. The managing partner obtained copies of the checks and determined that the paralegal's story was true. The managing partner then met with the lawyer in the estate planning group. The lawyer admitted writing the checks, but said he was only paying himself fees that were due under the firm's partnership agreement. As the managing partner knew, however, the trust account was used only to hold client funds. No attorneys' fees or partnership shares were ever paid out of the trust account. The lawyer also asked for the managing partner's understanding, admitting that he had a serious drinking problem and needed the money to pay debts he had incurred. The managing partner asked the

lawyer to repay the amount taken from the trust account and to resign from the law firm, which he did. No client funds were permanently converted. The managing partner also referred the lawyer to the state's lawyer assistance program, which helps lawyers deal with alcohol and drug abuse problems. The lawyer began an alcohol abuse treatment program and has been sober for six months.

Is the managing partner subject to discipline?

A. Yes, because she did not report the lawyer's misconduct to the appropriate professional disciplinary authority.

B. No, because she referred the lawyer to the state's lawyer assistance program for treatment of his alcohol abuse.

C. No, because no clients were harmed as a result of the temporary withdrawal of funds from the trust account.

D. No, because the managing partner did not have actual knowledge that the lawyer had committed a violation that raises a substantial question as to his trustworthiness.

Don't Be a Jerk

4. A male attorney is taking the deposition of a witness. The opposing counsel, a woman, is defending the deposition. As sometimes happens, the atmosphere became heated, as the attorney taking the deposition (the man) grew frustrated with a constant barrage of objections from the other lawyer. The deposition eventually recessed for lunch. As the parties and their lawyers were filing out of the room, the male attorney ostentatiously held open the conference room door for the female lawyer, saying "Ladies first!" Would the male attorney be subject to discipline for this conduct?

Explanations

Sticky Fingers

3. See *Board of Bar Overseers v. Warren*, 34 A.3d 1103 (Me. 2011). In that case, the Maine supreme court was bound by the factual findings of the hearing officer (interestingly, a single justice from the supreme court—I guess that's how it works in small states like Maine). The hearing officer found, bizarrely in my view, that the managing partner did not have subjective knowledge that the misappropriation of funds was conduct raising a substantial question as to the lawyer's honesty. On that view, the answer would be D. The hearing officer relied on the fact that the lawyer seemed remorseful and agreed to pay the money back, and that the managing partner seemed genuinely surprised by the conduct. The hearing officer was correct that the *mens rea* standard under Rule 8.3(a) is actual (that is, subjective) knowledge—see Rule 1.0(f)—and not an objective, "a

reasonable person would have known" standard.[6] Remember, though, that actual knowledge can be inferred from circumstances, and given conduct this serious, it's pretty hard to disclaim knowledge that the lawyer engaged in serious wrongdoing that calls his honesty into question.

I don't buy D as the answer, but it's the one given by the court. I would answer A. Once the managing partner knew the lawyer had his hands in the till, so to speak, he had a duty to report him to the appropriate disciplinary authorities. Violations of the duty to safeguard clients' funds are taken extremely seriously by regulators. Misappropriating client funds is almost a per se disbarment offense in many jurisdictions.

B is the best distractor, and arguably should be the right answer. But it isn't. Read Rule 8.3(c) carefully. It says that volunteer lawyers who work for state lawyer assistance programs do not have a duty to report, but it does not say that the lawyer assistance people are an "appropriate professional authority" for the purposes of Rule 8.3(a). Cases and ethics opinions tend to hold that they are not appropriate authorities because (1) participation in them is voluntary and (2) their mandate is to help lawyers with substance abuse problems, not to protect the public. I know, I know—the public would probably be better protected if lawyers with substance abuse issues were more likely to get treatment, but that isn't the way Rule 8.3(a) is generally interpreted. Do note, however, that a drinking problem by itself is not reportable conduct within Rule 8.3(a)—it has to result in interference with the lawyer's fitness in other respects.

Don't answer C, ever. The principle "no harm, no foul" is not found anywhere in the rules of professional conduct. True, a plaintiff in a legal malpractice action has to show harm (damages) and a causal connection with the attorney's negligence, but this isn't malpractice—it's professional discipline. There are no disciplinary rules which make harm an element of the violation.

Don't Be a Jerk

4. Under Rule 8.4(g) the question is whether this is "conduct that the lawyer knows or reasonably should know is harassment or discrimination on the basis of . . . sex." It is clearly related to the practice of law, and is not "advice or advocacy" since it is merely an interaction between counsel. The "ladies first" comment is based on the sex of the lawyer defending the deposition. However, does the conduct rise to the level of harassment or discrimination? The definitions in Comment [3] are interesting, because they say discrimination *includes* certain conduct, and harassment

---

6. The analysis was actually under the Maine version of the rule, which at the time had an idiosyncratic numbering system, but the substance of the rule was the same as Rule 8.3.

includes certain conduct. It does not say discrimination is such-and-such, and harassment is such-and-such. The definition of discrimination does say it is *harmful* verbal or physical conduct that manifests bias or prejudice. Maybe the male lawyer is a sexist jerk and is in fact biased against women lawyers, but was the single stray comment harmful? The lawyers had been mixing it up pretty good in the deposition, and it seems likely that the woman lawyer has endured worse in her career. Still, the text of the rule does not require a showing of harm, and as Stephen Gillers notes in his article about Rule 8.4(g), this omission was intentional:

> There is good reason not to require proof that the words or conduct described in Rule 8.4(g) harmed a targeted lawyer. That requirement would turn the inquiry into a question about the fortitude (or lack thereof, the sensitivity) of the lawyer, which in turn will discourage reporting. No lawyers will relish cross-examination asking whether they were unable "to take it."

Stephen Gillers, *A Rule to Forbid Bias and Harassment in Law Practice: A Guide for State Courts Considering Model 8.4(g)*, 30 Geo. J. Legal Ethics 195, 223 (2017). It is less likely that the conduct will be deemed harassment, particularly if the limitation in Comment [3] is followed, and harassment is defined with reference to hostile-environment caselaw under Title VII. The conduct is one-off, not a pervasive pattern of comments or actions, and it is nowhere close to being sufficiently severe to satisfy the Title VII standard. The male lawyer may also argue from mens rea, contending that a reasonable person would not know that a single comment, albeit sexist, could amount to harassment or discrimination on the basis of sex.

Whose Law Is It Anyway?

A lawyer admitted to practice in Texas has a nationally renowned practice representing plaintiffs in products liability cases. A medical device, manufactured by a company located in Ohio, is implanted by a surgeon in Oregon. The device malfunctions and injures the patient, who by now is living in Georgia. The patient hires a Georgia attorney who suggests associating with the lawyer from Texas, to obtain the benefit of her expertise in complex products liability cases. The lawyers file the lawsuit in Ohio. In the course of taking the deposition of the surgeon in Oregon, the Texas lawyer engages in abusive, uncivil conduct. In addition, the Texas lawyer never obtained the client's informed consent to sharing attorneys' fees with the Georgia lawyer. After a dispute with the client over the expenses of litigation, the Texas lawyer withdraws from the representation. The client is annoyed and wants to file a grievance with the relevant state disciplinary authority. Which state has the authority to impose discipline in the lawyer, and which state's law will apply, assuming there is a conflict among state laws?

Thankfully the first question is easy to answer. At the very least, a lawyer is always subject to discipline in the state of his or her admission to practice law. Rule 8.5(a). That means the Texas lawyer is always subject to discipline in Texas. In addition, she may also be subject to discipline in any state in which she provides or offers to provide legal services (that is, advertises or engages in solicitation). Rule 8.5(a). By associating with co-counsel in Georgia and representing the Georgia plaintiff, the Texas lawyer is also subject to discipline in Georgia. The idea is that professional discipline is aimed at the protection of the citizens of a state in which the lawyer practices. See Rule 8.5, cmt. [1]. What about Oregon? Taking a deposition is certainly within the definition of the provision of legal services, so let's include Oregon too; the surgeon is a resident of Oregon, and Oregon has an interest in protecting its citizens from abuse by out-of-state lawyers. What about Ohio? The lawsuit was filed in Ohio, so that state's professional disciplinary system also can reach the lawyer. That makes sense because one of the foundational policies of professional discipline is to safeguard the integrity of the litigation process.

Subsection (a) of Rule 8.5 deals with disciplinary jurisdiction, but there is still a question concerning the applicable law. Suppose there is a rule of professional conduct in Texas that prohibits the obnoxious conduct in which the lawyer engaged in the Oregon deposition.[7] The rule provides, among other things:

- Lawyers will be courteous, civil, and prompt in oral and written communications.
- Lawyers will not quarrel over matters of form or style, but will concentrate on matters of substance.
- Lawyers can disagree without being disagreeable. Effective representation does not require antagonistic or obnoxious behavior.
- Lawyers will not, without good cause, attribute bad motives or unethical conduct to opposing counsel nor bring the profession into disrepute by unfounded accusations of impropriety. Lawyers will avoid disparaging personal remarks or acrimony towards opposing counsel, parties, and witnesses. Lawyers will not be influenced by any ill feeling between clients. Lawyers will abstain from any allusion to personal peculiarities or idiosyncrasies of opposing counsel.

---

7. There really isn't any such rule. The provisions quoted in the text are taken from the Texas Lawyers Creed, promulgated in 1989 by the Texas Supreme Court and the Texas Court of Criminal Appeals. The Creed is purely voluntary.

There is no comparable rule in Oregon. Suppose the surgeon, annoyed at having been treated badly in the deposition, files a professional grievance against the Texas lawyer in Oregon. Rule 8.5(b) provides the choice-of-law analysis here. If there is a matter pending before a tribunal—and here there is, because there is a lawsuit file in Ohio—the rules of professional conduct of the jurisdiction in which the tribunal sits provide the applicable law. See Rule 8.5(b)(1). That means Ohio, not Oregon or Texas, law controls, because the conduct occurred at a deposition, which is in connection with the Ohio lawsuit.

The choice-of-law analysis is more difficult if there is no pending litigation. In that case, Rule 8.5(b)(2) says the governing law is provided by the rules of the jurisdiction in which the predominant effect of the conduct occurs. Let's modify the example slightly. Suppose the Texas lawyer learns of a pattern of failures of this medical device and also learns that, for whatever reason, a bunch of the devices were implanted in Iowa. The lawyer undertakes a targeted direct-mail advertising campaign in Iowa, seeking to retain clients who were injured by the device. Prior to the filing of a lawsuit, the predominant effect of the advertising campaign would be in Iowa, so that state's advertising rules would apply, even if the lawyer were subject to discipline in Texas.

Unauthorized Practice of Law (UPL)

All states have some sort of restriction on the right to practice law. In some jurisdictions, there are criminal statutes prohibiting the unauthorized practice of law; in other states, the restriction is found in a court rule. No matter what the source of authority, the rule is the same—certain kinds of tasks may be performed only by a licensed attorney who is admitted to practice in that jurisdiction. See Rest. §4. Note that unauthorized practice of law regulations apply only where one person performs a task on behalf of another person. People are permitted to represent themselves in legal matters. (Criminal defendants actually have a right under the U.S. Constitution to represent themselves at trial.) One may appear *pro se*—that is, without a lawyer—in court or may perform other legal tasks, such as drafting a will or a petition for an uncontested divorce, without running afoul of UPL regulations. Rest. §4, cmt. d; Wolfram §14.4.[8] The restrictions apply only where one person is representing another and performing tasks that constitute the practice of law.

---

8. As Wolfram observes, this right is limited to natural persons. Corporations, partnerships, and other entities may not appear in litigation *pro se* or be deemed to be self-represented for other purposes. The reason is that the entity is a separate legal "person," so the agent of the entity providing the services is effectively representing "another person" for the purposes of unauthorized practice of law restrictions.

Practicing law does not include only obviously "legal" activities like filing lawsuits and arguing motions in court. You do not need to enter a formal appearance before a tribunal to "practice law." Rather, the definition of practicing law is broad enough to encompass anything that can be characterized as the "application of legal knowledge, judgment, training, or skill in advising or otherwise assisting another to analyze or solve a particular legal problem or need." Frederick C. Moss, *A Law Professor's Cautionary Thoughts on Advising Students*, 42 S. Tex. L. Rev. 519, 522 (2001) (citing cases). The ABA's task force appointed to study the definition of the practice of law settled on a similar standard:

> The practice of law is the application of legal principles and judgment with regard to the circumstances or objectives of a person that requires the knowledge and skill of a person trained in the law.[9]

Applying this definition, if you tell your neighbor that she may sue a nearby pig farm under a recently decided nuisance case, you are practicing law. If you prepare a quickie promissory note to formalize a loan from one of your friends to another, you are practicing law. (Remember that you can draft this note for yourself, if you are borrowing money from a friend, because a person is permitted to represent herself.) In each of these cases, you are using your legal training and problem-solving ability and applying that judgment to a particular concrete problem.

Numerous nonlawyer professionals approach pretty close to the line between permissible activities and practicing law without a license. Financial planners may give advice about the estate tax consequences of a transaction; insurance adjusters interpret insurance policies, determine whether an event is covered by the policy, and negotiate settlements of insurance claims; title insurers perform title searches and render opinions about the validity of a deed to transfer title; real estate agents fill in blanks in standard-form contracts as part of land transactions; and accountants interpret the Internal Revenue Code when they prepare tax returns.[10] However, if a paralegal is self-employed, preparing legal documents may constitute the unauthorized practice of law. See, for example, *Florida Bar v. Brumbaugh*, 355 So.2d 1186 (Fla. 1978) (permitting nonlawyer to type up legal forms for clients based on their instructions but prohibiting her from answering questions put to her by clients and advising them on where to file the forms).

---

9. ABA Task Force on the Model Definition of the Practice of Law, Draft Report (Sept. 18, 2002), available online from the ABA's Center on Professional Responsibility, *www.abanet .org/cpr*.

10. Lawyers may employ nonlawyer assistants who interact with clients and may give them legal advice. Paralegals often do the bulk of advising and document drafting in estate planning and divorce matters, for example. This is permissible as long as a lawyer supervises the activities of the nonlawyer employee. Rest. §4, cmt. g.

A high-tech example is the marketing of self-help legal software, similar to tax preparation programs like TurboTax, which enables consumers to prepare documents like wills and divorce decrees by participating in an interactive "interview" structured by the software. In a rather notorious case, a federal district court in Texas granted an injunction against the sale in Texas of Quicken Family Lawyer software, which automated the process of preparing simple legal documents. *Unauthorized Practice of Law Committee v. Parsons Technology*, 1999 WL 47235 (N.D. Tex. 1999), *vacated*, 179 F.3d 956 (5th Cir. 1999).

Unfortunately, you will look long and hard for a bright-line test that separates the unauthorized practice of law from something that looks awfully close to practicing law, but is on the safe side of the line. The best you can do is keep in mind the basic definition—applying legal training and judgment to a particular problem—and think about the policy reasons for and against permitting a particular activity by nonlawyers.

On the side of restricting the activity, using UPL rules, is the argument from competence and client protection. The hurdles lawyers must surmount in order to become licensed and remain in good standing—that is, bar exam, law school, mandatory continuing legal education programs, etc.—keep some incompetent people from providing legal services. Also, the requirement of having a license to practice law means that the state has regulatory authority over the activity, in the form of the grievance and disciplinary procedures. On the other hand, licensure seems to be a rather clumsy method for enforcing competence. Surely there are many accountants who are much better informed about the tax consequences of some transactions than the vast majority of lawyers. I am licensed to practice law, but you should not rely on me to do a competent title search—a nonlawyer employee of a title insurance company would do a much better job. Wouldn't it make more sense to regulate competence directly, in the form of tort actions against incompetent service providers, rather than assuming that competence tracks licensure? Furthermore, requiring licensed lawyers to perform certain activities drives up the cost, as compared with nonlawyer service providers. Many consumers would prefer to pay less for a nonlawyer to do the very same job.

Examples

No Good Deed Goes Unpunished

5. Your friend went to the emergency room for what he believed was an acute medical emergency, and now his health insurer is unwilling to cover the expense, claiming he should have seen his regular primary care physician. You are a second- or third-year law student, and you, your friend, and the insurance company are all domiciled in the State of Perplexity. You

write a strongly worded letter for his signature, addressed to his health insurer. The letter cites a Perplexity Insurance Commission regulation on the payment of claims for emergency room visits, threatens to report this case to the Insurance Commission if it is not resolved promptly, and hints that a lawsuit for bad faith denial of coverage may be a possibility. Which of the following descriptions applies to this situation?

A. You have committed the unauthorized practice of law in the State of Perplexity, because writing the letter for your friend's signature requires the application of legal training and judgment to the problems of another, and you are not admitted to practice in Perplexity.

B. Writing the letter is not unauthorized practice of law because no lawsuit has yet been filed and you have not entered an appearance before a tribunal.

C. You would have committed the unauthorized practice of law if you had charged a fee, but since you did it as a favor for a friend, there is no problem here.

D. Because writing the letter required nothing more than looking up one section of the insurance regulations, it was not an action that can be performed only by skilled lawyers; therefore, it was not the unauthorized practice of law.

Leveling the Playing Field

6. The legislature in the State of Perplexity has long been concerned with the cost of legal services and the inability of people of average income levels to afford a lawyer. As part of its attempt to address this problem, the legislature enacted a statute creating a class of "certified public adjusters," who are authorized to represent individuals in dealing with their insurance companies. For example, if an insurer refuses to pay a claim for property damage, or authorizes an amount too small to cover the loss, the policyholder can hire a certified public adjuster to estimate the cost of the damage, document the loss, and act as a go-between in negotiations with the adjuster employed by the insurance company. As the legislative history of the statute shows, the legislature believed it was only fair to permit individuals to employ adjusters, since insurance companies have their own in-house adjusters, that they employ when dealing with individual policyholders.

   A group of lawyers in Perplexity has challenged the statute, claiming it violates the prohibition on the practice of law by nonlawyers. The professional association representing certified public adjusters intervened to defend the statute, pointing out that it gives a great deal of protection to consumers. To become a certified public adjuster, a person must pass a written examination covering subjects such as the Perplexity Insurance Code, appraisal procedures, building construction and fire code principles, and the basic principles of insurance law applicable to coverage issues. As the adjusters argued, a certified public adjuster is much less likely to make a mistake in a complex insurance coverage dispute than a general-practice lawyer, who may have no experience and training specific to insurance coverage issues.

Should the statute be struck down as the unauthorized practice of law?

Explanations

No Good Deed Goes Unpunished

5. Answer is A. Doing a bit of legal research and writing a letter may not sound like a big deal, but it falls within the broad definition of the practice of law. You do not need to appear before a tribunal to practice law (so B isn't the answer). Practicing law doesn't require accepting fees (so C isn't the answer), and it doesn't have to involve dealing with complicated legal problems that require great deal of specialized experience (so D isn't the answer). If you apply legal knowledge to the problems of another, you are practicing law. Even something as simple as looking up a few state insurance regulations is the application of some (fairly minimal) level of legal skill.

Leveling the Playing Field

6. This example is based on *Professional Adjusters, Inc. v. Tandon*, 433 N.E.2d 779 (Ind. 1982). The court held that the evaluation of insurance claims and the representation of a policyholder in negotiations with the insurance company is the practice of law. Insurance coverage disputes inevitably concern the legal rights and liabilities of persons, so any attempt by a nonlawyer to evaluate an insurance claim and represent another person in dealing with an insurer requires knowledge and training in the law. For example, determining whether a particular loss falls within the insurance policy requires interpretation of the contract between the insurer and insured. Certified insurance adjusters are performing tasks that usually are handled by lawyers, such as setting a value on a claim and advising their clients on whether to accept an offer of settlement from the insurance company.

Remember that the ABA's proposed Model Definition of the Practice of Law is as follows: "The practice of law is the application of legal principles and judgment with regard to the circumstances and objectives of a person that requires the knowledge and skill of a person trained in the law." This definition can be interpreted very broadly indeed. Giving tax advice requires some knowledge of tax law, but accountants provide tax advice all the time. More to the point of this example, the adjusters employed by insurance companies have to know something about insurance law in order to deal with their policyholders' claims. Yet nonlawyer insurance adjusters usually are not deemed to be practicing law, as long as they are employed by insurance companies. Isn't that unfair to individuals? Unauthorized practice of law rules are justified on the basis of the need to protect clients from incompetent or unethical providers of complex services. But doesn't the required exam for certified public adjusters guarantee a high level of competence? It certainly seems to be more narrowly tailored than the bar exam and legal education requirements used to screen out incompetent lawyers. A lawyer may be highly skilled in some other area of law—say, criminal defense—but not have any clue about insurance coverage issues. Ironically, though, that lawyer would be permitted to represent policyholders in disputes with an insurance company, but a certified public adjuster would not.

I am highly skeptical of the public-protection rationale usually offered in defense of UPL rules. Many lawyer "traditionalists" defend the rules vigorously, and the recent experience with the ABA's proposed model definition shows that the organized bar is still motivated to protect its monopoly over the provision of certain kinds of services. Interestingly, though, some of the skeptical arguments are beginning to influence the public debate over UPL. For example, the Federal Trade Commission and the antitrust division of the U.S. Department of Justice recently submitted a joint comment on the ABA's proposed definition. It is available online at *http://www.usdoj.gov/atr/public/comments/200604.pdf* and is worth reading if you would like to learn more about this controversy. In a nutshell, the joint comment expresses concern over the anticompetitive effects of prohibiting nonlawyers from providing certain kinds of services. In particular, routine residential real estate closings and the preparation of wills, trusts, and other legal documents could be handled by nonlawyers or by document-preparation software without compromising the quality of the services. As the comment argues, the public good would be better served by permitting competition from nonlawyers, which will lower the cost of obtaining these services, without any loss of consumer protection. This is an important challenge to the bar's attempt to enforce UPL rules, and this issue is likely to continue to be prominent in public debate.

Multijurisdictional Practice

It is a cliché to observe that our economy has become increasingly national in scope, particularly as technology such as fax machines, e-mail, and videoconferencing facilitates interacting with others at a distance. The practice of law is no different, and many lawyers work with clients all over the country. Significantly, they may do work that has an impact in several different jurisdictions, including states in which they may not be licensed to practice law. Some lawyers attract clients from all over the country, but even practices that seem localized at first may turn out to have multijurisdictional components. A domestic relations lawyer may work primarily with clients in the local area, but if one of the parents moves out of state and a dispute arises over child custody, the lawyer may be involved in a deposition or trial in another state. Local business transactions may involve parties from other states, and lawyers may meet with them or talk with them on the telephone when the parties are not in the "home" jurisdiction.

In addition to the nationalization of law practice, two other trends have put pressure on the traditional system of state-by-state regulation of lawyers. The first is the increasing *specialization* of the practice of law. Many lawyers are experts in particular subjects that cut across jurisdictional boundaries, such as white-collar criminal law, securities regulation, or environmental compliance. There is no necessary correspondence between these specialized fields and state borders. A complex product liability lawsuit in Nevada has more in common with a complex product liability lawsuit in Virginia than a sophisticated estate plan or a multiparty commercial real estate transaction in Nevada. The second trend is the *uniformity* of many areas of law. Perhaps the best-known example is the Uniform Commercial Code (UCC), which was specifically drafted to be applicable across state boundaries. Commercial transactions cross borders, so the law ought to be as uniform as possible to reduce transaction costs. As a result, lawyers who are competent in the UCC essentially are capable of working with any state's law. The increasing tendency of Congress to *federalize* a subject of concern also increases the uniformity of law across state borders. Federal law is the same all over, at least within the geographic circuits, and appellate courts in the various circuits try to harmonize their decisions with those of other federal courts. (In serious cases of disuniformity, the Supreme Court may take the case and issue a uniform national rule.)

The *Birbrower* Bombshell

Lawyers have been aware of these trends, and probably never thought much about the issue of whether transactional practice (as opposed to litigation) across state borders constitutes the unauthorized practice of law until the California Supreme Court refused to enforce a fee agreement between a California client and a New York Law firm. *Birbrower, Montalbano, Condon & Frank, P.C. v. Superior Court*, 949 P.2d 1 (1998). California Client (CC) was involved in a dispute over a software development and marketing agreement it had entered into with another company. The New York lawyers (NYL) helped CC in its dispute, which was governed by an arbitration provision in the marketing agreement. NYL did the sorts of things you would expect lawyers to do in a dispute that was heading for arbitration. They flew out to California and met with CC and its accountants, discussed strategy regarding the dispute, made recommendations and gave advice, met with the opposing party regarding the settlement discussions, interviewed potential arbitrators at the San Francisco office of the American Arbitration Association, made an oral or written demand for $15 million in settlement of CC's claim, and discussed a proposed settlement agreement with opposing party.

The case eventually settled, but there was a falling-out between NYL and CC. Disputes upon the termination of an attorney-client relationship can be ugly indeed. If the client refuses to pay the fee, the lawyer has to be very careful in trying to collect, because an action to collect the fee invariably will provoke a counterclaim for legal malpractice. That is exactly what happened here, although in addition to claiming malpractice, CC threw in the novel defense that the contract was void for illegality, because NYL were involved in the unauthorized practice of (California) law.

If this had been litigation — that is, a dispute before a court — the firm would have been able to protect itself from accusations of unauthorized practice of law. It could do this by being admitted pro hac vice under the rules of the tribunal. Most courts permit a lawyer to become temporarily admitted to practice in that court for the purposes of the pending litigation. (Sometimes the court will require that the lawyer associate with local counsel, presumably to ensure familiarity with local procedures, in order to be admitted pro hac vice.) The lawyer is then permitted to do anything that a lawyer licensed in that state would do, as long as it is related to the litigation. The lawyer could give advice, negotiate a settlement agreement, take depositions, argue before the court, and even try the case. Because it is a relatively routine matter to gain pro hac vice admission, courts are occasionally quite harsh with lawyers who fail to do so. The Virginia Supreme Court, for example, dismissed an otherwise timely and proper appeal because the notice was signed only by a Kentucky attorney. Wellmore Coal Corp. v. Harman Mining Corp., 568 S.E.2d 671 (Va. 2002). (The attorney had been admitted pro hac vice in the trial court, but not in the Supreme Court.) The court even refused to accept an amended notice of appeal signed by an attorney admitted in Virginia. There was no suggestion that the lawyer was incompetent, or that the client was prejudiced by his out-of-state status — in fact, the lawyer had represented the client at trial. This is an outrageous decision, because there is no conceivable harm to the client, and the rules against the unauthorized practice of law are justifiable only as a means to protect clients from incompetent lawyers. Nevertheless, it does show how seriously some states take unauthorized practice, even by otherwise perfectly competent lawyers.

The problem in Birbrower, of course, is that there is no way to get admitted pro hac vice for a nonlitigated matter. If NYL wants to do legal work in

California for CC, the only option is to associate with local counsel—that is, a lawyer admitted to practice in California—if associating with an in-state lawyer is permitted under the state's UPL statute. The problem with hiring local counsel, even if it avoids the application of UPL rules, is that the California lawyer will be on the hook for a malpractice claim by the client, so she will insist on doing a thorough review of any legal work performed by NYL. That means the client ends up paying for two lawyers (or sets of lawyers) doing essentially redundant work. If NYL is truly an expert on the law of software licensing, which is assumed to be basically uniform nation-wide with minor state-by-state variations, there seems to be no upside for CC. The client, in effect, gets one lawyer's expertise for the price of two!

That is exactly the result entailed by *Birbrower* because of the court's application of the California UPL statute. The statute restricted the practice of law in California to lawyers who were duly licensed in California. So, the question for the court was twofold: (1) did NYL "practice law," and if so, (2) did the lawyers practice law "in California"?

The answer to the first question should be easy, in light of the previous discussion. Representing a client in the negotiations surrounding the collapse of a licensing agreement, writing a demand letter, considering the possibility of arbitration, and interviewing prospective arbitrators involves the application of one's legal training, experience, and judgment to the particular legal problems of a client. It is true, as the dissent argues in *Birbrower*, that nonlawyers may represent parties in an arbitration proceeding, but it does not follow that what the lawyers did here is permissible. The lawyers went way beyond what a nonlawyer may do in connection with arbitration. Discussing strategy with CC, making recommendations and giving advice, meeting with the opposing party, writing a demand letter, and negotiating the settlement of a case certainly constitute the practice of law.

What about the "in California" element? Here, the court underscores an important point related to technology—one does not have to be physically present in California to practice law in California. As long as the lawyer has sufficient contacts with CC, engages in sufficient activities in the state, or creates an ongoing relationship with CC, the lawyer is practicing law in California. These contacts and relationships may be created and sustained entirely from the lawyer's New York office. The lawyer may communicate by phone, fax, e-mail, overnight courier, or carrier pigeon, but need not set foot in California to run afoul of state UPL rules. Merely advising a client outside of California on California law is probably not enough to constitute the practice of law in California, but the lawyers' frequent contacts with a California client, in that state, satisfied the second prong of the test in *Birbrower*.

Thus, the court held that the fee agreement between NYL and CC was void to the extent that it covered work performed for CC in California by NYL. The lawyers were entitled to recover on the contract for work performed in New York, and may have had a claim in *quantum meruit* against

CC to prevent unjust enrichment for the rest of the legal services, but the lawyers could not recover the lion's share of the over $1 million in fees for the legal work performed, because it was mostly performed in California, in violation of the UPL statute. Ouch.

Multijurisdictional Practice Reform

The *Birbrower* case focused the organized bar's attention on the uneasy fit between traditional state-by-state licensing of lawyers and the increasingly national, or cross-border, practice of law. The ABA appointed a commission to study the issue, which heard various proposals for reform, including a "driver's license" scheme in which a license to practice law in, say, New York would entitle the lawyer to act as an attorney in any state, as if she were licensed there. The commission rejected the most sweeping reform proposals, but did recommend adoption of a new version of Model Rule 5.5, which the ABA House of Delegates approved in August 2002. The revised rule reaffirms the basic principle of state-by-state licensing, and makes a lawyer subject to discipline for establishing a "systematic or continuous presence" for the practice of law in a jurisdiction in which he is not licensed. Rule 5.5(b). Significantly, though, the new rule provides some safe harbors for occasional practice in a jurisdiction in which the lawyer is not licensed. A lawyer not licensed in Jurisdiction X may provide legal services on a temporary basis in that state in one of four circumstances:

1. *Lawyer associates with local counsel.* Rule 5.5(c)(1). The rule specifically provides that the local lawyer must "actively participate" in the matter, not just serve as what is sometimes pejoratively called a "bag boy" local counsel—that is, someone who takes pleadings to the clerk's office for filing but otherwise has no substantial role in the representation.
2. *Lawyer is admitted* pro hac vice. Rule 5.5(c)(2). The rule extends to lawyers who reasonably expect to be admitted *pro hac vice* but have not yet been admitted. In a litigation matter, this means that a lawyer may fly out to Jurisdiction X before a lawsuit is filed, interview witnesses, review documents, advise the client, and do other acts that constitute the performance of legal services, as long as the lawyer reasonably believes that he will be admitted *pro hac vice* by the court once the lawsuit is filed.
3. *ADR proceedings.* Rule 5.5(c)(3). For lawyers in litigated matters, pro hac vice admission has always provided a way to avoid violating UPL statutes. But many disputes are resolved not through lawsuits, but through mediation, arbitration, or some other alternative dispute resolution (ADR) procedure. In the *Birbrower* case, for example, the software licensing agreement included a clause providing that

any dispute arising under the agreement would be submitted to arbitration—that is, a process resulting in a binding decision by someone other than a judge. Arbitration tribunals do not have the authority to admit lawyers *pro hac vice* because they are not part of the state court system; in fact, the appeal of alternative dispute resolution is that it avoids entanglement with the courts. Under the new rule, a lawyer appearing in Jurisdiction X to provide services "in or reasonably related to" an alternative dispute resolution procedure does not commit the unauthorized practice of law if (and note this condition) the services arise out of the lawyer's practice in a jurisdiction in which he is admitted.

To illustrate this latter condition, assume a lawyer admitted in Tennessee advises a Tennessee client on a transaction with someone from Michigan. The two parties may agree to a contract provision subjecting any disputes between them to arbitration, with the proceedings to be held in Detroit. If a dispute does arise and the Tennessee lawyer flies to Detroit to select an arbitrator and represent the client at the hearing, the lawyer's activities do not constitute the unauthorized practice of law because of the ADR exception, Rule 5.5(c)(3).

4. *Catch-all*. Rule 5.5(c)(4). A lawyer occasionally may practice in Jurisdiction X in any matter—for example, transactional, counseling, advising, regulatory work, etc.—without committing the unauthorized practice of law if the work in Jurisdiction X reasonably relates to the lawyer's practice in a jurisdiction in which he is licensed. This rule is similar to paragraph (c)(3), but it is not limited to ADR matters. It covers activities such as advising an affiliated company, located in Jurisdiction X, of a corporate client based in the lawyer's home jurisdiction, or negotiating a deal between a client based in the lawyer's home jurisdiction and another party based in Jurisdiction X. This exception does *not* permit a lawyer to represent clients with no relationship to a representation ongoing in the lawyer's home jurisdiction. Thus, a North Carolina lawyer could not handle a transaction for a South Carolina client, taking place entirely in South Carolina. That matter would constitute the unauthorized practice of law in South Carolina, even though it is an occasional rather than continuous presence in South Carolina.

The new version of Model Rule 5.5 also contains separate provisions for in-house counsel—that is, lawyers employed directly by a corporation or other organization, rather than being employees of a law firm that is retained on an occasional basis by clients. In-house lawyers may be transferred from one office to another, often in different states, and it would be a real hassle for them to take a new bar exam in each jurisdiction. Furthermore, to the extent that the rationale for requiring local admission for lawyers is to ensure competent representation of clients, these interests are satisfied for the clients of in-house lawyers, because the lawyer is licensed in some jurisdiction, and the client, as the lawyer's employer, can supervise the quality of the lawyer's work. For these reasons, Model Rule 5.5(d) permits a lawyer to perform legal services in any jurisdiction for a client that employs the lawyer as in-house counsel, as long as the lawyer is duly licensed in some jurisdiction.

Please remember that these safe harbors are only for truly temporary practice in a jurisdiction. If a lawyer establishes a systematic and continuous presence in a state for the purposes of practicing law, the lawyer had better get admitted to practice in that state.

Examples

Systematic and Continuous Sunshine

7. Shira Snowbird is admitted to practice in New York. She has a successful practice advising financial institutions on employer noncompete agreements. Her clients are busy and sophisticated, so all her work is over the phone, by videoconference, or e-mail, and never involves in-person meetings. Having grown tired of high taxes and harsh winters in New York, she moves to Florida and, from a condo overlooking the beach, performs the exact same legal work for the exact same clients. She does no work for clients in Florida, nor does she hold herself out as admitted to practice in Florida. Is Shira subject to discipline?

Back to *Birbrower*

8. Would the lawyers in *Birbrower* be able to take advantage of any of the safe harbors in the new version of Model Rule 5.5?

Explanations

Systematic and Continuous Sunshine

7. If Shira represented Florida clients or held herself out as admitted there she'd be in trouble for violating Rule 5.5(b). On the facts as given, however, it's a closer call. Paraphrasing a bit, Rule 5.5(b) says a lawyer not admitted in Florida may not establish an office or other systematic and continuous presence in Florida for the practice of law, or hold out or represent herself as admitted to practice in Florida. The word "or" is important here, because otherwise it might seem that the test for UPL in Florida is establishing a systematic and continuous presence for the

practice of law, which means holding oneself out as authorized to practice in that jurisdiction. Shira hasn't done that, and one might wonder what Florida regulators care if a New York lawyer represents only New York clients, but does so from Boca Raton? But can you get that conclusion out of the rule and comments? Comment [4] to Rule 5.5 notes that presence in a jurisdiction may be systematic and continuous even if the lawyer is not physically present there. If Shira weren't admitted in New York, she'd be in trouble. Clearly her practice in New York is systematic and continuous. Can we flip around the analysis in Comment [4] to support the conclusion that Shira's presence in Florida is not systematic and continuous *because* she is systematically and continuous representing clients only in New York? Maybe, and the result makes sense. The purpose of UPL regulations, which vary from state to state, is to protect citizens of that state from incompetent legal services provided by nonlawyers or out-of-state lawyers. The interest of Florida UPL regulators is protecting Florida citizens. The fact that Shira is soaking up the Florida sun while providing legal services in New York is irrelevant from the point of view of the purpose underlying UPL regulation.

I'm inclined to say Shira is okay here, although the disjunctive structure of Rule 5.5(b) makes me a bit hesitant. A lawyer can establish a systematic and continuous presence without holding herself out to the public as admitted to practice in Florida. I believe, however, that the way a lawyer would do this is by representing Florida clients. That is the crucial element in establishing a systematic and continuous presence in the state.

Back to *Birbrower*

8. The natural place to turn seems to be Model Rule 5.5(c)(3), on ADR proceedings, because the lawyers' activities in California related to an arbitration of a dispute between the two parties to a software licensing agreement. The lawyers were in California only in connection with the dispute that had arisen under the agreement, which was required to be submitted to arbitration. The advice, demand letters, negotiations, and eventual settlement were "reasonably related to a . . . potential arbitration" (the case settled before going to arbitration), so everything seems okay for the lawyer. But, do not forget the requirement in this rule that the arbitration proceeding arise out of, or be reasonably related to, the lawyer's practice in a jurisdiction in which the lawyer is admitted. If the lawyer had been representing a *New York* client in the licensing deal, the rule would apply and save the lawyer from a UPL violation. But the lawyer in *Birbrower* was representing a *California* client. The lawyer's work on the licensing agreement was not "practice in a jurisdiction in which the lawyer is admitted to practice," so the exception in Model

Rule 5.5(c)(3) does not apply. (The same analysis goes for Model Rule 5.5(c)(4), the catch-all rule, which also requires that the episodic practice in a jurisdiction in which the lawyer is not licensed is reasonably related to practice in a jurisdiction in which the lawyer is licensed.)

Pro Bono Representation

Coming in the last section of the last chapter on the duties of lawyers, the discussion of pro bono is bound to feel like a bit of an afterthought. Unfortunately, that seems to be the way most lawyers think of it. Lawyers like to talk about the importance of access to justice and ensuring that lawyers are available to everyone, not just the well-to-do. More theoretically, the special privileges of the profession, including the monopoly over the provision of anything that can be deemed "legal services" (which you know from this chapter to be very broad), are justified by the commitment of the legal profession to public service.[11] The organized bar has a long-standing commitment to the ideal of providing legal services free or at a reduced cost to those who cannot afford a lawyer. This effort to increase access to justice generally goes by the Latin name *pro bono publico*—for the public good—or pro bono for short.

It's one thing to talk about providing pro bono representation, but should it be made mandatory? The Kutak Commission that drafted the 1983 Model Rules of Professional Conduct originally proposed a requirement that lawyers provide 40 hours per year of pro bono representation. Deborah Rhode, one of the leading academic advocates for pro bono representation, tells the rest of the story:

> Outraged opposition prompted the commission to propose instead that lawyers simply make an annual report of pro bono work, and that the rule leave unspecified what would qualify as "pro bono." Even this minimal obligation proved unacceptable. About four-fifths of surveyed lawyers opposed any pro bono requirement. Accordingly, the Model Rules as initially adopted included only an aspirational mandate calling for an unspecified amount of "public interest legal service."[12]

Successive versions of the Model Rules have continued to pay lip service to the importance of pro bono without making it mandatory. Rule 6.1 begins by observing that "[e]very lawyer has professional obligation to provide legal services to those unable to pay," but then says only that lawyers "*should*

---

11. See American Bar Association Commission on Professionalism, "*In the Spirit of Public Service:*" *A Blueprint for the Rekindling of Lawyer Professionalism* (1986), reprinted in 112 F.R.D. 243 (1987).
12. Deborah L. Rhode, "Pro Bono in Principle and in Practice," 53 J. Legal Educ. 413, 426 (2003).

aspire to render at least (50) hours of pro bono public legal services per year." That's not much of an obligation. I "should aspire" to train for a marathon or learn to play drums like Questlove, but here I sit . . .

Even though Rule 6.1 has no teeth, you should still know what it says. There are a couple of features worth noting. The first is that it does require that one's civic-minded volunteer activities be *legal* in nature. Packing meals to feed needy children is admirable, but does not count toward the 50-hour requirement. Second, the rule requires that a substantial majority of the 50 hours be devoted to serving persons of limited means, either directly (Rule 6.1(a)(1)) or by the provision of legal services to "charitable, religious, civic, community, governmental and educational institutions" that are aimed at addressing the needs of persons of limited means (Rule 6.1(a)(2)). That means serving on the board of the local opera company or providing legal services of a general nature to one's church or synagogue do not count. In all cases these services must be delivered without any expectation of receiving a fee. The remainder of the 50-hour requirement, after the substantial majority of services have been provided as described in Rule 6.1(a), can be in one of three categories:

1. Free legal services, or legal services at a substantially reduced fee, to organizations seeking to protect civil rights, civil liberties, or public rights, or to charitable, religious, civic, community, governmental, and educational organizations in furtherance of their organizational purposes, where paying for legal services would significantly deplete the organization's resources. Rule 6.1(b)(1). This would include, for example, advising a small church with a shoestring budget on a zoning matter, or providing services at a reduced fee to a local environmental group.
2. Providing legal services at a substantially reduced fee to persons of limited means. Rule 6.1(b)(2).
3. Participation in activities designed to improve the law, the legal system, or the legal profession. Rule 6.1(b)(3). This would include service on a commission to study proposed amendments to the state rules of professional conduct, or teaching a continuing legal education (CLE) program. Rule 6.1, cmt. [8].

It is okay to provide financial support to any of these causes, but Rule 6.1 contemplates satisfying the 50-hour requirement by providing legal services. Judges and government lawyers, who may be restricted by statute or otherwise (see, for example, CJC Rule 3.10, which prohibits judges from practicing law) from providing pro bono legal services, may perform the services described in Rule 6.1(b)(3) to satisfy their requirement. See Rule 6.1, cmt. [5]. Judges may also encourage lawyers to perform pro bono services, as long as they do not use means that are coercive. ABA Formal Op. 470 (2015).

Student readers may appreciate the irony that the organized bar has not made pro bono service mandatory for lawyers, but in many instances it has seen no problem with making it mandatory for law students. Applicants seeking admission to practice in New York must demonstrate that they have provided 50 hours of pro bono service before applying for admission. Other states, including California, are considering adopting a pro bono requirement for admission. Many law schools also have their own pro bono requirements. Some states require annual reporting by lawyers of their time spent on pro bono matters.

Example

Does It Count?

9. Let's see if you read Rule 6.1 and the comments carefully. Do the following activities count toward the lawyer's aspirational goal of performing 50 hours per year of pro bono services? Assume the State of Perplexity requires lawyers to report pro bono activities annually on their licensing form.

   A. A lawyer has spent five hours assisting a woman whose income is just above the poverty line in obtaining a temporary restraining order against an abusive partner. The lawyer and client had a written fee agreement providing that the client would pay the lawyer's customary fee of $150 per hour. (The client told the lawyer that her parents would help her with her legal expenses.) At the conclusion of the representation, however, the client could not pay and told the lawyer that she made up the story about her parents helping her with the expenses. The lawyer decided to write off the $750 as uncollectable and not attempt to recover it from the client. May the lawyer report having performed five hours of pro bono service for the client?

   B. A lawyer represents several plaintiffs suing a landlord for violating a state statute prohibiting discrimination in rental housing. The lawyer works for Equal Housing Now, a non-profit legal services organization, funded by grants from the state Interest on Lawyers' Trust Accounts (IOLTA) fund. Equal Housing Now represents only clients whose incomes fall below the poverty level, as defined by federal law. The state housing discrimination statute includes an attorneys' fees provision, giving the trial court discretion to award attorneys' fees in addition to damages if the court finds that the discrimination was particularly egregious. Plaintiffs represented by Equal Housing Now are told that under no circumstances will they be required to pay for the services of the organization's lawyers. After a trial concluded with a judgment in favor of the plaintiffs, the trial court entered an award of $50,000 in attorneys' fees, payable to Equal Housing Now, concluding that the landlord's conduct was outrageous.

C. A lawyer serves on the board of Primitive Pathways, a local non-profit organization that provides wilderness survival and leadership training for teenagers. Fees for the summer Primitive Pathways program are $200 per week. The kids served are mostly middle-class, although a few families with more modest incomes pay no fee. An annual chicken barbecue raises money to provide scholarships for these families. Recently Primitive Pathways was sued by a family who claimed that its programming was not suitable for teenagers with certain types of disabilities. With the consent of the other members of the board, the lawyer represented Primitive Pathways in the litigation. She agreed to do so for no fee. After the lawyer worked approximately 200 hours on the matter, the lawsuit was settled and Primitive Pathways agreed to make changes to its activities. May the lawyer report any of this time on her license renewal form? Does it matter whether she has performed a substantial majority of 50 hours of pro bono service in other matters?

Explanation

Does It Count?

9. Although a lawyer is not subject to discipline for failing to live up to the aspiration to render 50 pro bono hours per year, in a mandatory reporting state the lawyer must be truthful on her license renewal form. See Rule 8.4(c). Do these matters satisfy the tests set out in Rule 6.1?

A. Nope. Rule 6.1(a) defines pro bono services as those performed with no expectation of a fee. That means no *ex ante* belief that the client will be able to pay. In this case, the lawyer thought the client had someone to help her pay her bills, so the lawyer had an expectation of receiving a fee. See Rule 6.1, cmt. [4] ("services cannot be considered pro bono if an anticipated fee is uncollected"). The situation also does not come within Rule 6.1(b)(2), because the lawyer charged her customary fee. If the facts had been different, and the lawyer had offered to charge a modest fee of, say, $25 per hour, then the lawyer may report the five hours as part of the "category (b)" hours—not a substantial majority, but filling out the remainder of her 50-hour requirement. See Rule 6.1, cmt. [7].

B. Yes. This is the flipside of the previous example. Go through the requirements of Rule 6.1(a): The lawyer is providing legal services to persons of limited means, and is doing so for no fee. What about the language, "expectation of a fee?" Here, the lawyer had no *ex ante* expectation of receiving a fee. Comment [4] clarifies the effect of the court's award of attorneys' fees: "[T]he award of statutory attorneys' fees in a case originally accepted as pro bono would not disqualify such services for inclusion under [Rule 6.1(a)(1)].

C. This is a close call. Look carefully at Rule 6.1(a)(2) and Rule 6.1(b)(1). The first rule, covering services that can make up a substantial majority of a lawyer's reported *pro bono* hours, pertains to legal services to organizations "that are designed primarily to assist the needs of persons of limited means." See Comment [3], which mentions homeless shelters, domestic violence centers, and food pantries as examples of this type of organization. While outdoor leadership is important, it is not the same type of basic interest as food or shelter, and in any event Primitive Pathways is not primarily aimed at meeting the needs of persons of limited means. Thus, the case does not fall within Rule 6.1(a)(2). As for (b)(1), there are a similar limitation, but the language is somewhat broader. To qualify for pro bono under Rule 6.1(b)(1), an organization must be aimed either at meeting *legal* needs, such as "First Amendment claims, Title VII claims and environmental protection claims," Rule 6.1, cmt. [6], or at charitable, religious, civic, etc., purposes, *and* it must be the case that the payment of standard legal fees would "significantly deplete the organization's economic resources." Primitive Pathways fails the first prong of this test, but it may be the case that paying the lawyer for 200 hours of work would significantly deplete the organization's resources. The example does not say so explicitly, but it was written to make Primitive Pathways sound like a modest community-based organization with a relatively limited budget.

PART V

Judicial Ethics

The Judicial Role

INTRODUCTION

How Lawyers and Judges Are Different

If you've gotten this far in the book, you can probably boil down the duties of lawyers to a couple of basic principles. These constitute the normative foundation of legal ethics, and serve to explain and justify the specific provisions making up the law of lawyering. The central principle of legal ethics may be referred to as *partisanship*.[1] It is the idea that the lawyer's first object of concern is her client. The principle of partisanship includes the duty of loyalty, which underlies the numerous provisions of the conflicts of interest rules, including Rules 1.7, 1.8, and 1.9. The value of loyalty requires

---

1. This term is frequently used in theoretical legal ethics, as one of three principles making up the so-called standard conception. (The other two are neutrality and nonaccountability, which refer respectively to the lawyer's obligation to "screen out" moral considerations such as the undesirability of the client's objectives and to the evaluative perspective to be adopted by those who observe the lawyer's actions.) For important early articles setting out the standard conception, see, for example, Murray Schwartz, "The Professionalism and Accountability of Lawyers," 66 Cal. L. Rev. 669 (1978); Gerald J. Postema, "Moral Responsibility and Professional Ethics," 55 NYU L. Rev. 63 (1980). If you're interested in theoretical legal ethics, I have written an introduction for law and philosophy students called *Law and Ethics: An Introduction* (Cambridge University Press 2014). Chapter 3 talks about the standard conception.

the lawyer to put the client's interests first, and not to be influenced by a personal financial, reputational, or other interest, or the representation of other current or former clients. Partisanship also entails competence (Rule 1.1): The lawyer is the legal agent of the client and must act to protect the client's interests. Serving the client's interests effectively requires the lawyer to have sufficient skill and knowledge to handle the client's legal problems. Finally, partisanship includes the duty of confidentiality (Rule 1.6). The lawyer must keep the client's secrets, subject to certain well defined exceptions, even if disclosing them would contribute to justice, as considered from the point of view of society as a whole. (Remember Bentham's critique of the attorney-client privilege, from Chapter 7?) The principle of partisanship is often summarized by lawyers as the duty of zealous advocacy, although it is meant also to apply to lawyers counseling clients and representing them in transactions.

The principle of partisanship is not unqualified. Lawyers must be zealous advocates only *within the bounds of the law*. Limitations on zealous advocacy include the obligation of candor to the tribunal (Rule 3.3), the duty not to pursue frivolous claims or defenses (Rule 3.1), and the obligation not to lie to third parties (Rule 4.1). Although zealous advocacy is a qualified duty, the core idea remains that lawyers' duties are primarily oriented around the client's interests. Lawyers are agents of their clients, their clients define the objectives of the representation (Rule 1.2(a)), and lawyers provide the expertise necessary for clients to accomplish their goals. Legal ethics is fundamentally client-centered.

Judicial ethics is a different kettle of fish. The central normative ideal that structures the ethics of the judicial role is *impartiality*. As Chief Justice John Roberts famously stated in his Senate confirmation hearing, a judge should be like a baseball umpire, just calling the balls and strikes. As the Supreme Court has said, a judge must decide cases based on "proper controlling factors" and not "some personal bias or improper consideration." *Caperton v. A.T. Massey Coal Co.*, 556 U.S. 868, 883 (2009). Working out the difference between proper and improper considerations can be a thorny issue. For example, can a judge decide a case about the constitutional right to same-sex marriage when his religious commitments include the belief that same-sex marriage is morally wrongful? *See Cheney v. U.S. District Court*, 541 U.S. 913, 927-28 (2004) (Scalia, J.) (denying motion to recuse due to his friendship with Vice President Cheney, and observing that his impartiality had also been questioned because of his Roman Catholic faith). The confirmation process for Justice Sotomayor featured a little skirmish in the press over President Obama's statement that she would bring her life experience and empathy to the Supreme Court. Alabama Senator Jeff Sessions, then the ranking Republican member of the Judiciary Committee, responded in terms that usefully highlight the value of impartiality and the distinction we are discussing here between proper and improper grounds for judicial decisions:

> "I will not vote for, and no senator should vote for, anyone who will not render justice impartially," Sessions said. "Call it empathy, call it prejudice, or call it sympathy, but whatever it is, it's not law," he said. "In truth, it's more akin to politics, and politics has no place in the courtroom."

See Robert Barnes, Amy Goldstein & Paul Kane, *In Senate Confirmation Hearings, Sotomayor Pledges "Fidelity to Law,"* Washington Post (July 14, 2009).

Senator Sessions's reference to the law-politics distinction is fundamental to judicial ethics. Consider this line from a U.S. Supreme Court opinion: "Judges are not politicians, even when they come to the bench by way of the ballot." *Williams-Yulee v. Florida Bar*, 135 S.Ct. 1656, 1662 (2015). That's true—judges aren't exactly like politicians, and presumably some "political" considerations would be improper as grounds for a judicial decision. Judges are not supposed to follow the preferences of their supporters. *Id.* at 1667. The trouble is, many states have elections for judicial offices, and the Supreme Court has held that candidates for judicial office may state their opinion on contested political issues. *See Republican Party of Minn. v. White*, 536 U.S. 765 (2002). If judges aren't supposed to follow the preferences of their supporters, what is the point of stating, for example, that they are "tough on crime," will approach the job with empathy, favor a strict interpretation of the constitution, or whatever? More generally, no one thinks judges are or should be robots, lacking community ties, ordinary human emotions, and beliefs and convictions about issues of significance to the public. Which side of the law/politics distinction do values fall, like favoring the free market over government regulation, believing that consumer products should be made safer rather than relying on users to take additional care, or prioritizing expressive freedom over the right to privacy? Right off the bat it seems that the fundamental ideal of judging is too vague to serve as the basis for regulating judicial conduct.

The Code alludes frequently to the value of impartiality, generally defining it negatively—that is, by what impartiality is not. For example:

> "Rather than making decisions based upon the expressed views or preferences of the electorate, a judge makes decisions based upon the law and the facts of every case." CJC Rule 4.1, cmt. [1].

This passage captures nicely the value of impartiality. Judges are very likely to have views about most matters of public importance. Few people reach adulthood without forming beliefs about issues such as the role of government regulation in a market economy or the balance between individual liberties and the public interest. No one really believes Chief Justice Roberts's umpire analogy. Unlike balls and strikes, issues in litigation are not clearly one thing or another.[2] A certain amount of judgment is required to decide whether to exclude evidence, grant summary judgment, reduce an award of damages, interpret a provision of a contract, and so on. That is to be expected, and judicial ethics does not attempt to turn judges into machines. Nor could it, consistent with the First Amendment rights that judges, no less than other citizens, have to participate in the process of democratic self-governance. But the law still recognizes a distinction between considerations that are properly relevant to decisions made in a case and those that are not.

In marginal cases it may be difficult to draw this distinction. What do you think, for example, about a judge whose religious beliefs cause her to oppose capital punishment, notwithstanding the support of a majority of voters in her state for the death penalty? Fortunately, in the great majority of cases, the distinction between proper and improper considerations is clear. A judge may not, for example, decide a case involving a company in which her spouse owns an equity interest. ABA Code of Judicial Conduct ("CJC") Rule 2.11(A)(3) & cmt. [6]. The reason should be obvious: The judge might have an incentive to rule for the party in which her spouse is an investor, so that the spouse's investment will increase in value, and that is not a proper reason for ruling in favor of a party to a legal dispute. The most important rules of judicial ethics are aimed at safeguarding the process of judicial decisionmaking from certain clearly defined risks to impartiality.

Speaking of "the rules," you may be wondering where they come from and how they're enforced. The development of rules of judicial ethics roughly parallels the trajectory of legal ethics rules. The ABA first promulgated Canons of Judicial Ethics in 1924. Following a scandal (in this case, the collapse of Abe Fortas's nomination to the U.S. Supreme Court after revelation of financial improprieties), the Canons were formalized into a Code of Judicial Conduct, issued in 1973. The Code was revised in 1990, 2007, and 2010, and like the Model Rules for lawyers, it now resembles a statute, with a definitions section and duties stated in explicit black-letter rules with

---

2. I know virtually nothing about baseball, but my baseball-loving friends tell me that calling balls and strikes requires a certain amount of judgment, too. That makes sense; I'm more of a basketball fan, and realize that something like a charge/block/no-call judgment can vary from one ref to another and, notoriously, according to whether one of the players involved is a superstar. But really that's the point: Are there standards that can be used to evaluate the judgments made by umpires, refs, and judges? To the extent there are standards external to the decision-maker, we can coherently formulate the idea of bias, in the literal sense of a deviation from the proper direction of a cut. Calling a charge on the opponent of a player who flops reflects either bad refereeing or bias in favor of the flopper. This is consistent with a range of reasonable calls, however. One could imagine a situation in which one-third of refs would have called a charge but two-thirds would not. A decision to call a charge in that situation is not necessarily evidence of bias. Similarly, just because two-thirds of refs would not have called a charge is not conclusive evidence of lack of bias. To bring the discussion back to judicial ethics, the law tries to regulate bias indirectly, using proxies such as financial interests and participation in certain activities.

carefully enumerated exceptions, as opposed to a statement of ideals or best practices. Citations here to the Code of Judicial Conduct ("CJC") are to the version adopted in 2010. For this history, and for much other helpful discussion, see the leading treatise in the area, Charles Gardner Geyh, et al., *Judicial Conduct and Ethics* §1.03 (5th ed. 2013).

As always, however, your mileage may vary—that is, your state may have adopted an earlier version and not changed it in the meantime, or it may have specifically opted to deviate from the ABA's model. All states and the District of Columbia have established some type judicial conduct commission that is empowered to investigate allegations of misconduct by judges and impose an appropriate sanction. These commissions are controlled to a significant extent by judges, to protect the independence of the judiciary and safeguard against political meddling. Decisions by a state commission are generally appealable to a state court. See Geyh, *supra* §1.05. Some states have advisory committees that issue opinions on judicial ethics issues.

In addition to state rules of judicial conduct, enforced by a judicial conduct commission, state statutory and regulatory law often includes conflict of interest and other ethical rules for government officials, including judges. CJC Rule 1.1 requires judges to comply with the law, so a violation of a state statute prohibiting, for example, receipt of certain campaign contributions, would also be a violation of Rule 1.1.

Federal judges are governed by the Code of Conduct for United States Judges. It is similar in substance to the ABA Code of Judicial Conduct, but differs in the numbering of the rules and some specific language. Complaints against federal judges are handled by circuit-based judicial councils. See Geyh, *supra* §1.06. Discipline of federal judges is made more complicated by Article III of the U.S. Constitution, which prohibits the removal or reduction in salary of judges, except via the impeachment process. The judicial councils have other remedies available, however, including censure and the temporary suspension of a judge's duties. The conduct of federal judges is also regulated by statute, particular 28 U.S.C. §144 and §455. Section 144 permits a party to file an affidavit of prejudice, thereby compelling the judge to recuse herself from the case. Section 455 requires a judge to recuse herself in any proceeding in which her impartiality may reasonably be questioned.

The discussion of judicial ethics will mostly make reference to the ABA Code. These are the rules tested on the MPRE. According to the current MPRE subject matter outline, 2–8 percent of questions on any given exam administration will cover judicial ethics.

General Principles of Judicial Ethics

Stated positively, the rules seek to maintain the image and reality of judges as the heroes of our legal system. I'm not being entirely facetious here.

American legal education tends to valorize certain judges as exemplars of a type of virtuous person—wise, resolute, incorruptible, prudent, creative where appropriate, but also humble and aware of the risk of abusing their power. Names like Benjamin Cardozo, Learned Hand, Henry Friendly, Thurgood Marshall, John Minor Wisdom, and Ruth Bader Ginsburg recur in casebooks, and lawyers are tacitly encouraged to emulate these great judges. What, then, are their ethical characteristics? According to the Code of Judicial Conduct, a judge shall be courageous—"not . . . swayed by public clamor or fear of criticism" (CJC Rule 2.4(A)); not capable of being influenced by "any person or organization" (CJC Rule 2.4(C)); competent (CJC Rule 2.5); patient and courteous (CJC Rule 2.8, cmt. [1]); free from bias or prejudice (CJC Rule 2.3); and above all, a person of integrity, that is, characterized by "probity, fairness, honesty, uprightness, and soundness of character" (CJC Terminology). That's a lot to live up to! The ideal of judges as secular saints is important to understand, however, because it helps explain the results in many judicial disciplinary cases. Judges really are expected to be a bit better than the rest of us.

Another major concern for judicial ethics is avoiding the abuse of the office of judge. See CJC Rule 1.3. Judges are pretty powerful, and there is a risk that they may use their authority for purposes unrelated to the activity of deciding cases. See, for example, In re Mosley, 102 P.3d 555 (Nev. 2004) (judge reprimanded for writing on official judicial letterhead to his child's school, to inform school officials that his ex-girlfriend had lost custody of the child). The classic example of abuse of the prestige of judicial office is the judge who gets pulled over for speeding and asks the police officer, "Do you know who I am?" In some cases "abuse" may be too strong a word, because some misuses of the judicial office can be for seemingly good purposes. For example, a judge might send around letters to local lawyers soliciting donations for her favorite charity. Even if the judge's intentions are admirable, however, there is some possibility that lawyers will feel coerced into supporting the judge's charity. Who wants to say no to a judge and then appear in front of that judge the next week in court? For that reason, judges may participate in many charitable activities, but they may not solicit contributions, except from their family members and their colleagues on the bench. CJC Rule 3.7(A)(2).[3] Judges also may not impliedly invoke the prestige of their office to assist candidates for public office, by making speeches, endorsing candidates, or contributing to candidates or political organizations. CJC Rule 4.1. Judges may write recommendation letters or provide references, however, as would be the usual practice for their former

---

3. "Member of the judge's family" is a defined term that recurs in the Code. It refers to a spouse, domestic partner, child, grandchild, parent, grandparent, or other relative with whom the judge maintains a close familial relationship. See CJC Terminology.

law clerks, even though this conduct arguably lends the prestige of the office to the recommendation. CJC Rule 1.3, cmt. [2].

Finally, rules of judicial ethics regulate the conduct of proceedings in the judge's court. They are in some ways the counterpoint to the three-series rules governing the conduct of litigation by lawyers. For example, Model Rule 3.5(b) prohibits lawyers from communicating *ex parte* with judges. The counterpart rule for judges, CJC Rule 2.9, prohibits judges from communicating *ex parte* with lawyers.

The Code is organized around four Canons, with the first digit in the Rule number referring to the overarching Canon. Canon 1 contains general principles; Canon 2 relates to the conduct of litigation and the business of court; Canon 3 regulates extrajudicial activities; and Canon 4 deals with political and campaign activities. As another principle of organization, note the defined terms in the Terminology section at the beginning of the Code. If a term used in the Code is defined, it is followed by an asterisk. When you see an asterisked term, be sure to flip over to the front of the Code and read the definition carefully.

When applying the rules of judicial ethics, beware of one of the differences between them and the rules of professional conduct for lawyers. Lawyers must avoid impropriety, as defined in various ways (having a conflict of interest, failing to communicate with clients, etc.).[4] Judges, on the other hand, must also avoid the *appearance* of impropriety. CJC Rule 1.2. An independent, impartial judiciary is vital to the rule of law, which is one of the underpinnings of our democratic society. It is also important that citizens believe in the impartiality of the judiciary, and for this reason the rules require judges to avoid acting in a manner that creates an appearance of impropriety. Public confidence in the courts may be diminished if the public believes something untoward is going on. Most reported disciplinary cases seem to use appearance of impropriety as a makeweight; that is, the judge's conduct is found to violate one of the specific prohibitions in the CJC's, but the judicial conduct commission also notes, for good measure, that the conduct created an appearance of impropriety. See Raymond J. McKoski, *Judicial Discipline and the Appearance of Impropriety: What the Public Sees Is What the Judge Gets*, 91 Minn. L. Rev. 1914 (2010). As you become more familiar with the rules, see if you can think of a situation in which there would be no actual impropriety—defined as a violation of one of the specific provisions of the CJC—but would nevertheless be an appearance of impropriety.

The following discussion surveys some of the issues in judicial ethics that you should be familiar with as part of your education in Professional

---

4. Canon 9 of the Model Code required lawyers to avoid the appearance of impropriety, but the Model Rules eliminated that requirement. The overwhelming trend of modern authority regarding lawyers is to focus only on actual impropriety. See Restatement §121, cmt. c(iv).

Responsibility. The subject is quite a bit deeper and more fascinating than this brief treatment suggests.

Who Counts?

Before getting into the rules in detail, we have to know to whom they apply. Most cases are easy: A full-time, salaried government employee serving on a trial or appellate court of general jurisdiction is a judge. In addition, however, there is a bewildering array of judicial or quasi-judicial officials: Magistrates, court commissioners, special masters, administrative law judges, and judges on courts of limited jurisdiction, such as town, justice of the peace, and small-claims courts. Many judge-like officials serve only part time; they may spend most of their time practicing law. (In many states, including New York, "judges" on these limited-jurisdiction tribunals need not be lawyers.) Do the rules in the Code of Judicial Conduct apply at all, always, or only when part-time judges are serving as judges? Retired judges may also serve as private mediators or arbitrators. (Active judges are prohibited from serving as private mediators—see CJC Rule 3.9.) Finally, in many jurisdictions judges are elected, not appointed. One may therefore ask whether the rules apply to candidates for judicial office.

The Code has a fairly straightforward approach to this jurisdictional question. Anyone—even a non-lawyer—who is "authorized to perform judicial functions" is a judge subject to the provisions of the Code. See CJC, Application, Rule I. The interesting issues are in the application of the Code to part-time judges and candidates for judicial office, who are likely to be lawyers as well as judges. As the introduction to this chapter emphasizes, lawyers and judges play very different roles. Lawyers are supposed to be loyal partisans of their clients, while judges above all are supposed to be impartial. It is thus important to know which side of the lawyer/judge line someone falls on.

Example

Either/Or, or Both/And?

1. A lawyer is a civil litigator with a firm located in Big City. She lives in Pleasant Village, about an hour's drive from her office in Big City. Under state law, minor parking and traffic matters in Pleasant Village are handled by volunteer judges who hear cases on Saturday afternoons. The lawyer wants to know whether she can serve as a volunteer judge in Pleasant Village and, if so, whether it will require her disqualification as counsel in a class action lawsuit pending against the state, alleging a pattern of civil rights violations in several state correctional facilities. The

lawyer once wrote a column in the Pleasant Village Gazette in which she bemoaned the traffic congestion caused by the numerous visitors from Big City who come out to Pleasant Village on the weekends to fish and hike. Can the lawyer serve as a part-time volunteer judge?

Explanation

Either/Or, or Both/And?

1. Look at Rule I in the Application section of the CJC. It states that the Code applies to all full-time judges. As for part-time judges, some of the rules do not apply, but the remainder do apply. Structurally, Rules II-V of the Application section carve out bits of the Code, depending on the type of part-time judge. In this case the lawyer would be serving repeatedly as a part-time judge, so her situation is covered by Rule II.

Rule III carves out, among other provisions of the CJC, the prohibition on practicing law in Rule 3.10 and the rule against participating as an employee of a business entity (the law firm) in Rule 3.11(B). The only restriction on practicing law is that the judge/lawyer may not practice law in the court in which she serves or act as counsel in any proceeding related to one in which she has served as judge. CJC Application, Rule III(B). That rule does not prohibit the lawyer from representing the class of plaintiffs in the civil rights litigation. Would the attorney conflicts rules prohibit this dual service? It seems unlikely that the lawyer's weekend work as a volunteer judge would create the kind of interference with her loyalty to the plaintiffs that would rise to the level of a material limitation on her representation under Model Rule 1.7(a)(2). The former government attorney rule, Model Rule 1.11(a), would disqualify the lawyer only from representation in a matter in which she participated personally and substantially. In this case, that would be only the traffic and parking matters.

The fact about the lawyer's annoyance at weekend traffic congestion is silly, but was included to make the point that the remainder of the Code, if not carved out by Application Rule III, applies to all part-time judges. We'll talk later in the chapter about disqualification for bias, but look at the numerous provisions that may apply in light of the judge's preconceptions concerning out-of-towners: CJC Rule 1.2 (judge must avoid the appearance of impropriety); Rule 2.2 (judge must perform duties fairly and impartially); Rule 2.3(A) (judge must perform duties without bias or prejudice); Rule 2.4(AB) (judge must not permit other interests to influence judicial conduct or judgment); Rule 2.11(A)(1) (disqualification required if the judge has a personal bias concerning a party). The lawyer should carefully consider whether she can set aside her irritation at weekend drivers and apply the law impartially, and expect a motion to disqualify her for bias if a defendant from out of town discovers her newspaper article.

Affiliations, Memberships, and Activities

Judges should safeguard their impartiality and avoid the appearance of impropriety by avoiding extrajudicial activities that might create conflicts with their duties as judges. CJC Rule 3.1. Potential threats to impartiality include financial investments and business activities, outside government service and the practice of law, participation in civic and charitable activities, and friendships. Because these are also activities from which people derive satisfaction, the rules seek to accommodate the interest in having a life off the bench. That's why Rule 3.1 begins with a permission, which is kind of unusual for a rule of professional conduct. The rule states that "[a] judge may engage in extrajudicial activities," except to the extent prohibited by other law or the CJC.

The area of most active concern for judges is probably outside financial activities, including investments. As a very rough general rule, active participation in outside business activities (with the exception of family businesses) is prohibited, while passive investment is permitted. See CJC Rule 3.11. Passive investment includes owning stocks, bonds, shares in a mutual fund, life insurance, or other financial assets. However, while passive investment is generally permissible, a specific investment may require the judge's disqualification from presiding over a particular proceeding. A judge who has an "economic interest" (a defined term) in the subject matter of the litigation or a party to the proceeding must disqualify herself. CJC 2.11(A)(3). Suppose a local real estate developer sells limited partnership shares to finance construction of a golf course. Limited partners contribute $50,000 in exchange for a share of the potential profits, but play no role in managing the enterprise. A judge may, under CJC Rule 3.11, take advantage of this investment opportunity. But suppose an environmental protection organization files a petition for a preliminary injunction to halt construction of the golf course, maintaining that it will have an adverse impact on a vital wetland area. The judge may not consider this action for the almost-too-obvious reason that she will have a financial incentive to favor the developer's position in order to protect her investment.

Despite the general permission to engage in passive investment, a judge should not invest her assets in a way that will lead to frequent disqualification of the judge, even if the investments would otherwise be permissible. See CJC Rule 3.11(C)(2); compare Rule 3.1(B). A judge is permitted to purchase 1,000 shares of stock in ABC Corporation, located on the other side of the country. However, a judge should not purchase 1,000 shares of XYZ Corporation, whose headquarters in the county in which the judge's court is located, and which is a frequent party in litigation in that county's courts.

The rules are considerably less permissive when it comes to active participation in a business. Judges are expected to be judges first, and to give precedence to the duties of the judicial office over other activities. CJC Rules 2.1. 3.1(A). Considerations of time management, as well as the need to avoid conflicting financial entanglements, support a prohibition on engaging in outside business activities. The rules prohibit judges from serving in any capacity — as an "officer, director, manager, general partner, advisor, or employee" — of any business entity other than one that is closely held by the judge or the judge's family, or is engaged primarily in investing the financial resources of the judge or the judge's family. CJC Rule 3.11(B). Judges similarly may not serve as a fiduciary (trustee, executor of an estate, guardian, etc.) except for their family members. CJC 3.8. In addition, even if you think the practice of law is a profession and not a business, judges are not permitted to practice law. CJC Rule 3.10. Again, there are limited exceptions for self-representation and for performing legal work for one's own family. In the latter case, however, only out-of-court representation, such as drafting documents and giving legal advice, is permitted. Some business activities, such as writing and speaking, are permitted subject to the requirement that the judge's compensation be reasonable and not create the appearance to a reasonable person that the judge's impartiality has been compromised. CJC Rule 3.12.

Judges may be involved in a wide variety of civic, charitable, religious, and other non-profit organizations, and may play many roles within those organizations. CJC Rule 3.7 is written as a list of permissions, as long as an exception does not apply. In general the exceptions are justified by concerns that a judge's impartiality may be compromised or that the judge may use the prestige of the judicial office to exert undue pressure on others. See CJC Rule 1.3. For example, suppose a judge wants to ride in a 100-mile bicycle race to raise money for a local AIDS charity. Riders must solicit at least $500 in contributions to be eligible to ride. The judge may solicit those donations from members of her family, or from other judges not subject to the judge's supervisory or appellate authority. CJC Rule 3.7(A)(2). The concern here, obviously, is that a judge might hit up a bunch of local lawyers for donations, and the lawyers might worry (reasonably or not) that the judge will be displeased if they do not donate to her fundraising efforts. Also related to the concern about abusing the prestige of office, judges are permitted to solicit memberships in organizations or be publicly identified with an event put on by an organization only where that organization's purposes relate to the law, the legal system, or the administration of justice. CJC Rule 3.7(A)(3),(4). Read the exceptions in Rule 3.7 carefully, but also understand that, in general, judges are allowed to have the kind of civic and charitable involvement that ordinary folks do. They can be scout leaders, kids' soccer coaches, members of the board of religious organizations, and so on. Judges are similarly permitted to accept ordinary social hospitality, gifts from family members, and various goodies available to the general public. CJC Rule 3.13.

To explore the details of the rules on associations and extrajudicial activities, most of which are contained under Canon 3 of the Code, consider the following examples.

Examples

Extrajudicial Entanglements

2. Janet was recently appointed to be a judge on a state trial court after a long and distinguished career as a business lawyer. She has a busy life and would like to know which of the following activities she may continue now that she is a judge. Please cite the relevant provision of the Code of Judicial Conduct when advising her.

   A. Membership in the Santa Lucia Society, a civic organization whose membership is limited to those of Swedish descent. Janet is proud of her Swedish heritage and would like to continue to help plan and run the Society's annual Santa Lucia Dinner, where young women wearing wreaths of candles on their heads give gifts to their families.

   B. Working pro bono for five hours per month during the spring tax season, helping people with modest incomes fill out federal and state tax returns at a legal aid clinic sponsored by the local bar association. Janet had significant experience with tax law in her previous law practice, but now given the jurisdiction of her court, she will never consider tax issues.

   C. Serving on the volunteer board of directors of St. Gertrude's Home for Orphan Cats, a non-profit animal shelter.

   D. Serving on the volunteer board of directors of Save the Lake!, a non-profit foundation dedicated to preventing excessive development along the lakeshore. The foundation has filed numerous lawsuits against property developers which have been tried in the county in which Janet is a judge.

   E. Teaching a continuing legal education (CLE) program on "new developments in business law" at a conference held annually in February at a five-star resort in the Bahamas. The organizers of the conference pay roundtrip airfare, hotel, and meal expenses for lawyers and judges who teach CLE programs. The fair market value of the plane ticket, hotel rooms, and meals is approximately $3,000. In addition, the organizers waive the registration fee of $500. The conference runs for a long weekend and Janet works diligently during the preceding week to ensure that it does not result in a backlog in her caseload.

F. Same facts as in E, only in addition the organizers also pay presenters a $1,000 honorarium.

G. Same facts as in F, only in addition most of the expenses of the conference are underwritten by an organization called Reflections of America (ROA). Although the details are murky, ROA is funded primarily by a wealthy liberal hedge fund manager who has stated in an interview with National Public Radio that she will "use her fortune to advance the cause of racial and ethnic diversity in corporate America." It is widely believed that one of the purposes of the conference is to allow lawyers to schmooze with judges at cocktail parties, dinners, and on the golf course.

H. Janet travels frequently to see her grandchildren, who live on the other side of the country. As a result she has attained elite status with an airline's frequent-flier program. One day as she was checking in for a flight, the gate agent (who recognized her from a recent newspaper article) said, "Oh, congratulations Judge Janet, you got upgraded to first class!" The difference in airfare between the coach and first-class cabin is substantial. Upgrades are available at no cost to elite frequent fliers if there are unused first-class seats on a flight. Priority for upgrades is determined by a computer, and gate agents have no way of jumping a passenger to the head of the queue for upgrades.

I. Janet is registered as a member of the New Bull Moose Party, a statewide organization dedicated to running candidates as alternatives to the entrenched two-party system. As a fundraiser for the New Bull Moose candidate for Governor, the local party committee has organized a dinner. For $250 per person, attendees will enjoy food cooked by a prominent local chef and music by a popular jazz band. May Janet attend the dinner? Must she change her political registration from N.B.M. to "independent"?

J. When Janet's father-in-law passed away, she and her husband inherited a large old house that had been converted into apartments rented by students at the local university. Given her experience as a business lawyer, Janet would like to help her husband run the family rental-property business. For tax reasons the house would be owned by a limited liability corporation, 123 Main St., LLC, in which Janet and her husband would each own 50 percent of the shares. Janet's husband would be the president of the corporation and Janet will be the treasurer. A lower-level court in town, on which Janet does not sit, deals with most legal matters involving students, including landlord-tenant disputes and citations for drunk and disorderly conduct.

K. After a tragic fire, the town council requested public comment on a proposal to limit the number of occupants of rented houses. The proposal would substantially reduce the number of students who could live in the house owned by 123 Main St., LLC. Janet believes that the council's proposal should be modified to permit a greater number of occupants if there is an exterior fire escape on the second or higher floor of a house. May she testify at the council hearing on the proposal?

L. Janet and her husband have a long-standing friendship with another couple, who are serious wine collectors. Every year the couple has a dinner, to which they invite Janet and her husband, along with two other people, and have a tasting of classified-growth Bordeaux. The fair-market value of wine consumed at the dinner is generally in excess of $2,000.

M. Janet occasionally officiates at wedding ceremonies. She believes, as a matter of deeply-held religious conviction, that a "marriage" is limited to a union of a man and a woman. Thus, when a friend asks Janet if she will officiate at his wedding to his long-time partner, a man, Janet is uncertain whether she is permitted to refuse.

Explanations

Extrajudicial Entanglements

2. Poor Janet is going to be spending a lot of time with the Code of Judicial Conduct! Most of the results make a certain amount of common sense, but it is important to read the rules carefully. There are many traps for the unwary, including exceptions to permissions or prohibitions, and the dreaded "exception-to-exception" structure in which many rules are qualified by an overarching analysis of whether the judge's independence and impartiality will be affected.

A. This is probably fine, but this issue can be a minefield for judges. You've probably heard of the prohibition on judges belonging to organizations that discriminate on the basis of sex, race, ethnicity, national origin, religion, sexual orientation, and the like. There is such a rule—see CJC Rule 3.6(A)—but notice that it prohibits membership in organizations that practice *invidious* discrimination on prohibited grounds. What, then, is meant by invidious discrimination? I would define it as something like, excluding prospective members with malice or hostility based on their ethnicity or national origin. The Code is a bit vague, however. See Rule 3.6, cmt. [2], which doesn't quite get around to defining "invidious" very precisely, but says it is "a complex question to which judges should be attentive."

Why all the tiptoeing around the definition of "invidious?" Because, it's not hard to imagine a 1950s version of this organization called something like the "European-American Heritage Association" whose membership criteria excluded applicants of African descent.

The whole awful history of white flight and massive resistance to school desegregation shows that the flipside of inclusion of one group is exclusion of another. The rules try to recognize the existence of common and inoffensive groups like Garrison Keillor's fictional Sons of Knute, while remaining sensitive to the continuing presence of truly invidiously discriminatory groups. The controversy not long ago over the exclusion of women by the Augusta National Golf Club shows that this is an ongoing controversy.[5] In this case, my made-up Santa Lucia Society is not dedicated to putting down people other than Swedes (although they may occasionally make fun of Norwegians); it is an innocuous association of people who want to celebrate their common heritage. Thus, the judge's membership is permissible.

Note the difference between the judge rule, prohibiting belonging to organizations that engage in invidious discrimination, and Model Rule 8.4(g) for lawyers, which prohibits "conduct that the lawyer knows or reasonably should know is harassment or discrimination on the basis of race, sex, religion, national origin, ethnicity, disability, age, sexual orientation, gender identity, marital status or socioeconomic status in conduct related to the practice of law."

What about membership in a church, synagogue, mosque, or other organization which excludes members on one of the prohibited grounds, such as sexual orientation, or separates members by sex? Comment [4] simply excludes religious organizations by fiat, perhaps not wanting to attempt to sort out the Free Exercise Clause of the First Amendment, statutory protections for religious liberty (such as federal and state Religious Freedom Restoration Acts), and the difficult normative issue of the relationship between religious commitments and a liberal society.

B. It seems like Janet ought to be able to do this, but there is an absolute prohibition on judges practicing law, with the narrow exceptions of acting *pro se* and giving out-of-court assistance to family members. See CJC Rule 3.10. Lawyers are encouraged to perform pro bono service, but judges may not practice law at all, even pro bono and even under circumstances in which there is no chance that the judge will ever be in a position to make a decision about the work she performed for the clients. It seems a pity, but the rule is quite clear. A judge may, however, encourage lawyers to perform pro bono services. CJC Rule 3.7(B) & cmt. [5]. ABA Formal Op. 470 (2015) has interpreted that exception to permit judges to send letters to state bar associations supporting pro bono, provide lists of available pro bono

---

5. Look at CJC Rule 3.6(B). Janet would have been prohibited from even having lunch at Augusta National before its decision in 2012 to admit women as full members of the club.

opportunities, and participate in programs recognizing lawyers for performing pro bono services.

C. This is okay. See CJC Rule 3.7(A)(6). I included this example to set up the next one, which illustrates an exception to the rule.

D. Nope. Notwithstanding the general encouragement offered by CJC Rule 3.7 to participate in the activities of "educational, religious, charitable, fraternal, or civic organizations," judges have to ensure that their participation will not lead to frequent requests for disqualification. If Save the Lake! appears as a plaintiff in a lawsuit seeking an injunction to halt a development, Janet would have to disqualify herself under CJC Rule 2.11(A)(1). Service on the board of the organization shows that she is biased in its favor. That's fine, but if the organization is likely to be a litigant in the judge's court, Janet's service on the board will result in her frequent disqualification. For that reason this service is prohibited by CJC Rule 3.1(B), which prohibits judges from participating in activities that will require their frequent disqualification. See also CJC Rule 3.7(A)(6), limiting the general permission to participate in civic activities if the organization is likely to be engaged in proceedings that will frequently come before the judge's court. These rules flesh out the general duty stated in CJC Rule 2.1, which requires a judge to give precedence to the duties of the judicial office over all of the judge's personal and extrajudicial activities.

E. Nice work if you can get it! As CJC Rule 3.14, cmt. [1] recognizes, "[e]ducational, civic, religious, fraternal, and charitable organizations often sponsor meetings, seminars, symposia, dinners, awards ceremonies, and similar events. Judges are encouraged to attend educational programs, as both teachers and participants, in law-related and academic disciplines, in furtherance of their duty to remain competent in the law." Judges, including Justices on the U.S. Supreme Court, do this sort of thing all the time.[6] This boondoggle is probably permissible, but Janet will have to satisfy several requirements.

First, she must comply with CJC Rule 2.1, requiring her to give precedence to her judicial duties. It is stipulated in the facts that she works hard to clear her desk before taking the trip to the Bahamas, so that rule is likely satisfied. What about the reimbursement of expenses? CJC Rule 3.14(A) permits judges to accept reimbursement for "necessary and reasonable expenses for travel, food, lodging, or other incidental expenses." Comment [2] notes that organizations that sponsor these educational programs often waive the registration

---

6. See, for example, editorial, "The Justices' Junkets," Wash. Post (Feb. 20, 2011).

fee (as occurred here) and also reimburse speakers for "necessary travel, food, lodging, and other incidental expenses."

So it looks like everything is hunky-dory, but keep reading the Comment: "The judge must undertake a reasonable inquiry to obtain the information necessary to make an informed judgment about whether acceptance [of reimbursements] would be consistent with the requirements of this Code." What's that all about? All of the rules on expense reimbursement, receipt of gifts and honoraria, and compensation for permissible extrajudicial activities are qualified by an overarching requirement. It must not appear to a reasonable person that acceptance of the invitation, reimbursement, compensation, etc., would "undermine the judge's independence, integrity, or impartiality." See CJC Rules 3.1(C), 3.12, 3.13(A), and 3.14(A) (incorporating by reference Rule 3.1 and 3.14(A)). Impartiality, integrity, and independence are all defined terms in the CJC—see the Terminology section at the beginning. Look carefully at the definitions. I would boil them down to the idea that a judge must be able to decide a case on the merits, without being swayed by bias or prejudice in favor or against one of the parties or any other irrelevant considerations.

The facts so far merely allude vaguely to "the conference organizers," so for now assume that a well-respected, non-partisan, non-profit group organizes these seminars. Given the overall tenor of the rules, which encourage judges to participate in educational activities, a reasonable person should not question Janet's independence or impartiality just because she got a weekend in a swanky resort in the Bahamas.

Note that, in addition, Rule 3.15(A)(3) requires public reporting of the reimbursements.

F. Rule 3.12 permits reasonable compensation for extrajudicial activities, and Comment [1] clarifies that this permission includes acceptance of stipends and honoraria, "provided the compensation is reasonable and commensurate with the task performed." An honorarium of $1,000 for teaching a CLE program is pretty generous, but not outside the bounds of reasonableness. As noted above, Janet must ensure that acceptance of the honorarium would not appear to a reasonable person to undermine her independence, integrity, or impartiality. CJC Rule 3.12.

G. Now this is starting to look like a real issue that judges have been facing. I made the funding group a liberal organization, but much of the controversy has centered on conservative (mostly free-market, anti-regulation) organizations funding these judicial junkets. It doesn't matter: Whether it is conservative or liberal, an organization may be quite keen to sponsor "educational" programming not only to reinforce and disseminate its position on matters of public importance, but also to strengthen networks of like-minded lawyers, judges, and scholars. In terms of the Code of Judicial Conduct, the issue is whether a reasonable person would believe that attending an expenses-paid seminar in a posh resort would "undermine the judge's independence, integrity, or impartiality." CJC Rule 3.14, cmt. [3]. What do you think? Arguments can be made on both sides:

- Pro (that is, these trips should be permitted): Judges generally have a great deal of legal experience before coming to the bench, and often have spent many years as judges; they have made up their minds long ago on issues of public importance. It's highly unlikely that a fancy dinner or a presentation by a scholar at a think tank affiliated with some special interest group is going to change the judge's mind. Anyway, judges should not have to isolate themselves from the give-and-take of politics. They are ordinary citizens, too, and should be expected to have their own values and beliefs. As a society we expect them to set their own commitments aside when deciding cases.

- Con (that is, these trips are a problem): Even if judges' views aren't swayed by attendance at these seminars, if they are put on by special interest groups, it may look like the sponsor is buying influence. Public confidence in the independence of the judiciary may be undermined if it appears that judges are being wined and dined by powerful people whose cases may be coming before the courts on which the judges sit. Organizations dedicated to some cause are not in the business of spending money for genuinely altruistic reasons like improving judges' understanding of the law; they run these seminars because they believe it will cause judges to look favorably on their arguments in court.

Comment [3] to Rule 3.14 sets out factors that can be used to determine whether attending a conference like this one would cause a reasonable person to doubt the judge's independence, integrity, or impartiality. Read those factors carefully. To summarize, they emphasize the nature of the sponsoring organization (an educational institution or bar association versus a trade association or for-profit entity); the source of funding; whether the identity of funders is disclosed; the ideological balance on panels of speakers; the balance of educational activities and recreational pursuits like golf and cocktail parties; and (perhaps most importantly) whether the sponsoring organization is associated with parties or positions that are likely to be in controversy in the judge's court.

This example is almost too easy, because as a state trial court judge, Janet is unlikely to rule on matters of great national political significance. In the real world, however, this is one of the most important ethical issues for state appellate judges and federal district court and court of appeals judges.

H. No problem with this. See CJC Rule 3.13(B)(4). The key fact is that Janet's upgrade is "made available on the same terms to similarly situated persons who are not judges." See also Rule 3.13, cmt. [3]. If the facts were different and the gate agent had discretion to upgrade passengers, imagine that Janet had walked up and said, "Hello, I am Judge Janet, and I was wondering if there are any upgrades available on the flight today." That could arguably constitute a violation of CJC Rule 1.3, which states that "[a] judge should not abuse the prestige of judicial office to advance the personal or economic interest of the judge . . . "

I. The answers under the Rules are fairly straightforward, but this Example again raises the issue of the balance between the rights of political participation that belong to all citizens and the special requirements of independence and impartiality that characterize the judicial role. Suppose Janet is genuinely able to set aside her commitments to New Bull Moose positions when ruling on matters that come before her. Should she be required to renounce any affiliation with the party? Without getting to any consideration of the strength of Janet's commitments to the party, Rule 4.1, cmt. [3] permits her to "register to vote as members of a political party." A contrary rule, prohibiting judges from registering as members of a party, would probably be invalid as a violation of the First Amendment right of association. The rule does, however, prohibit most activities that go beyond registering as a New Bull Moose Party member. Janet cannot be a leader in the local party organization, CJC Rule 4.1(A)(1), nor can she make speeches on behalf of the party or endorse N.B.M. candidates. Rule 4.1(A)(2), (3). Similarly, attending the dinner crosses the line. Judges are prohibited from making contributions to political organizations or candidates, Rule 4.1(A)(4), and also may not "attend or purchase tickets for dinners or other events sponsored by a political organization or candidate for public office." Rule 4.1(A)(5). Sorry, Janet—no rubber chicken for you.

J. Judges are generally discouraged from involvement in outside business activities, and may not serve as an "officer, director, manager, general partner, advisor, or employee of any business entity," with limited exceptions. CJC Rule 3.11(B). One of the exceptions is for a business closely held by the judge or the judge's family members. Rule 3.11(B)(1). Another exception is for a business that is primarily engaged in investment of the judge's family's assets. Rule 3.11(B)(2). Finally, a judge is permitted to manage investments of the judge and her family. Rule 3.11(A). All of these exceptions apply to owning and managing the rental property. As in other cases, however, you should be aware of exceptions-to-exceptions. Activities that are otherwise permissible may be prohibited in some cases. If the judge's business activities would "lead to frequent disqualification of the judge" they are prohibited. See Rule 3.11(C)(2). Here, however, the facts stipulate that most landlord-tenant matters are considered by a different court, so Janet's disqualification would not be required every time there was some dispute over a student's lease.

K. Yes, because the matter involves Janet's economic interests. See CJC Rule 3.2(C). In general, however, judges should refrain from voluntarily giving public testimony before government bodies. The concern is that a judge may receive excessive deference, due to the prestige of her office. Comment [3] attempts to mitigate this risk by reminding judges of the general prohibition in Rule 1.3 on abusing the prestige of office.

L. Nice friends if you can get them! CJC Rule 3.13 contains a long and surprisingly detailed prohibition on the receipt of many types of gifts. Numerous exceptions in Rule 3.13(B) list gifts that a judge *may* receive, including knickknacks like trophies and plaques with no intrinsic value, prizes in random drawings that are open to the public, and "ordinary social hospitality." The annual wine dinner, notwithstanding its lavish price tag, probably falls within the exception in Rule 3.13(B)(3). See also Rule 3.13, cmt. [2] ("Gift-giving between friends and relatives is a common occurrence, and ordinarily does not . . . cause reasonable persons to believe that the judge's independence, integrity, or impartiality has been compromised."). There's that language again! Comment [2], as well as the text of Rule 3.13(A), is another example of an exception-to-exception; even though ordinary social hospitality is generally an exception to the prohibition on receiving valuable gifts, it may be prohibited if a reasonable person would conclude that it interferes with the judge's impartiality. If the family friend is Montgomery Burns, a local business tycoon whose power plant is the subject of frequent litigation in Janet's court, the wine dinner looks rather different.

A "friendship" case that generated a great deal of discussion involved a duck-hunting trip taken by Supreme Court Justice Scalia with his good buddy, Vice President Dick Cheney. See *Cheney v. U.S. District Court*, 541 U.S. 913 (2004). Various environmental groups had brought a lawsuit seeking to obtain records of a White House energy-policy task force headed by Cheney. When the lawsuit found its way to the Supreme Court, the plaintiffs moved to disqualify Justice Scalia. The motion appealed to the federal disqualification statute, 28 U.S.C. §455, but the language of the statute is identical to CJC Rule 2.11.(A), that is, disqualification is required when a judge's "impartiality might reasonably be questioned." In an entertaining memorandum order,

Justice Scalia listed numerous examples of friendships between judges and government officials, including Justice William O. Douglas playing poker with FDR and "Justice Stone toss[ing] around a medicine ball with members of the Hoover administration mornings outside the White House," surely a sight to behold. 541 U.S. at 916-17.

M. Following the Supreme Court's decision in *Obergefell v. Hodges*, 135 S.Ct. 2584 (2015), holding that states are required by the Due Process and Equal Protection Clauses to perform and recognize same-sex marriages, this would seem easy. Judges are state officials, so they are similarly required to officiate at same-sex weddings. But some judges have raised religious-freedom claims similar to those asserted by some bakers, photographers, florists, etc. The difference is that judges are state officials and bound by the Constitution and the Code of Judicial Conduct, while non-judge participants in weddings are subject to state anti-discrimination statutes. Nevertheless, there is a similar issue presented by the conflict between the First Amendment and generally applicable anti-discrimination laws.

The relevant provision is CJC Rule 2.3(A) and (B), prohibiting bias or prejudice in the performance of judicial duties, on the basis of numerous protected classifications including sexual orientation. If Janet performed other weddings, but refused to officiate at her friend's wedding to his boyfriend, wouldn't she be engaging in prohibited discrimination? The ABA, in Formal Op. 485 (2019), said yes. If a judge performs weddings at all, she must not refuse to officiate at same-sex marriage ceremonies. In a footnote, the ABA committee said a judge's First Amendment rights in this context are subordinated to the duty to perform the duties of the judicial office impartially and without bias.

Disqualification and Recusal

The judicial-ethics issue with the most significance for lawyers—that is, the vast majority of you who are not planning to become judges, at least not right away—is when judges should not sit to decide a particular case. The terms "disqualification" and "recusal" are often used interchangeably. See CJC Rule 2.11, cmt. [1]. Some commentators say that recusal referred to a judge's *sua sponte* decision not to consider a case, while disqualification resulted from a motion or affidavit of prejudice filed by one of the parties. I don't know if that's technically true, and most secondary sources on judicial ethics use the terms as synonyms. In any event, the disqualification rule requires a judge to determine whether to step aside from a case whether or not a motion is filed seeking the judge's disqualification. Rule 2.11, cmt. [2].

As is often the case in judicial ethics, the underlying ideal is the independence of the judge from extraneous factors that might bias the decision she makes—that is, the judge's *impartiality*. Rule 2.11(A) states that a judge should disqualify herself "in any proceeding in which the judge's impartiality might reasonably be questioned," and follows that general prohibition with a non-exclusive list of circumstances in which disqualification is required. Note carefully the structure of this rule: The operative prohibition is on a judge presiding over any matter in which her impartiality might reasonably be questioned. The enumerated cases that follow in Rule 2.11(A)(1)-(6) are illustrative, but there may be circumstances not covered by those enumerated provisions in which the judge's impartiality might reasonably be questioned. The test for disqualification is an objective one: Disqualification is required if "an objective, disinterested observer fully informed of the relevant facts would entertain a significant doubt" concerning the judge's impartiality. Geyh, *supra* §4.05.

The rules governing disqualification should be read as exceptions to the so-called duty to sit, stated in CJC Rule 2.7. Unless disqualification is required by Rule 2.11 or other law, a judge shall preside over matters assigned to her. Without the duty to sit, judges might be tempted to duck hard or controversial case assignments.

Rule 2.11 has many bright-line provisions that are fairly easy to apply. For example, it should be clear when a judge's family member, within a specified degree of relationship, is a party to the proceeding, is acting as counsel, is likely to be a material witness in the case, or has more than a *de minimis* interest that may be affected by the proceeding. Rule 2.11(A)(2). Similarly, it should not be hard to figure out when the judge knows that she or a member of her family, residing in her household, has an economic interest, either in the subject matter of the litigation or in one of the parties. Rule 2.11(A)(3) (remember that "economic interest" is a defined term). Rule 2.11(A)(4), covering situations in which one of the lawyers has made a contribution to the judge's campaign, Rule 2.11(A)(5) on statements made in the course of campaigns for judicial office, and Rule 2.11(A)(6), dealing with successive conflicts of interest, are similarly straightforward. You have to know these rules, but for the most part they do not require you to make difficult judgment calls.

Disqualification that is otherwise required may be waived by the parties, provided the judge goes through the procedures set out in CJC Rule 2.11(C). Two important requirements are that the basis for disqualification and the agreement of the parties be stated on the court record, and that the judge provide an opportunity for the parties and their lawyers to confer outside the judge's presence about whether to waive disqualification. Like the subset of nonwaivable attorney conflicts of interest (see Model Rule 1.7(b)), some cases requiring judicial disqualification are nonwaivable. These are the situations set out in CJC Rule 2.11(A)(1), where the judge has a personal bias or prejudice concerning a party or the party's lawyer, or has personal knowledge of the facts in dispute in the matter.

The hard, but really interesting part of the disqualification rule is CJC Rule 2.11(A)(2), on bias and prejudice, and the catch-all language of Rule 2.11(A) on cases where the judge's impartiality might reasonably be questioned. The cases are hard because we believe judges are people, too, and have attachments, relationships, community ties, personal histories, and philosophical, political, and religious beliefs, all of which they necessarily bring to their work as judges. At the same time, however, we expect judges to remain open to persuasion, and to consider only the facts and law pertinent to the cases before them. Imagine that a newly-appointed judge had worked for fifteen years as a lawyer defending companies against claims of discrimination in employment. Over the course of her practice career, she became convinced that many of the plaintiffs' claims lacked merit and were merely a way of settling scores with management. A certain amount of weariness and cynicism may be expected after a long career in practice in a contentious area of litigation, but the former lawyer, now judge, must not allow that experience to cause her to form preconceptions about the result of any particular case. In *Catchpole v. Brannon*, 42 Cal. Rptr. 2d 440 (Ct. App. 1995), the appellate court criticized the trial judge for manifesting sexist attitudes and gender bias toward the plaintiff in an employment discrimination action, tried without a jury. The court reversed the trial judge's finding that no harassment had occurred, because the judge's impartiality was reasonably subject to doubt. The trial judge made numerous remarks that demonstrated his belief that most claims of sexual harassment were unfounded. What about the judge in our hypothetical case? It's a close call, but it is likely that, without more, a history of practice in a particular area, or another type of association with clients having a specific viewpoint, is not sufficient to require a judge's disqualification. It is okay for a judge to have a point of view, *as long as* the judge can set it aside and preside with impartiality. The judge in *Catchpole* demonstrated that he was not able to set aside his biases, and therefore should have disqualified himself. Without specific reasons to believe that a judge cannot be impartial, however, do not jump too quickly to a conclusion that a judge should be disqualified under the general Rule 2.11(A) standard.

An interesting, evolving area of law is the relationship between judicial ethics and constitutional due process. An early case, *Tumey v. Ohio*, 273 U.S. 510 (1927), established the principle that the Due Process Clause incorporates the common law rule that a judge should disqualify herself for bias. The Supreme Court's due process jurisprudence focuses on actual, objective bias. The test is whether the circumstances of a case are such that "experience teaches that the probability of actual bias on the part of the judge or decisionmaker is too high to be constitutionally tolerable." *Withrow v. Larkin*, 421 U.S. 35, 47 (1975). Most of the Court's cases focus on either financial interests or the judge's personal interest when the judge presides over a contempt proceeding involving conduct that had previously occurred before that judge. See, for example, *Aetna Life Ins. Co. v. Lavoie*, 475 U.S. 813 (1986) (justice on the Alabama Supreme Court should have disqualified himself from appeal involving punitive damages against an insurance company; judge was simultaneously plaintiff in an action raising similar issues); *Ward v. Monroeville*, 409 U.S. 57 (invalidating conviction where town mayor served as judge, and fines were paid into the town treasury); *In re Murchison*, 349 U.S. 133 (1955) (contempt proceedings must be heard by a judge other than the one presiding over action in which conduct occurred).

In an important recent case, the Court held that while not every contribution to a judge's campaign requires disqualification, there may be extraordinary circumstances in which a judge should be disqualified from a proceeding in which a party or a lawyer's contribution had a "significant and disproportionate influence" in the campaign. See *Caperton v. A. T. Massey Coal Co.*, 556 U.S. 868 (2009). In that case, one donor contributed $3 million to the campaign of a judge who was elected to the West Virginia Supreme Court. That contribution required the judge's disqualification from a case involving a company of which the donor was the chairman, president, and chief executive officer. The ABA model version of CJC Rule 2.11(A)(4) allows states to fill in a dollar figure for individual and aggregate contributions to a judge's campaign that would require the judge's disqualification. It does not necessarily follow, however, that disqualification is required as a matter of constitutional due process merely because it is required under a state version of Rule 2.11(A)(4). A judge may be subject to discipline under the rule, but the contribution may not violate the "significant and disproportionate influence" standard of *Caperton*.

Example

Yer Out!

3. Must the following judges disqualify themselves in the proceedings before them? Cite the appropriate CJC provisions, including definitions if applicable, in your answer.
   A. Judge A practiced in a private law firm before becoming a judge. Her retirement savings are invested, through a 401(k) plan, in several mutual funds managed by Big Rock Capital, Inc. Like many investors, Judge A relies on Big Rock's reputation for honesty and performance, and does not know details concerning the funds in which her savings are invested. As it happens, one of the Big Rock funds holds 10,000 shares of stock in Gargantuan Motors Corp. Judge A is currently presiding over a products liability case involving a Gargantuan truck

whose brakes allegedly failed, causing a fatal crash. If the plaintiff is successful in the action, recoverable damages may be as much as $500,000. The net income of Gargantuan Motors in the previous year was $3.95 billion.

B. Judge B is presiding over a complex case involving a corporate take-over. Shareholders in XYZ Corporation have alleged that the corporation's directors breached their fiduciary duty by accepting an offer to purchase the corporation that was below its fair market value. Under state corporate law, XYZ Corp. is the named defendant in the action. In the course of the litigation, Judge B realized that one of the directors of XYZ Corp. is Norbert, the husband of his wife's brother's daughter. Judge B's wife is not close to her brother, Judge B has not seen his niece since she was six years old, and he has never met Norbert.

C. Judge C is a state trial court judge. His brother-in-law owns a trucking business. At 4:00 P.M. on Friday afternoon, a lawyer representing the local bank comes rushing in with a motion for a temporary restraining order (TRO). The motion papers show that the bank lent $500,000 to the business to buy new trucks, and has reason to believe that the business may default and at least one of the trucks is about to be driven across the state line. The TRO would prohibit any trucks from leaving the state. Judge C naturally recognizes the name of his brother-in-law's business, so he quickly calls around other judges' offices to see if someone else can consider the TRO motion. Unfortunately, no other judges are available because it is the beginning of a holiday weekend.

D. Same facts as C, except assume that after Judge D makes the required disclosure on the record of his brother-in-law's relationship with the proceeding, the lawyer representing the bank says, "Your Honor, I have appeared before you many times and believe that you will always act with the utmost integrity and fairness, even in a case involving a member of your family." Judge C responds, "Counsel, why don't you go discuss that outside the courtroom with your client and see what she thinks?" The lawyer agreed, stepped outside to call the bank's vice-president, and returned a few minutes later to state that she had agreed to waive disqualification.

E. Judge E and her partner have a long-term, long-distance intimate relationship, but are not married. Judge E's partner lives in another state where he works for a venture capital firm. Judge E and her partner see each other every other weekend. A small startup company filed a lawsuit in Judge E's court, alleging theft of trade secrets and tortious interference with contract by a large company. Judge E did not know that her partner had made a substantial financial investment (with his personal funds) in the startup company. Naturally she could not disqualify herself, but is she subject to discipline if subsequently her partner's investment is discovered?

F. Judge F is considering a lawsuit, filed under the state administrative procedure act, to invalidate a set of regulations recently promulgated by the State Department of Environmental Conservation (DEC). The DEC rules prohibit a type of natural gas drilling technique called horizontal hydrofracturing, or "fracking." Judge F's wife is a researcher and lobbyist for an organization called Affordable Energy Now, which strongly supports fracking.

G. Judge G was appointed to the Perplexity Court of Appeals one year ago. Before becoming a judge she was a partner at the law firm of Wyman & Wood, in the commercial litigation department. One of her partners, Stewart, represented a paper mill in an action against an insurance company, seeking a declaration that the insurance company had an obligation to cover the paper mill's defense costs in an environmental lawsuit. Lawyer G, now Judge G, did no work on the coverage litigation, learned no material confidential information of the paper mill, and was apportioned no part of the fee from the firm's representation of the paper mill. The insurance company appealed the trial court's decision to the Perplexity Court of Appeals. The appeal was filed after Lawyer G terminated her association with Wyman & Wood and became Judge G. Must Judge G disqualify herself from participating in the appeal?

A. No, because she did not participate personally and substantially in the litigation while at Wyman & Wood.

B. No, because she did not learn any material confidential information of the paper mill while at Wyman & Wood.

C. No, because she terminated her association with Wyman & Wood before the appeal was filed.

D. Yes, because Stewart participated substantially in the litigation while Lawyer F was at Wyman & Wood.

Explanation

Yer Out!

3. Some of the results here are counterintuitive, so be sure to read the applicable rules carefully.

A. This should be easy, but make sure you cite the applicable definitions. CJC Rule 2.11(A)(3) governs disqualification for having an economic interest in a party to a proceeding. In a literal, albeit attenuated sense, Judge A has an economic interest in Gargantuan Motors. However, "economic interest" is defined in the Terminology section of the CJC to *exclude* "an interest in the individual holdings within a mutual or common investment fund." That definition is repeated in Rule 2.11, cmt. [6]. The result here makes perfect sense, because the impact of any given legal proceeding on any given company in which a mutual fund is invested is so infinitesimally small that even dishonest judges have no incentive to "throw" a case to improve the bottom line of their investments.

B. I'm not sure this result makes a whole lot of sense, but it does illustrate the sometimes technical nature of applying the rules. See CJC Rule 2.11(A)(2)(a). Norbert is the director of one of the named parties to the proceeding, XYZ Corporation. Actually, in a so-called shareholder derivative action like this, XYZ Corp. is only the nominal party, and the allegedly unfaithful directors are the real defendants. In any case, Norbert is within the list of persons to whom the judge might potentially be too closely related. How close is too close? The rule says a family member within the third degree of relationship (defined term!) to the judge or the judge's spouse, or the spouse of that person. Third degree includes nieces and nephews; the judge's wife's brother's daughter is the judge's niece; and Norbert is her spouse. Thus, Judge B is disqualified even if he doesn't know Norbert from the man on the moon. This is an example of the sometimes over-inclusive nature of bright-line rules.

C. Ordinarily Judge C would be disqualified—that should be clear. See CJC Rule 2.11(A)(2)(c): His brother-in-law is within the enumerated list of persons, and he has a more than *de minimis* (defined term!) interest that may be affected by the issuance of a TRO. But look at Comment [3]. It says the "rule of necessity" may override the rule of disqualification in some cases, and gives temporary restraining orders as an example. The rule of necessity is actually an ancient common law doctrine, with roots traceable at least to an English case in 1430. See Geyh, *supra* §4.04. It would be helpful if it were part of the text of this rule and not merely the comments, however. Comment [3] goes on to say that Judge C should disclose on the record the grounds for disqualification and seek to transfer the case to a different judge as soon as possible.

D. One of the recurring issues in the law governing lawyers is the waivability of various rules, but waiver does not come up that often in the Code of Judicial Conduct. Most of the restrictions on judges' conduct are nonwaivable. Many of the disqualification rules, however, are waivable—the only exception being disqualification for bias or prejudice. See CJC Rule 2.11(C). Judge D in this case followed the correct procedure, and as long as the disclosure and agreement are incorporated into the record of the proceedings, the bank's waiver of Judge D's disqualification will be effective.

E. There are a couple of things going on in this scenario, including once again a defined term—this time, "domestic partner." It means someone with whom the judge "maintains a household and an intimate relationship" other than a spouse. See CJC, Terminology. Pre-*Obergefell* the primary significance of adding domestic partner to spouse in the list of relationships in Rule 2.11(A)(2) might have been to acknowledge the possibility of a relationship tantamount to a legal marriage in a state in which same-sex marriage was not permitted. But does it broaden the list of relationships to include a long-term, monogamous relationship that could be a marriage but is not? And what about the fact that Judge E and her partner do not share a household, as required by the text of the definition of "domestic partner"? In a case of uncertainty like this, go back to the policies underlying the rules. The whole point of Rule 2.11 is to protect the integrity and impartiality of the judiciary. Rule 2.11(A)(2) recognizes that a judge's impartiality may be affected by concern for the interests of an intimate partner. Does it really matter whether they share a household and are married? Well, it probably wouldn't require disqualification if Judge E and the investor were just friends, or had only recently begun casually dating, but if they are truly a long-term, monogamous couple, then Judge E might quite understandably not want to see her partner lose a lot of money.

The other wrinkle in this problem is that Judge E didn't know about the investment. The disqualification rule kicks in only when a judge *knows* about the conflicting interest. Notice, however, that Rule 2.11(B) says that a judge "shall . . . make a reasonable effort to keep informed about the personal economic interests of the judge's . . . domestic partner." There aren't enough facts here to say for sure whether Judge E made a reasonable effort. It would be unrealistic, not to mention intrusive, to require her to insist that her partner provide an up-to-the-moment list of investments he makes. Depending on the industry in which he invests, and Judge E's caseload, it may be highly unlikely that one of his companies would ever end up in Judge E's courtroom. Of course, a judge cannot disqualify herself if she does not know of the grounds for disqualification. That suggests that Rule 2.11(B) is meant to encourage judges to keep abreast of their family's financial interests, but a grievance committee might exercise discretion and not discipline a judge *ex post* who did not know of her partner's financial interests.

F. This problem is based on the controversy over the association of Supreme Court Justice Clarence Thomas's wife, Ginni, with the Heritage Foundation, which had lobbied against the Affordable Care Act. Justice Thomas, of course, was on the Court that twice considered challenges to that legislation. The technical rule-interpretation point here is that the term "interest" in CJC Rule 2.11(A)(3) is qualified by the adjective "economic." It does not include the kind of ideological or philosophical interest represented by the spouse's organization in this problem. See Geyh, *supra* §4.15[5]. Thus, even if Judge F's spouse feels quite passionately about the issue of fracking and is a member of a pro-fracking organization, Judge F's disqualification is not required ... under this specific rule. Remember, however, that Rule 2.11(A) list *non-exclusive* examples of situations in which a judge's impartiality might reasonably be questioned. It would be helpful if the Terminology section or the comments contained a definition of "impartiality ... reasonably ... questioned." The definition from the leading treatise on judicial ethics is as follows: If "an objective, disinterested observer fully informed of the relevant facts would entertain a significant doubt" concerning the judge's impartiality. Geyh, *supra* §4.05.

What's the answer, then, under the "impartiality reasonably questioned" standard? It's a tough question, but probably should be resolved against disqualification. As a comment to the impartiality rule observes, judges come to the bench with their own background and set of beliefs and commitments. CJC Rule 2.2, cmt. [2]. Having a general philosophical predisposition toward one side or another of an issue does not mean a judge is not open to persuasion. (On many occasions I saw the judge for whom I clerked hold his nose, so to speak, and write an opinion that followed the law to reach a result contrary to his prior philosophical leanings.) A disqualification rule that looked to a judge's background values would be unworkable, since all judges would be subject to motions to disqualify on this ground. Additionally, in this case, the relevant commitments are those of Judge F's spouse. Maybe the judge and his spouse agree about fracking, but without more one cannot know whether they are of the same mind about this issue.

G. The answer is D. See CJC Rule 2.11(A)(6)(a). Option A plays off the language of Model Rule 1.11(a)(2), which deals with former government lawyers moving into private practice. Lawyer G/Judge G is moving in the opposite direction. Option B picks up on Model Rule 1.9(b), which disqualifies a lawyer from representing a person in the same or a substantially related matter when a firm at which the lawyer had previously been associated represented a client whose interests are materially adverse to the person, but only if the lawyer had acquired material confidential information. This rule is inapplicable here, however, because once Lawyer G becomes Judge G, she is not "representing" anyone. Her obligation is to act impartially, not to be a loyal, partisan representative of clients. Option C does not say so explicitly, but it suggests a narrow definition of "matter" — that is, that there are two separate matters, the trial proceedings and the appeal. "Matter" is not a defined term in the Code of Judicial Conduct, but it is defined in the lawyer disciplinary rules, in Model Rule 1.11(e). Comment [10] to that rule states that a matter may continue in another form, so the evaluation of whether two matters are the same involves consideration of whether they "involve the same basic facts, the same or related parties, and the time elapsed." The trial and appeal are the same matter under this analysis, and that makes sense when you think about it—the degree to which Judge F can be impartial does not vary according to whether the trial-level litigation has terminated. The point is that she has a prior association with a firm associated with the proceedings as a whole, including the various levels of trial and appeal.

Conduct of Litigation

The value of impartiality comes up in a couple of different ways in connection with proceedings in the judge's courtroom. These are not addressed by the procedure of disqualification because they occur in the course of litigation. They therefore cannot be anticipated by the parties and made the subject of a disqualification motion, or anticipated by the judge as part of a *sua sponte* evaluation of disqualification. One potential violation of impartiality is back-channel communication with one of the parties or its lawyer, giving that party an opportunity to present a misleading version of the facts or law. Another violation of impartiality is rude, bullying, or insensitive behavior toward one of the participants, including parties, witnesses, and counsel. CJC Rule 2.8(B). This conduct may include the manifestation of bias or prejudice based on gender, race, ethnicity, and other suspect classifications. CJC Rule 2.3.

The judiciary as a whole has not always had a particularly good record when it comes to treating women and people of color with respect, whether as parties or as attorneys appearing in court. Numerous reported cases involve allegations of judges making comments such as referring to a women's rights organization as a "one-sided, man hating bunch of females, a pack of she-dogs,"[7] and alluding to "another n—in the woodpile" when sentencing two black defendants."[8] The Code requires that judges must in all respects avoid manifesting bias or prejudice on the basis of various protected classifications, including race, ethnicity, national origin, sex, gender, religion, disability, age, sexual orientation, marital status, socioeconomic

---

7. In re Greene, 403 S.E.2d 257 (N.C. 1991).
8. In re Agresta, 476 N.E.2d 285 (N.Y. 1985). For a depressing litany of similar examples, see Geyh, supra §3.03.

status, and political affiliation. See CJC Rule 2.3(B). This includes manifesting bias through "facial expressions and body language." Rule 2.3, cmt. [2]. See also Rule 3.1, cmt. [3], admonishing judges to avoid "jokes or other remarks that demean individuals" based upon the same set of suspect classifications. Judges must ensure that court staff similarly refrain from bias, CJC Rule 2.3(B), and must even require lawyers appearing before them to avoid manifesting bias or prejudice, Rule 2.3(C). The prohibition on manifesting bias or prejudice is supported by the rule requiring a judge to disqualify herself from any proceeding in which the judge has a personal bias or prejudice against a party or a party's lawyer. Rule 2.11(A)(1).

The list of suspect classifications in Rule 2.3(B) is not exclusive (see the language "including but not limited to"), but in any event there is a general duty in Rule 2.3(A) to perform all duties of the judicial office, including the conduct of in-court proceedings, without bias or prejudice. That means that if a judge has an irrational hatred of, say, fans of heavy metal music or redheads, she must avoid manifesting this bias and may, in cases in which her impartiality might reasonably be questioned as a result, disqualify herself from the proceedings. See Rule 2.11(A)(1). In addition to avoiding manifestations of bias or prejudice, judges have an obligation to treat all participants in the process with dignity and courtesy. CJC Rule 2.8(B).

The rule of judicial impartiality in connection with litigation that most frequently involves lawyers is the prohibition on *ex parte* communications between judges and others. CJC Rule 2.9. Compare the provision of the lawyer conduct rules, Model Rule 3.5(b). You can see the reason for the rule more clearly by looking at all the conduct that is prohibited — not just private communication with one side, but also receiving advice from outside experts on the law or making independent investigations into the facts. See CJC Rule 2.9(A)(2), Rule 2.9(C). This rule shows that judges must not only be impartial, in the sense of keeping an open mind, but must also be willing to learn about the facts and law pertaining to a matter through the procedures of the adversary system. Think back to Chief Justice Roberts's umpire analogy. It has force because, in a common-law system, judges do not initiate the actions or direct the investigation into facts and law. They are relatively passive, allowing the parties (acting through their lawyers, in most cases) to develop and present factual and legal theories. Judges respond to requests for relief from the parties, but they do not control the direction of the litigation. The various provisions of CJC Rule 2.9, which you should study carefully, can be understood as keeping judges in their umpire role.

One little wrinkle on the *ex parte* communication rule has considerable significance in practice. If the parties consent, a judge may meet and confer separately with the parties and their lawyers for the purpose of attempting to settle a case. CJC Rule 2.9(A)(4). Many cases do not need to go to trial; if the positions of the parties are close enough, they may be able to negotiate a settlement and avoid the expense and delay of trial. The parties may use a mediator to help them settle, and in fact many judges will order the parties to go through mediation before trial. (See generally Model Rule 2.4 on service by lawyers as third-party neutrals, including mediators.) The parties may prefer to use the trial judge as a mediator, however, particularly if the judge is familiar with the factual record and the claims and defenses of the parties. Since mediation often involves so-called shuttle diplomacy, with a mediator going back and forth between the parties in an attempt to bring them closer together, the consent of the parties is required to permit what would otherwise be *ex parte* communications with the judge.

For the application of these and other rules on the conduct of litigation, consider the following example.

Example

The Honorable Judge Klutz

4. Judge Klutz is a newly appointed trial court judge. One of the cases to which he is assigned involves a contract dispute between a general contractor, a subcontractor, and a real estate developer at the site of a new downtown building. The developer sued the general contractor for extensive delays in the construction, and the general contractor filed a cross-claim against the subcontractor who was supposed to perform concrete fabrication work. The subcontractor defended on the grounds of commercial impracticability, claiming that the type of prestressed steel reinforcing bars ("rebar") specified in the contract was unavailable and that there were no feasible substitutes. The subcontractor counterclaimed against the general contractor, claiming a breach of the latter's obligation to install pumps to keep the site free of accumulations of water. The general contractor denied that the pumps were necessary given the location of the site on high ground.

    One evening after a torrential rainstorm, Judge Klutz decided to drive by the construction site to see if water was accumulating. When he arrived, he noticed numerous deep pools of water. He decided that the general contractor was full of it, and should have installed pumps to dry out the site. He also had his doubts about the claim that no other types of rebar would have sufficed for the concrete construction, so he called a civil engineer who taught at Perplexity Tech University. The engineer spent an hour talking with Judge Klutz about the finer points of building with concrete. He agreed that the rebar specified in the contract would have been the best choice, but that the subcontractor could have used a different type. "If you want to know what I think," said the engineer, "I think the subcontractor was just stalling, hoping the price for the specified type of rebar would go down—that's the oldest trick in the book for these guys." To double-check the engineer's opinion, Judge Klutz ran several Google searches for information about different types of rebar.

The subcontractor moved for summary judgment on the commercial impracticability issue. The motion was fully briefed by lawyers for the subcontractor and the general contractor. Judge Klutz remembered that his law school contracts professor had said something helpful about commercial impracticability, so he called her. The professor explained the doctrine in detail and stated confidently that it would not be available as a defense in a case such as this. Judge Klutz denied the motion and scheduled a jury trial to begin in three months.

Around the same time, a reporter from the local newspaper called Judge Klutz's law clerk. She stated that she was writing a story about the building delays at the construction site, which had become an eyesore and the subject of much public speculation. She asked the law clerk if he could help explain the reason for the delay. The law clerk gave a brief, "on background" explanation of the litigation between the general contractor and the subcontractor. He also said that the judge would be looking closely into allegations of "funny business" with rebar. The reporter subsequently published a story entitled, "Faulty Reinforced Concrete Used in New Building?"

A month before the scheduled start of trial, Judge Klutz got a call in his chambers from the lawyer representing the general contractor. She requested an extra week to submit proposed jury instructions, because she was currently in trial in another case in federal court. Judge Klutz agreed to this request. Realizing that he enjoyed talking to this lawyer, Judge Klutz sent her a "friend" request on a popular social network site. The lawyer ignored the request.

A week before trial was set to begin, Judge Klutz held a pre-trial hearing to hear arguments about jury instructions and motions in limine on evidentiary matters. One of the lawyers for the developer appeared to be intoxicated. He slurred his speech, frequently lost the thread of his argument, and looked disheveled. When Judge Klutz mentioned this performance later to his law clerk, the clerk replied, "Oh yeah, that guy drinks like a fish—I'm surprised his firm hasn't fired him yet."

On the morning of the second day of trial, Judge Klutz began by announcing to the courtroom that he had gone the previous evening to see a famous stand-up comedian performing at a local theater. He retold one of his jokes, thinking it was pertinent to the trial. "If you ever missed your fifth grade graduation because you had jury duty . . . you might be a redneck!" No one in the courtroom laughed.

After a week of trial, the jury returned a verdict against the subcontractor. It specifically found in a special verdict form that it would not have been commercially impracticable to secure substitute rebar. After listening to the jury foreperson return the verdict, Judge Klutz effusively thanked the members of the jury for their service and thanked them specifically for "seeing to it that justice was done in this case."

Describe the violations of the Code of Judicial Conduct committed by Judge Klutz during the litigation, with cites to the applicable CJC provisions.

Explanation

The Honorable Judge Klutz

4. Back to judicial training school for you, Judge Klutz! Go through his numerous violations in order they're described.

Judges are prohibited from conducting independent investigations into the facts in a matter. CJC Rule 2.9(C). The permission to consult disinterested experts pertains only to experts on the applicable law. CJC Rule 2.9(A)(2), and in any event that testimony must be in writing. Put simply, Judge Klutz should not have driven by the site to see if water was accumulating. For all he knows, it may have run off before morning, but more to the point, his decision should be based on properly admitted evidence, not his own freelance investigation. The same goes for calling the engineer to obtain expert testimony on different types of rebar. Rules of evidence and civil procedure have elaborate provisions governing expert discovery and the admissibility of expert testimony. A judge cannot make an end-run around these rules by calling people they think will be knowledgeable. It may have been a bit heavy-handed, but the bit where the engineer speculates about the subcontractor's motives was intended to show the risk of conducting expert discovery without an orderly process to ensure its reliability and relevance. Comment [6] to Rule 2.9 clarifies that the prohibition on independent investigation extends to Googling information about rebar. Rules of evidence permit judges to take judicial notice of facts that are not in dispute, but these rules generally require that the accuracy and reliability of the source of the facts cannot be reasonably subject to question. See Geyh §5.04. That means a judge may be able to consult an almanac to determine the time of sunset on a particular date, but no reliance on Wikipedia!

The communication with the former professor about the commercial impracticability defense would have been okay if Judge Klutz had given advance notice to the parties, indicating who he was consulting and giving them an opportunity to object and respond to the substance of the advice received. CJC Rule 2.9(A)(2). See also Comment [3], stating that the prohibition on *ex parte* communications includes law teachers.

Judges may not make public statements that might reasonably be expected to affect the outcome or impair the fairness of a pending matter. CJC Rule 2.10(A). Here, however, the statement to the reporter was made by the judge's clerk. Rule 2.10(C) requires judges ensure that their staff not make statements that the judge would be personally prohibited from making. The problem says nothing about whether Judge Klutz trained his law clerks, but this clerk seems pretty clueless about the dangers of talking to the press. Was the clerks' statement one that might affect the fairness of the proceeding? The counterpart rule for lawyers, Model Rule 3.6, focuses on extrajudicial statements that are likely to affect a jury's decisionmaking. In this case, there may be some reasonable possibility that prospective jurors will have read about shenanigans with the concrete rebar, and might therefore be predisposed to agree with one of the parties. The likelihood of prejudice is not entirely clear here, but a prudent judge would have advised his law clerk not to give interviews to the press about a pending case.

One well known case led to the disqualification of the trial judge for making statements to the press. See *U.S. v. Microsoft Corp.*, 253 F.3d 34 (D.C. Cir. 2001). The district judge had given extensive media interviews in which he strongly suggested that he would find that Microsoft had violated antitrust laws by integrating the Internet Explorer browser with its Windows operating system. The judge questioned the credibility, and even the ethics, of several of Microsoft's witnesses, and explained his thinking about the case with a folksy story about a mule trainer:

> He had a trained mule who could do all kinds of wonderful tricks. One day somebody asked him: "How do you do it? How do you train the mule to do all these amazing things?" "Well," he answered, "I'll show you." He took a two-by-four and whopped him upside the head. The mule was reeling and fell to his knees, and the trainer said: "You just have to get his attention."

253 F.3d at 111. The D.C. Circuit found that the district judge had violated the Code of Conduct for federal judges, but the provision at issue applied to all comments on the merits of pending cases—it did not have the qualification " . . . that might reasonably be expected to affect the outcome or impair the fairness of a matter." If it had, however, the judge's comments would likely have satisfied that standard. In addition, the judge was disqualified because the comments to the press gave the reasonable impression that he was not impartial. Compare CJC Rule 2.11(A).

Ex *parte* communications with lawyers representing the parties are generally prohibited. CJC Rule 2.9(A). Judges may communicate ex *parte* for scheduling purposes, as long as two requirements are satisfied: The communication must not address substantive matters, Rule 2.9(A)(1)(a), and the judge must promptly notify the other parties and give them an opportunity to respond, Rule 2.9(A)(1)(b). The word "substantive" is not defined. You may be accustomed to thinking in terms of the distinction between substantive and procedural legal rules, but I think the word here is meant to be broader than that. Many procedural matters, even scheduling issues, can make a difference to the outcome of the case, or at least be important to one of the parties. The category of permissible non-substantive *ex parte* communications is best understood as communications on matters that are unlikely to affect the rights of other parties. An extension of a day or two to file a reply brief, for example, is unlikely to make much difference. Even so, other parties deserve notice of the communication and an opportunity to respond.

The prohibition on *ex parte* communications also potentially applies to friend or connection requests on social media sites such as Facebook and LinkedIn. See, for example, In re Terry (Texas Judicial Comm'n 2009). Judges are people, too, and it is perfectly permissible for them to waste time on Facebook looking at cat videos or pictures of their high school classmates' kids. Numerous state ethics opinions have addressed the issue of whether it is permissible to be connected with lawyers in town on social media. See Geyh, *supra* §10.05 (reviewing opinions from California, Florida, Kentucky, Maryland, Massachusetts, New York, Oklahoma, and South Carolina). The emerging majority position seems to be that judges and lawyers can be Facebook friends, but if the lawyer is appearing before the judge, *either* (1) the judge should disqualify herself or (2) the social media connection may not be used to have *ex parte* communications specifically about the case. As always, if the lawyer-judge relationship is sufficiently close that the judge's impartiality may reasonably be questioned, then the judge should disqualify herself, whether or not the relationship includes social media connections. CJC Rule 1.11(A). Similarly, whether via Facebook or some other application, judges may not have *ex parte* communications with lawyers appearing in a proceeding before them. CJC Rule 2.9(A). You should have spotted the mirror image issue for the lawyer—that is, whether she was permitted to accept the judge's friend request. See Model Rule 3.5(b). Here the lawyer did the prudent think by ignoring it during the pendency of the proceedings.

Judges having a *reasonable belief* that a lawyer's performance is impaired by alcohol (or are otherwise suffering from a physical or mental disability that interferes with their performance) must take "appropriate action," including referral to a lawyers' assistance program, if one is available. CJC Rule 2.14. Other appropriate actions include speaking directly to the impaired lawyer and contacting the lawyer's supervisor. Rule 2.14, cmt. [1]. The judge's belief must be reasonable, however. The law clerk's gossipy report may not be enough on its own, but the lawyer's visible intoxication might prompt Judge Klutz to ask around with some of his colleagues to learn more about whether the lawyer in question has a drinking problem. If Judge Klutz had *knowledge* (a term defined as actual knowledge; and note the difference in the *mens rea* standard from the rule on lawyer impairment) that the lawyer had committed a violation of the applicable attorney rules of conduct, he would have an obligation to report the lawyer to the state disciplinary authorities, provided that the conduct raised a substantial question regarding the lawyer's honesty, trustworthiness, or fitness as a lawyer in other respects. CJC Rule 2.5(B).

The Jeff Foxworthy "you might be a redneck" jokes are familiar and mostly inoffensive clichés, but on a literal application of the rule Judge Klutz's retelling of the joke could fall within prohibited manifestation of bias based on socioeconomic status. See CJC Rule 2.3(B); Rule 3.1, cmt. [3] (prohibiting "jokes . . . that demean individuals based upon their . . . socioeconomic status"). Some reported cases involve socioeconomic bias that are no laughing matter. See, for example, *In re Michelson*, 591 N.W.2d 843 (Wis. 1999). Would a judge get into trouble in the real world for telling a relatively harmless joke that trades on stereotypes about people in a particular socioeconomic group? Maybe, maybe not, but the prudent thing would be for judges to keep their attempts at humor to themselves. Consider also the mule trainer joke told by district judge in the Microsoft antitrust case. It's best to leave comedy to professionals.

A judge may not commend jurors for their verdict, except in a written order or opinion. CJC Rule 2.8(C). The reason given for this rule is bizarre—jurors might think they are expected to somehow read the judge's mind and reach the "right" verdict in future cases. (Really, that's what it says—read Comment [2].) The weirdness of this rule is underscored by the permission to commend jurors in a court order or opinion. Granted, jurors are unlikely to read the opinion resulting from the case in which they participated, but they might, and in that case wouldn't they also have the expectation that the judge in a future case wanted them to do the right thing? More to the point, what is the likelihood in any sizeable community that a person will (1) be a juror in another case in front of the same judge; (2) believe that the judge remembers him or her from the last case; and (3) believe that the judge really thinks jurors should be able to discern the judge's view about how the case should come out?

Table of Cases

Table of Cases

Table of Cases

Index

Index

Index

Index